Art of Japan

紀貫之

むすふての
しつくに
にこるやまの井の
あかても人に
わかれぬるかな

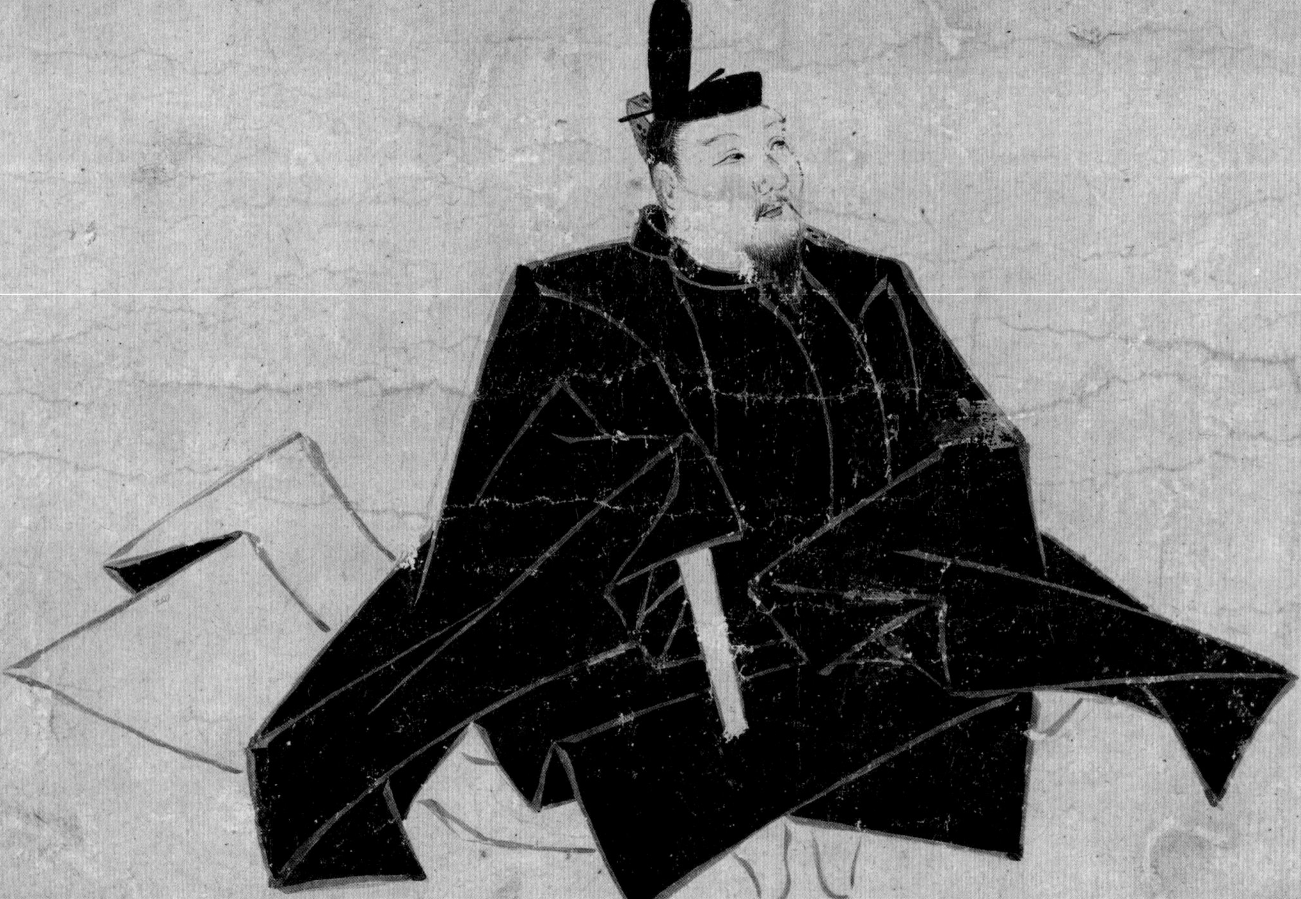

Edited by
Felice Fischer
Kyoko Kinoshita

Essay by
Felice Fischer

Contributions by
Naoko Adachi
Dilys Blum
Monique D'Almeida
Julie Nelson Davis
Felice Fischer
H. Kristina Haugland
Jeannie Kenmotsu
Kyoko Kinoshita
Eri Mizukane
Nicholas Purgett
Maria Puzyreva
Quintana Heathman Scherer
Harrison Schley
Xiaojin Wu
Yue Xiu

Art of Japan

HIGHLIGHTS FROM THE PHILADELPHIA MUSEUM OF ART

Philadelphia Museum of Art
Distributed by
Yale University Press
New Haven and London

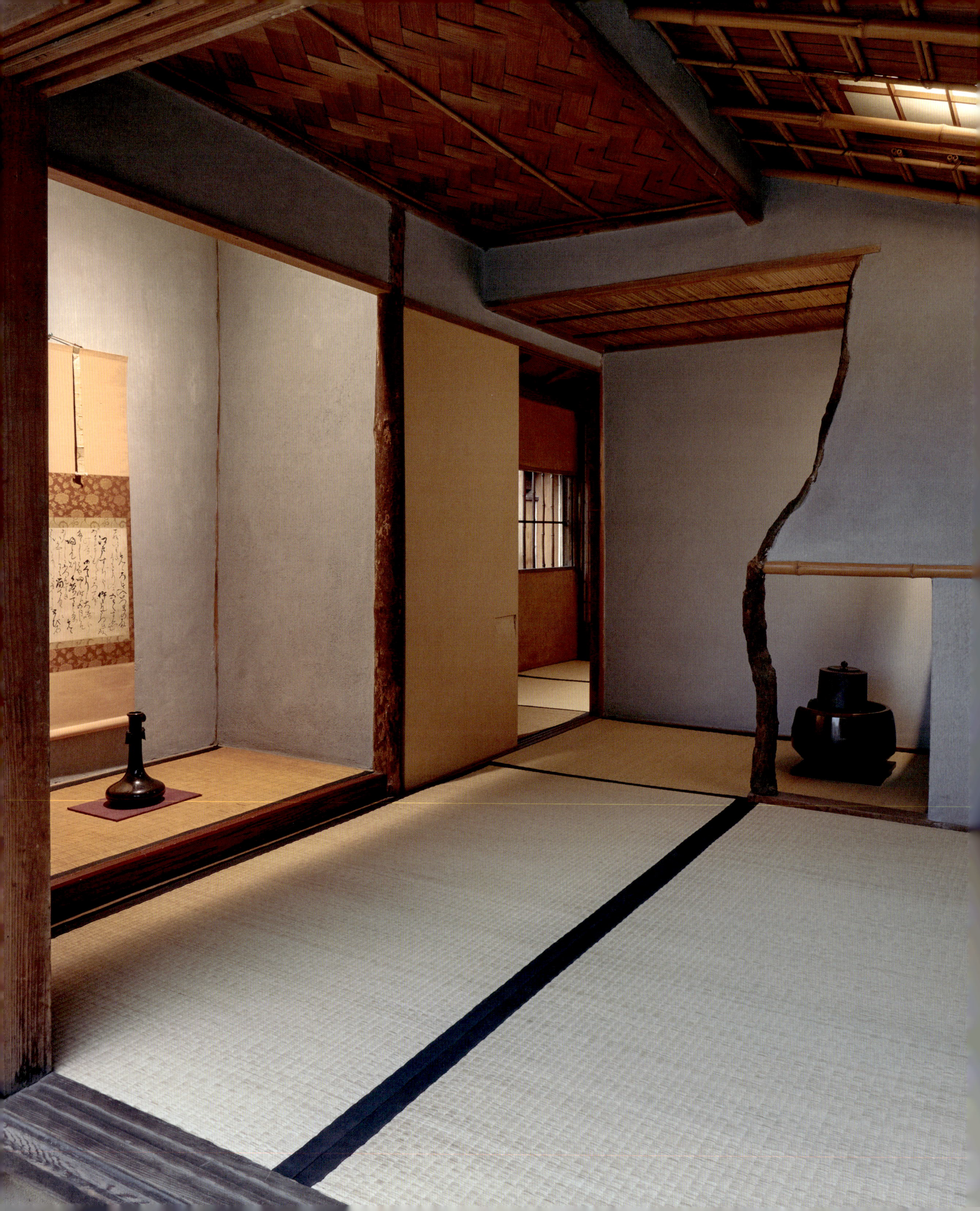

Contents

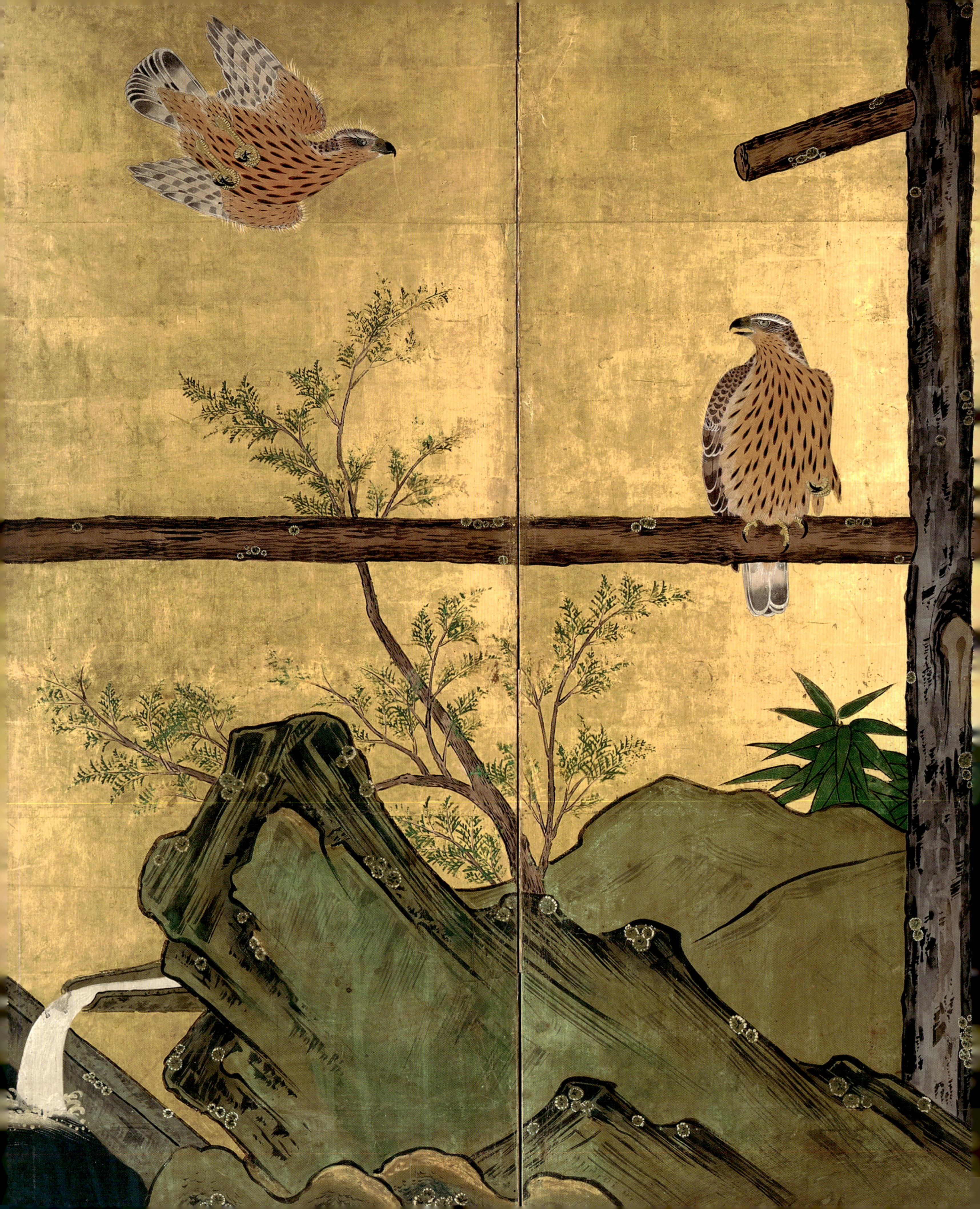

Foreword

The Philadelphia Museum of Art (then the Pennsylvania Museum and School of Industrial Art) was founded in 1876 on the occasion of the city's Centennial Exhibition, a seminal event that also hosted Philadelphia's first exhibition of Japanese art and craft. It was there that American audiences were introduced to a wide assortment of Japanese material culture and where prominent Philadelphians such as General Hector Tyndale were inspired to begin the collections that would later be donated to form the foundation of the museum's East Asian holdings.

Early additions to the collection include the Temple of the Attainment of Happiness and the beloved ceremonial teahouse by Ōgi Rodō, which remain must-sees for visitors today. Both works were acquired in 1928 under the museum's first curator of Asian art, Horace Jayne, and during Fiske Kimball's tenure as director. Since then, the collection of Japanese art has expanded to more than nine thousand works spanning prehistory to the present and is especially strong in works of the Edo and Meiji periods, as well as contemporary crafts.

The latter is due largely to the visionary curatorial work of Dr. Felice Fischer, who began her career at the museum in 1972. Dr. Fischer started as a curatorial assistant, rising through the ranks and becoming the Luther W. Brady Curator of Japanese Art in 1996 and the Senior Curator of East Asian Art in 2001. The museum benefited from Dr. Fischer's unrivaled knowledge of the collection and her leadership until she retired in 2020. Among Dr. Fischer's greatest contributions during her tenure was her ability to gain the trust and collaboration of colleagues in Japan. This allowed the museum to borrow Japanese National Treasures for exhibitions, and ultimately earned Dr. Fischer the Order of the Rising Sun, Gold and Silver Rays, from the Japanese government. I am grateful to Dr. Fischer for her scholarly contributions to the museum and her stewardship of the collection and her teams. This book is a recent manifestation of those contributions and represents only a fraction of Dr. Fischer's achievements. Even so, it will bring considerable knowledge and insight to those who spend time with it.

Together with Dr. Fischer, I thank her coauthors, in particular Kyoko Kinoshita, with whom she has collaborated closely for many years, including on the major exhibitions and catalogues *Ike Taiga and Tokuyama Gyokuran: Japanese Masters of the Brush* (2007) and *Ink and Gold: Art of the Kano* (2015). I also join her in thanking her colleagues in the departments of East Asian Art; Costume and Textiles; Prints, Drawings, and Photographs; the Photography Studio; Publishing; and throughout the museum for their contributions toward the realization of this volume. Institutional teamwork is among the great joys of museum work, and Dr. Fischer was its stalwart champion.

I want to express our sincere gratitude to the Japan Foundation and the Tokyo National Research Center for Cultural Properties for funding and carrying out the conservation of Japanese works of art over the years. In addition to material and financial support, these relationships yielded important international collaborations that continue to facilitate critical cultural exchange.

Finally, I want to express the museum's sincere gratitude to East Asian Art Advisory Committee member Jeanette Lerman-Neubauer and the Neubauer Family Foundation, whose generosity and commitment to art and education made this book possible.

Sasha Suda
The George D. Widener Director
and Chief Executive Officer

Acknowledgments

This publication on the highlights of the Philadelphia Museum of Art's Japanese art collection would not have been possible without the support, assistance, and advice of many individuals.

Among institutions and colleagues in Japan who lent their time and expertise, we wish to acknowledge Kiyomizu-dera Temple, Kōfuku-ji Temple, Nara National Museum, Sakai Teruhisa, and Yamaguchi Ryūsuke.

We also thank all who contributed entries on the works included in these pages: Naoko Adachi, Dilys Blum, Monique D'Almeida, H. Kristina Haugland, Jeannie Kenmotsu, Eri Mizukane, Nicholas Purgett, Maria Puzyreva, Quintana Heathman Scherer, Harrison Schley, Xiaojin Wu, and Yue Xiu, with special thanks to Julie Nelson Davis for her expertise in coordinating the entries on our Japanese prints, in addition to writing her own.

Colleagues at the museum to whom we owe thanks include, in the Conservation department, Sally Malenka, Katherine Cuffari, and Peggy Olley, conservators of decorative arts, furniture, and sculpture; Thomas Primeau, paper conservator; and Kate Duffy and Beth Price, conservation scientists, for their care of the collection and research assistance in identifying materials. For access to works in their collections and help with research, thanks go to Louis Marchesano, Monique D'Almeida, and Amanda Bock in the Prints, Drawings, and Photographs department, and to Dilys Blum and Kristina Haugland in Costume and Textiles. For ensuring that every item in the book was beautifully represented with the best possible photography, special thanks go to Justyna Badach and photographers Joseph Hu and Tim Tiebout. Dave Gallagher and his team of art handlers provided safe movement for the artworks to and from the Photography Studio. In the Development department, we thank Ann Kirschner for her advocacy of this project. For assistance with locating archival materials and images, we thank Margaret Huang and Susan Nolan in Library and Archives. In East Asian Art, we were fortunate to have had the research assistance of Maria Puzyreva, Harrison Schley, and Yue Xiu, as well as the organizational skills of Holly Chen, Jessica Kwasniak, and Gabrielle Niu in attending to the many details required behind the scenes. We also thank Hiromi Kinoshita for her support and assistance and Xiaojin Wu, successor to the post of curator of Japanese art. For approving and encouraging this book project, we are indebted to Katie Reilly, under whose leadership the first four volumes in the museum's highlights series were published. For their work in realizing the current volume, we thank Mary Cason and Sarah Noreika, editors, and most especially Kathleen Krattenmaker, director of Publishing, and Richard Bonk, production manager, for shepherding the book throughout two years of Covid hurdles. We owe thanks to Joseph Cho and Stefanie Lew of Binocular for the elegant design of the book.

Finally, we warmly thank the East Asian Art Advisory Committee and its chair, Maxine Lewis, for their support in acquiring and exhibiting the Japanese art collection, and we gratefully acknowledge the generosity of the Neubauer Family Foundation that enabled this publication.

Felice Fischer
Curator Emerita of Japanese
and East Asian Art

Kyoko Kinoshita
Project Associate Curator
East Asian Art

Note to the Reader

Japanese and Chinese names are listed throughout with last name first, as is customary, except when those cited commonly use or used a Western name order. Dimensions are given in the order height by width by depth. For cylindrical or round objects, the two dimensions indicate height and diameter. The conventions for describing materials and techniques differ depending on the type of object. For example, *color* is used to describe paint on silk, while *paint* or *painted decoration* is used for sculptures, furniture, and architecture. Materials were generally identified and are described by visual characteristics. In some cases, scientific analysis was done to further identify a material. References cited in the object entries and the Documentation (pp. 247–61) are given in full under References, which are divided into exhibitions and their catalogues (pp. 263–67) and other types of publications (pp. 267–71). In the Documentation, the provenance of an object prior to its acquisition by the museum has been provided when known. The sequence of entries is roughly chronological, incorporating groups of objects loosely associated by theme, much as in Japanese linked verse (*renga*).

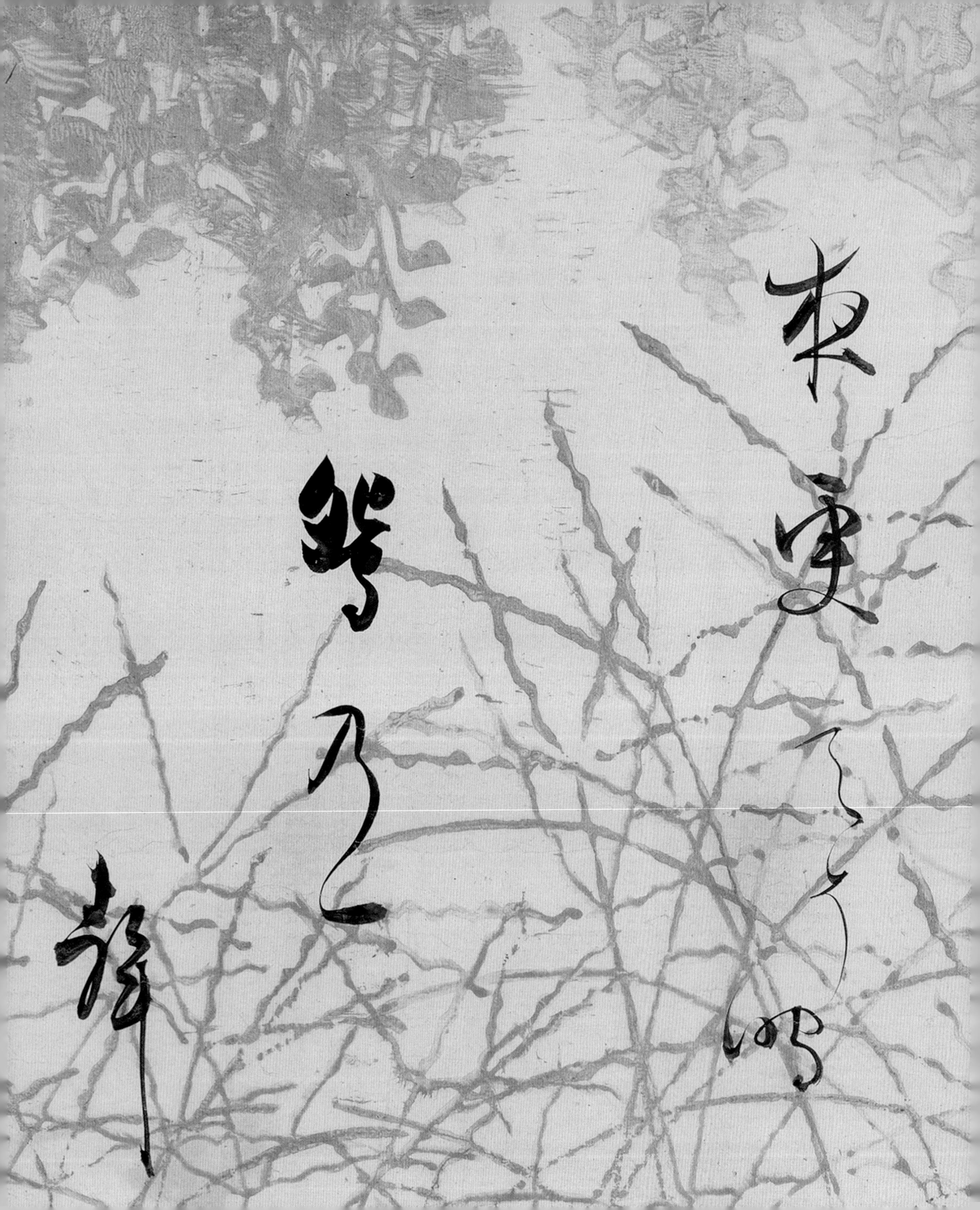

Philadelphia and the Art of Japan

Felice Fischer

Philadelphians experienced their first live glimpse of Japan on June 9, 1860, with the arrival of a diplomatic embassy to ratify the Treaty of Amity and Commerce (fig. 1). Some one hundred thousand citizens lined Broad Street to cheer the visitors, who stayed for a week and attracted crowds wherever they went, including the Philadelphia Mint, the ironworks of Morris, Tasker & Co., and numerous smaller businesses and shops.[1] The delegation brought gifts to US President James Buchanan, among them Japanese crafts that were praised in contemporary accounts.[2]

However, it was at the 1876 world's fair, the Centennial International Exhibition in Philadelphia, that Americans were introduced to Japanese crafts on a large scale. The Japanese government had gathered examples of crafts nationwide and shipped about seven thousand packages to Philadelphia. The timbers for two Japanese buildings and the workmen to assemble them arrived in late 1875 and aroused considerable attention (fig. 2). During the six-month run of the exhibition, Japanese crafts, particularly ceramics, garnered the lion's share of awards among foreign exhibitors.

An important figure in promoting the Japanese wares was General Hector Tyndale (1821–1880; fig. 3), the retired partner of Tyndale & Mitchell, a ceramics importer and manufacturer, whose store the embassy members of 1860 had visited.[3] Owing to his background, Tyndale was appointed a judge of the Centennial Exhibition's ceramics section, in which capacity he lauded the Japanese entries most highly. At the close of the exhibition he purchased a wide-ranging collection of Japanese ceramics, bequeathed in 1897 to the Pennsylvania Museum and School of Industrial Art (renamed the Philadelphia Museum of Art in 1938) (see no. 70).[4]

The Pennsylvania Museum and School of Industrial Art opened on May 10, 1877, in Memorial Hall, which had been built as the Centennial Exhibition's art gallery, with the aim of housing a permanent new museum after the fair's close. The museum's goal, according to its charter, was to collect instructive models for "the development of the art industries of the State" and for "the improvement and enjoyment of the people of the Commonwealth."[5] Japanese ceramics and lacquerware were acquired by the museum directly from

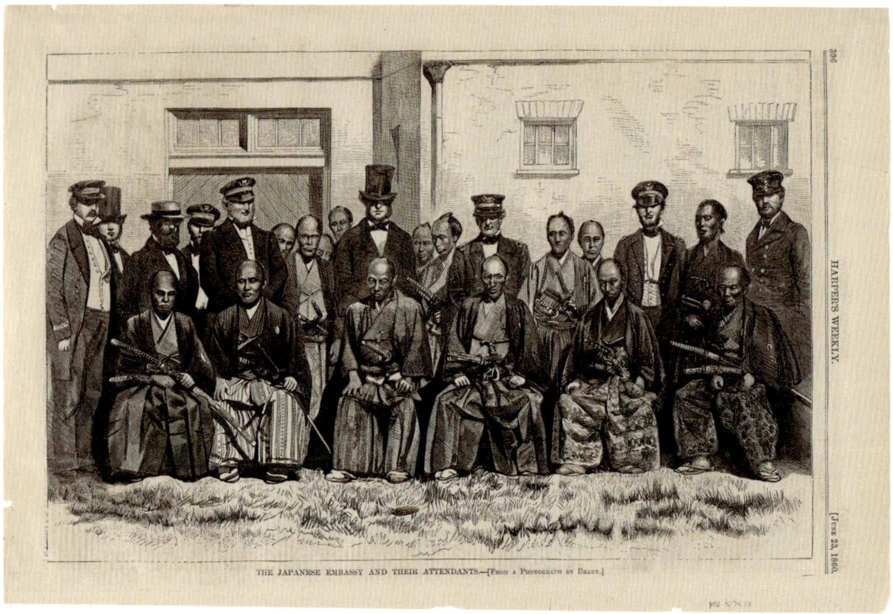

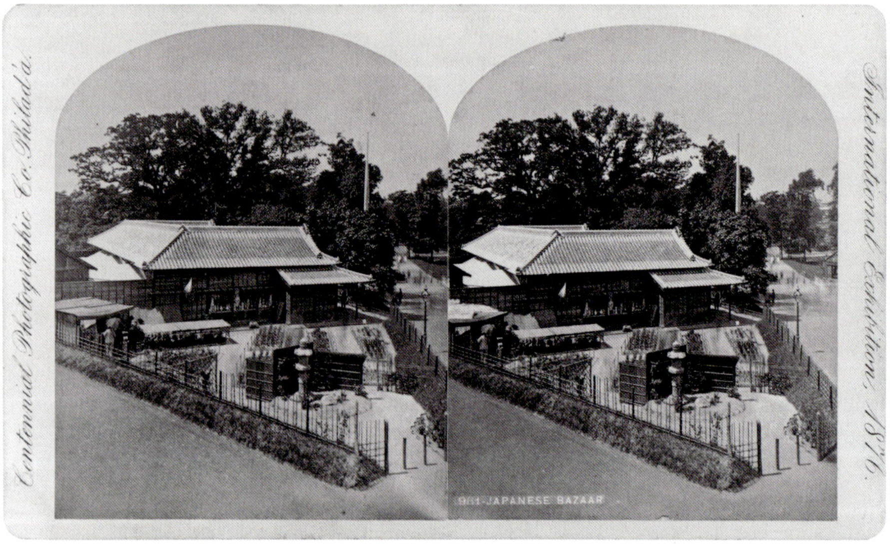

FIG. 1 Japanese Embassy and Their Attendants. Engraving after a photograph by Mathew B. Brady (American, 1823–1896). Published in *Harper's Weekly* 4, no. 182 (June 23, 1860). Originally published in *Frank Leslie's Illustrated Newspaper* 10, no. 237 (June 9, 1860)

FIG. 2 Japanese bazaar, Centennial International Exhibition, Philadelphia, 1876. Stereograph by the Centennial Photographic Company, Philadelphia. Albumen silver print, overall: 3⅞ × 6¼ in. (9.8 × 15.9 cm). Private collection

exhibitors (fig. 4; see also no. 68). Tyndale aggressively subscribed to the ideal promoted in the museum's charter, and his bequest to the museum numbered several hundred objects, including Japanese wares as well as Chinese and European ceramics.[6]

Among the visitors to the 1876 exhibition was John T. Morris (1847–1915), who became an avid supporter of the new museum in his native city and whose family's iron factory had been visited by the 1860 Japanese delegation. Morris became a member of the Pennsylvania Museum in 1879, and in 1892 he was elected to the board of trustees, on which he served until his death.[7] There is no record of Morris or his sister Lydia T. Morris (1849–1932) purchasing any Japanese objects at the Centennial Exhibition, but they visited Japan during their 1889–90 world tour. The two traveled there for nearly two months, with a base in Yokohama, and seem to have been thoroughly smitten with Japanese culture.[8] Many purchases were made, including an album of photographs, and Lydia posed in a kimono for a commemorative picture. The largest purchase John made was a Japanese-style teahouse that he commissioned from carpenters in Tokyo and subsequently erected at Compton, the summer estate he and Lydia owned in the Chestnut Hill section of Philadelphia.[9] After their return, Morris continued to purchase Japanese art, including a group of arms and armor in 1911 for the museum's collection, and other items that later came to the institution by bequest (fig. 5).[10] Morris also installed a Japanese garden at Compton and was involved in the planning (and funding) of a lotus garden at the site of a Japanese temple gate in Fairmount Park (see no. 5). For the planning of the latter project, Morris consulted Ernest F. Fenollosa (1853–1908; fig. 6), the first curator of Asian art at the Museum of Fine Arts, Boston, and adviser to Charles Lang Freer (1856–1919), whose extensive collection of Asian art was bequeathed to the Smithsonian Institution in Washington, DC.[11]

Fenollosa had attended the Centennial Exhibition while a student at Harvard and was impressed by the Japanese display. Two years later, in 1878, he was invited by the Japanese government to teach Western philosophy at the newly established University of Tokyo as part of the government program to modernize the country.[12]

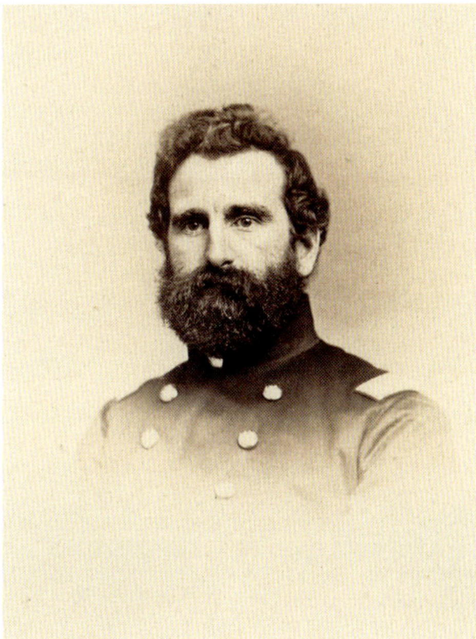

FIG. 3 Brigadier General Hector Tyndale, 28th Pennsylvania Infantry Regiment and US Volunteers Infantry Regiment, in Uniform, c. 1861–65. Photograph by J. E. McClees (American, 1821–1887). Albumen print on card mount, overall: 3 15/16 × 2 1/2 in. (10 × 6.3 cm). Library of Congress, Prints and Photographs Division, Washington, DC

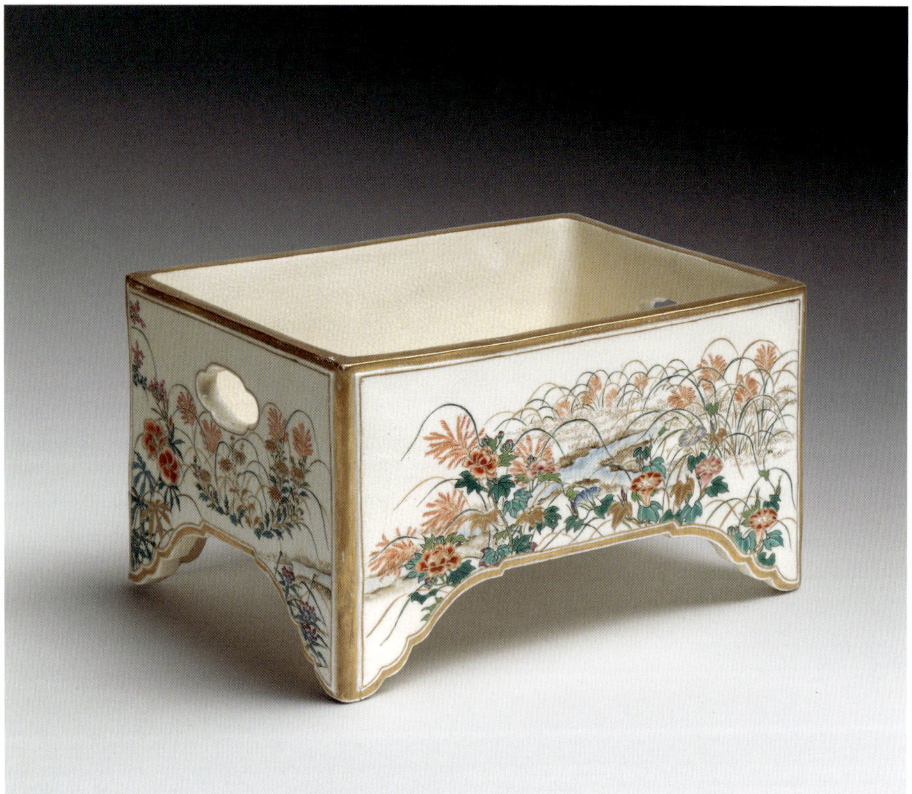

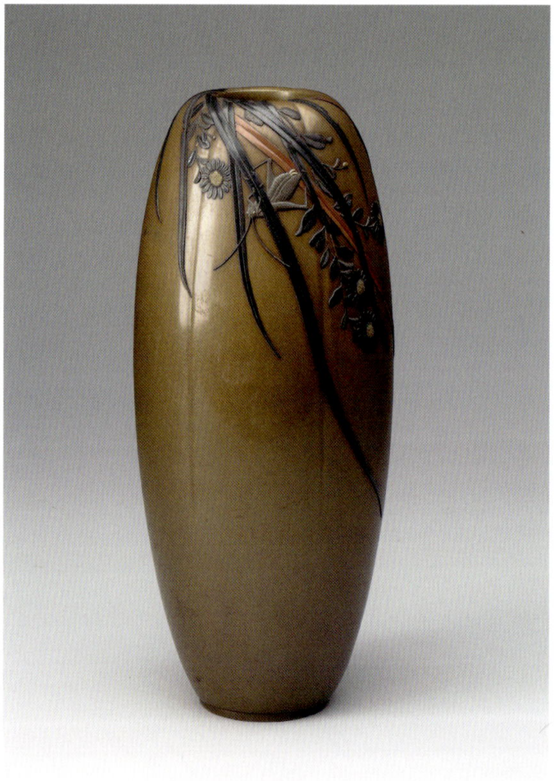

FIG. 4 Ri Seisho (Japanese, life dates unknown). Tray. Manufactured and decorated by Nakashima Ryokei. Meiji period (1868–1912), late 19th century. Earthenware with enamel and gilt decoration (Satsuma ware), 4¼ × 5¼ × 7¼ in. (10.7 × 13.3 × 18.5 cm). Philadelphia Museum of Art: Purchased with Museum funds, 1876-1665

FIG. 5 Vase. Meiji period (1868–1912), late 19th century. Bronze, silver, and copper, 9½ × 3⅞ in. (24.1 × 9.8 cm). Philadelphia Museum of Art: Gift of Lydia Thompson Morris, 1925-27-126

Fenollosa soon became interested in Japanese art and advocated for the promotion of traditional Japanese ink painting and sculpture, which he thought in danger of becoming overwhelmed by Western practices.[13] He encouraged and supported the artists of the Kano school, who were struggling to continue their artistic heritage in the face of a very changed world. Fenollosa collected their paintings, as well as applied arts with which he furnished his Tokyo home (see no. 76). These were inherited by Fenollosa's daughter, Brenda Fenollosa Biddle (1883–1959; fig. 7), who donated the collection to the Philadelphia Museum of Art in 1940 and 1941, in hope that despite the United States being at war with Japan, the importance and richness of Japanese culture — which Fenollosa had first introduced to US audiences — would continue to be recognized.[14]

One of Fenollosa's students in Tokyo, and his successor to the post of curator of Asian art at the Museum of Fine Arts, Boston, was Okakura Kakuzō (1863–1913), who became a household name in the United States with the publication of *The Book of Tea* in 1906, which introduced US audiences to the aesthetics of simplicity, imperfection, and community espoused by tea practitioners. That same year the Boston museum's administration selected two young men to train to work with Okakura in the Department of Asiatic Art. One of them was Langdon Warner (1881–1955; fig. 8), a 1903 graduate of Harvard.[15] Warner met Okakura in Japan at the latter's Japan Art Institute (Nihon Bijutsuin). Okakura assigned his younger brother, Yoshisaburō, to tutor Warner in the Japanese language, and the sculptor Niiro Chūnosuke to take Warner on at his conservation studio in Nara to study the techniques and aesthetics of traditional Buddhist sculpture, which became Warner's field of expertise. In 1910 Warner served as assistant to Okakura to prepare the Japanese works of art and the English-language catalogue for the fine arts displayed at the Japan-British Exhibition in London. The exhibition included some of the most important early Buddhist sculptures, paintings, and decorative arts, and constituted a deep immersion in the arts of Japan for Warner.[16] During this time he also formed many lasting friendships with Japanese scholars and collectors, which would prove important in his future work with Japanese art. After his

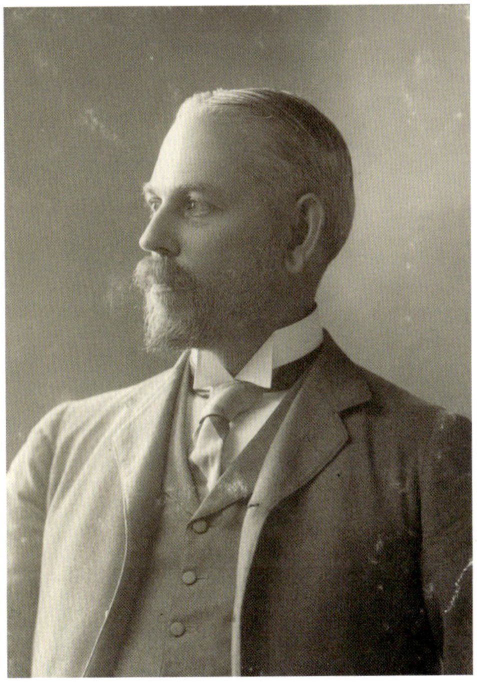

FIG. 6 Ernest F. Fenollosa, c. 1890. National Museum of Asian Art Archives, Washington, DC

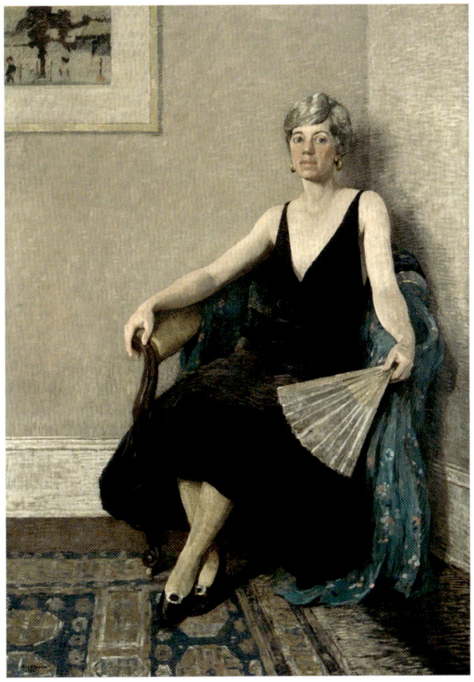

FIG. 7 Robert Spencer (American, 1879–1913). *Portrait of Brenda Biddle*, 1926. Oil on canvas, 60⅛ × 42⁹⁄₁₆ in. (152.7 × 108.1 cm). Philadelphia Museum of Art: Gift of Owen Biddle and Peyton R. Biddle, 1978-12-1

return to Boston and a stint as associate curator there until 1913, Warner went to China to establish the American School of Archaeology on behalf of the Smithsonian Institution. This project was supported by Freer, who several years later encouraged Warner to accept the position of director of the Pennsylvania Museum.

Although Warner's tenure in the role was short, from 1917 to 1923, and he took several leaves of absence for archaeological field trips to Asia, he proved to be an energetic and foresightful director. In 1919 he established the first children's museum in Philadelphia, located in the basement of Memorial Hall (which since 2008 has housed another children's museum, the Please Touch Museum). Even more significant to the future of the Pennsylvania Museum, that same year Warner accepted as a gift a sixteenth-century South Indian temple hall from Madurai, which he installed in Memorial Hall as the museum's first architectural unit from Asia.[17] Warner also installed the W. P. Wilstach Collection of Western painting that Wilstach's widow, Anna, bequeathed to the city of Philadelphia. He organized the first loan exhibition of Oriental carpets, and in 1920 he hired the first full-time staff photographer. Warner was also deeply involved in planning for the move of the museum's collections to its new building at the site of the former waterworks in the Fairmount section of the city. To help with the expansion of the collections, Warner hired the institution's first curator of Asian art, Horace H. F. Jayne (1898–1975; fig. 9), in 1921. Jayne's interest lay with Chinese art, and he joined Warner on expeditions to China.[18] Warner resigned his position as director in 1923 to join Harvard University's Fogg Museum, where he served in various capacities as an influential curator and charismatic teacher to several generations of specialists in Asian art until his retirement in 1950. He served as an honorary adviser for the Pennsylvania Museum in 1923–25, and he continued a long and warm friendship with Jayne.[19]

When Fiske Kimball (1888–1955) was named the museum's director in 1925, he further built the collection of Asian art on the foundation Warner had established, sending Jayne to Japan and China in 1928 to acquire additional representative structures to be installed in the new museum building. Kimball's "walk through

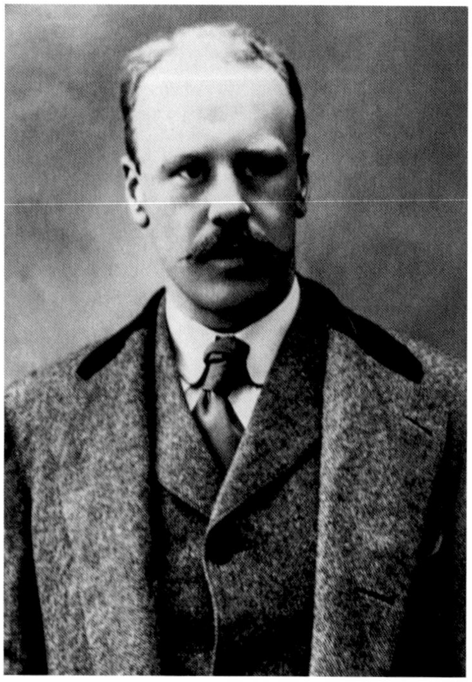

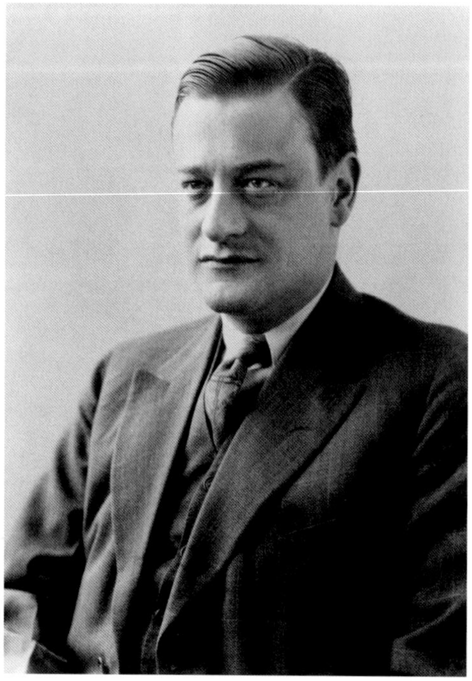

FIG. 8 Langdon Warner, c. 1905. Philadelphia Museum of Art Library and Archives

FIG. 9 Horace H. F. Jayne, 1929. Philadelphia Museum of Art Library and Archives

time" was to constitute a series of "period rooms" to give context to the American, European, and Asian works of art on display.[20] Warner was in Japan in 1928, working on his book on eighth-century Buddhist sculpture of the Tempyo period, when Jayne arrived to look for a Japanese temple and traditional teahouse. Through Warner's connections Jayne met Takahashi Yoshio (tea name, Sōan; 1861–1937), an expert on tea ceremony and its history who introduced Jayne to Ōgi Keiichirō (tea name, Rodō; 1863–1941). Ōgi Rodō was an architect of traditional teahouses and had erected one for his own use, called Sunkaraku (Evanescent Joys), which Jayne was able to acquire for the museum (see no. 24).[21] A formal farewell tea gathering was held on September 23, 1928, before the teahouse was disassembled for shipment to Philadelphia (fig. 10). Jayne was equally successful in his quest for a Buddhist temple building, most likely also through introductions from Warner (see no. 23). These were the first two complete Japanese structures of this type acquired for display in a US museum, although economic and political contingencies delayed their debut to the public until 1957.

The world's fairs in the United States that followed the 1876 Centennial International Exhibition, including the 1893 World's Columbian Exposition in Chicago and the 1904 Louisiana Purchase Exposition in Saint Louis, featured Japanese pavilions that served Japanese tea. These stimulated an interest not only in Japanese architecture but also in ceramics for tea. One Philadelphia collector active in the 1920s and 1930s was Mrs. John Reilly, who had a specific interest in tea-related ceramics. Among the 104 ceramics that she bequeathed to the museum in 1941 were twenty-eight teabowls, including an unusual seventeenth-century black Oribe piece (see no. 27); ceramics for *sencha*, the Chinese-style steeped tea; and teapots used to brew tea, forty of which came to the museum. We do not know if Mrs. Reilly ever traveled to Japan, but we do know from her correspondence that she purchased some pieces at Yamanaka & Co. in New York, and she often quotes a Mr. Tanaka of that firm in her notes on particular objects.[22] Yamanaka & Co. was a dealer in Japanese art, with stores in both the United States and Europe, having opened its first store in New York

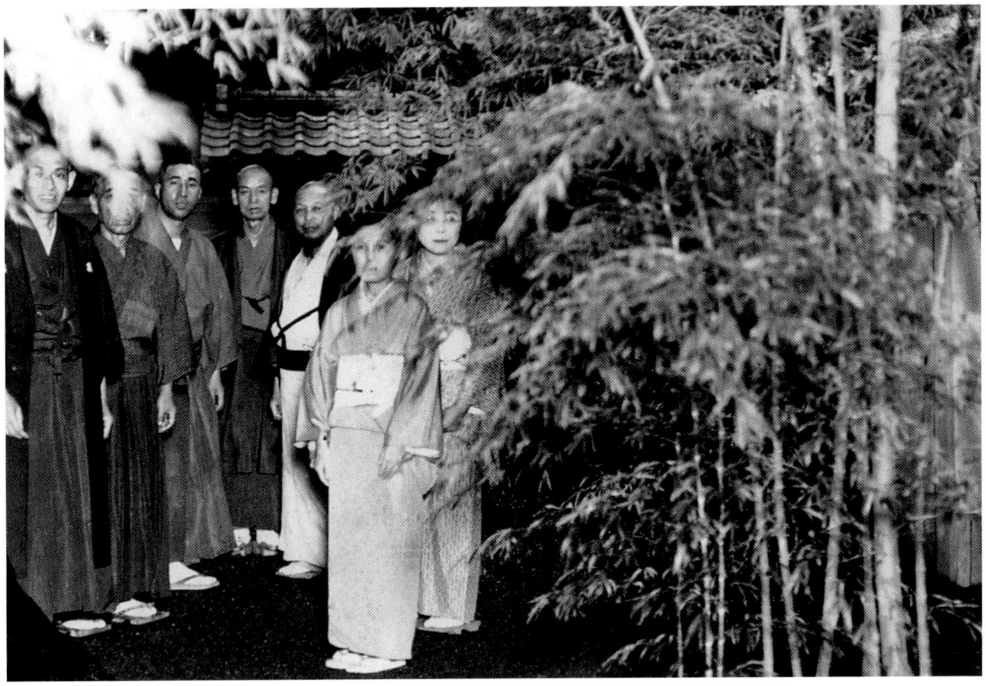

FIG. 10 Farewell tea ceremony at the Sunkaraku Harajuku, Tokyo, September 23, 1928. Ōgi Rodō is third from right. Philadelphia Museum of Art Library and Archives

in 1894. Among its clients were Freer and members of the Rockefeller family, and museums such as the Museum of Fine Arts, Boston, also acquired Japanese art from the dealer.[23]

Several early collectors were businessmen whose travels to Japan led to their interest in Japanese art. Edmund Louis Gray Zalinski (1849–1909; fig. 11) had a military background and became renowned for his expertise in artillery with his invention of a new type of pneumatic "dynamite torpedo-gun" for shipboard use. In 1889 Zalinski toured a group of visiting dignitaries from Japan, showing his invention at the Philadelphia shipyard of William Cramp & Sons.[24] Zalinski made two trips to Japan, the first in 1895 and the second in 1896, the latter on behalf of Bethlehem Steel Works to expand the company's business into the country, which was increasing its military forces. While there he acquired a large collection of over two hundred Japanese swords that he had appraised by experts in Tokyo (see no. 61). Zalinski's sword collection remained in the family until the 1960s, when his grandson, Edmund L. Zalinski II, donated it to the Philadelphia Museum of Art.

Another contributor to the museum's holdings of Japanese art was Samuel S. White 3rd (1876–1952; fig. 12), whose grandfather founded the S. S. White Dental Manufacturing Company of Philadelphia, one of the exhibitors at the 1876 Centennial Exhibition. Born the year of the Centennial, he was heir to the family fortune and worked for the firm from 1903. That year he traveled to Japan on his first official business trip for the company, and he subsequently returned several times. Recent research indicates that he purchased most, if not all, of his Japanese paintings during that first sojourn (see no. 79). At least four of the paintings now in the museum's collection were exhibited in Tokyo at an exhibition in late 1902 that was sponsored by the Japan Art Institute. It is not clear how or where White saw these paintings, since the exhibition had closed the year before his stay in Japan. He may have been alerted to them by the artist Yoshida Hiroshi (1876–1950), whose studio he visited and from whom he commissioned a painting. The two may have met previously in the United States when Yoshida's work was in a group show touring the country.[25] White's wife, Vera

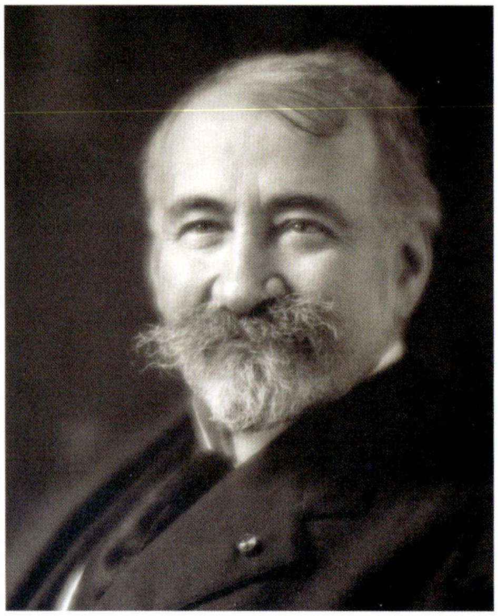

FIG. 11 Edmund Louis Gray Zalinski, c. 1900. Photograph by Pirie MacDonald (American, 1867–1942). Philadelphia Museum of Art Library and Archives: Gift of Mathilda Davidson, 2020

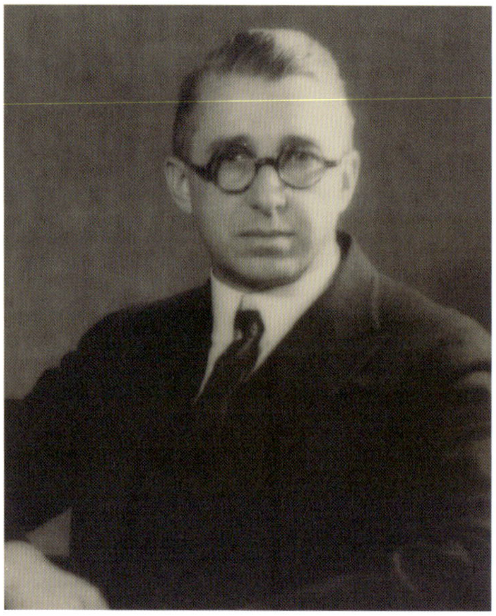

FIG. 12 Samuel S. White 3rd, early 1930s. Photograph by Man Ray (American, 1890–1976). Philadelphia Museum of Art Library and Archives

FIG. 13 Altered Noh Robe. Meiji period (1868–1912), early 20th century. Silk twill weave with silk and metal thread, weft-patterned, brocaded lampas. Philadelphia Museum of Art: The Samuel S. White 3rd and Vera White Collection, 1967-30-329

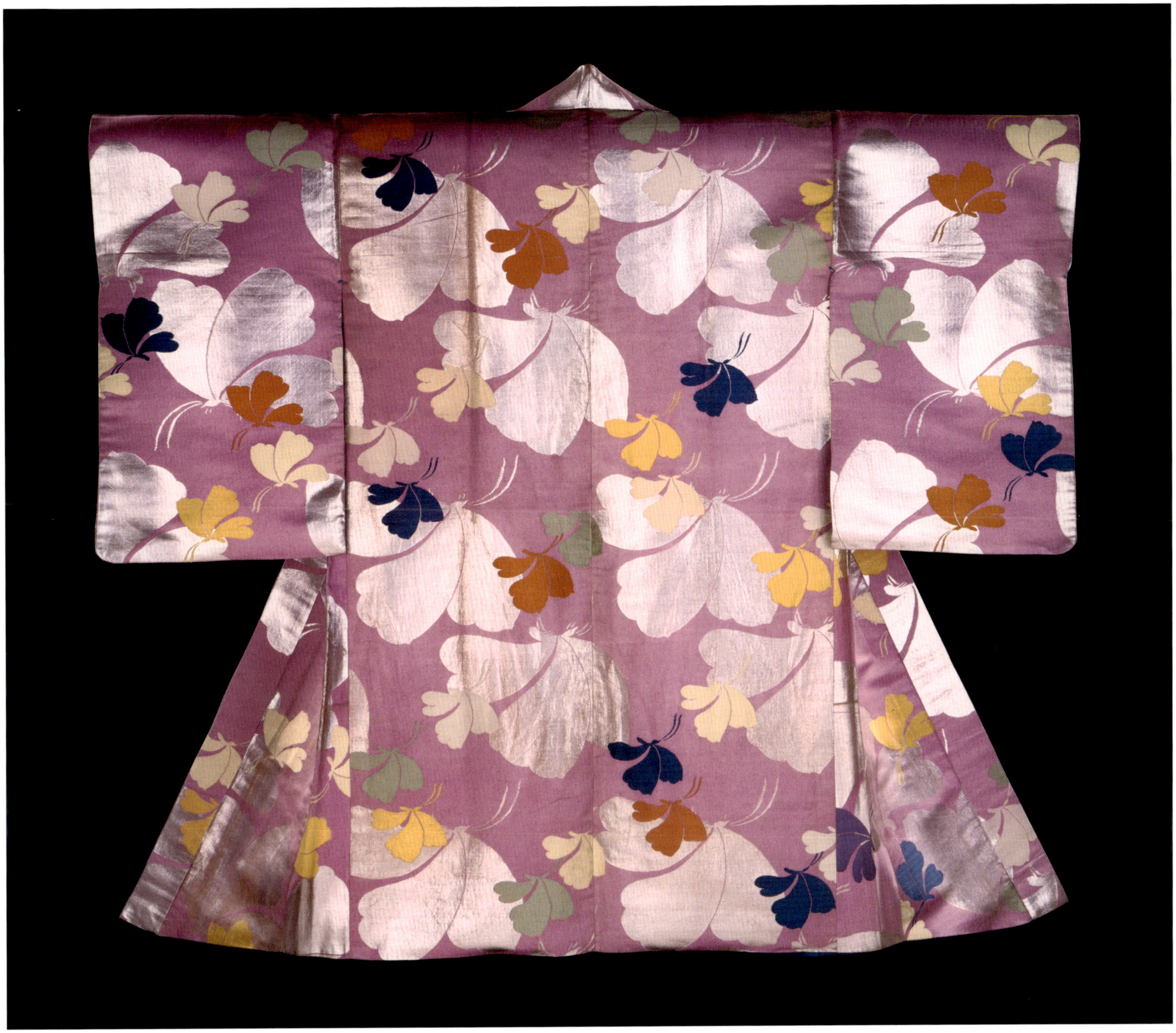

(1888–1966), collected Japanese textiles (fig. 13), and their collection was featured at the museum in 1935 in the exhibition *Art of Japan*, installed by Horace Jayne. The group of seven paintings White purchased in 1903 was bequeathed to the museum in 1967, along with nearly one hundred Japanese prints and decorative arts that he and his wife had collected over the years.[26]

Jayne continued to oversee the Asian art holdings until 1940, returning as acting head of the department from 1953 to 1954 and co–vice director of the museum from 1955 to 1957.[27] His successor was Jean Gordon Lee (1916–1997; fig. 14), who oversaw the installation of the Japanese temple and teahouse as part of the opening of the Far Eastern Wing in 1957, which completed Kimball's plan for the suite of period rooms (fig. 15).[28]

The post–World War II period ushered in renewed interest in the architecture and art of Japan. In 1953 the Japanese government sent the extraordinary exhibition *Japanese Painting and Sculpture* to the National Gallery of Art in Washington, DC, and four additional venues.[29] Langdon Warner, who had served as an expert consultant to the Arts and Monuments Division under the Supreme Commander for the Allied Powers in Japan in 1946, was on the selection committee for the exhibition. A second survey, *Art Treasures from Japan*, traveled to venues in the United States and Canada in 1965–66, including the Philadelphia Museum of Art (fig. 16).[30] On the US side, the Rockefeller Foundation funded artistic and cultural exchange programs, which in 1959 sponsored Munakata Shikō's visit to teach printmaking workshops and exhibit in New York. Munakata came to Philadelphia to work with Arthur Flory (1914–1972) on producing his first lithographs and was invited by prints curator Carl Zigrosser to visit the museum (see no. 92). US interest in Zen Buddhism, fueled in part by the lectures of Daisetz Suzuki at Columbia University in New York, spilled over into related arts such as painting and calligraphy (see no. 93).

Similar to circumstances during the Meiji period (1868–1912), increased travel by Americans to Japan and the availability of important works of art in the postwar years encouraged the collecting of Japanese art. The holdings in Edo-period (1615–1868) art especially were greatly strengthened by purchases and donations

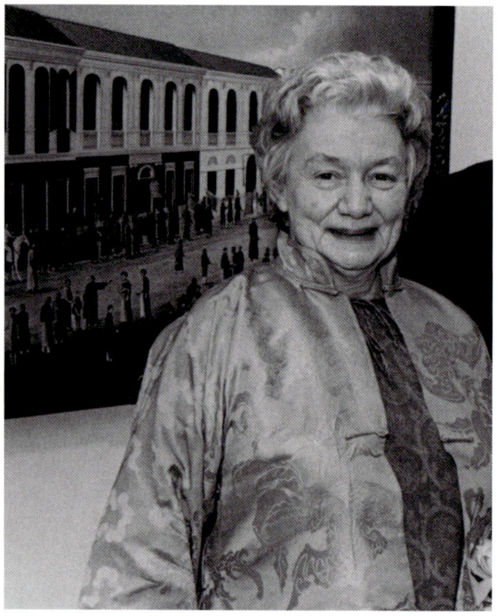

FIG. 14 Jean Gordon Lee, 1984. Philadelphia Museum of Art Library and Archives

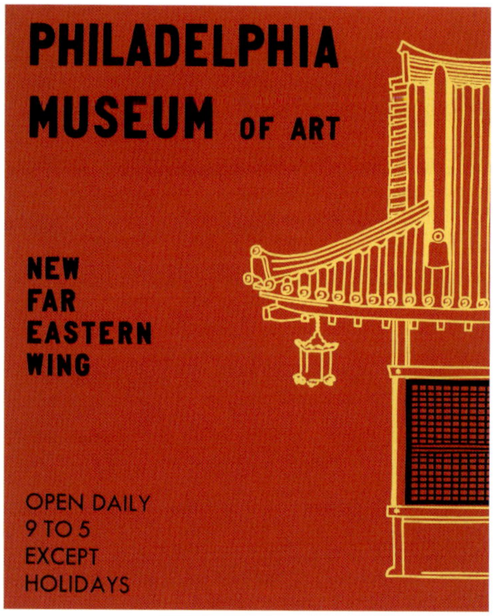

FIG. 15 Poster for the newly opened Far Eastern Wing at the Philadelphia Museum of Art, 1957. Philadelphia Museum of Art Library and Archives

FIG. 16 *Art Treasures from Japan*, Philadelphia Museum of Art, February 13–March 27, 1966. Philadelphia Museum of Art Library and Archives

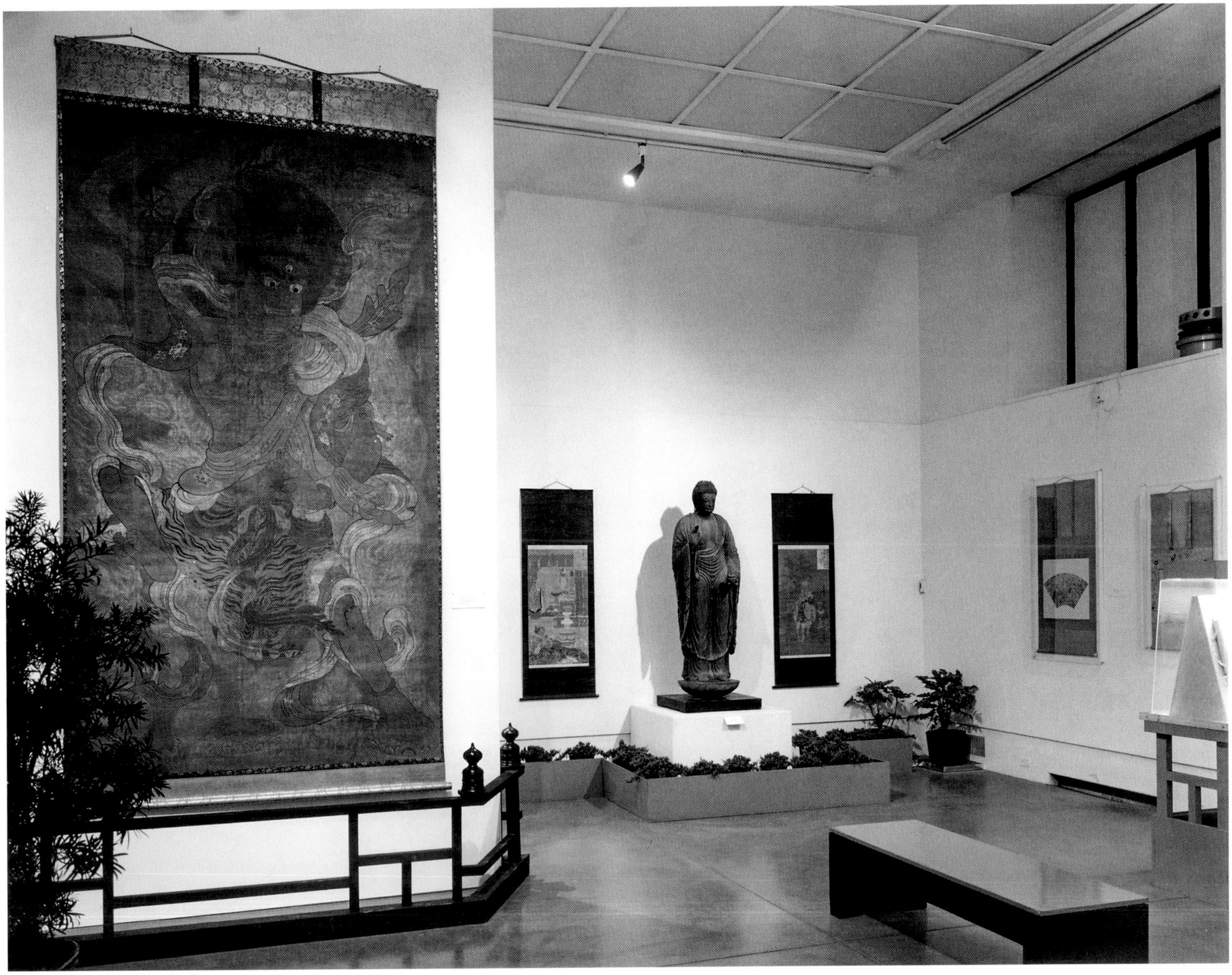

to the museum from the 1960s. In 1965 the Far Eastern Art Committee was formed at the museum, with Henry B. Keep as its first chair, to advise and support the expansion of the department's holdings (see, among others, nos. 16, 18). Many of the important Japanese acquisitions since then came through the gift or funding of committee members, especially William M. Hollis and Andrea M. Baldeck (for example, nos. 4, 21, 22, 26, 28, 40, 41, 48, 51, 53, 58, 71, 80, 85). Three curatorial positions in the department have been endowed by committee members, including in 1996 the Luther W. Brady Curator of Japanese Art, the position I held until my retirement in 2020.

By 1993 the collection had grown to the extent that it became the subject of the third publication in the series Catalogue of Japanese Art in Foreign Collections.[31] During the years that Anne d'Harnoncourt (1943–2008; fig. 17) served as director of the museum, from 1982 to 2008, several major exhibitions of Japanese art were organized by the department that further stimulated interest in painting and related arts and led to significant acquisitions. *Japanese Design: A Survey Since 1950* was developed in collaboration with Kathryn B. Hiesinger, curator of European decorative arts, and presented the first-ever comprehensive overview of modern and contemporary Japanese design (fig. 18). After premiering in Philadelphia in the fall of 1994, the exhibition traveled to the Galleria dell'Triennale in Milan, the Städtische Kunsthalle in Düsseldorf, and the Centre Pompidou–Musée national d'art moderne in Paris, before ending its tour at the Suntory Museum Tempozan in Osaka, Japan, in 1996. *The Arts of Hon'ami Kōetsu: Japanese Renaissance Master*, which opened at the museum in July 2000, revealed the multifarious talents of one of Japan's greatest artists. The majority of objects had never before been shown outside Japan, and the exhibition led to the acquisition of a masterpiece of Kōetsu's calligraphy (fig. 19; see also no. 38). In 2007 the department organized another significant presentation of paintings from Japanese collections, *Ike Taiga and Tokuyama Gyokuran: Japanese Masters of the Brush*. These two artists are now also well represented in the museum's collection owing to interest in their work aroused by this exhibition (fig. 20; see also nos. 50, 51).

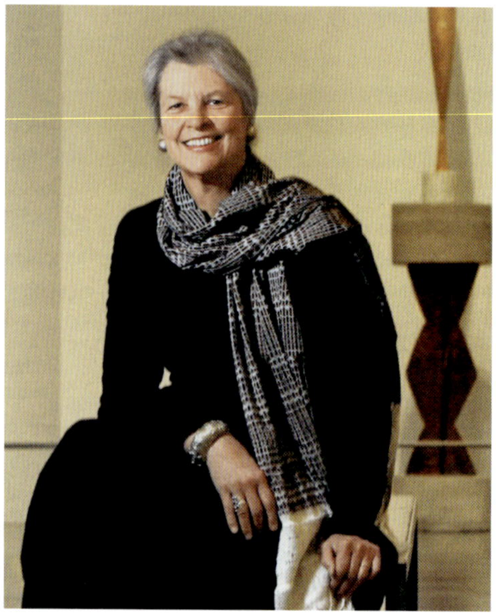

FIG. 17 Anne d'Harnoncourt, 2008. Photograph by Michael Bryant / *Philadelphia Inquirer*

FIG. 18 *Japanese Design: A Survey Since 1950*, Philadelphia Museum of Art, September 5–November 27, 1994. Philadelphia Museum of Art Library and Archives

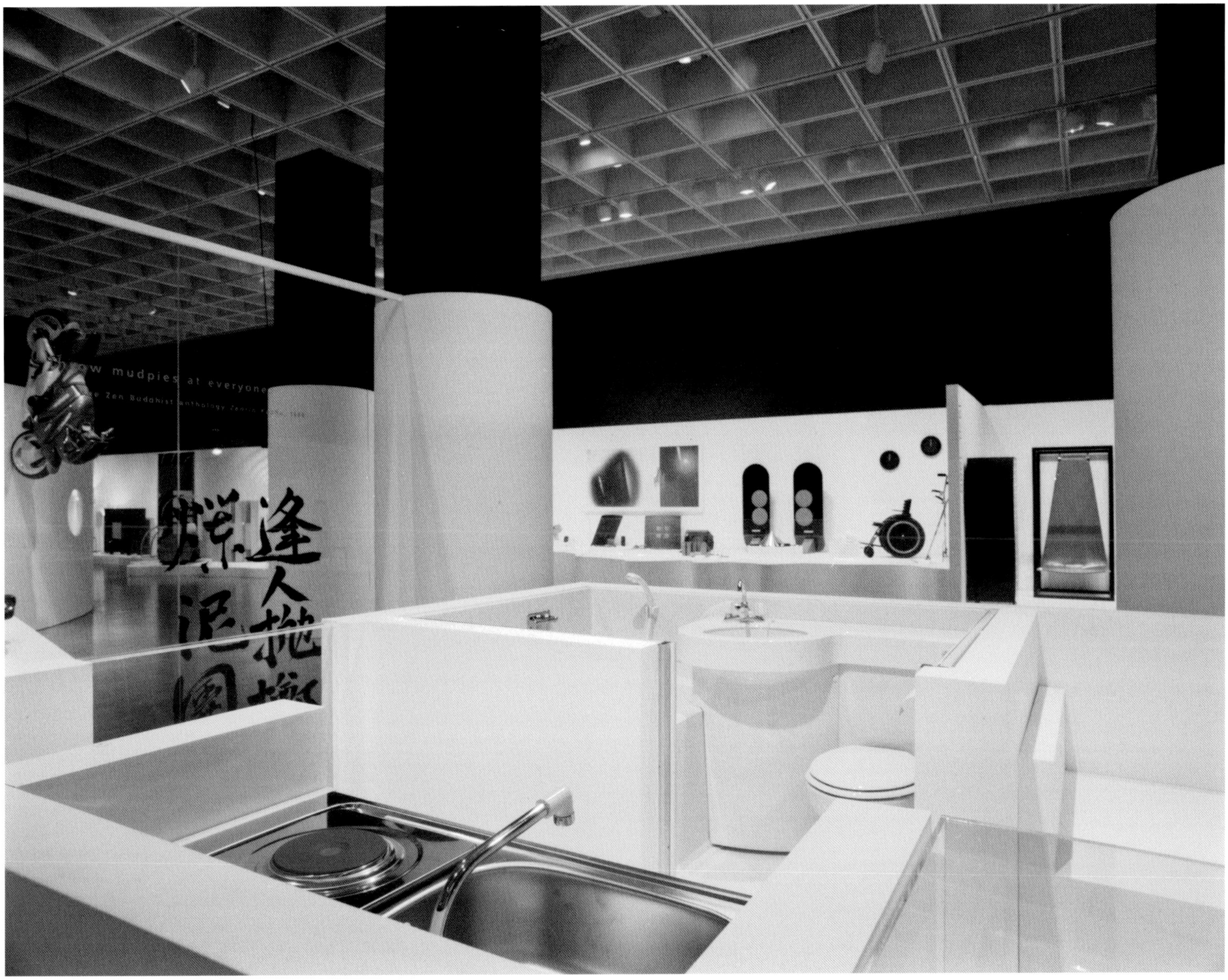
mudpies at everyone
Zen Buddhist anthology

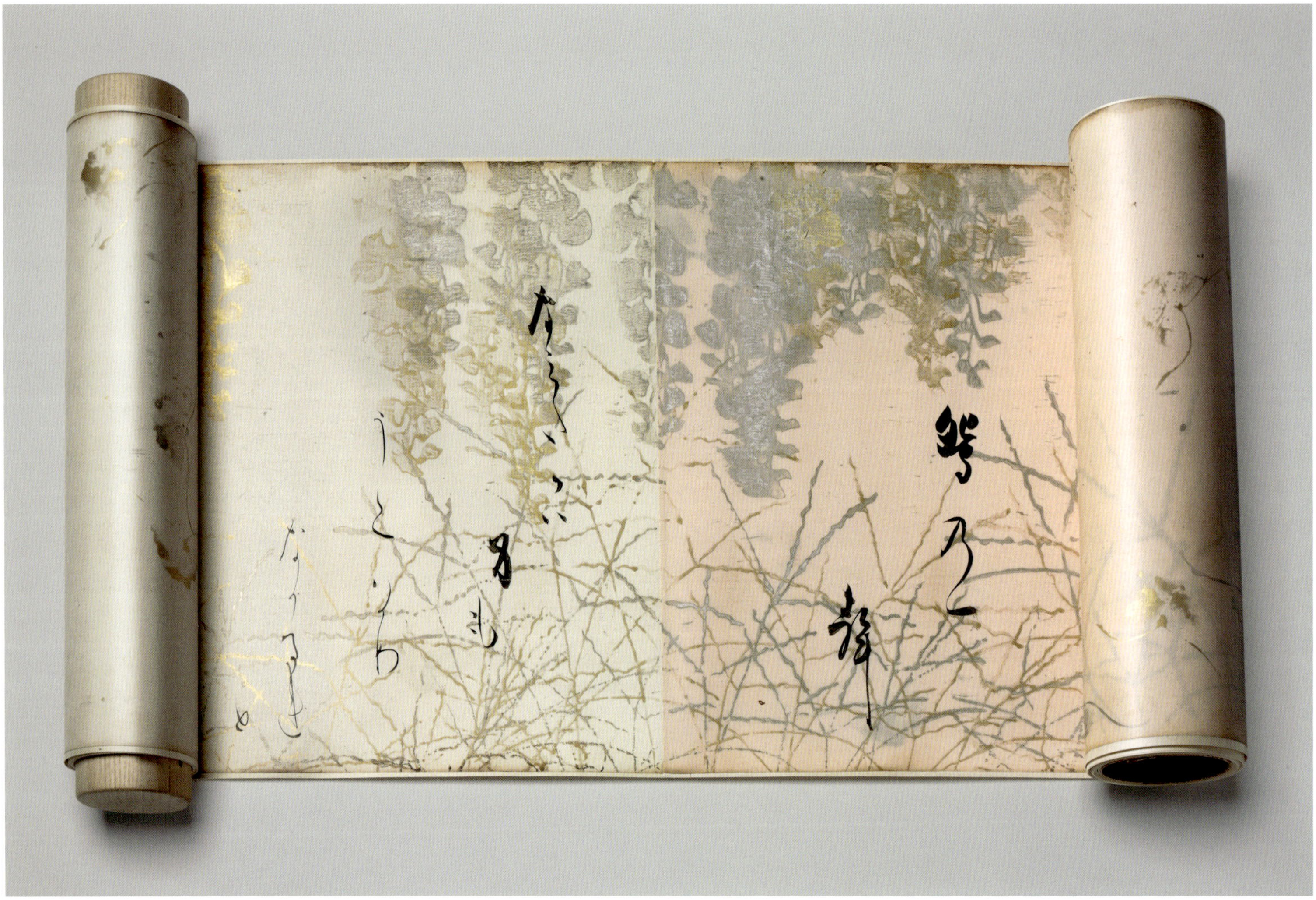

FIG. 19 Hon'ami Kōetsu (Japanese, 1558–1637). Poems from the *Shinkokin wakashū*. Edo period (1615–1868), early 17th century. Ink, gold, and silver on paper, mounted as a handscroll; 13⁵⁄₁₆ in. × 27 ft. 2¾ in. (33.8 × 830 cm). Philadelphia Museum of Art, 125th Anniversary Acquisition: Purchased with funds contributed by the members of the Committee on East Asian Art, 1999-39-1

FIG. 20 Ike Taiga (Japanese, 1723–1776). *Calligraphy and Chinese Figures*. Edo period (1615–1868), 18th century. Ink and color on paper, mounted as a six-panel screen; 65¾ in. × 12 ft. ⅞ in. (167 × 368 cm). Philadelphia Museum of Art: Purchased with the Hollis Fund for East Asian Art Acquisitions, 2016-194-1a

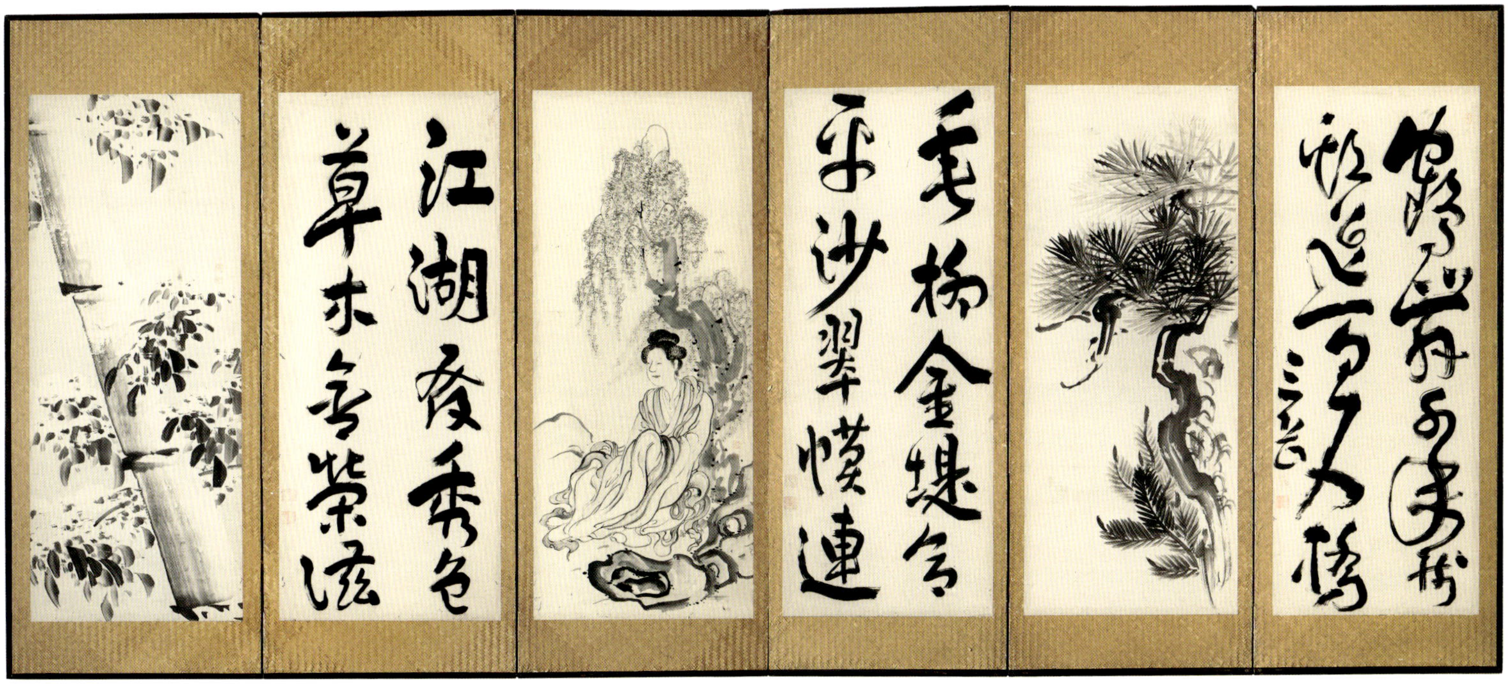

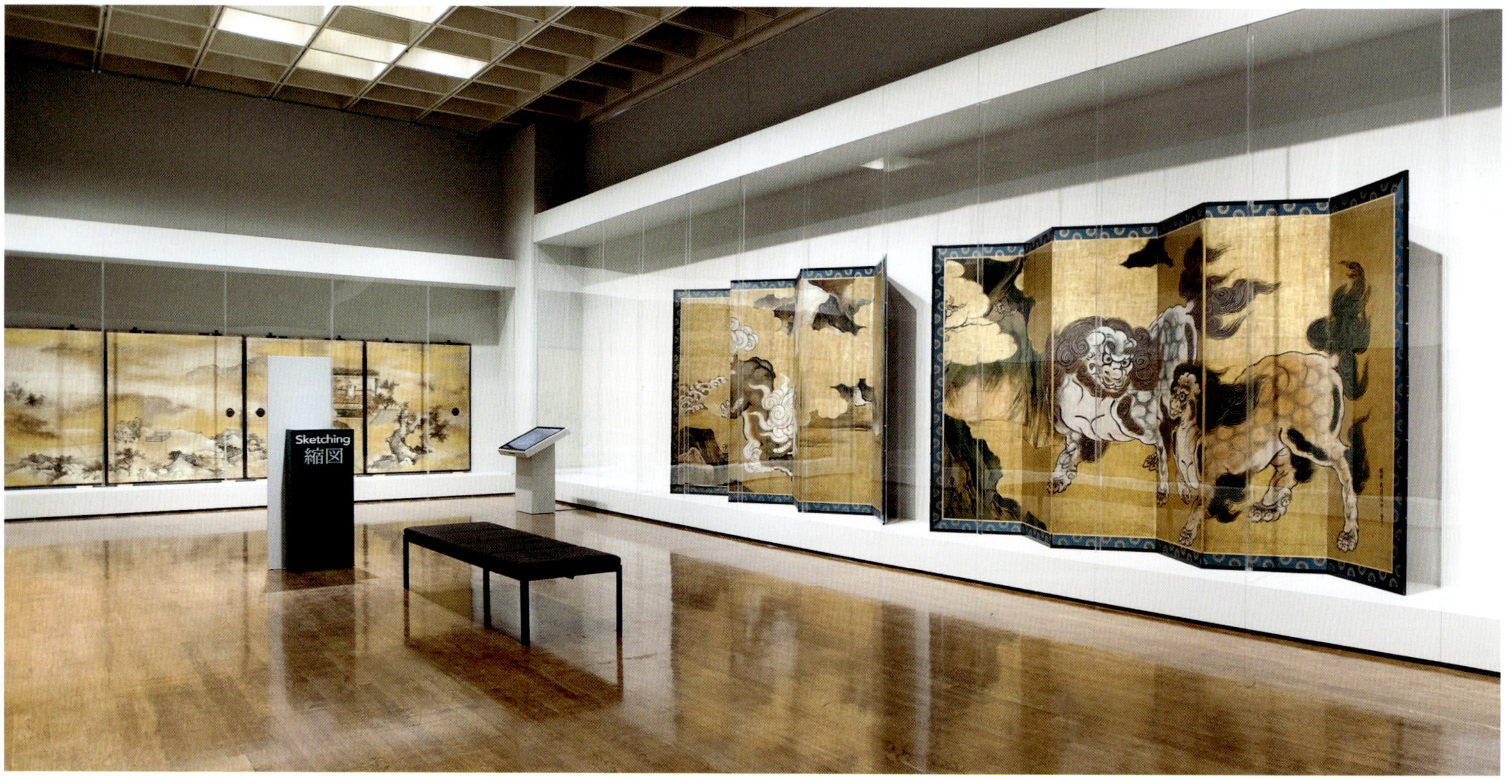
Sketching
縮図

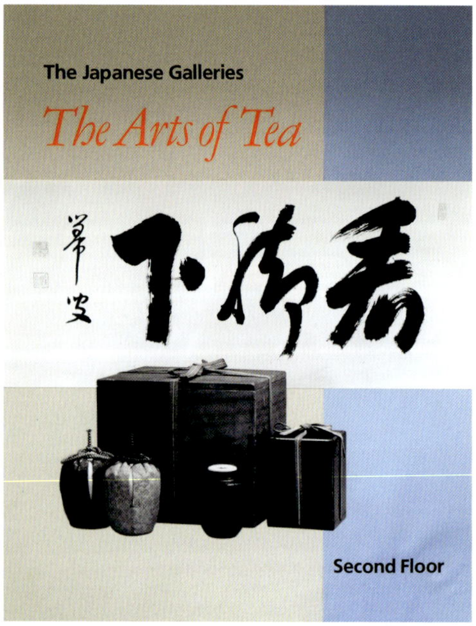
The Japanese Galleries
The Arts of Tea
Second Floor

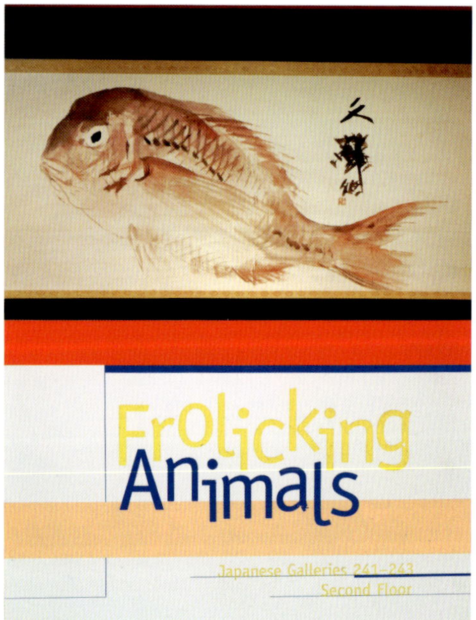
Frolicking
Animals
Japanese Galleries 241–243
Second Floor

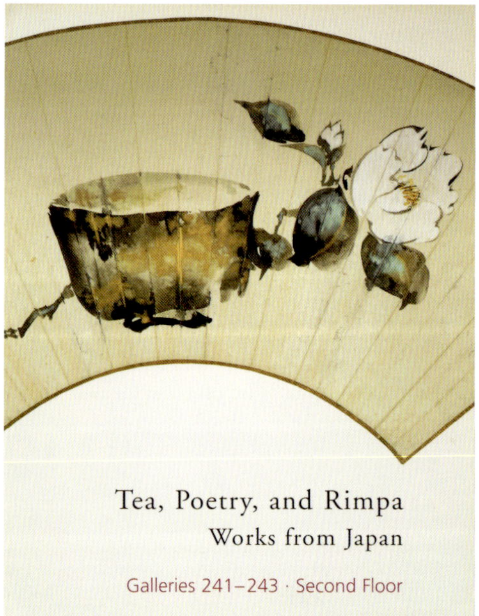
Tea, Poetry, and Rimpa
Works from Japan
Galleries 241–243 · Second Floor

FIG. 21 *Ink and Gold: Art of the Kano*, Philadelphia Museum of Art, February 16–May 10, 2015. Philadelphia Museum of Art Library and Archives

FIGS. 22A–C Posters for annual installations of Japanese art from the permanent collection of the Philadelphia Museum of Art: (left to right) *The Arts of Tea*, September 1988–July 1989; *Frolicking Animals*, September 26, 1997–August 2, 1998; *Tea, Poetry, and Rimpa: Works from Japan*, July 1, 2000–April 29, 2001

FIG. 23 Okada Kenzō (Japanese, b. 1948). Dish. Shōwa period (1926–89), c. 1981. Glazed stoneware (Mashiko kiln), 1½ × 17 in. (3.8 × 43.2 cm). Philadelphia Museum of Art: Purchased with funds contributed by Dr. Luther W. Brady, 1983-79-1

In some instances, existing strengths of the collection have led to major exhibitions, such as *Ink and Gold: Art of the Kano*, held in 2015. Building on the base of the Meiji-period Kano paintings from the Fenollosa collection, the exhibition traced the school's history back to its beginnings in the fifteenth century (fig. 21; see also nos. 76, 78). Because many of the works in the museum's Japanese collection cannot be on view permanently due to conservation concerns such as light sensitivity and climatic conditions, the department also organizes annual thematic exhibitions in the galleries adjacent to the Japanese teahouse garden (figs. 22a–c).

An area of contemporary art in which Japanese artists have had important global influence is crafts, especially ceramics (fig. 23). Many of the early postwar cultural exchanges involved ceramics, including the first exhibition dedicated to works by the eminent potter Kitaōji Rosanjin (1883–1959), at the Museum of Modern Art in New York in 1954. The extensive collection of twentieth-century Japanese crafts donated by Frederick R. McBrien III in 2008 forms the core of what is now one of the major areas of strength in the Philadelphia Museum of Art's Japanese holdings (see no. 87; also no. 86). The Norma Gene Lykes collection of Japanese bamboo baskets and sculpture constitutes another significant group of objects (see no. 97).

Since the first Japanese object entered the museum's collections nearly 150 years ago, the growth of its holdings of the art of Japan has been sporadic yet encompassing, resulting in a collection that represents the wide range and full variety of Japanese art. These objects reflect the interests of individual collectors and curators, as well as changes in aesthetic and social preferences over a century and a half. This publication aims to provide an overview of the highlights of the collection. We encourage visitors to come to the museum for repeat visits to view rotating installations and exhibitions, and we hope that perhaps some will be inspired to become appreciators, collectors, or scholars of Japanese art.

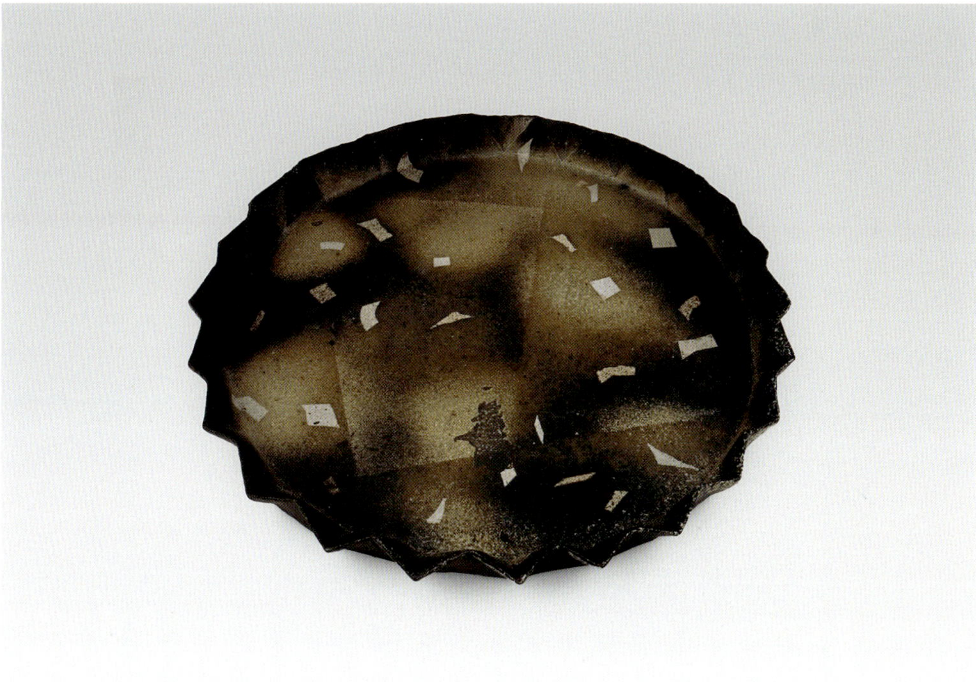

1. Reports appeared in the *Philadelphia Daily News*, June 9 and 11, 1860; the *North American and United States Gazette* (Philadelphia), June 11, 1860; and the *New York Journal of Commerce*, June 11 and 16, 1860. *Frank Leslie's Illustrated Newspaper* 10, no. 237 (June 9, 1860) published an engraving of the embassy members after a Mathew Brady photograph (see fig. 1). When the diplomats arrived in New York, the parade in their honor moved Walt Whitman to write "A Broadway Pageant," later published in *Leaves of Grass*. He described them as "two-sworded princes," as their high daimyo noble rank required these "Princes of Asia" to carry samurai swords.

2. *Scientific American* reported that Japanese craftsmen were "skillful in carving" and manufactured "silk fabrics of every kind, [and] lacquered articles"; "The Japanese, Their Proficiency in Mechanics, Agricultural Sciences, & C.," *Scientific American*, n.s., 2, no. 26 (June 23, 1860): 407. Three lacquer braziers that were among the gifts to President Buchanan are preserved in the National Museum of Natural History, Smithsonian Institution, in Washington, DC. Philadelphians were more familiar with objects imported from China, as direct trade between Philadelphia and China had been thriving since 1784. See Jean Gordon Lee, *Philadelphians and the China Trade, 1784–1844*, exh. cat. (Philadelphia: Philadelphia Museum of Art, 1984).

3. For a detailed account of Tyndale's role in Philadelphia and the Centennial Exhibition, see Felice Fischer, "The Centennial Exhibition, the Philadelphia Museum of Art, and Hector Tyndale," *Magazine Antiques* 161, no. 3 (March 1, 2002): 96–103.

4. "Philadelphia Museum of Art Accession Records, 1897–1902," vol. 4, Registrar's files, Philadelphia Museum of Art.

5. *General Guide to the Collections of the Pennsylvania Museum and School of Industrial Art in Memorial Hall, Fairmount Park, Philadelphia, PA*, rev. ed. (Philadelphia: printed for the Museum, 1910).

6. Early collections of Japanese ceramics in Philadelphia were formed under the influence of then prevalent scientific discoveries and attitudes. Charles Willson Peale (1741–1827) established the first museum in Philadelphia in 1786. Peale's Museum, as it was named, contained both natural history collections as well as paintings. As far as we know, its holdings did not include any examples of Japanese ceramics. One of the earliest and largest extant collections of Japanese pottery was formed by the naturalist Edward Sylvester Morse (1838–1925). Morse, who spent much of his life in Salem, Massachusetts, resided in Japan in 1877, having traveled there to study and teach marine biology. He applied his scientific method of categorizing objects to his collection of more than seven thousand pieces of Japanese ceramics, now housed at the Museum of Fine Arts in Boston and at the Peabody Essex Museum in Salem.

7. For a detailed account of Morris's role in developing the museum's American and European decorative arts collections after Edwin Atlee Barber became director in 1892, see Kathryn Bloom Hiesinger, *Collecting Modern: Design at the Philadelphia Museum of Art Since 1876* (Philadelphia: Philadelphia Museum of Art, 2011), 41–71.

8. I am grateful to Joyce Munro for making me aware of the diary of the trip kept by the Morrises' travel companion, Louise Kellner. The details of their travels and purchases are based on this source; "Around the World," 1889–90, Louise Kellner diaries, Historical Society of Pennsylvania, Philadelphia.

9. The Morrises' photographic travel albums survive and are housed at the Hagley Museum and Library in Wilmington, Delaware; for the Japan album, see "Volume 2: Japan; Trip Around the World, 1889–90," Morris travel albums, Archival Collections at Hagley Museum and Library, box 5, album 5, 1976.432. The teahouse was destroyed in a hurricane in 1955. The Compton estate was bequeathed to the University of Pennsylvania upon Lydia's death and is now known as the Morris Arboretum.

10. See Mrs. Cornelius Stevenson, "Collection of Japanese Helmets," *Bulletin of the Pennsylvania Museum* 9, no. 35 (July 1911): 37–41. These objects were purchased for the museum at the auction of the Klauder Collection held at Samuel T. Freeman and Company in Philadelphia in May 1911. In her will, Lydia carried out other wishes of her brother—namely, that the museum and school each receive $25,000. The John T. Morris Fund enabled the museum to acquire approximately 1,300 objects, beginning in 1938 and continuing through 2011, in combination with other funds.

11. The Morris party and Fenollosa were on the same ship from Yokohama to San Francisco in 1890, although it is not clear that they were acquainted with one another at the time. Fenollosa gave a series of lectures in Philadelphia in the winter of 1904–5, which Morris may well have attended.

12. The Meiji government also invited legal, medical, military, industrial, and scientific specialists to advise and train the Japanese. More than five hundred foreigners were employed by the government at the height of the program in 1875. Edward Morse had been hired by the university to teach zoology in 1877, and he recommended Fenollosa to the school.

13. For details on Fenollosa's activities in Japan, see Felice Fischer, "Meiji Painting from the Fenollosa Collection," special issue, *Philadelphia Museum of Art Bulletin* 88, no. 375 (Autumn 1992): 1–24.

14. Brenda Fenollosa Biddle to Fiske Kimball, November 18, 1940, Fiske Kimball Records, Philadelphia Museum of Art Library and Archives. Biddle was born in Japan and retained fond memories of her early years in Tokyo. See Brenda Fenollosa Biddle, manuscript, October 12, 1952,

Archives Reference Files, Philadelphia Museum of Art Library and Archives.

15. The other was John Ellerton Lodge (1876–1942), who became head of the Boston museum's Asian art department in 1916 and later was the first director of the Freer Gallery of Art in Washington, DC, a position he held from 1920 to 1942.

16. *An Illustrated Catalogue of Japanese Old Fine Arts Displayed at the Japan-British Exhibition, London, 1910*, 2 vols., exh. cat., White City Stadium, London (Tokyo: Shimbi Shoin, 1910). The Japan-British Exhibition was held from May 14 through October 29, 1910. Between the catalogue's two volumes there are a total of ninety pages of text listing seven hundred exhibited objects with 525 of them illustrated on 324 pages of plates.

17. For the complete, complex story of this structure, see Darielle Mason, *Storied Stone: Reframing the Philadelphia Museum of Art's South Indian Temple Hall* (Philadelphia: Philadelphia Museum of Art, 2022).

18. Warner was an inveterate letter writer, and accounts from his travels were published in the museum's *Bulletin*. See "Announcement," *Bulletin of the Pennsylvania Museum* 16, no. 62 (July 1918): 35–37; and "Letters from Mr. Warner and Mr. Jayne," *Bulletin of the Pennsylvania Museum* 19, no. 81 (December 1923): 54–57. See also James Bowie, ed., *Langdon Warner through His Letters* (Bloomington: Indiana University Press, 1966). On Warner's role in building the Chinese collection at the museum, see Hiromi Kinoshita, "Collecting China at the Philadelphia Museum of Art," in *Art of China: Highlights from the Philadelphia Museum of Art*, ed. Hiromi Kinoshita (Philadelphia: Philadelphia Museum of Art, 2018), 19–21.

19. Warner and Jayne collaborated on editing the journal *Eastern Art*. For Warner's role as adviser to the Nelson-Atkins Museum of Art in Kansas City, Missouri, see Patricia J. Graham, "Langdon Warner's Vision for the Japanese Collection at the Nelson-Atkins Museum of Art, 1930–1935," *Journal of the History of Collections* 28, no. 3 (November 2016): 367–82.

20. See David B. Brownlee, *Making a Modern Classic: The Architecture of the Philadelphia Museum of Art* (Philadelphia: Philadelphia Museum of Art, 1997). See also Hiesinger, *Collecting Modern*, 79–87.

21. See Felice Fischer, "Sunkaraku-an: A Teahouse for Philadelphia," *Orientations* 48, no. 6 (November/December 2017): 1–7.

22. Reilly Correspondence file, Registrar's files, Philadelphia Museum of Art.

23. For details on the activities of dealers such as Yamanaka & Co. and the Boston-based dealer Matsuki Bunkio (1867–1940), see Constance J. S. Chen, "Merchants of Asianness: Japanese Art Dealers in the United States in the Early Twentieth Century," *Journal of American Studies* 44, no. 1 (February 2010): 19–46.

24. "Japanese at Cramp's: The Royal Party's [*sic*] Visit the Shipyard and Inspect the Cruisers," *Philadelphia Inquirer*, March 30, 1889.

25. Yoshida was related by marriage to Matsuki Bunkio, who arranged the exhibition of Yoshida's work. At least three drawings by Yoshida dating to before White's 1903 trip were in the latter's collection and are now in the museum's collection; these include *Rokan Buzen* (1901; acc. no. 1960-45-3), *Near Yabe Village Chikugo* (1887; acc. no. 1960-45-4), and *Buildings by Water's Edge* (1902; acc. no. 1960-45-5). See Henry G. Gardiner, "The Samuel S. White, 3rd, and Vera White Collection," *Philadelphia Museum of Art Bulletin* 63, nos. 296–97 (January 1, 1968): 137, nos. 273–75. Yoshida later concentrated on printmaking, for which he is now best known (see no. 83).

26. See Gardiner, "Samuel S. White, 3rd," 71–150. Japanese print collections came under the aegis of the Prints Department, which was headed by Carl Zigrosser (1891–1975) from 1941 until his retirement in 1963. He was succeeded by Kneeland McNulty (1922–1991), who had joined the staff as Zigrosser's assistant in 1952 and was instrumental in enlarging the Japanese print collection.

27. For the history of the Chinese collection of the Philadelphia Museum of Art, see Kinoshita, "Collecting China," 13–31.

28. See *Bulletin of the Pennsylvania Museum* 30, no. 164 (November 1934): 2–31; and *Handbook of the Far Eastern Wing* (Philadelphia: [Philadelphia Museum of Art], 1958).

29. The exhibition was on view at the National Gallery of Art from January 25 to February 25, 1953. It then traveled to the Metropolitan Museum of Art, New York (March 26–May 10, 1953); the Seattle Art Museum (July 9–August 9, 1953); the Art Institute of Chicago (September 15–October 15, 1953); and the Museum of Fine Arts, Boston (November 15–December 17, 1953).

30. The exhibition venues included the Los Angeles County Museum of Art (September 29–November 7, 1965); the Detroit Institute of Arts (December 5, 1965–January 16, 1966); the Philadelphia Museum of Art (February 13–March 27, 1966); and the Royal Ontario Museum, Toronto (April 24–June 5, 1966). It was a class outing from Columbia University to the Philadelphia Museum of Art to see this exhibition that ultimately guided me to pursue the field of Japanese art history and, after I graduated in 1972, employment at the museum. As successor to Jean Lee, I served as department head until my own retirement in 2020.

31. See Association of Scientific Research on Historic and Artistic Works of Japan, *Painting and Sculpture of Philadelphia Museum of Art*, Catalogue of Japanese Art in Foreign Collections 3 (Tokyo: Tokyo National Research Institute of Cultural Properties, 1993).

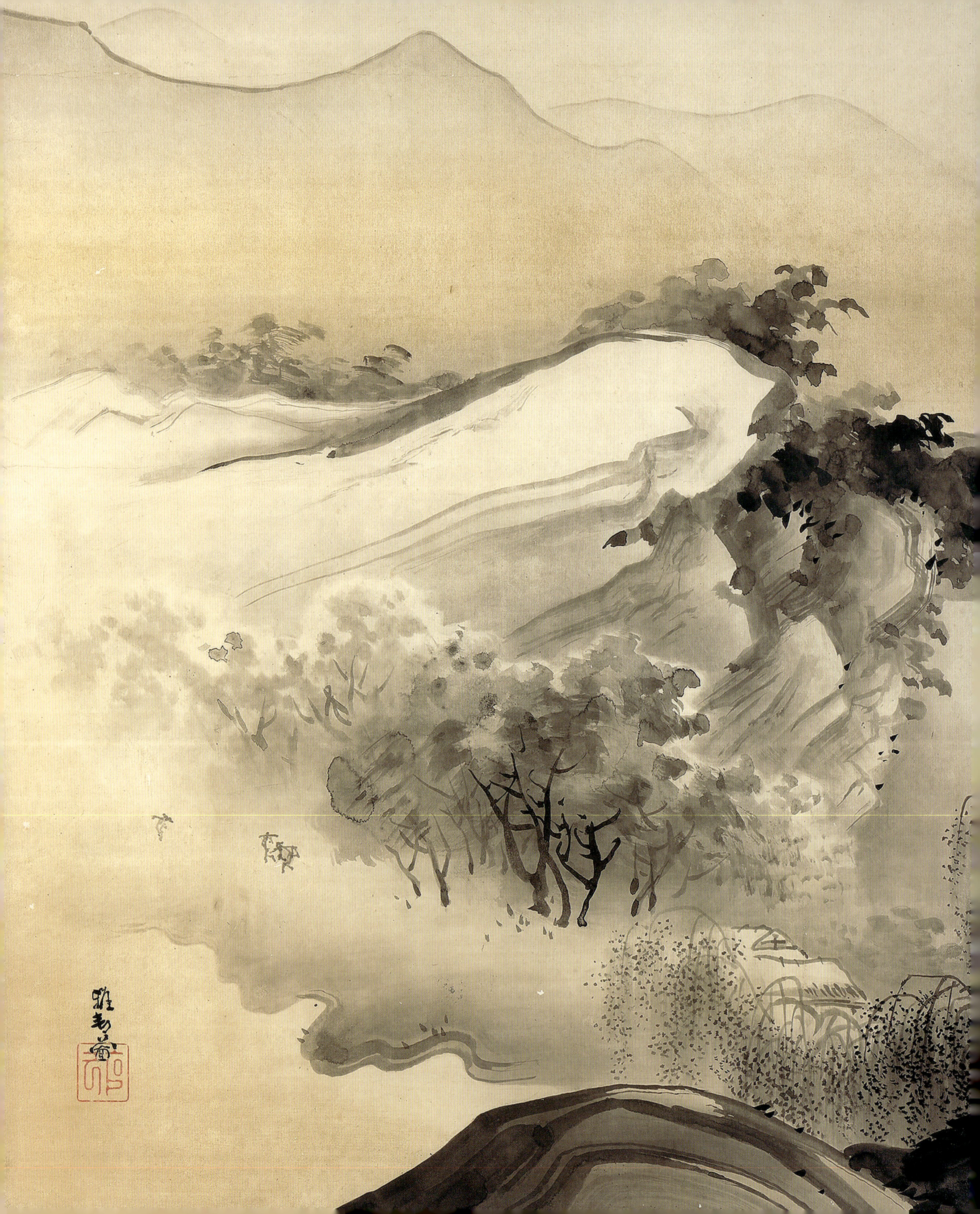

Highlights from the Collection

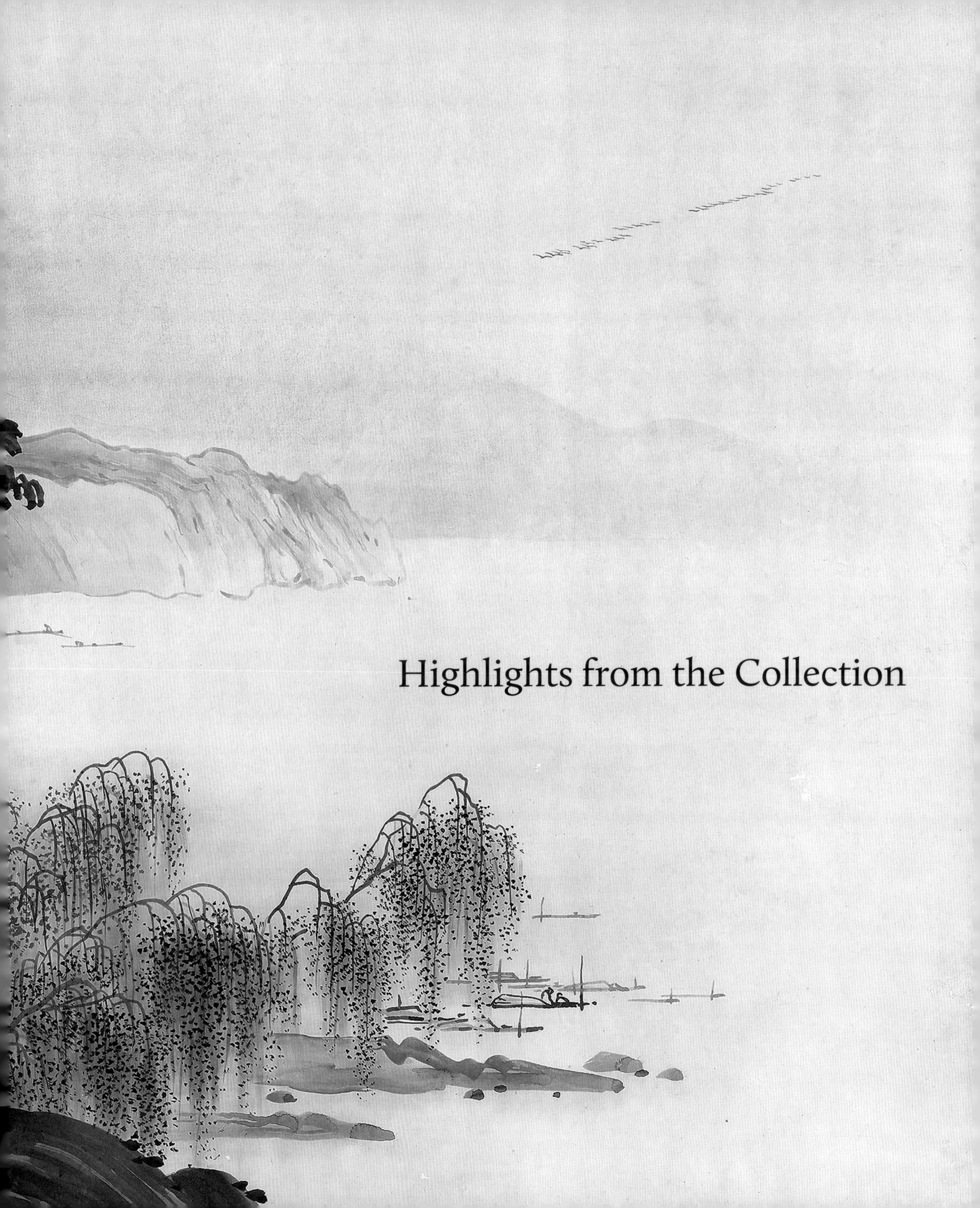

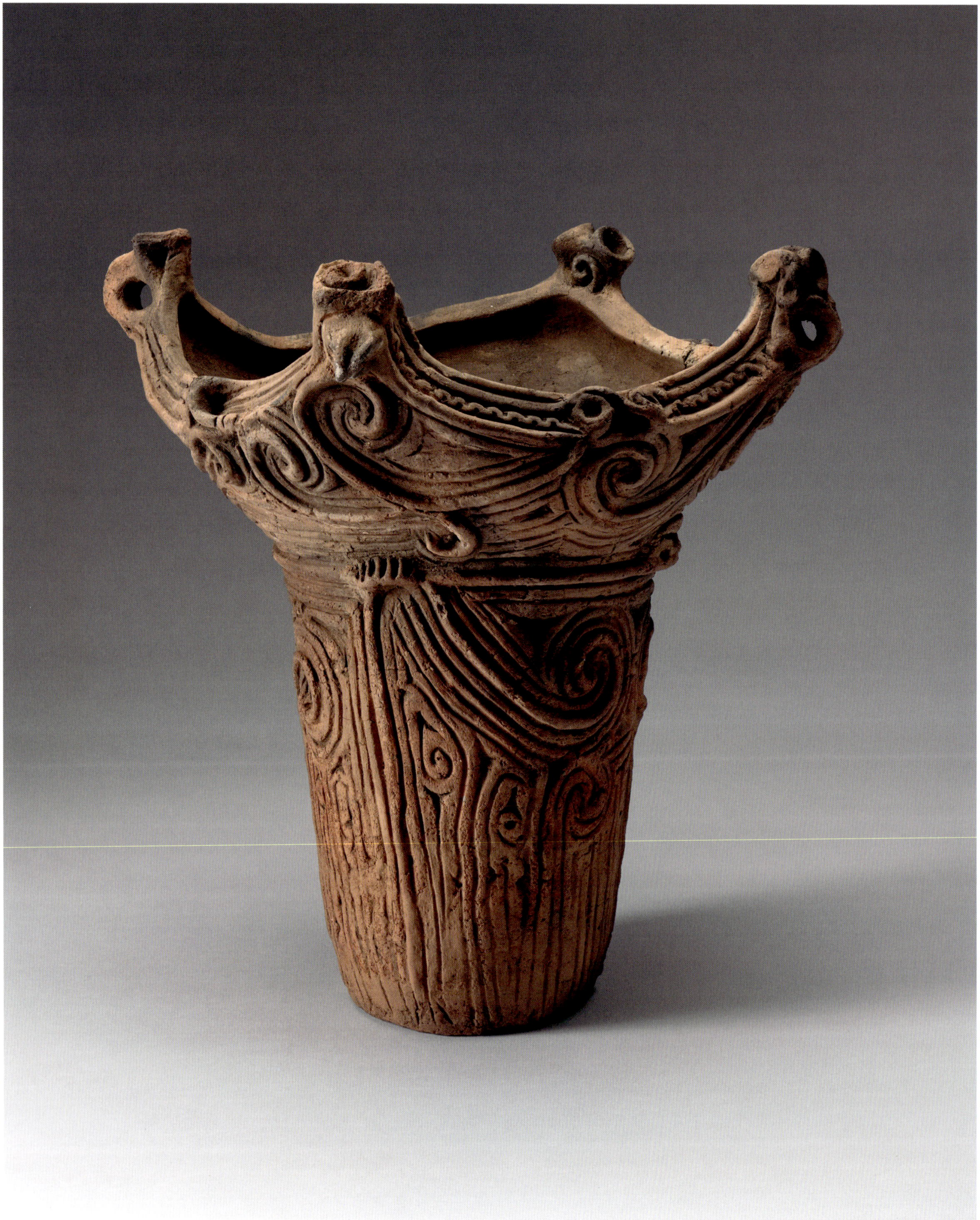

1

Jar

Middle Jōmon period
(3000–2000 BCE)

Earthenware with applied
and incised decoration
H. 14⅛ in. (35.9 cm)

125th Anniversary Acquisition.
Purchased with the Hollis Family
Foundation Fund, the Henry B.
Keep Fund, and the East Asian
Art Revolving Fund, 1999-130-1

Earthenware made in the Japanese archipelago during the period from around 11,000 BCE to 300 BCE is collectively called Jōmon pottery.[1] The American naturalist Edward Sylvester Morse (1838–1925), who was appointed the first professor of zoology at the University of Tokyo in 1877, learned of the Ōmori Shell Mounds and initiated their excavation along with the study of archaeology and anthropology in Japan.[2] The word *Jōmon* is a direct translation of Morse's term "cord marked" and refers to the decorative surface of the vessels that was produced by impressing cords (straw ropes) into the wet clay before firing. This type of pottery was oxidation fired in the open, without using a kiln, at relatively low temperatures, ranging from 1100 to 1500 degrees Fahrenheit.

According to the inscription on the box that accompanied this piece when it was acquired by the museum, the jar was made during the Middle Jōmon period and excavated from a site in Naka-Uonuma, Niigata Prefecture, that is well known for wares dated to that era. During the Incipient and Initial Jōmon phases, the bottoms of vessels were tapered, but from the Early Jōmon period they became flat. This piece, with its flat bottom and stable shape, is representative of Middle Jōmon jars. Circular sloping sides rise to a circular neck that flares upward and outward, ending with a squared-off lip with four corners, three with loops and the fourth with incised decoration. Applied across the surface of the jar's body are coil decorations of vertical cones and scrolls. These decorations are interrupted at the neck by a horizontal line and continue again with additional horizontal motifs of scrolls and swirls. The mouth has a slightly inward curve at the top. The jar's interior is smooth and somewhat darker in color than its exterior. KK

---

1. The Jōmon period is divided into six phases: Incipient (11,000–8000 BCE), Initial (8000–4000 BCE), Early (4000–3000 BCE), Middle (3000–2000 BCE), Late (2000–1000 BCE), and Final (1000–300 BCE).
2. See Morse 1901.

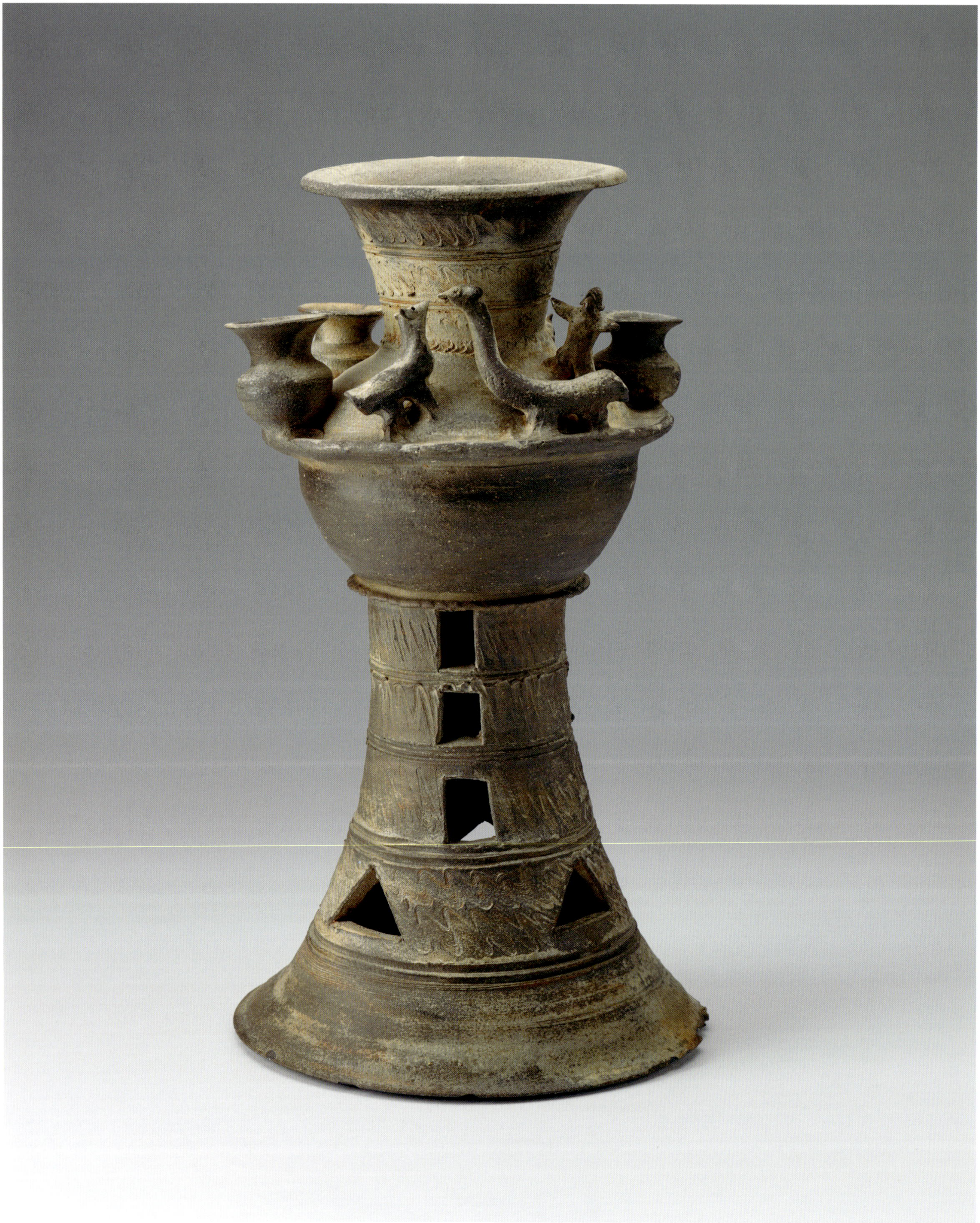

2

Pottery Jar with Pedestal and Animal Decoration

Kofun period (250–538), 6th century

Stoneware (Sue ware)
H. 17¹¹⁄₁₆ in. (45 cm)

Purchased with the Henry B. Keep Fund, 2009-80-1

The technology for producing high-temperature earthenware began in the Jiangnan region of China and was passed on to the Korean peninsula. The *Nihon shoki* (Chronicles of Japan), completed in 720 and the second-oldest book of classical Japanese history, asserts that Sue ware was produced by a migrant from Baekje, one of the Three Kingdoms of Korea. It also states that Prince Amenohiboko of the Silla kingdom and the craftspeople who followed him came to Japan around the first century BCE, during the reign of Emperor Suinin (r. 29 BCE–70 CE). The technology for this type of pottery is believed to have been transmitted from Baekje to the Japanese archipelago via the Kaya region of southern Korea.

Sue pottery is formed with a potter's wheel and fired at high temperatures up to 2500 degrees Fahrenheit using an underground or semiunderground climbing kiln called an anagama. The etymology of the word *sue* for these vessels is not well understood, but one theory is that they were considered hard like iron, *sue* being the Korean word for "iron." An anagama kiln is closed, and thus the reduced oxygen supply requires high heat for combustion. Due to the high firing temperature, the clay not only is harder after baking but takes on a dark blue-gray color.

The pedestal base of this tall jar consists of five tiers; the upper four tiers are decorated with a comb-shaped wavy pattern, and the lower tier is plain and undecorated. Each of the top three tiers has three incised rectangular cutouts that are vertically aligned, while the bottom section has three triangular cutouts spaced between the stacked rectangles. The neck of the jar has three bands of incised decoration and a flaring lip.

Arranged on the shoulder rim are figurines of a human, a long-necked animal, a horse-like animal, and a wild female pig with two piglets, as well as three small jars. According to the *Higo no Kuni no fudoki* (Gazetteer of the northern Kyushu area), edited in 713, these human and animal figures were meant as offerings to gods to calm natural disasters and epidemics. KK

Detail of the jar's shoulder rim, showing three small jars and figurines of a human and a wild female pig with two piglets

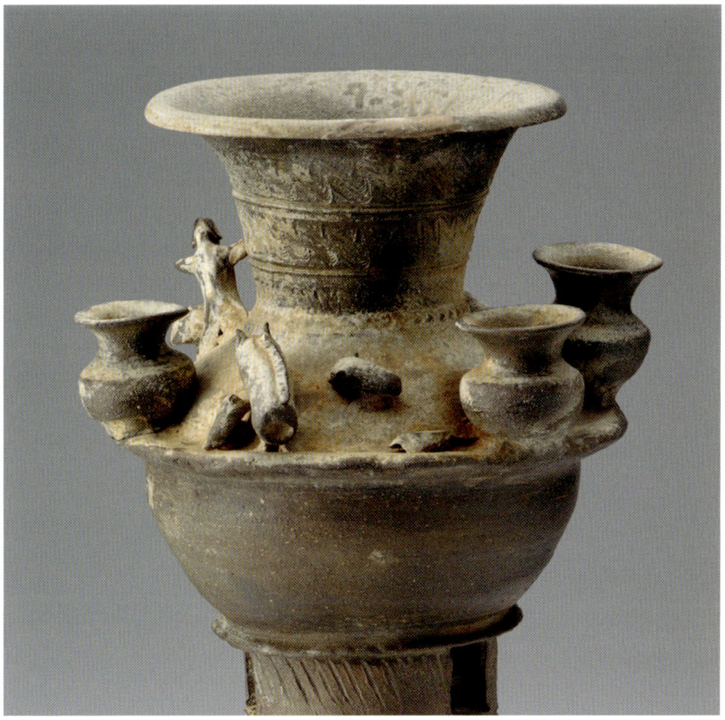

3

Tomb Guardian (*Haniwa*)

Kofun period (250–538), 6th century

Ceramic, H. 25¾ in. (65.4 cm)

Gift of Mrs. John Wintersteen, 1963-46-1

During the years from roughly 250 to 538 CE, referred to as the Kofun period in Japan, large tombs called *kofun* were built for members of the ruling class. Formed of unglazed pottery, *haniwa*, or tomb guardians, are unique to Japan and were used to decorate grave mounds. With the nationwide spread of these burial mounds, *haniwa* eventually took the form of various kinds of buildings, weapons, birds, and animals, and were also used for funeral ceremonies.

According to the *Nihon shoki* (Chronicles of Japan), when a member of the nobility died during the reign of the legendary emperor Suinin (r. 29 BCE–70 CE), it was customary to bury the people who had served them within the tomb. Legend recounts that those who were buried alive cried day and night, and it was unbearable for those left among the living. Nomi no Sukune (life dates unknown), who is believed to have served the emperor, suggested that pottery figures of human beings and animals such as horses and dogs should replace the living people and be set up around the grave mound. The emperor was pleased with this idea and immediately adopted the practice for the tomb of Princess Hibasuhime no mikoto. Additional types of animal- and human-shaped *haniwa* appeared at the end of the fifth century and probably were used to represent various scenes related to funeral rituals.

The museum's *haniwa* is known as a *bujin haniwa* (tomb-guardian warrior) because it has a sword at its waist. The figure also wears a beaded necklace. Its hair is abstractly represented in the ancient Japanese male style of *mizura*, in which the hair is divided at the back of the head and tied at each ear in the shape of the numeral eight. It is hypothesized that full-body *haniwa* were primarily used to represent the deceased, and half-body ones represented those who supported the deceased while alive. KK

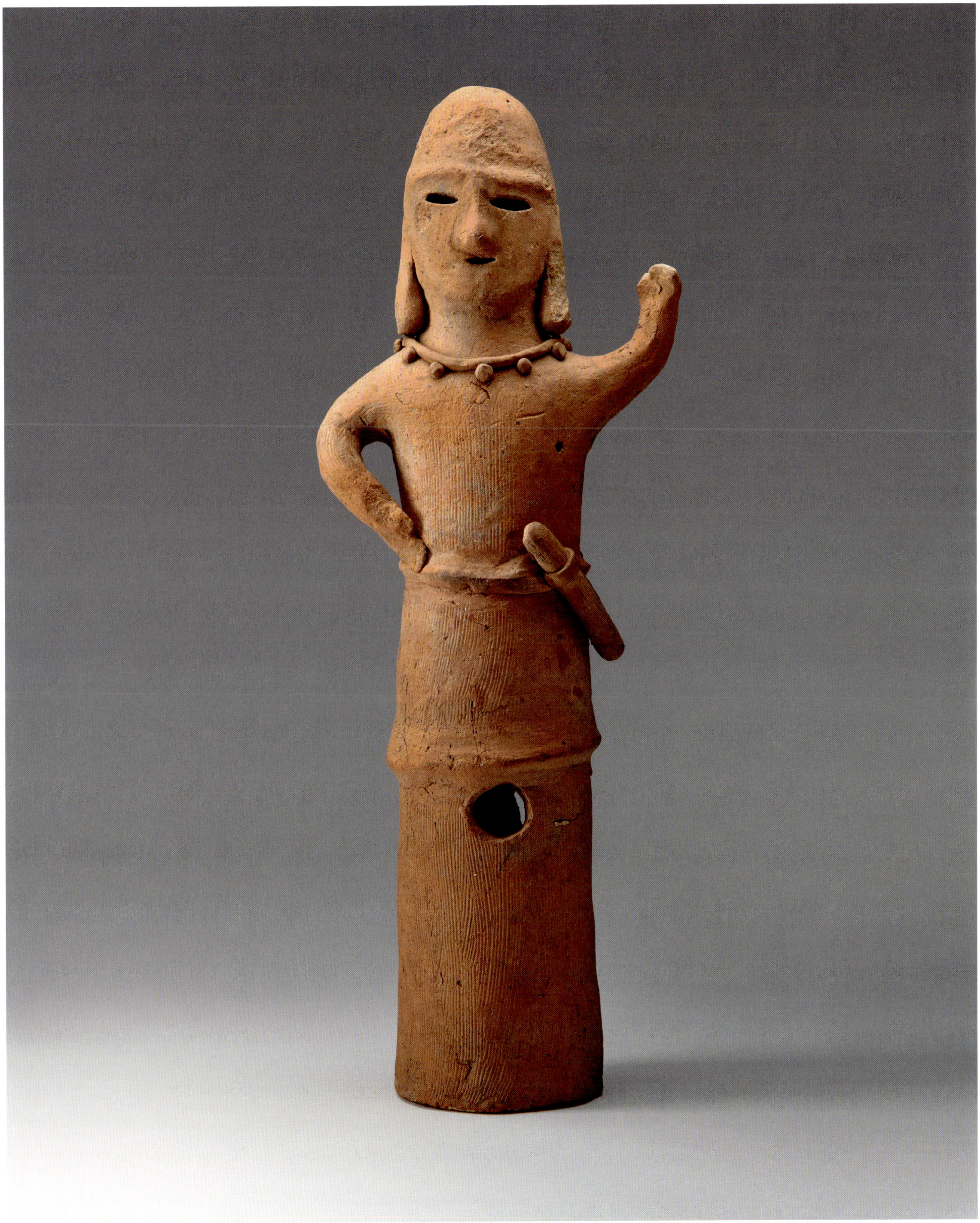

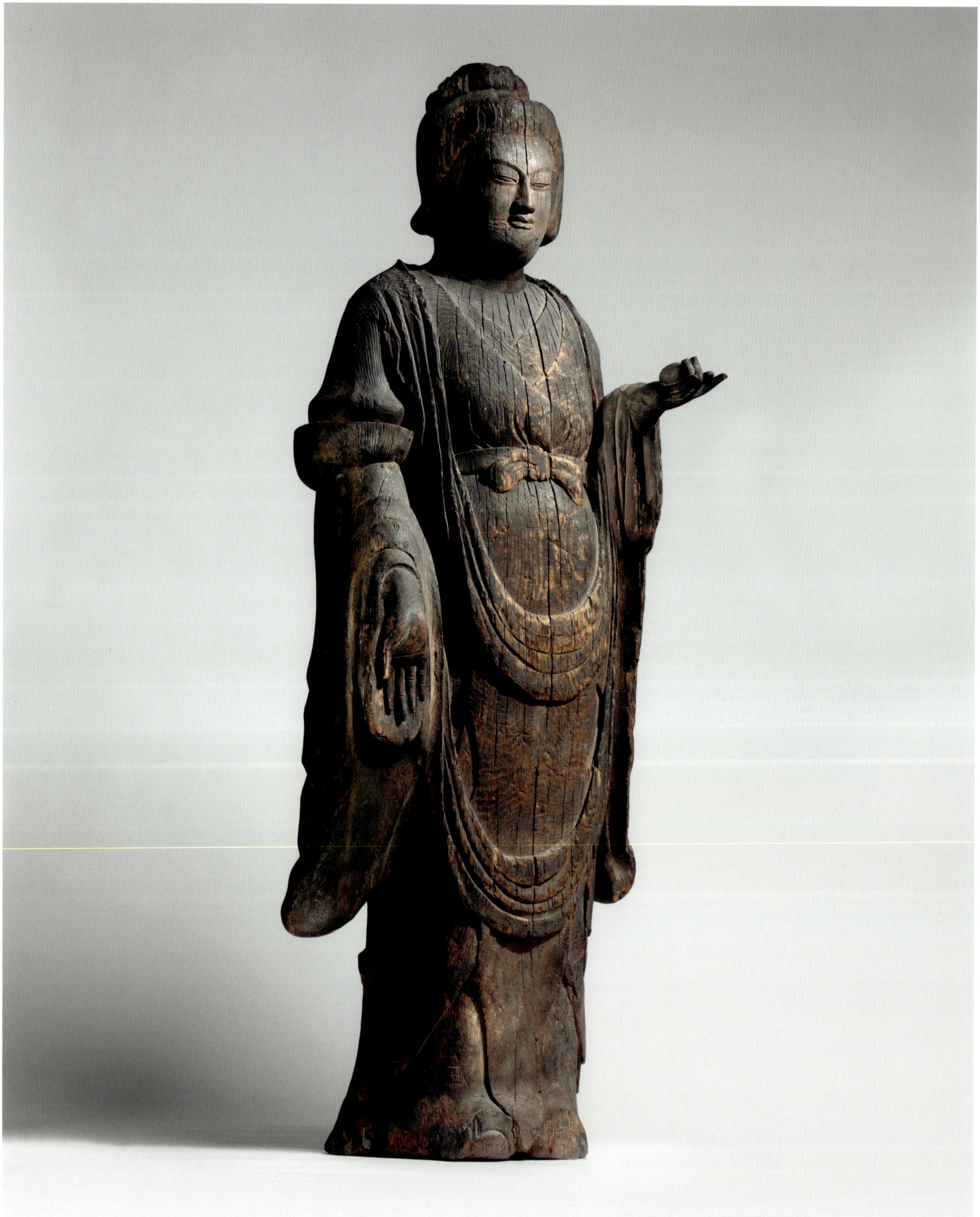

4
Kisshōten

Heian period (794–1185),
late 9th–10th century

Japanese cypress (hinoki)
H. 42⅞ in. (119 cm)

Purchased with funds contributed by Andrea M. Baldeck, M.D., in honor of Felice Fischer, the Luther W. Brady Curator of Japanese Art and Curator of East Asian Art, 2009-78-1

This monumental image of the Buddhist deity Kisshōten was carved from a single block of Japanese cypress (hinoki).[1] Only the hands were carved and added as separate elements. The anonymous sculptor must have had a massive log available, as the diameter of the carved statue reaches nineteen inches (forty-eight centimeters). During the Heian period, when this sculpture was made, most of the hinoki wood was harvested from the mountains of the Kumano region, southwest of Kyoto, the seat of the imperial government and aristocratic patrons of Buddhism.

Buddhism itself had been introduced to Japan from the Chinese mainland via Korea in the mid-sixth century. By the eighth century Japanese priests traveled directly to China, and several important Chinese clerics came to Japan to transmit the Buddhist doctrines. The Chinese monks brought with them not only scriptures and religious artifacts, but also groups of craftspeople who painted and sculpted the Buddhist icons for the newly founded temples in Japan. The early sculptural tradition reflects the Chinese origin, as can still be discerned in this depiction of Kisshōten.

Kisshōten (or Kichijōten; Sanskrit: Srilaksmi) was worshipped in Japan from the eighth century as the goddess who provided abundant harvest, good fortune, and happiness. She appeared in both painted and carved form as a Chinese beauty in the Tang-dynasty (618–907) style, wearing a V-neck robe with long, wide sleeves and tied at the waist with a ribbon. The only accessory is a narrow scarf that extends from the shoulders and wraps around the arms. The hair is also in the Chinese style, with a flattened chignon at the top.

The sculptor used the grain of the wood to accentuate the vertical lines of the hair and flowing robe, as can be seen now, but which would originally have been covered with pigments over a layer of white gesso. The dignified solidity of the torso is counterbalanced by the deeply carved, sinuous curves of the sleeves and scarf, as well as by the hands and face. The hands are most likely later replacements, but they reflect the original iconography. The right hand is held in the gesture (mudra) known as *segan-in*, indicating Buddhist charity or granting of desires. In the raised left hand, Kisshōten holds the wish-granting jewel (*nyoi-shu*), symbolizing her power to bring happiness by granting her devotees' prayers for good fortune and wealth.

Kisshōten's beneficent nature is best evoked in the carving of the face, by the eyes gazing down at the worshipper and the smile at once reserved yet tender. Indeed, as the cult of Kisshōten grew, this deity transcended the role as spelled out in the Buddhist scriptures, such as the *Konkōmyō saishō-ō-kyō* (*Golden Splendor Sutra*), to become part of the daily lives of the Japanese people. Her worshippers spread beyond the Heian court women to lowly farmers praying for a good harvest. She became the ideal of beauty and wealth, often appearing in Japanese popular lore as one of the seven gods of good fortune. In this statue the artisan has captured both the awe-inspiring dignity of a goddess, and the solid, down-to-earth quality of approachable generosity for which Kisshōten remains revered to this day. FF

1. Hinoki or white cedar (*Chamaecyparis obtusa* [Cupressaceae]) is a species native to Japan, widely grown for its high-quality building timber.

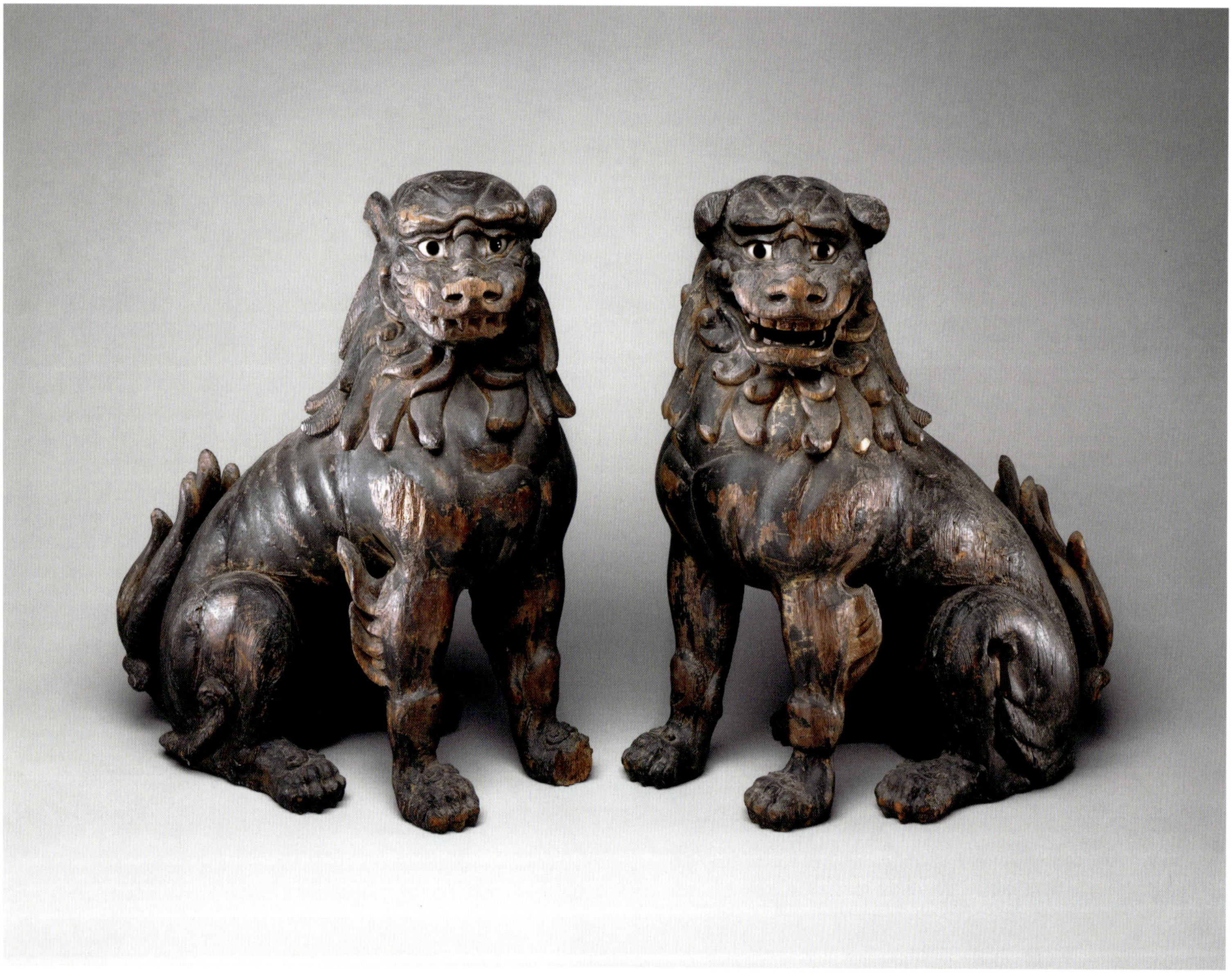

5

Pair of Guardian Lions

Kamakura period (1185–1333), 14th century

Wood with traces of lacquer and gilt decoration, each: 22 13/16 × 9 13/16 × 19 11/16 in. (57.9 × 24.9 × 50 cm)

Gift of John H. Converse and Samuel M. Vauclain, F1906-2-1a,b

In India, where the animal was indigenous, the lion was used as a symbol of Shakyamuni, the historical Buddha, who was called "lion of the Sakya clan." The lion imagery is believed to have been brought to Japan from Korea along with the introduction of Buddhism, and statue pairs such as this are often referred to as *kara shishi* (lion of China) and *koma inu* (dog of Korea).[1] They were placed as symbolic guardians at the door to Buddhist sanctuaries. Typically, one lion has its mouth open, and the other has a closed mouth.

Skillfully employing the joined-wood (*yosegi*) technique (see no. 8), the sculptor of this lion pair has endowed them with large, powerful chests and naturalistically rounded torsos narrowing at the haunches. There is a hint of movement in the paws placed slightly forward and the turn of the heads. The artist's focus is on the heads, with their full, flowing manes curling down the shoulders, and their alert, keen expressions, emphasized by inset crystal or glass eyes. Yet, there can be little doubt that the sculptor who created these lions was imagining an animal he had never seen in the flesh and instead relied on other sculptures for his models.

These lions represent a relatively rare instance in which we can clearly trace the route by which an object of such antiquity came to the museum. The first reference to them is a 1906 article in the museum's *Bulletin*.[2] The sculptures were part of an ensemble of Buddhist statuary and ritual implements displayed in a temple gate exhibited at the Louisiana Purchase Exposition held in Saint Louis in 1904.[3] At the close of the exhibition, the Philadelphians Samuel M. Vauclain and John H. Converse purchased the temple gate with its contents and donated it to the city's Fairmount Park.[4] The gate was reassembled in the park, near the site of the 1876 Centennial Japanese bazaar, and the contents were deposited with the museum in 1906 (figs. 24, 25). FF

---

1. *Kara shishi* (or *agyō*, female) and *koma inu* (or *ungyo*, male). The *a* and *un* of the alternative terms represent the first and last letters of the Sanskrit alphabet.
2. "Nio-Mon" 1906. This notice describes them as "two sacred dogs (*koma-inu*) said to be the work of the famous Unkei who lived in the thirteenth century."
3. The Seion-ji is a Rinzai-sect Buddhist temple located in Ibaraki Prefecture (Shimo Furuuchi town). It was dedicated in 1344 (Kanei 3) by the daimyo Satake Yoshiatsu I (1311–1362) to honor his father Sadayoshi (d. 1352). A Buddhist triad dated to 1352 was the central statuary and is now housed at Hōkō-ji in Shizuoka Prefecture. The temple gate itself was built around 1600 by "Lord Satake, Minister of Justice," a descendant of the temple founder. The information about the temple is from a brochure published by the temple's owner, "K. Sano," after the close of the Saint Louis exposition.
4. Samuel M. Vauclain (1856–1940) was a museum trustee and served on the Fairmount Park Commission. John H. Converse (1840–1910) was likewise on the commission and was Vauclain's partner at Baldwin Locomotive Works, which exhibited at the Saint Louis exposition.

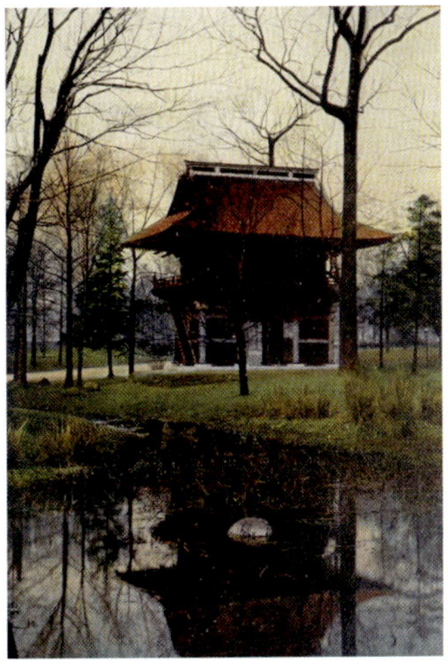

FIG. 24 Temple gate, Fairmount Park, Philadelphia, c. 1908. Hand-colored postcard by the Hugh C. Leighton Co. Private collection

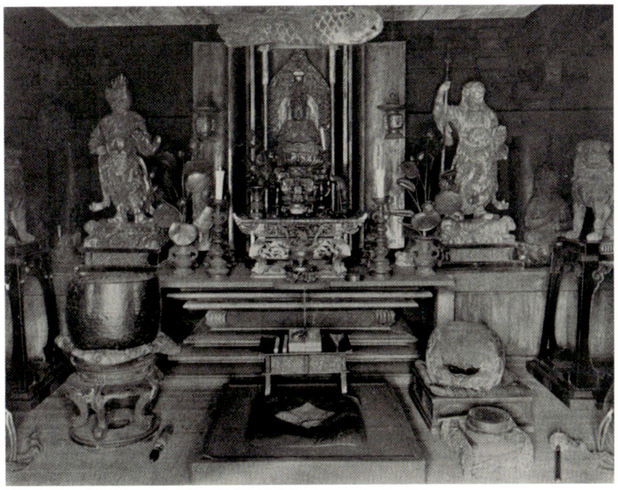

FIG. 25 Memorial Hall installation of the pair of guardian lions from the temple gate in Fairmount Park, Philadelphia, 1906. Philadelphia Museum of Art Library and Archives

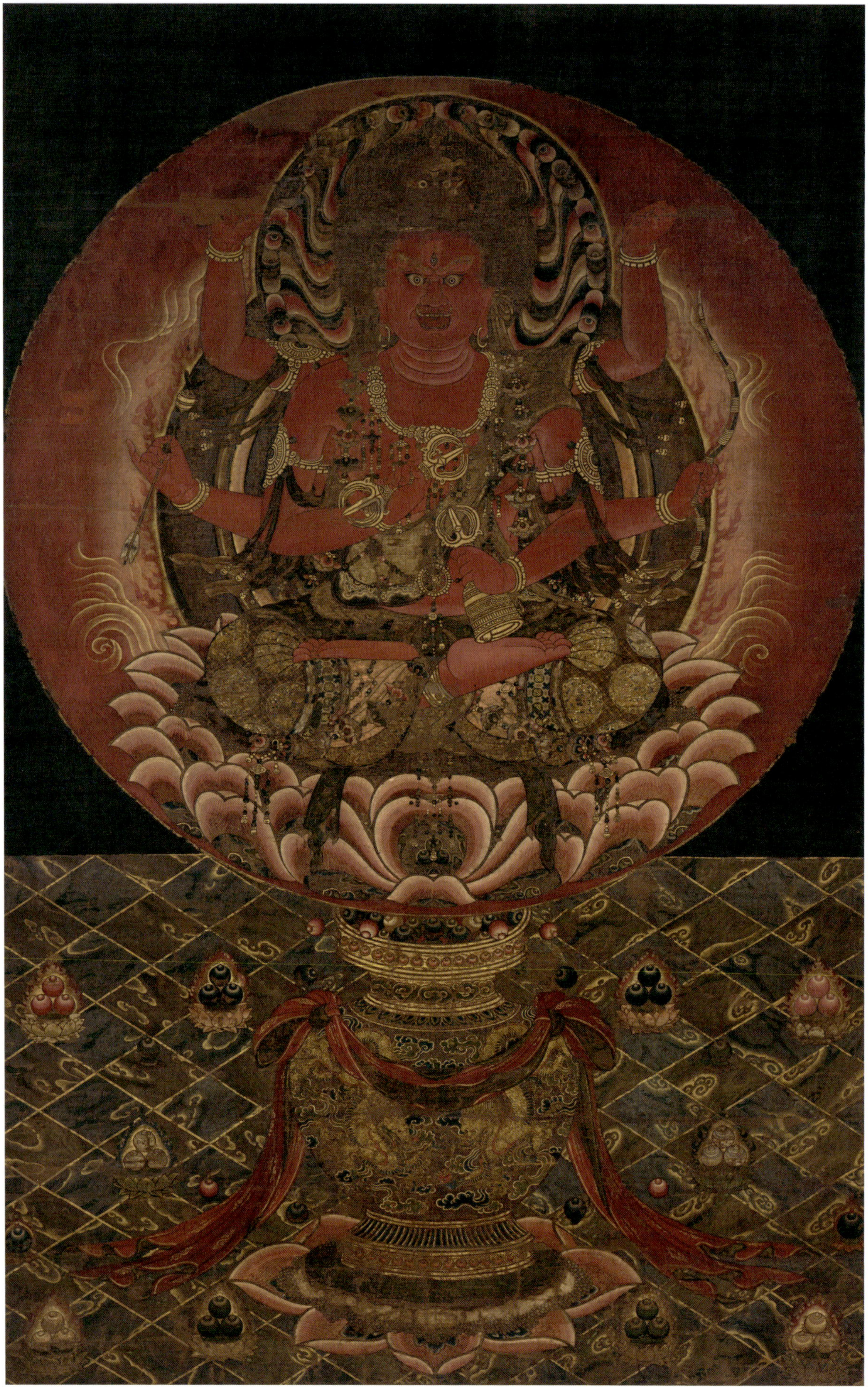

6

Aizen Myōō

Nambokuchō period (1333–92), 14th century

Colors and cut gold on silk, mounted as a hanging scroll
45 × 27¾ in. (114.3 × 70.5 cm)

Purchased with the John T. Morris Fund, 1960-7-1

Aizen Myōō (Sanskrit: Rāgarāja) is the avatar of Kongōsatta Bodhisattva (Vajrasattva), a deity venerated in the Esoteric and Vajrayana Buddhist traditions. As described in the *Kongōburōkaku-issaiyugayugyō-kyō* (Scripture of all the yogas and yogis of the Vajra-peak pavilion), Aizen Myōō has three eyes and six arms, and wears a head of a lion as a crown. His red skin color is described as "like the shining sun," and his hair rises like flames. The furious eyes with raised eyebrows and the open mouth with fangs express his fierce determination to defeat evil. Each of the ten petals of the lotus throne on which he sits has three jewels. Beneath the throne, colorful jewels of good fortune are stored in a treasure vase, also placed on lotus petals and decorated with a pair of dragons in clouds. Additional jewels are depicted on the floor.

Images of Aizen Myōō commonly include a lotus flower and a jewel, or a fist without a weapon, in the upper hands; a bow and an arrow in the middle hands; and a *vajra* (the diamond that cuts through illusion) and a *vajra* bell in the lower hands. Unfortunately, here the paint that depicted Aizen Myōō's attributes in his upper hands has peeled off, but his upper-right hand appears to be held in a fist. The deity wears a *jōhaku* (cloth) on his left shoulder and *kun* (skirt) that are decorated with *kirikane* (gold leaf cut into strips) and various beautiful patterns. All elements of the composition are delicately and elegantly depicted with gold and high-quality mineral pigments.

Retired Emperor Shirakawa (1053–1129) instituted the ritual of Nyohō Aizen Ōhō at the imperial palace in 1080 to pray for peace, safe childbirth, and so on, with jewels placed next to a sculpture or painting of Aizen Myōō. As the ritual continued to be practiced until 1371,[1] this painting may have been made for the imperial court. KK

1. Kanagawa Kenritsu Kanazawa Bunko 2011, 4–8.

Detail of cut-gold decoration at lower left

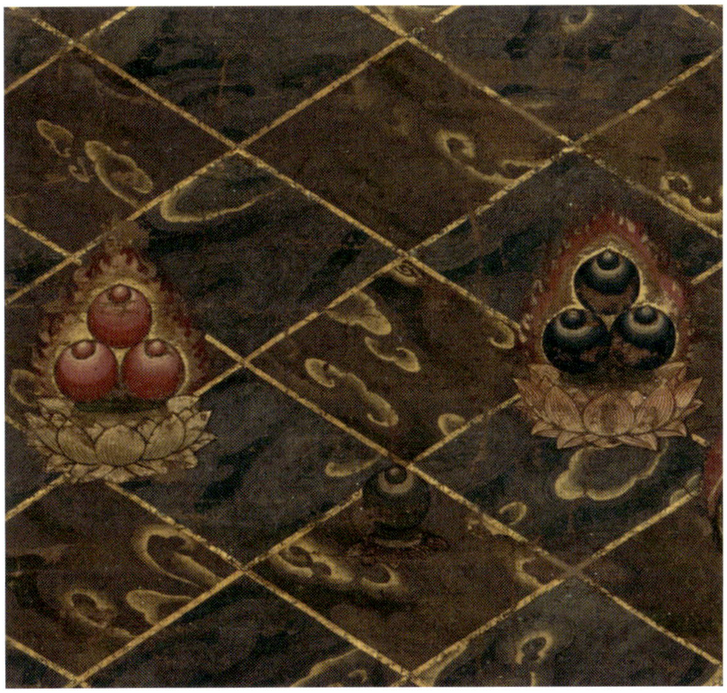

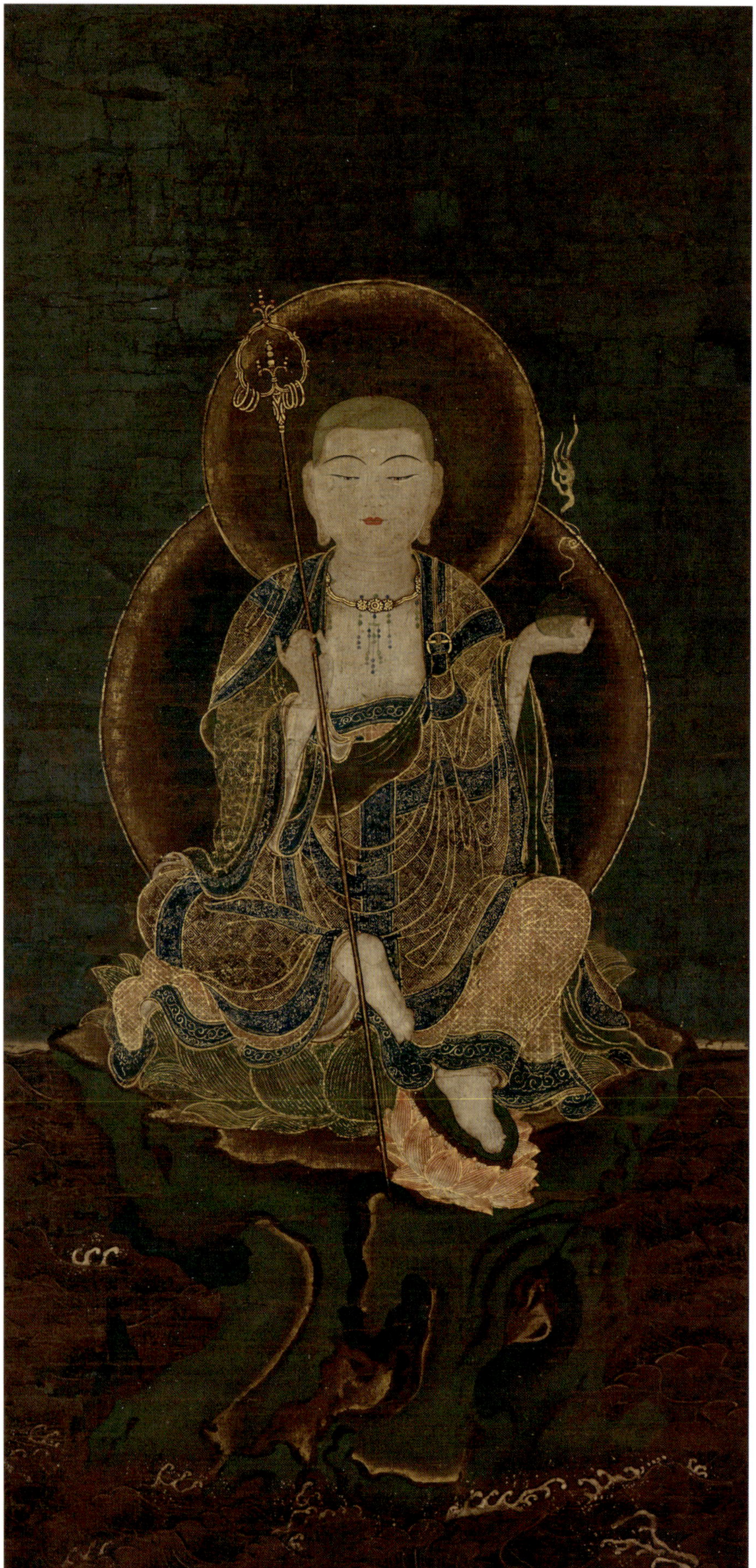

7

Seated Jizō

Kamakura period (1185–1333), early 14th century

Ink, colors, and cut and reverse-stamped gold on silk, mounted as a hanging scroll; 33⅜ × 15¾ in. (84.8 × 40 cm)

Gift of the Friends of the Philadelphia Museum of Art, 1983-16-1

Jizō, or Ksitigarbha in Sanskrit, has been venerated in Japan since the tenth century as the bodhisattva who saves the sentient beings wandering the six realms of existence (*rokudō*) into which humans might be reborn if they do not attain salvation. Because of this association, Jizō became the protector of the vulnerable or weak, such as children, women in childbirth, and travelers. Jizō is most often depicted in the form of a Buddhist monk with a shaved head, wearing priestly robes and holding a staff in his right hand, a standard possession of mendicant priests to announce their approach. The rich cut-gold design of his robes and the luminous gold of the double halo attest to Jizō's divinity, and the jewel (*cintamani*) in his left hand symbolizes his power to respond to the prayers and invocations of the faithful. Jizō sits on a lotus pedestal, the lotus being symbolic of rebirth. Its petals defined by thin gold-leaf strips, the lotus rests on a rocky promontory amid a sea of rolling waves topped by whitecaps, which may be a reference to Jizō's legendary abode, Mount Kharadiya.[1]

The ample use of gold leaf and the luminous gold of the double halo create an aura of otherworldliness, an effect enhanced by the application of gold leaf from the back of the silk, a technique known as *urahaku.* The white coloration of the bodhisattva's skin has likewise been painted from the reverse, with the facial features and fingers brushed in delicate, wirelike red lines. In the subtle balance between the intricacy of the cut gold and the simplicity of the brushstrokes in the face and hands, the anonymous artist has achieved a felicitous harmony of elements, transmitting both the divine spirituality and the humane compassion that are the essence of Jizō's role in the Japanese Buddhist cosmology.

Among the known previous owners of this painting is Viscount Takahashi Korekiyo (1854–1936), who served as prime minister of Japan in 1921–22. His fame rests on his role as minister of finance in reviving the Japanese economy after the 1929 Great Depression. Takahashi sold this painting at the Tokyo Art Club in 1917, and it reappeared at another sale there in 1968, where it was exhibited by S. Yabumoto. FF

---

1. This is a rather unusual rendering, more often associated with the bodhisattva Kannon; most Jizō figures depict him standing, not seated, although the museum also owns a sculptural rendering of a seated Jizō (fig. 26). Called Enmei Jizō, these statues depict Jizō with one leg on the ground, as if he is getting ready to stand up and immediately depart on a rescue mission (*hankafuza*).

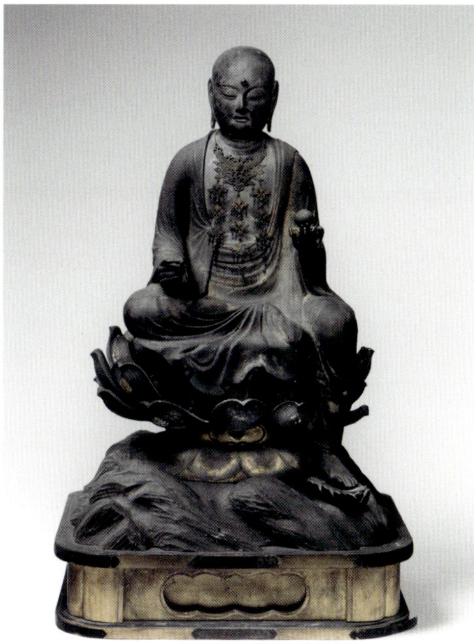

FIG. 26 Seated Jizō. Late Kamakura period, late 13th–early 14th century. Wood with traces of paint, lacquer, and gilt decoration; glass; H. 64 in. (162.6 cm). Philadelphia Museum of Art: Purchased with funds contributed by Andrea M. Baldeck, M.D., and William M. Hollis, Jr., 2007-128-1

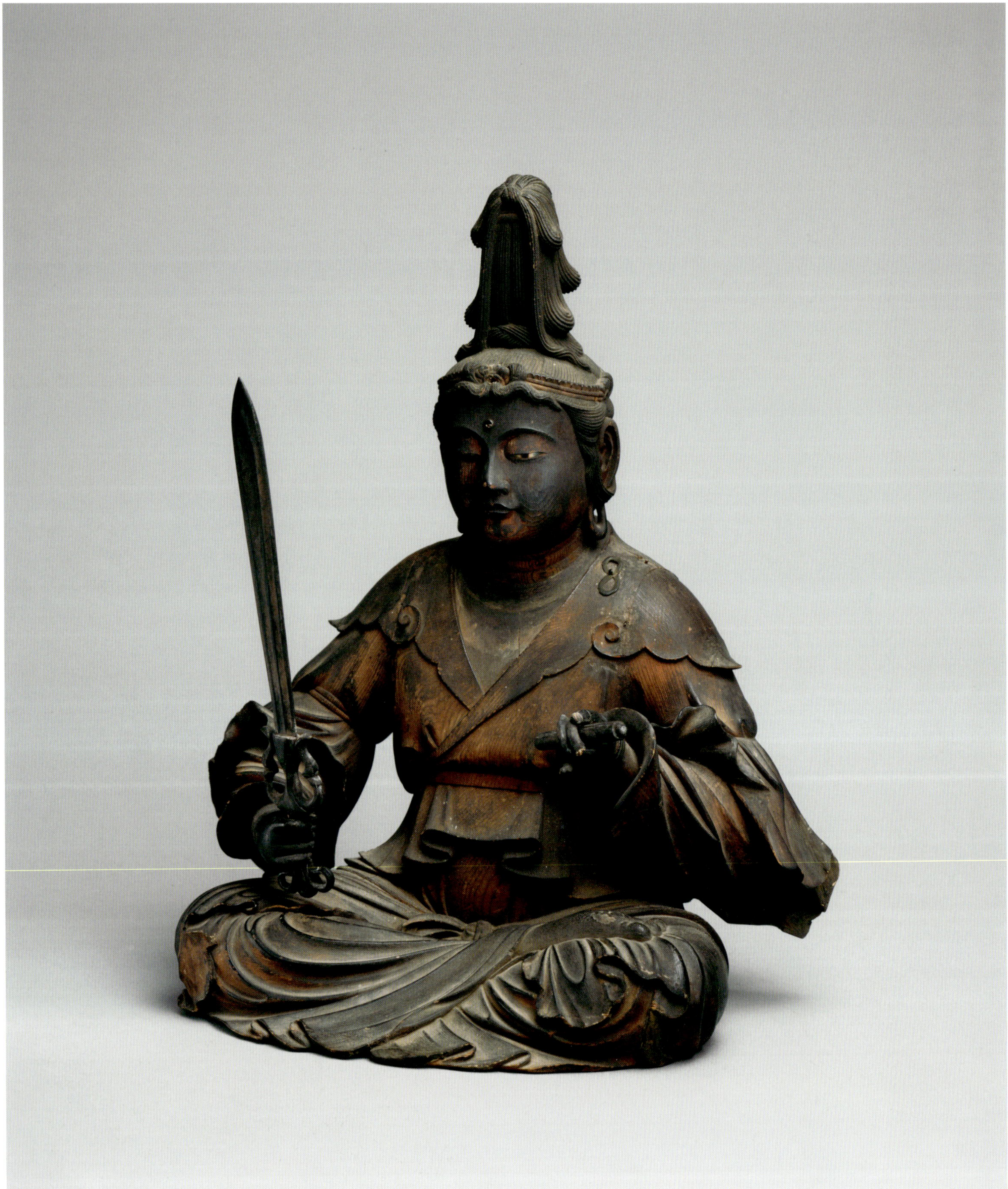

8

Seated Monju

Kamakura period (1185–1333), early 14th century

Japanese cypress (hinoki)
H. 14⅝ in. (37.2 cm)

Purchased with the Katharine Levin Farrell Fund, the Haney Foundation Fund, the Margaretta S. Hinchman Fund, the Bloomfield Moore Fund, the John T. Morris Fund, the Edgar Viguers Seeler Fund, the George W. B. Taylor Fund, and with funds contributed by Mrs. Rodolphe Meyer de Schauensee, 1979-57-1

Monju is the bodhisattva worshipped as the manifestation of the Buddha's wisdom. Bodhisattvas are enlightened beings, but in their selfless compassion they forgo entering the state of full extinction (Nirvana) to intervene on behalf of the faithful in seeking salvation. Monju (Sanskrit: Manjusri) is one of the most important bodhisattvas in the Buddhist cosmology, first introduced to Japan from China in the ninth century. The cult of Monju was particularly strong during the Kamakura period, when this sculpture was made.

Whereas earlier sculptors carved from a single block of wood (*ichiboku*; see no. 4), the artist who created this Monju used several blocks of wood joined together in a technique called *yosegi*. The joined-block technique allowed artists to create large-scale sculptures, with complicated elements such as lions' manes and tails (see no. 5). The craftsperson hollowed out the interior to make the statue a lighter weight and less prone to cracking. Inscriptions or consecrated items such as sutras could be placed inside these sculptures, providing important clues to dating and provenance. The *yosegi* method allowed the sculptor to choose the best woods with the finest grain, as seen here on Monju's face and in the lines of the jacket. The vigorous carving of the deep folds of the drapery, as well as the naturalistic rendering of the hair, contrasts with the serene gaze of the figure. The inlaid eyes, probably crystal, were inserted from the back of the hollowed-out head before the front and back sections were joined. The scroll in Monju's left hand symbolizes the sacred writings, the sutras (see no. 10). The sword represents the victory of wisdom over ignorance, leading to the path to enlightenment. The Chinese-style jacket was probably inspired by paintings or sculptures brought from Song-dynasty (960–1279) China, with which Japan had renewed contact from the late twelfth century.[1]

Monju is often depicted seated on a lion, as can be seen in a photograph taken in 1906 showing this sculpture (fig. 28).[2] The whereabouts of the lotus pedestal and lion are not known, but the carving of the seated Monju is ample evidence of the virtuosity of Japanese sculptors in wood. FF

---

1. Iconographic drawings that were used as models (fig. 27) usually depict Monju in robes and jewels that reflect the Indian origins of the historical Buddha as a royal prince.
2. See Yamaguchi and Miyazaki 2018, 24–25. There are two photographs in the archives of Kōfuku-ji (temple) in Nara, taken on July 1, 1906, showing groups of Buddhist sculptures outside the temple storehouse. The photograph illustrated here includes the Philadelphia Museum of Art's Monju, seated on a lotus pedestal atop a lion. A select group of the statuary found its way into the possession of Masuda Eisaku (1865–1921). This Monju sculpture with its lotus pedestal but without the lion is pictured in a 1941 catalogue of the Ikeda family collection; Ikeda 1941, 2, no. 39.

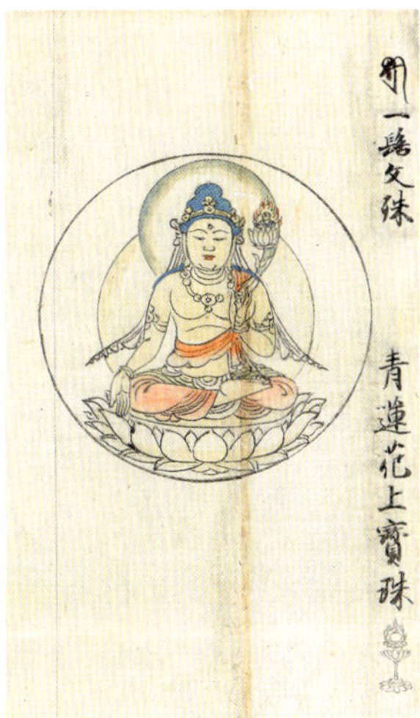

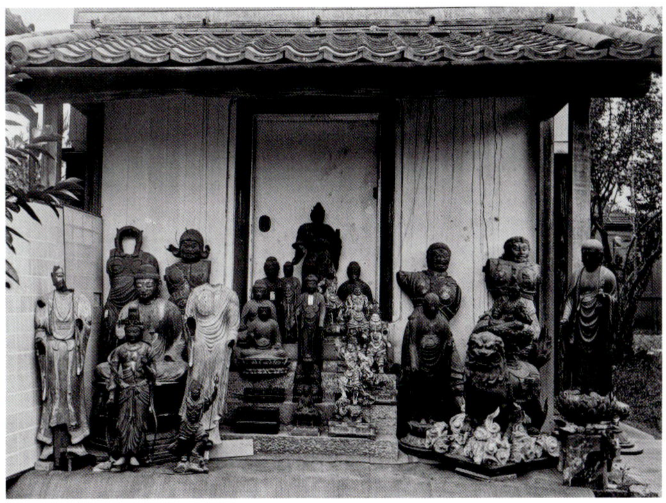

FIG. 27 *Monju Bosatsu*. Kamakura period (1185–1333). Ink and colors on paper, mounted as a *kakemono*; silver scroll ends; 10¾ × 6⅜ in. (27.3 × 16.2 cm). Philadelphia Museum of Art: Gift of Hosomi Ryoichi, 1965-4-1

FIG. 28 A group of Buddhist sculptures outside the Kōfuku-ji storehouse, Nara, Japan, 1906. The Philadelphia Monju can be seen at right, seated on a lotus pedestal atop a lion. Philadelphia Museum of Art Library and Archives

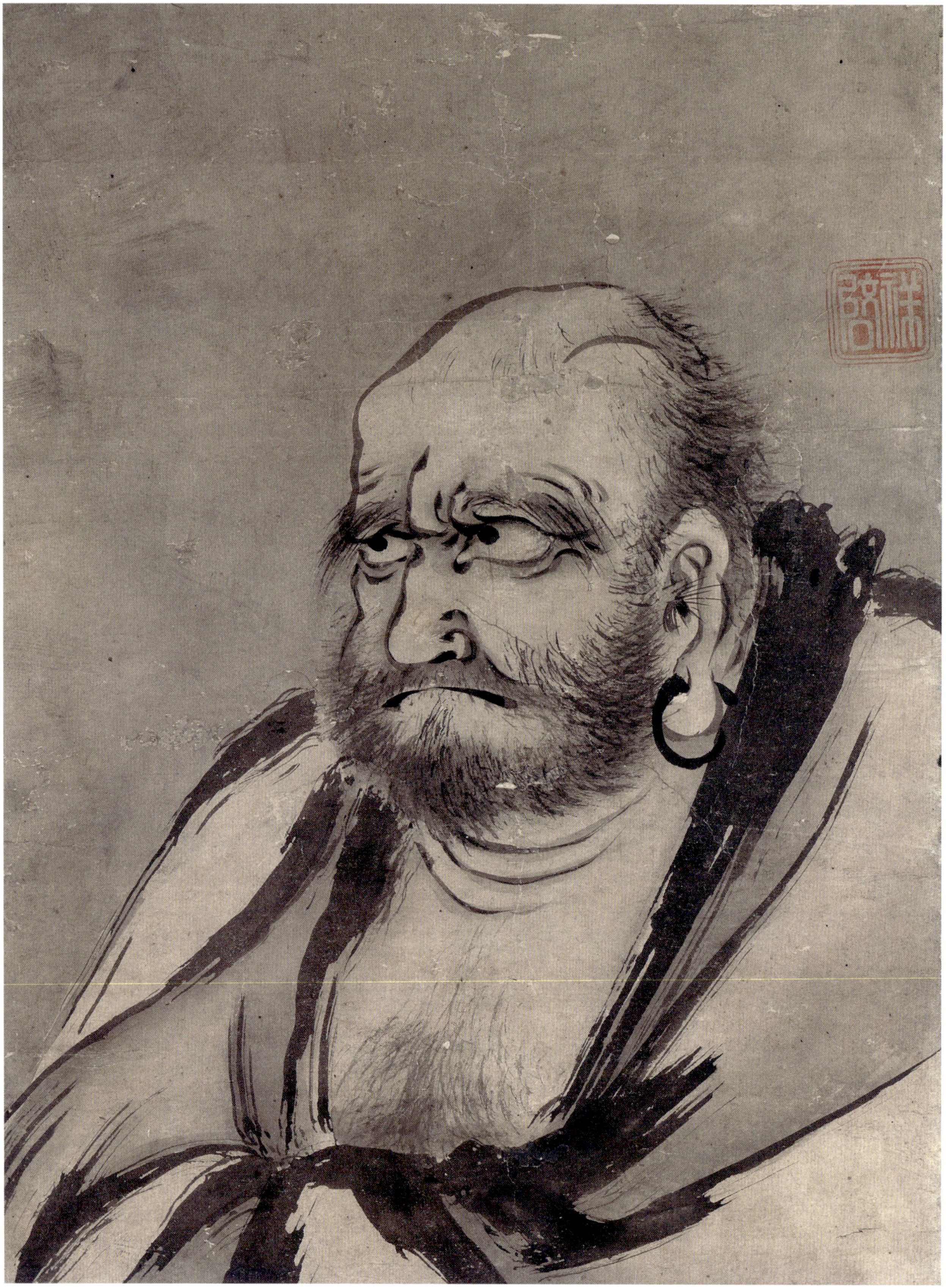

9

Ideal Portrait of Daruma

Kenkō Shōkei
(d. 1523)

Muromachi period (1392–1573), early 16th century

Ink on paper, mounted as a hanging scroll; 13¾ × 8⅞ in. (35 × 22.5 cm)

Purchased with Museum funds, 1928-104-1

The Zen priest and Buddhist painter Kenkō Shōkei was born in Utsunomiya, Shimotsuke (now Tochigi Prefecture), and his father was a painter who has been identified only as "Mr. Maruyoshi."[1] Active in the Muromachi period from the late fifteenth to the early sixteenth century, Shōkei is considered to be a representative painter of the Kanto region (Tokyo and the surrounding area). He is believed to have learned to paint at Kenchō-ji (temple) in Kamakura from the priest Chūan Shinkō (life dates unknown), whose painting followed the tradition of Minchō, a master of painting the figures of Daoism and Buddhism. Shōkei moved to Kyoto in 1478 and studied under Geiami (1431–1485), while also studying the Song-dynasty (960–1279) paintings of the Higashiyama *gomotsu* (treasure), a collection of Chinese paintings and ceramics held by the Ashikaga shogun. Before Shōkei's return to Kamakura, Geiami presented him with a *kanbakuzu* (hermit viewing a waterfall) painting made in 1480 as recognition of his student's expertise.[2]

In 1493 Shōkei once again moved to Kyoto, where he lived in Shōkoku-ji and interacted with high-ranking literary priests such as Ōsen Keisan (1429–1493) and Keijo Shūrin (1440–1518). He also continued to study the Higashiyama *gomotsu*. At Shōkoku-ji he studied under Shūbun (life dates unknown) and also learned from Sesshū-style and Kano-school paintings.

The subject of this painting, Daruma (Bodhidharma), was a semilegendary monk who had physically trained and meditated for nine years to achieve enlightenment on China's Shaolin Mountain during the fifth and sixth centuries. Regarded as the first patriarch of the Zen sect of Buddhism, Daruma became one of the most important subjects in Zen Buddhist painting. Shōkei used both delicate and bold brushstrokes for this figure. The direction of each hair, including those in his eyebrows and beard, was carefully depicted with a fine-point brush, while Daruma's robe was created with powerful, quick brushstrokes in dark ink. Daruma's eyes are sharp and strong, suggesting a powerful presence. KK

—

1. Kanō 1693, 19–20.
2. In the twentieth century the work was designated by Japan's Agency for Cultural Affairs as Important Cultural Property; it is now in the collection of Nezu Museum in Tokyo.

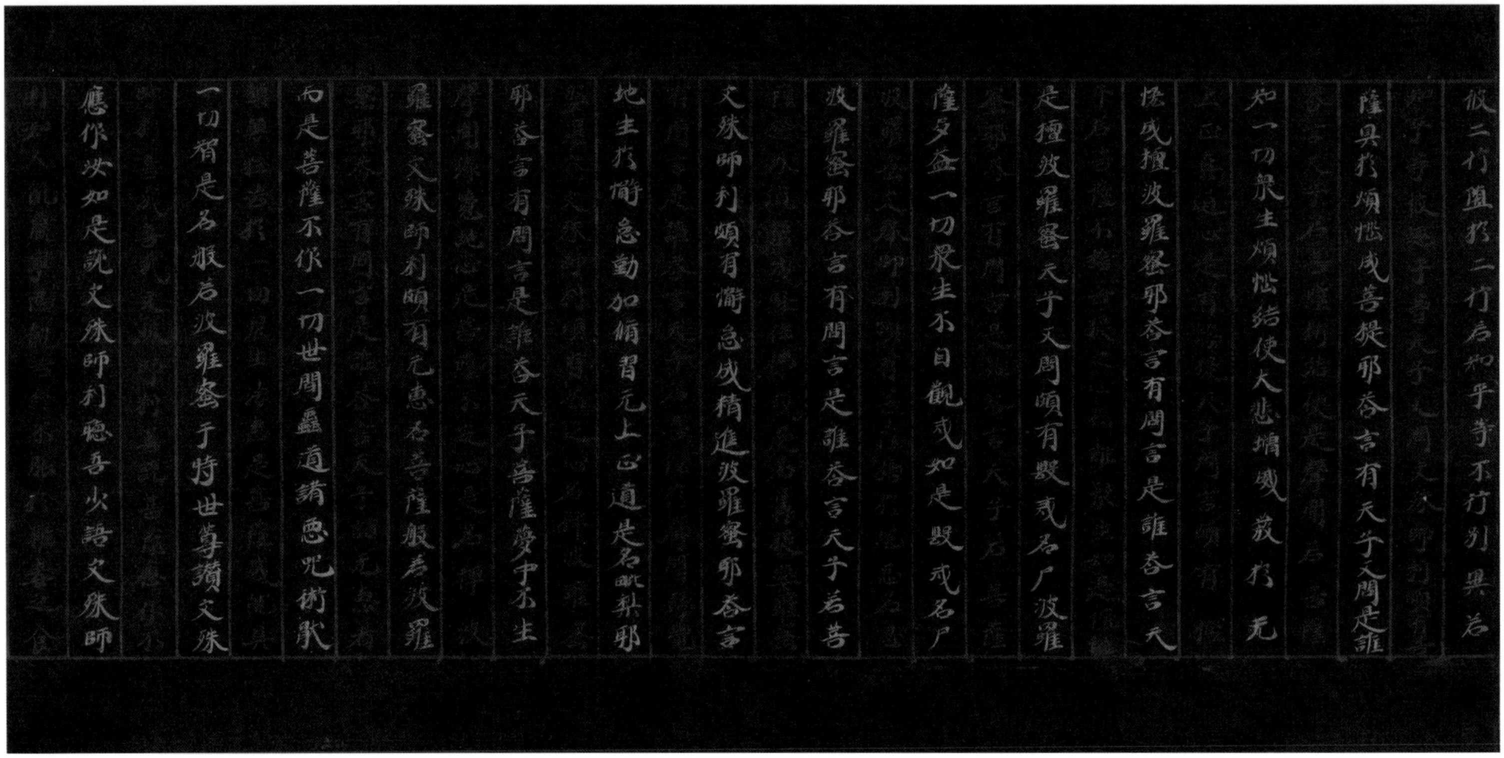

彼二行道於二行名知平等不行別異名
薩異於煩惱成菩提邪答言有天子文殊是誰
知一切衆生煩惱結使大悲增盛故於无
惱成種波羅蜜邪答言有問言是誰答言天
是種波羅蜜天子又問頗有毀戒名尸波羅
薩多益一切衆生不自觀戒如是毀戒名尸
波羅蜜邪答言有問言是誰答言天子若菩
文殊師利頗有懈怠成精進波羅蜜邪答言
地生於懈怠勤加脩習无上正道是名毗梨邪
邪答言有問言是誰答天子菩薩夢中不生
羅蜜文殊師利頗有无恵名菩薩般若波羅
而是菩薩不作一切世間蠱道諸惡咒術就
一切智是名般若波羅蜜于時世尊讚文殊
應作汝如是說文殊師利聽吾少語文殊師

10

Sutra Fragment

Heian period (794–1185),
12th century

Silver and gold ink on paper, mounted as a hanging scroll
8¾ × 20 in. (22.2 × 50.8 cm)

Gift of Mr. and Mrs. Lessing J. Rosenwald, 1959-93-89

The great Asian religion of Buddhism reached Japan in several successive waves from the Chinese continent. Japanese historical records describe the arrival of an embassy from the Korean kingdom of Baekje, which brought Chinese Buddhist texts and artifacts to Japan in 552. Buddhism was already one thousand years old and had developed a complex canon of thought, as well as a rich and sophisticated artistic heritage that reflected both its Indian origins and the transformations it underwent in China. After initial resistance to the new faith in Japan, Buddhism was adopted by the imperial family and the nobility. Temples were built and official scriptoria established for the copying of sutras (scriptures), which were written in Chinese.[1]

The copying or commissioning of sacred texts was considered an act of piety, and many aristocratic families vied to donate lavishly decorated sets of sutras. The head of the Fujiwara clan in northern Japan, Fujiwara Kiyohira (1056–1128), is known to have commissioned a complete set of the texts comprising the Buddhist canon (*issaikyō*), numbering over five thousand scrolls. The copying work began in 1117 and took several years. The completed scriptures were dedicated in 1126 at the tutelary temple Chūson-ji in Hiraizumi (present-day Iwate Prefecture).[2]

This fragment of a sutra dates to about the same time. The text is from the regulations of monastic codes and discipline known as vinayas in Sanskrit and takes the form of a dialogue with the bodhisattva Monju (Sanskrit: Manjusri) about the correct behavior of bodhisattvas.[3] Like the Chūson-ji texts, it is written in alternating lines of gold and silver (*kingin kōsho*) on indigo-dyed dark blue paper framed by a silver border. The formal calligraphy required great concentration and control to achieve the perfectly balanced columns of seventeen characters each. The practice of mounting fragments of sutra texts as hanging scrolls grew out of the displays of calligraphy used in tearooms in the late nineteenth century.[4] FF

---

1. The first Buddhist texts imported to Japan in the sixth century were Chinese translations of Indian Sanskrit and Pali scriptures. The complete canon (*issaikyō*) consists of three types of texts: the sutras, the vinayas (rules and procedures that govern the Buddhist monastic community), and scholastic expositions of the texts (*shastras* or *abhidharma*).
2. The Chūson-ji complex was decimated by a rival warlord in 1189, and over 4,500 of the scrolls were transferred to temples in Kyoto and Osaka in the late sixteenth century. Scrolls and fragments from the set have found their way into US and European museums in the last century. See New York 1979, nos. 9–11; and Saunders 1964.
3. For a translation, see Takakusu et al. 1977; and "Vaipulya Sūtra of the Pure Vinaya," Buddha Sutras, accessed September 27, 2022, sutrasmantras.info/sutra30.html. See no. 8 for more on the bodhisattva Monju.
4. See Guth 1993 for collecting practices of Masuda Takashi and his circle. An 1868 government edict proclaiming the separation of Buddhism from the native Shinto religion resulted in the defrocking of Buddhist clergy, the closing of many Buddhist temples, and the sale of sculptures, paintings, and even sacred texts to fund the upkeep of surviving temples. As a result, collectors including Masuda and Ernest Fenollosa (see nos. 13, 76) were able to acquire important works during the later decades of the nineteenth century.

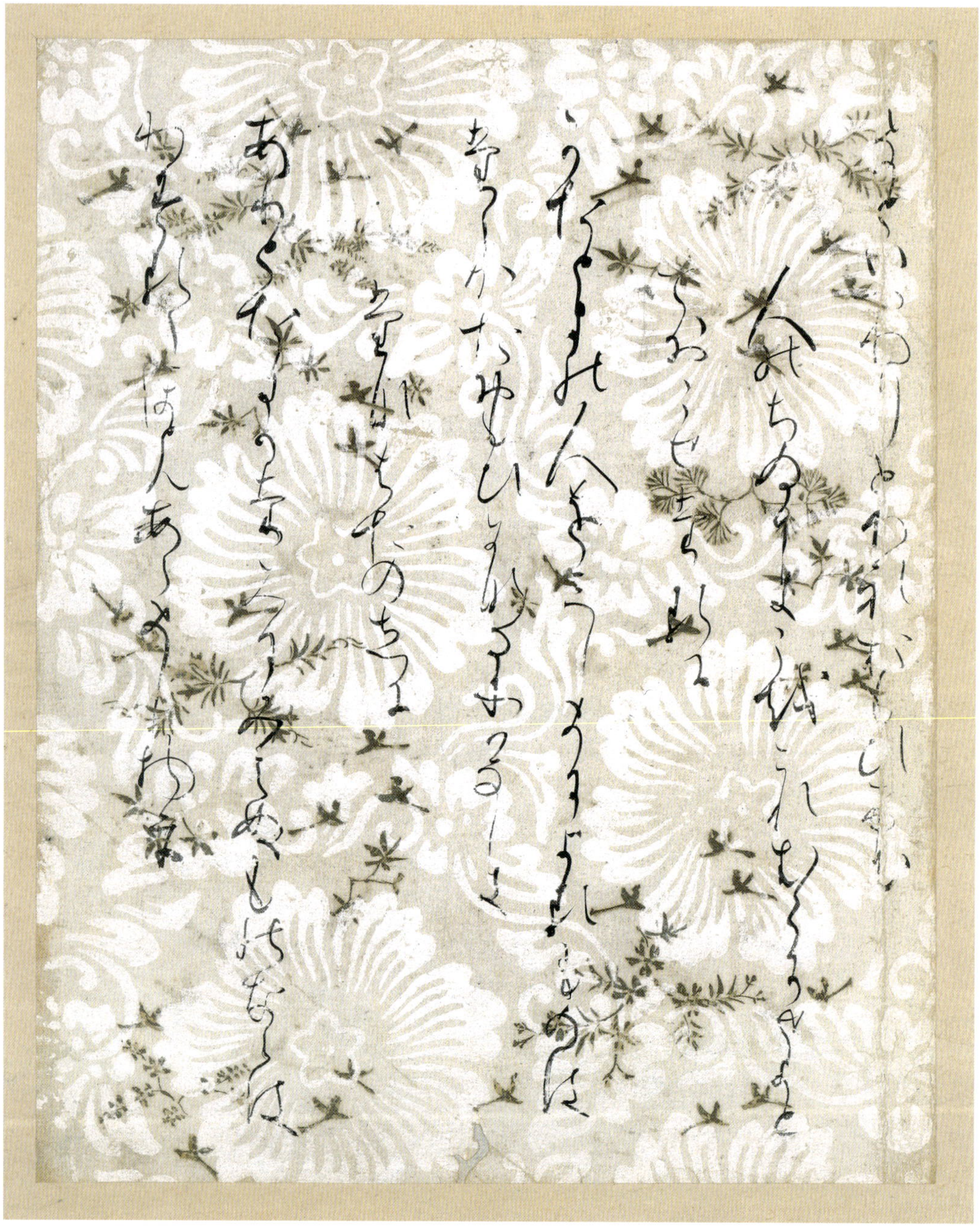

11

Page from the *Anthology of Poems by Thirty-Six Immortal Poets*

Heian period (794–1185), c. 1112

Ink and silver over mica woodblock printing on paper, mounted as a hanging scroll; 8 × 6¼ in. (20.3 × 15.9 cm)

Gift (by exchange) of Mrs. Henry W. Breyer, Sr., 1965-77-1

Poetry played a central role in the lives of Heian-period aristocrats, and the grouping of poets into sets has a long history in Japan, beginning with the six poets singled out by Ki no Tsurayuki (872–945) in his preface to the earliest imperially commissioned poetry anthology of 905.[1] This scroll shows a page from the *Anthology of Poems by Thirty-Six Immortal Poets* (*Sanjū rokkasen*) that is believed to have been commissioned for the sixtieth-birthday celebrations of the emperor Shirakawa (1053–1129) in 1112. Some twenty of the leading calligraphers of the time worked on this anthology, and the elegant brushwork evident here is typical of the transcriptions of the entire thirty-nine-volume set.[2] The paper of this page, inscribed with poems by Lady Ise, features mica-printed peonies, over which birds, ferns, and pine needles are painted and stamped in silver.

Lady Ise (c. 870–940; fig. 29), the author of these verses, was one of the well-educated aristocratic women of her time, many of whose poetic and prose works have survived to the present day.[3] She is one of five women included in the original selection of the anthology of thirty-six noteworthy poets compiled by Fujiwara Kintō (966–1041), who was himself a noted poet and critic of his day.

This page includes one partial and two complete poems with their headnotes by Lady Ise:

[Having heard
That the color of tears
Has turned crimson,]
Why should I have
Thought it a lie?

In response to a message proposing that a young son marry another person's daughter:

Sad would it be
If from a moment's meeting
Came
One-sided love.

Composed for a picture depicting Tanabata (the Lover's Festival on the seventh day of the seventh month, when the Cowherd and the Weaving Girl, two stars in the Milky Way, are permitted to meet on a bridge of magpies' wings):

Were there no
Reminder of you
In the features of this child,
Forgetfulness
Might come.[4]

FF

1. See no. 12 for Ki no Tsurayuki and no. 37 for the Thirty-Six Immortal Poets.
2. The thirty-nine volumes of this set of the anthology were rediscovered in 1896 in the storage of the Nishi-Hongan-ji (temple) in Kyoto. It had been donated by the imperial household in 1549. In 1929 the volumes of Lady Ise and the Ki no Tsurayuki poetry collections were dismembered and sold by the temple. Other pages from the collections, all mounted as hanging scrolls, are extant at the Museum of Fine Arts, Boston; the Metropolitan Museum of Art, New York; and the Seattle Art Museum.
3. Among Lady Ise's contemporaries were women such as Murasaki Shikibu, the author of *The Tale of Genji*.
4. Translated by Edwin A. Cranston and Fumiko E. Cranston in New York 1984–85, 56.

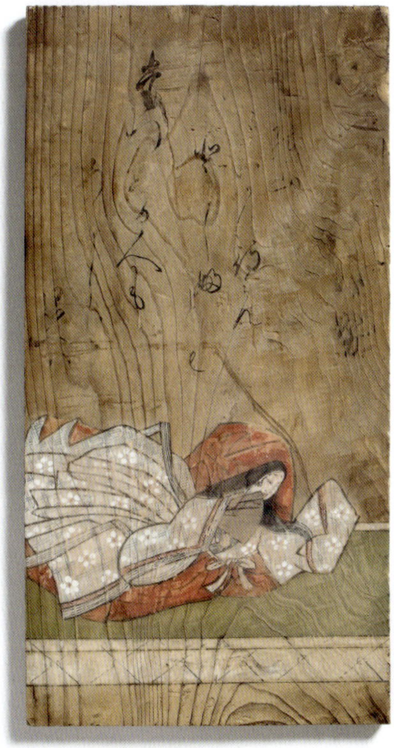

FIG. 29 *Lady Ise*. Edo period (1615–1868), 1698. Ink and color on wood, 19½ × 9⅞ in. (49.5 × 25.1 cm). Philadelphia Museum of Art, 125th Anniversary Acquisition: Gift of Dr. Luther W. Brady, Jr., 2008-257-20

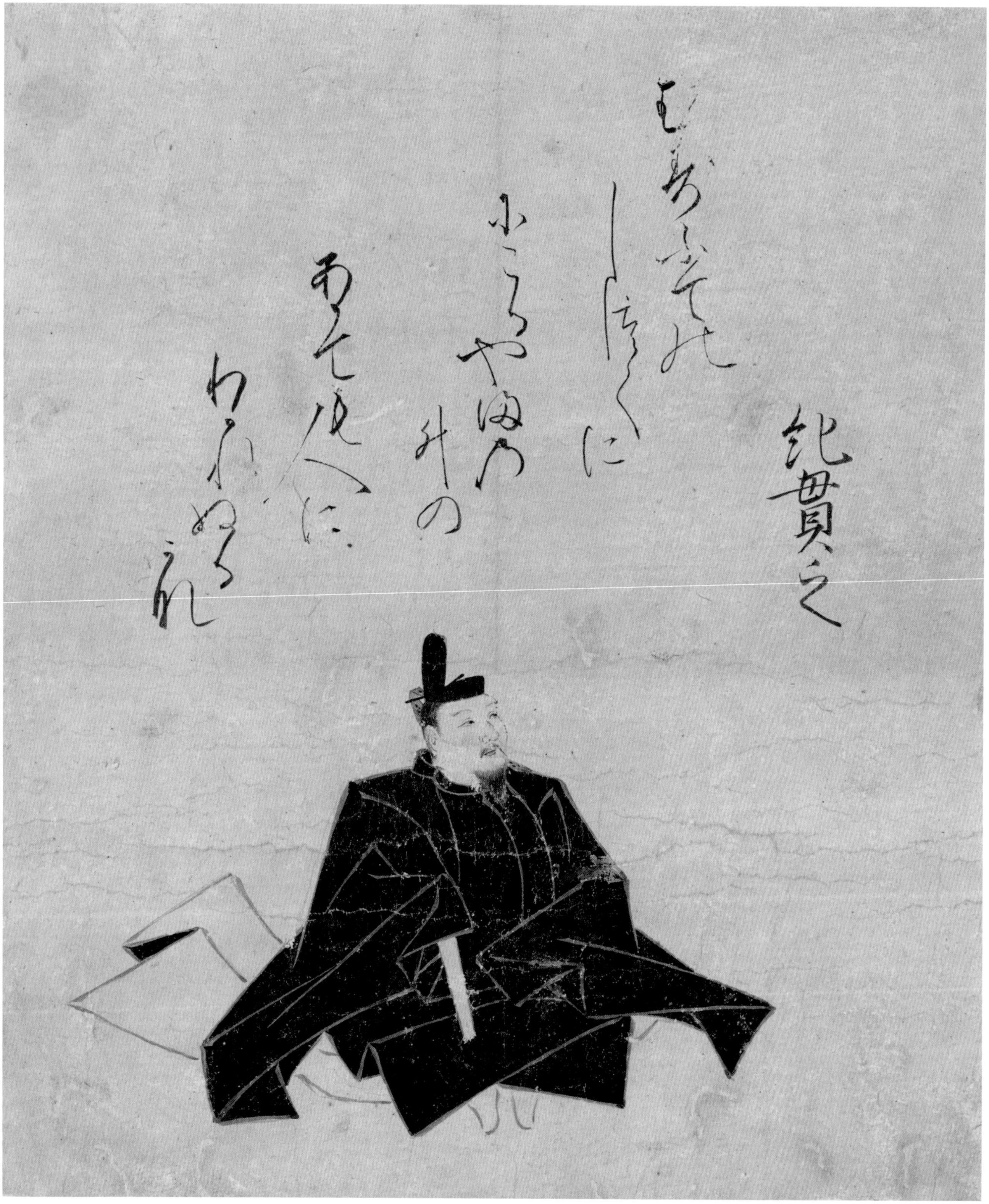
紀貫之

12

Ki no Tsurayuki

Kamakura period (1185–1333), early 14th century

Ink and color on paper, mounted as a hanging scroll; 11⅛ × 9⅛ in. (28.3 × 23.2 cm)

Purchased with funds contributed by Mr. and Mrs. Howard H. Lewis and the Henry B. Keep Fund, 2013-24-1

Ki no Tsurayuki (872–945) was a famed poet of his day, and one of the four compilers of the first imperially commissioned anthology of Japanese poetry, the *Kokin wakashū* (Collection of poems from ancient and modern times), completed in 905. Tsurayuki wrote the preface to the collection, in which he singled out Six Immortal Poets (*rokkasen*), a grouping that was later further expanded to thirty-six poets (see no. 37).[1] Tsurayuki was included in the latter set, and the poem on this fragment is from the *Kokin wakashū*.

"Composed on parting from someone with whom he had chatted at Ishii Spring on Shiga Pass"

Unsatisfied as
Someone who scoops water from
A spring so shallow
It clouds with drops from her hands
She went away and left me.[2]

Luxurious manuscript versions of the Thirty-Six Immortal Poets were commissioned by aristocrats, such as the thirty-nine-volume edition of about 1112, produced with imperial patronage (see no. 11). By the late twelfth century, imaginary portrait images of the thirty-six poets from different eras were combined with their poems.[3] This "portrait" of Tsurayuki shows him in the formal robes and headgear of a court official, holding an ivory ceremonial tablet. The three characters at the right are his name, followed to the left by his poem, with the delicate Japanese script floating above him like a canopy or "thought bubble."

This is a section of a longer handscroll that included images and verses of all Thirty-Six Immortal Poets. The calligraphy has traditionally been attributed to Fujiwara Tameuji (1222–1286), and the manuscript from which this section is taken is known as the Tameuji-bon (Tameuji edition). Scholars now believe the handscroll was produced in the early fourteenth century, and there are four additional known sections extant.[4] The lavish gold-and-silver-stamped textile mount and the ivory scroll ends testify to the esteem in which this fragment was held. FF

1. Fujiwara Kintō (966–1041) is credited with the first anthology of selections of verses by the Thirty-Six Immortal Poets, compiled around 1010. In the early thirteenth century, an expanded anthology of *One Hundred Poems by One Hundred Poets* was assembled by Kintō's descendant, Fujiwara Teika (1162–1241).
2. Translated in Keene 1993, 25.
3. See Graybill 1983.
4. For other sections of the scroll, see Tokyo 1986, nos. 59, 60, and 61.

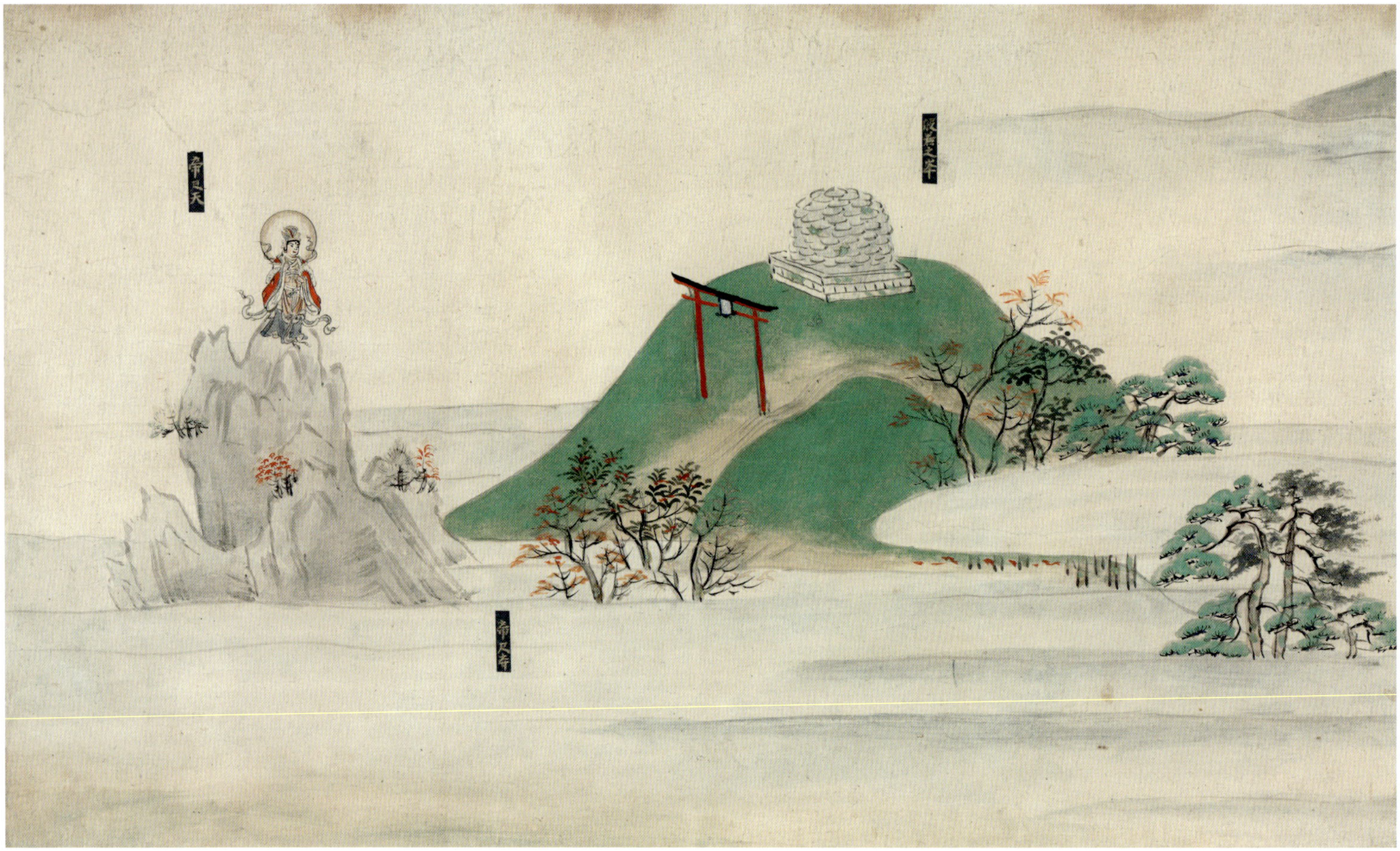

13

Jino-ji engi (*Legends of Jin'o-ji*)

Nambokuchō period (1333–92), 14th century

Ink and colors on paper, mounted as hanging scrolls
1962-18-1: 13½ × 21⅛ in. (34.3 × 53.7 cm)
1962-18-2: 13¼ × 21⅛ in. (33.7 × 53.7 cm)

Gift of Mrs. Moncure Biddle in memory of her father, Ernest F. Fenollosa, 1962-18-1,2

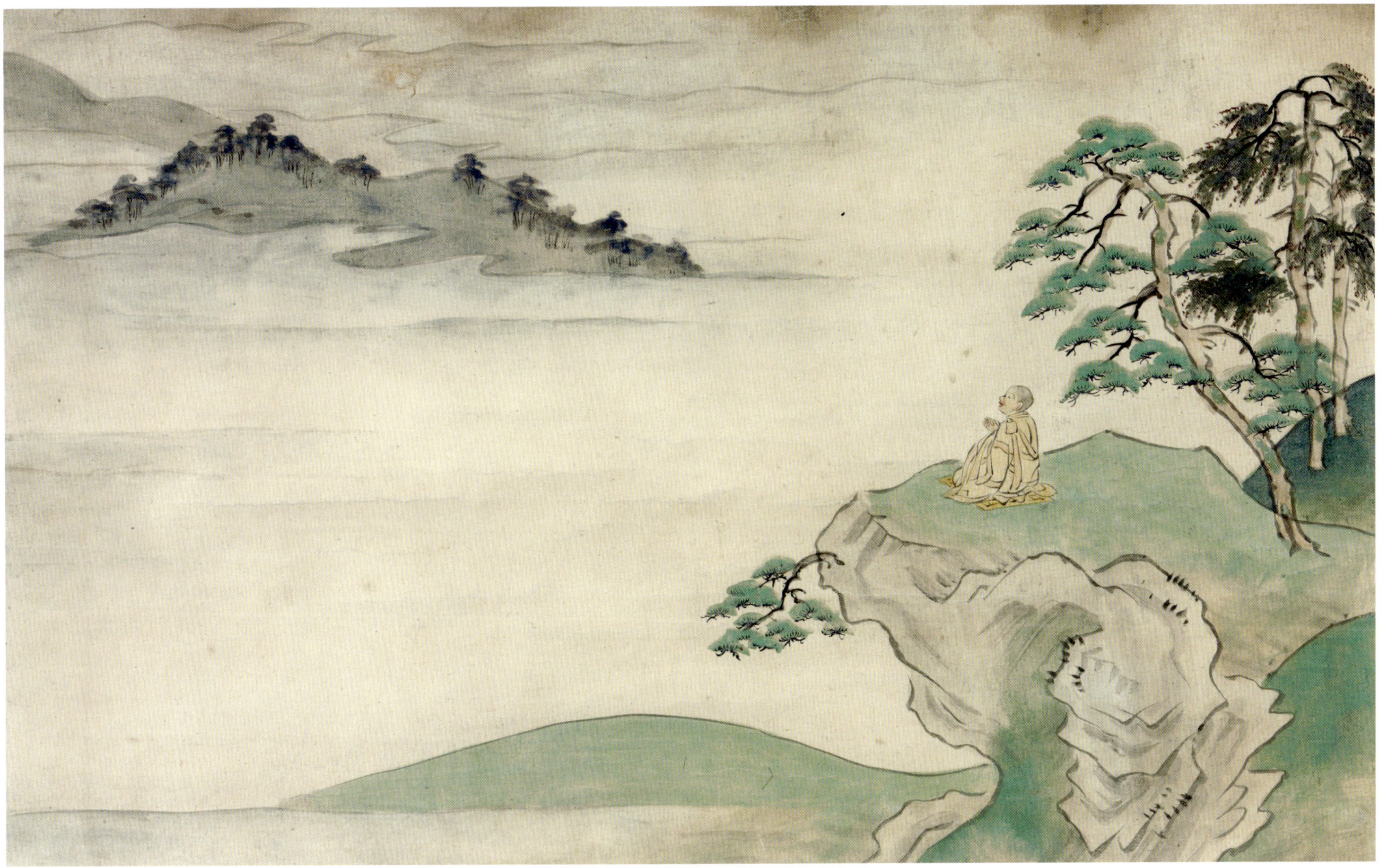

Handscrolls of illustrated histories (*engi*) of temple origins and of famous monks or founders of sects became popular during the Kamakura period (1185–1333) with the rise of numerous new Buddhist sects. The scrolls were often commissioned by wealthy patrons and adherents of the temple, and were produced by monks working in Buddhist painting studios. The images were accompanied by texts that explicated the stories.[1]

Now mounted as hanging scrolls, these two images were originally part of a pair of long handscrolls depicting the history of the Jin'o-ji, a Buddhist temple near Osaka. The narrative is also known as the *Kōnin shōnin eden* (Illustrated biography of the monk Kōnin), as the second scroll deals with the legend of the Korean priest Kōnin's revival of the temple, which had fallen into neglect and disrepair. By the time of Kōnin's death in 775, the temple had been restored to its former state as a center for worship. The two sections shown here are consecutive images from the second scroll, near the end of episode twelve.

In the first scene (reading right to left) the cleric Kūkai (774–835) is depicted during a visit to the temple in 833 to dedicate a copy of the *Hannya rishu kyō* (*Sutra of the Perfect Wisdom*) that he had previously copied there. Kūkai is seated on a cliff near the temple, where in the second scene what may be the figure of Taishaku-ten (Guardian of the East, one of the Twelve Guardian Kings, or Jūniten) miraculously appears to accept Kūkai's offering. The original scrolls were dismembered and sections, including these two scenes, were remounted as hanging scrolls sometime after World War II.[2] The latter fragment retains the small blue cartouches identifying the subjects.[3]

The style of these scenes is typical of mid-fourteenth-century narrative scroll painting: vivid colors applied in washes for the landscape elements, combined with detailed lines for the figural depictions. The colors of these fragments are in excellent condition, probably owing to the fact that since Jin'o-ji was a small, out-of-the-way temple, they were not frequently displayed. FF

---

1. The earliest extant example in Japan is the mid-eighth-century *E inga-kyō* (*Illustrated Sutra of Cause and Effect*), which treats the life of the Buddha. See no. 16 for an example of a complete scroll narrating the biography of the famed priest Kūkai.
2. Numerous sections of the scroll are extant in museums outside Japan and illustrated in Akiyama 1969, which includes an essay on the history of Jin'o-ji. Before the sale of the handscrolls, the temple had modern copies made of both, which include portions of the narrative text.
3. The section showing Kūkai originally had one such "label" and a section of text, both of which were cut off when it was mounted as a scroll. The labels on the second section identify Taishaku-ten, Hannya no mine (Wisdom Sutra Hill), and Taishaku-ji.

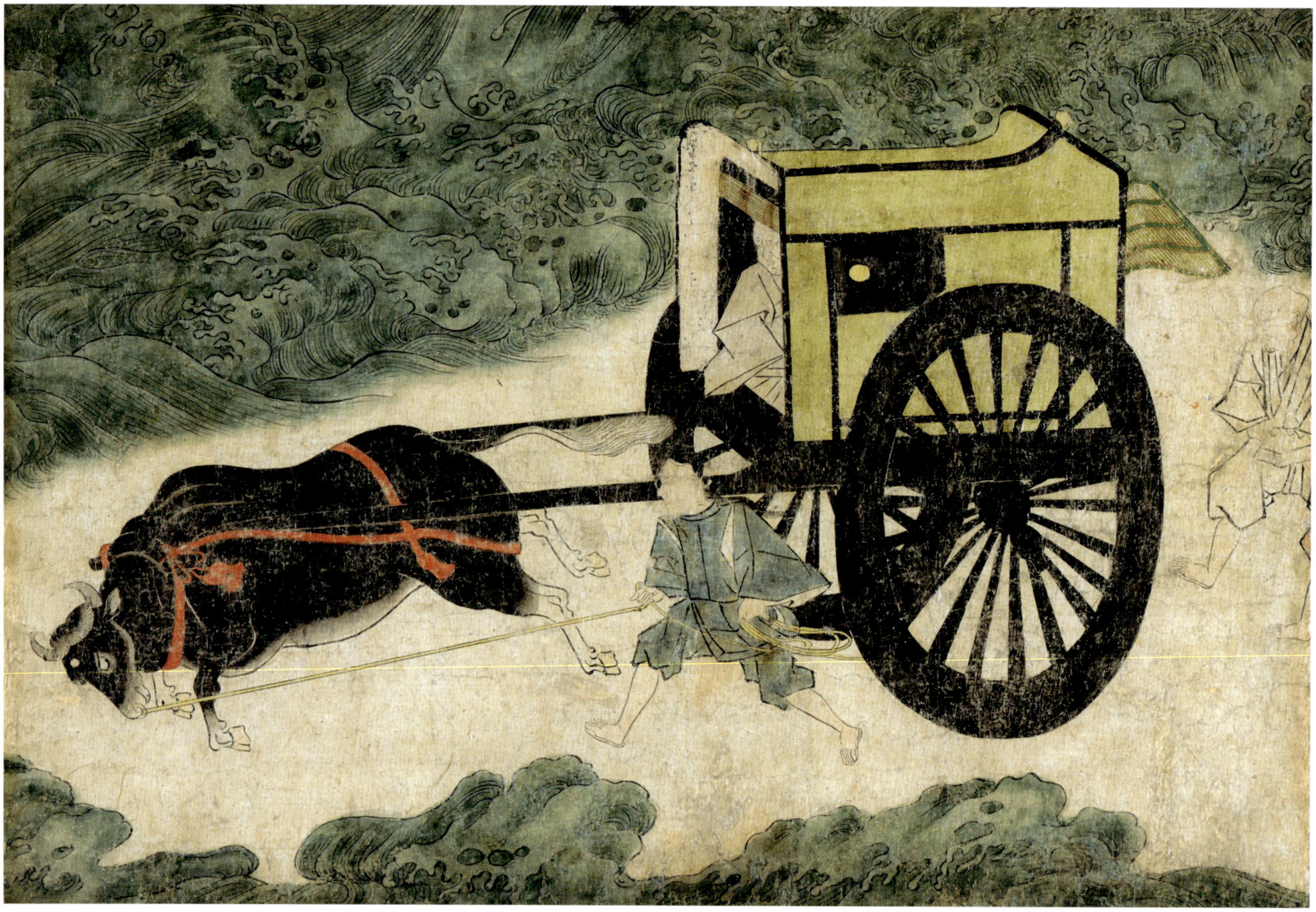

14

Priest Son'i's Visit to the Imperial Palace, from the *Kitano Tenjin engi* (*Legends of Kitano Tenjin Shrine*)

Muromachi period (1392–1573), late 14th century

Ink and colors on paper, mounted as a hanging scroll; 11¾ × 16½ in. (29.8 × 41.9 cm)

Purchased with Museum funds from the Simkhovitch Collection, 1929-40-222

Sugawara no Michizane (845–903) was a poet, a scholar of literature, and a politician in the Heian period (794–1185). Emperor Daigo (r. 897–930) appointed Michizane "minister of the right" (*udaijin*), the second-most important ministerial position. However, the emperor favored Michizane's rival Fujiwara no Tokihira (871–909), who convinced the emperor that Michizane was plotting treason. Michizane was banished from the court and relegated to an administrative post in Dazaifu, Kyushu, far from the capital of Kyoto. According to legend, following his death in Dazaifu, he became a vengeful spirit and the object of worship as Tenjin. Since Michizane was well known as the most intelligent person of his era, he became the god of learning.

The *Kitano Tenjin engi* (*Legends of Kitano Tenjin Shrine*) is an illuminated scroll depicting the life of Michizane, stories of miraculous efficacy attested to him, and the foundation of the namesake shrine in Kyoto. Copies of handscrolls of the *Kitano Tenjin engi* were made and distributed in Tenjin shrines all over Japan. The Kitano Tenjin shrine in Kyoto owns eight volumes of the handscrolls referred to as the "Jōkyū version" as they were made during the Jōkyū era (1219–22). They are considered to be the oldest and highest-quality handscrolls in existence, and have been designated a National Treasure in Japan.

The museum's segment of the *Kitano Tenjin engi* was probably produced in the Muromachi period. It depicts a visit to the imperial palace by Son'i (866–940), a head priest of Enryaku-ji of the Tendai sect. In this scene he hastens to the palace to placate Michizane, who has turned into a thunder god and is attacking the Seiryō-den, the emperor's residence. Using the power of Buddhism, Son'i parts the waters of the Kamo River, which is raging due to a thunderstorm, and rushes across in an ox-pulled cart. This scene subsequently became an independent theme for painting, as seen on a screen in the collection of the Idemitsu Museum of Arts in Tokyo (fig. 30). KK

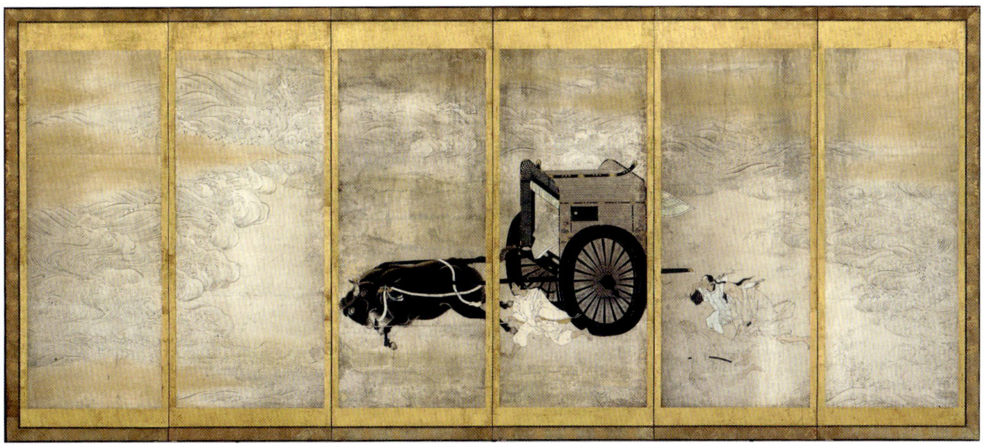

FIG. 30 *Priest Son'i's Visit to the Imperial Palace*. Muromachi period (1392–1573). Ink and gold on paper, mounted as a six-panel screen; 54⁷⁄₁₆ in. × 10 ft. 10⅜ in. (138.3 × 331.1 cm). Idemitsu Museum of Arts, Tokyo

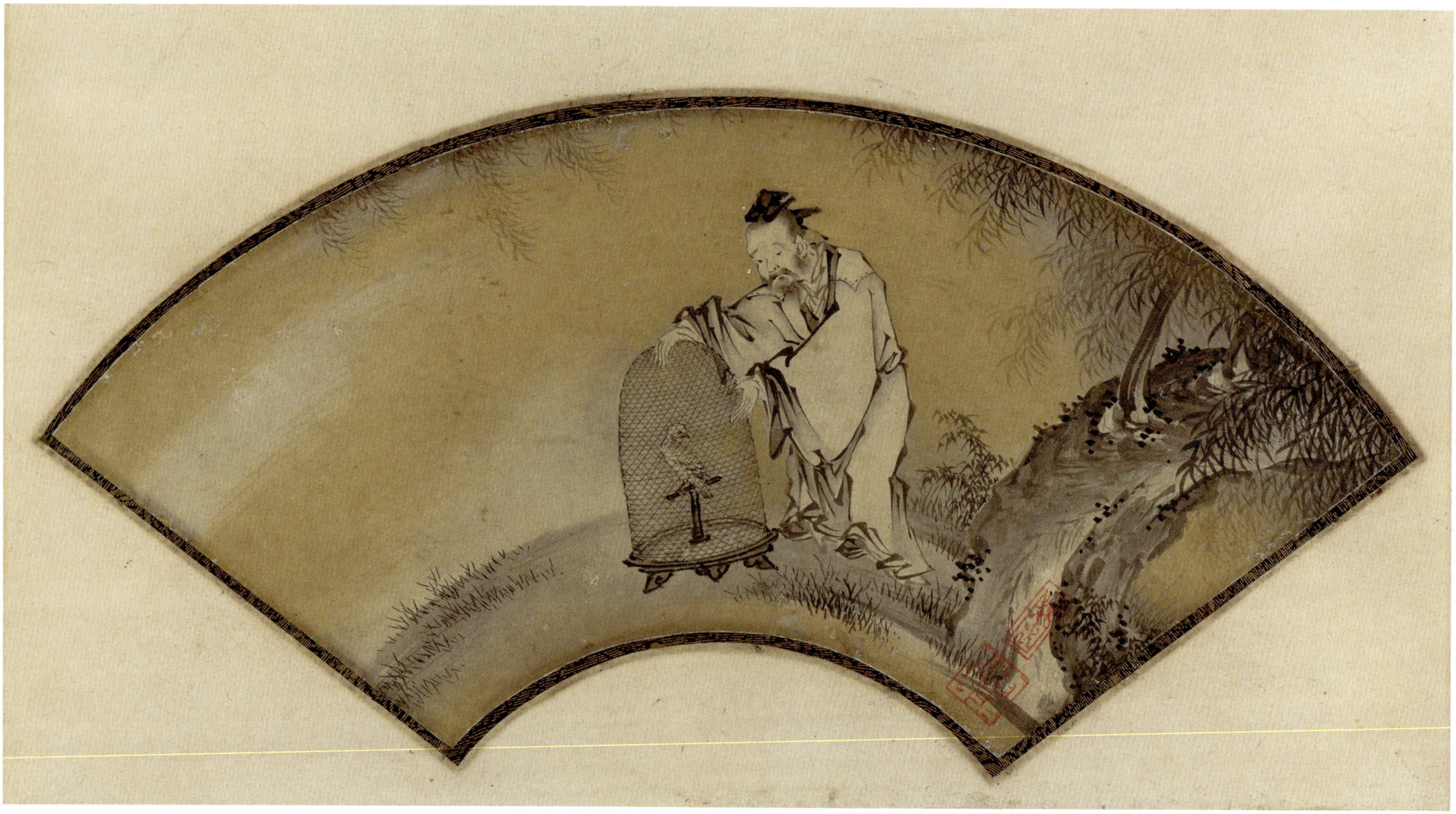

15

Chinese Man Releasing a Bird from a Cage

Shikibu Terutada
(act. mid-16th century)

Muromachi period (1392–1573), mid-16th century

Ink and gold on paper, mounted as a hanging scroll; 7¾ × 20 in. (19.7 × 50.8 cm)

Purchased with the Henry B. Keep Fund, 1989-78-1

On paper brushed with gold wash, Shikibu Terutada depicted an intriguing scene: a Chinese man standing under a willow tree is about to open a cage to release the pet bird kept inside. The subject could be an allusion to a poem by the Chinese recluse poet Tao Yuanming (365–427), who wrote, "The caged bird longs for the old trees. . . . Too long a prisoner, captive in a cage. Now I can get back again to nature."[1]

The fan-shaped painting, currently mounted as a hanging scroll, bears no signs of use as a folding fan. Research has revealed that a group of sixty fan paintings were mounted on a pair of six-panel folding screens formerly in the Hisamatsu collection; the screens were remounted with thirty of the fans, and the other thirty were remounted as hanging scrolls.[2] It is unclear whether the Philadelphia Museum of Art's painting was originally among the sixty, but stylistically, it is close to the ones currently mounted as hanging scrolls in the British Museum in London and in the Minneapolis Institute of Art (formerly in the Burke collection) (fig. 31). The curved shape of the fan provided the artist with a unique pictorial space to work with and an opportunity to create a sense of movement and spatial depth.

We have little biographical information about the artist. Yamashita Yūji's research has provided the most detailed accounts to date of this painter.[3] Shikibu's oeuvre encompasses landscape, bird-and-flower, and figural paintings. His large-scale work is exemplified by the landscape screens of the four seasons in the collections of the Seikadō Bunko Art Museum in Tokyo and the Asian Art Museum in San Francisco. Fan painting constitutes a good proportion of his extant work. A distinctive feature of his screens and fan paintings is the use of gold wash in the background as both a decorative and compositional element.

The rugged lines on the Chinese man's robe recall a stylistic feature in Kano school paintings, suggesting Shikibu's affinity with that school. The soft brushstrokes on the willow trees and ink wash on the ground show his connection with painters of the Kanto region (eastern Japan). In this regard, it is interesting that the label on the painting's storage box notes "Kei shōki," attributing the work to the fifteenth-century painter Kenkō Shōkei (see no. 9), a central figure in the development of Kanto ink painting and an artist who influenced Shikibu. XW

1. Kline 2000, 122.
2. Yamashita 1992.
3. Yamashita 1985 and Yamashita 1992.

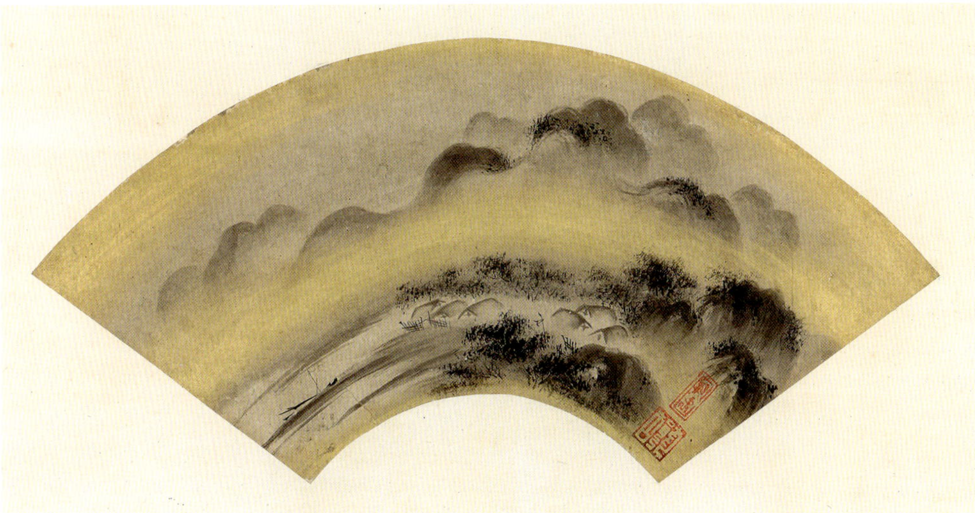

FIG. 31 Shikibu Terutada. *Fishing Village in Evening Glow*, one of the *Eight Views of Xiao-Xiang*. Muromachi period, 16th century. Ink and gold on paper, mounted as a hanging scroll; 10½ × 20⅞ in. (26.7 × 53 cm). Minneapolis Institute of Art: Mary Griggs Burke Collection, gift of the Mary and Jackson Burke Foundation, 2015.79.57

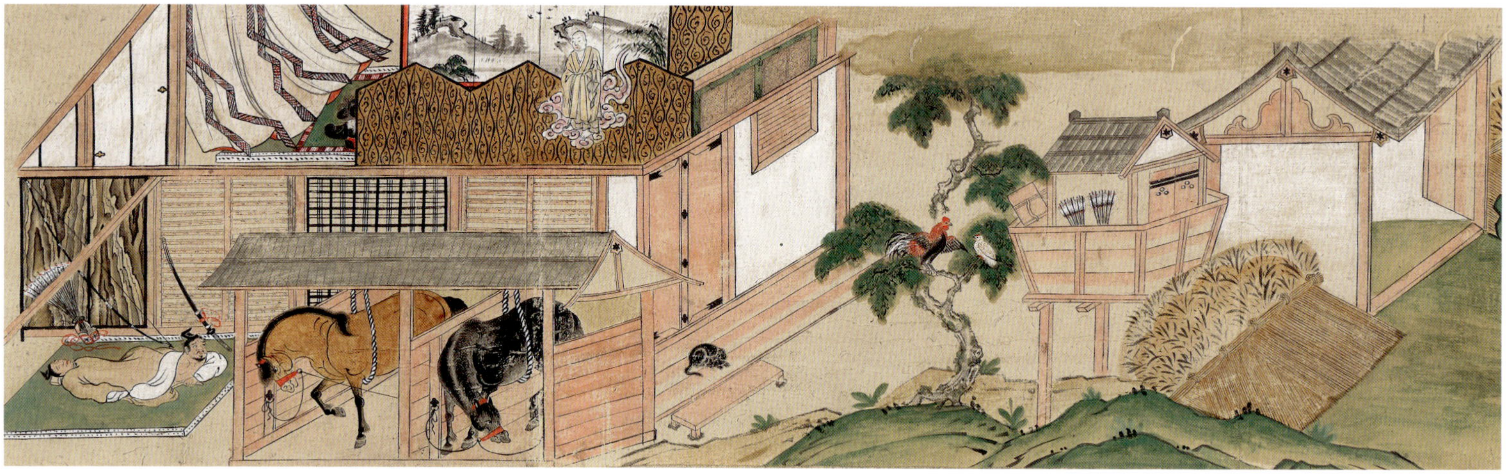

A: Kūkai's miraculous birth

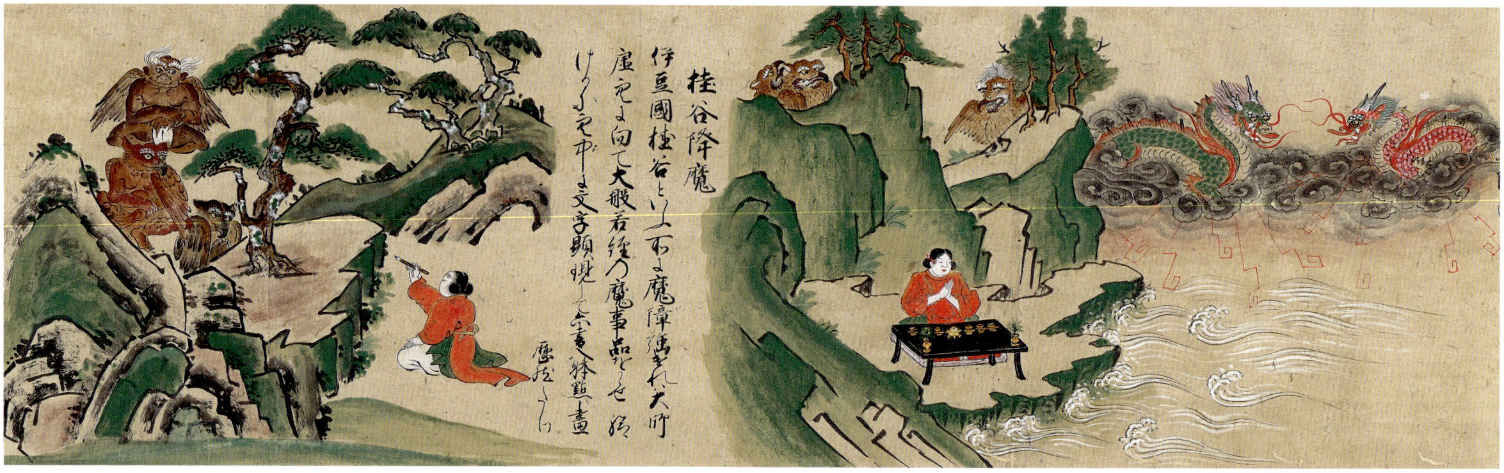

C: Kūkai subduing monsters of the Katsura Valley

B: Kūkai quelling the evil dragons

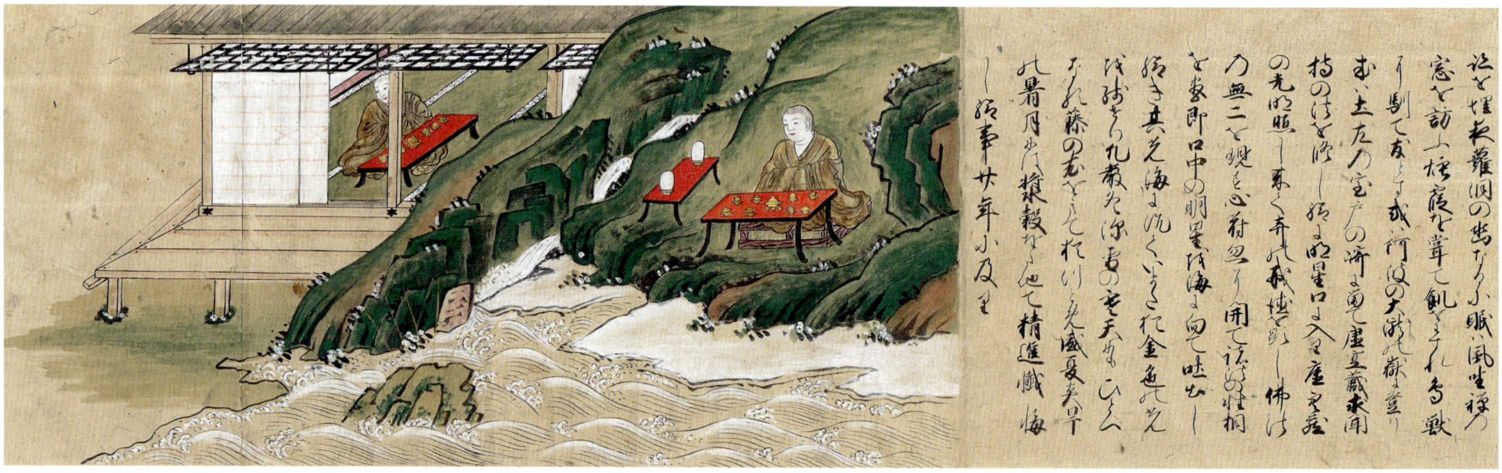

D: Morning star entering Kūkai's mouth

16

Biography of the Great Teacher of Mount Kōya (Kōya Daishi Gyō-jō-e)

Momoyama period (1568–1615), second half of 16th century

Ink and colors on paper, mounted as a handscroll; 12½ in. × 41 ft. 9 in. (31.8 × 1272.5 cm)

Bequest of Henry B. Keep, 1983-83-6

Over the centuries, the Japanese priest Kūkai (774–835) has been revered as a Buddhist master, poet, and calligrapher, whose religious prestige transformed him into a cultural icon. Kūkai traveled to China in the year 804 and studied under the seventh patriarch of the Shingon sect, Huiguo (746–805). Two years later, he returned to Japan as the eighth patriarch, designated by his master to preach esoteric Buddhist teachings.

As the founder of Japan's Shingon school of Buddhism, Kūkai was also known posthumously as Kōbō Daishi, meaning "Grand Master Who Propagated the Buddhist Dharma." In the year 816, Kūkai established his monastic training complex on Mount Kōya, which is now considered a pilgrimage site for Buddhist practitioners. This sacred mountain also served as the source of Kūkai's other sobriquet, Kōya Daishi, as indicated in this painting's title. This handscroll was probably the first of a set of ten depicting Kūkai's life and religious career. With calligraphic texts accompanying didactic biographical scenes, the scroll portrays him in childhood as a bodhisattva-like figure who performed miracles.

Kūkai's story begins with his miraculous birth portended by a priest (A). Standing on clouds, the priest appears in a dream to Kūkai's mother, who sleeps behind a standing screen. Alongside this vision, the painting conveys a sense of tranquil realism with details such as a sleeping cat on the veranda and two horses tethered in a stable; their grooms, one of whom appears captivated by the sacred appearance, rest quietly on nearby mats. In the next scene, three Buddhas reveal themselves to Kūkai, signifying the boy's spiritual awareness. This divine encounter inspires him to create clay Buddha images to worship and eventually leads to his lifelong pursuit of Buddhist truth.

The scroll's imagery gradually unveils Kūkai's childhood, which culminates with scenes of the young priest demonstrating his Buddhist ability by subduing the evil dragons and grotesque monsters of the Katsura Valley. In one such scene (B), the young priest, sitting on the seashore in prayer at a small altar table, is disturbed by dragons from the sea in the middle of the night. Kūkai quells the evil by spitting on the sand and stones, making them shine bright as stars. In the next image (C), three long-nosed *tengu* forest demons attempt to interrupt Kūkai's Buddhist practices but soon surrender when the monk brushes Mahāyāna sutras in the air that magically reveal in front of their eyes. The narrative ends with the spectacle of the morning star entering Kūkai's mouth, symbolizing his enlightenment (D). After the awakened one expels the star into the sea, its illumination remains, as indicated by the golden rays over the rock.

The beauty of the classical calligraphy together with the luxurious use of gold and saturated colors indicates that this work was commissioned by a high-status patron. The lyrical drawing of the mountainous landscape and the individualized facial expressions of the various figures enliven the calligraphic texts to persuade viewers of their truth. YX

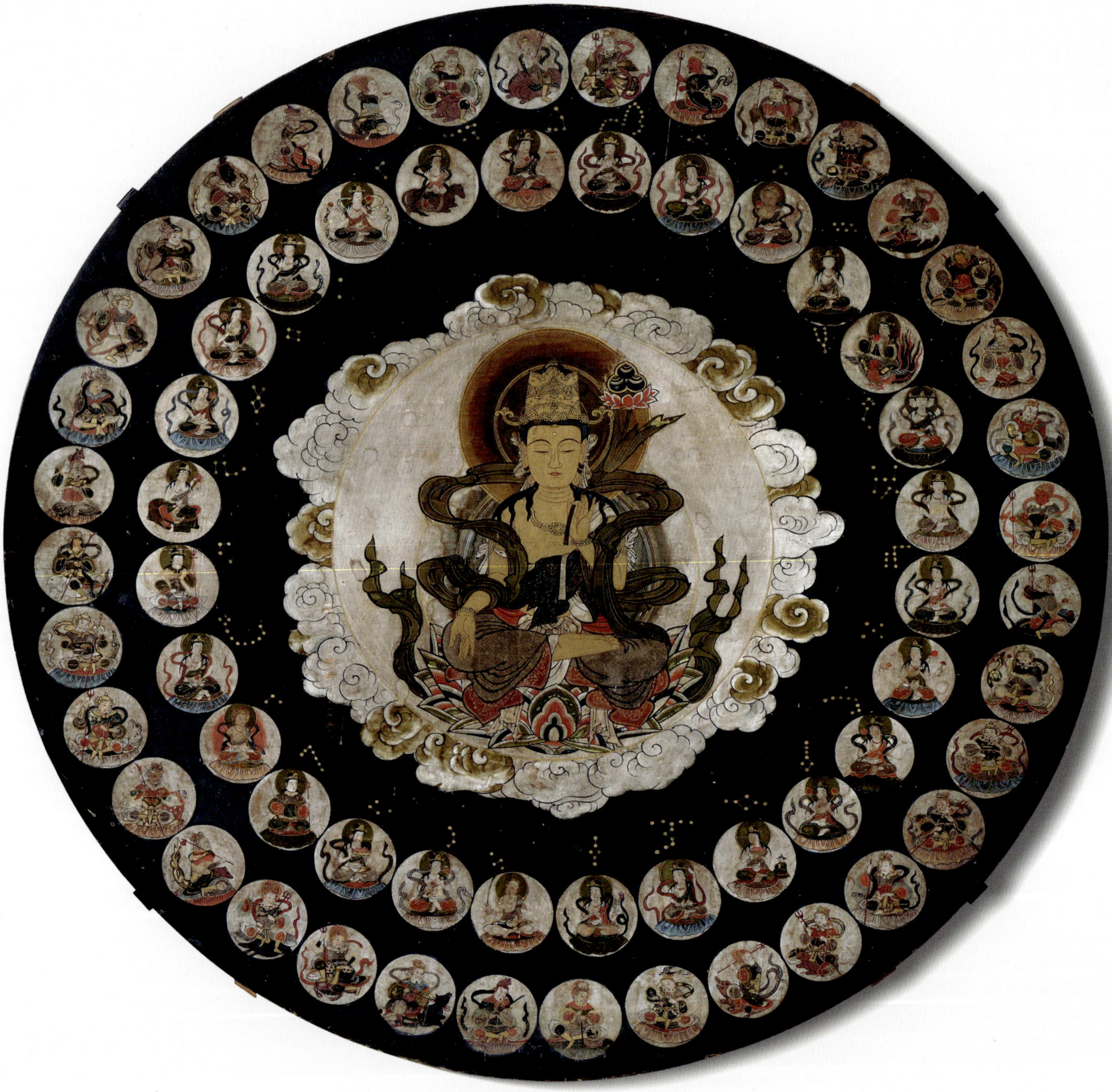

17

Star Mandala

Edo period (1615–1868), 17th century

Wood, gold, colors
Diam. 21½ in. (54.6 cm)

Gift of the Friends of the Philadelphia Museum of Art, 1978-45-2

Mandalas, visual representations of the Buddhist cosmos, are found throughout Asian art.[1] At the center of this mandala, the bodhisattva Kokūzō (Sanskrit: Akasagarbha; Chinese: Xukongzang) sits on a lotus-shaped throne and holds a lotus flower topped with three flaming jewels that have the power to fulfill wishes. Kokūzō, who is associated with Venus and the rising sun, is encircled by a celestial disk and swirling clouds set against a deep blue-green background representing the night sky. Popular among Japanese adherents of esoteric Buddhism, such as the Shingon and Tendai sects, Kokūzō is often counted among the Eight Great Bodhisattvas, who serve the Buddhas, guard the faithful, and answer prayers for worldly needs.[2]

Star mandalas frequently depict a Buddha or bodhisattva, such as Kokūzō, surrounded by supporting deities to represent the astral order. Two groups form the outer rings of this mandala. The inner circle shows twenty-eight bodhisattvas, each paired with one of the twenty-eight constellations, known as lunar mansions (Japanese: *shuku*; Chinese: *xiu*), that are central to East Asian astrology. This system divides the night sky into twenty-eight constellations surrounding Ursa Major and the North Star.[3] The outermost ring depicts thirty-six guardian deities shown in military garb. These warriors are playfully depicted with various animals, including the twelve animals of the Chinese zodiac.

Painted on a circular wood panel, the form of the mandala is reminiscent of *kakebotoke*, round plaques that typically feature embossed or relief representations of Buddhist deities.[4] Made from bronze, iron, or, less commonly, wood, *kakebotoke* derive from the use of bronze mirrors in early Japanese rituals and are often associated with Shugendō sects of esoteric Buddhism. This mandala may have been used in such esoteric Buddhist rites to venerate celestial bodies, to ward off natural catastrophes, or to pray for worldly needs such as good health and harvests.[5] HS

1. See New York 1997–98a.
2. Images of the Eight Great Bodhisattvas surrounding a central Buddha are among the oldest and most common examples of mandala imagery and played a key role in the development of this artistic format. See New York 1997–98a, 26. For a painting of Jizō (Sanskrit: Ksitigarbha; Chinese: Dizang), another of the Eight Great Bodhisattvas, see no. 7.
3. For more on the origins of East Asian astrology, see Pankenier 2013, 1–11.
4. Blair 2011, 6.
5. In Japan, Kokūzō is associated with the divine protection of crops. The Japanese pronunciation of Kokūzō (literally "treasury of empty space") is similar to the word *kokuzō* (granary). Castiglioni 2015, 327.

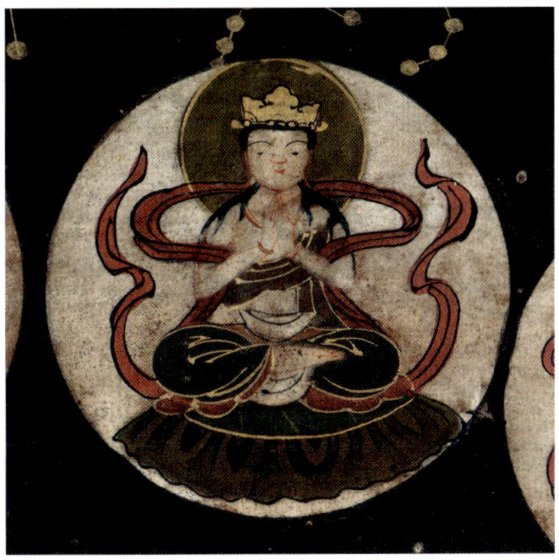

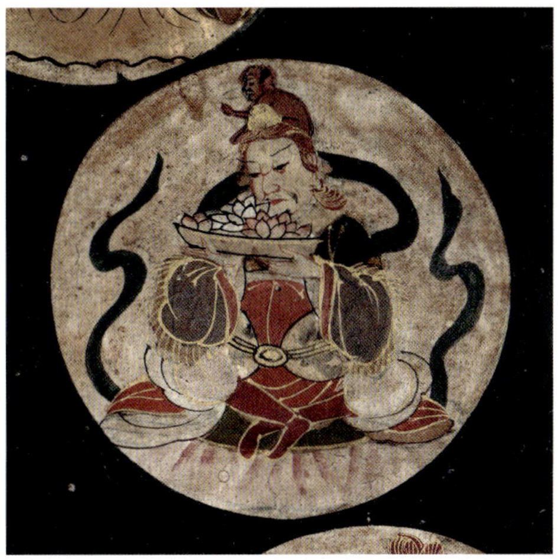

Details of a bodhisattva and a lunar mansion of the western sky (left) and a guardian figure with a monkey perched on his head (right)

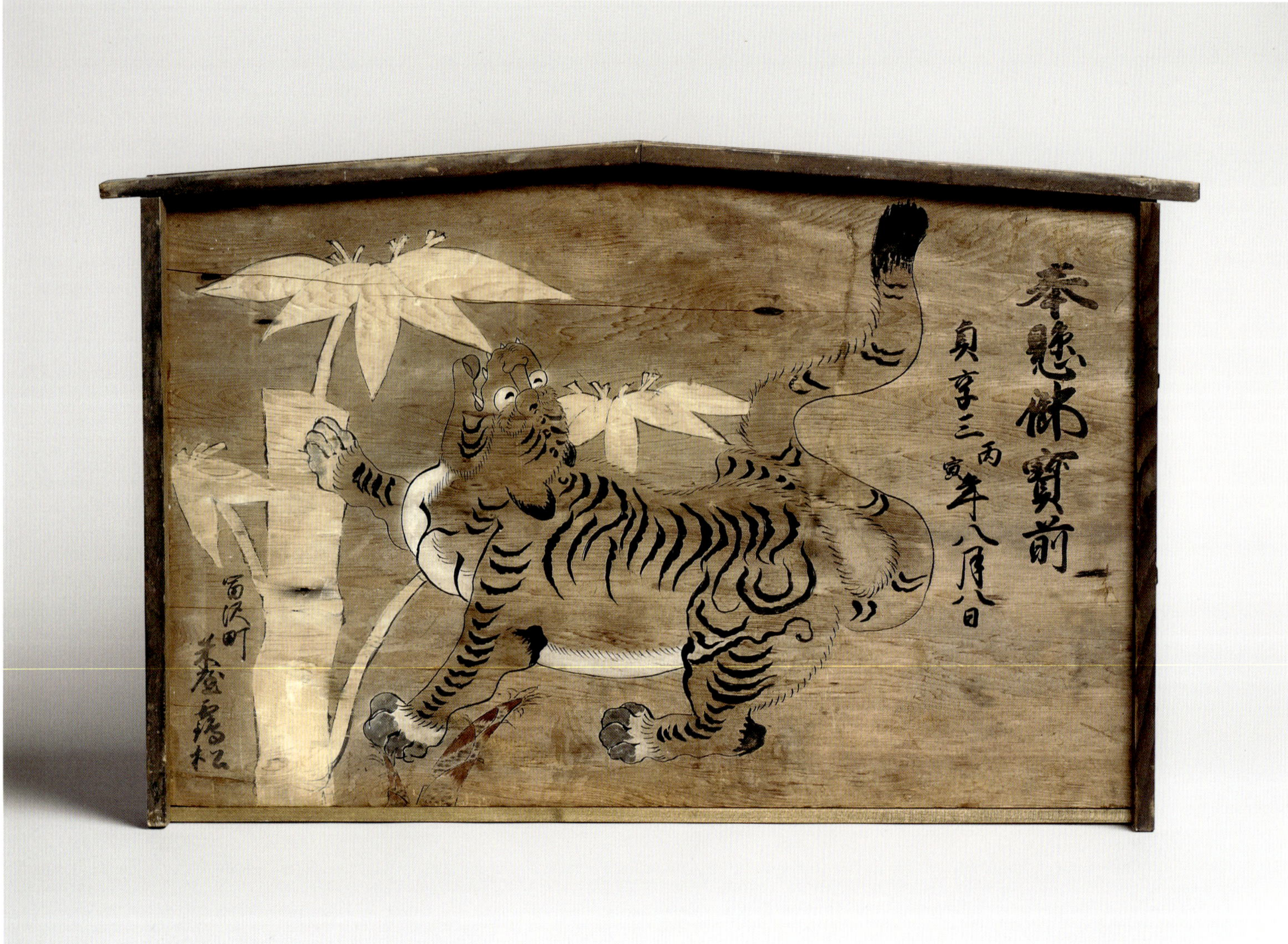
奉懸御寶前
貞享三丙寅年八月八日

18

Votive Plaques (*Ema*) of a Tiger

Edo period (1615–1868), 1686

Ink and color on pine wood, overall (including frame): 19 × 28¼ × 15/16 in. (48.3 × 71.8 × 2.4 cm)

Purchased with funds contributed by Henry B. Keep, 1966-118-2

For many centuries in Japan, the donation of painted wooden tablets to temples and shrines has been a common practice for worshippers to pray for good fortune and protection. Such votive plaques are called *ema*, or "horse pictures," because they were used as substitutes for the presentation of an actual horse as a sacred offering to the gods. In the Edo period, the motifs of *ema* expanded to include a plethora of subjects beyond horses, and the sizes of the plaques varied. This large *ema* (a type known as *ōema*) depicting a tiger was likely commissioned by donors from a professional local artist in order to assure a promising and successful future in the coming year.

Made of pine wood, this tablet was donated by a rice shop named Tsuyumatsu in the town of Tomizawa. The work is inscribed with the date of the eighth day of the eighth month in the Year of the Tiger, which probably accounts for the subject. In the center of the plaque is a tiger playfully pawing a bamboo stalk. In the folk tradition, tigers are the gods of mountains who guard peace on earth. The animal looks up cheerfully, a position echoed by its upward-pointing tail that vividly suggests the creature's vigor. The bamboo stalk on the left is boldly executed in outline, and two young brown shoots grow at the tiger's feet. A favored theme in Asian art, bamboo symbolizes prosperity and strength. The pairing of tiger and bamboo was popularly celebrated by Edo townspeople and aristocrats alike for its auspicious connotation (fig. 32). Embedded with the donor's wishes for a good harvest and prosperity in business, the work also functions as a medium for expressing vows and displays the contemporary skills of rural artists. YX

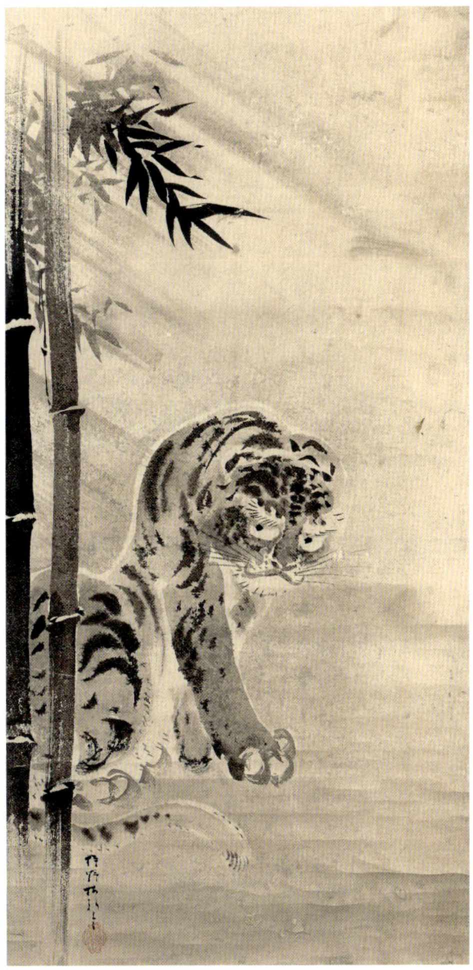

FIG. 32 Kano School. Detail of *Tiger and Bamboo*. Edo period, c. 1750. Ink on paper, mounted as a hanging scroll; 35⅛ × 14⅞ in. (89.2 × 37.8 cm). Philadelphia Museum of Art: Gift of Helen Cunningham in memory of Ted Newbold, 2019-13-4

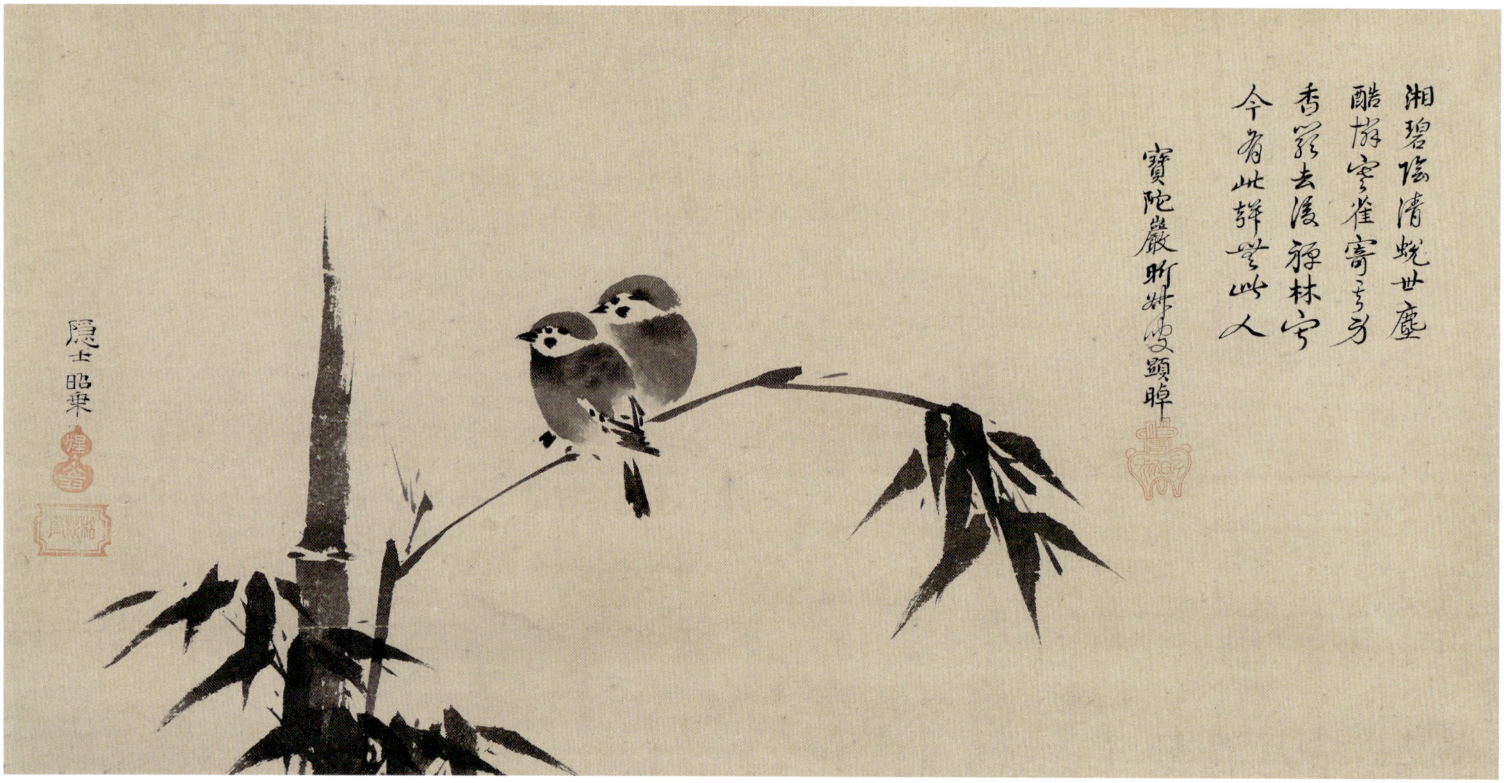

19

Bamboo and Sparrows

Shōkadō Shōjō
(1584–1639)

Edo period (1615–1868), c. 1638

Calligraphy by Kinshuku Kentaku (1610–1658)

Ink on paper, mounted as a hanging scroll; 11⅞ × 21⅛ in. (30.2 × 53.7 cm)

Purchased for the W. P. Wilstach Collection, W1972-1-1

Shōkadō Shōjō was a prominent artist and priest of the Shingon sect. Born Nakanuma Shikibu, he adopted his current name in 1637 when he retired to a mountain retreat named Shōkadō (Pine Flower Hall). There he devoted himself wholeheartedly to the realms of art and Zen, producing a volume of twenty-four paintings, titled *Yahata meibutsu* (Famous works of Yahata),[1] with a circle of scholars, monks, and artists as collaborators. *Bamboo and Sparrows* is one of Shōkadō's works from this collection (see also fig. 33).[2]

Praised as one of the *Kanei sanpitsu*, the Three Brushes of the Kanei era (1624–45),[3] Shōkadō demonstrated exceptional skill in calligraphy. While his painting style does not belong to a specific school, it shows a harmonious atmosphere that correlates to the Zen appreciation of nature. The motif of *kachō-ga*, or bird-and-flower paintings, flourished in Japan since the fourteenth century, following an influx of prestigious Chinese art brought in by the Ashikaga shogun. Japanese monks, who were often cultural pioneers, applied this genre to Zen and tea cultures to represent the Buddhist way of life. In this scroll, two plump sparrows perch on a branch of bamboo. As one of the Four Gentlemen (along with plum trees, chrysanthemums, and orchids), bamboo was favored by scholar-artists as a symbol of integrity and prosperity. The sparrows may signify the condition of enlightened beings, with their free and spontaneous movement.

This scroll is distinguished for the collaborative efforts embellished by Shōkadō's painting and the calligraphy of Kinshuku Kentaku, the abbot of Shōkoku-ji, a Zen monastery in Kyoto. The verse reads:

Among the bamboo lucid and green,
free of worldly dust,
Sojourning sparrows lodge.
In the silent woods, lingering fragrances
And the murmuring of human voice,
There is no one.

The imagery, accompanied by thought-provoking Buddhist poetry, makes this work an ideal object of appreciation for the tea ceremony. YX

1. Yahata (or Yawata) was the name of the town near Shōkadō's retreat.
2. The series was originally mounted as a single handscroll but was dismembered after World War II, with sections remounted as individual hanging scrolls.
3. The other two were Konoe Nobutada (1565–1614) and Hon'ami Kōetsu (1558–1637). For the latter, see no. 38.

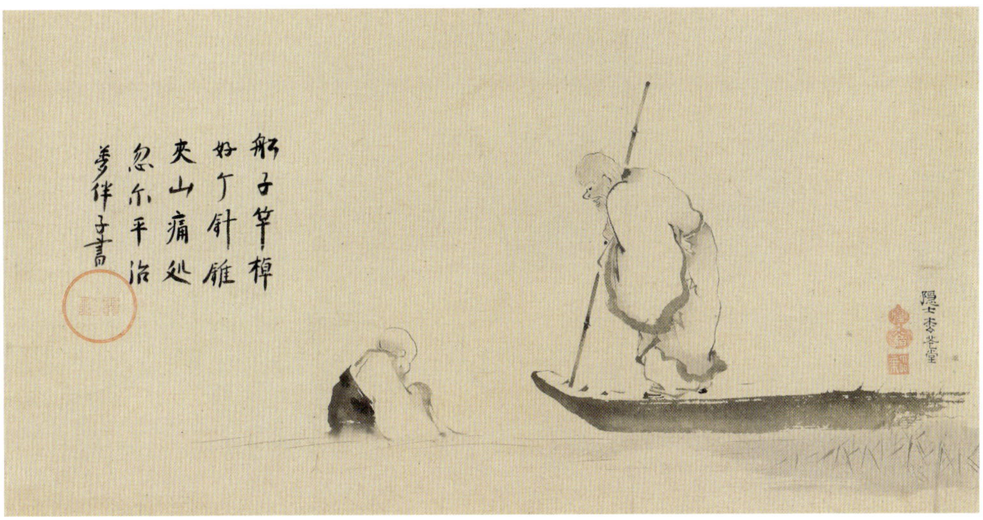

FIG. 33 Shōkadō Shōjō. *Chia-shan and the Ferryman*. Calligraphy by Tenyū (1586–1666). Edo period, c. 1638. Ink on paper, mounted as a hanging scroll; 11¼ × 21¼ in. (28.6 × 54 cm). Philadelphia Museum of Art: Purchased with the Fiske Kimball Fund and the Marie Kimball Fund, 1970-44-1

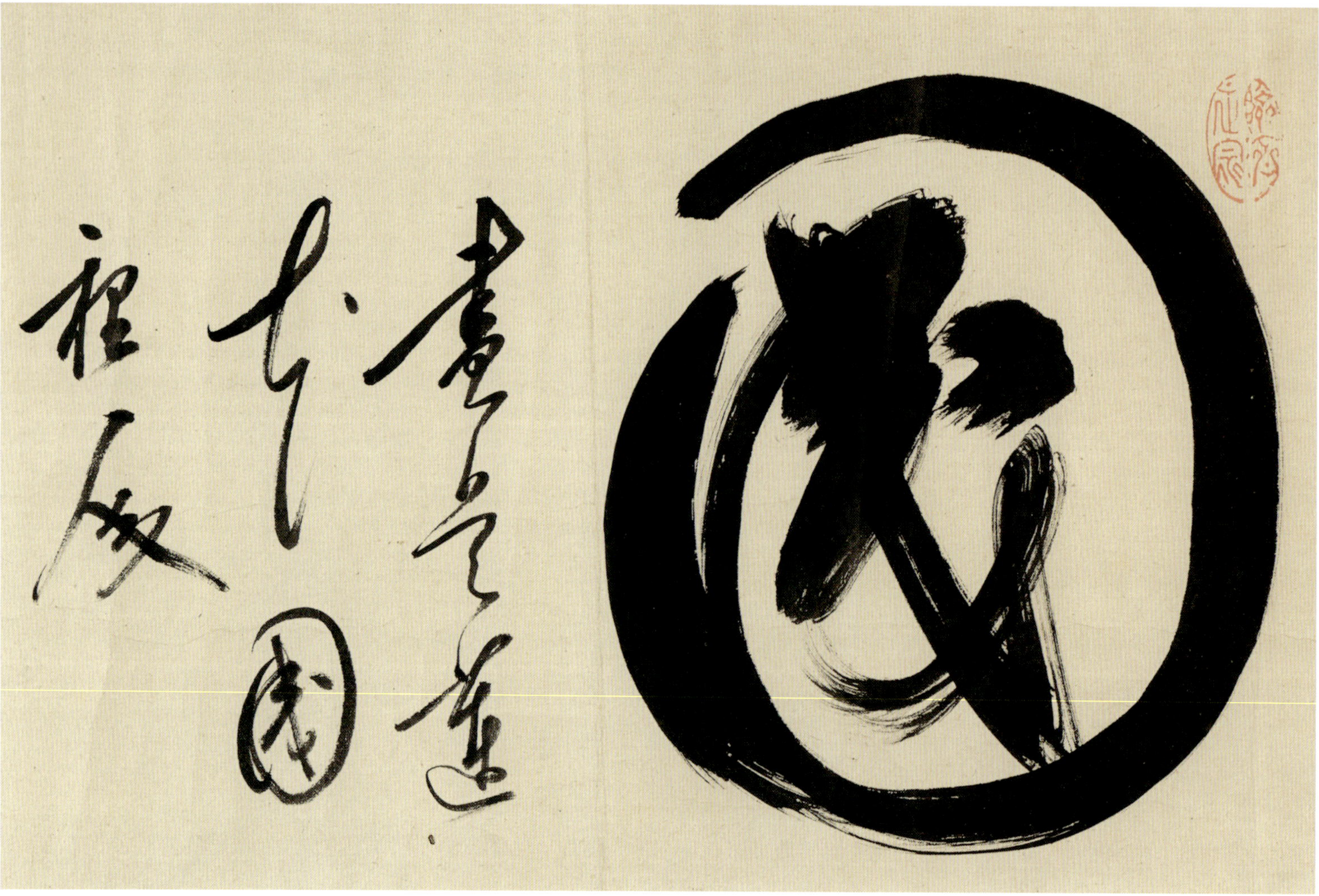

Detail of Kōsen Shōton (1633–1695; see p. 75)

20

Ink Traces (*Bokuseki*)

Edo period (1615–1868), c. 1679

Ink on paper, mounted as a handscroll; 12 in. × 37 ft. ½ in. (30.5 × 1129 cm)

Purchased with the Edward and Althea Budd Fund, 1977-164-1(1–15)

In 1654, ten years after the fall of the Ming dynasty (1368–1644) in China, a group of Zen Buddhist monks led by their abbot Ingen (1592–1673) traveled from southern China to Nagasaki, Japan.[1] The Zen Buddhism they brought is known as Ōbaku (Chinese: Huang-Po), named after the mountain where the sect's first monastery was located in China. The Ōbaku school of Zen in Japan was distinguished by the Chinese characteristics of its cultural and religious practices. Its main temple, Manpuku-ji, was constructed entirely in the Ming-dynasty style and furnished with paintings and sculptures brought by the monks from their homeland. The arts of painting, poetry, and calligraphy were considered a means to guide practitioners toward enlightenment through disciplined practice and meditation. This remarkable handscroll consists of fifteen Zen ink traces (*bokuseki*) by early leaders of the Ōbaku sect in Japan, including six of the first seven abbots of Manpuku-ji.[2]

While the meaning of the Zen phrases and poems are often deliberately paradoxical, the strong and fluid brushwork of the Ōbaku monks serves to reveal their dynamic personalities. This is evident from the opening section of three bold and well-composed characters by Ingen's successor, Mokuan Shōtō (1611–1684). The horizontal format, often used for signboards in temple buildings, here reads (from right to left), "Changes outside the frame." The harmony between the powerful brushwork and empty space suggests the balanced ideal of the Zen spirit. The second section is a Buddhist verse brushed by Sokuhi Nyoitsu (1616–1671), quoting words of the Chinese Zen master Baso Dōitsu (709–788): "That which is mind is precisely Buddha," to highlight the Buddha nature that lies within each individual.[3] Ingen, Mokuan, and Sokuhi were praised as *Ōbaku sanpitsu*, the three most excellent calligraphers of the Ōbaku school. Another horizontal format popularized by the Ōbaku monks is the use of a large emphatic opening character (*okiji*), as in Kōsen Shōton's section. The first word, "land," fills the entire height of the paper, with the remainder of the seven-syllable couplet in a smaller yet distinctive calligraphy. The influence of the Ōbaku calligraphers extended to their use of boldly carved individualistic seals.

For Zen disciples, the master's writings serve as visual koan to provoke meditation and eventual "awakening" (*satori*). In some examples here, motifs such as the moon, flowers, or clouds serve as reminders of life's transience; others celebrate the newly established Ōbaku sect's beliefs. Their dynamic brushwork stimulated Japanese interest in Ming-dynasty calligraphy and culture, which had a lasting impact. YX/FF

---

1. Ingen is the Japanese pronunciation of his Chinese name Yinyuan. He came at the invitation of another Chinese monk, who was the abbot of a temple in Nagasaki, where there was a resident Chinese community. See Lawrence and New Orleans 1978, n.p.
2. All the calligraphers represented in this scroll were Chinese immigrant monks.
3. See the Documentation (pp. 249, 251) for translations of the fifteen calligraphies.

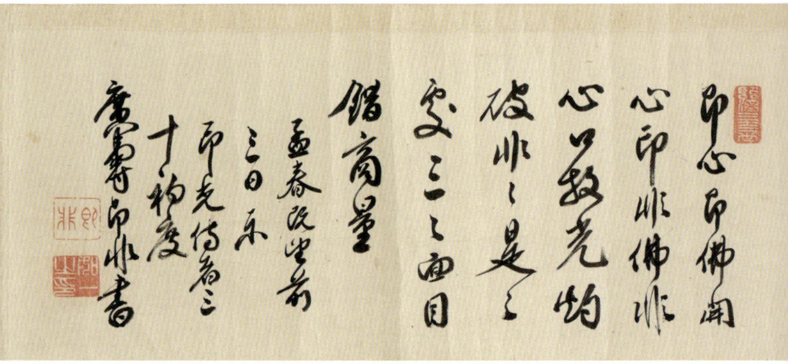

2. Sokuhi Nyoitsu (1616–1671)

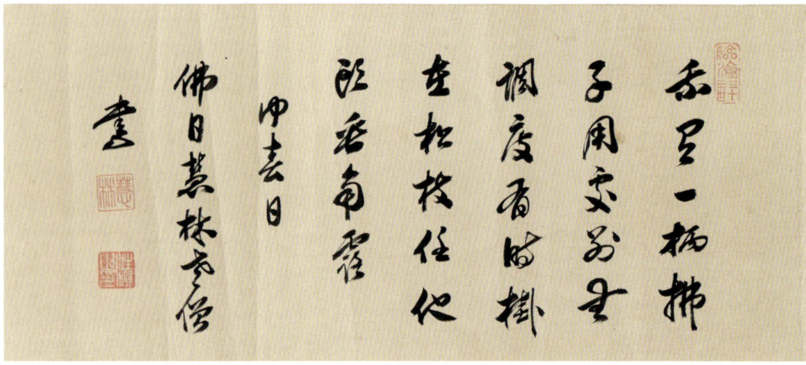

3. Erin Shōki (1609–1681)

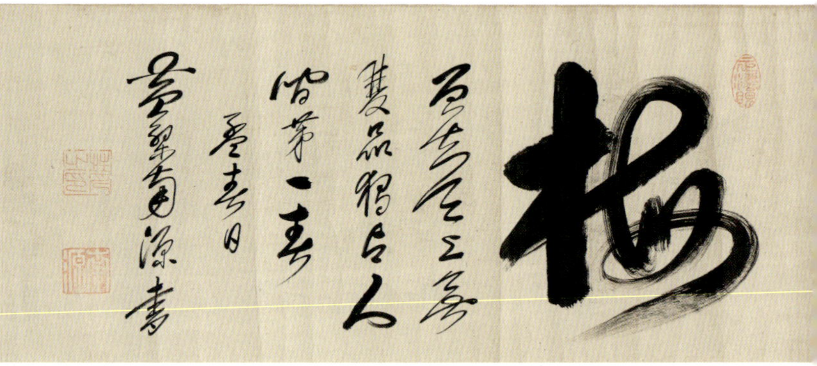

6. Nangen Shōha (1631–1692)

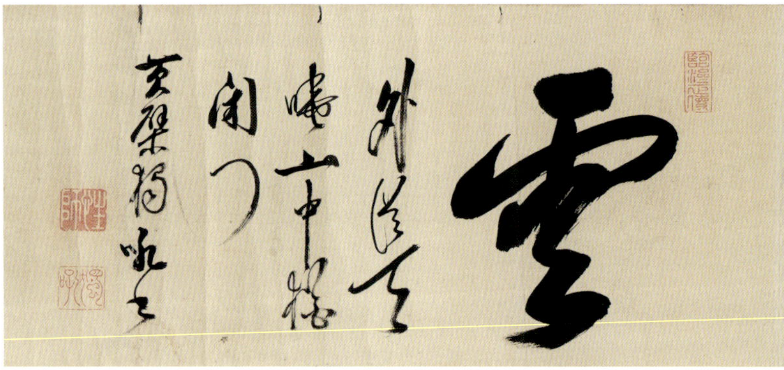

7. Dokku Shōshi (1624–1688)

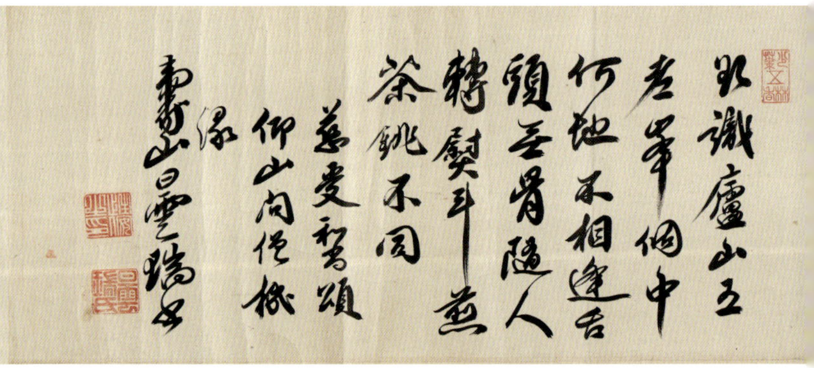

10. Donzui Shōan (1636–1705)

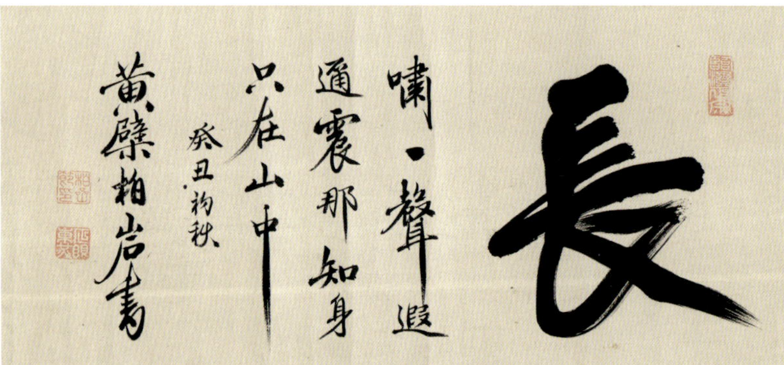

11. Hakugan Shōsetsu (1634–1673)

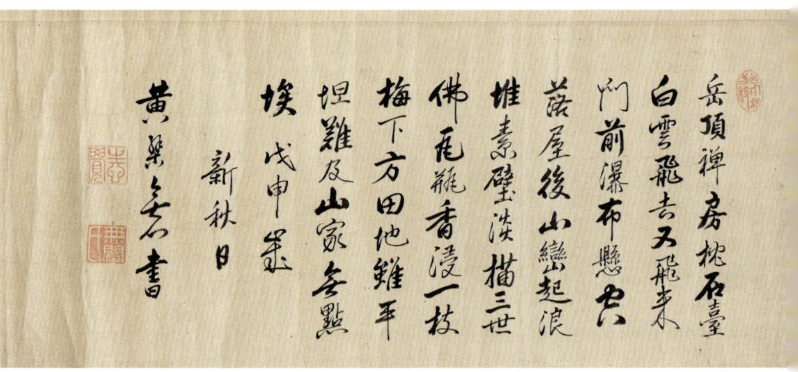

14. Mushin Shōkaku (1613–1671)

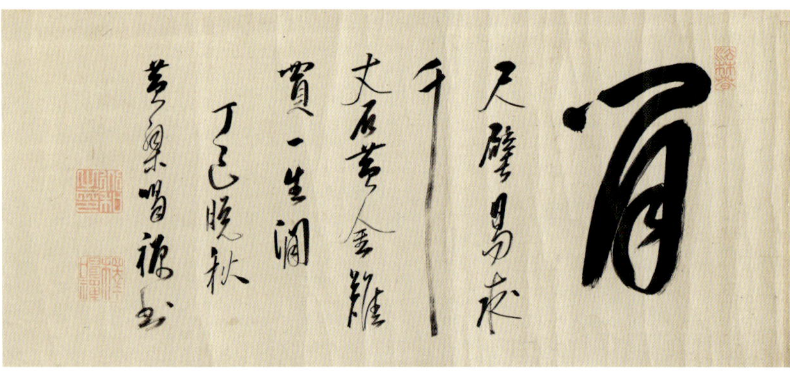

15. Katsuzen Dōwa (1634–1707)

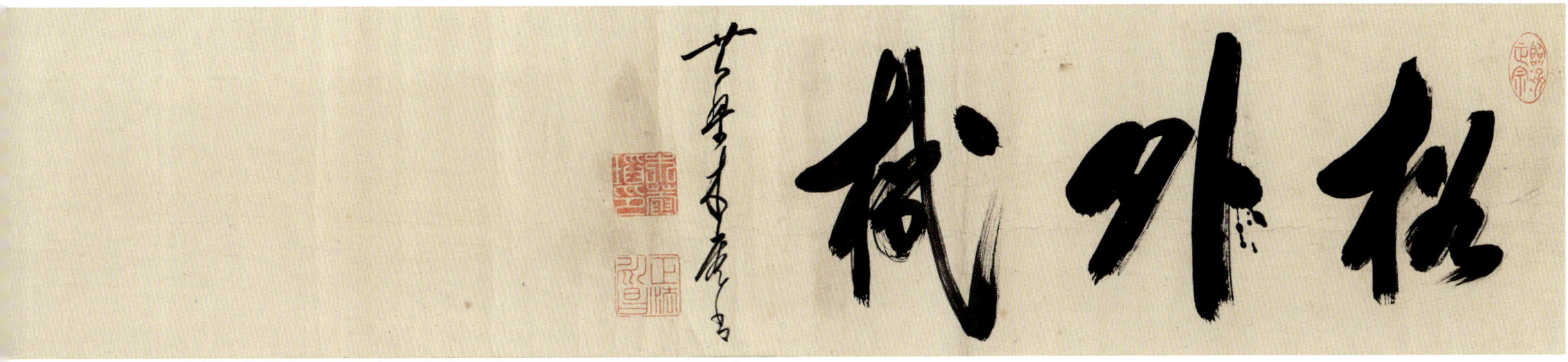

1. Mokuan Shōtō (1611–1684)

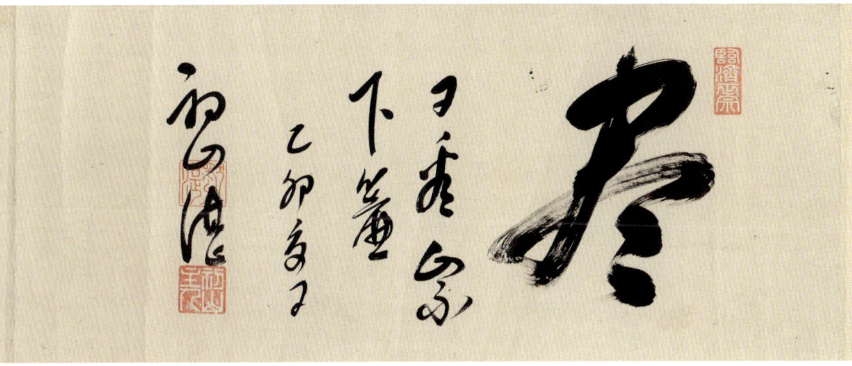

4. Dokutan Shōkei (1628–1706)

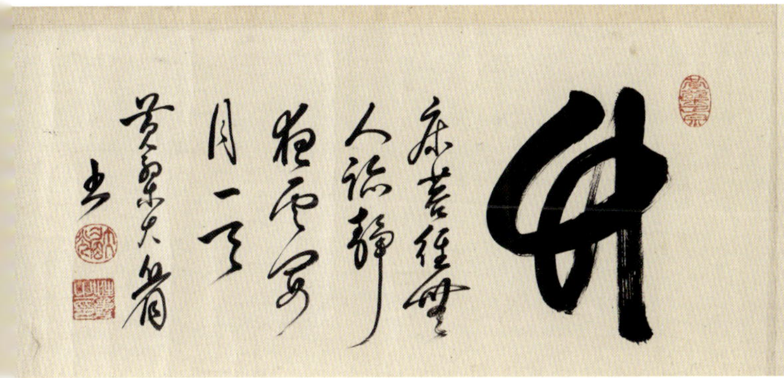

5. Daibi Shōzen (1616–1673)

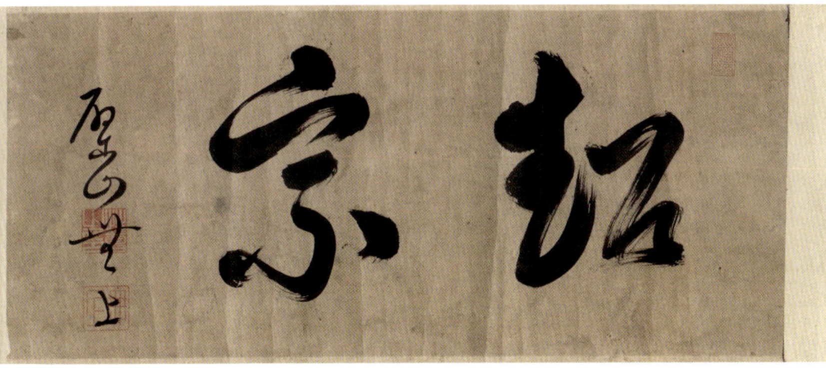

8. Mujō Shōson (1631–1660)

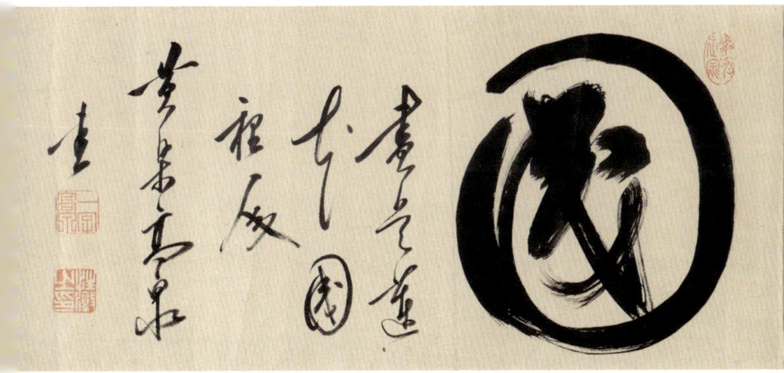

9. Kōsen Shōton (1633–1695)

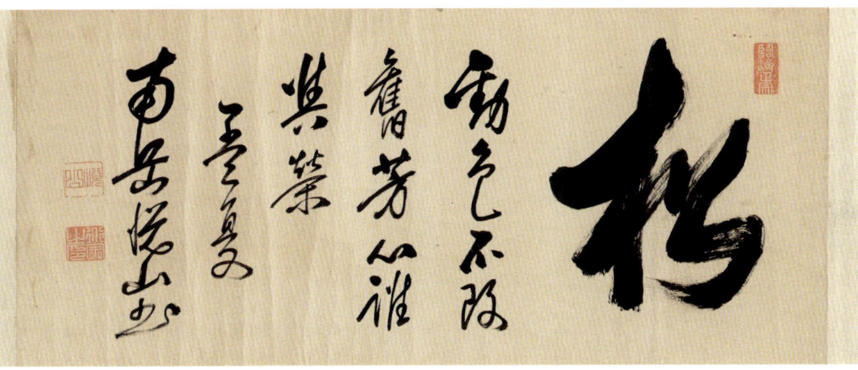

12. Essan Dōshū (1629–1709)

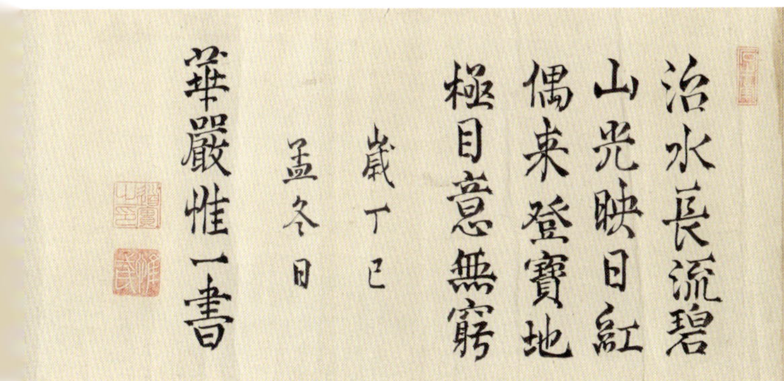

13. Yui'i Dōjitsu (1620–1692)

21

Myōhō Renge-kyō (Lotus Sutra of the Wonderful Law)

Onkō Jiun
(1718–1804)

Edo period (1615–1868), late 18th century

Ink on paper, mounted as a hanging scroll; 48 7/16 × 22 5/8 in. (123 × 57.5 cm)

Purchased with the Hollis Family Foundation Fund, 2002-198-1

One the most talented and individualistic of Edo-period calligraphers, Onkō Jiun was trained as a Buddhist monk. He became renowned for his scholarship and devotion, and even started his own eclectic Buddhist sect. Jiun's calligraphy was most influenced by the brushwork of the Ōbaku Zen monks, known as *bokuseki* (ink traces), although he seemed consciously to ignore the rules of calligraphy in his free and idiosyncratic handling of ink and brush.[1]

The five-character inscription of this calligraphy reads *Myōhō Renge-kyō*, or *Lotus Sutra of the Wonderful Law*, referring to the canonical Sanskrit Buddhist text more popularly known simply as the *Lotus Sutra*. It relates the final sermon given by the historical Buddha Shakyamuni at Vulture Peak. Jiun's quest to read the sutras in their original language led him to study Sanskrit, becoming its foremost scholar and translator of his day.

This enormous, four-foot-tall calligraphy is Jiun's homage to the sutra, and at the same time provides a focus for meditating on its significance. Starting at the upper right and dominating the whole is the large character *myō* (wonderful). Jiun shows his mastery of the brush, beginning with this powerful sweep of ink, going from very wet, deep black at the top to the "flying white" dry tail that extends almost the entire length of the paper surface. The pressure of Jiun's brush in the dry section reveals the pattern of the ribbed tatami mat underneath the paper. The small character at lower right is *hō* (law) and serves as a stolid anchor for *myō* above it. The three characters to the left, *renge-kyō* (lotus sutra), are comfortably nestled in the embrace of the large *myō* and bring a sober balance to the whole.

Jiun spent the final decades of his long life in retirement at a temple near Osaka. It was during this period, between 1781 and 1804, that he produced most of his calligraphies, including this example. The depth of his religious fervor is revealed in the strength of his extraordinary brushwork. FF

1. See no. 20, where large emphatic initial characters (*okiji*) are frequently employed.

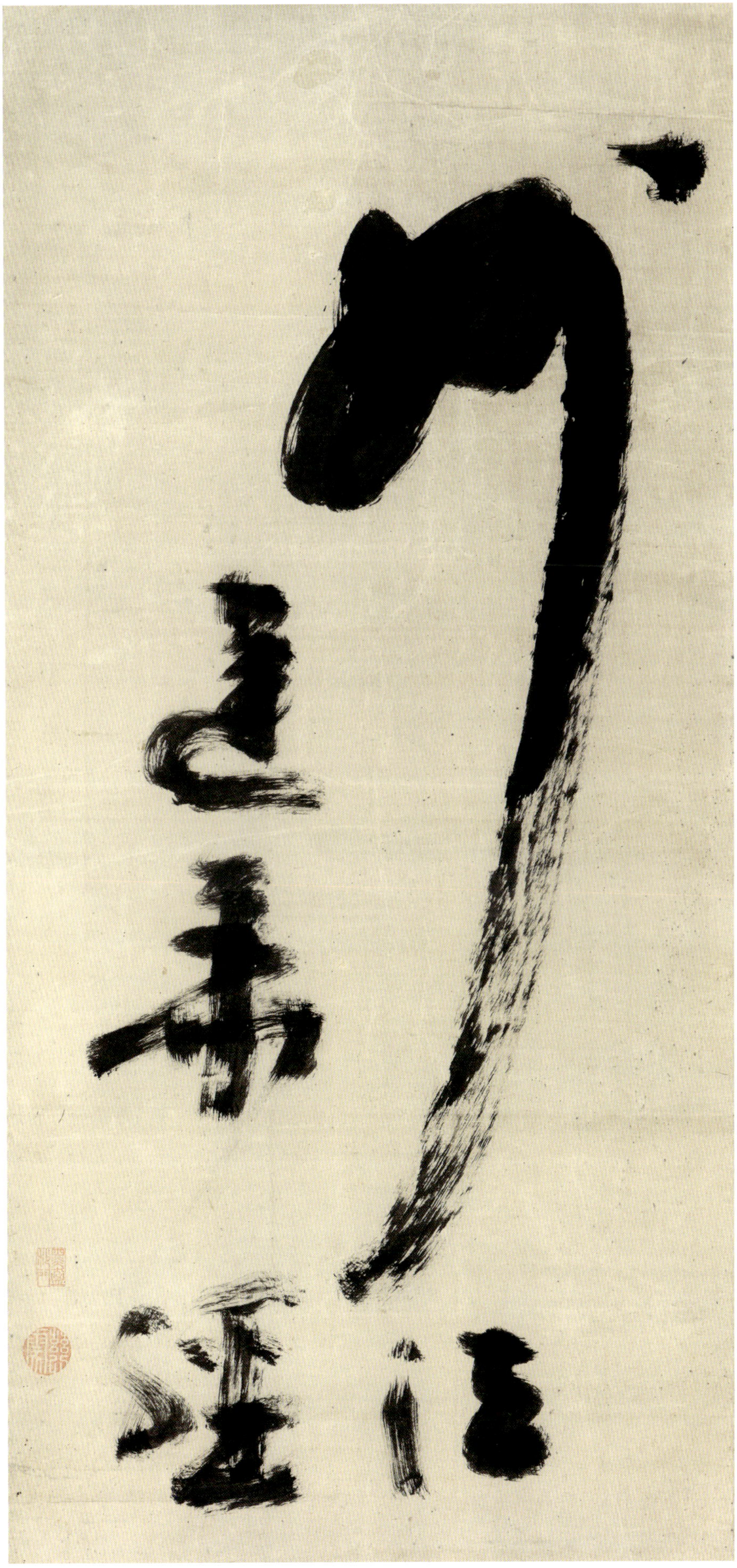

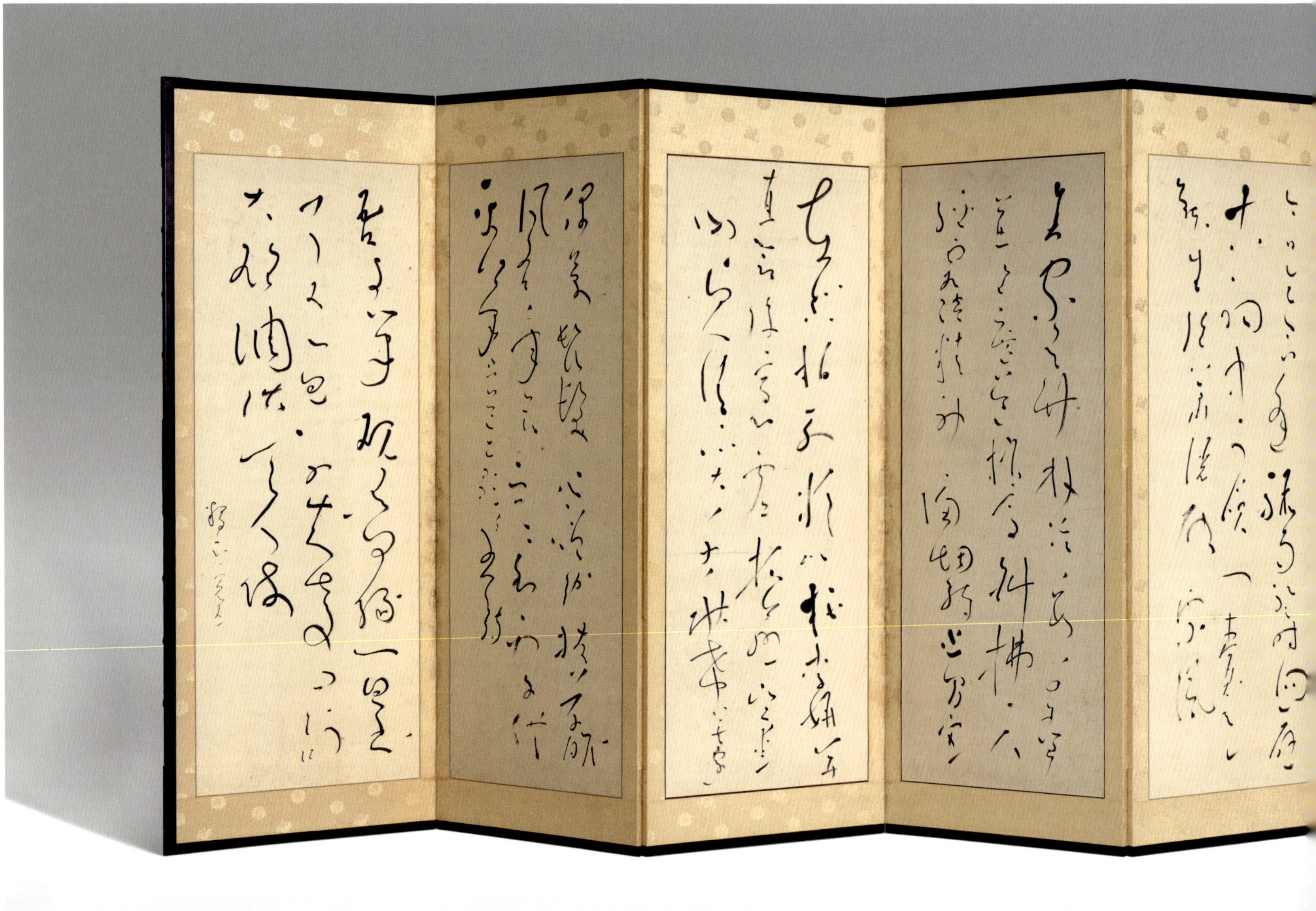

22

Five Poems

Ryōkan
(1758–1831)

Edo period (1615–1868),
c. 1816–26

Ink on paper, mounted as a six-panel screen; each panel: 50 9/16 × 18 15/16 in. (128.4 × 48.1 cm)

Purchased with funds contributed by members of the East Asian Art Committee, the Hollis Endowment for East Asian Art acquisitions, and other donors in honor of Felice Fischer, 2021-112-1

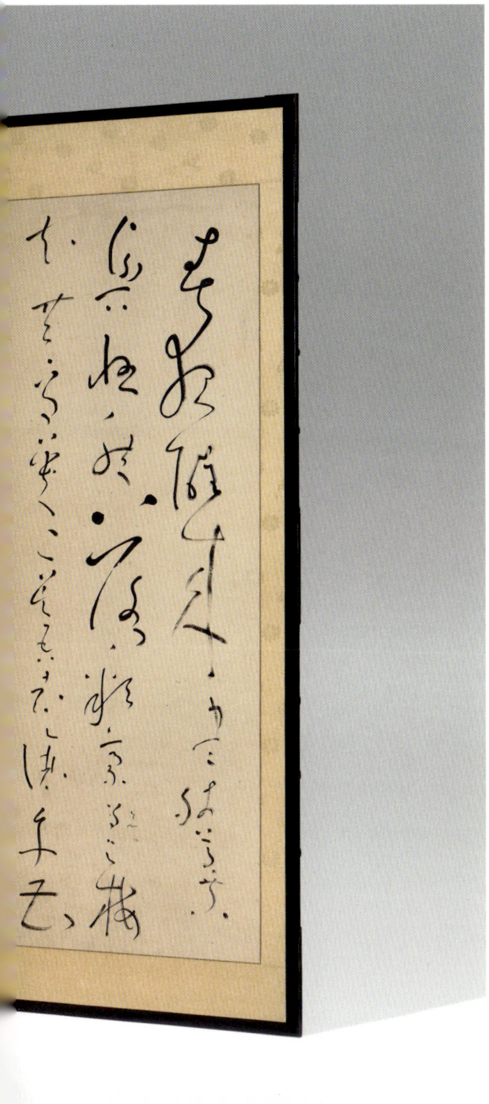

Ryōkan was born in Niigata Prefecture in northern Japan and entered a Zen monastery at the age of seventeen. In his twenties he moved to Okayama to study with a famous Zen master, and subsequently spent years traveling throughout Japan as an itinerant monk in the mode of predecessors such as Matsuo Bashō (1644–1694). Ryōkan eventually returned to his hometown and lived in a one-room hut on the nearby mountainside before moving to a lodging at the foot of the mountain in 1816. His relatively quiet life would have remained unknown were it not for his talents as a poet and calligrapher. His fame seems at times to have been a burden to this gentle, modest man.

He wrote verses in Chinese in the manner of Ike Taiga (1723–1776; see no. 50), an artist whom Ryōkan much admired. He too was inspired by the Chinese poets of the Tang dynasty (618–907), and by the Chinese calligraphy mode called "untrammeled." The calligraphy on this screen is a superb example of Ryōkan's style: while avoiding the more bombastic mode of famous Zen monks such as Onkō Jiun (see no. 21; also no. 20), Ryōkan's brushwork seems spontaneous in its fluidity and nervous energy. The lustrous inking is subtly modulated between thick and thin; the characters between are sinuous and stolid.

Ryōkan's poetic subject matter ranges widely but most often focuses on his everyday life as a monk who went out daily to beg for his food among the families and children of the village near his hermitage. This screen includes five Chinese verses, one on each of the four outer panels, and a single twelve-line verse that straddles the two center panels.[1] This arrangement indicates that the calligraphy was originally intended as a screen, a relatively rare format for Ryōkan.

This was the right-hand screen of a pair that originally belonged to, and was most likely commissioned by, the brothers Suzuki Tōken (1794–1851) and Suzuki Buntai (1797–1870), who anthologized Ryōkan's poetry (*Sōdōshū*).[2] FF

1. See the Documentation (p. 251) for translations of the five poems.
2. See Sōma 1928, nos. 83a, 83b. The missing left-hand screen featured Japanese verse. Ryōkan first met Buntai in 1813. Buntai was a scholar of Confucian studies who opened his own private academy. For a chronology of Ryōkan's life, see Kojima and Sekiya 2017, vol. 3.

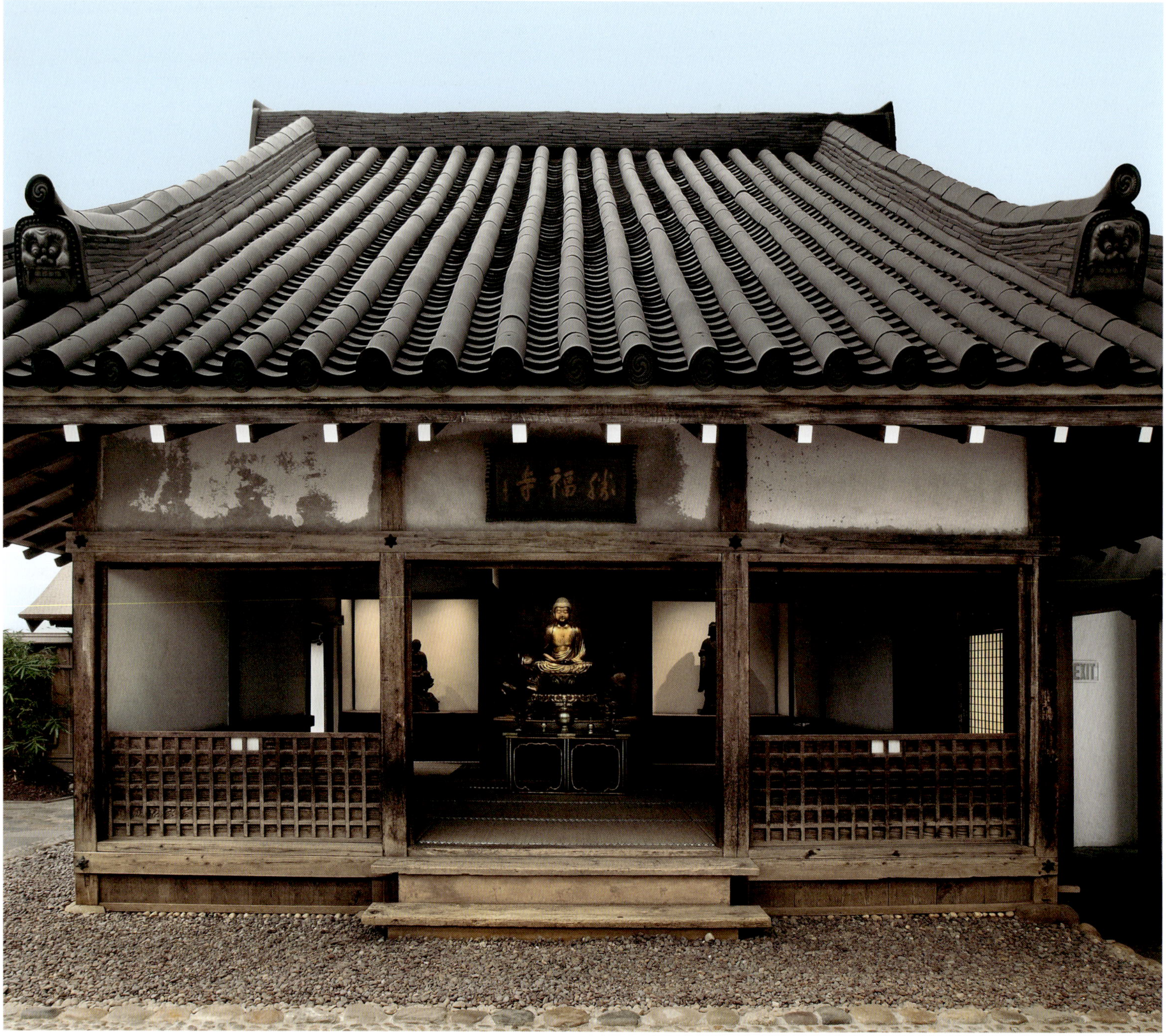
EXIT

23

Shōfuku-ji (Temple of the Attainment of Happiness)

Muromachi period (1392–1573), 1398

Wood and plaster, 19 × 22 ft. (579.1 × 670.6 cm)

Purchased with Museum funds, 1929-58-1

When Buddhism became the official religion of Japan in the eighth century, temples of worship were built in great numbers, particularly in and around the capital city of Nara, with support of the imperial family. The architectural style, like other arts imported with Buddhism, followed Chinese precedent, emphasizing an imposing tiled roof and formal symmetry throughout. Although this Buddhist temple was built in 1398 and extensively repaired in the latter half of the seventeenth century, it serves as a time capsule of the earlier style. It stood originally in Katagiri village in Nara Prefecture as a subsidiary part of Hōryū-ji, the great Buddhist temple. When the Shōfuku-ji building was dismantled in 1928, the museum acquired its wooden elements as part of the plan to display religious and secular architecture of the world.[1]

The name of the temple, Shōfuku-ji, is inscribed on a signboard above the central bay. The building is supported by twelve cypress posts resting on stone bases, with white plaster walls on three sides. The three-bay front can be closed off by wooden latticed doors (*shitomi-do*), the upper halves of which open horizontally inward and are held open by hooks from the ceiling. There are also two side entrances with sliding wooden doors (*ama-do*). The hipped roof is covered with pottery tiles and two demon-mask tiles (*oni-ita*) intended to frighten away evil spirits. Iron lanterns hang from the corners of the eaves.

The center of the temple interior holds the main altar (*butsudan*), where a lacquered and gilt wood statue of Amida Buddha presides. The side niches (*tokonoma*) are used as subsidiary altars.[2] Although modest in size, the building, with its imposing roof and formal symmetry, has a monumental quality in the space that it shares with the Sunkaraku teahouse (see no. 24). FF

1. See Felice Fischer, "Philadelphia and the Art of Japan," in this volume, esp. 18–19.
2. The contents on display are not original to the temple but are intended to approximate what the interior might have looked like. The pottery tiles are modern, made in the traditional style by Nara craftspeople in 1955.

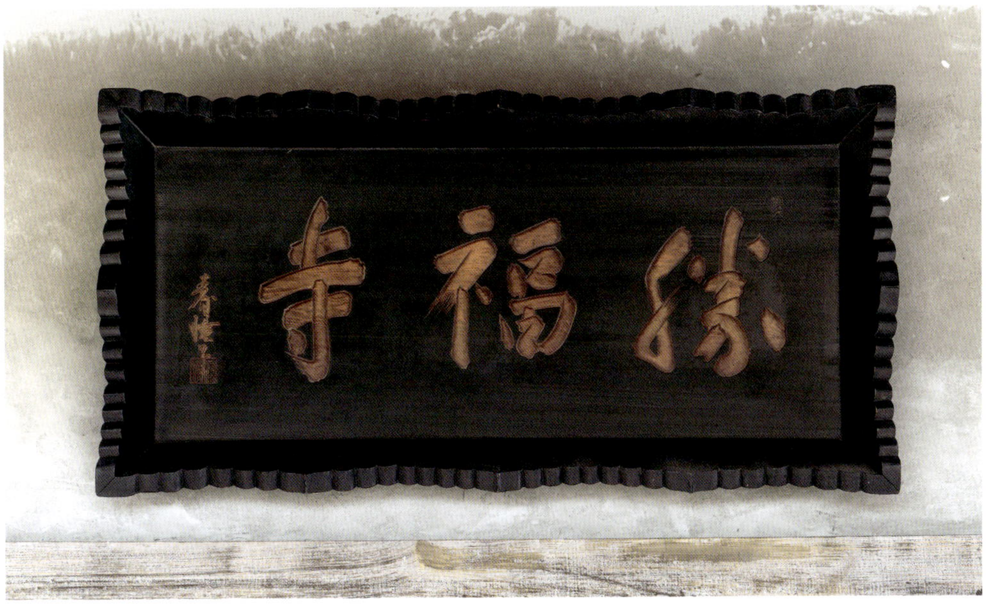

Signboard inscribed with the temple's name, Shōfuku-ji

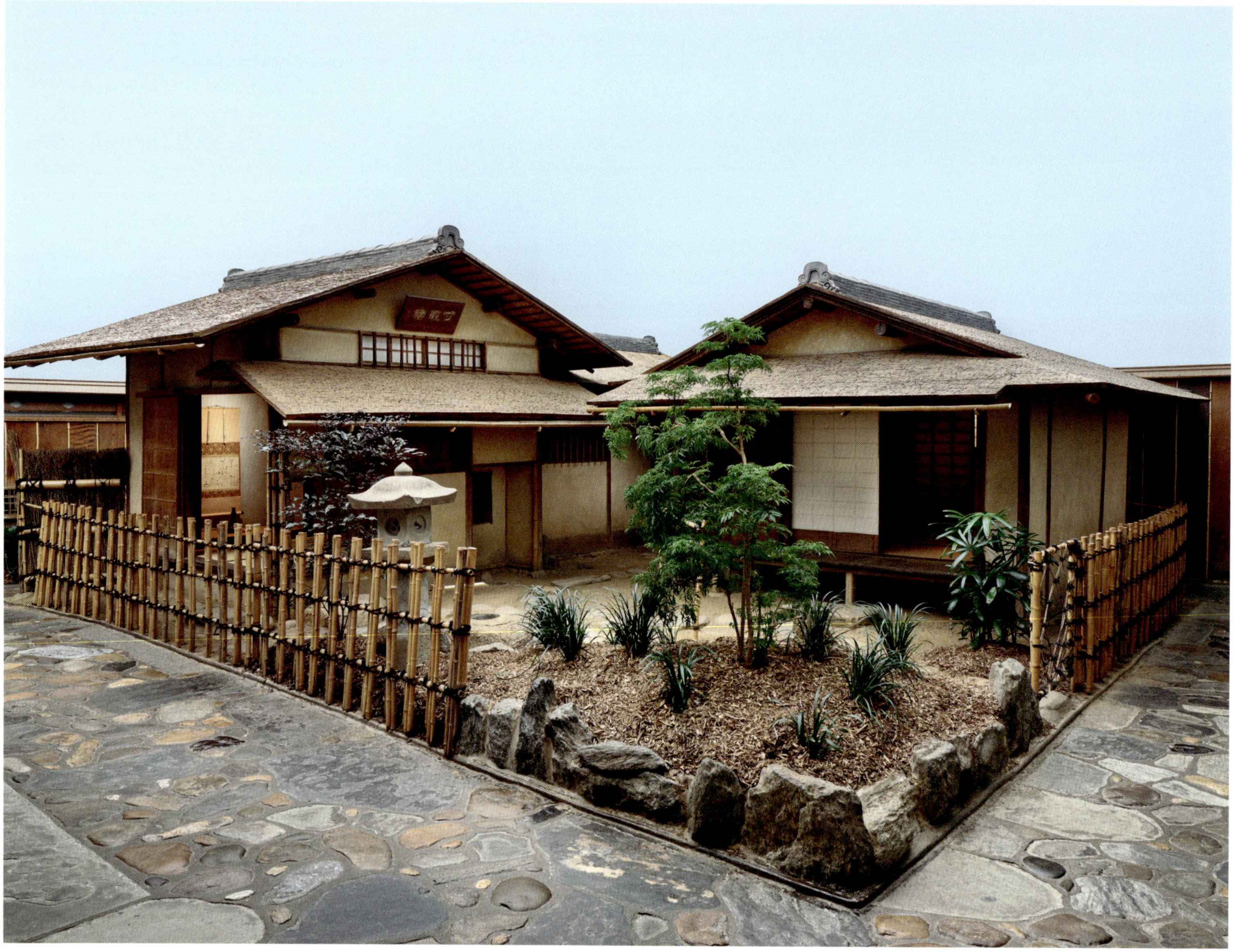

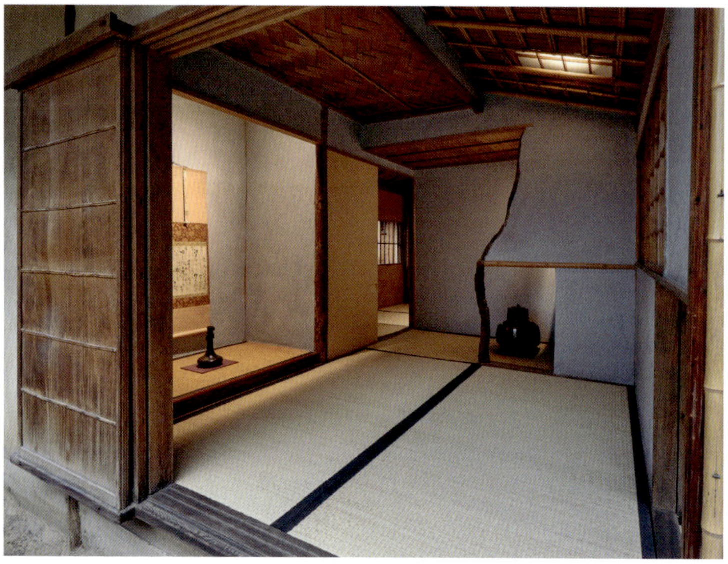

24

Sunkaraku (Evanescent Joys) Ceremonial Teahouse

Ōgi Rodō
(1863–1941)

Taishō period (1912–26), c. 1917

Wood, bamboo, stone, metal, rush, plaster, paper, ceramic, fabric, and mulberry bast cord

Purchased with Museum funds, 1928-114-1

The teahouse named Sunkaraku (Evanescent Joys) was built over one hundred years ago in Tokyo as a private setting for the practice of the tea ceremony. The ritual drinking of tea in Japan has its roots in the Zen Buddhist temples, where it served as a stimulant for the monks to keep alert during long hours of meditation.[1] Tea gatherings became popular in the secular realm in the fourteenth century with the spread of *cha-awase* (tea-matching) events, which took place in aristocratic homes, and can be likened to wine tasting in modern terms. About two centuries later a separate teahouse structure was introduced, with the intent of returning tea drinking to the Zen ideal of a meditative retreat from the world, shared by two or three participants. The figure most instrumental in establishing and codifying the tea ceremony as it is practiced today was Sen no Rikyū (1522–1591). He advocated what is called *wabi-cha* (austere tea), based on a taste for poverty, humility, and restraint.

The tea ceremony gradually expanded to include a meal and two rounds of tea, requiring additional utensils and food dishes. Tea aficionados vied to commission potters, lacquer artists, and chefs to produce the most memorable objects and meals. Among the architectural adaptations was the addition of a second structure, the *yoritsuki*, which serves as a waiting room for guests while the host prepares the tearoom.

Designed by the architect Ōgi Keiichirō, better known by his tea name, Rodō, Sunkaraku incorporates the historic features of teahouse architecture, including a small alcove for displaying art (*tokonoma*). The signboard proclaiming its name, Sunkaraku, features the calligraphy of an earlier tea master, Matsudaira Fumai (1751–1818). Using parts from an older structure, Rodō erected the teahouse at his residence in Tokyo (fig. 34). The natural materials are primarily wood, bamboo, and paper, with no extraneous decoration or paint, and are assembled by joinery techniques requiring no nails. A farewell tea ceremony was hosted by Rodō on September 23, 1928 (see fig. 10), after which the teahouse was disassembled and shipped to Philadelphia, where it still is used for tea gatherings on special occasions.[2] FF

1. The monk Eisai (also pronounced Yōsai; 1141–1215) is credited with bringing back tea-plant seeds and tea practices to Japan when he returned from Buddhist studies in China in 1191. Unlike the steeped tea most familiar in the United States and Europe, the Zen tea is a powdered form (matcha) that is whisked into a frothy beverage with hot water.

2. The crates containing the teahouse elements arrived in Philadelphia in 1928, but it would be another three decades before they were reassembled, owing to the 1929 stock market crash, warfare in the Pacific in the 1930s, and World War II. It was not until the spring of 1955 that the Sunkaraku teahouse was unpacked, and a trial construction was begun in the museum's garage. The official dedication of the teahouse and garden space took place on November 28, 1957.

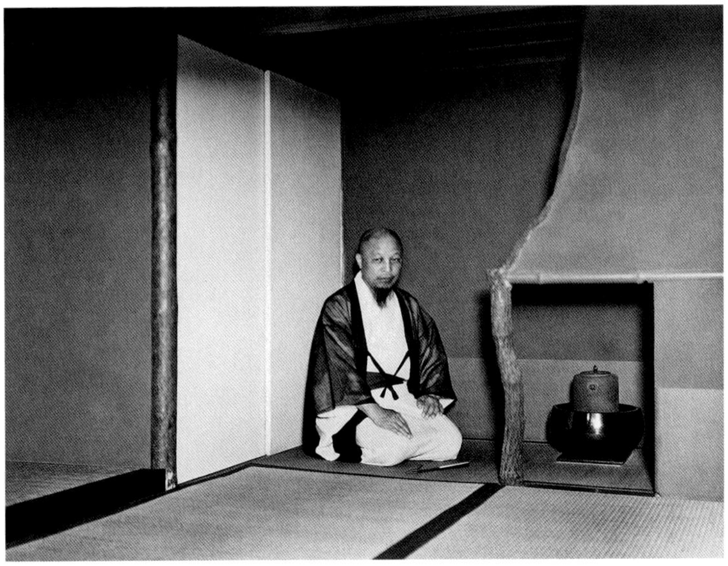

FIG. 34 Ōgi Rodō seated inside his tearoom, Tokyo, 1928. Philadelphia Museum of Art Library and Archives

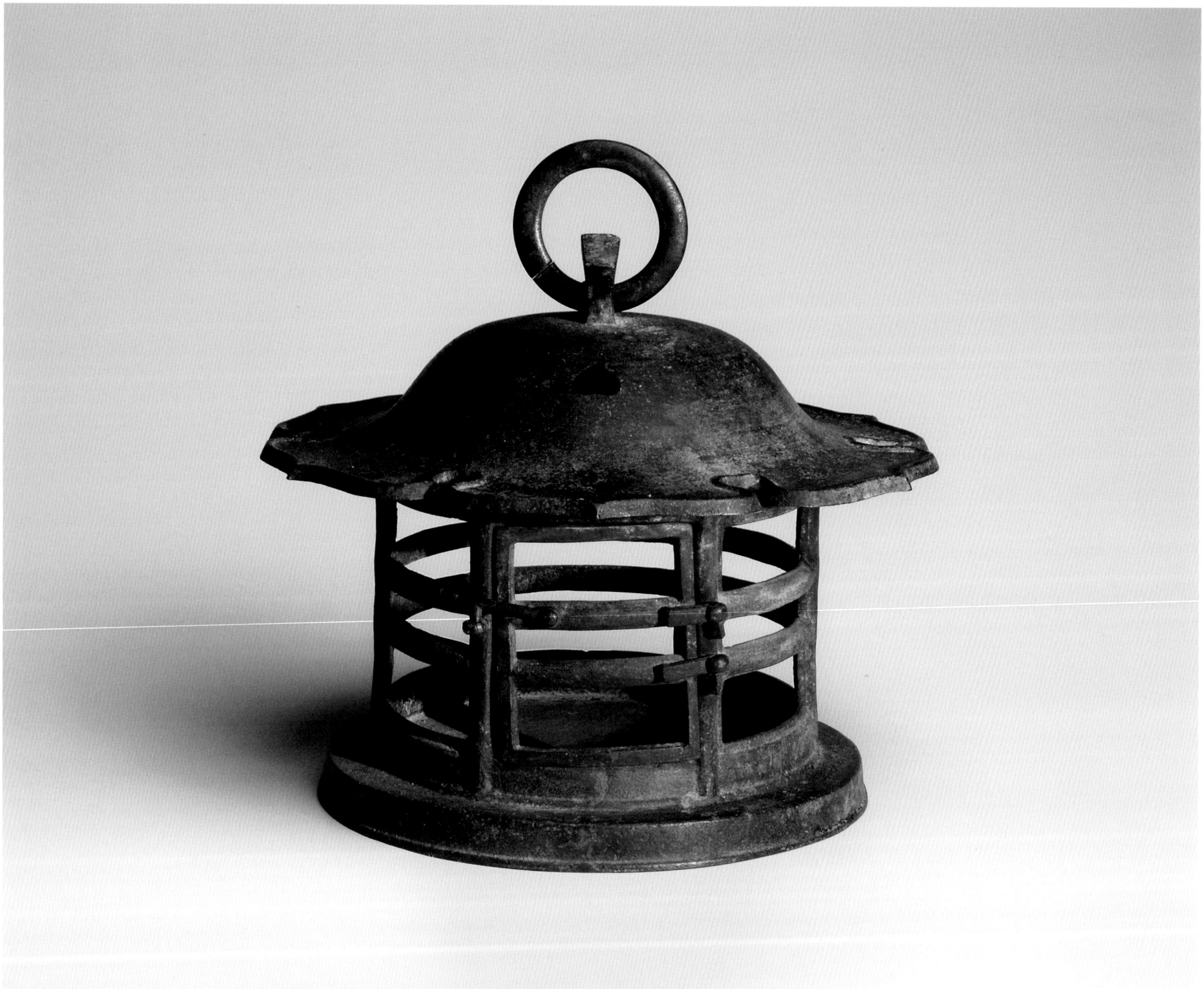

25

Lantern

Muromachi period (1392–1573), 16th century

Bronze, 9½ × 12 × 9 in. (24.1 × 30.5 × 22.9 cm)

Purchased with the Henry B. Keep Fund and the John T. Morris Fund, 2004-179-1

Lanterns were used to light the pathways leading to Buddhist temples in Japan beginning in the Nara period (710–94). Most were made of stone for durability, although the famed bronze lantern in front of the Buddha Hall at Tōdai-ji dates to the eighth century. The great Shinto shrine Kasuga Taisha displays three thousand lighted lanterns during the annual festivals of Setsubun (marking the beginning of spring) and O-bon (marking the return of ancestral spirits). Smaller wood or metal versions like this one, a type known as *tsuri-tōrō* (hanging lanterns), could be hung from the eaves of temple buildings as well.[1] Although there is a ring on top of this example for suspending it, the flat base of its hexagonal shape suggests that it was originally mounted on a pedestal or used along the ground to light garden paths at a temple or shrine.

The simple cast form with a foliate cap and the patination of the bronze over time would have appealed to the "rustic" taste of tea masters.[2] The six sides were originally lined with handmade paper to give off a warm, soft light. One side has a hinged door to give access to the interior, and a small heart-shaped opening at the top allows smoke to escape. When lanterns were periodically replaced or sold by temples, tea aficionados would often acquire the old ones for use in evening tea ceremonies. The creative repurposing of objects for tea gatherings started with Sen no Rikyū's use of Korean rice bowls to serve tea, and this lantern likewise was given new life by the anonymous tea collector who had a paulownia-wood storage box made for it to protect the lantern when not in use. FF

1. For an example of such a temple, see no. 23.
2. The ideal of *sabi*, espoused by tea masters since Sen no Rikyū (1522–1591), literally means "rust."

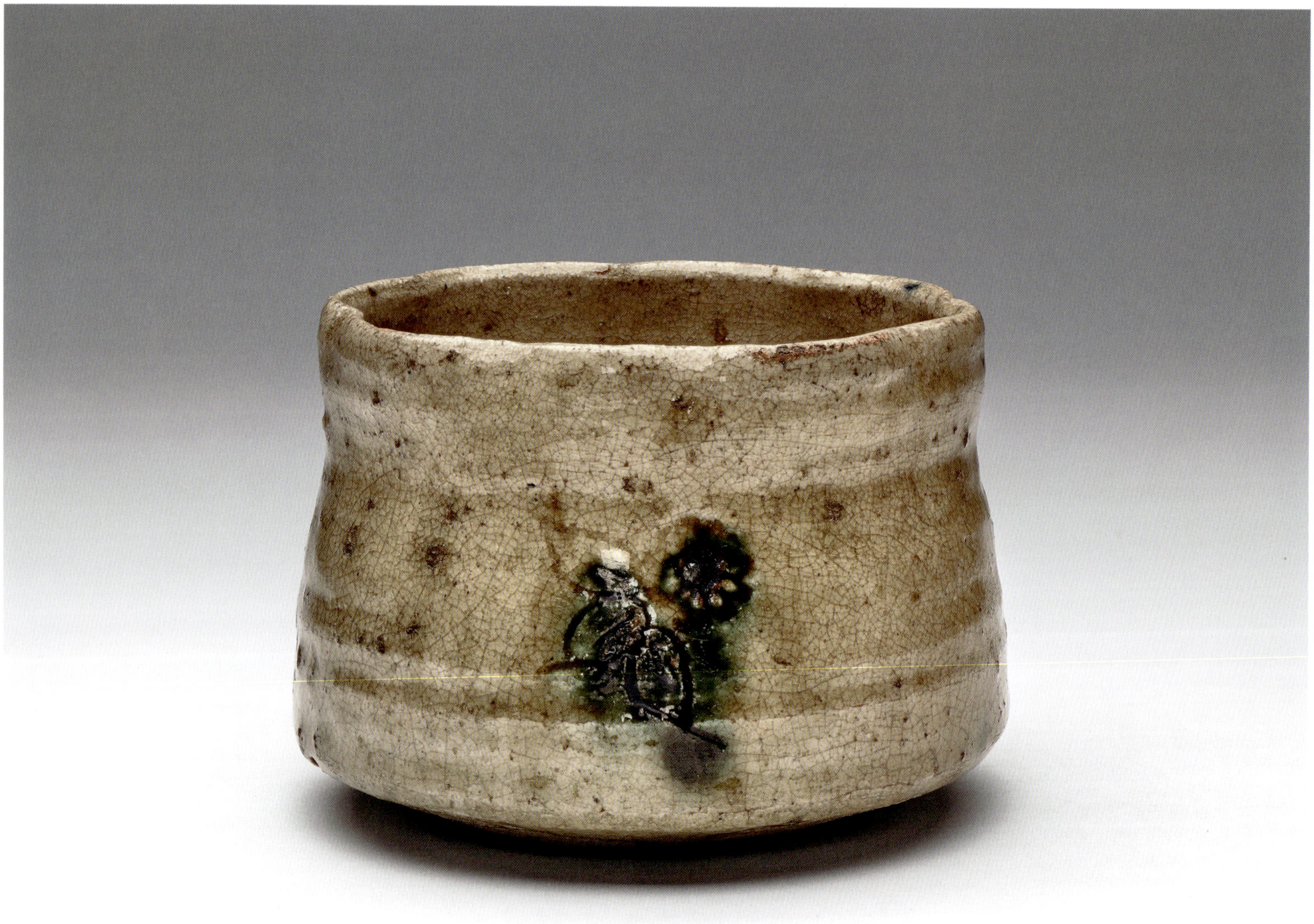

26

Teabowl

Momoyama period (1568–1615), late 16th–early 17th century

Glazed stoneware (Kiseto ware)
3¾ × 4¾ in. (9.5 × 12.1 cm)

Purchased with the Hollis Fund for East Asian Art Acquisitions, 2011-47-1

Artisans in Seto and Mino, north of Nagoya, mixed wood ash, water, and iron-rich clay to create the honey-yellow glaze of this Kiseto, or Yellow Seto, teabowl. Formed on a wheel, the finely potted bowl shows traces of the potter's fingers, which left rippling lines on the vessel's thin walls. In one's hand, the bowl feels lighter than its sturdy, squat form would otherwise suggest.

Kiseto wares are typically decorated with stamped or incised floral designs highlighted by a dab of copper-based green enamel. This bowl has green chrysanthemum-like flowers on the front and back. Seen from above, the vessel's undulating rim combined with a touch of copper enamel in the center of the interior suggests a yellow flower with a green pistil. The yellow, green, and occasionally rust-red coloring of Kiseto ware has led some scholars to speculate that the style was inspired by earlier three-color ware (Japanese: *sansai*; Chinese: *sancai*) made in southern China.[1]

In the late sixteenth and early seventeenth centuries, artisans in Seto and Mino exported ceramics in an array of new styles to markets in the tea centers of Sakai, near Osaka, and Kyoto.[2] Tea gatherings were popular among wealthy merchants and warriors and served as forums to build social, commercial, and political relationships. To this day, tea is a popular practice in Japan and tea events range in formality, depending on the season and occasion, from quick impromptu encounters to elaborate full-day affairs. At formal gatherings, ceramic dishes are used to serve a light meal as well as two courses of both sweets and tea. Like many Kiseto wares, this bowl was probably intended to serve a side dish, such as pickled vegetables, during the meal at these gatherings and was later repurposed to serve the tea itself. HS

1. Gifu 2005, 41.
2. For more on this trade, see Tokyo 2018.

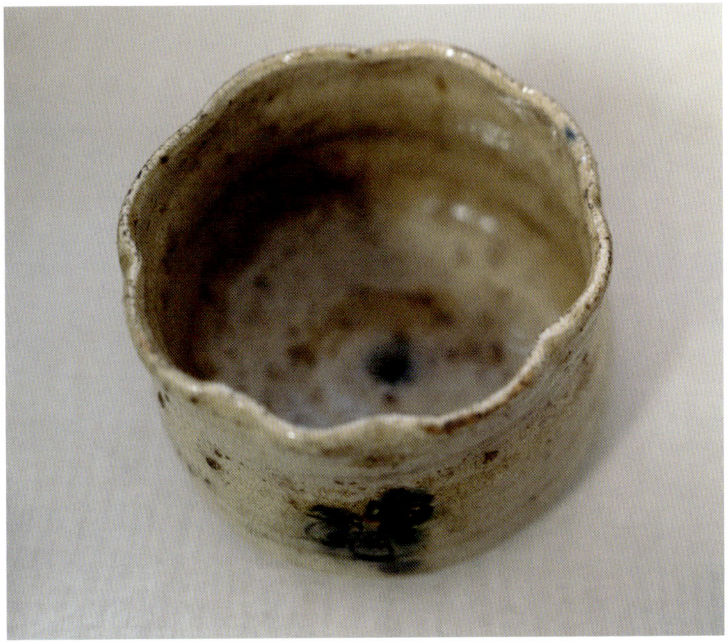

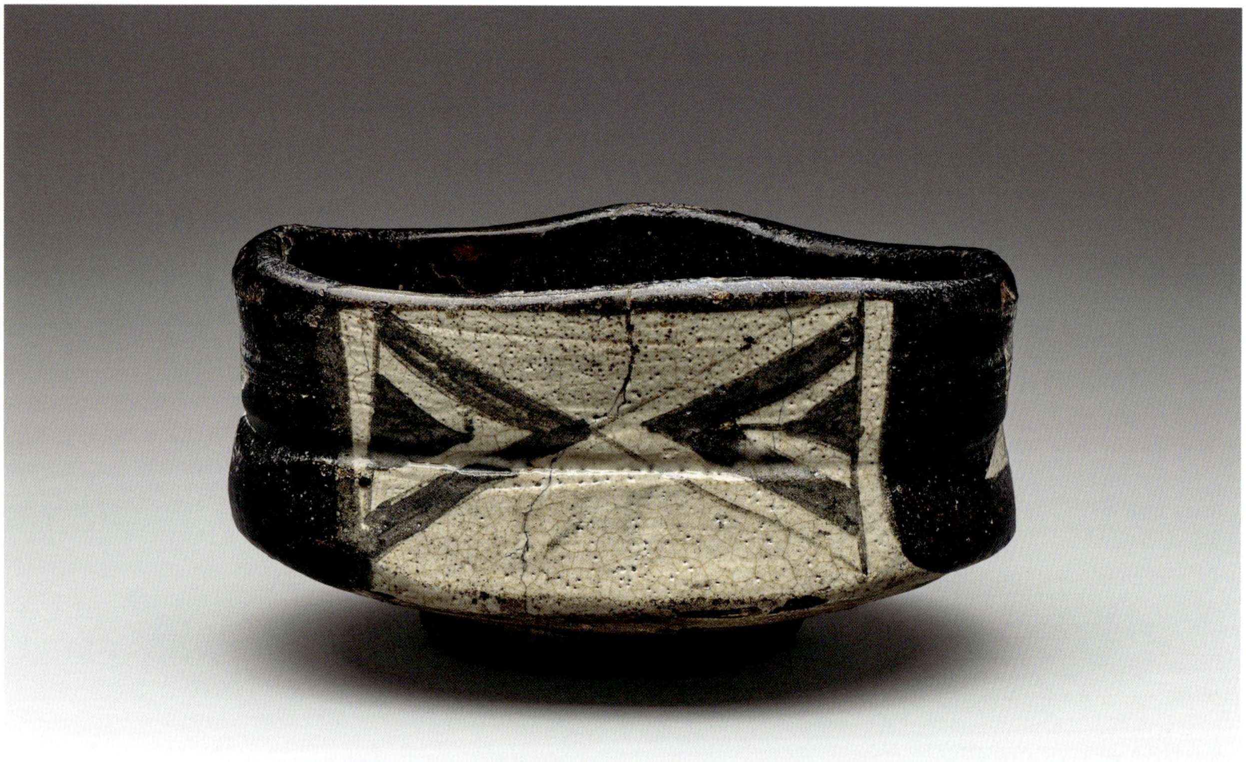

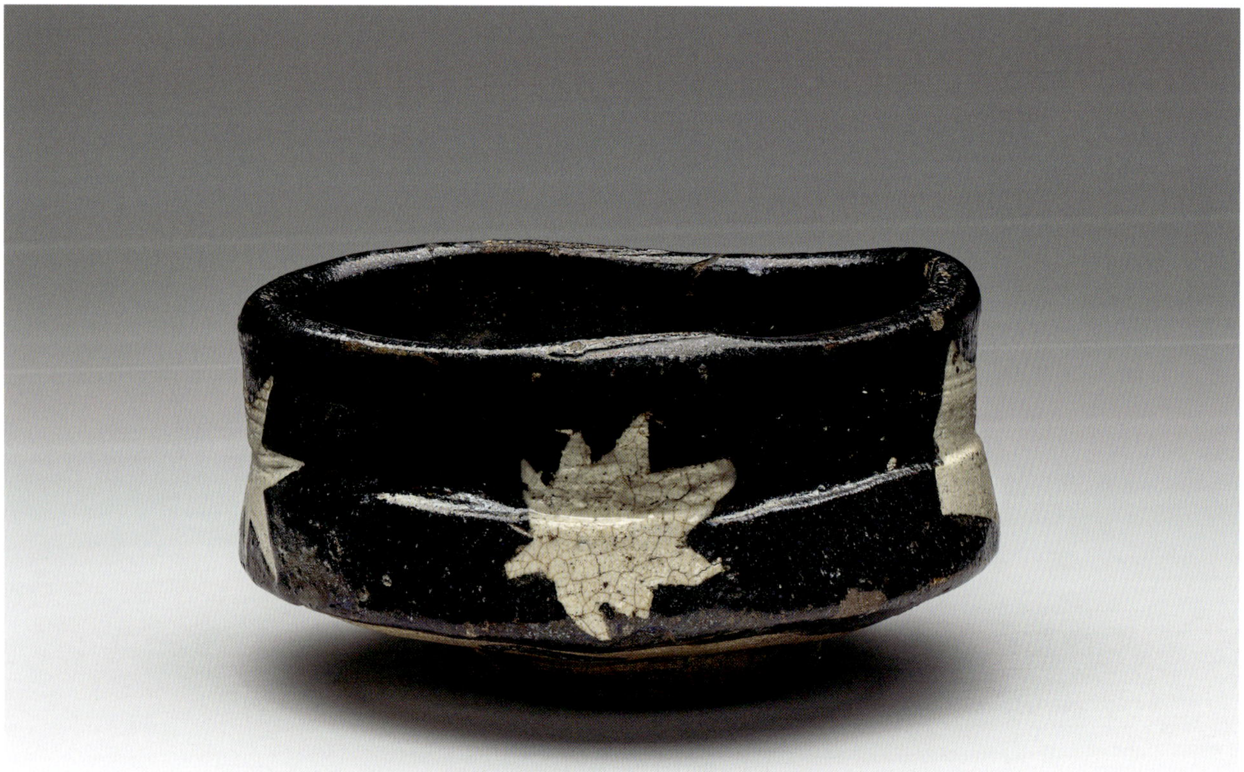

27

Teabowl

Edo period (1615–1868),
17th century

Glazed earthenware (Oribe ware)
2⅝ × 5⅛ in. (6.7 × 13 cm)

Gift of Mrs. John Reilly,
1941-87-45

Japanese tea gatherings are social events that link participants to the art assembled. The service centers around a teabowl in which matcha (powdered green tea) is whisked with hot water into a frothy, pleasantly bitter beverage. Originally, tea culture, or *cha-no-yu* (literally "hot water for tea"), was practiced by monks and aristocrats who served tea in bowls imported from China. Domestic bowls gained in popularity during the sixteenth century, when tea practice flourished as a conduit for social, commercial, and political connections between merchants and the ruling warrior class.

A potter formed the thick walls of this teabowl on a wheel before hand-molding the vessel into its slightly triangular form, known as *kutsugata* (shoe shaped). To create the stark black-and-white design, an artisan first dipped the bowl into white slip and then applied maple leaf–shaped and abstract stencils before coating the surface with a thick black glaze.

The bowl's design and abstract form is representative of the Kuro-Oribe (Black Oribe) style of tea ceramics named for the famed tea master Furuta Oribe (1544–1615).[1] Oribe was a disciple of Sen no Rikyū (1522–1591), one of the founders of modern *cha-no-yu* and one of Japan's most prominent tea men in the sixteenth century. At that time, artisans in the Seto and Mino regions produced many tea ceramics with abstract shapes and styles that later came to be known categorically as Oribe ware. Contemporaries described Oribe himself as a flamboyant individual with unconventional taste, and archaeological evidence indicates that he collected and used these novel tea wares. Despite this, there is no evidence that Oribe was directly involved in designing these ceramics.[2] HS

1. New York 2003–4.
2. Kaminishi 2021.

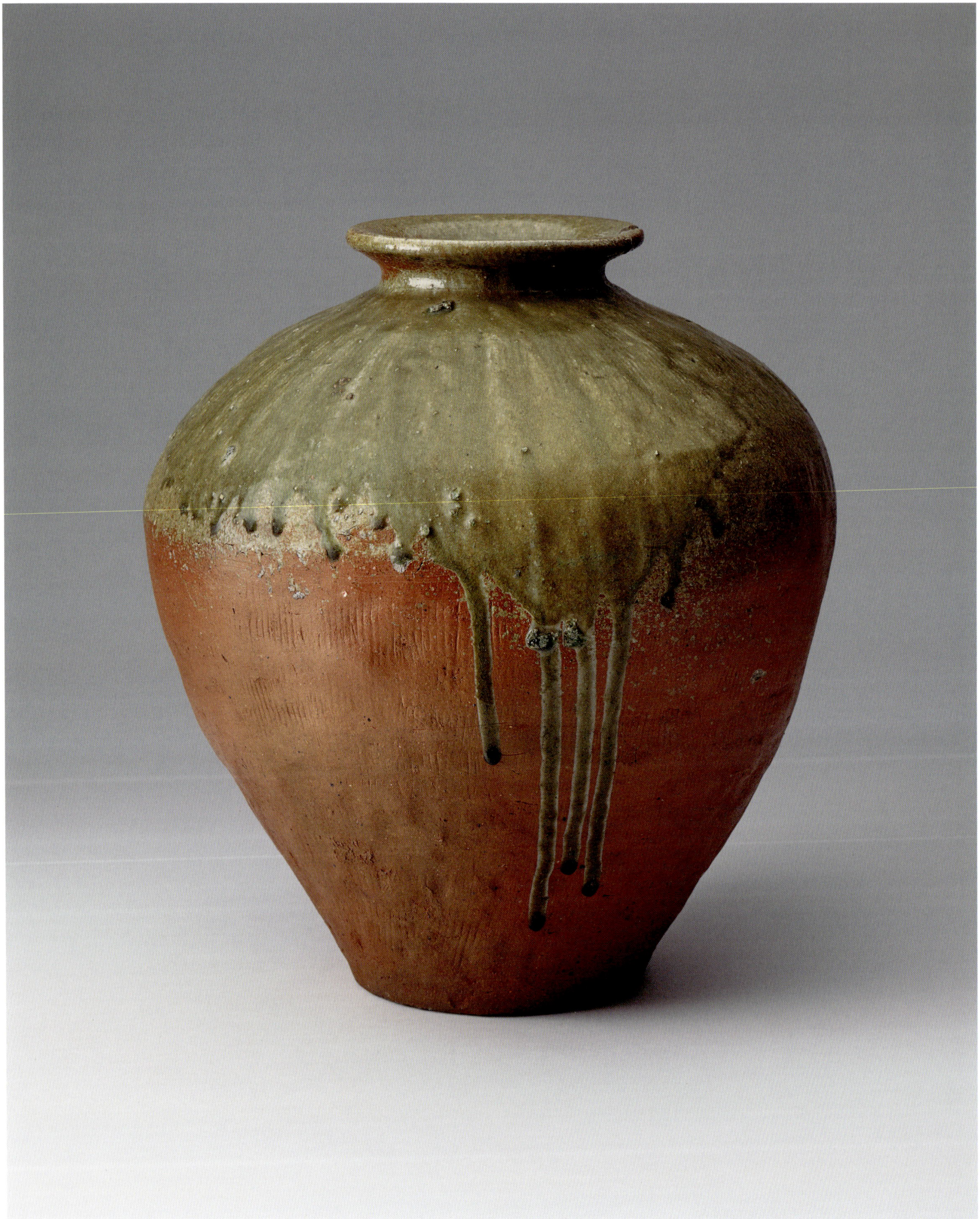

28

Jar

Nambokuchō period (1333–92)

Stoneware with ash glaze
17¾ × 14¹³⁄₁₆ in. (45.1 × 37.7 cm)

Purchased with the Hollis Fund for East Asian Art Acquisitions, 2013-25-1

Tamba, west of Kyoto, is one of Japan's oldest ceramics centers. Since the late Heian period (794–1185), artisans have used the region's iron-rich clay to make utilitarian goods such as cups, bowls, and storage jars.

This large vessel was made to store pickles or dry goods. First, the potter rolled ropes of clay and coiled them into the jar's general form. Next, they placed the coiled clay on a wheel to smooth the coils together. Thin lines in the walls show where the potter beat the vessel with a string-wrapped paddle to make its body thinner and stronger. In the kiln, wood ash from the fire liquefied at the high temperatures needed to make nonporous stoneware and dripped down the sides of the jar, decorating it with a naturally occurring, deep-green glaze. A prominent X mark on the shoulder identified the jar's owner among the many vessels fired in the communal kiln (see detail below).

In the late fifteenth century, the famed tea master Murata Jukō (1423–1502) started the practice of incorporating domestic ceramics in tea gatherings alongside imported Chinese wares. Among these domestic wares were Bizen and Shigaraki jars that Jukō repurposed to decorate the tearoom and to store tea leaves until they were ready to grind and serve as powdered tea, or matcha. Such reimagined or "found" objects (*mitate*) are a key aesthetic element in Jukō's *wabi-cha* ("austere tea") practice, which continues to the present day.

It was not until the seventeenth century that the tea master and tastemaker Kobori Enshū (1579–1647) popularized Tamba ware for tea caddies and freshwater vessels, and as tea-leaf storage jars.[1] It was probably around that time that this jar was reinterpreted from a utilitarian object into a prized vessel for tea. HS

1. Nakanishi 2009, 10.

Detail of shoulder, showing the X mark that would have identified the jar's owner

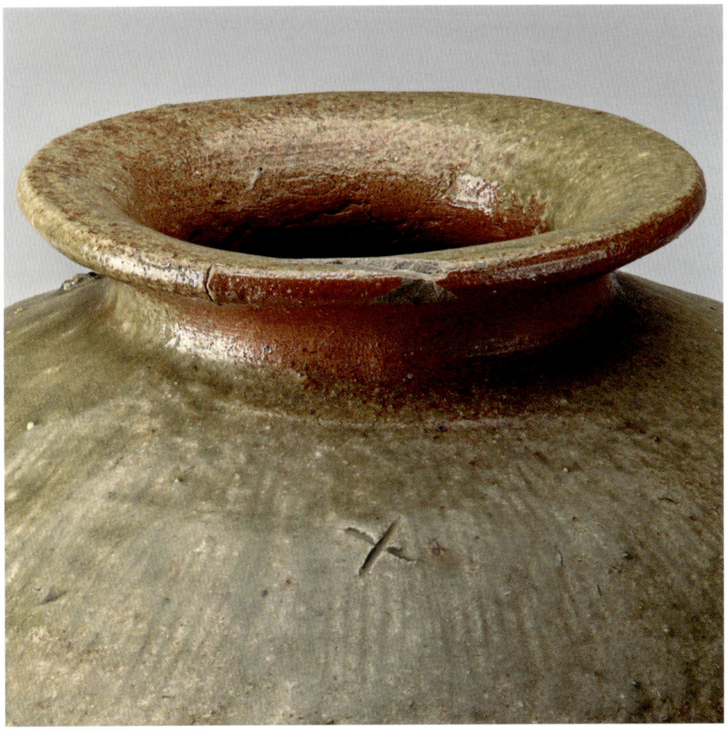

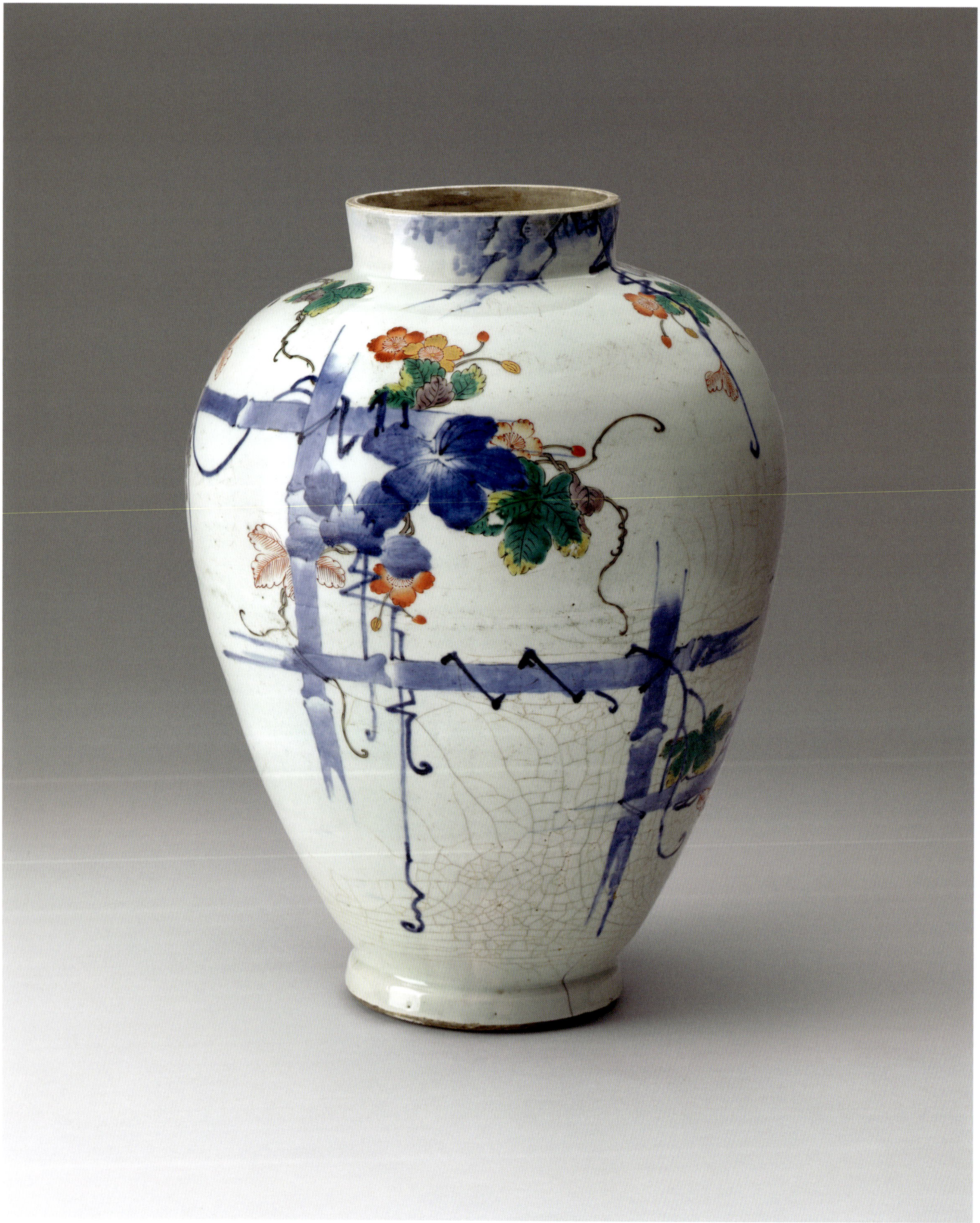

29

Tea Storage Jar (*Chatsubo*)

Edo period (1615–1868), 18th century

Porcelain with underglaze blue and overglaze enamel decoration (Arita ware), 17¾ × 12 1/16 in. (45.1 × 30.7 cm)

Purchased with the George W. B. Taylor Fund, 1955-10-1

This large porcelain jar was made in Arita, on Japan's southernmost island. In the mid-seventeenth century, Arita had become the country's center for porcelain manufacture and export, renowned for its superb blue-and-white and enamel decoration in the Imari, Kakiemon, and Nabeshima styles. Jars of this type, called *chatsubo* (tea storage jars), were used to store fresh tea leaves in a cool place, such as in the ground or in the mountains, following the spring harvest. In early October of the lunar calendar, around November 7 or 8 in our current calendar, the new season of tea begins and the *ro* (sunken hearth) is used for the first time, marking the start of the winter season and the beginning of a new season of tea. The seal of the jar with the previous spring's tea is broken in a ceremony known as *kuchikiri*, and the tea leaves are then mashed with a stone mill to make green tea powder.

Tea jars are usually made of breathable pottery baked at a lower temperature than that of porcelain, which is less suitable for the storage of tea leaves. In late seventeenth-century Kyoto, Nonomura Ninsei (act. second half of the seventeenth century) created large tea storage jars decorated with landscapes and flowers such as wisterias, cherry blossoms, and poppies in various colors, and with gold and silver. His pottery was appreciated more for its aesthetic qualities than for its practical use, which may have led to the production of large, decorated tea jars made of colored porcelain in Arita.

This porcelain tea jar is a rare surviving example of this type of Arita ware. It has a delicate decoration of a fence with flowering vines, a popular subject during the Edo period that evokes painting as well as contemporary kimono design. In the tea ceremony tradition, bamboo fences and gutters are renewed for the new tea season. The decoration on this jar might have been intended to suggest this annual celebration. KK

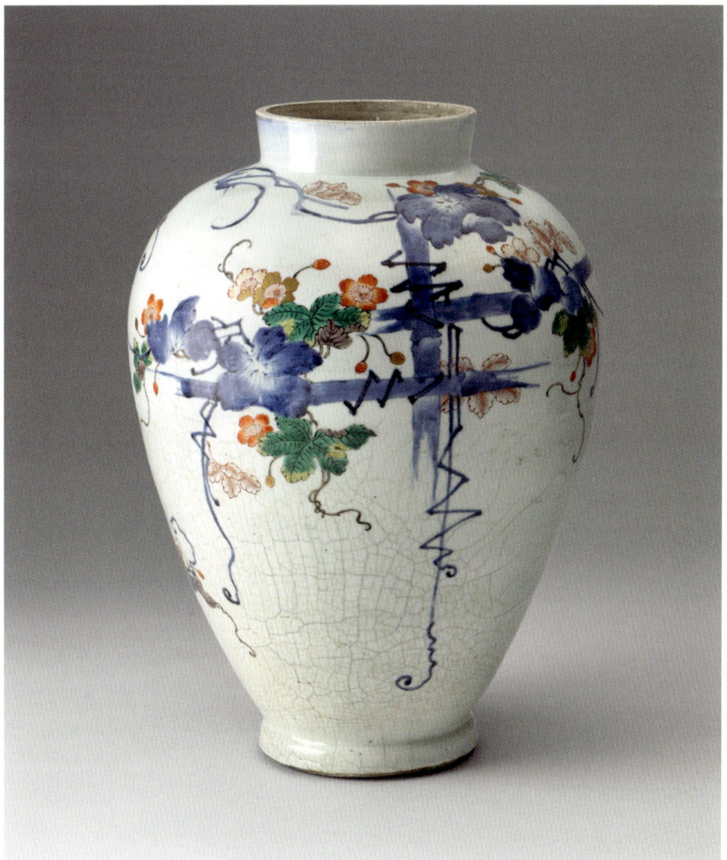

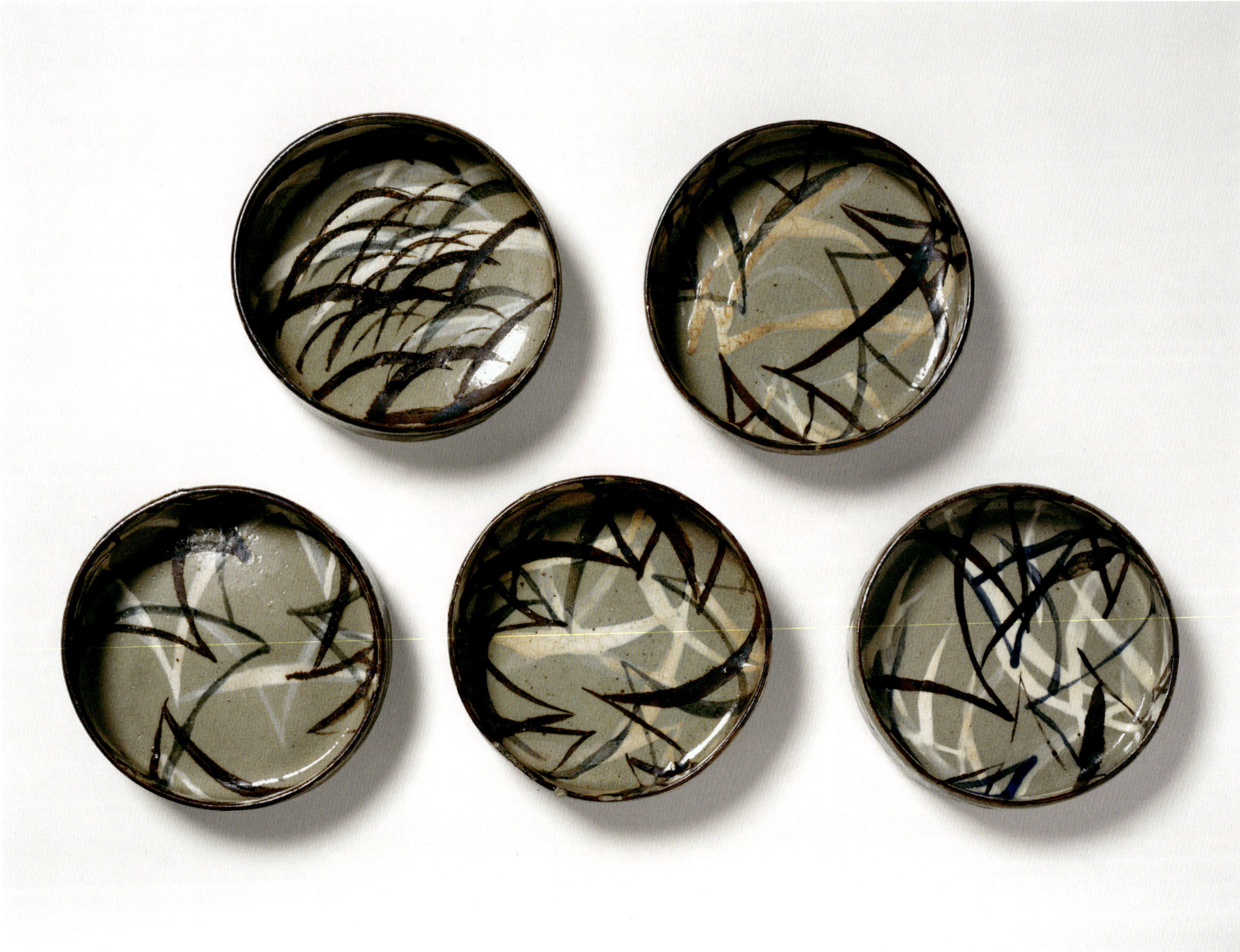

30

Dishes

Ogata Kenzan

(1663–1743)

Edo period (1615–1868), 1712–31

Glazed stoneware, each: 1⅝ × 5½ in. (4.1 × 14 cm)

125th Anniversary Acquisition. Purchased with funds contributed by Marguerite and Gerry Lenfest, Maxine and Howard H. Lewis, Maude de Schauensee, Alexandra Q. and Fred C. Aldridge, Jr., the Joseph E. Temple Fund and the Hollis Family Foundation Fund, 2002-75-1–5

Ogata Kenzan opened his first workshop in Narutaki, on the outskirts of Kyoto, in 1699.[1] Working with his brother, the artist Ogata Kōrin (1658–1716), he translated the styles of Rimpa painting, which emphasizes bold, often simplified renderings of natural motifs, to the surfaces of ceramic dishes, cups, and plates. Kenzan cultivated a brand as an innovative artist and potter who was intimately involved in making the wares that bore his signature. His wares have influenced Japanese ceramics up to the present day, and Kenzan is considered one of the Edo period's greatest potters.

This set of five dishes was made at Kenzan's second workshop, in Chōjiyamachi, in the heart of Kyoto, which he opened in 1712. Each dish has a slightly different form: some are thicker and heavier, the body of one is slightly warped, and the walls of three are ovular. The outer walls and interiors are decorated with a pampas-grass motif painted with blue cobalt, red iron oxide, and white clay slip under a clear glaze. Like most Chōjiyamachi dishes, the unglazed bottom is marked with the artist's signature, "Kenzan."[2]

In Chōjiyamachi, Kenzan worked as a merchant as well as an artist, and he made numerous innovations to emphasize mass production. For example, to produce this set Kenzan cut costs by buying pre-bisque-fired dishes that the workers in his shop decorated and glazed before sending them to a communal kiln to be refired. The lighter coloring of one of the dishes indicates that it was fired separately from the others, possibly as a distinct production.

Similarly shaped plates and other dishes with simple forms were routinely made with an array of different decorations that could be mixed and matched according to the customer's wishes. Although this set shows only pampas grass, similar sets in the National Museum of Asian Art in Washington, DC, and the Miho Museum in Shiga Prefecture, Japan, each include a vessel of the same shape with various designs including plum and paulownia (fig. 35).[3] HS

1. For more on Kenzan, see Wilson 1991; and Washington 2001–2.
2. For an illustration of the signature, see the Documentation (p. 252).
3. Koka 2004, 159.

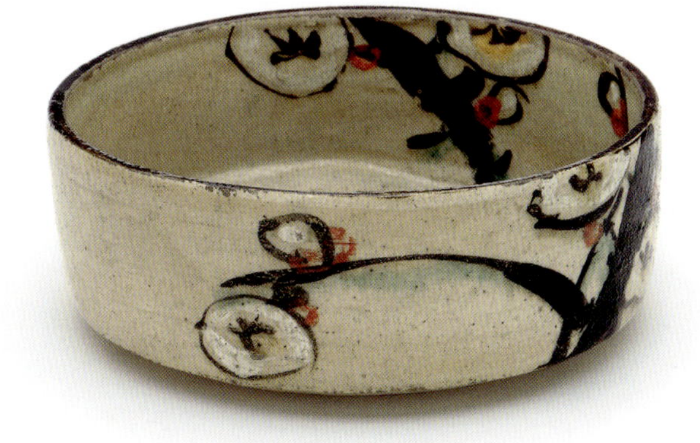

FIG. 35 Ogata Kenzan. Food Dish with Design of Plum. Edo period, 1712–31. Glazed stoneware, 2 1/16 × 5¼ in. (5.2 × 13.3 cm). National Museum of Asian Art, Freer Gallery of Art, Washington, DC: Gift of Charles Lang Freer, F1905.323

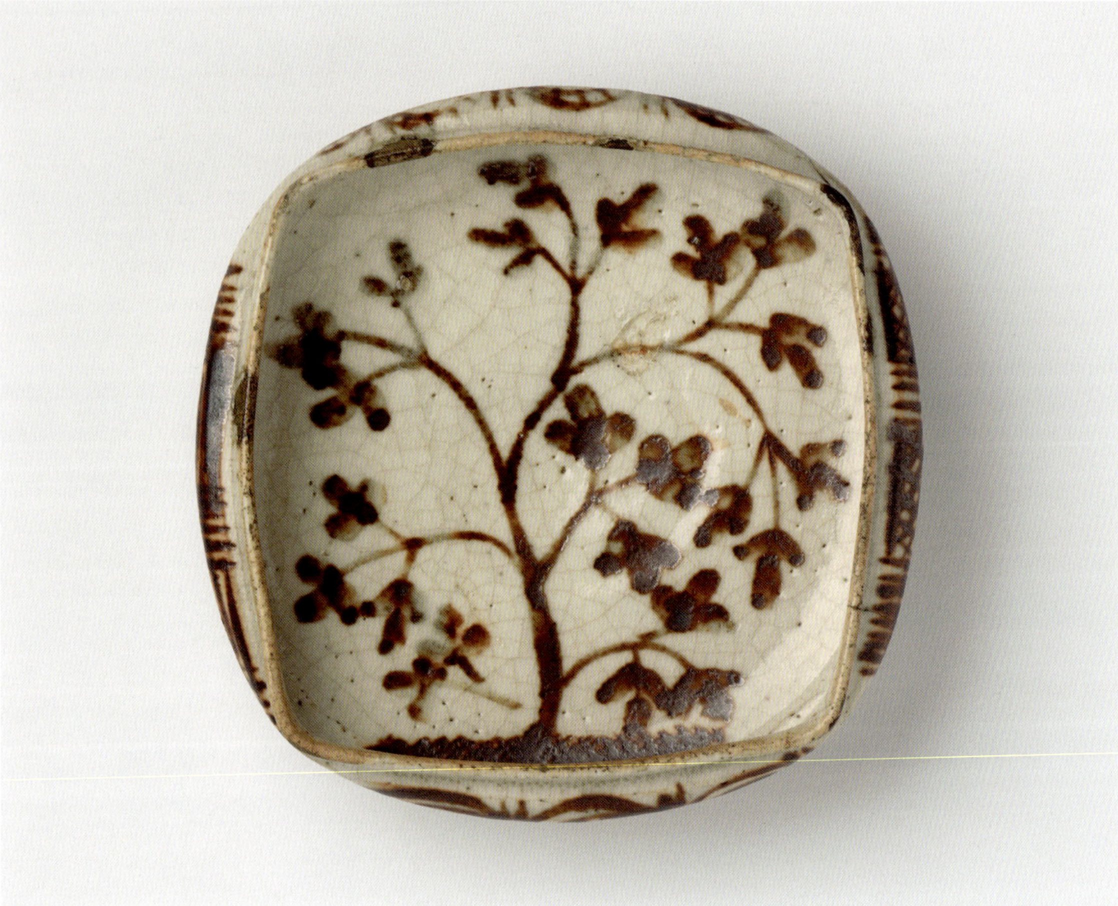

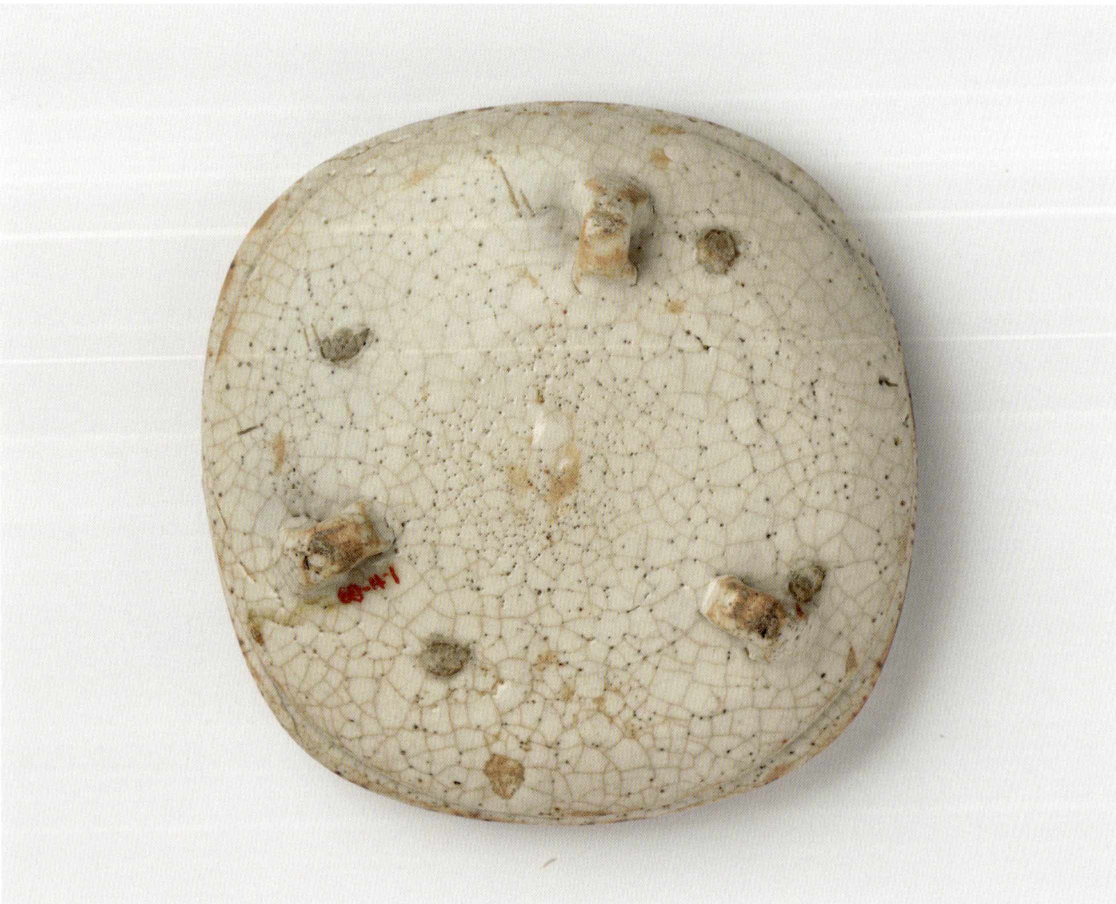

31

Dish

Momoyama period (1568–1615), late 16th–early 17th century

Stoneware with underglaze iron oxide decoration (Shino ware)
2 × 6⅞ in. (5.1 × 17.5 cm)

Purchased with the Edgar Viguers Seeler Fund, 1968-4-1

In the sixteenth century, tea masters reimagined Japanese aesthetics when they turned away from imported Chinese ceramics to emphasize simple, domestic wares in their tea gatherings. This form of "austere tea," or *wabi-cha*, looked to the historic kilns in the Seto and Mino regions in central Honshu. Originally these potters emulated Chinese designs, but they soon turned to new domestic styles such as this dish, named for its clear white Shino glaze.[1]

The artisan, possibly at Mino's Motoyashiki kiln where similar dishes were excavated, formed this dish into a circular bowl on a potter's wheel before pressing and trimming the lip to create a square opening.[2] The square in a circle shape was common in Seto and Mino ceramics and evokes the phrase "round sky and square Earth" (Japanese: *ten en chi hō*; Chinese: *tian yuan di fang*), an auspicious representation of the cosmic order. After bisque firing, a painter used iron-rich glaze to draw the flowering tree in the bowl's interior and parallel depictions of fences on the outer walls to suggest an enclosed garden. Finally, the dish was dipped in a vat of Shino glaze made from white clay mixed with water and refired.

The dish was initially intended for one of Japan's major tea centers, such as Sakai, near Osaka, or Kyoto, where it would have been sold to a wealthy merchant or a member of the warrior class. During the Momoyama period, a network of merchants communicated orders from tea practitioners to potters for certain styles and designs, and transported the finished wares to urban markets.[3] A similar dish in the National Museum of Asian Art in Washington, DC, indicates that this was a popular style that was probably produced regularly by Mino potters for a growing market of tea practitioners eager to display the most up-to-date fashions (fig. 36). HS

1. For more on Seto and Mino wares, see Cort 1992.
2. Cort 1992, 103.
3. Tokyo 2018.

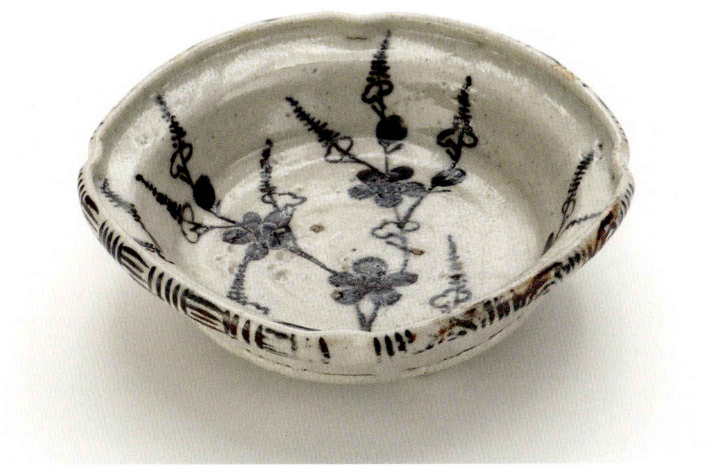

FIG. 36 Individual Serving Dish with Design of Flowering Quince. Momoyama period, 1607–15. Stoneware with iron pigment under feldspathic glaze (Mino ware, Shino ware), 2³⁄₁₆ × 6⅝ × 6⅝ in. (5.5 × 16.9 × 16.9 cm). National Museum of Asian Art, Freer Gallery of Art, Washington, DC: Purchase by Charles Lang Freer Endowment, F1962.20

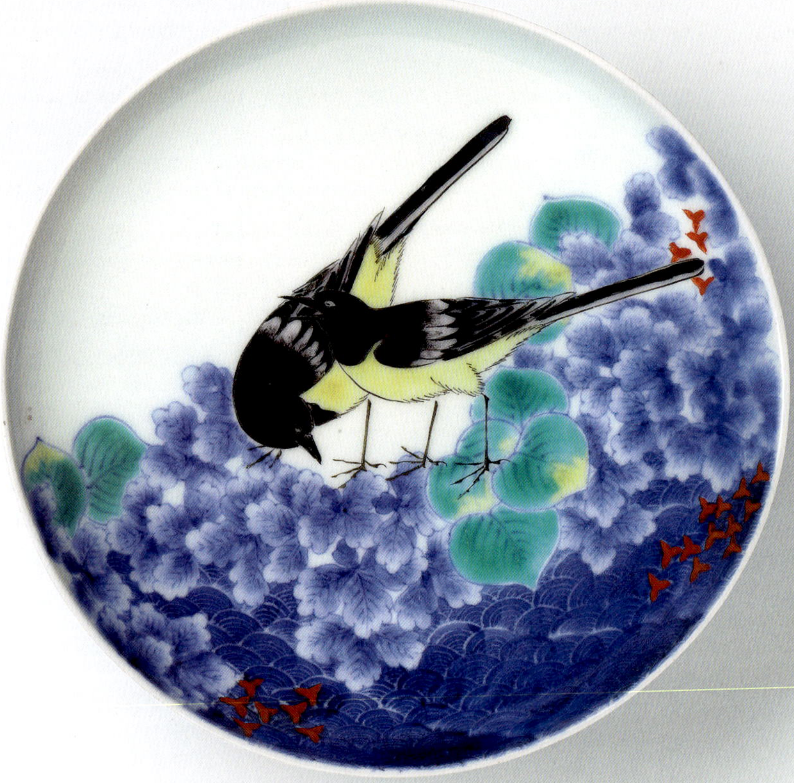

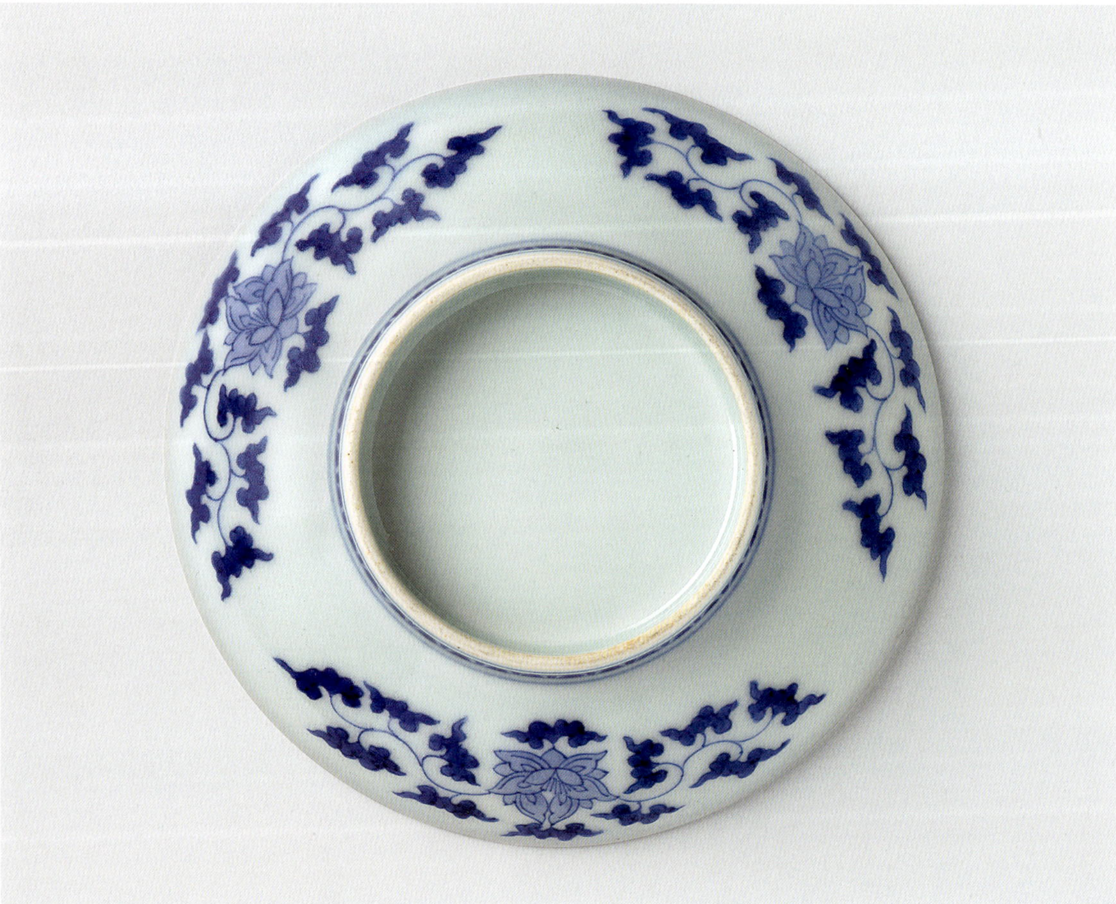

32

Dish with Design of Birds

Edo period (1615–1868), c. 1650–75

Porcelain with underglaze blue and overglaze enamels (Nabeshima ware)
Diam. 5 15/16 in. (15.1 cm)

Purchased with the Henry B. Keep Fund, 2013-20-1

This small porcelain dish shows a pair of magpies nestled amid a floral design and rolling waves. Its production required the collaboration of a team of artisans. First, a potter shaped it on a wheel using refined porcelain clay, a mixture of kaolin, and volcanic stone. After the dish was bisque fired, a painter used cobalt blue to draw the flowers, possibly hydrangeas, and waves before applying a clear glaze. Finally, a second painter added thick layers of red, yellow, green, and aubergine-black enamel over the glaze to create the slightly raised, tactile forms of the leaves and magpies. The body of the dish is thick and feels sturdy in one's hand.

During the Edo period, the Japanese archipelago was governed by some two hundred semiautonomous domains under the general hegemony of the Tokugawa shoguns, military rulers based in Edo, now Tokyo. As part of this system, many daimyo (domanial rulers) sent annual tributes to the shogunal court. This plate's design of turquoise hollyhock leaves, the symbol of the Tokugawa family, indicates that it was commissioned by the Nabeshima daimyo, the rulers of Saga domain in modern Saga Prefecture, as a gift to the shogun.[1] Although porcelain had been made in Saga since about 1520, Nabeshima initially sent imported wares from China, and only switched to domestic dishes after the fall of China's Ming dynasty (1368–1644) interrupted the international porcelain trade. The dish's simple design and short foot indicate that it is from the period shortly after the Nabeshima transitioned to domestic gifts (for another example, see fig. 37).

The Saga domain workshop where this dish was made comprised primarily Korean artisans who worked exclusively for the Nabeshima daimyo. Between 1592 and 1598, the Japanese ruler Toyotomi Hideyoshi (1537–1598) led an invasion in Korea known as the Imjin War. At that time Korean pottery was highly valued in Japan, and numerous daimyo fighting in Korea, including Saga domain's Nabeshima Naoshige (1538–1618), brought back Korean potters. Although some potters who sided with the Japanese forces came willingly, many were captured in order to open new workshops in Japan.[2] HS

1. Arita 2012.
2. See Clements and Sang 2022. Rebekah Clements leads the project "Aftermath of the East Asian War of 1592–1598" at the Universitat Autònoma de Barcelona, which explores the effects of the Imjin War with a special focus on its impact on Japanese ceramics.

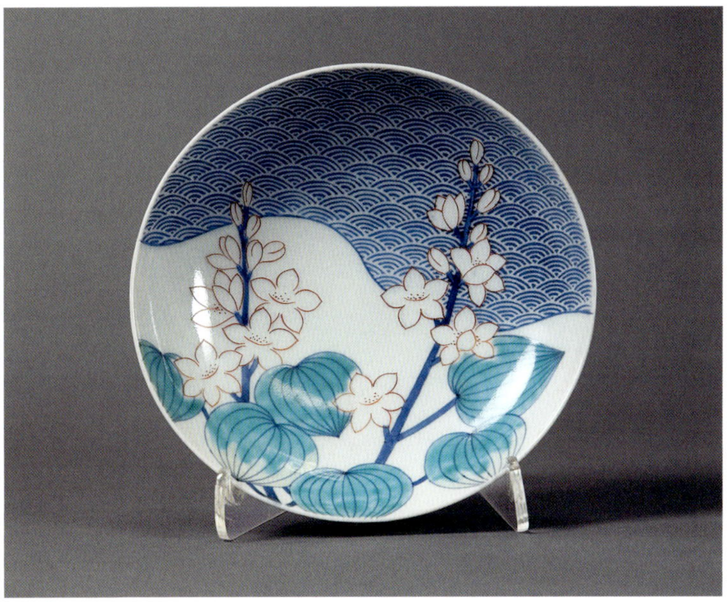

FIG. 37 Dish with Design of Waves and Water Plants. Edo period, early 18th century. Porcelain with underglaze blue and overglaze enamels (Nabeshima ware), diam. 5 7/8 in. (14.9 cm). The Metropolitan Museum of Art, New York: The Harry G. C. Packard Collection of Asian Art, Gift of Harry G. C. Packard, and Purchase, Fletcher, Rogers, Harris Brisbane Dick, and Louis V. Bell Funds, Joseph Pulitzer Bequest, and The Annenberg Fund Inc. Gift, 1975.268.564

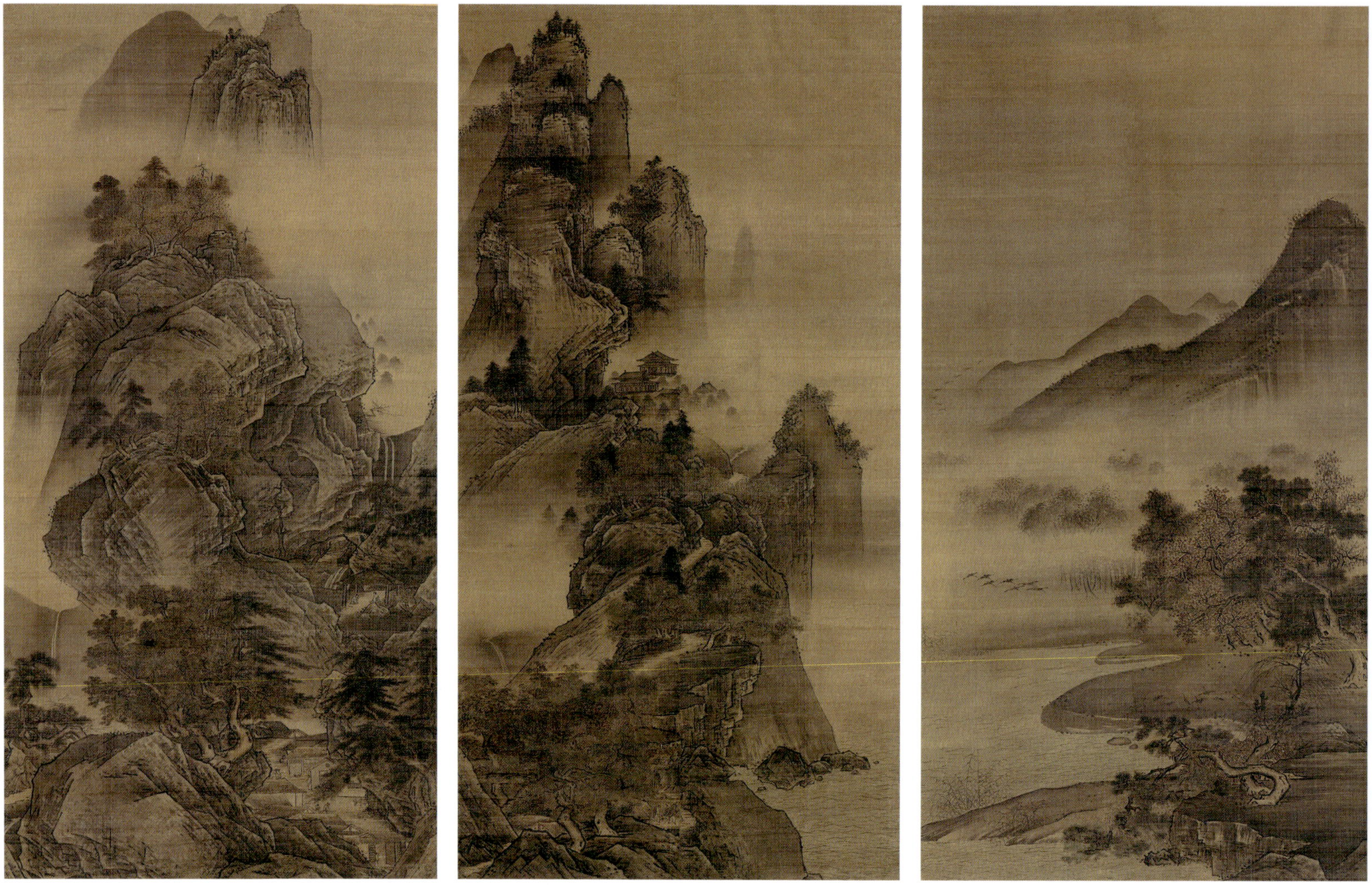

33

Landscapes of the Four Seasons

School of Sesshū Tōyō
(1420–1506)

Muromachi period (1392–1573), 15th century

Ink and colors on silk, mounted as a hanging scroll; each: 57$\frac{5}{16}$ × 30$\frac{5}{16}$ in. (145.5 × 77 cm)

Purchased with Museum funds from the Simkhovitch Collection, 1929-40-237–40

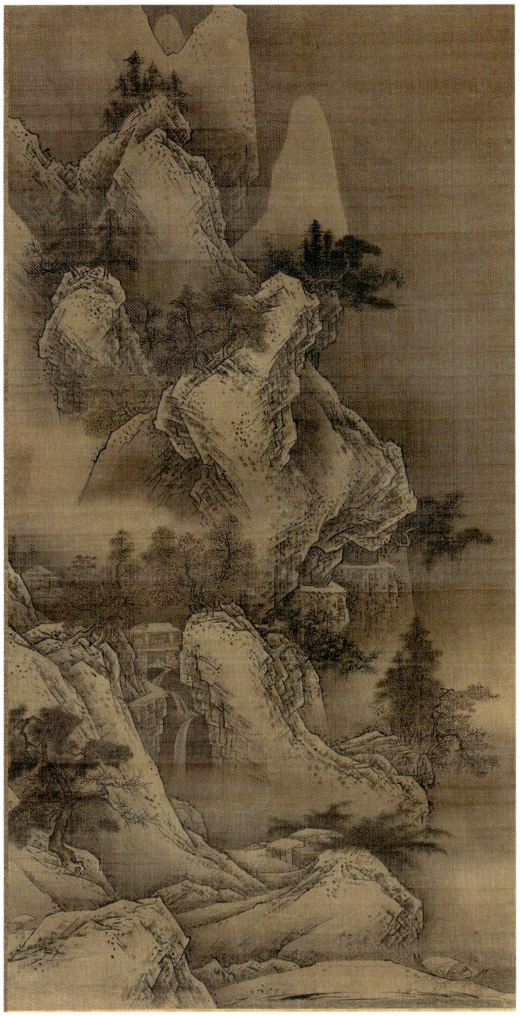

This set of four hanging scrolls once belonged to the Date daimyo in Sendai, which was founded in the early Kamakura period (1185–1333) and continued to be one of the powerful families after Date Masamune (1567–1636) became its head. Three other paintings from the Date family are also in US collections, one in the Museum of Art of the Rhode Island School of Design (RISD) in Providence and two in the Cleveland Museum of Art. These seven landscapes depict scenes related to the Eight Views of Xiao and Xiang, a poetic motif that refers to the scenery in present-day Hunan Province where the Xiao and Xiang Rivers converge into Dongting Lake (see no. 82). It is believed that the original format for the paintings was a pair of four-panel *oshiebari* screens — in which each painting is pasted on a single panel — and that seven of the paintings were transformed into hanging scrolls before export to the United States.

The Philadelphia Museum of Art's paintings follow a seasonal sequence comprising the scenes known as "Mountain Market Clear with Rising Mist" (spring), "Evening Bell from Mist-Shrouded Temple" (summer), "Wild Geese Descending to a Sandbar" (autumn), and "River and Sky in Evening Snow" (winter). The RISD landscape is likely "The Rain at Night on the Xiao and Xiang," and the two landscapes in Cleveland depict "Fishing Village in Evening Glow" and "The Sailing Ship Returning Home." The eighth view, "The Moon in Autumn on Dongting Lake," is currently unlocated.

As there is neither a seal nor a signature on any of the extant paintings, it is difficult to identify the artist. The compositions appear to have been strongly influenced by the style of the Chinese artist Li Tang (c. 1050–1130), and it has been argued that they were painted by Sesshū Tōyō in his youth because of their refined depictions and faithful reproduction of landscape paintings by court painters of the Northern and Southern Song dynasties.[1] Together, the seven paintings are important works for understanding what Chinese models Sesshū may have studied and absorbed in developing his own style. KK

1. Kyoto and Tokyo 2002, 232–37.

34
"Red-Seal" Ship

Edo period (1615–1868), early 17th century

Ink, color, and gold on paper, mounted as one of a pair of six-fold screens; 67 in. × 12 ft. 4½ in. (170.2 × 377.2 cm)

Gift of Mrs. Francis E. Green, 1953-32-1

35
"Red-Seal" Ship

Edo period (1615–1868), early 17th century

Ink, color, and gold on paper, mounted as one of a pair of six-fold screens; 67 in. × 12 ft. 4½ in. (170.2 × 377.2 cm)

Gift of Mrs. G. Brinton Roberts, 1938-31-1

In the late Momoyama through the early Edo period, between 1604 and 1635, foreign trade with Southeast Asian countries was conducted by ships carrying a *shuinjō*, a red-sealed letter patent issued by the Tokugawa shogunate. *Shuinjō* were given to several daimyo and wealthy merchants in Kyoto, Nagasaki, and Sakai to promote imports of silk, sharkskin, deerskin for armor, agarwood, sugar, and spices, and the export of silver, copper, sulfur, swords, and other artifacts. A so-called red-seal ship was a unique sailing vessel that fused the technology and design of a galleon with a junk ship, and carried an international crew and passengers.[1] In the 1620s, against a background of conflicts at sea and the increasing influence of Christianity, the Edo shogunate strengthened its control over trade. After Tokugawa Iemitsu (1604–1651) became shogun, he proceeded in 1633 with the development of Nagasaki as the base for management and control of trade, and in 1635 he prohibited all Japanese from traveling abroad. As a result, trade via red-seal ship ended.

During the time that trade via these ships flourished, shipowners and traders in

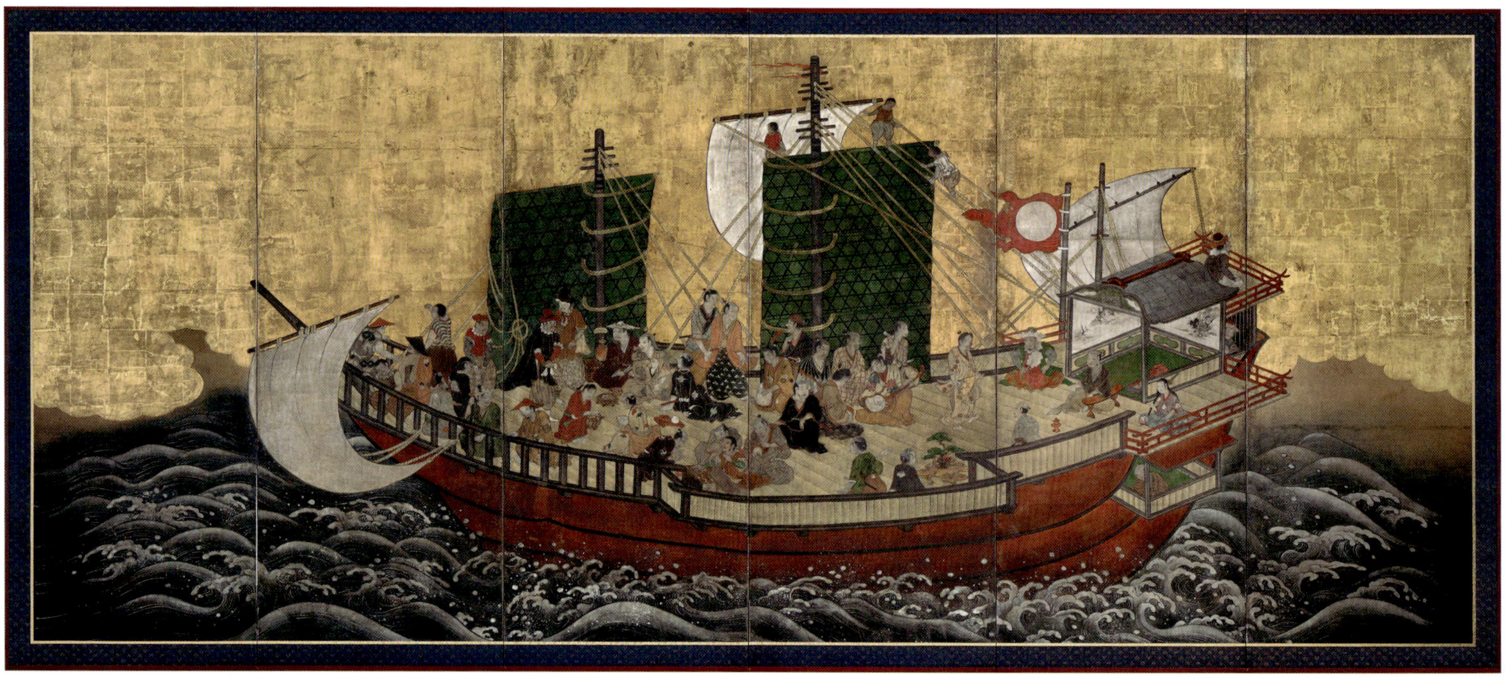

1953-32-1

Kyoto, Nagasaki, and Osaka made votive tablets that they dedicated to shrines, praying for the safety of their ships and for the success of their trade. There are six extant votive tablets illustrating red-seal ships.[2] Among them is a tablet depicting a *karafune* (white Chinese-style ship), symbolizing a treasure ship, that was dedicated to the Kiyomizu temple in Kyoto in 1634 by Suminokura, a wealthy merchant in Kyoto, who had commissioned the work from a skillful Kano artist (fig. 38). The Kiyomizu temple has another three of the six tablets, and the one by Kitamura Chūbei (life dates unknown; fig. 39) especially has several points of iconographical similarities to the museum's pair of *nanban* screens, which depict a red-seal ship sailing to Southeast Asia (1953-32-1) and its return voyage to Japan (1938-31-1). In all three works, the figures on board are vividly depicted. Sailors play on the masts and riggings, while on deck below people dance and play musical instruments, wrestle, play backgammon, or enjoy bowls of sake. The types of flags on the ships are almost identical, and the shape of the hulls is comparable. Each of the three works has an image of an elderly man holding a boy's hand, which, together with an illustration of a similar ship, also appears in the *Hengaku kihan* (Model of tablets) by Aikawa Min'wa (d. 1821) and published in 1819.[3] Similar kimono patterns and eared owl designs can be found in screen 1938-31-1 and the Chūbei tablet (figs. 40a,b; 41a,b), whereas screen 1953-32-1 shares with the tablet a scene of two young men playing shamisens (figs. 42a,b).

Before the edicts banning Christianity, *nanban* screens mainly featured scenes of Portuguese ships arriving in Japan, including the unloading of their crews, the landing of their admirals, and missionaries welcoming them. But when Christianity was banished in 1612, motifs such as the Nanban-ji (Catholic Church in Japan) and missionaries were removed from the paintings and replaced with images reflecting auspicious wishes for business prosperity and nautical safety. During the Kanei era (1624–45), *nanban* screens focused on subjects relating to trade with foreign countries and imagery emphasizing the desire for wealth among the emerging commercial and manufacturing segments of the population. However, this pair of screens is the only known example of screens illustrating the subject of red-seal ships, and it was probably a special commission.

The original owner of the screens was the grandfather of Laurance P. Roberts (1907–2002), a scholar of Chinese art and director of the Brooklyn Museum. Roberts graduated from Princeton University in 1929 and worked for a short time in the Far Eastern Art department at the Philadelphia Museum of Art.[4] He was the author of *A Dictionary of Japanese Artists: Paintings, Sculpture, Ceramics, Prints, Lacquer*, a standard work in the field first published in 1976. According to registrarial records, Roberts's grandfather purchased the screens when he traveled to Japan around 1900. The right screen was bequeathed to Roberts's father, Brinton, and the left screen to his aunt, Mrs. Francis Green. Each was then donated to the museum. KK

1. Iwao 1985.
2. Kinoshita 2019, 508–18.
3. Aikawa 1819a, n.p.; Aikawa 1819b, n.p.
4. "Memorial" 2002.

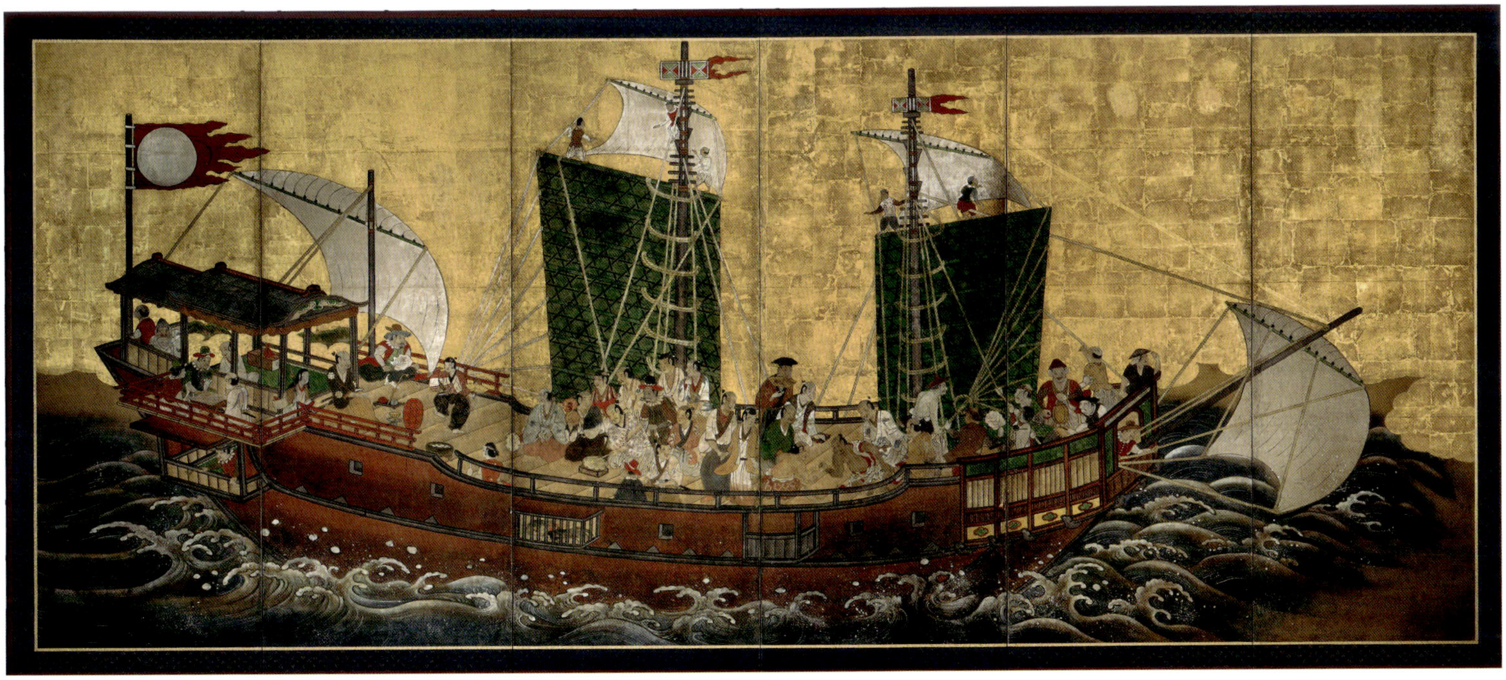

1938-31-1

FIG. 38 *The Suminokura Ship Votive Tablet*. Edo period, 1634. Ink and color on wood, 6 ft. × 7 ft. 6½ in. (182.9 × 229.9 cm). Kiyomizu Temple, Kyoto. Important Cultural Property

FIG. 39 Kitamura Chūbei (life dates unknown). *The Sueyoshi Ship Votive Tablet*. Edo period, 1634. Ink and color on wood, 6 ft. × 7 ft. 6½ in. (182.9 × 229.9 cm). Kiyomizu Temple, Kyoto. Important Cultural Property

FIGS. 40A,B Details of screen 1938-31-1 (top) and fig. 39 (bottom), showing men wearing kimono with similar patterns

FIGS. 41A,B Details of screen 1938-31-1 (top) and fig. 39 (bottom), showing kimono with similar eared owl designs

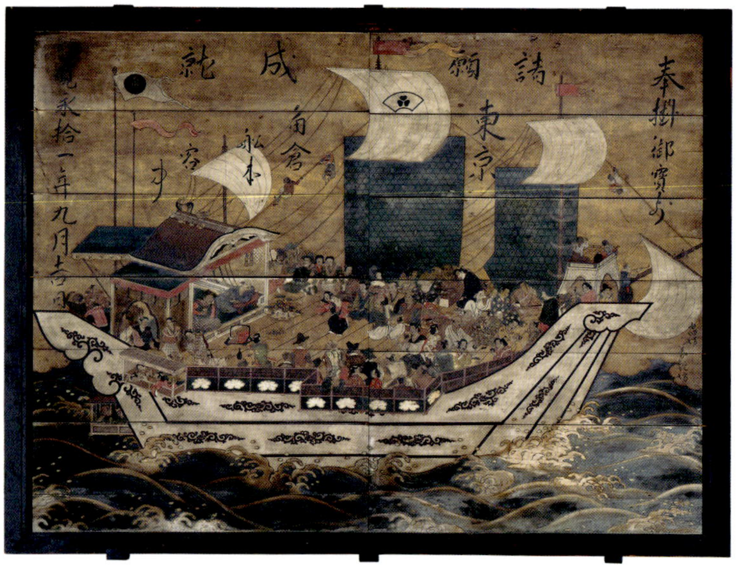

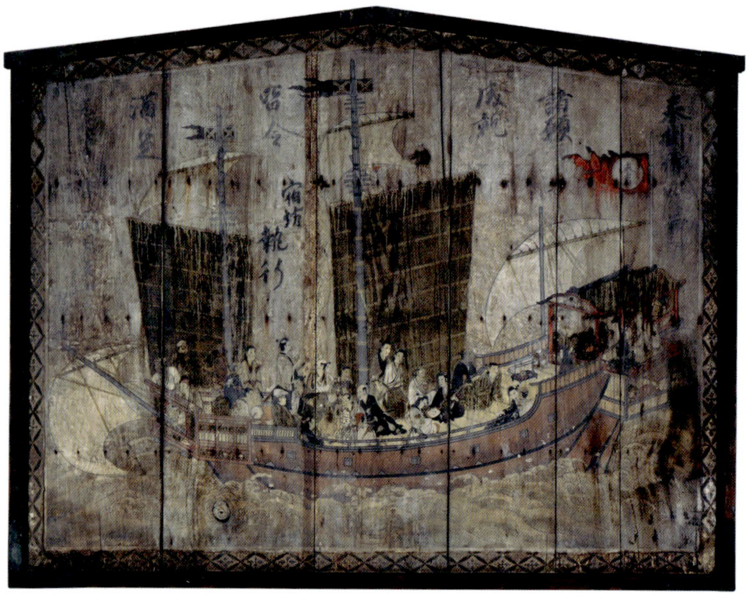

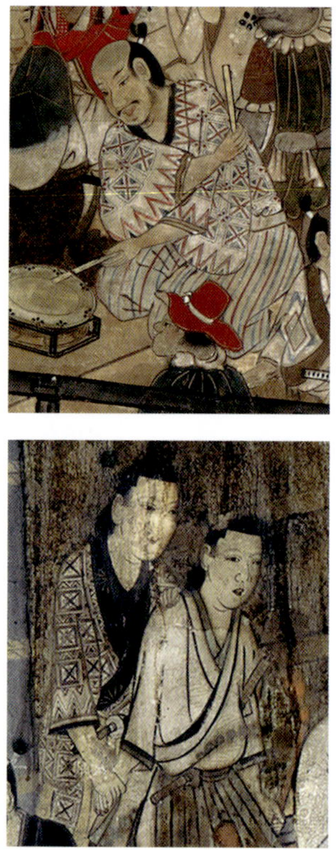

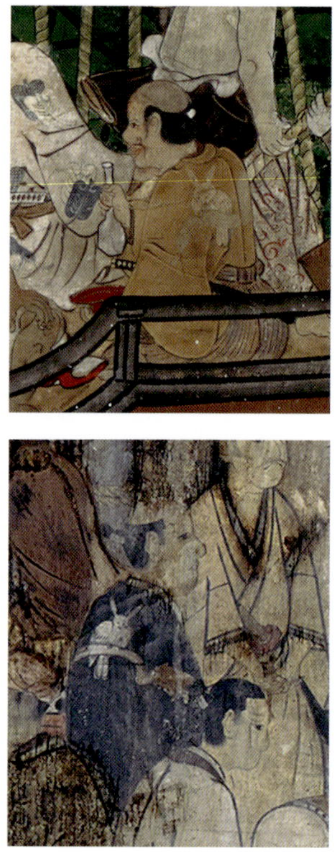

FIGS. 42A,B Details of screen 1953-32-1 (top) and fig. 39 (bottom), showing young men playing shamisens

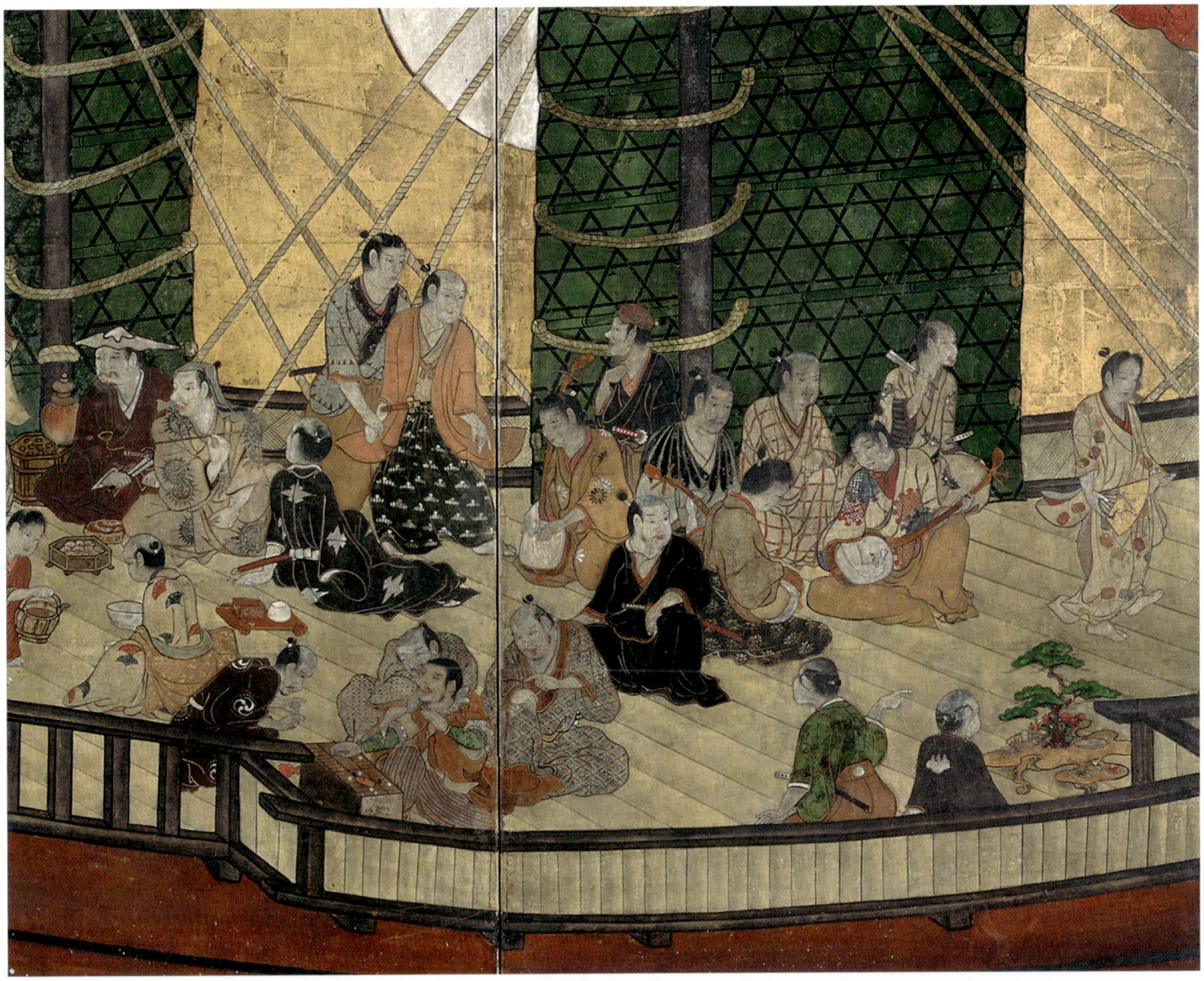

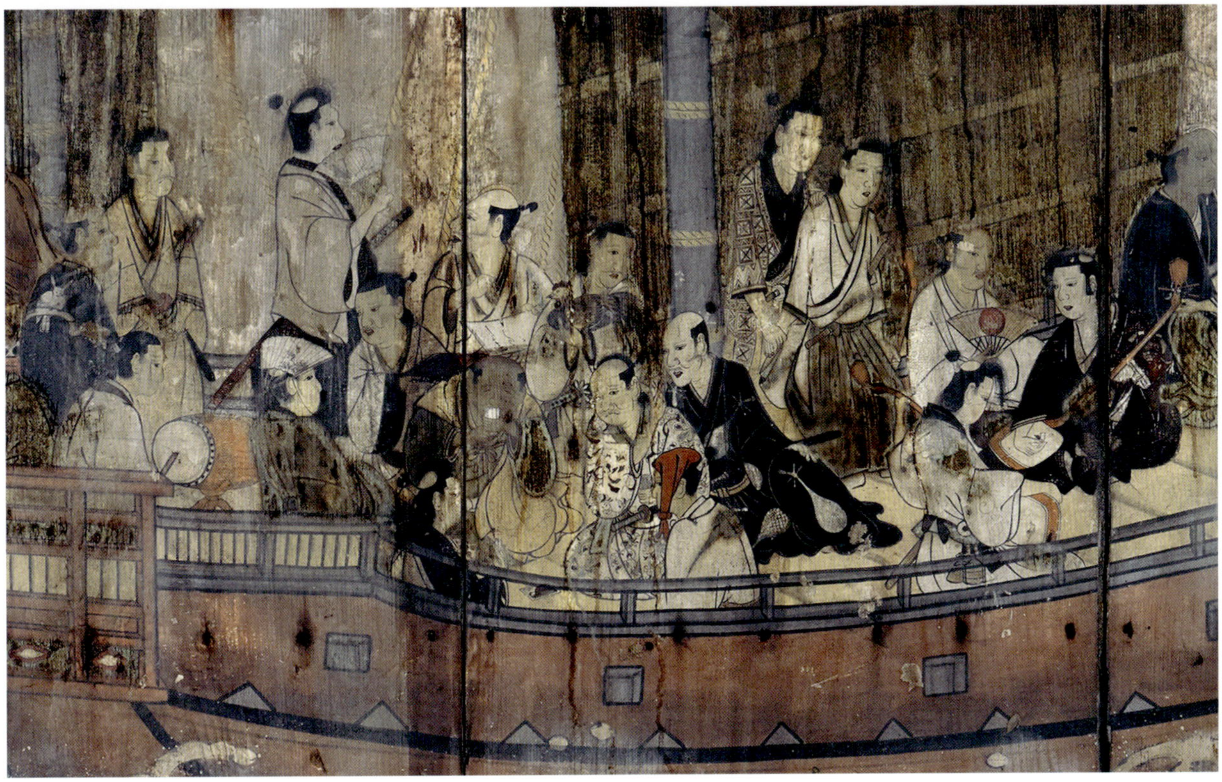

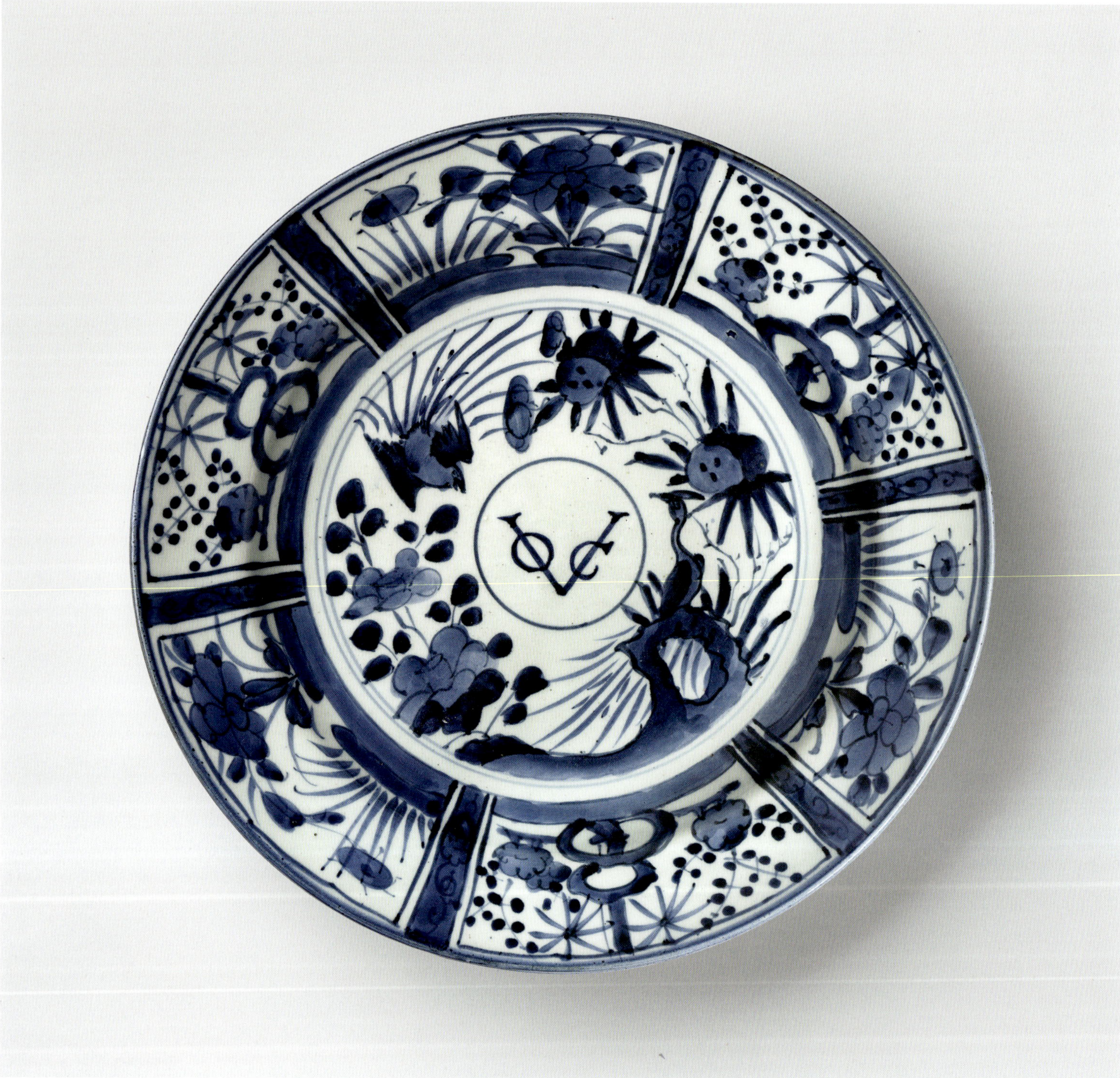
VOC

36

Dish

Edo period (1615–1868), c. 1660–80

Hard-paste porcelain with underglaze blue decoration
2⅛ × 15⁹⁄₁₆ in. (5.4 × 39.5 cm)

Purchased with funds contributed by The Women's Committee and the Craft Show Committee of the Philadelphia Museum of Art, 1969-135-1

This rather unassuming, large dish speaks to an important chapter in the history of Japanese ceramic production. The VOC initials at the center of the dish are those of the Dutch international conglomerate, the Vereenigde Oostindische Compagnie (Dutch East India Company), which had a Japanese trading post at Hirado (Nagasaki) from 1609. Before the Japanese government instituted an isolationist policy in 1639, the Spanish and Portuguese were also active in commerce with Japan. The latter were excluded from trade, and only the Dutch were permitted an outpost from 1641 on the island of Dejima.[1]

When the Dutch trade with China was interrupted after the fall of the Ming dynasty in 1644, the Dutch turned to the potters in Arita to fill the gap in ceramic production. This porcelain plate copies the underglaze blue decorations of Chinese wares, with its plant-motif cartouches around the segmented rim, and the central rondel of long-tailed birds and pomegranates.[2] The VOC initials indicate that the Dutch intended these wares not for sale, but as presentation pieces or for use by their staff in Hirado or other outposts. They were among the earliest export porcelains made in Japan for the European market. FF

1. The only other foreign nationals permitted residence and trading rights were the Chinese, confined to Nagasaki.
2. The Chinese versions were known as *Kraak* wares by the Dutch. The central design on the Philadelphia dish is a somewhat misunderstood version of the original. See, for example, Seattle 2007–8, pl. 139.

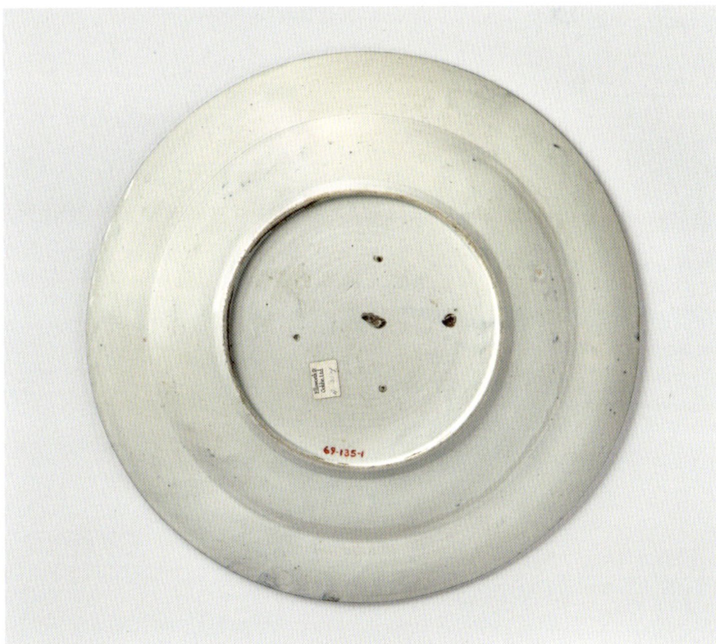

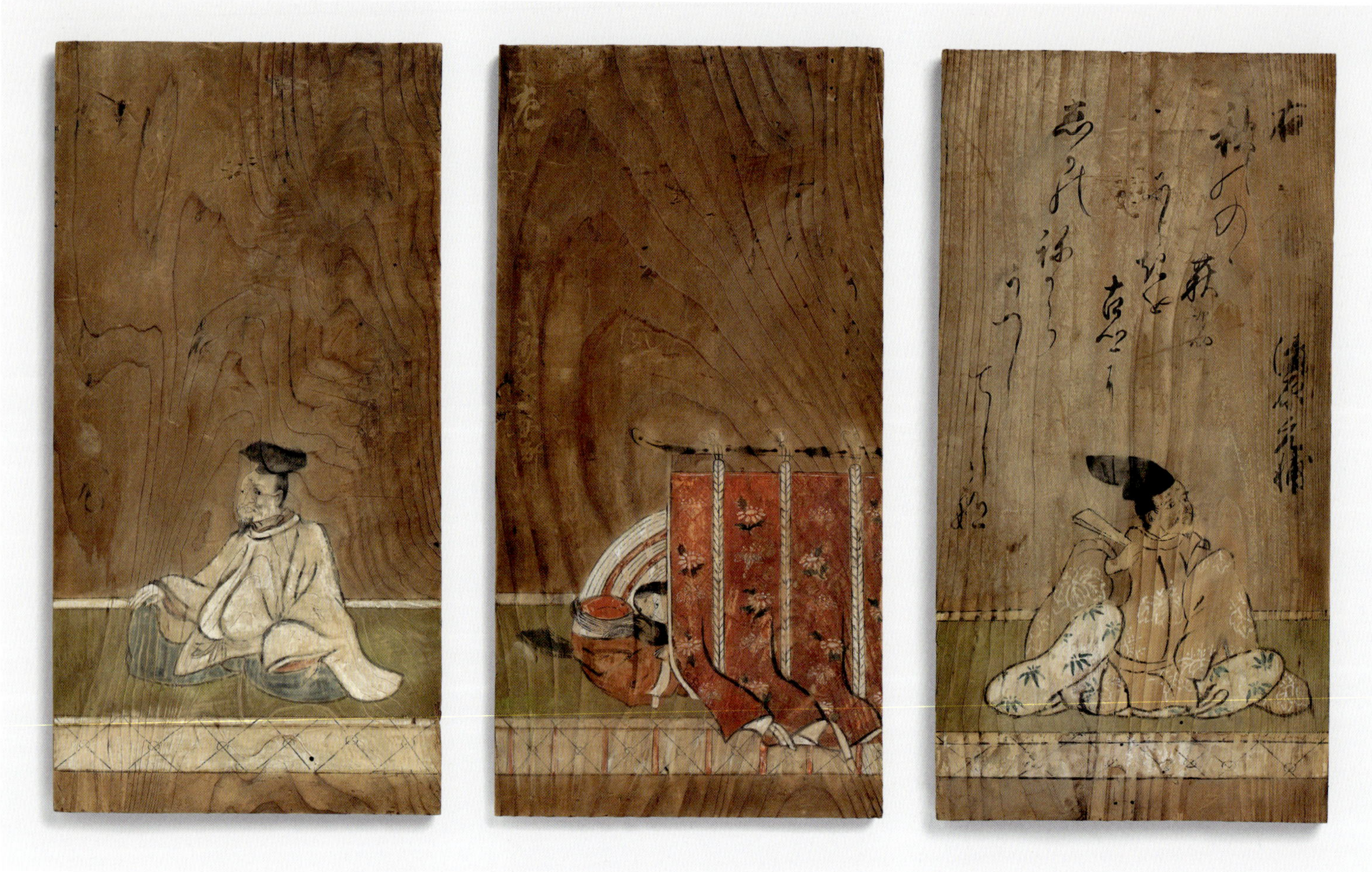

A: Hitomaro

B: Saigū no Nyōgo (Princess Kishi)

C: Kiyohara Motosuke

37

Votive Plaques (*Ema*) of Thirty-Six Immortal Poets

Edo period (1615–1868), dated to 1698

Ink and color on cryptomeria wood (*sugi*), each: 19½ × 9⅞ in. (49.5 × 25.1 cm)

125th Anniversary Acquisition. Gift of Dr. Luther W. Brady, Jr., 2008-257-1–36

Poetry and poets have been highly revered in Japan for over one thousand years. As early as the tenth century, Japanese emperors commissioned anthologies of the works of famous poets of the past and present (see no. 11). By the twelfth century, aristocrats had begun illustrating handscrolls made of paper or silk with imaginary portraits of poets. The majority of such handscrolls depict members of a group known as the Thirty-Six Immortal Poets, who were among the popular authors of the past (see no. 12). In the fifteenth century, low-ranking rural aristocrats and village associations began to donate portraits of poets painted on wooden votive plaques (*ema*), such as those seen here, to shrines and temples.[1]

The sequence of images of the thirty-six poets from different eras became standardized with minor variations and followed that found in the earlier handscrolls, although the verses chosen show variations. With the rise of printing, the verses and iconography of the Thirty-Six Immortal Poets reached a wider audience.[2] Here each poet is shown with their poem brushed directly above and around the figure. The dedicatory inscription for this set, dated to 1698, is brushed in ink on the reverse of each tablet.

Because these votive plaques were actually hung for many centuries, the painting and calligraphy have faded, as in the *ema* of Hitomaro (c. 653/55–707/10?). But because the images were standardized — Hitomaro, for example, is always depicted in a Chinese scholar's cap and robe (A; see also fig. 43) — they can fairly confidently be identified. The five women in the group wear the elaborate multilayered robes of the nobility of the Heian period (794–1185). The sole woman from the imperial line, Saigū no Nyōgo (Princess Kishi; 929–985?) is usually depicted behind curtains, in deference to her higher rank (B). Some plaques retain enough of the calligraphy to identify the poem, as with the *ema* of Lady Ise (c. 870–940; see fig. 29). Several of the *ema* preserve enough of the ink to discern a notation of "right" or "left" at their upper corners, as seen in the portrait of Kiyohara Motosuke (908–990) (C). These designations refer to the format of aristocratic poetry contests, with eighteen poets ranged on the left and eighteen on the right. The poets on the left are headed by Hitomaro, and those on the right by Ki no Tsurayuki (872–945?). The brushwork by the anonymous calligrapher is fluid and graceful, despite the difficulty of writing directly on the grained wood. The reverse of the final plaque gives the name Fujita, but it has not been possible to trace this artisan, who most likely worked at a regional painting studio. FF

1. See Kanazawa 2003. The first examples of single votive plaques were dedicated to Hitomaro, and the earliest known set of thirty-six poets in this format is dated to 1436. A noted patron in this regard was Ishikawa Jōzan (1583–1672), who in 1641 commissioned Kano Tan'yū (1602–1674) to paint a set of votive plaques featuring thirty-six Chinese poets (sometimes referred to as *hengaku kasen-e*, or "framed images of immortal poets") for his retreat, Shisendō, in Kyoto. The set is still extant. The Philadelphia Museum of Art's set of *ema* of Thirty-Six Immortal Poets is complete, and the only one known to be outside Japan.
2. See Philadelphia 2000, no. 39 for a printed version and no. 59 for translations of the thirty-six poems. A further expansion of the grouping to the *Hyakunin isshu* (*One Hundred Poems by One Hundred Poets*) remains popular today in the form of a New Year's card game.

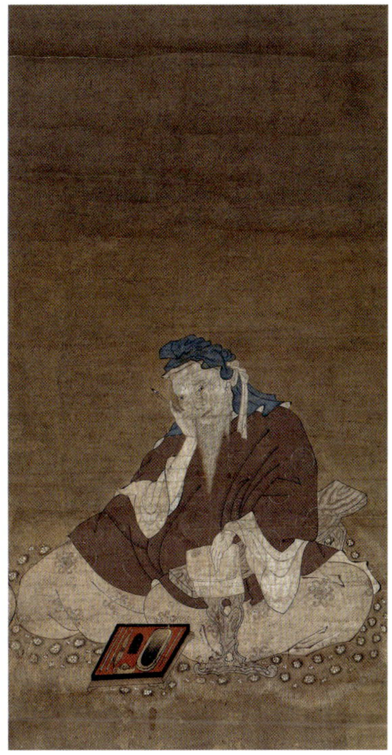

FIG. 43 *Portrait of Hitomaro*. Muromachi period (1392–1573), 16th century. Ink and color on paper, mounted as a hanging scroll; 30¾ × 15¼ in. (78.1 × 30.3 cm). Philadelphia Museum of Art: Gift of Edward B. Robinette, 1930-106-2

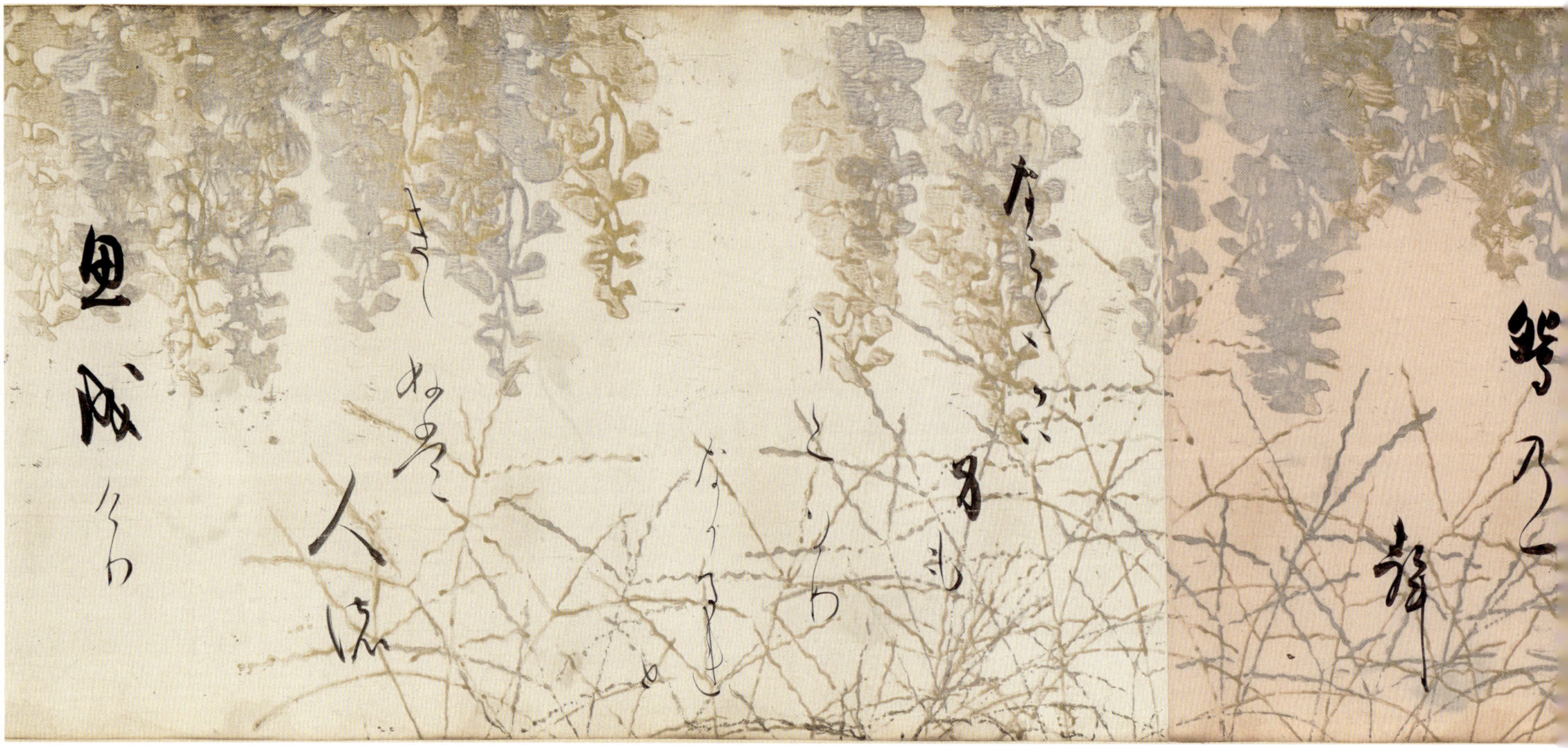

38

Poems from the *Shinkokin wakashū*

Hon'ami Kōetsu
(1558–1637)

Edo period (1615–1868),
early 17th century

Ink, gold, and silver on paper, mounted as a handscroll; 13$\frac{5}{16}$ in. × 27 ft. 2$\frac{3}{4}$ in. (33.8 × 830 cm)

125th Anniversary Acquisition. Purchased with funds contributed by the members of the Committee on East Asian Art, 1999-39-1

Hon'ami Kōetsu was a central figure in Japanese art at the turn of the seventeenth century. He was what would now be termed an "art director," bringing together talented artists from the Kyoto cultural arena. Kōetsu worked with lacquer artisans to make writing boxes after his designs; he was active in the world of tea, both as a participant in tea ceremony and as a potter of teabowls; he joined a project to print classical texts such as *The Tales of Ise* and Noh libretti; and his collaborations with the artist Tawaraya Sōtatsu (act. c. 1600–1640) resulted in handscrolls of classical poetry such as this one that are among the most beautiful works of any period of Japanese art.[1]

Each handscroll represents a unique assemblage of painting, calligraphy, and poetry, and each has many layers: the physical object, that is, the paper, the mica coating, and the weight and feel of the scroll; the images of painted or printed designs; the variations in the color of the ink of the calligraphy, from gray to jet black; and finally, the meaning of the poetic text. Kōetsu created an entirely new approach to seeing and using space, taking advantage of the characteristics of the handscroll as an artistic medium.

Normally the viewer can see only about one of the 21- to 24-inch sections at any single time, and the movement of the scroll itself is an essential element for both its creation and its appreciation. The handscroll is in effect an "interactive" medium, controlled by the viewer as one rolls the scroll forward or back, quickly or slowly. The perceptual dynamic is both immediate and cumulative. There is a balance and tension between what has come before, what is being viewed at that moment, and what is still to come. Kōetsu often created a deliberate sense of alienation, so that each layer is separate, and neither painting nor calligraphy fades out or into the other, making the viewer continually conscious of both. The logic of the progression of each

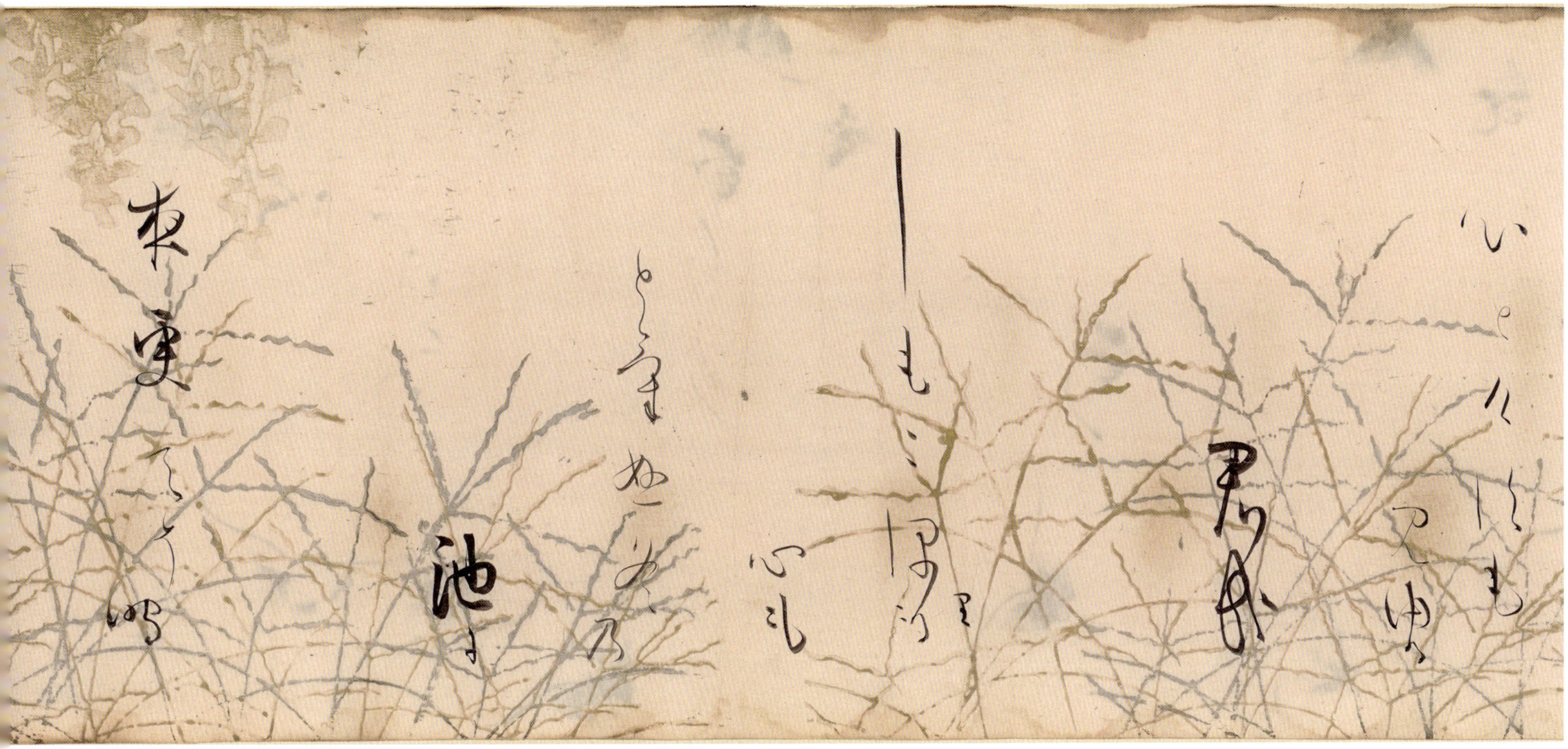

layer is also not necessarily synchronized or complementary.

This work consists of nine sections of paper dyed in varying colors, made and mounted as a handscroll by Kamishi Sōji, whose rectangular seal appears on the backing where the papers are joined.[2] There is also a random pattern of butterflies stamped in silver and gold on the reverse, creating another visual layer as the scroll is unrolled. Kōetsu often collaborated with this papermaker to assure the highest quality paper for his handscroll projects. Kōetsu's other collaborator was Sōtatsu, whose designs were carved into small wood blocks and stamped individually by hand in gold and silver onto the prepared paper.

Onto this 27-foot-long surface, Kōetsu brushed twelve poems from the early thirteenth-century imperial poetry anthology, the *Shinkokin wakashū* (New collection of poems from ancient and modern times), in his elegant calligraphy.[3] Kōetsu's transcription of the verses shows his characteristic variations of dark and light ink, broad and fine brushstrokes, and the "scattering" of the words among the grasses, providing lovely, irregular visual patterns. His brushwork is particularly effective in sections such as the wisteria and grasses that span the blue and pink sheets of paper. The poems are all on the subject of love, written in the traditional thirty-one-syllable format called *waka*. FF

1. See no. 39 and Philadelphia 2000 for examples of the range of Kōetsu's creativity. Sōtatsu collaborated with Kōetsu on other projects such as printed Noh libretti. See Philadelphia 2000, 56–60, 62–70, 173–75, nos. 29–35.
2. Kamishi Sōji's life dates are unknown; the seal used on this handscroll is believed to predate 1615.
3. Now some twenty-seven feet in length, the scroll may originally have been longer, but it suffered fire damage at an unknown date. Its careful restoration, undertaken in Japan in the 1980s, deliberately retained some signs of damage, emphasizing the beauty of age and wear, rather than denying or disguising the work's history.

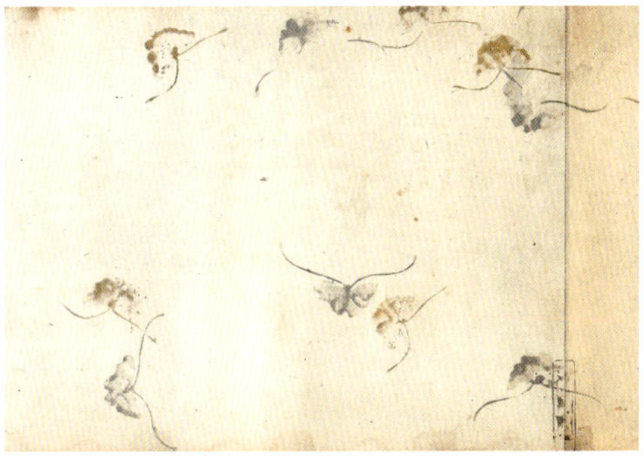

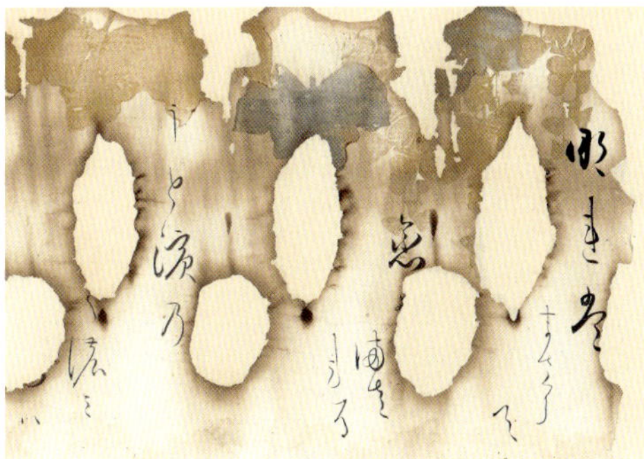

Detail of the backing paper, with butterfly stamps and Kamishi Sōji's seal

Detail of the first section of the scroll, showing fire damage

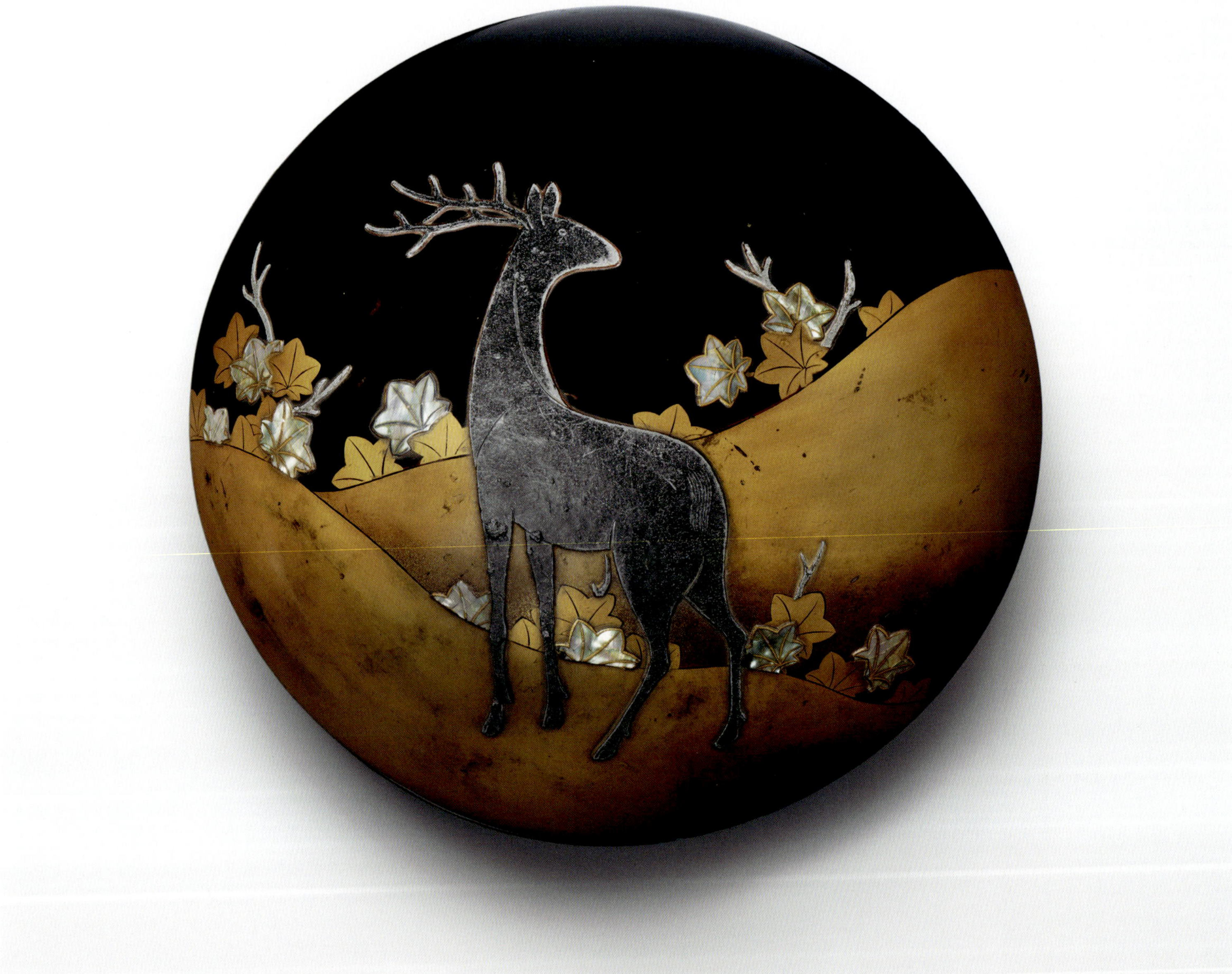

39

Writing Box (*Suzuri-bako*) with Design of a Deer

Attributed to Hon'ami Kōetsu (1558–1637)

Edo period (1615–1868), early 17th century

Wood, lacquer, gold *maki-e*, lead, and *raden* (mother-of-pearl)
Diam. 11⅝ in. (29.5 cm)

Gift of the Friends of the Philadelphia Museum of Art, 1992-7-1a–d

Hon'ami Kōetsu's fame rests primarily on his calligraphy (see no. 38), but his creativity extended into many areas of Japanese art, including designs for writing boxes.[1] This *suzuri-bako* (literally "ink-stone box") contains the essentials for producing the ink used to brush calligraphy: a rectangular ink stone, on which ink sticks are ground to a fine powder and mixed with water to form the liquid ink; and a square iron water dropper. These two elements are set into the bottom of the box, which is decorated with scattered gold-lacquer maple leaves on a black lacquer ground. The interior of the lid shows the gnarled trunk of a maple tree with gold leaves. Writing boxes essentially function as storage cases for writing tools, but they also serve as objects for aesthetic appreciation. While the calligrapher slowly grinds the ink, he can contemplate, and draw inspiration from, the motifs of the *suzuri-bako.*

In this example, the maple design finds its full expression on the domed lid, with a single stag gazing out over the autumnal landscape. The bold image recalls the classical poetic theme of solitary longing. The stag, its head turned in search of its mate, is made of lead, silhouetted against the black lacquer sky and the gold hillocks that are scattered with leaves in gold and mother-of-pearl. The arched dome of the lid and the use of lead and mother-of-pearl reflect the work of a highly skilled artisan, fulfilling the dramatic design of and for a master calligrapher. FF

---

1. By 1615 Kōetsu had moved to Takagamine, near Kyoto, where he established a small community that attracted numerous craftspeople to settle, including lacquer artisans of the noted Igarashi family. In an extant letter to one lacquer artist, Kōetsu gives his specific instructions about the design of a writing box. See Philadelphia 2000, 20, 200–201, and no. 72.

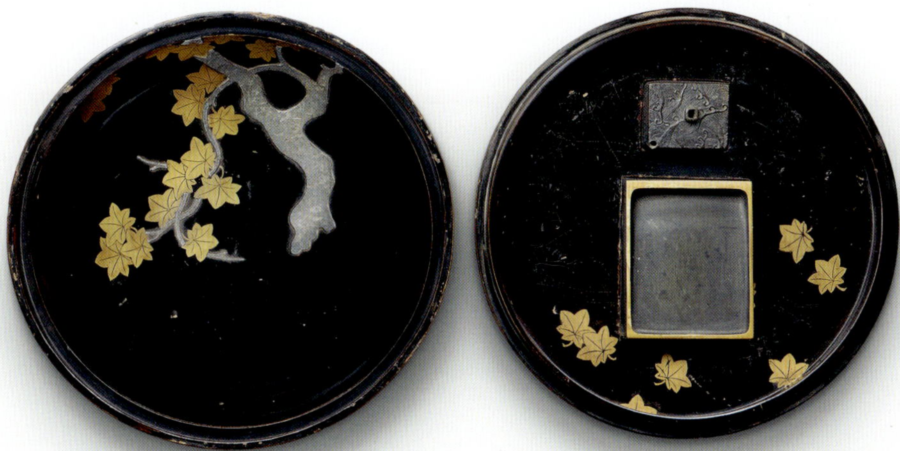

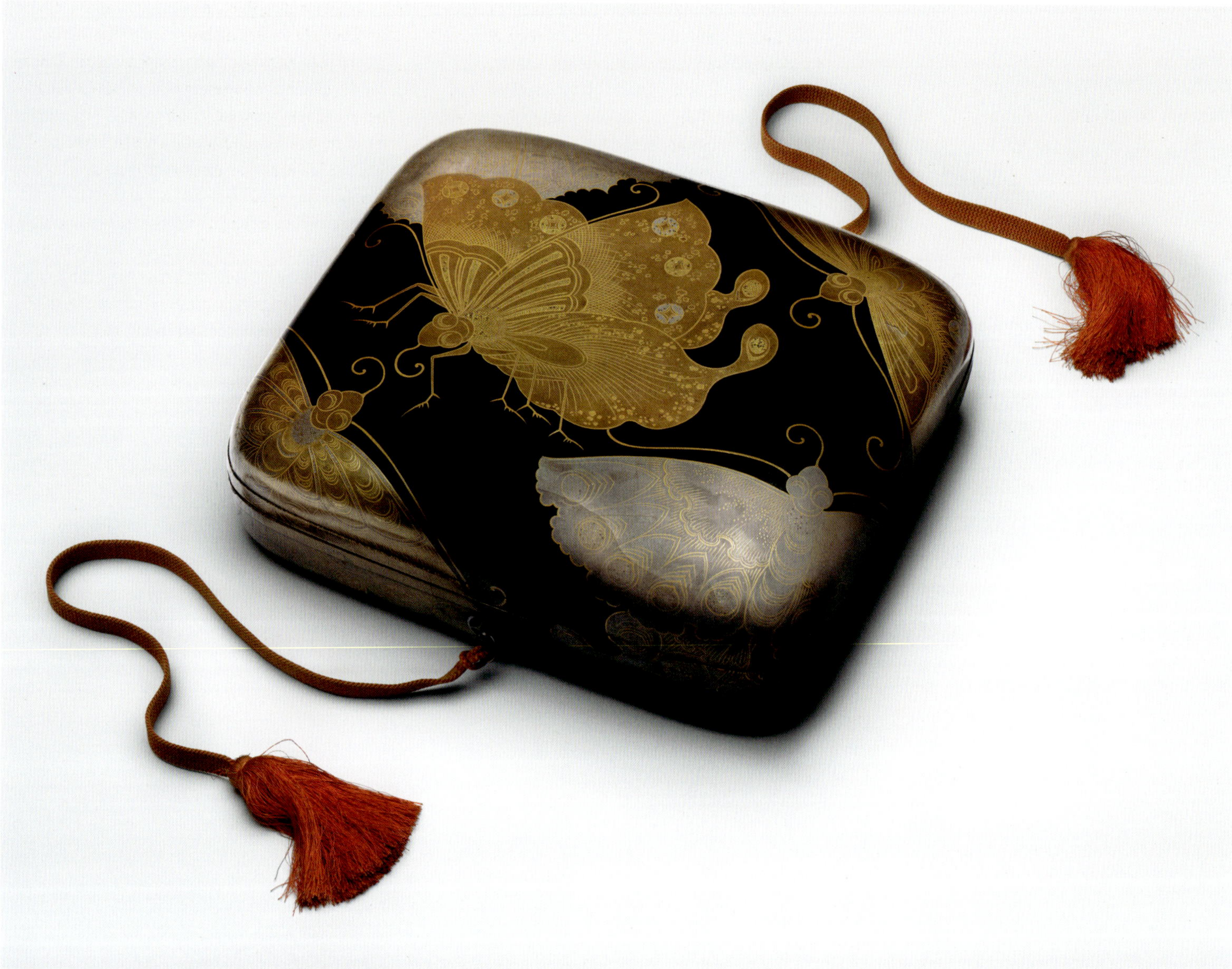

40

Document Box with Design of Five Butterflies

Edo period (1615–1868), 17th–18th century

Deer hide with black lacquer, silver and gold *maki-e*; metal ring fittings; $5\frac{1}{8} \times 11\frac{13}{16} \times 13\frac{3}{8}$ in. (13 × 30 × 34 cm)

Purchased with the Hollis Fund for East Asian Art Acquisitions, 2004-83-1a,b

The bold design of five gold and silver butterflies on a polished black ground, as well as the slightly domed shape of the box lid, reveals the strong influence of Hon'ami Kōetsu (see nos. 38, 39). This lavishly produced document box features the "sprinkled picture" (*maki-e*) technique using gold and silver powder and particles to create the motifs. Often referred to as Kodai-ji (after the temple where it first appeared), this style is characterized by striking, elegant motifs such as these swallowtail butterflies flying into all corners and sides of the box. Butterflies, as symbols of renewal and longevity, were frequently used design elements. Their renderings on this box were inspired by the butterfly crest of the Taira family, a motif that was widely employed in the seventeenth century and popularized by printed Noh texts.[1]

The material of the box, deer hide covered in multiple layers of black lacquer, is unusual, as most such pieces have a wood base. The craftsmanship displayed here is of the highest order: while maintaining a sophisticated harmony between the shape of the box and the overall design, the anonymous artisan employed a variety of finely detailed patterning on each butterfly. The box can be tied shut with tasseled cords attached to metal rings at either side. The multiple layers of lacquer provide a durable coating to protect against dampness or insects, ideal properties for a box used to store documents such as letters or poetry cards to ensure their longevity. FF

1. The motif was called *ageha chō* (butterfly with raised wings); see Atami 1999, nos. 21, 81.

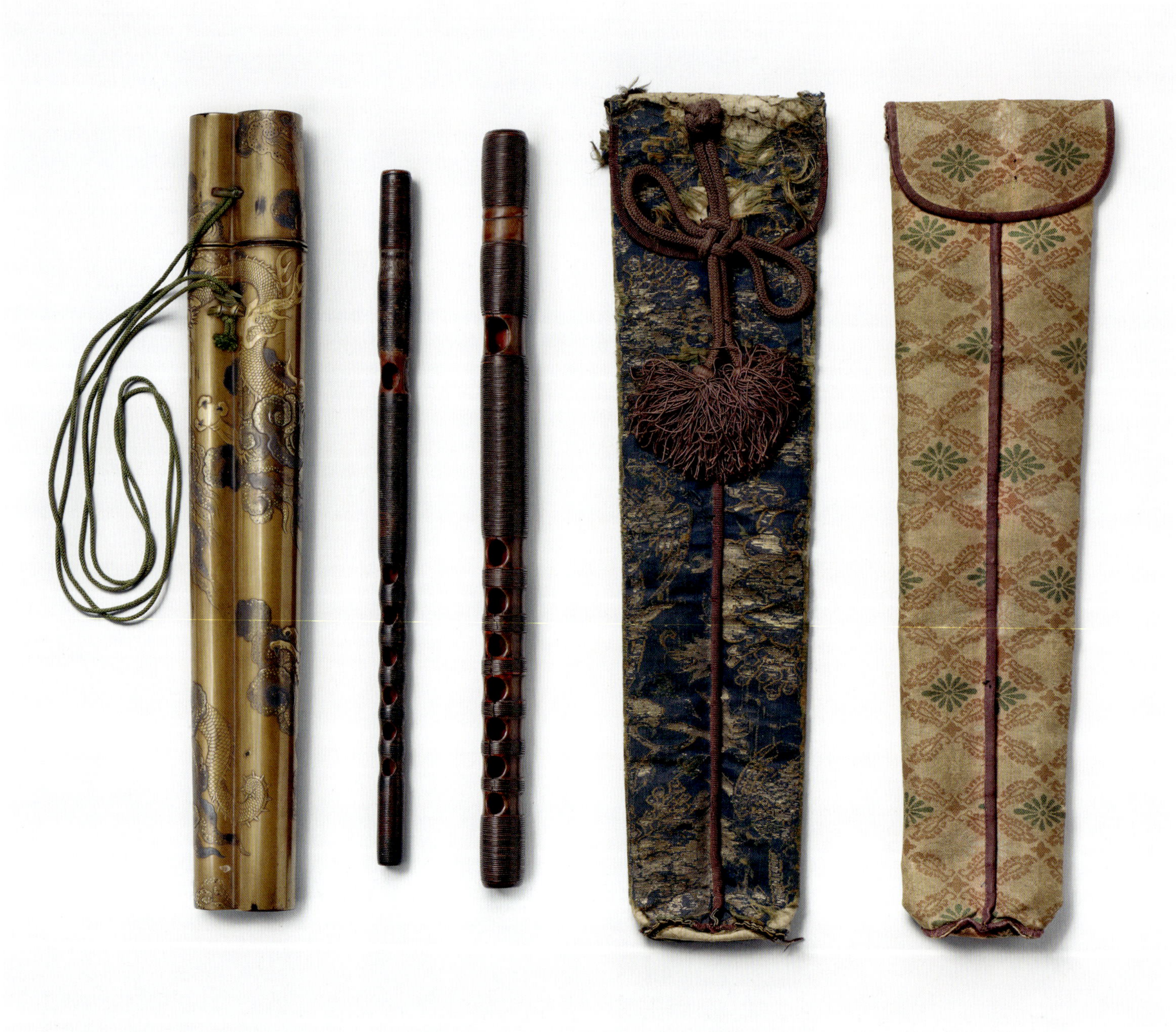

41

Pair of Flutes (*Nōkan*)

Edo period (1615–1868), 18th century

Lacquered bamboo, cherry wood bark, and ivory
Flute A: L. 15¾ in. (40 cm), diam. 1³⁄₁₆ in. (3 cm)
Flute B: L. 14⁹⁄₁₆ in. (37 cm), diam. ¹³⁄₁₆ in. (2 cm)

Purchased with funds contributed by Andrea M. Baldeck, M.D., 2009-86-1a,b

This pair of transverse flutes are of the type used for Noh theater performances, as is reflected in the Japanese name *nōkan* (literally "Noh tube"). The flute is the sole wind instrument used in the accompaniment for Noh theater, but like the hand drum, it functions as a rhythm instrument. The text in Noh plays is usually sung by the actors, and the flute often serves to punctuate or heighten a passage with its high, shrill notes.[1] The effect is that of disembodied sounds, evoking the spirit world to which the main characters in Noh plays often belong.

The flutes are made from lacquered bamboo wound with thinly split cherry bark. The bamboo preferred for these flutes is so-called smoked bamboo, or bamboo that has been naturally aged from smoke over a charcoal fire, giving it a rich, dark color. In addition to the mouth hole, the smaller flute has six finger holes, while the larger, standard one has seven.

The artisan created a double case for the flutes, covered with gold and silver lacquer and decorated with a three-clawed golden dragon rising vertically amid silver-gray swirling clouds. The top and bottom of the cases have circular family-crest motifs (crossed falcon feathers and a three-petaled blossom; see details below). The combined family crests may indicate that the flutes were part of a wedding dowry. Costly textiles were employed for the protective cloth cases. Many of the wealthy daimyo lords of the Edo period, such as the Sakai, sponsored their own Noh theater troupes, and would have commissioned the musical instruments as well.[2] FF

1. The secret to the construction of these flutes can be detected through X-ray photography. Each flute seems weighted at the neck, and a smaller tube has been inserted into the hollow between the mouthpiece and the first finger hole. This constricts the passage of air, allowing only for the high-pitched notes. The inside of the flute is furthermore covered in multiple layers of a mixture of lacquer and polishing powder (*tonoko*).
2. Also employed in Noh plays are small hand drums with lacquer-decorated surfaces (see fig. 44).

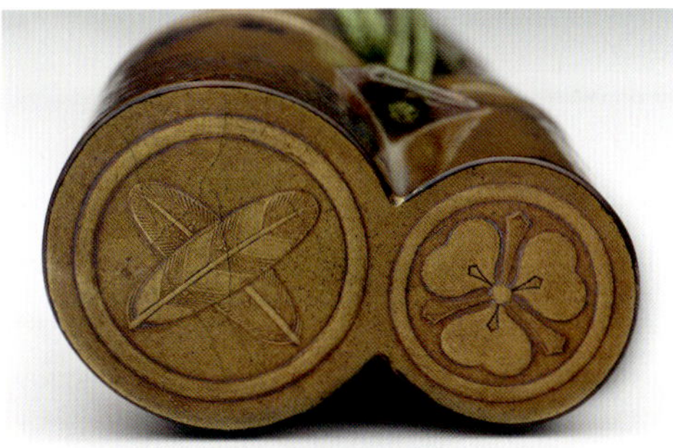

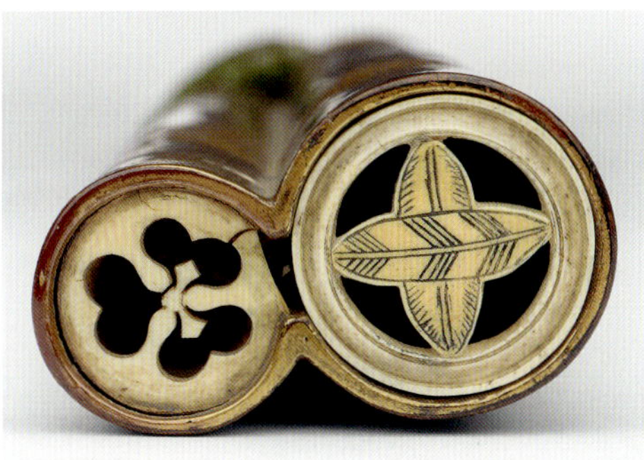

Details of the family crests on the top and bottom ends of the flute case

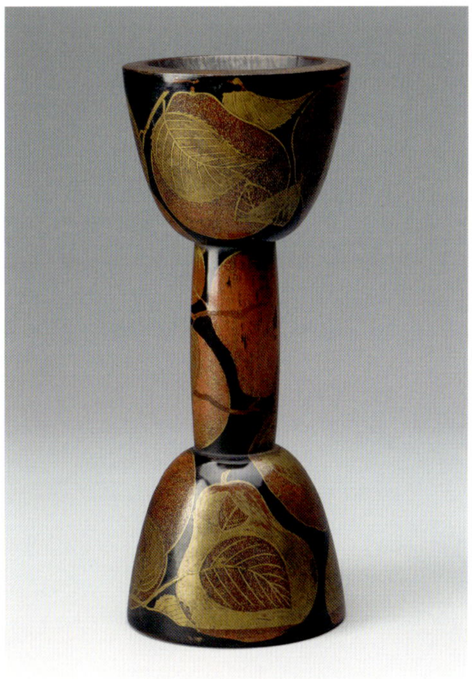

FIG. 44 Hand Drum. Momoyama period (1568–1615), 17th century. Black and gold lacquer on wood, 10 × 3¾ in. (25.4 × 9.5 cm). Philadelphia Museum of Art, 125th Anniversary Acquisition: Purchased with the Hollis Family Foundation Fund and with funds contributed by the Mary Livingston Griggs and Mary Griggs Burke Foundation, The Annenberg Foundation, Priscilla Grace, Colonel Stephen McCormick, the Honorable Ida Chen, Mr. and Mrs. Gary Graffman, Hannah L. and J. Welles Henderson, 2002-95-1

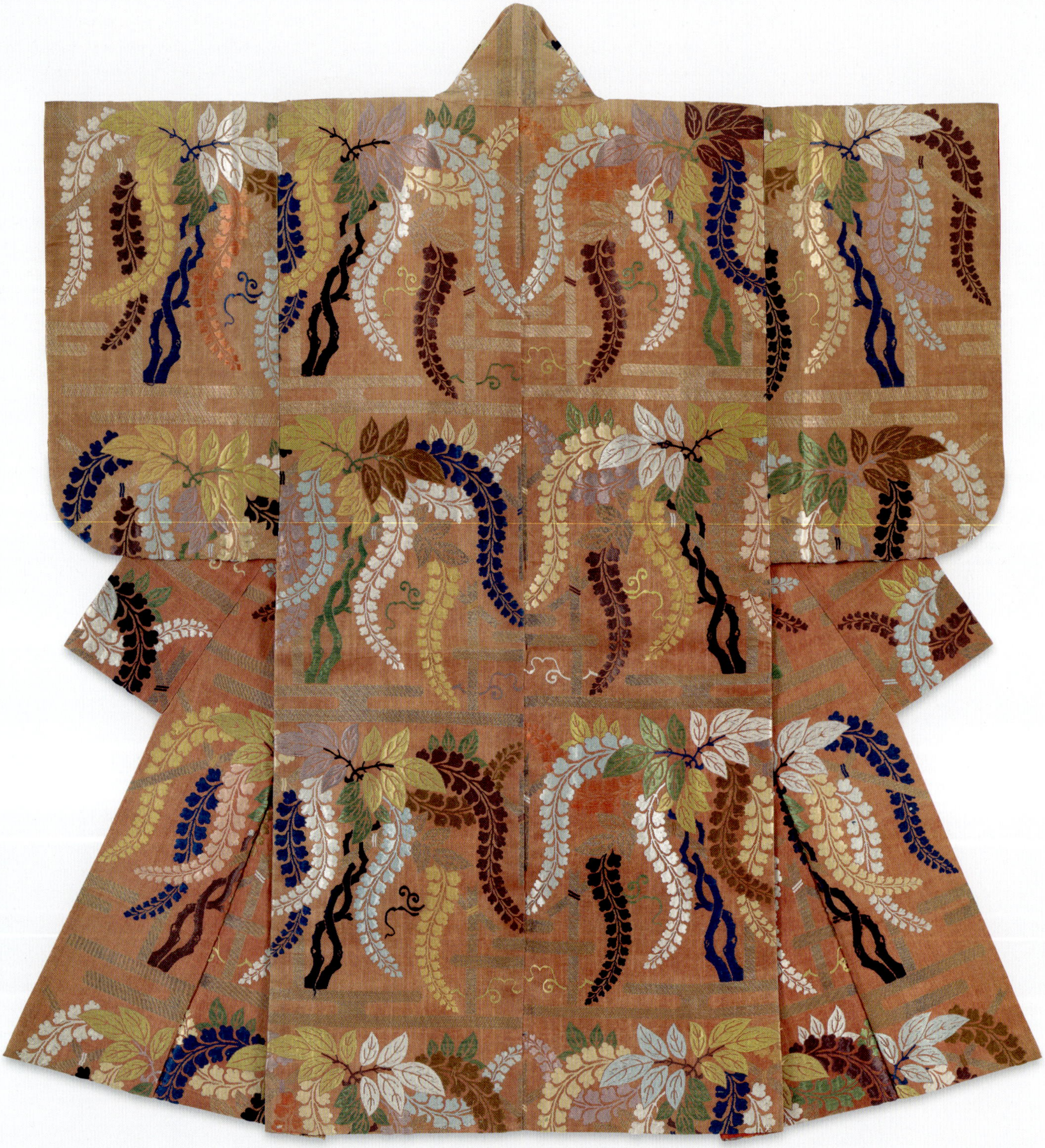

42

Noh Robe, *Uwagi* (Outer Garment for Female Role), *Karaori* Type

Edo period (1615–1868), 1750–1850

Silk twill weave with silk- and gilt-thread pattern wefts

Gift of Henry B. Keep, 1964-218-1

Traditional Japanese Noh theater combines elements of dance, drama, music, and poetry to create an art form that focuses on the expression of emotion and emphasizes the aesthetic and the symbolic. The plots of Noh performances — often centered on a historical, literary, or supernatural protagonist — are minimal. Splendid costumes are a vital part of the drama. Their brilliant colors and intricate patterns provide the primary visual interest on an otherwise austere stage, where the stylized movements of the performers (all male) display the garments' majestic forms. While each character in a Noh drama wears a prescribed style of costume to convey status and state of mind, actors make specific choices within these conventions to give esoteric nuances to the performance.

Noh drama developed in the fourteenth and early fifteenth centuries, when costumes both mirrored everyday Japanese dress and included expensive, fashionable garments donated by members of the aristocratic samurai (warrior) class. By the seventeenth century, Noh had become the official ceremonial entertainment of the military shogunate regime. During the Edo period, Noh costumes evolved as a distinct variety of stage dress that reflected upper-class dress traditions from previous centuries, contrasting with the new court fashions. Noh robes are classified into several categories of outer and inner garments worn for various male and female roles; each has its own characteristics, but all Noh robes show a sumptuousness that accords with the elegance and evocative beauty of this theatrical art.

This Noh robe is made from continuously patterned, woven fabric known as *karaori* (literally "Chinese weaving"), a term applied to an intricate weave type in which untwisted silk wefts float across the surface of the fabric, giving the impression of elaborate embroidery. After the technique went out of favor for fashionable garments, it continued to be used for Noh costumes; robes such as this — also known as *karaori* — are generally worn as an outer garment for female roles. They are stiff and heavy and when worn give the character a regal effect appropriate for the slow and considered movements of Noh drama. This robe's wisteria and lattice motif is typical of the "feminine" pictorial patterns of *karaori*; the use of red indicates that the robe was intended for roles portraying young women. HKH

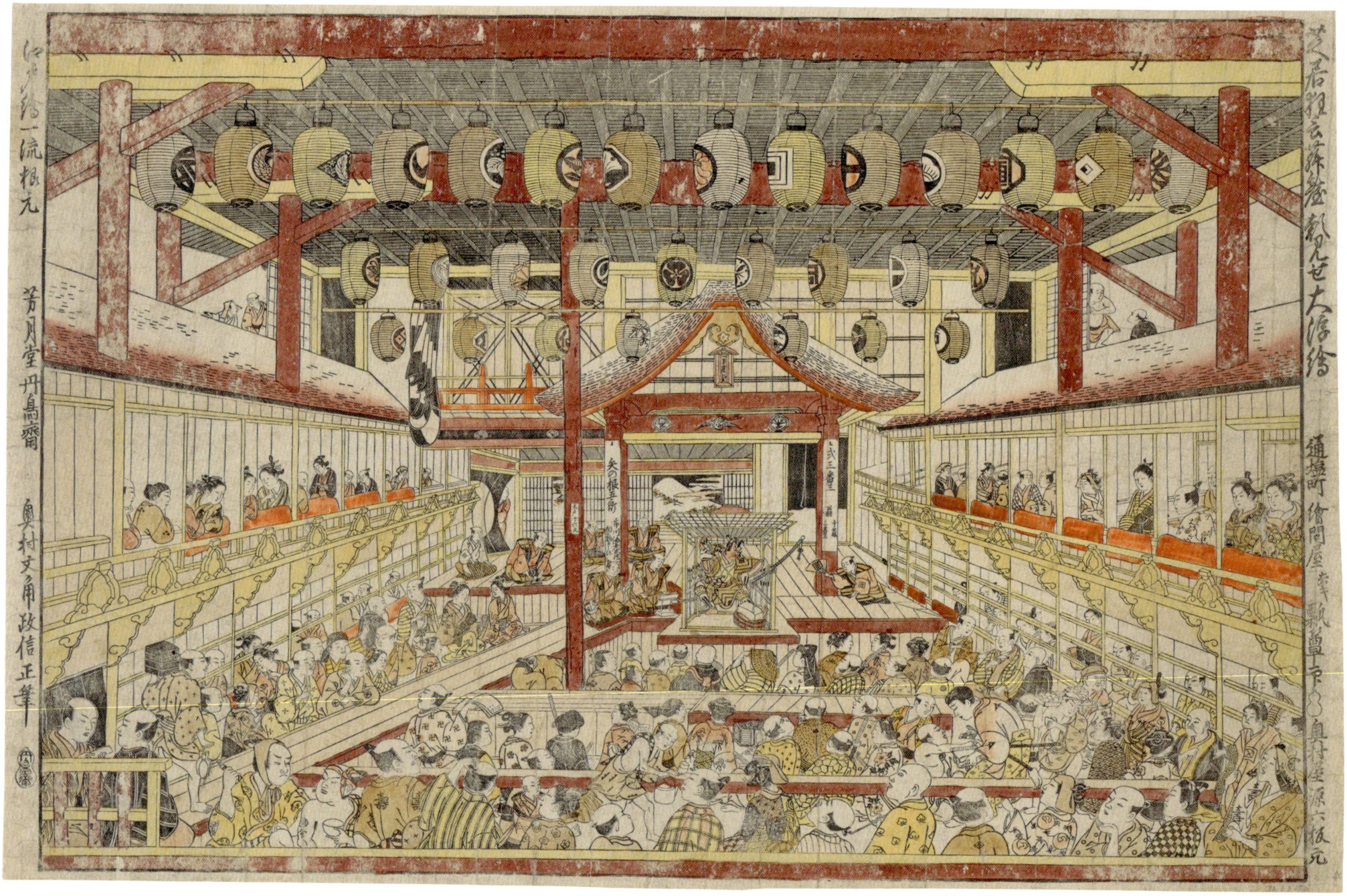
芝居狂言舞台顔見世大浮絵
江戸繪一流根元
芳月堂 丹鳥齋
奥村文角政信正筆

43

Large Perspective Picture of the Face-Showing at the Stage Performance of a Drama (*Shibai kyōgen butai kaomise ōukie*)

Okumura Masanobu
(1685–1764)

Edo period (1615–1868), 1745

Hand-colored woodblock print
17½ × 26¼ in. (44.5 × 66.7 cm)

Gift of Elizabeth Matthews Jayne for the Henry LaBarre Jayne Collection, 1926-63-20

The theater is packed on the opening day of the annual kabuki season. Actor Ichikawa Ebizō (Danjūrō II; 1688–1758) is on stage in one of his most famous roles, the warrior Soga Gorō Tokimune. He pauses while polishing an arrowhead, momentarily freezing to emphasize the drama of the moment. Die-hard fans are rapt in admiration. Yet much of the crowd is otherwise occupied — lounging, posing, chatting, people watching, or drinking tea — enjoying the outing as much for socializing as for the performance. The theater is fully described in this work, showing the center stage and connecting walkway (*hanamichi*), box and bench seating, lanterns with actors' crests, and shoji doors opened to light and air.

Yet what was most striking to viewers of this print when it was made — as well as to viewers today — is the presentation of the scene using European-style perspective. This mode of representing space came to Japan via Dutch and Chinese trade, and it was considered such a novelty that it was called *uki-e*, or "floating picture." The term suggests that for period viewers a picture such as this seemed visually unstable, as if it were about to float up or even fall away. Okumura Masanobu often used linear perspective for interiors in this period of his career, with varying results depending on the scene, as found in other examples in the museum's collection.[1]

On the right side of the print, the title includes the term *ōuki-e* ("large floating picture"). This is a rare example from the period of a print made using an entire sheet of paper; it was printed with a single woodblock, with color applied by hand. The publisher's address and name are listed along the lower-right edge, and he is promoted as a "first-class publisher of Edo pictures" at upper left. Masanobu's studio name and his signature also appear along the left, followed by the term "true brush," assuring the work's authenticity.

Uki-e prints were popular through the eighteenth century and were often viewed with lensed devices that enhanced their special effects. Some images showed famous places around Edo, as can be seen in a later example by Utagawa Toyoharu (1735–1814; fig. 45); others presented imagined views of distant lands. In Toyoharu's print, other visual conventions, such as the lower horizon line and shading in the trees, mimic conventions present in period copperplate prints imported from Europe. These innovations in perspective were adapted by later artists, including Katsushika Hokusai (1760–1849) and Utagawa Hiroshige (1797–1858), for landscape studies in the first half of the nineteenth century. JND

1. See, for example, PMA acc. nos. 1946-66-13 and 1970-35-1.

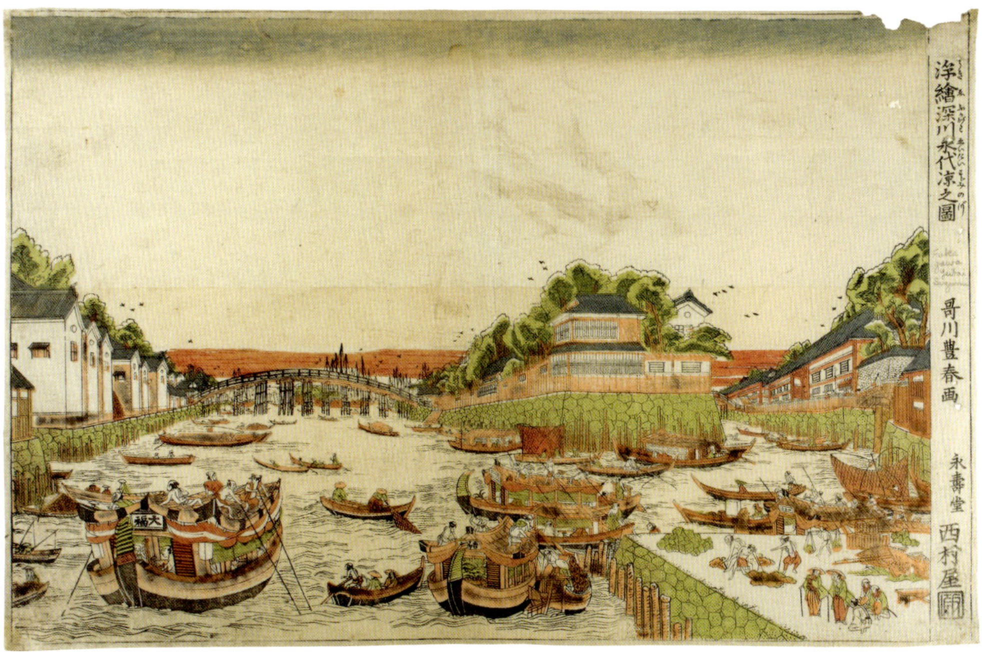

FIG. 45 Utagawa Toyoharu (1735–1814). *Perspective Picture of a Summer Evening at Eitai in Fukagawam* (*Ukie Fukagawa Eitai suzumi no zu*). Edo period, c. 1771. Color woodblock print, 9¾ × 14¾ in. (24.8 × 37.5 cm). Philadelphia Museum of Art: Gift of Mrs. Anne Archbold, 1946-66-50

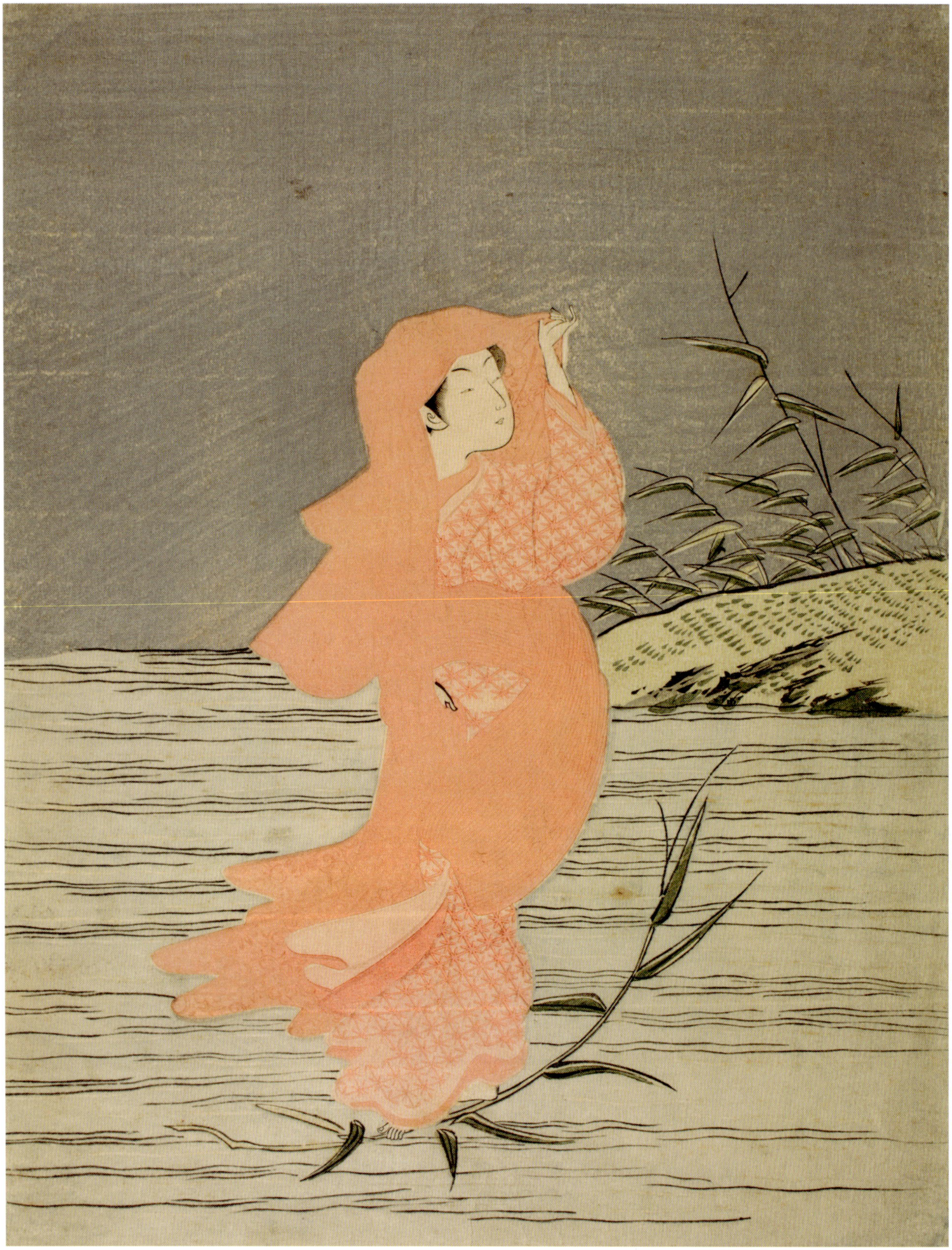

44

Courtesan as Daruma Crossing the River

Suzuki Harunobu
(1725?–1770)

Edo period (1615–1868),
c. 1765–67

Color woodblock print
(*chūban tate-e*), 10⅞ × 8¼ in.
(27.6 × 21 cm)

Gift of Mrs. Emile Geyelin
in memory of Anne Hampton
Barnes, 1960-17-1

Poised upon a floating reed, a beautiful young woman peers out from an enveloping hood. Her voluminous, pinkish-red robes stand in contrast with the flat, gray-blue sky and pale blue water below. Contemporary viewers would have recognized in this figure a parody of the great Zen patriarch Bodhidharma (Daruma), credited with the transmission of Chan (Zen) Buddhism to China and later said to have crossed to Japan on a reed (see no. 9). The juxtaposition of such an elevated subject with contemporary culture was popular in Edo-period woodblock prints, although it was more common to find pictures of Daruma enjoying the pleasures of the floating world's brothels and theaters.[1] Here Suzuki Harunobu took the appropriation a step further, replacing the Zen master in his characteristic red robes with the delicate figure of a young woman.[2] Harunobu stood at the center of the pivotal transition in ukiyo-e printmaking from limited-color to full-color prints made with five or more color woodblocks.[3] In collaboration with patrons and skilled carvers and printers, Harunobu produced elegant and witty prints that quickly became known as *nishiki-e*, or brocade pictures, for their lush, multihued imagery.

Beyond the clever transposition of subject matter, this print demonstrates the exquisite technical printing achieved by Harunobu and his circle in the early Meiwa era (1764–72). Especially impressive is the figure's clothing, for which blind printing was used to suggest the texture of the obi and to create the fabric's starburst designs and embossed floral patterns. Notably, the black line of the key block was used only to contour the woman's hands, face, and feet. The diminished presence of line emphasizes the virtuosic printing techniques and highlights the delicacy of the figure — and perhaps gestures to the otherworldliness of the Zen patriarch for whom she substitutes.

This impression — a rare first state of the design — is especially notable for its well-preserved red colorants, which are probably derived primarily from *beni* (safflower).[4] JK

---

1. The artist revisited the theme of Daruma in the pleasure quarters in numerous print designs, often picturing the sage in amusing and compromising situations with the *yūjo* (sex workers). He also re-created the scene of Daruma's crossing as a pillar print, which was probably made after this version. Examples can be found at the Museum of Fine Arts, Boston (acc. no. 11.21286), and the Brooklyn Museum (acc. no. 62.79.7).
2. The conceit of substituting a prostitute of the pleasure quarters in Daruma's guise may have been inaugurated by the artist Hanabusa Itchō (1652–1724), as related in the *Koga bikō* (Biographies of painters). For a discussion in English, see Waterhouse 2013, 1:108.
3. Color printing was already in use in single-sheet prints of two or three colors, known as *benizuri-e*, as well as in illustrated books; the development of full-color prints is usually assigned to the calendar prints produced by Harunobu and his circle for the New Year of 1765.
4. Another impression of the first state is in the collection of the Museum of Fine Arts, Boston; the Philadelphia impression is superior. Later states feature thin or scalloped cloud forms at the top edge of the sheet, which may indicate damage to the original block. An impression of the second state is in the Worcester Art Museum in Massachusetts; impressions of the third state are in the British Museum, London, and the Museum für Asiatische Kunst, Berlin.

45

Woman's Kimono (or Robe) (*Kosode*)

Edo period (1615–1868), late 17th–early 18th century

Silk figured satin weave (*rinzu*) with stencil resist dyeing (*kata kanoko*), painting (*kaki-e*), and silk floss embroidery in couching and satin stitches, silk- and gilt-thread embroidery in couching and satin stitches, and metallic embroidery in couching stitch; silk crepe

Gift of Mr. and Mrs. Rodolphe Meyer de Schauensee, 1951-42-1

The T-shaped Japanese garment has proven to be both adaptable and almost all-purpose. Worn since the eighth century, these robes have been known as kimono (meaning "thing to wear") since the mid-nineteenth century, but earlier forms included *kosode* (meaning "small sleeves," a reference to the size of the wrist openings). By the sixteenth century, *kosode* had become the main attire for all classes and genders in Japan.

Simply constructed from lengths of fabric stitched together, the flat form of *kosode* was ideal for showing off beautiful textiles and diverse designs made with sophisticated weaving, dyeing, and decorative techniques. Some *kosode* were enriched with grid-like filling patterns made by a laborious method of tie-dyeing called *kanoko shibori*, or "fawn-spot dyeing," which produced dense fields of small white dots with raised colored centers; on others, such as this example, the dotted effect—although not the dimensionality—was imitated by a less expensive method of stencil resist dyeing known as *kata kanoko*.

This *kosode* exemplifies the refined and richly decorated style favored by wealthy merchants of the Genroku era (1688–1703). The soft and supple figured silk (*rinzu*) gives the garment a relaxed silhouette, and the fabric's monochrome woven pattern—a key fret sprinkled with floral motifs—adds a textural quality to the embroidered, painted, and resist-dyed embellishment. The asymmetrical decorative scheme leaves empty one front side, which would be hidden when worn, as well as the waist area of the opposite back side, but the rest of the robe is covered with auspicious imagery. Meandering branches of a mandarin orange tree are laden with fruit and intermingled with sprightly paulownia flowers, while bamboo hedges of various heights rise from the hem forming graphic verticals. Broad banana leaves drape over the tops of these hedges, and several small gilt cages or lanterns perch on these soft coverings, an indication of the harmonious interaction between humans and nature. HKH

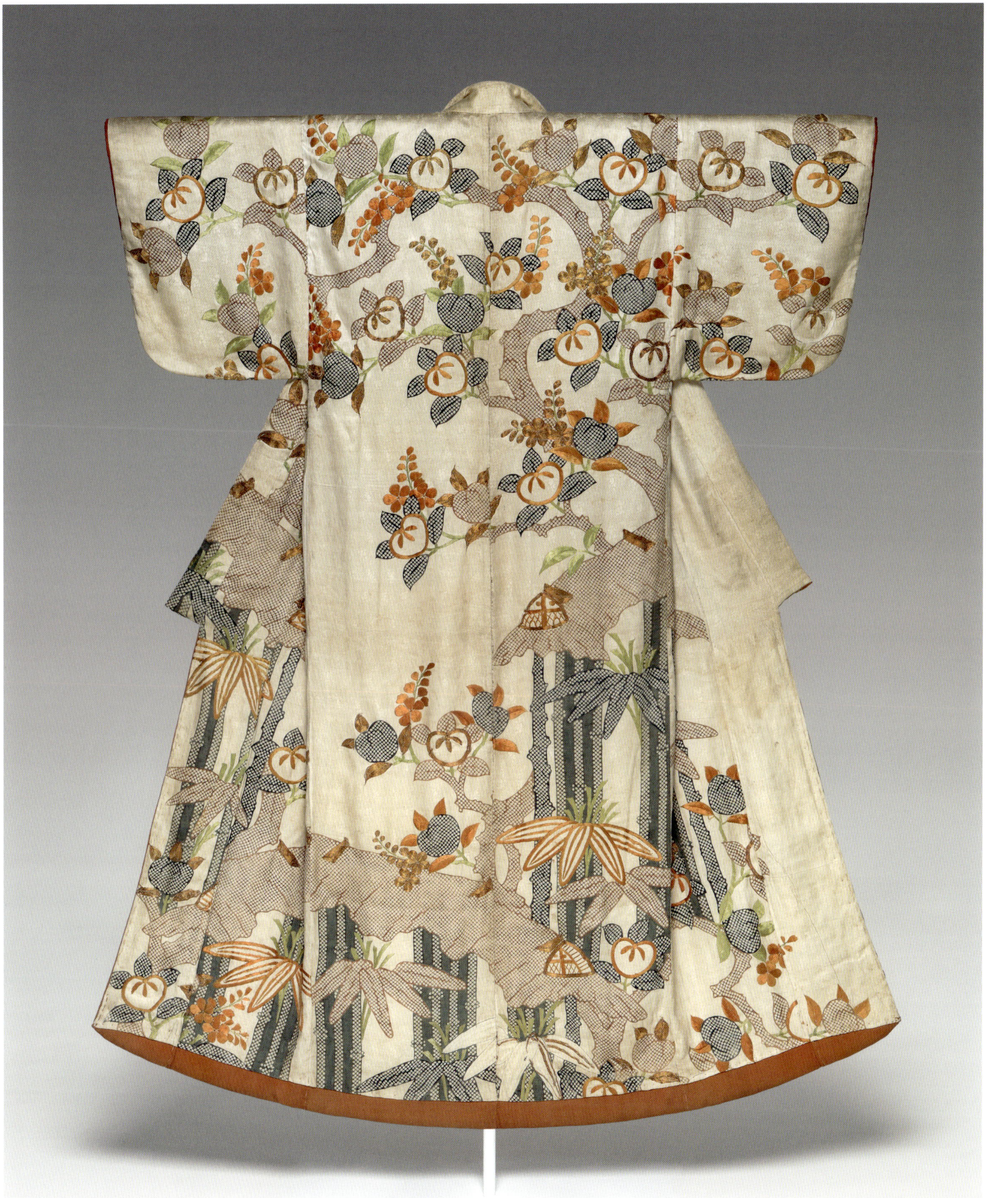

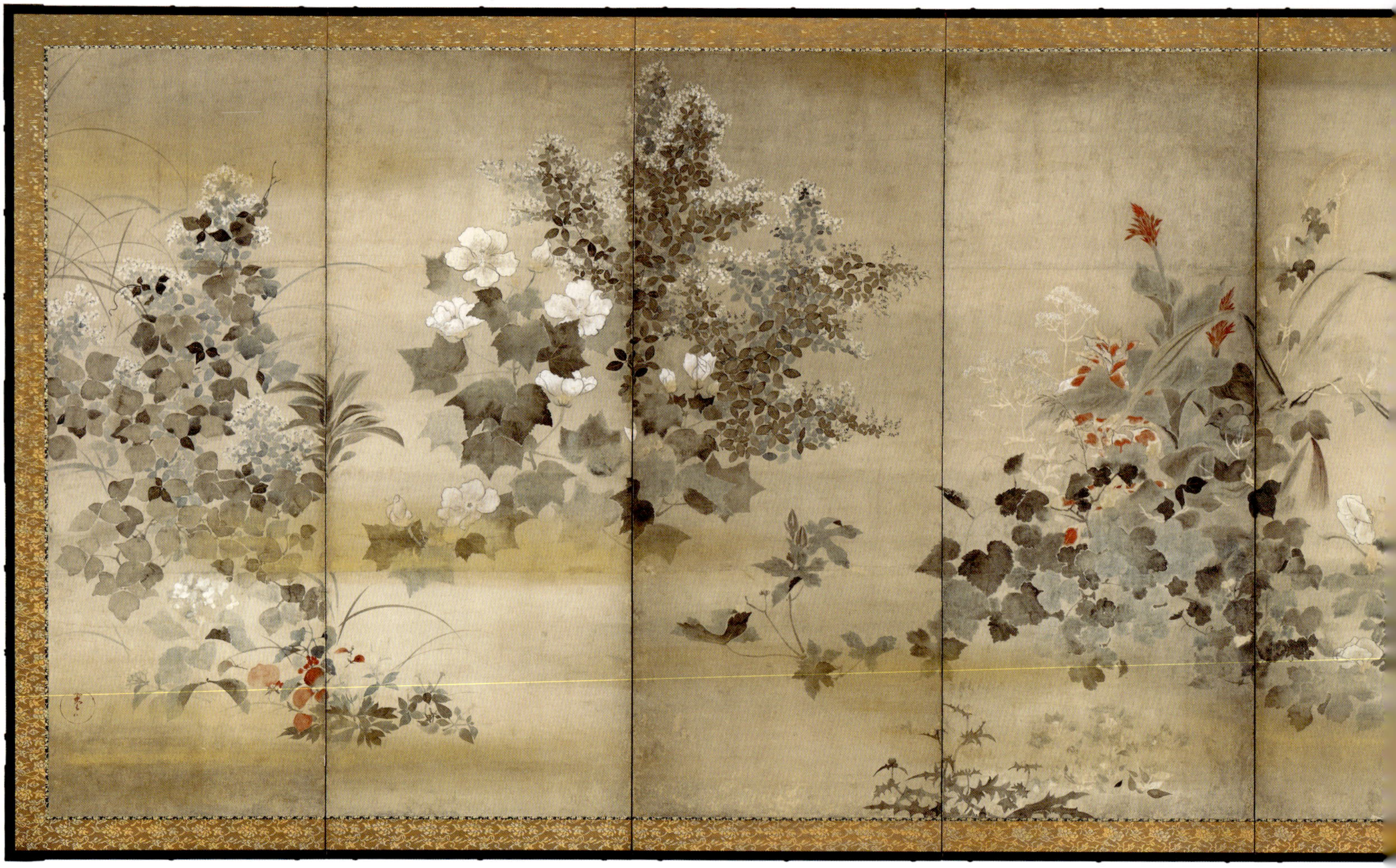

46

Autumn Flowers

Kitagawa Sōsetsu
(act. mid-17th century–
early 18th century)

Edo period (1615–1868),
mid-17th century

Ink and colors on paper, mounted
as a six-fold screen; 63½ in. ×
11 ft. 6 in. (161.3 × 350.5 cm)

Gift of Mrs. Horace Binney Hare,
1966-100-1

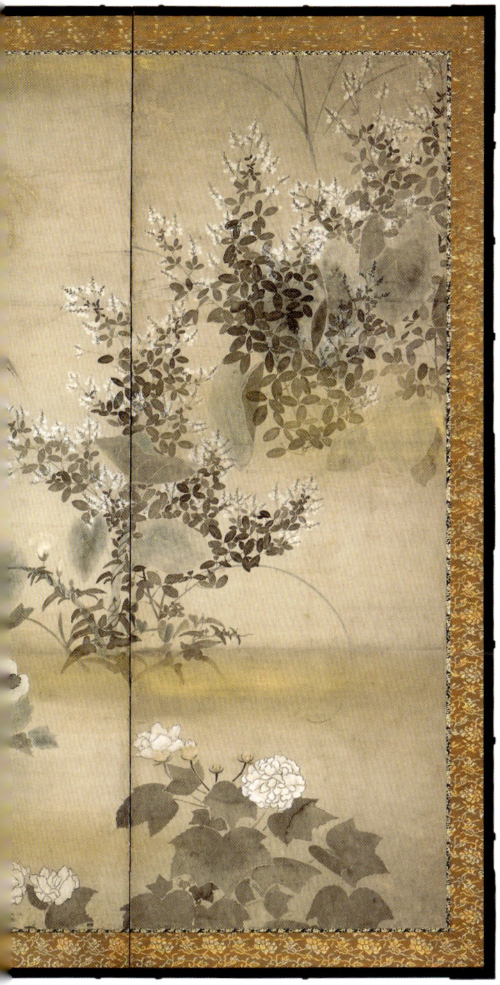

The details of the life of Kitagawa Sōsetsu, including the year of his birth and death, are unknown. Based on his painting style, he is believed to have been a disciple of Tawaraya Sōsetsu (whose life dates are also unknown).[1] Tawaraya Sōsetsu was either a younger brother, a son, or a disciple of the famed early seventeenth-century Rimpa-school painter Tawaraya Sōtatsu (act. c. 1600–1640). Inscriptions on paintings by Kitagawa Sōsetsu at the Ishikawa Prefectural Museum of Art and the Kuroda City Art Museum in Toyama indicate that he was designated as *Hokkyō* (literally "Bridge of the Law"), an honorific given to accomplished Buddhist artists since 1022.[2] Kitagawa may have worked for the family of Maeda Toshiie, who was daimyo of the Kaga domain (now Ishikawa Prefecture).[3]

Kitagawa was proficient at flower painting using pale sumi ink and light colors, as seen on this screen. Here he depicted ivy, bush clover, mallow, cockscomb, and grasses on a gold wash using two techniques: *mokkotsu-hō*, drawing with color but without contour, and *tarashikomi*, adding a successive layer of paint before the previous layer dries (see also nos. 47, 48). The result is an elegant work full of emotion. At the lower-left corner, Kitagawa's seal reads "Taiseiken"; he may have inherited the inscription from Tawaraya or his studio, but the seal's shape differs from those used by the elder artist.[4]

It is well known that the Philadelphia artist Mary Cassatt (1844–1926) was influenced by Japanese woodblock prints. She formerly owned this screen as well as *Flowers of the Four Seasons* attributed to the school of Ogata Kenzan (1663–1743; fig. 46). KK

1. The same pronunciation is used for "Sōsetsu" in the names of Kitagawa and Tawaraya, but the Chinese characters are different. It was once believed that they were the same person, but now Kitagawa is considered to be a member of the generation that followed Tawaraya.
2. The first artist to be designated *Hokkyō* was the sculptor Jōchō (d. 1057).
3. Okada 2014.
4. Tawaraya Sōtatsu used a round *Inen* seal as well as *Taisei* and *Taiseiken* seals in his later years.

FIG. 46 School of Ogata Kenzan (1663–1743). *Flowers of the Four Seasons*. Edo period, 17th century. Ink and color on paper, mounted as a six-fold screen; 69½ in. × 12 ft. 2 in. (176.5 × 370.8 cm). Philadelphia Museum of Art: Purchased with the George W. B. Taylor Fund, 1943-16-1

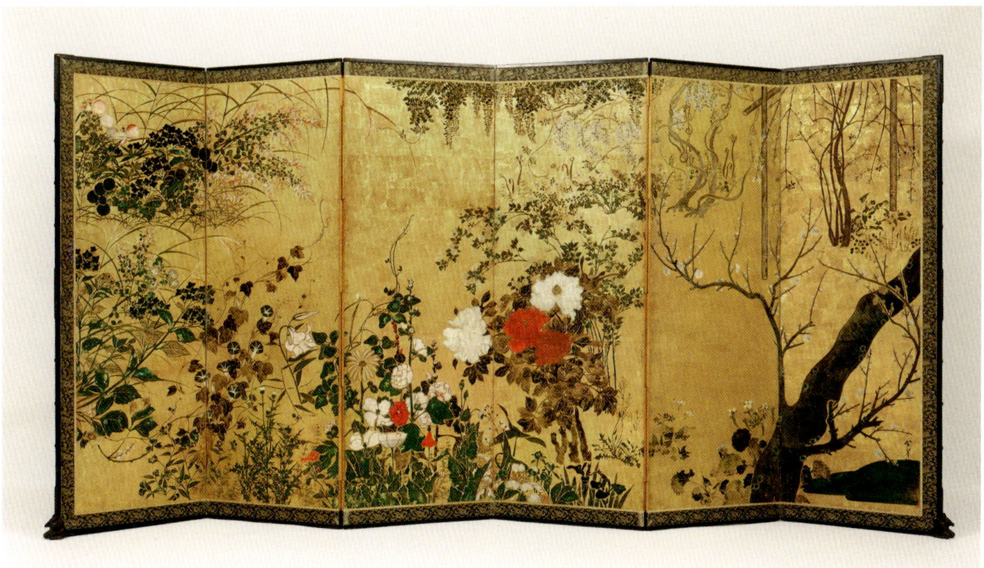

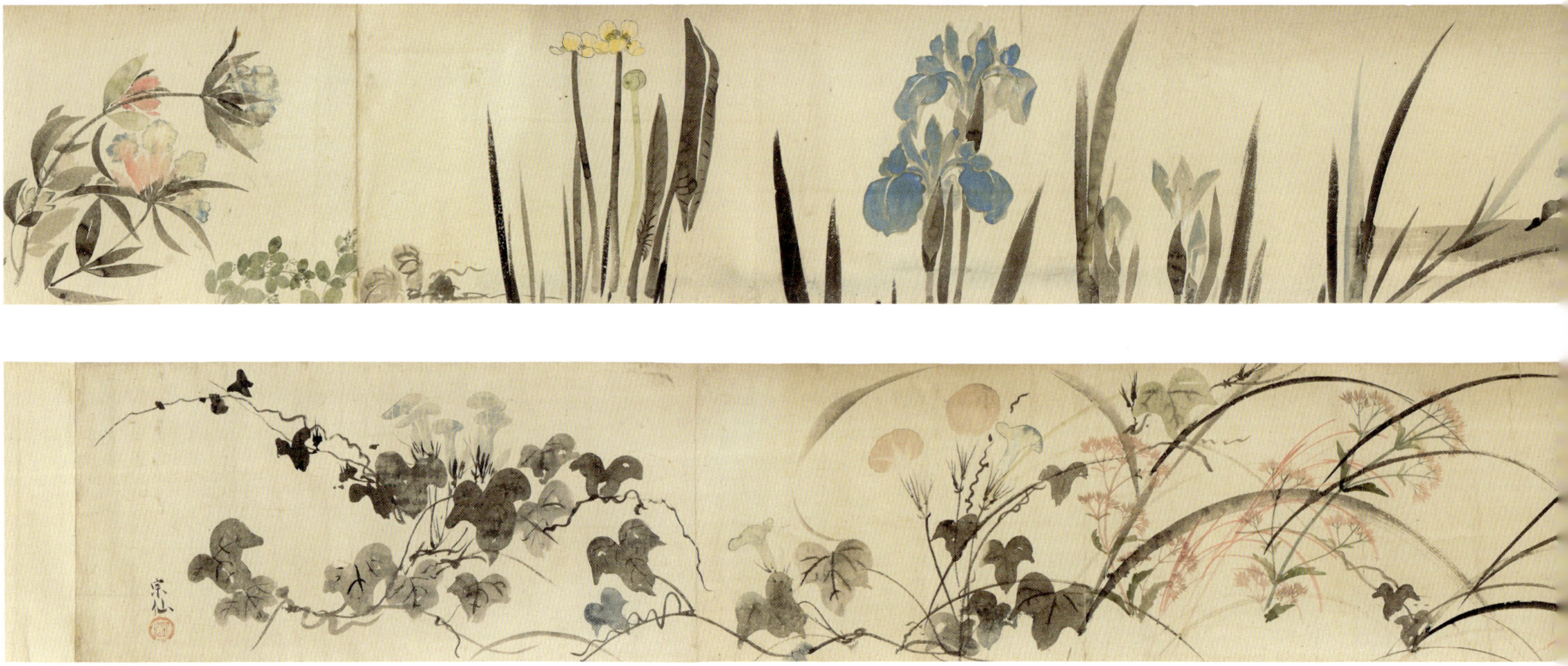

47

Flowers of Spring and Summer

Sōsen
(act. 1624–43)

Edo period (1615–1868),
17th century

Ink and colors on paper, mounted
as a handscroll; 11½ in. × 19 ft. 11⅞ in.
(29.2 × 609.3 cm)

Purchased with funds contributed
by Mrs. John C. Atwood, Jr.,
1965-21-1a,b

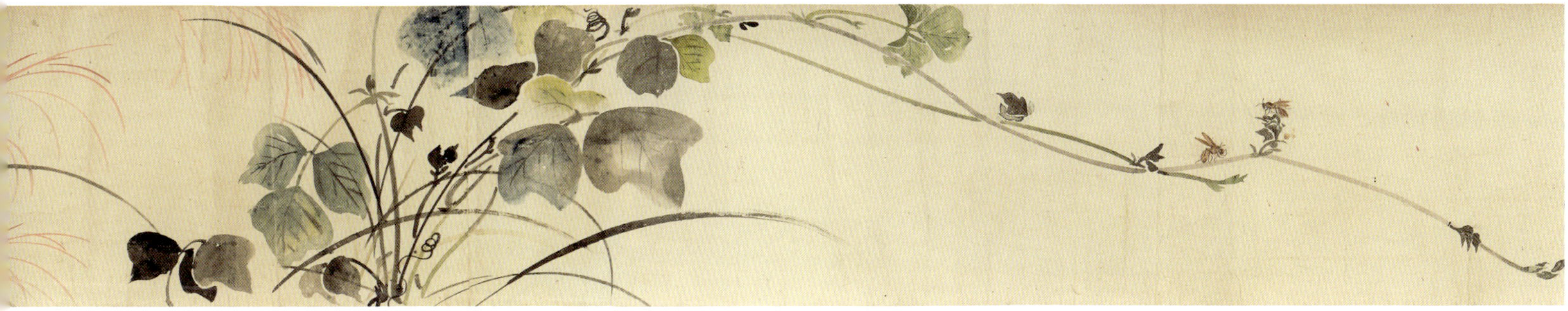

The six sheets of paper that make up this handscroll depict various kinds of flowers in spring and summer. The primary images are drawn using dark and light ink, with some colors on flowers, leaves, and grasses. In the first section (reading right to left), a large rock is drawn in the foreground with rough brushstrokes; daffodils bloom behind it, and a plum branch with white buds extends to the left. Three horsetails on the ground announce the arrival of spring. The second section depicts the flowers of summer — wisteria in soft shades of pinks and blues, yellow dandelions, blue irises, and yellow poppies — along with grasses and lotus leaves. Oleander, bush clover, and pale pink patrinias feature in the third section. Two wasps settle on a long tendril that extends to the right. The leaves seem to be changing their colors at summer's end. Japanese bindweeds, which flower from June to August, appear in the final section. A peduncle emerges from the base of a leaf, and a funnel-shaped, pale pink flower blooms at the tip of the vine.

Sōsen used a painting technique called *tarashikomi*, which involves the application of a drop of color, ink, or water to painted or inked areas that have not yet dried, to achieve an effect of blotting (see also nos. 46, 48). This method was frequently used by one of the founders of the Rimpa school, Tawaraya Sōtatsu (act. c. 1600–1640), and his successors actively incorporated the technique into their works.

There are few records about Sōsen, but his seals are listed and mentioned as "Hokkyō Sōsen" in the *Ogata-ryū ryaku-inpu*, a collection of Ogata-school seal impressions by Sakai Hōitsu (1761–1828) first published in 1815.[1] In addition, Sōsen is mentioned as "Juntei; Gō Sōsen" ([his name is] Juntei; artist's name is Sōsen) in the Kōetsu school's *Koga bikō*, a collection of painters' biographies compiled by Asaoka Okisada (1800–1856) and published in 1850.[2] The seal on *Flowers of Spring and Summer* is similar to that for "Sōsen" listed in the *Koga bikō*. However, there was also a Kano-school artist named Kano Sōsen, who worked on the mural paintings in the Imperial Palace under Kano Tan'yū (1602–1674) in 1662 and Kano Yasunobu (1614–1685) in 1675. It has been argued that Sōsen was not satisfied with the formalized techniques of the Kano school and that he turned to Sōtatsu-style painting.[3]

The box inscription was written by Ikeda Shigeaki (1867–1950), a politician, cabinet minister, and businessman before World War II. KK

---

1. *Ogata-ryū ryaku-inpu* was reprinted in 1892.
2. Asaoka Okisada, son of Kano Isen'in Naganobu (1775–1828), began to write painters' biographies in 1850. Following Okisada's death, his manuscripts were supplemented by Ōta Kin (d. 1925) and published as the *Koga bikō* in fifty-one volumes between 1903 and 1905.
3. Aimi 1938.

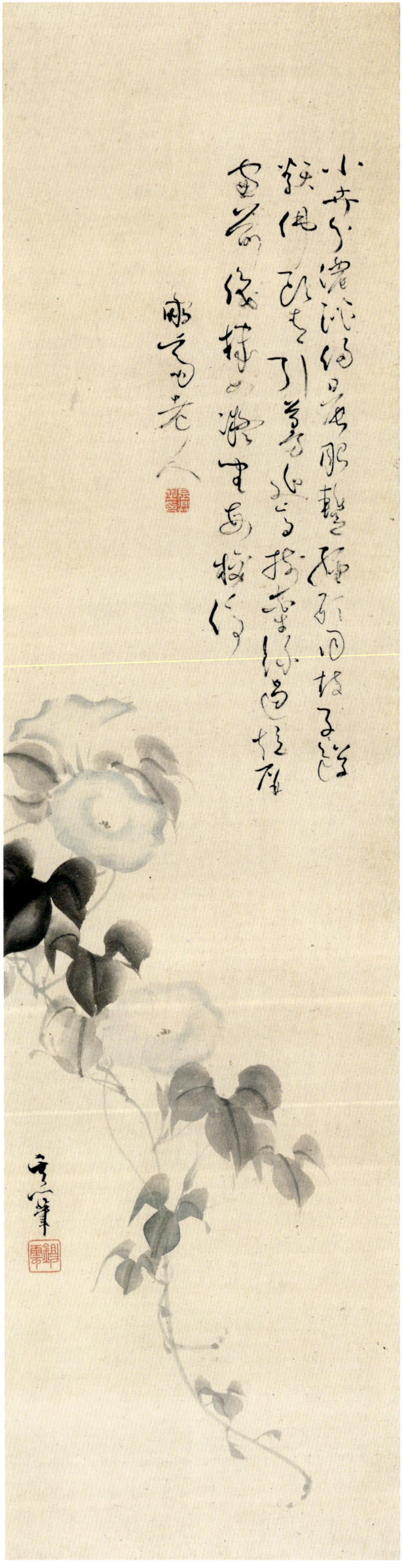

48

Morning Glories

Suzuki Kiitsu
(1796–1858)

Kameda Bōsai
(1752–1826)

Edo period (1615–1868), before 1826

Ink and light color on paper
39½ × 10¼ in. (100.4 × 26 cm)

Purchased with the Hollis Fund for East Asian Art Acquisitions, 2016-194-7

Suzuki Kiitsu was born into a family whose business was indigo dyeing. As a child his talent as a painter was discovered by the artist Sakai Hōitsu (1761–1828), famed as the founder of the Edo-period Rimpa school. At the age of eighteen, Kiitsu became an apprentice of Hōitsu, from whom he also learned tea ceremony and haiku. For his haiku, Kiitsu used the pseudonym Ōsu (warbler's nest), borrowing the Chinese character Ō (warbler) from his teacher's haiku name, Ōson (warbler's village). Hōitsu's relationships were wide-ranging and included the Confucian scholar Kameda Bōsai, with whom Kiitsu became acquainted and began to collaborate, as in this painting.

Kiitsu's signature in the cursive style on this painting is associated with his early work.[1] A pair of screens depicting morning glories in the collection of the Metropolitan Museum of Art in New York (acc. no. 54.69.1,.2) was probably made during his mature period, from 1844 until 1858, and is considered representative of his work. The painting in the Philadelphia Museum of Art suggests that Kiitsu portrayed morning glories from early on. While the flowers of the New York screens are painted in brilliant blue and green colors on gold, the morning glories here are depicted using the *tarashikomi* technique in ink and pale color (see also nos. 46, 47). Kiitsu's elegant composition and confident brushwork harmonize well with Bōsai's calligraphy for the inscription he composed:

Lovely small flowers,
of deep or pale shades,
Burst into bloom at dawn,
though for only a short while.
In form, they resemble squatting
"drummer boy" flowers,
But in [color] they are tinged blue
as the Buddha's head.
Tendrils of the vines
stretch up to tall trees,
While climbing over
the edges of low trellises.
In front of a window,
the maiden at the loom
Stops her shuttle every time
she gazes out upon them.[2]

KK

1. Okano 2017, 320–24.
2. Translated in New York 2012–13, 192.

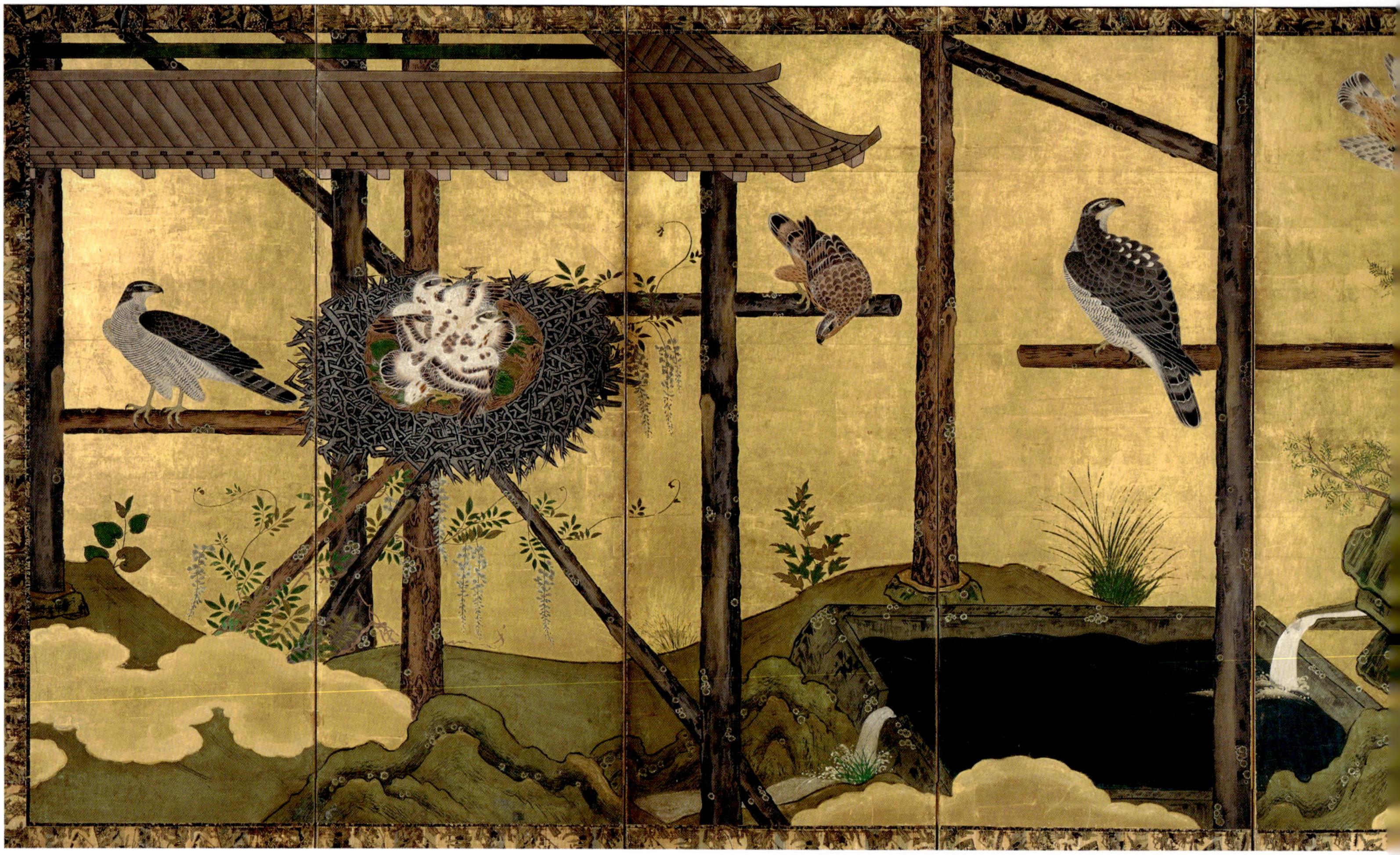

49

Goshawk Mews

Edo period (1615–1868), c. 1675

Ink, color, and gold on paper, mounted as a six-fold screen
66⅝ in. × 12 ft. (169.2 × 365.8 cm)

Gift of Mr. and Mrs. Douglas J. Cooper, 1978-122-1

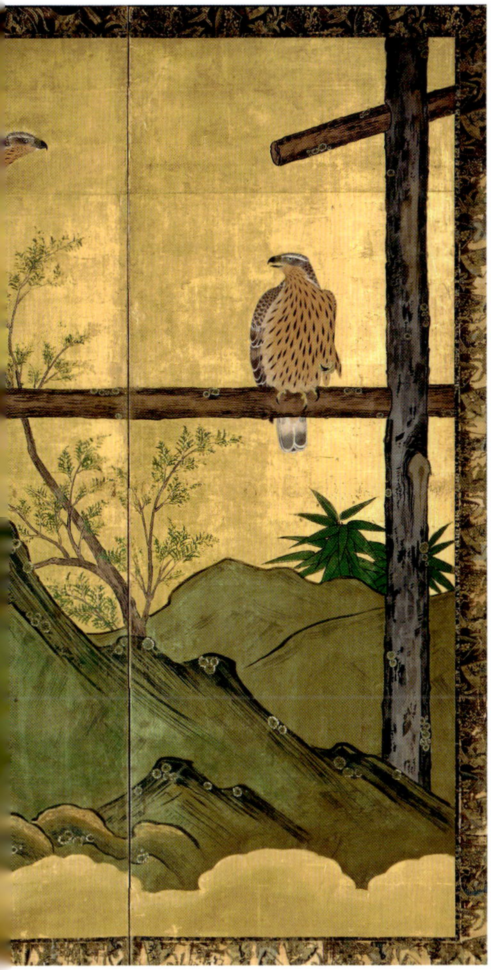

Hawks and falcons served as symbols of courage and perseverance and were considered kings of the avian world.[1] *Takagari* (falconry or hawking) was introduced to Japan from the Asian continent, and clay figures (*haniwa*) of falconers were produced for sixth-century burial sites. The emperor and aristocracy engaged in falconry during the Heian period (794–1185), and it became a favorite sport of the military elite as well. They commissioned painted depictions of falconry, as seen in a pair of screens by Kano Sanraku (1559–1635): one screen shows a hawk pursuing a crane, and the other, a male and female hawk tending a nest of chicks in a pine tree.[2] The latter may reflect the new era of peace (and domestication) under the rule of the shogunate, when the raising and training of hawks for hunting moved to designated shogunal lands. Chicks were usually removed from nests in the wild and brought to mews specifically designed to house them for falconry training.

The *Goshawk Mews* screen is a rare depiction of such an enclosure.[3] The birds are expertly rendered, including three reddish-brown younger ones, an adult pair, and a nest of chicks under a protective roof. The anonymous Kano-school painter complemented the design of the simple wood structure with rocks, a pool with running water, and wisteria and other delicate blooms. The gold background serves as a plain but rich backdrop. The artist has carefully aligned the birds so that the paired panels form an independent image when the screen is partially folded. *Goshawk Mews* represents a superb example of animals and plants closely observed and rendered.[4] FF

1. For a discussion of the symbolism and depiction of hawks in Chinese art, see Cincinnati 2009–10, 7–38; fig. 21 (*Eagle*) shows a similar composition, attributed to Emperor Huizong (1082–1135), at the Musée Cernuschi in Paris.
2. See Doi 1980, pl. 3.
3. I know of only one other such six-panel screen (sixteenth century; ink on paper), at the Tokyo National Museum. See Bonn 2003, no. 101.
4. If there was a companion screen to this one, it may have depicted a hawking scene, as in the Sanraku pair.

50

Flowering Plum Trees in Mist

Ike Taiga
(1723–1776)

Edo period (1615–1868), c. 1750

Ink and color on paper, mounted as a pair of six-fold screens; each: 60 in. × 11 ft. 9¼ in. (152.4 × 358.8 cm)

Purchased with the George W. Elkins Fund, E1969-1-1,2

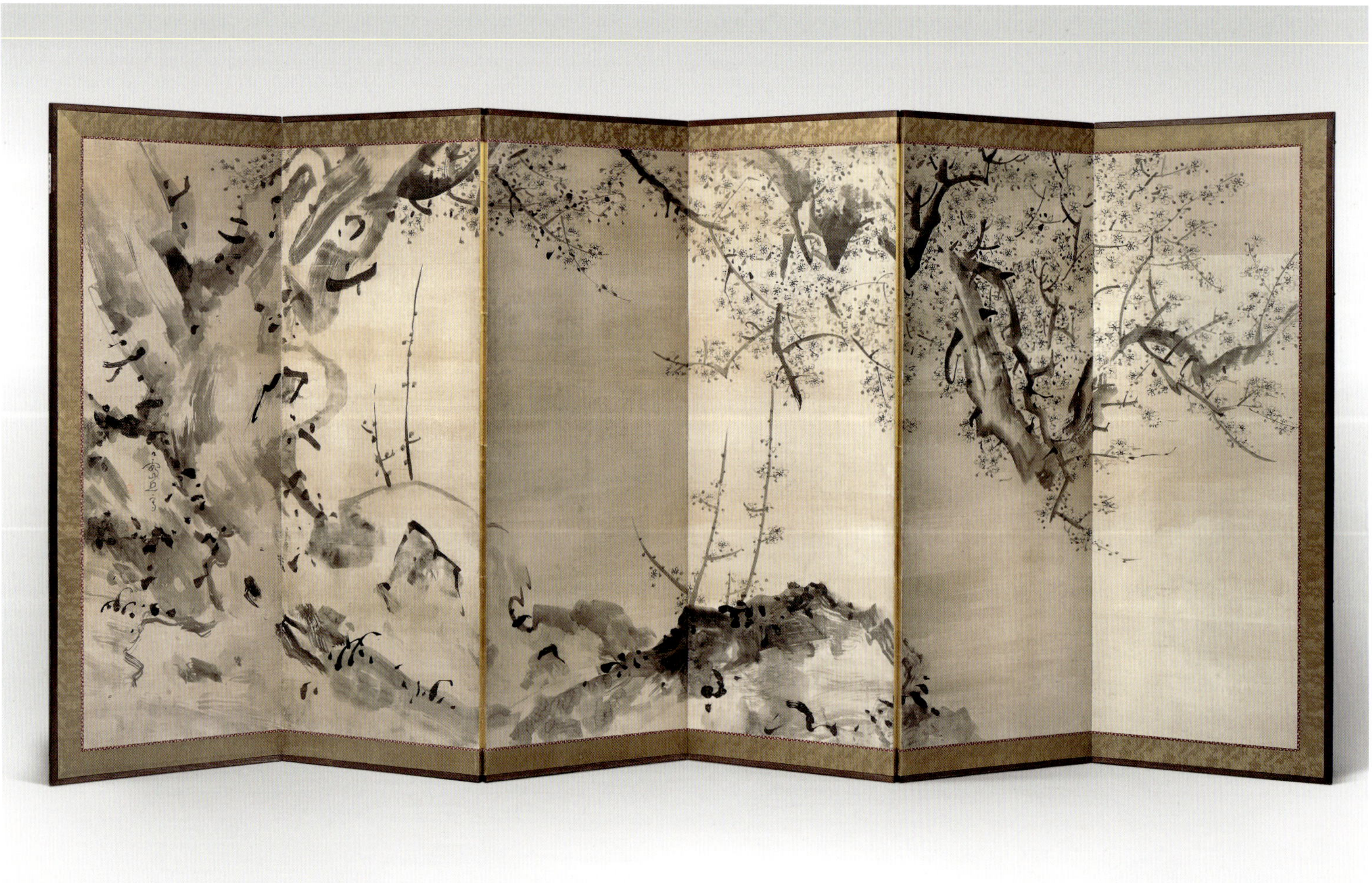

During a prodigious career that spanned four decades, Ike Taiga produced over one thousand calligraphies and paintings in an impressive range of styles, techniques, compositions, and subject matter. To his contemporaries he was an eccentric marvel, indifferent to the worldly preoccupations of those around him. He helped develop the visual language of the early eighteenth-century style of painting known as Nanga (Southern painting), the Japanese counterpart of a Chinese school of literati scholar-painters that flourished from the fourteenth century onward. Like their Chinese predecessors, Japanese Nanga painters were individualistic and nonconformist, both as artists and as people. Taiga's direct contact with Chinese culture and artistic modes came through his association with the Chinese clerics of the Ōbaku sect.[1]

In this pair of screens, Taiga rendered a favorite Chinese theme, plum blossoms, in one of his bravura displays of monochrome ink brushwork. The composition of the right screen is weighted to its right side, and the diagonal of the rocks in that portion is echoed by the plum branches — growing from a large, gnarled tree trunk that fills the center — that stretch to the left across the top of the painting. On the companion screen, a massive tree trunk rises from a jagged rock formation on the left. The rocks are outlined in thick, dark ink and filled in with quick, short, calligraphic brushstrokes and pools of ink. Areas of thick, rapidly applied strokes and washes are the foil for the precise and detailed depictions of the tiny five-petal plum blossoms that grow in profusion across the top of both screens.[2] The only color applied are highlights of pale gold wash over the whole, producing a shimmering reflection in changing light. The effect of sitting on the floor surrounded by these images, in the home where the screens were originally placed, must have been dazzling. FF

1. See no. 20; and Philadelphia 2007.

2. Taiga's composition and brushwork may have been inspired by screens of the same subject by Sakaki Hyakusen (1697–1752), painted in 1749. While Hyakusen's screens are smaller and on a gold ground, the approach used by Taiga is very similar. See Los Angeles 1985, no. 41.

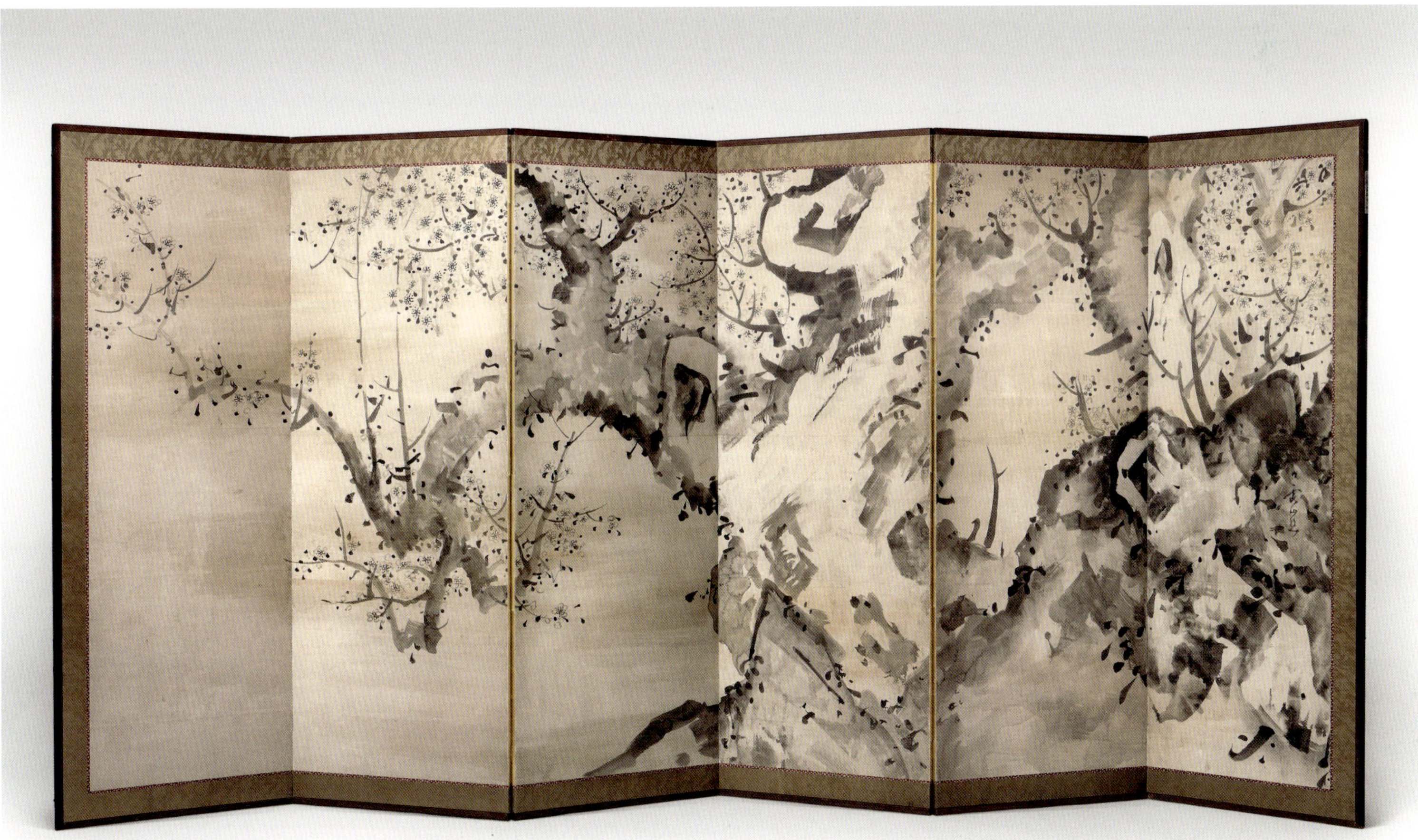

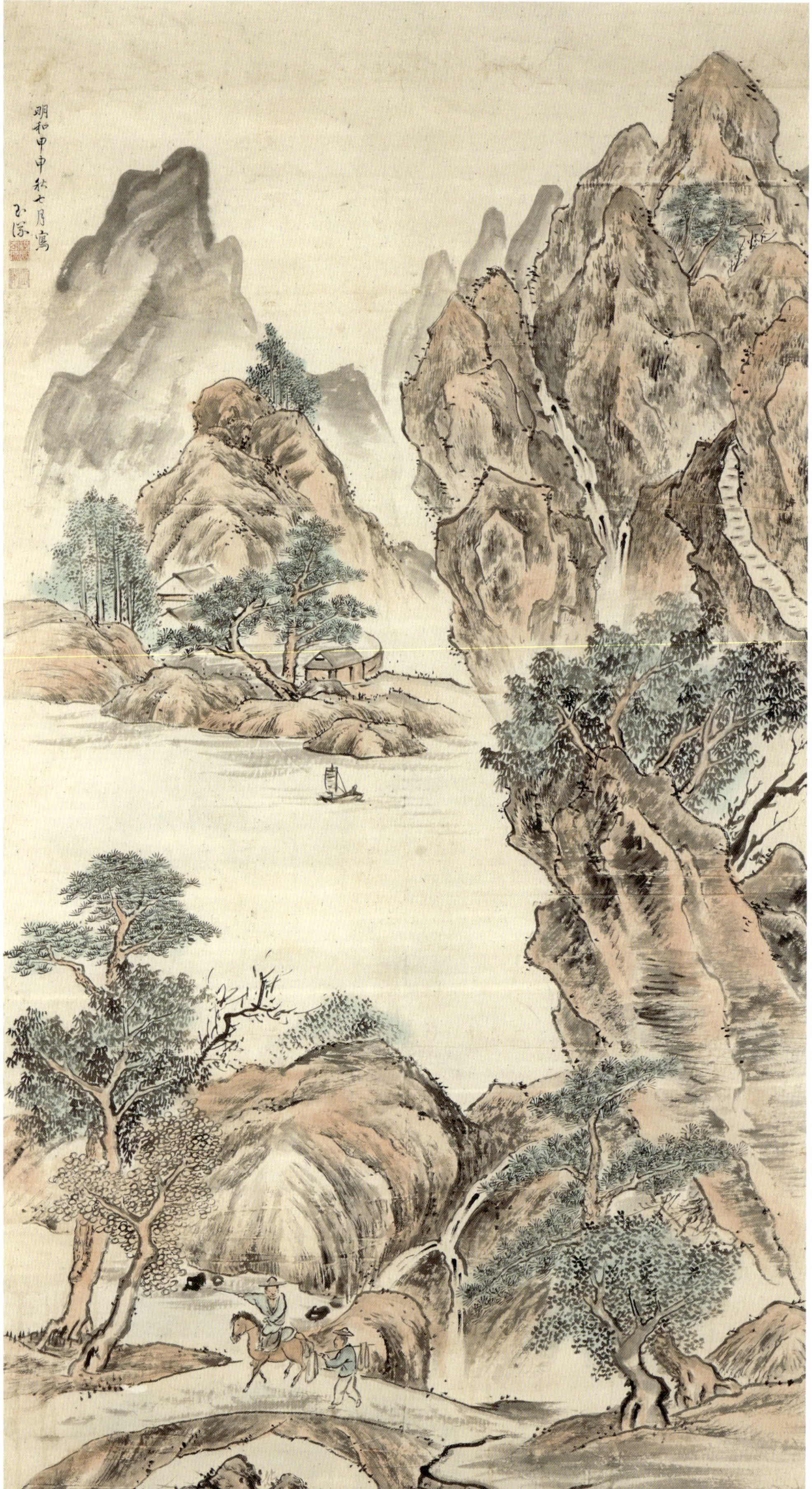
明和甲申秋七月寫
玉洲

51

Summer Landscape

Tokuyama Gyokuran
(1728–1784)

Edo period (1615–1868), 1764

Ink and color on paper, mounted as a hanging scroll; 66$\frac{1}{8}$ × 34$\frac{1}{2}$ in. (168 × 87.6 cm)

Purchased with funds contributed by Andrea M. Baldeck, M.D., in honor of Kyoko Kinoshita, 2010-51-1

Tokuyama Gyokuran was famous as a painter and a poet during her lifetime, but she is perhaps best known today as the wife of the legendary artist Ike Taiga (1723–1776). Gyokuran's mother, Yuri (1694–1764), and grandmother Kaji (act. early eighteenth century) were renowned poets in Kyoto and also ran a teahouse. Under the influence of her mother and grandmother, Gyokuran became familiar with the five-line genre of poems known as *waka*. She learned painting from Yanagisawa Kien (1704–1758), one of the pioneers of Japanese literati painting. In 1751 Gyokuran married Taiga (see no. 50), whom she had met through Kien, and began to study with her husband, whose influence can be seen most clearly in her landscapes.[1] Their congenial marital relationship was well known and even referred to in a biographical compilation, Mikuma Katen's *Kinseii kijinden*, published in 1790. Following her mother's death, Gyokuran took over the teahouse but continued her activities as a painter and a poet.

For *Summer Landscape*, Gyokuran used a wonderful combination of dry- and wet-brush techniques, particularly in rendering the rocks, mountains, and trees. Her name is listed at the end of the painters' section in three editions of *Heian jinbutsu-shi* (Who's who in old Kyoto), in 1768, 1775, and 1782, indicating that she was widely recognized as a painter at that time, an extremely unusual occurrence for a female artist. The museum has four other paintings by Gyokuran, including one of a pair that she created with Taiga (fig. 47).[2] KK

---

1. Kinoshita 2007, 37–38.
2. See also PMA acc. nos. 2004-86-1, 2013-22-1, and 2016-194-2.

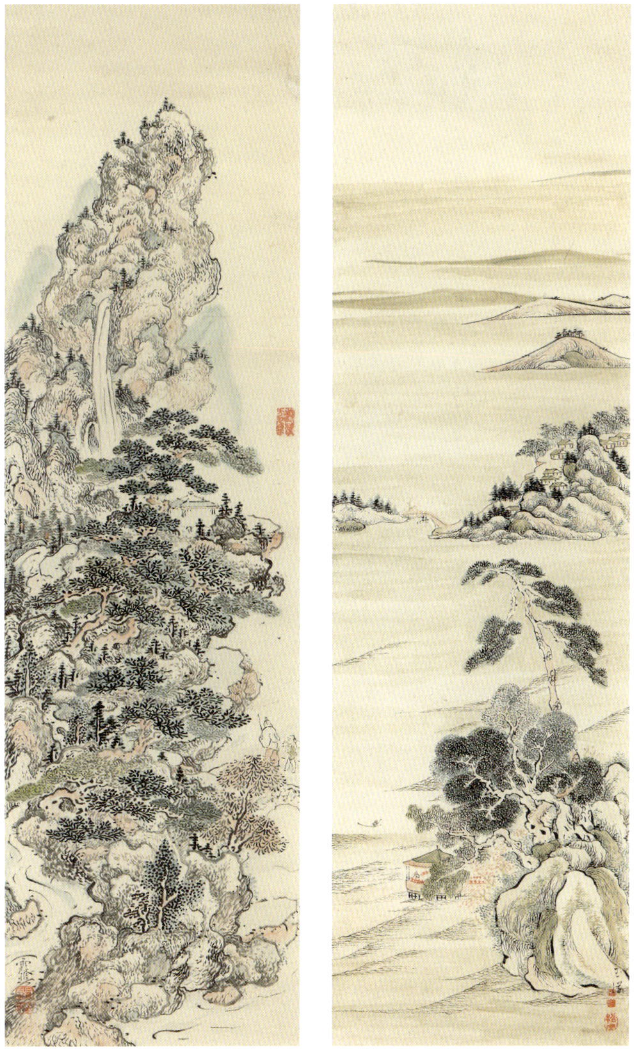

FIG. 47 Ike Taiga (1723–1776) and Tokuyama Gyokuran. *Landscape*. Edo period, 18th century. Ink and color on paper, mounted as a pair of hanging scrolls; each: 39$\frac{3}{16}$ × 11$\frac{7}{16}$ in. (99.6 × 29 cm). Philadelphia Museum of Art: Purchased with funds contributed by Andrea M. Baldeck, M.D., and William M. Hollis, Jr., 2007-9-1,2

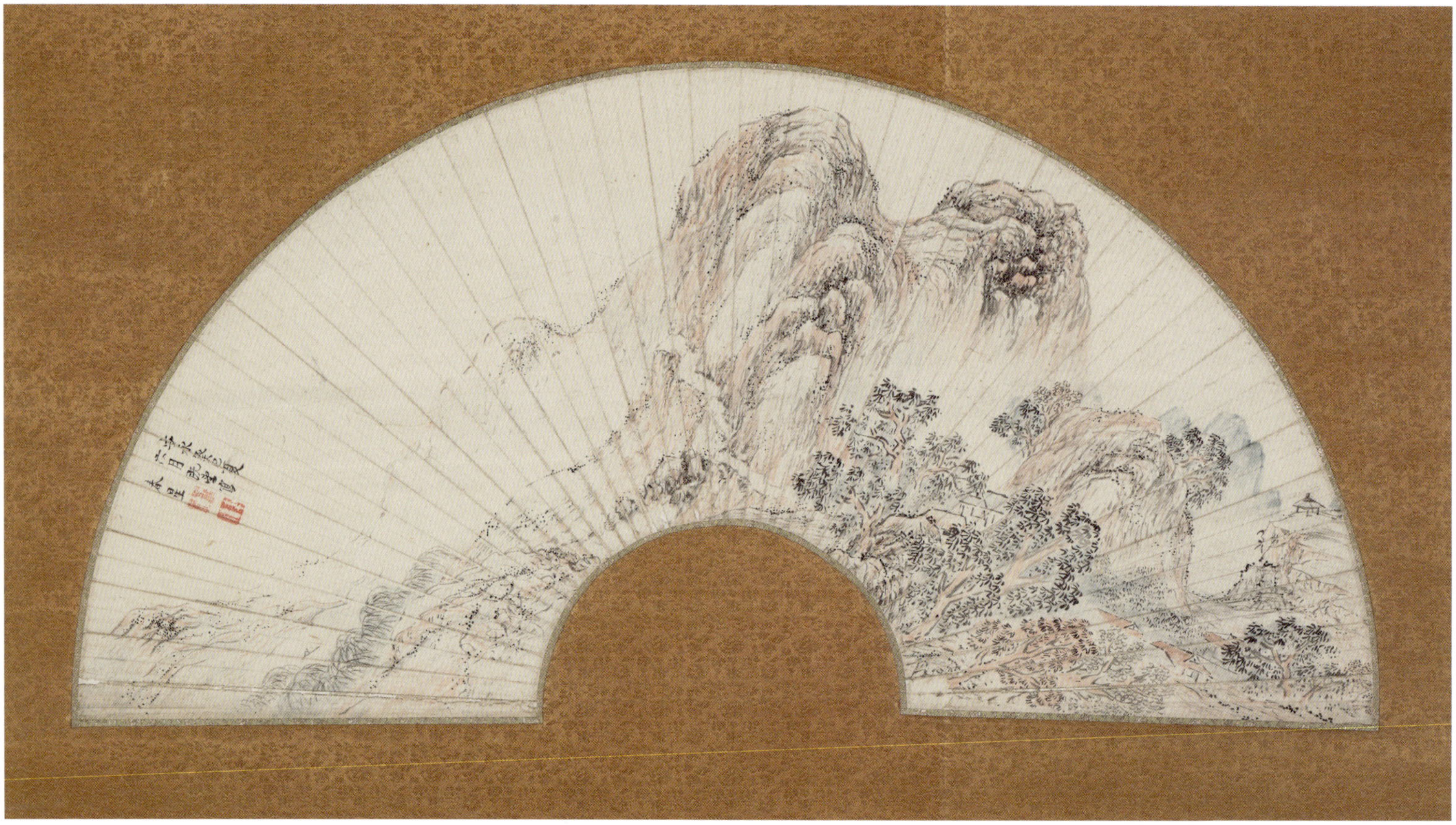

52

Mountain Retreat in Summer

Yosa Buson
(1716–1783)

Edo period (1615–1868), 1773

Ink and color on paper, fan mounted as a hanging scroll
10½ × 27½ in. (26.7 × 69.9 cm)

Purchased with the Henry B. Keep Fund, 2019-153-1

Born near Osaka, Yosa Buson spent most of his life in Kyoto, pursuing both painting and haiku poetry.[1] Along with his contemporary Ike Taiga (1723–1776), Buson is considered the principal literati artist (*bunjin*) of his time. The literati painting style was inspired by Chinese printed manuals for painting, as well as by Ming-dynasty (1368–1644) paintings transmitted directly to Japan. Buson was an inveterate traveler, and as such was able to view many original Chinese works in temple and private collections. These helped shape his own experiments with ink and brush. Buson's late period of activity was particularly rich in landscape painting, and this fan is among the works produced during the last decade of his career.

Buson was adept at working in small formats such as album paintings and fans, achieving a visual intimacy appropriate to their scale. Here Buson adroitly used the fan format to emphasize the small cluster of houses among the trees at the right, leading our gaze leftward to the mountain path at the center, as the foothills trail off to the cluster of willow trees at the far left. The hermit living in a mountain retreat away from the bustle of the world was one of the ideals of the literati artists, and Buson depicted both the grandeur of the natural scenery as well as the intimacy of the recluse's hut nestled among the hills. The stippled brushstrokes Buson employed for depicting the trees and the curved parallel strokes of the mountains were modeled on Chinese examples, and the variety of brush techniques lend a monumentality to the scene despite the small format. For a fan, however, it is larger than usual and was probably made as a presentation piece for a special occasion or patron. The fan was originally mounted on a bamboo framework but was remounted as a scroll to preserve it. FF

1. Buson's fame as a poet rests on his seventeen-syllable verses in the manner of Matsuo Bashō (1644–1694), and he was greatly influenced by the example of Sakaki Hyakusen (1697–1752), renowned both for his haiku poetry and for his Chinese-influenced paintings. See Fischer 2019.

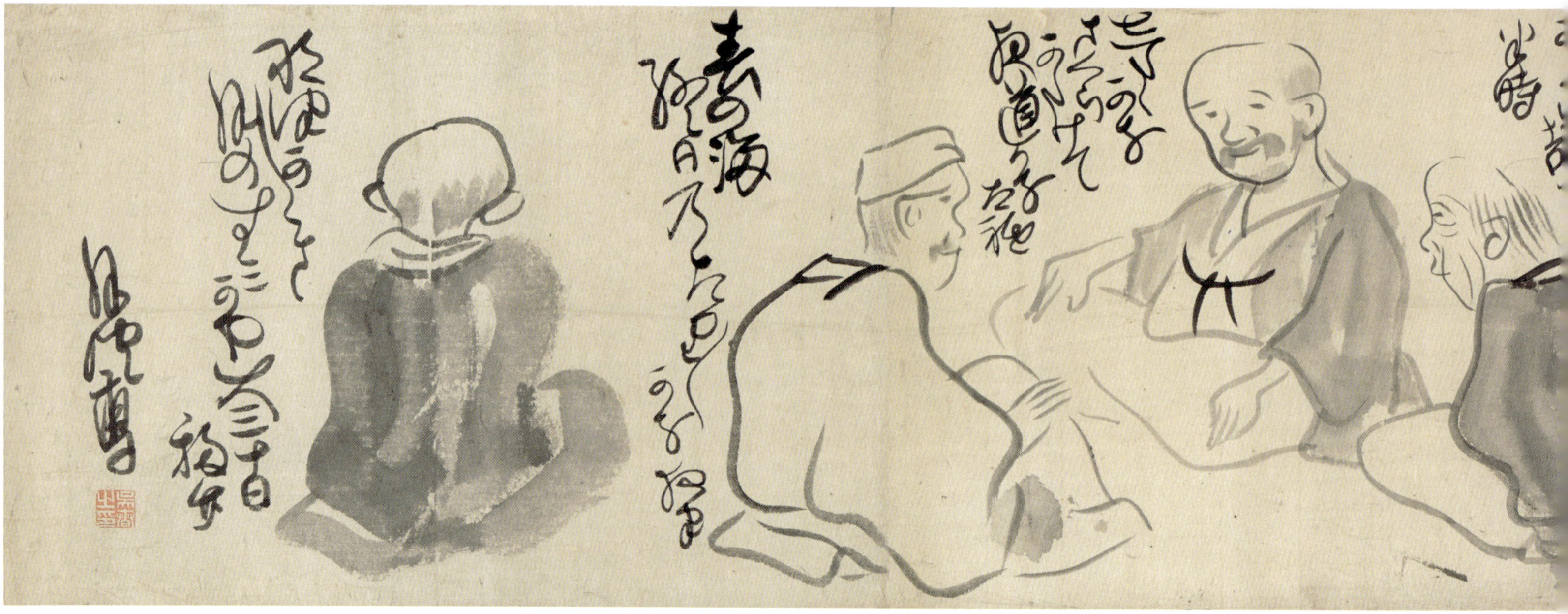

53

Seven Haiku Poets

Matsumura Goshun
(1752–1811)

Edo period (1615–1868), c. 1785

Ink on paper, mounted as a handscroll; 10½ × 54¾ in. (26.7 × 139.1 cm)

Purchased with funds contributed by Andrea M. Baldeck, M.D., and William M. Hollis, Jr., 1997-168-1

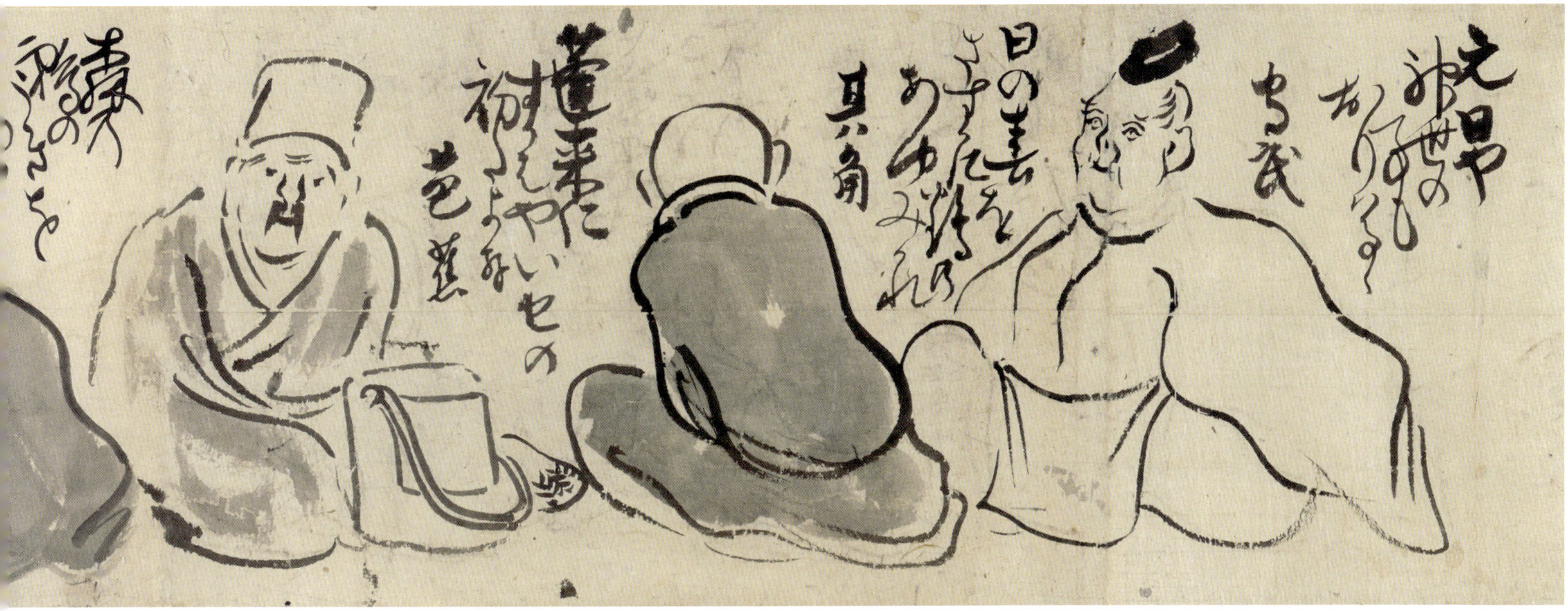

Lineage is perennially important in all aspects of Japanese cultural history, and claiming one's place in a line of haiku poets legitimized one's efforts in that vein. Here Matsumura Goshun proffered his lineage literally, with a scroll of poet portraits. Such works, often in groupings of six or thirty-six, were inspired by Heian-period (794–1185) examples, such as the Six Immortal Poets known as the *rokkasen*, and remained a popular theme (see also nos. 12, 37). Two editions of *Haikai sanjū rokkasen* (Thirty-Six Immortal Poets of haikai) were brought out in 1799 and featured printed images that were most likely based on a painted handscroll of the subject by Yosa Buson (1716–1783; see no. 52), who was Goshun's teacher in poetry and painting.

Goshun depicted seven poets in this handscroll. At the far right is Arakida Moritake (1473–1549), one of the key early practitioners of *renga* (linked verse), the antecedent of haikai. To the left, with his back to us, is Takarai Kikaku (1661–1707), a disciple of the great poet Matsuo Bashō (1644–1694). Bashō himself appears next in his traveler's outfit with knapsack. It is no coincidence that Goshun has placed Bashō, whom he considered the most important of the poets, near the center of the grouping. To his left is Matsuki Tantan (1674–1761), also known as Hantoki or Hanji, a follower of Kikaku and a contemporary of Buson. Tantan converses with Tan Taigi (1709–1771) and Buson. Buson was a close friend of the final figure, Tagawa Ichiku (1710–1760).[1] He sits apart from the other poets, his back turned toward the viewer.

Each verse deals with the New Year or early spring, so this scroll may have been painted as a New Year's presentation. Some traces of tatami matting show through the paper where brushstrokes form Ichiku's robe, indicating that perhaps Goshun did this as a performance piece (*sekiga*) at a New Year's gathering of haiku poets. FF

1. I thank Dr. Sonia Coman for identifying the final figure.

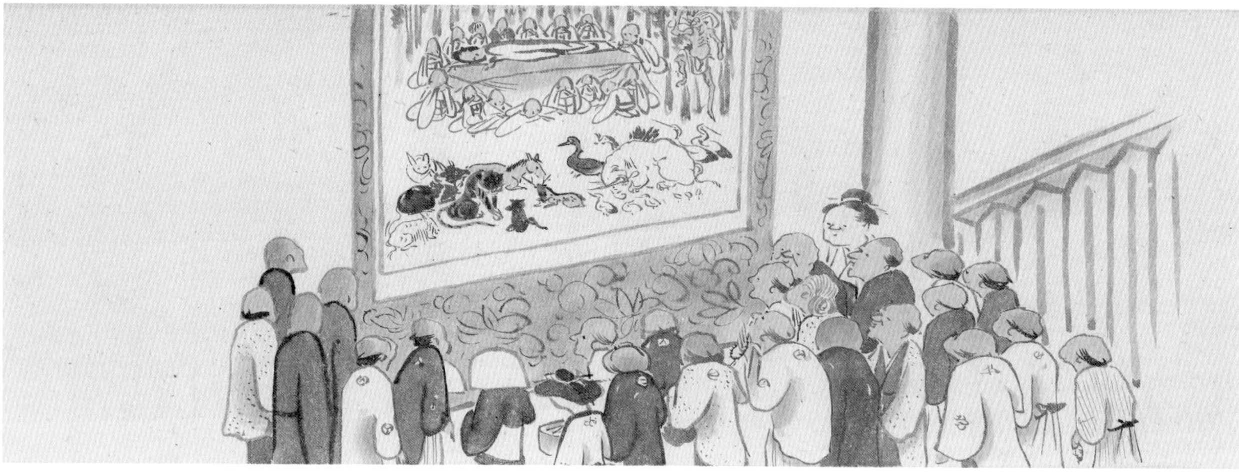

Worshippers gathering to commemorate the death of the Buddha on the fifteenth day of the second month

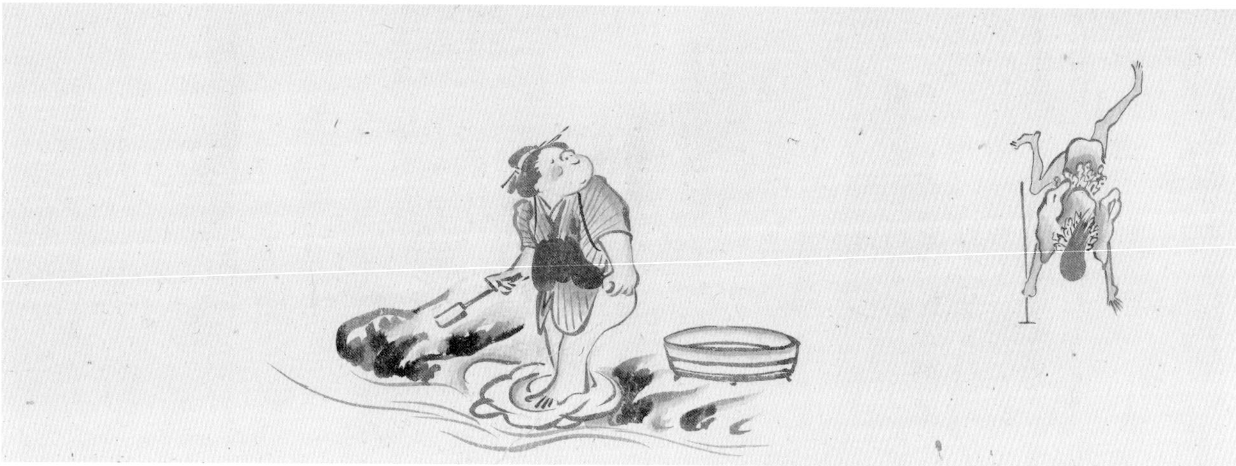

The legendary Kume no Sennin falling out of the sky after espying the bare legs of a young woman washing clothes, for the eighth month

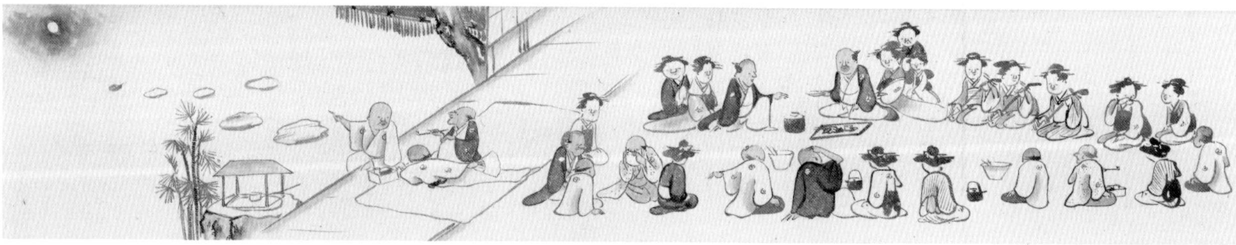

A gathering for the traditional moon viewing in the ninth month

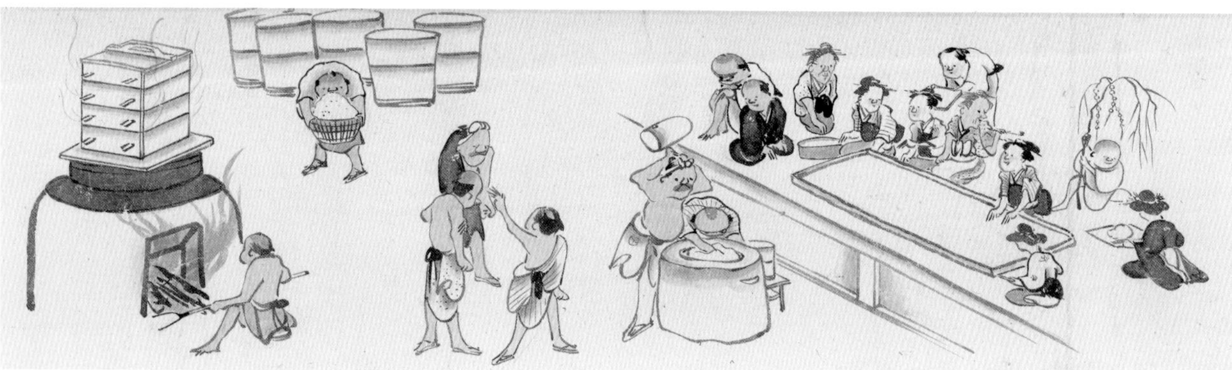

Preparing rice cakes for New Year's celebrations in the twelfth month

54

The Activities of the Twelve Months

Nichōsai (Matsuya Heizaburō or Hanzaburō)
(b. before 1751, d. 1802 or 1803)

Edo period (1615–1868), 1794

Ink and color on paper, mounted as a handscroll; 7¼ in. × 30 ft. (18.4 × 914.4 cm)

Gift of Henry B. Keep, 1964-5-1

Nichōsai was an ukiyo-e and caricature artist in Osaka during the Edo period. His surname is unknown, but his given name was Heizaburō (or Hanzaburō), and he is commonly known as Matsuya Hanzaburō. The name Nichōsai first appeared in 1780 as the author of *Ehon mizu ya sora* (Picture book of water and sky), which describes the winning roles of forty-three popular actors from Osaka, Kyoto, and Edo (Tokyo). According to the *Sōkō: Naniwa meika bosho-ki* (Draft of the record of famous families' cemeteries in Naniwa), edited by the journalist Miyatake Gaikotsu (1867–1955) in 1911, Nichōsai was born in a brewer's house in Osaka, but after his family business declined, he became an antique dealer. Self-taught as a painter, he studied the styles of the priest painters Toba Sojō (1053–1140) and (Myōyo) Kokan (1653–1717),[1] and became famous for his light and sophisticated caricature style with simple and rhythmic brushstrokes.

At the beginning of this handscroll is the title *Shikainami shizuka* (All quiet on the four seas), written by the well-known author Ōta Shokusanjin (or Nanpo; 1749–1823).[2] Shokusanjin served as a government official for the Tokugawa shogunate's sanctioned copper monopoly and guild (*za*) in Osaka in 1801 for a year,[3] and he might have visited Nichōsai during this time. What follows is the preface written by Nichōsai himself in 1794. After these two sections, Nichōsai depicted common customs and events that occur in Osaka during each of the twelve months in the lunar calendar (see no. 78 for another version), as well as a scene from the legend of Kume no Sennin of Nara. Known as *tsukinami-e* (literally "pictures of months in sequence"), such works are found in partition paintings from the Heian period (794–1185) onward. Nichōsai's lively renderings of humorous and animated figures taking part in various activities include the four scenes illustrated here as well as the first visit of the year to the shrine (first month) and the Dragon Boat Festival (sixth month).

The Japanese classical scholar Hagiwara Hiromichi (1815–1863), best known as the author of *Genji monogatari hyōshaku* (Commentary on *The Tale of Genji*), owned this handscroll and wrote the colophon at the end, which he dated 1863. The work was later owned by Sakai Shōtō (life dates unknown), a calligrapher and an art collector in Kobe, until it was sold at auction in 1924.[4] Nichōsai's hanging scrolls, handscrolls, fans, and picture books were particularly popular with the public in the nineteenth and early twentieth centuries. KK

---

1. Miyatake 1911, 62.
2. This four-character idiomatic compound is derived from a Chinese poem composed by the Southern Song poet Yang Wanli (1122–1206).
3. Ōta 1986, 75–140.
4. *Nada Sakai Shōtō-shi shozō-hin nyūsatsu* 1924, pl. 39.

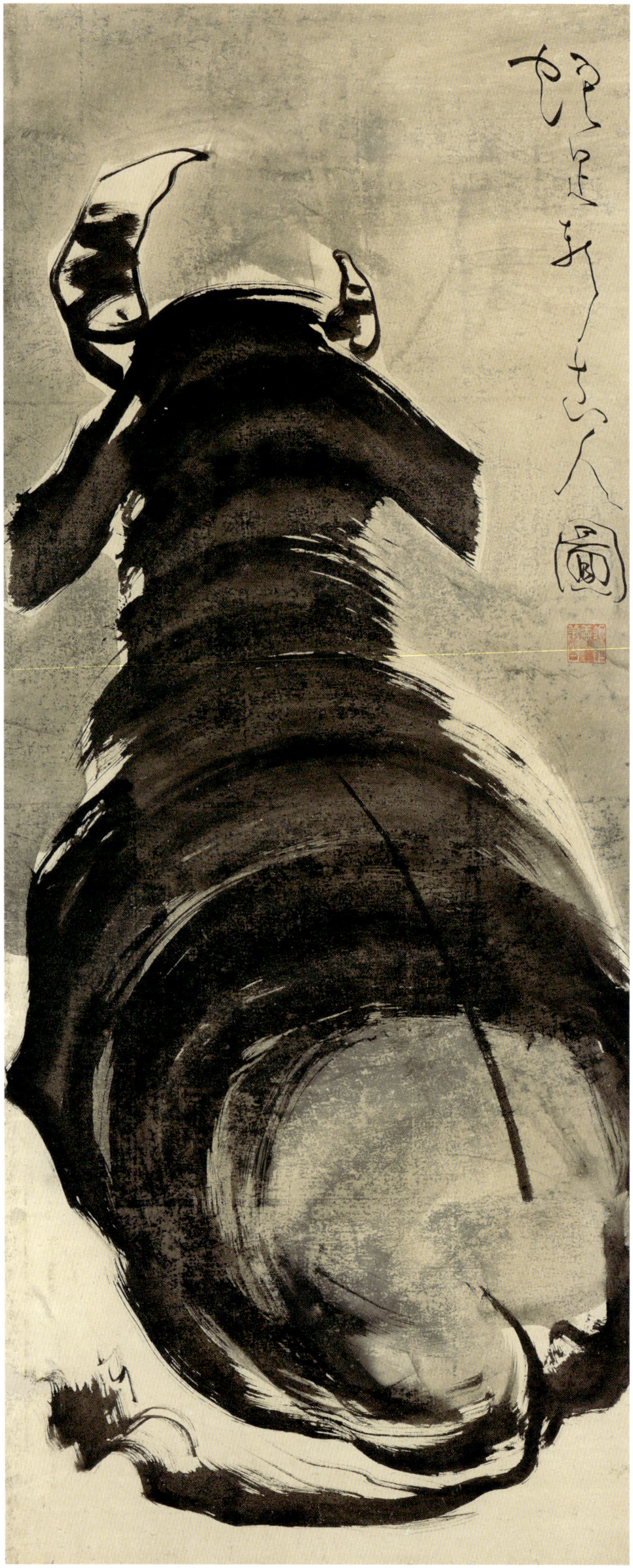

55

Recumbent Bull

Soga Shōhaku
(1730–1781)

Edo period (1615–1868), c. 1775

Ink on paper, mounted as a hanging scroll; 52¼ × 21 in. (132.7 × 53.3 cm)

Purchased with the New Members Fund, 1971-11-1

Soga Shōhaku swept a wide brush dynamically across the paper, and in about a dozen horizontal strokes created an abstracted yet unmistakable figure of a resting bull. The outlines of the animal's massive body and tail are defined by the dry-brush technique known as *hihaku* or *kasuri* ("flying white"). The left horn appears much larger than the right one, suggesting that the bull has tilted its head, perhaps to view the moon and stars in the sky above. A recumbent bull is a symbol of the Tenmangū shrine in Kyoto and refers to the legend of the historical figure Sugawara no Michizane (845–903; see no. 14). Shōhaku succeeded in transforming a traditional subject with his vigorous, unconventional brushwork, which extends to his signature, rendered in large, eccentric characters along the right edge.

Shōhaku was born into a merchant family named Tanba-ya (or Tango-ya) in Kyoto in 1730.[1] Although little is known about his early life or artistic training, Shōhaku was a disciple of Takada Keiho (1674–1755), who had studied painting under Kano Eikei (1662–1702).[2] The latter's influence can be seen in Shōhaku's style of ink painting, which consists of simple and realistic representations and gradations of dark ink that contrast with white.

The first record of Shōhaku's activity as a painter is the inscription "Gyōnen nijūkyū-sai Soga Shōhaku-zu" (Depicted by Soga Shōhaku at the age of twenty-nine years) on the *fusuma* (sliding door) painting *Seven Sages in the Bamboo Grove* of 1758 at Sairai-ji (temple) in Tsu, Mie Prefecture. Shōhaku's use of the name "Soga" in this early signature alludes to Soga Jasoku (life dates unknown), a legendary ink painter in the late Muromachi period (1392–1573). In the highly competitive world of eighteenth-century painting, Shōhaku used this fictitious lineage to assert his own artistic authority.[3] The signature and seal on this *fusuma* painting also mark Shōhaku's claim of a connection to the Soga painting lineage, despite the absence of proof.

Shōhaku seems to have led a life of an itinerant artist, painting *fusuma* and *sugito* (wooden sliding doors) on commission at temples and *ema* (votive plaques) at shrines in Mie as well as in Hyogo, Kyoto, and Shiga. By 1775, when he was forty-five years old, his reputation earned him a place in the painter's section of *Heian jinbutsu-shi* (Who's who in old Kyoto). Despite his concerns with artistic lineage, he did not have any prominent students or followers. KK

1. Kanō 2005.
2. Hickman 1998.
3. "*Ryaku-nenpu*" 2005.

56

Grapes

Itō Jakuchū
(1716–1800)

Edo period (1615–1868), 18th century

Ink on paper, mounted as a hanging scroll; 42 × 15½ in. (106.7 × 39.3 cm)

Gift of Maxine and Howard H. Lewis, 1965-70-1

57

Morning Glories

Itō Jakuchū
(1716–1800)

Edo period (1615–1868), 18th century

Ink on paper, mounted as a hanging scroll; 43 × 16⁵⁄₁₆ in. (109.2 × 41.5 cm)

Gift of Harry C. Nail, Jr., 1965-71-1

Itō Jakuchū is one of the representative painters of Kyoto active during the middle of the Edo period. He was born in 1716 as the eldest son of a vegetable wholesaler named Masuya who worked in the city's Nishiki Market. Jakuchū demonstrated excellent artistic talent from childhood, honing his painting skills by observing and sketching the vegetables that his father sold, the fish that lined the market stalls, and the chickens in the family's garden. At the age of twenty-three, after the death of Masuya, Jakuchū succeeded him in the family business. The name Jakuchū—meaning "what is very fulfilling looks like empty"—was given to him by Daiten Kenjō (1719–1801), a Zen priest at Shōkoku-ji (temple). Jakuchū lacked enthusiasm for commerce and handed over the vegetable wholesale business to his younger brother, retiring in 1755 to devote himself to painting. It appears that he never drank alcohol, never married, and took no interest in accolades for his art.[1]

Jakuchū's lively and dynamic style is exemplified by these two ink paintings. As they are close in size, they may have originally formed part of an *oshiebari byōbu*, a six-panel folding screen with one painting pasted on each panel. Jakuchū rendered the flowers, fruits, and leaves with *sujime-gaki*, a white-line drawing technique using pale gray and dark ink. For *Grapes*, wet brushstrokes were carefully applied to the soft and absorbent *gasenshi* (a type of high-quality Chinese paper) in such a way as to leave narrow, unpainted lines that delicately describe the forms of the fruits and leaves. In *Morning Glories*, the outlines of the flowers and the vines are drawn in pale ink while the leaves are filled in with strong, dark ink. Together these two works offer excellent examples of Jakuchū's contrasting painting and drawing techniques. KK

1. Daiten 1875, n.p.

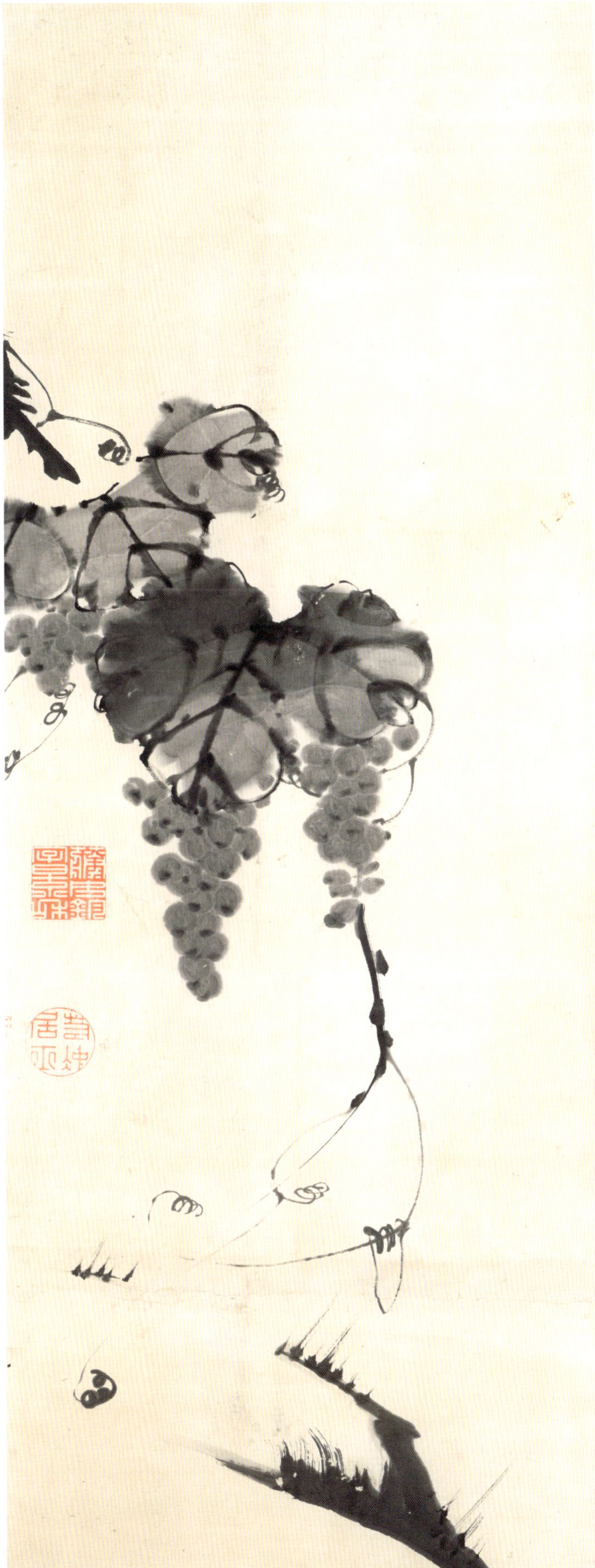

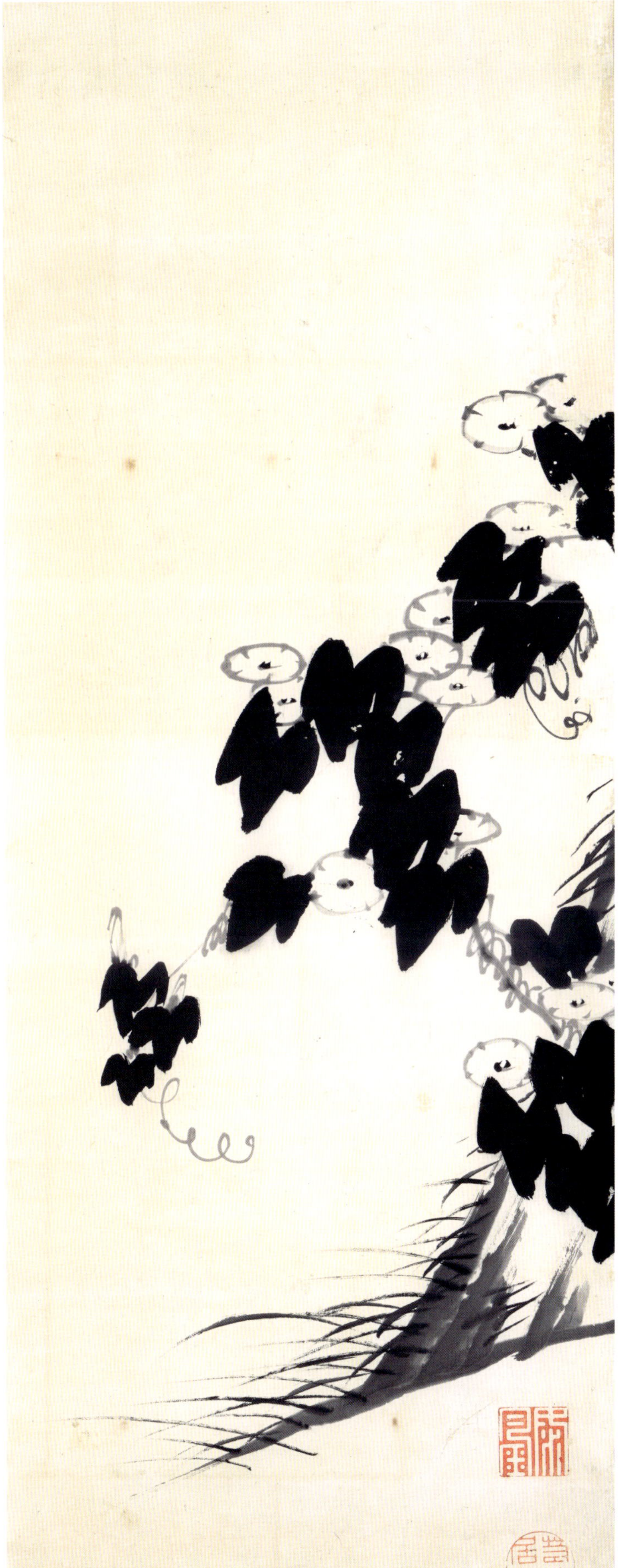

58

Woodcutter and *Fisherman*

Nagasawa Rosetsu
(1754–1799)

Edo period (1615–1868), c. 1794

Ink and color on silk with malachite and *gofun* (powdered shell), mounted as a pair of hanging scrolls; each: 49⅝ × 21⁵⁄₁₆ in. (126 × 54.1 cm)

Purchased with the Henry B. Keep Fund, the East Asian Art Revolving Fund, and the Baldeck/Hollis Fund for East Asian Art, 2010-27-1,2

Nagasawa Rosetsu was born Uesugi Hikouemon, a low-ranking samurai of the Sasayama clan in Tamba (now Hyogo Prefecture). During his childhood, Rosetsu's father moved the family to Yamashiro (Kyoto Prefecture) to work for the daimyo of the Yodo clan. By 1778 Rosetsu had gone to Kyoto, where he studied painting under Maruyama Ōkyo (1733–1795). The name Nagasawa Rosetsu appears in the painters' section of the 1782 edition of *Heian jinbutsu-shi* (Who's who in old Kyoto), published when he was twenty-eight years old, and he was regarded as a talented disciple of Ōkyo, who may have been the most popular painter in Kyoto. Unable to take on work for the *fusuma* (sliding door) paintings of temples in Wakayama, Ōkyo asked Rosetsu to do so. His work there on a large number of paintings gave Rosetsu a chance to break new ground.

The theme of the woodcutter and the fisherman is a traditional East Asian painting subject, based on a dialogue that can be summarized as follows: The woodcutter says, "Even if you carry as much firewood as you can, you will just fall and get injured," while the fisherman says, "Even if the fishing rod and line are perfect, catching or not catching fish is due to heaven." The moral of the tale is thus not to exceed one's limits as the life of every individual is ruled by fate. Rosetsu chose to depict the woodcutter and the fisherman individually in a pair of hanging scrolls, focusing on the human figures as if to reveal the inner nature of each.

In 1785 Rosetsu first used the *Gyo* (fish) seal, which is shaped like an ice crystal and appears on this pair of scrolls. This choice may be related to the following anecdote: On the way to Ōkyo's studio one cold winter morning, Rosetsu saw fish struggling in the water of a partially frozen stream. Returning home, he stopped by the stream to discover that the ice had melted and the fish were swimming freely. Rosetsu mentioned this story to his teacher the next day, and Ōkyo replied that what his student had observed was similar to the experience of a disciple who found their training difficult but eventually, as if the ice had begun to thaw, gained freedom in painting. For the rest of his life, Rosetsu kept this parable in mind and used the *Gyo* seal. However, the upper-right corner of the seal is missing in his works dated to around 1792 and later, which provides an index for roughly estimating dates for his works.[1] The seal Rosetsu used still exists and there is evidence that it was broken intentionally. It is thought that Rosetsu purposely cracked it as a statement of determination to gain freedom in painting.[2] KK

1. McKelway 2018.
2. Tsuji 2019, 267–68.

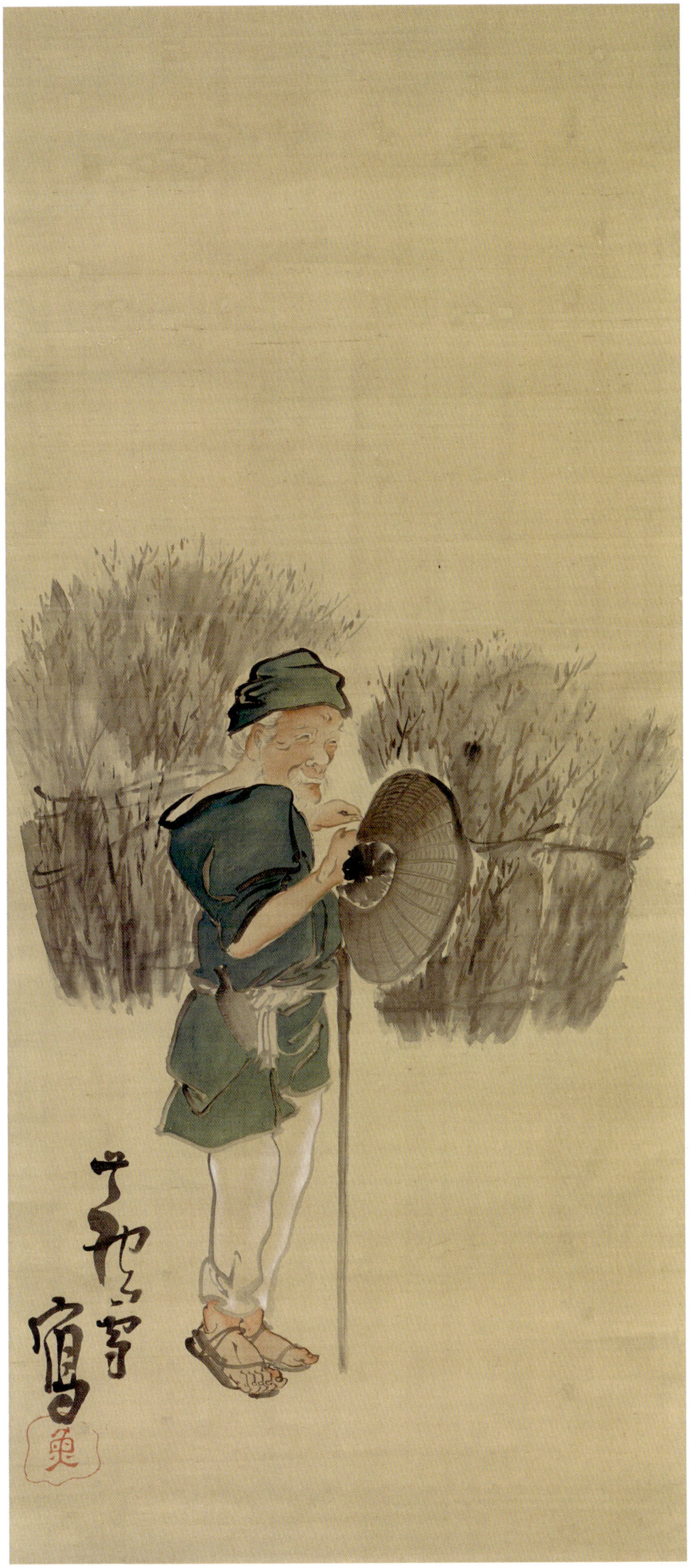

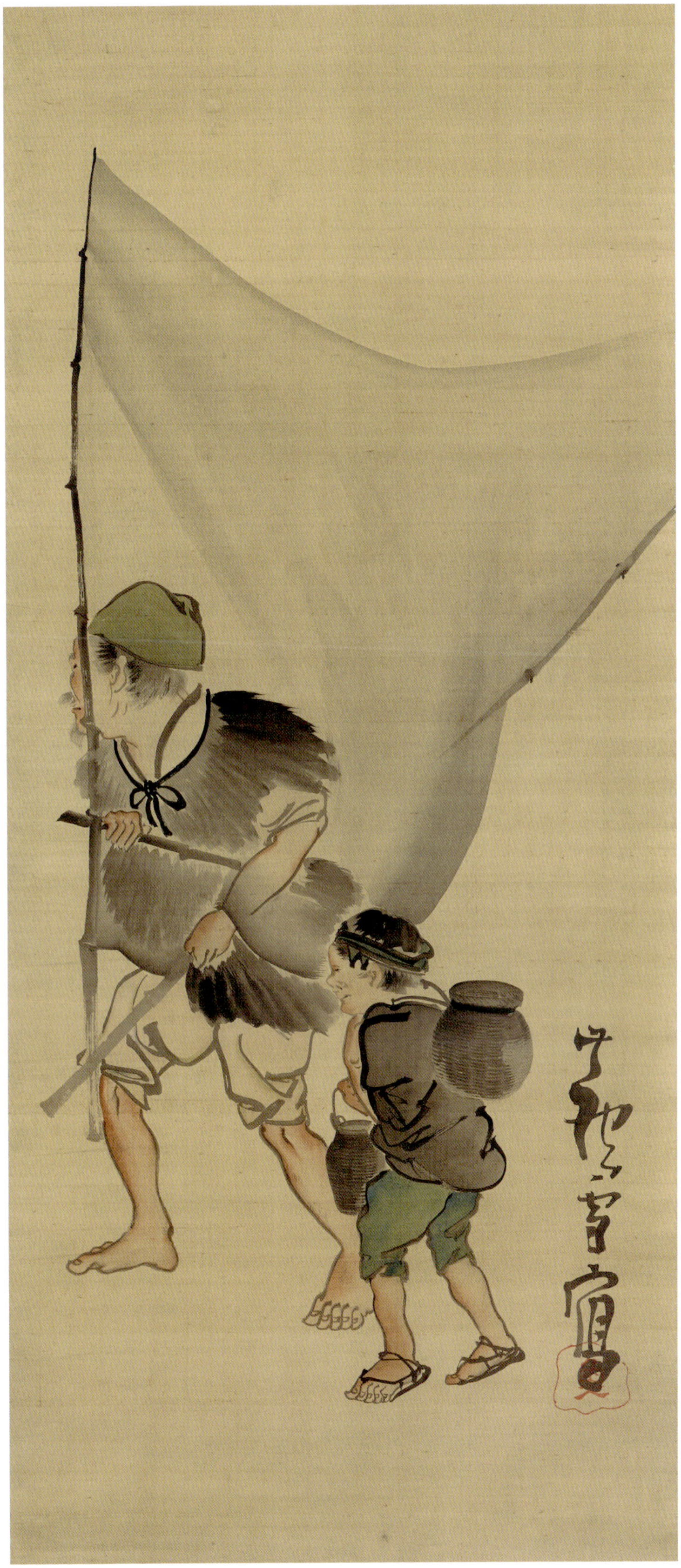

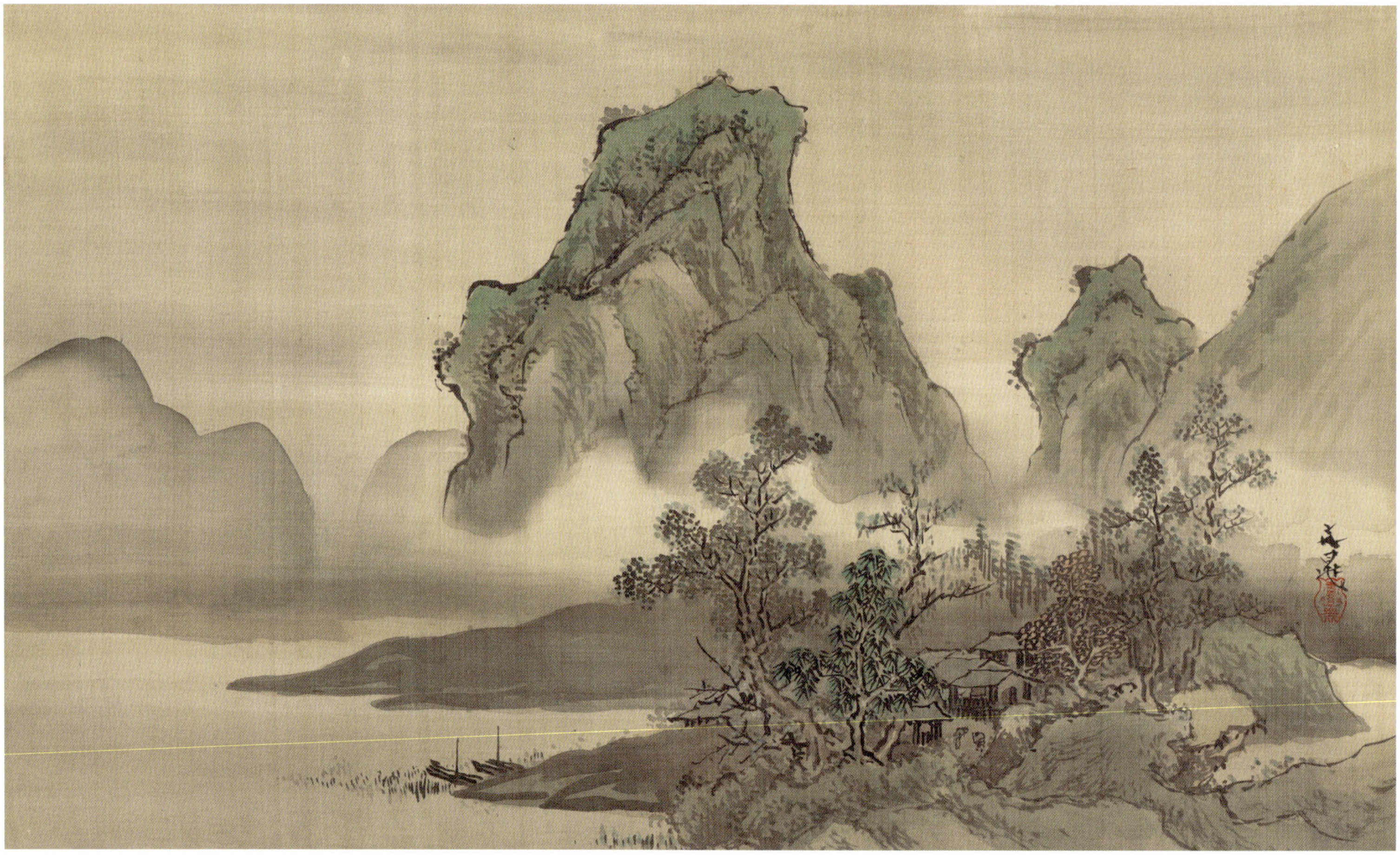

59

Summer Landscape

Tani Bunchō
(1763–1840)

Edo period (1615–1868),
early 19th century

Ink and color on silk, mounted
as a hanging scroll; 21⅜ × 34⅞ in.
(54.3 × 88.6 cm)

Gift of Mr. and Mrs. Ralph
Balestrieri, 1976-193-1

Tani Banchō was one of the representative and most highly appreciated painters of the late Edo period. He was born in Edo (present-day Tokyo) to a family of retainers of the Tayasu family, who were descendants of the eighth Tokugawa shogun. Around the age of twelve, he trained with Kato Bunrei (1706–1782) of the Kano school, and after Bunrei's death, he studied Chinese painting with the naturalized Chinese artist Kitayama Kangan (Ma Mengxi; 1767–1801), whose grandfather had immigrated to Japan at the end of the Ming dynasty (1368–1644) and whose father, Ma Daoliang (life dates unknown), was born in Japan and became a painter.

Bunchō went on to learn various Japanese painting styles, including ancient Yamato-e, Rimpa, and Maruyama-Shijō as well as Korean and European painting. When he was twenty-six years old, he went to Nagasaki for the purpose of studying contemporary Chinese painting with Zhang Qiugu (life dates unknown). Bunchō's talents were recognized by Matsudaira Sadanobu (1759–1829), a high-ranking member of the shogun's council of elders, who appointed the artist as an informal painter in attendance. In 1793 Bunchō accompanied Sadanobu on a trip along the Edo bay, and he produced a handscroll called *Kōyō tanshō-zu* (Paintings of scenic spots) that incorporates the perspective and shading methods of European painting. On the orders of Sadanobu, he also investigated the country's cultural properties, producing two compilations of its pictorial collections, *Shūko jisshu* (Ancient collection of ten kinds) and *Koga ruijū* (Old pictures of objects by category), and sketched important examples of traditional calligraphies and paintings.

Bunchō's eclectic style and wide-ranging subject matter reflect his exposure to various schools and styles, and this lyrical landscape is an excellent example of his work. Employing soft ink washes on silk, he depicted a Chinese-style landscape with a fishing village in the foreground and a jagged mountain looming in the background, separated by a horizontal band of morning mist. His use of perspective and modeling of the rocks and mountain speaks to his training in European-style painting. The signature on this scroll is known as "*Karasu* (Crow) Bunchō" because its characters recall the footprints of a crow and "*Chōchō* (Butterfly) Bunchō" because of its resemblance to a butterfly. His paintings with this style of signature are believed to have been made during the Tenpō era (1830–44), Bunchō's most productive period. Another superb painting by the artist in the museum's collection, *Tao Yuanming Seated under a Willow* (fig. 48), is dated 1812 and also has the "crow"-style signature. KK

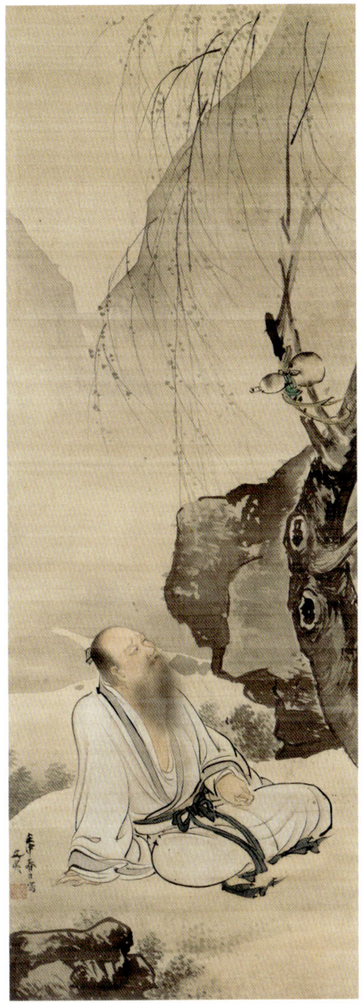

FIG. 48 Tani Bunchō. *Tao Yuanming Seated under a Willow*. Edo period, 1812. Ink on paper, mounted as a hanging scroll; 38½ × 13⅝ in. (97.8 × 34.6 cm). Philadelphia Museum of Art: Purchased with the Hollis Family Foundation Fund, 2003-179-1

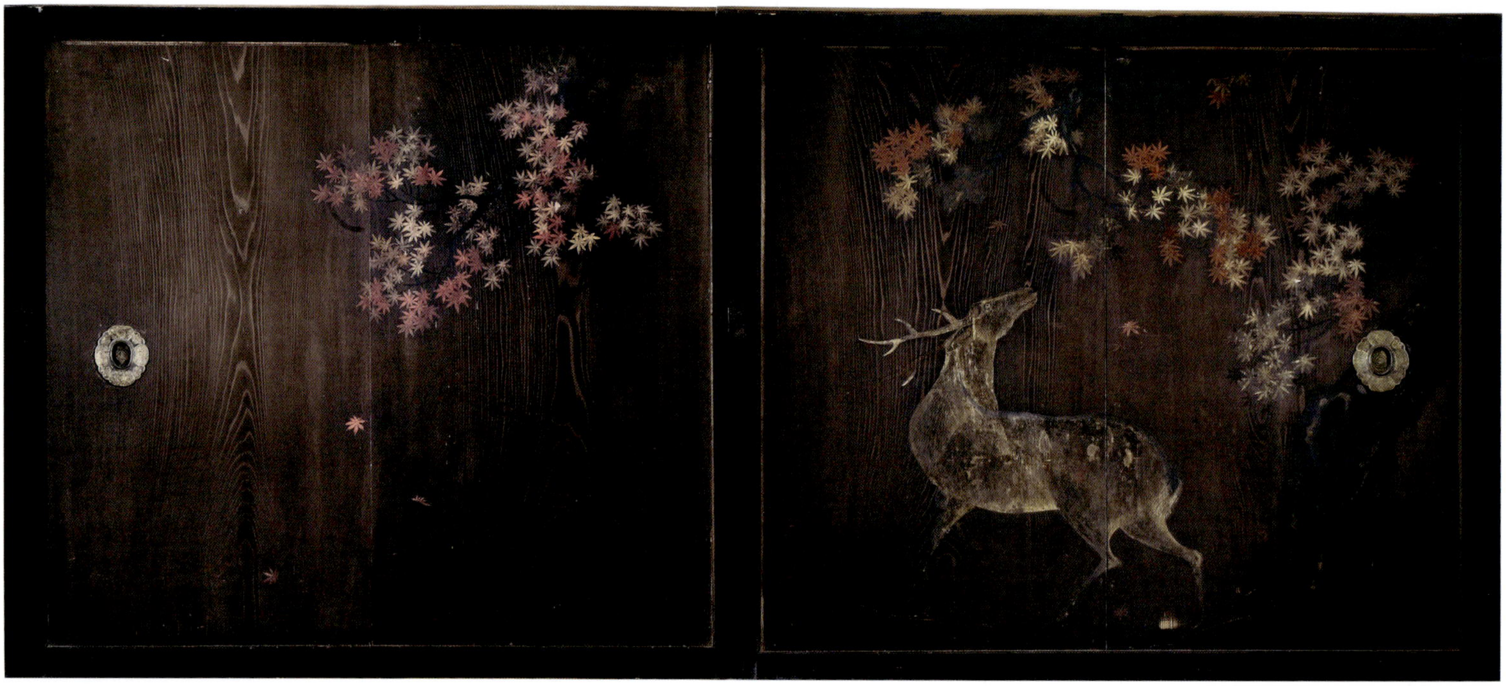

A (obverse): *Deer and Maple Leaves*

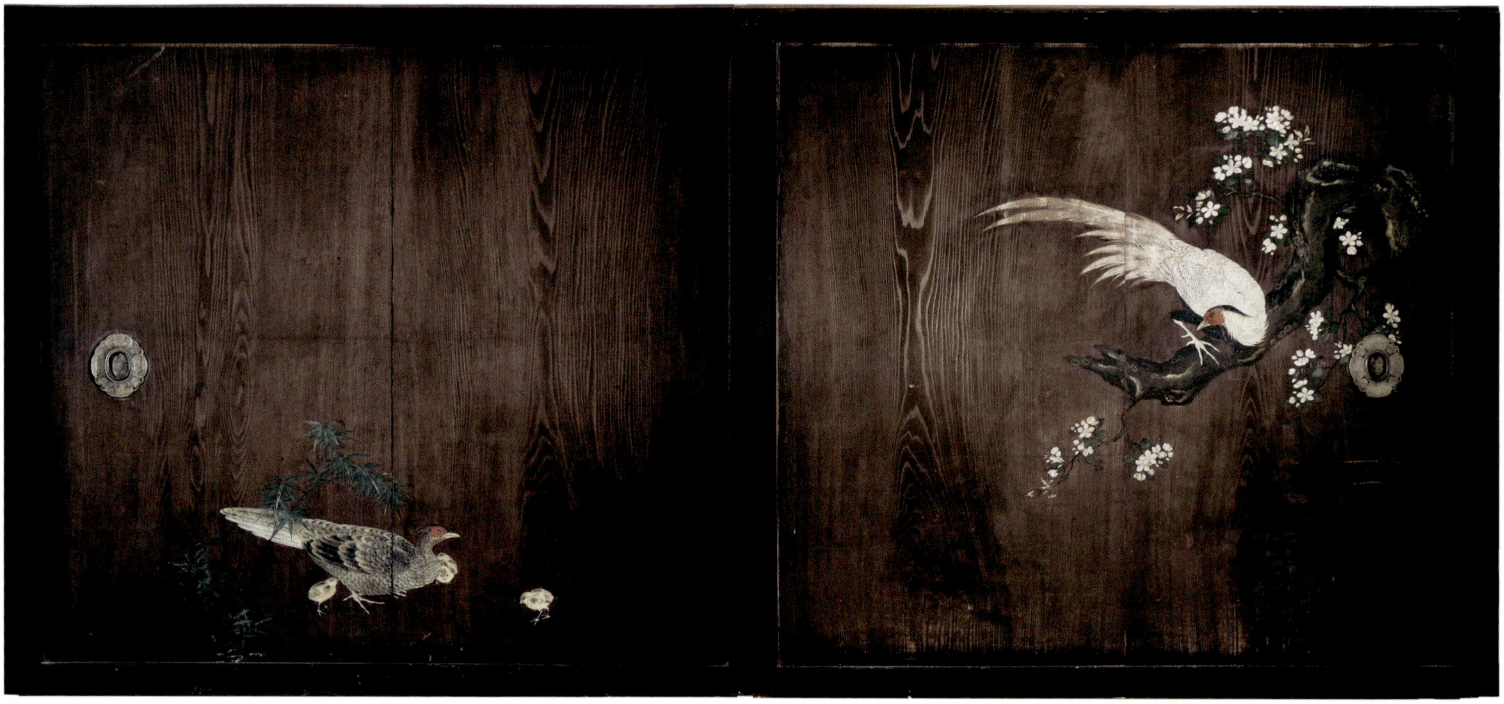

A (reverse): *Pheasant and Peahen with Chicks*

60

Three Pairs of Sliding Doors (*Sugito*)

A (obverse): *Deer and Maple Leaves*; (reverse): *Pheasant and Peahen with Chicks*
B: *Guan Yu, Zhou Cang, and Guan Yu's Attendant*
C: *Chinese Boys at Play*

Edo period (1615–1868), 18th century

Color on cryptomeria wood (*sugi*)
A: 69½ in. × 6 ft. 6⅛ in. (176.5 × 198.5 cm)
B: 62¾ × 56 in. (159.4 × 142.2 cm)
C: 64 × 62¾ in. (162.6 × 159.4 cm)

Purchased with the Fiske Kimball Fund and the Marie Kimball Fund,
A: 1966-211-7a,b;8a,b;
B: 1966-211-5b,6b;
C: 1966-211-15a,16a

Sugito is the Japanese term for a sliding door made of *Cryptomeria japonica* wood, which was historically an indispensable construction material for castles, *shoin* (reception rooms), and temples. The doors were installed around entrances and corridors to provide ventilation, light, and insulation against sound and the weather, as well as for security. Following the Meiji Restoration in 1868, the abolition of castles as residences was promulgated in 1873.[1] A total of 145 castles were handed over to the ministry of finance, and apart from those used by the prefectural office, the buildings and their interiors were sold by auction. Nagoya Castle of the Owari Tokugawa family, for example, came under the jurisdiction of the army, and the Ninomaru Palace was sold along with its architectural materials, including *sugito*.[2] The Meiji government also initiated a new policy of separating the Shinto and Buddhist religions, and abolished various privileges previously granted to Buddhist temples, making it difficult for the buildings to be maintained. Therefore, historical temples especially were forced to sell treasures such as *sugito* for protection of their principal Buddhist sculptures, ritual implements, main halls, and priests, and many of the sold objects were brought to foreign countries (see no. 8). Temple *sugito* by famed artists as well as *fusuma* (sliding door) paintings and screens were also exhibited at domestic expositions in Japan.

The museum owns twenty *sugito*, each with a front and a back side with door pulls. Twenty-one of the pulls are decorated with the Tokugawa family crest, called *mitsuba-aoi* (three leaves of hollyhock within a circle), indicating that the doors may have originally been part of a building associated with that family. The auspicious combination of deer and maple leaves, as seen on the obverse of one of these pairs of doors (A), is thought to derive from a Japanese poem by Sarumaru Dayū (life dates unknown) from the *Kokin wakashū* (Collection of poems from ancient and modern times), published during the early tenth century. The verso of the doors depicts two silver pheasants, one perched on a branch with peach blossoms, and the other, a peahen, surrounded by three chicks.[3] This pair of doors has pulls with paulownia flower and butterfly designs (p. 154, bottom left). The *sugito* in the museum's collection with images of the Chinese warriors Guan Yu and Zhou Cang and Guan Yu's attendant (B) have door pulls with decorations of *ura-aoi* (hollyhock surrounded by six leaves), a design also associated with the Tokugawa family (p. 154, bottom center). Another pair of doors features a scene of Chinese boys at play (C), a popular painting subject in Ōoku, the residence of the children of the shogun family, the lawful wife, and the inner maids of Edo Castle. Its door pulls include the Tokugawa *mitsuba-aoi* crest (p. 154, bottom right). Considering the size of the doors, the fine workmanship of the metal fittings, and the quality of the painting, the *sugito* in the museum's collection may have been from an abandoned castle or the main hall of a large temple related to the Tokugawa family. KK

1. Moriyama 2016, 88–124.
2. Nagoya 2013, pl. 14.
3. Silver pheasants became a common and significant motif after Kano Tan'yū (1602–1674) sketched and painted them. In 1658 Kuroda Mitsuyuki (1628–1707), daimyo of Chikuzen Province (Fukuoka Prefecture), presented a pair of silver pheasants to the shogun Tokugawa Ietsuna (1641–1680). Tan'yū most likely was asked to sketch these rare birds. Philadelphia 2015a, 274, pls. 81, 82.

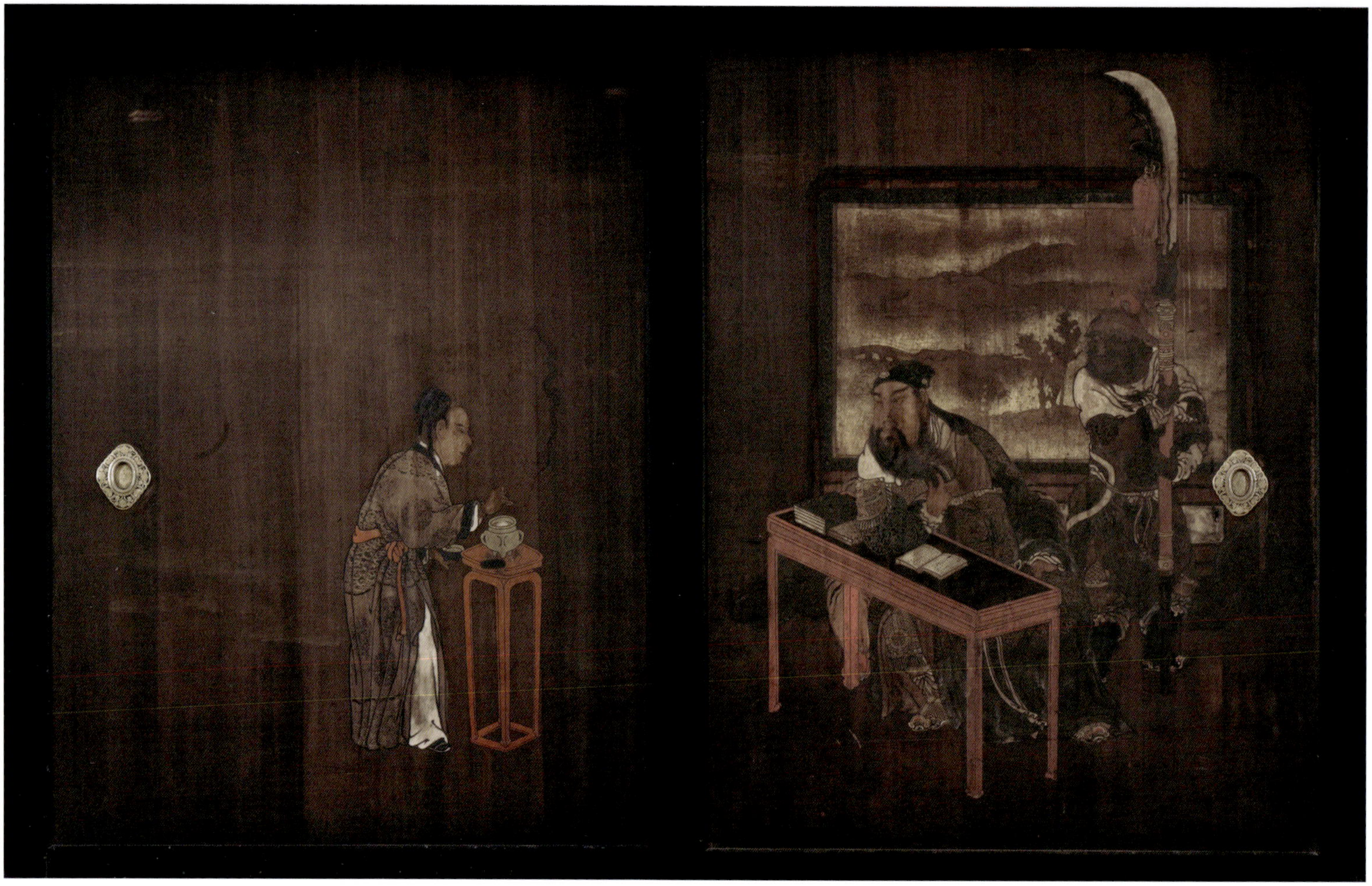

B: *Guan Yu, Zhou Cang* [both right panel], *and Guan Yu's Attendant*

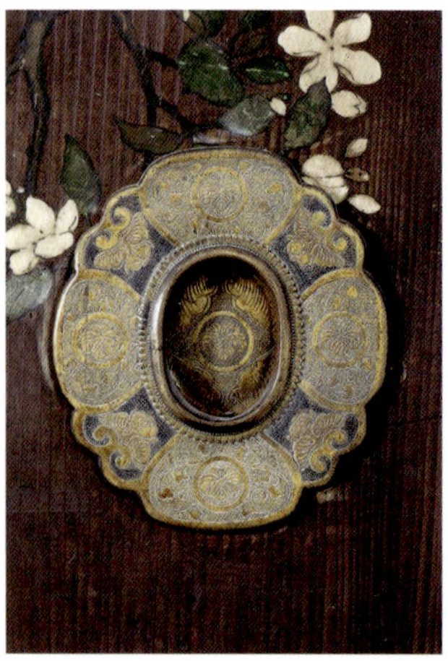

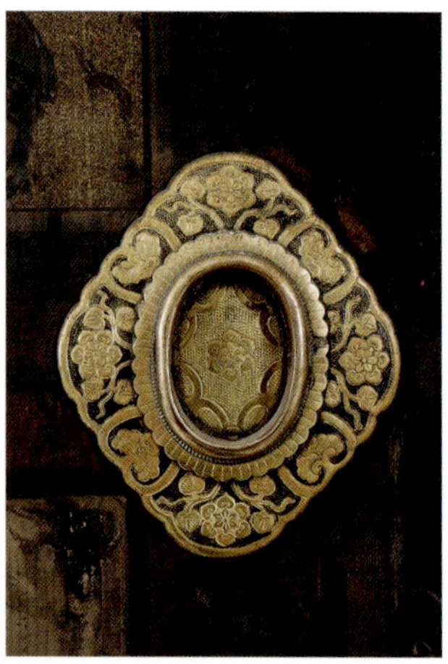

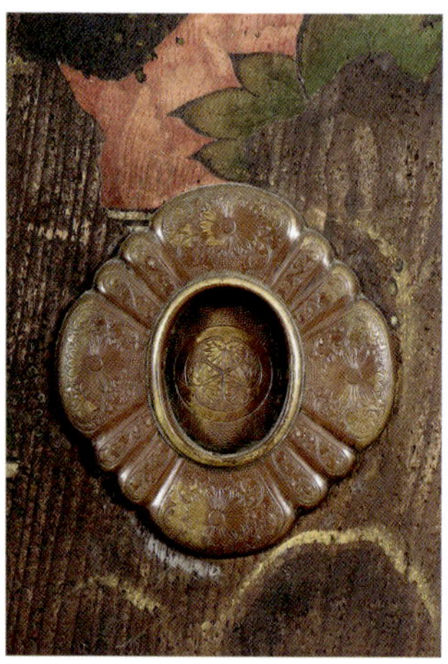

Detail of the right door pull of *Pheasant and Peahen with Chicks* (A), with paulownia flower and butterfly designs

Detail of the right door pull of *Guan Yu, Zhou Cang, and Guan Yu's Attendant* (B), with decorations of *ura-aoi* (hollyhock surrounded by six leaves)

Detail of the left door pull of *Chinese Boys at Play* (C), with the Tokugawa *mitsuba-aoi* crest surrounded by designs of chrysanthemums and leaves

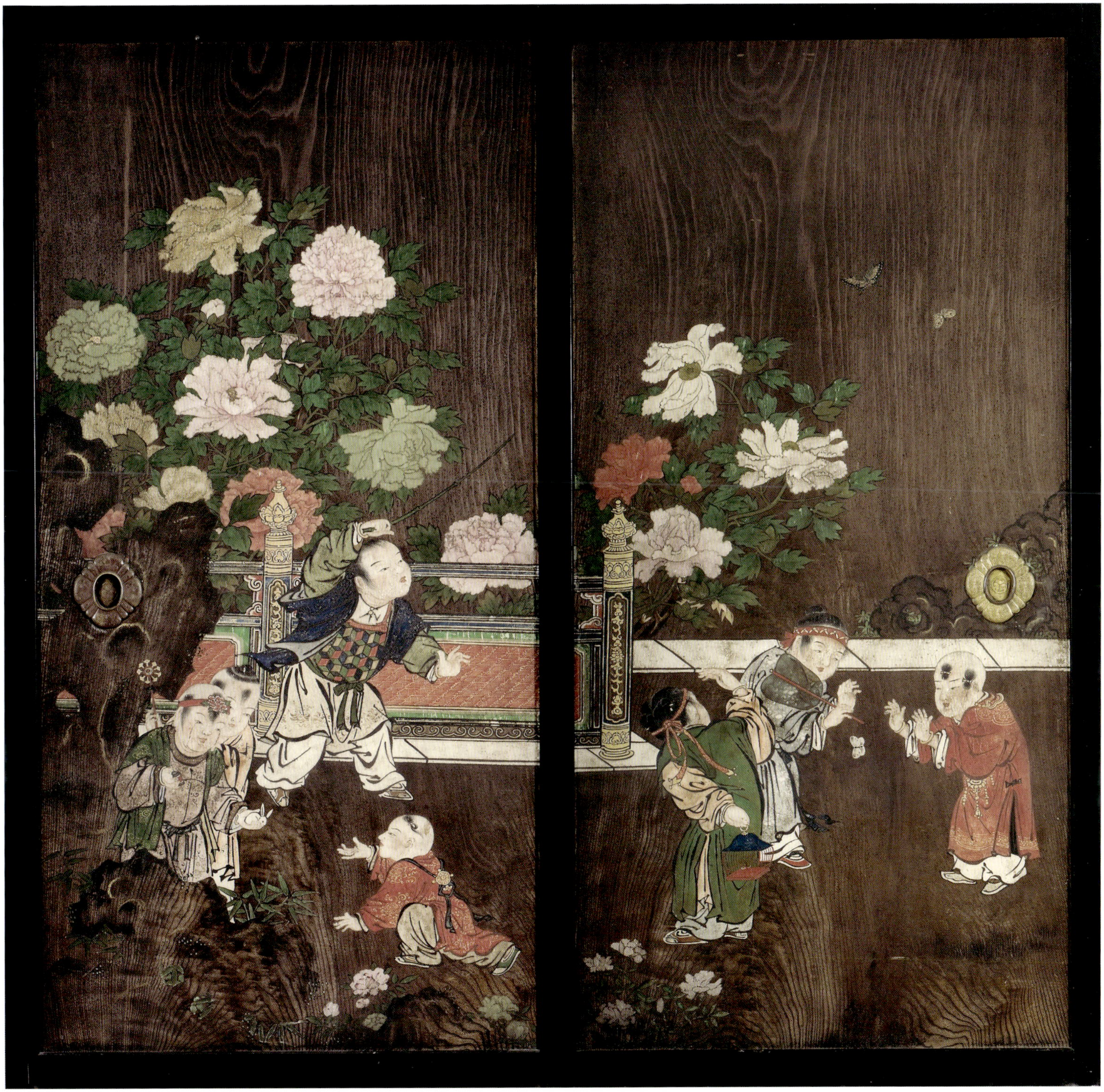

c: *Chinese Boys at Play*

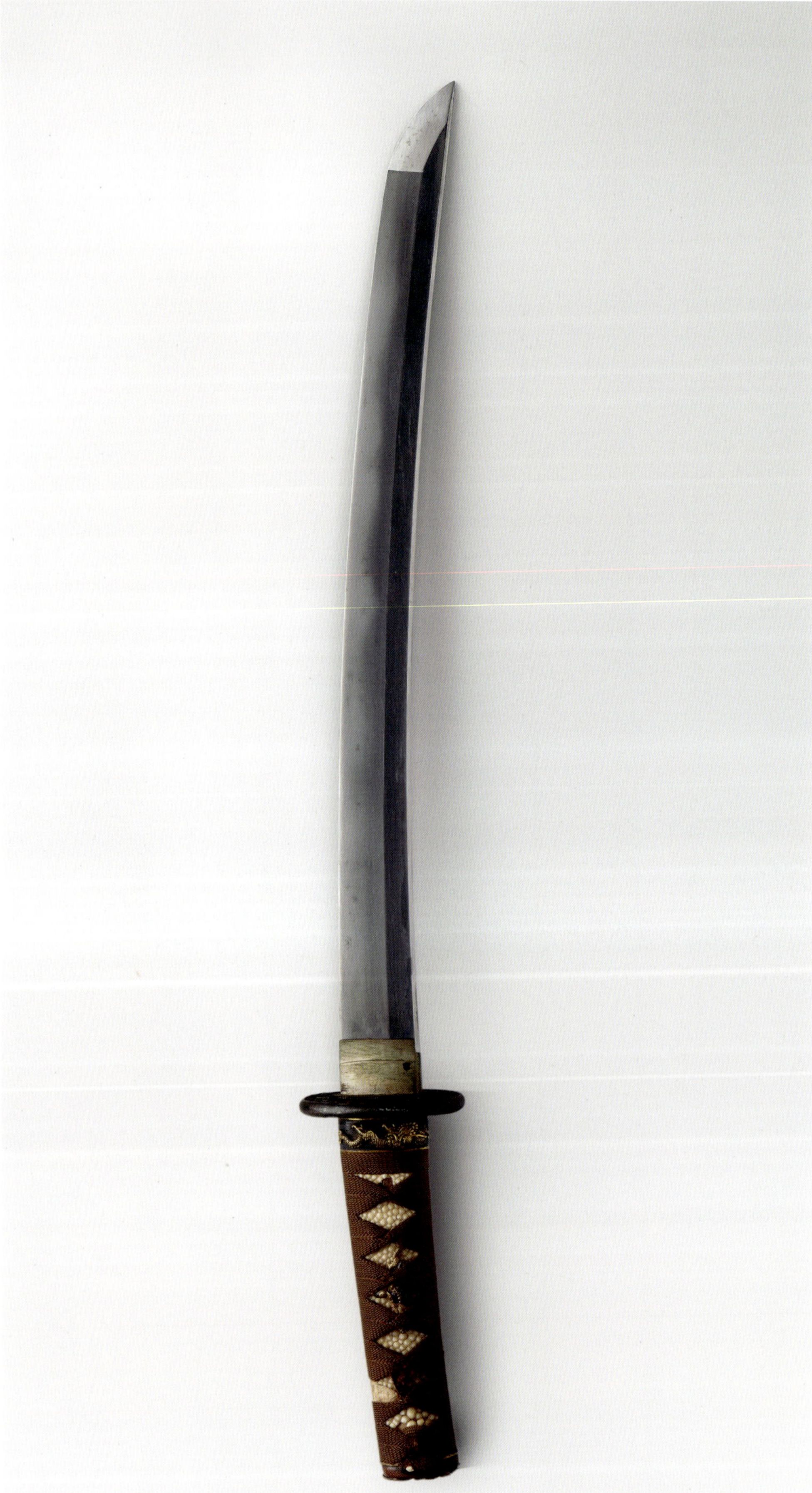

61

Short Sword (*Wakizashi*)

Attributed to Inoue Kunisada II
(1630–1682)

Edo period (1615–1868), c. 1650

Steel blade, iron hand guard, gold and *shakudō* fittings, sharkskin, and fabric (hilt); L. 15½ in. (39.4 cm)

The Edmund L. Zalinski Collection, 1964-178-30

In the early seventeenth century, the shogun Tokugawa Ieyasu (1543–1616) united Japan's regional daimyo into a governing coalition that ended decades of violence and warfare. The ensuing Edo period had a thriving economy and stable government that was ruled by a class of samurai, hereditary warriors turned administrators. Strict sumptuary laws restricted wearing swords in public to this warrior class.[1] By the time this *wakizashi*, or short sword, was forged as part of a pair with a longer katana, now lost, swords were rarely used in combat and had become symbols of prestige and political power.[2]

The exceptional quality of the blade and its fittings indicate that the original owner was of high status, even within the warrior class. The blade is attributed to Inoue Kunisada II, also known as Shinkai, a renowned swordsmith based in Osaka. Kunisada matched the gentle curve of the blade with an undulating temper line along the cutting edge, like a rolling fog or clouds. As if flying through this mist, dragons reappear throughout the sword's furnishings. On the iron handguard, a dragon wraps through a lattice of openwork, hand-chiseled clouds. The decorative pegs (*menuki*) on the hilt depict a Buddhist deity, probably Kannon (Sanskrit: Avalokitesvara; Chinese: Guanyin), seated on a flying dragon (see also no. 62). The bodhisattva of compassion, Kannon represents both protection in this life and the promise of rebirth in a paradisiacal Pure Land.

In the 1890s, Edmund Zalinski (1849–1909) purchased this sword while working in Japan. A lifelong soldier, Zalinski was among the world's leading experts on artillery and matériel in the late nineteenth century. He returned from Japan with a collection of over two hundred swords, which he displayed in New York and Philadelphia to teach about Japan and its history. HS

1. For a detailed discussion of Edo-period sumptuary laws, see Shively 1964–65.
2. For more on the history of Japanese swords, see New York 2009–10.

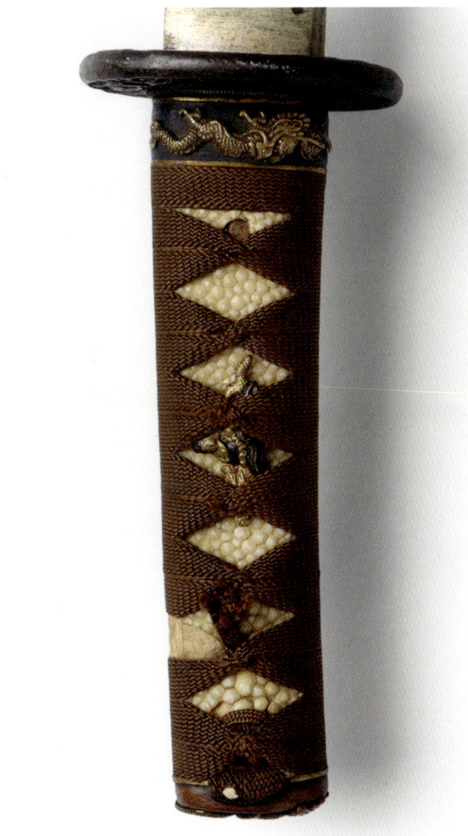

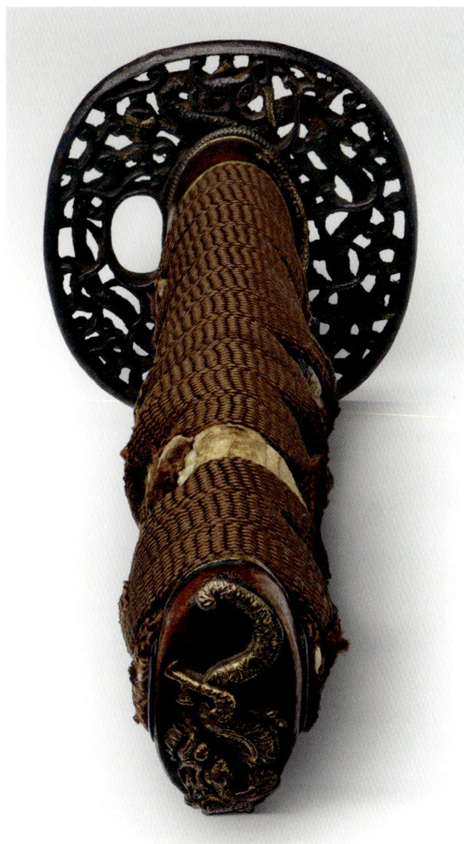

Details of the *menuki* and the handguard

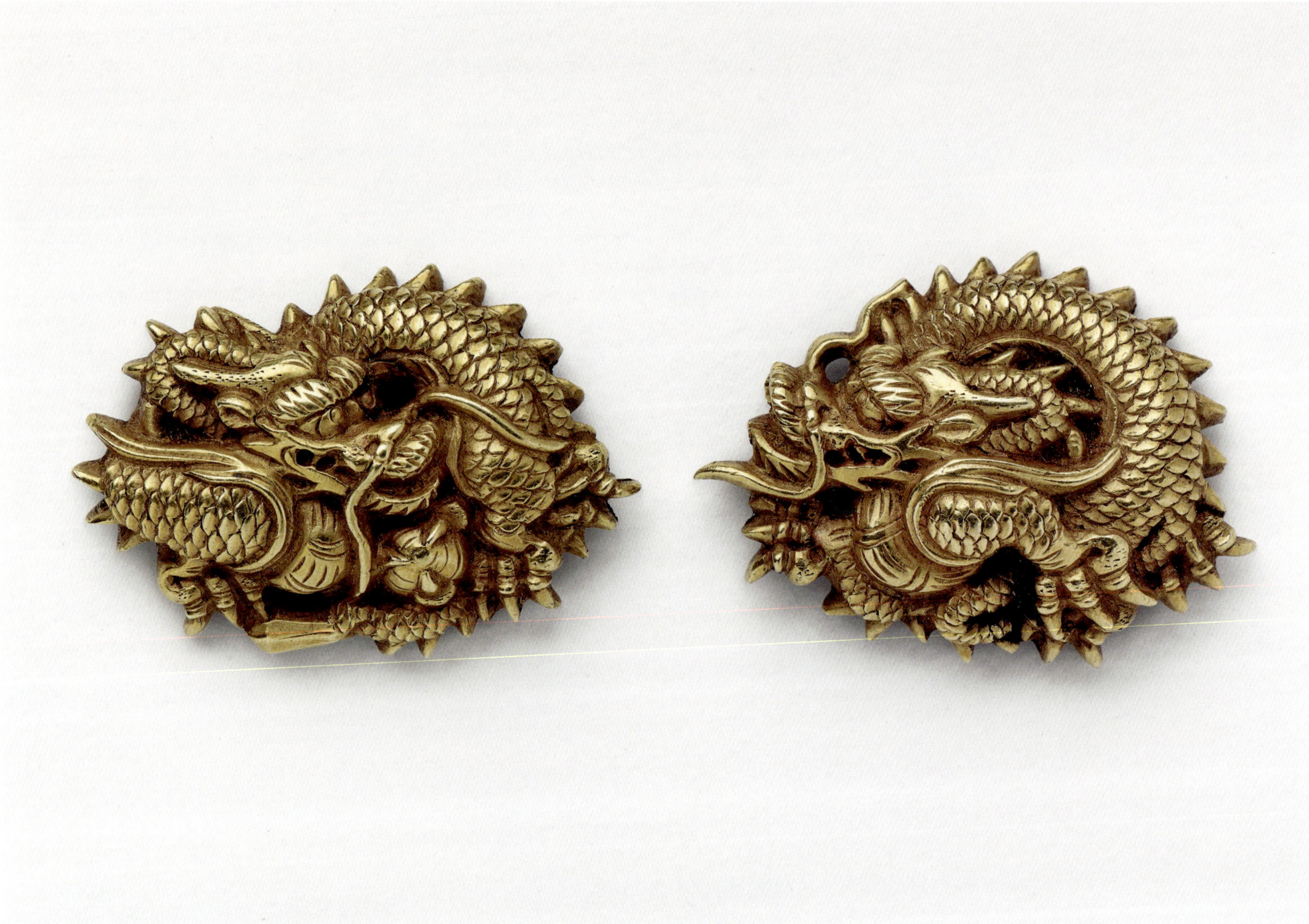

62

Dragon *Menuki*

Edo period (1615–1868), c. 1825

Gold, each: diam. 1⅛ in. (2.9 cm)

Gift of Alfred Wolkenberg, 1972-167-1a,b

On a Japanese sword, the blade is attached to the hilt via a small two-sided peg, or *menuki*. These pins are often highly decorative, despite being partially obscured by fabric wrapped around the wood and ray-skin hilt. This was especially the case during the peaceful Edo period, when swords became increasingly ornamental objects. For the ruling warrior class, ornate furnishings including *menuki*, handguards, and pommels, and even the blades themselves were elaborate markers of wealth, status, and power.[1]

To make this pair of *menuki*, the goldsmith first used a mold to create the general shape before chiseling and engraving the final openwork form and detail. The craftsmanship of the two coiling, three-clawed dragons extends to their individual scales and teeth, and even the clearly marked pupils on the dragons' eyes. One dragon holds a wish-fulfilling jewel in its front talons.

Dragons, one of the twelve animals of the zodiac and an auspicious symbol of strength, are a common motif on Japanese arms and armor (see no. 61).[2] A pair of two dragons, one holding a wish-fulfilling jewel, is a particularly common theme, and during the Edo period might have suggested numerous meanings. The imagery could evoke the bodhisattva of compassion Kannon (Sanskrit: Avalokitesvara; Chinese: Guanyin), who is often depicted riding a dragon, or the guardian deity Fudō Myōō (Sanskrit: Acala; Chinese: Budong Mingwang), who can be represented as a dragon coiling a sword. The wish-fulfilling jewel could allude to the legendary Dragon King, who keeps such jewels in his palace at the bottom of the sea. However, the theme of a dragon with a sacred jewel is in fact among the oldest armorial iconography in Japan and traces back to at least the Kofun period (250–538), likely predating these interpretations (fig. 49). HS

1. For more on Japanese swords, see New York 2009–10.
2. See Tokyo, Osaka, and Shizuoka 2017.

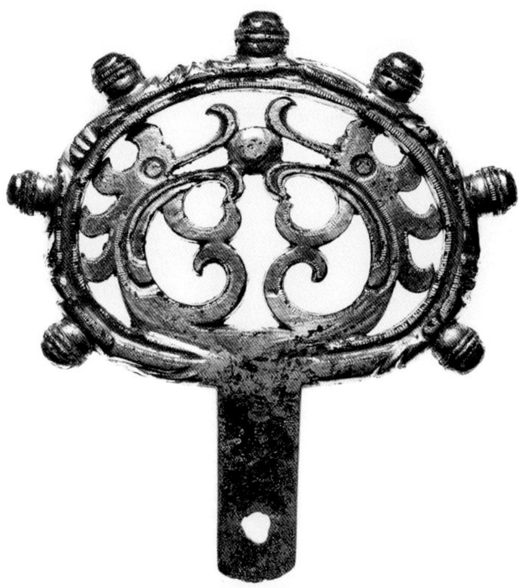

FIG. 49 Sword Ornament with Design of Dragons and Pearl. Kofun period (250–538). Bronze, 4¹³⁄₁₆ × 5⁹⁄₁₆ in. (12.3 × 14.1 cm). Museum of Fine Arts, Boston: John Ware Willard Fund, 58.315

63

Figure of a Beckoning Cat (*Maneki neko*)

Edo period (1615–1868), late 18th–early 19th century

Painted wood, 10½ × 6½ × 5¾ in. (26.7 × 16.5 × 14.6 cm)

Gift of Tsuyoshi Yanai in memory of Edwin D. Hewitt, 1984-107-1

The *maneki neko*, or "beckoning cat," made its appearance as a fixture in urban Japan in the nineteenth century, when it was displayed by inn- and shopkeepers as a talisman for good fortune (*engi-mono*). A variety of materials were used in fashioning *maneki neko*, from stone and wood to ceramic and papier-mâché. This early example in wood has its left paw raised in a beckoning gesture, inviting prospective customers to enter the establishment. Its plump torso is carved from a single small-diameter log, with saw and chisel marks on the underside. Around the cat's neck is a collared bib showing the wood grain, while its body is painted a creamy white that has darkened with handling over time.[1] Black paint was applied to the ears and eyes, and to create whiskers and spots on the body. The overall carving is minimal but beguilingly effective and shows the hand of a skilled craftsperson at work. The naive charm of *maneki neko* has made them popular among Western collectors as well.[2]

A relatively recent phenomenon, the interest in Japanese "folk crafts" was given its philosophical and aesthetic underpinnings by Yanagi Sōetsu (1889–1961) in the early twentieth century, culminating in the opening of Tokyo's Nihon Mingeikan (Japan Folk Crafts Museum) in 1936.[3] Scholars of Japanese art such as Langdon Warner have seen in folk art "an enduring quality that places it beyond the whims of fashion," which certainly applies to this charming sculpture of a cat.[4] FF

1. Analysis of the paint determined that the white coloring is *gofun* (crushed oyster shell), a relatively inexpensive material. See Conservation Examination Report, October 31, 1984, East Asian Art archives, Philadelphia Museum of Art.
2. See, for example, the collection of over 150 *maneki neko* from the Billie L. Moffitt Collection at the Mingei International Museum in San Diego, California.
3. See no. 85 for folk art's influence on modern craft.
4. See Warner 1958, 76–84, for his paean to folk craft.

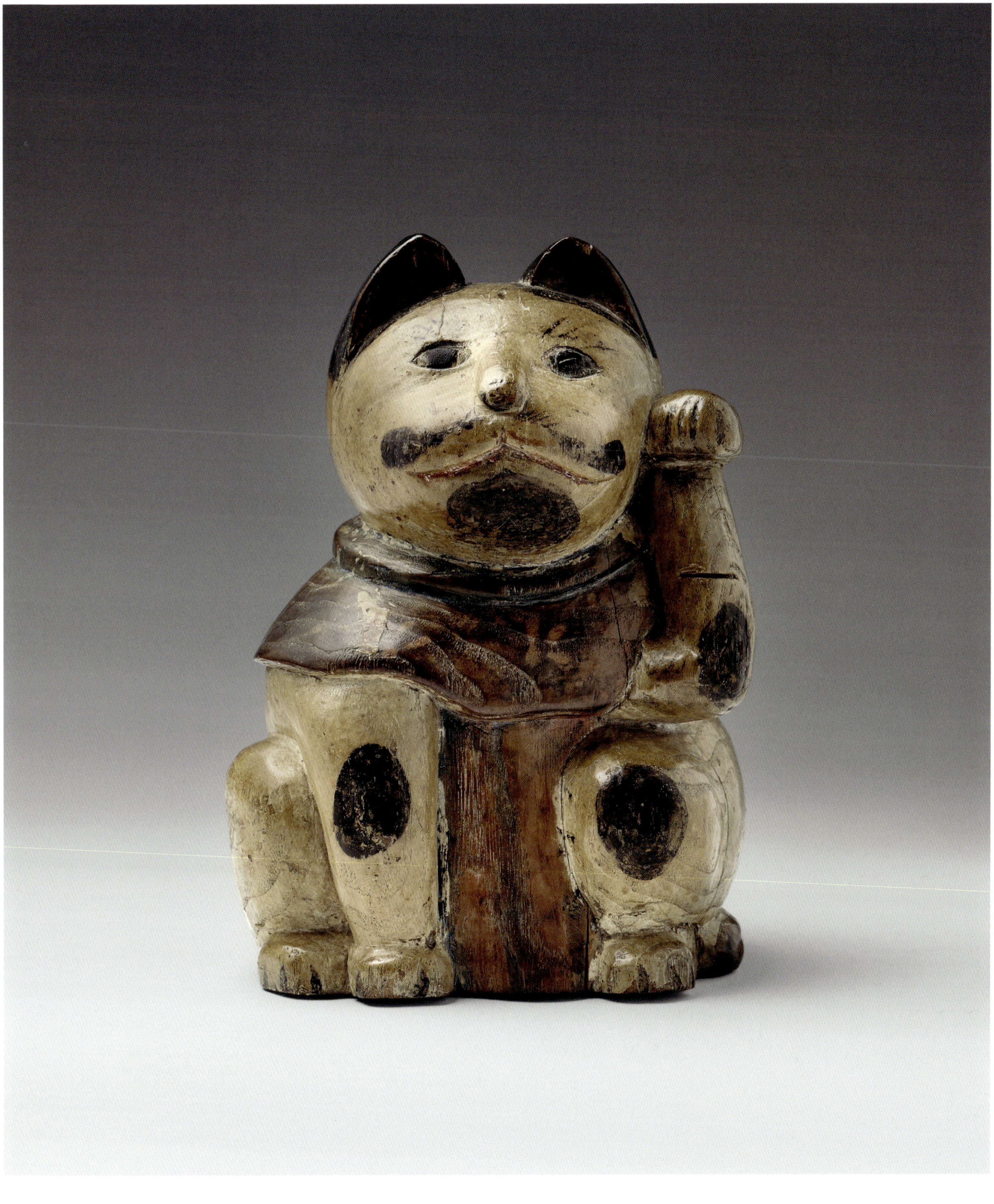

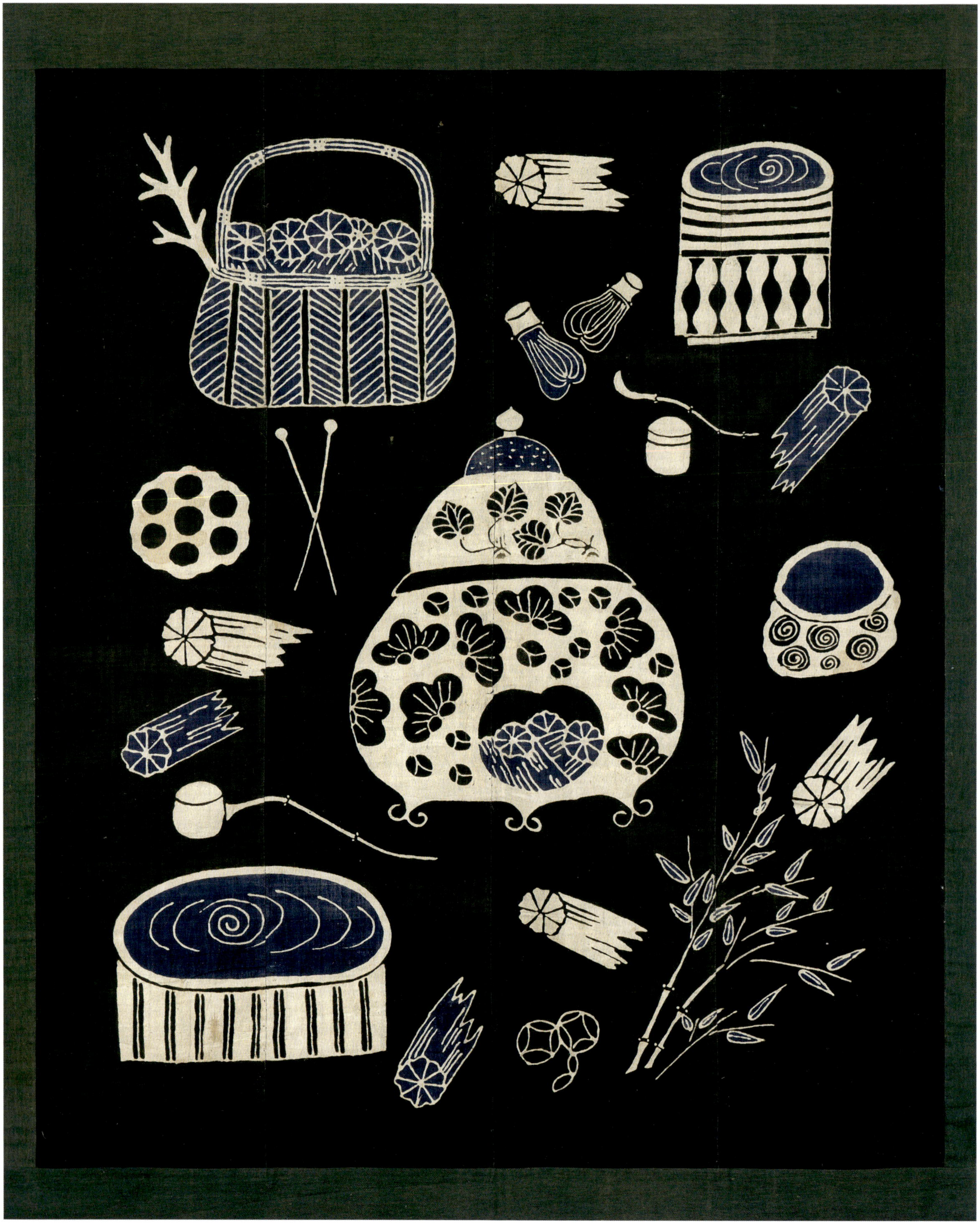

64
Futon Cover

Edo period (1615–1868) or Meiji period (1868–1912), 19th century

Cotton plain weave with rice-paste resist design (*tsutsugaki*), 65¾ × 52¾ in. (167 × 134 cm)

125th Anniversary Acquisition. Purchased with funds contributed by the Otto Haas Charitable Trust, The Women's Committee of the Philadelphia Museum of Art, Maude de Schauensee, Theodore R. and Barbara B. Aronson, Edna and Stanley C. Tuttleman, The Hamilton Family Foundation, and Maxine and Howard H. Lewis, 2000-113-35

For centuries, skilled Japanese craftspeople created beautiful objects for everyday use, but until the early twentieth century the aesthetic value of these crafts was largely ignored. As inexpensive, machine-made commodities proliferated, however, a new interest in and appreciation of time-honored folk crafts developed. This "art of the people" became known as *mingei*, a term coined in the mid-1920s by scholar and philosopher Yanagi Sōetsu (1889–1961), who combined "min" from *minshu*, meaning common people, and "gei" from *kōgei*, meaning crafts.

Decorative household textiles, including bedding and curtains that customarily formed part of a bride's trousseau, were an important segment of these traditional crafts. Such textiles were usually made using the *tsutsugaki* technique, in which designs are drawn in rice paste that resists indigo dye and colored pigments. Only one piece at a time can be produced, and designs are drawn freehand, encouraging bold and expressive patterns. Rural artisans, not restricted by the rigid protocol of the elite or by the need to follow the latest urban fads, commonly chose to depict auspicious subjects or utilitarian objects.

This bed covering, which would have been stuffed with cotton batting when used, illustrates the utensils used during a traditional tea ceremony. Rooted in the principles of Zen Buddhism, this ritualized occasion is an important aspect of Japanese life and culture that reflects reverence for the beautiful in everyday routines. Tea-ceremony implements, called *chadōgu*, include a brazier and kettle used to heat water, depicted in the center of this futon cover, as well as teabowls, pieces of charcoal, whisks, a tea caddy and scoop, and a water container and ladle. Each would have been specially selected and valued for its practical function and aesthetic quality. Other examples of futon covers in the museum's collection depict auspicious imagery, such as *noshi*, thin strips of dried abalone bound in a bundle that were attached to ceremonial gifts and allude to long life (fig. 50). HKH

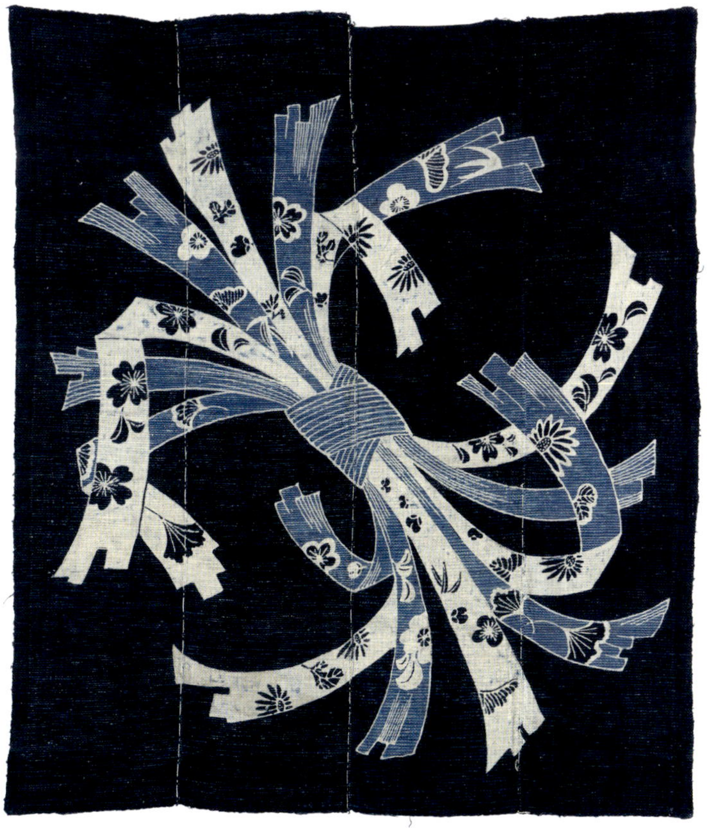

FIG. 50 Futon Cover. Edo or Meiji period, 19th century. Plain-weave cotton with rice-paste resist design (*tsutsugaki*), 64 × 54 in. (162.6 × 137.2 cm). Philadelphia Museum of Art, 125th Anniversary Acquisition: Purchased with funds contributed by the Otto Haas Charitable Trust, The Women's Committee of the Philadelphia Museum of Art, Maude de Schauensee, Theodore R. and Barbara B. Aronson, Edna and Stanley C. Tuttleman, The Hamilton Family Foundation, and Maxine and Howard H. Lewis, 2000-113-5

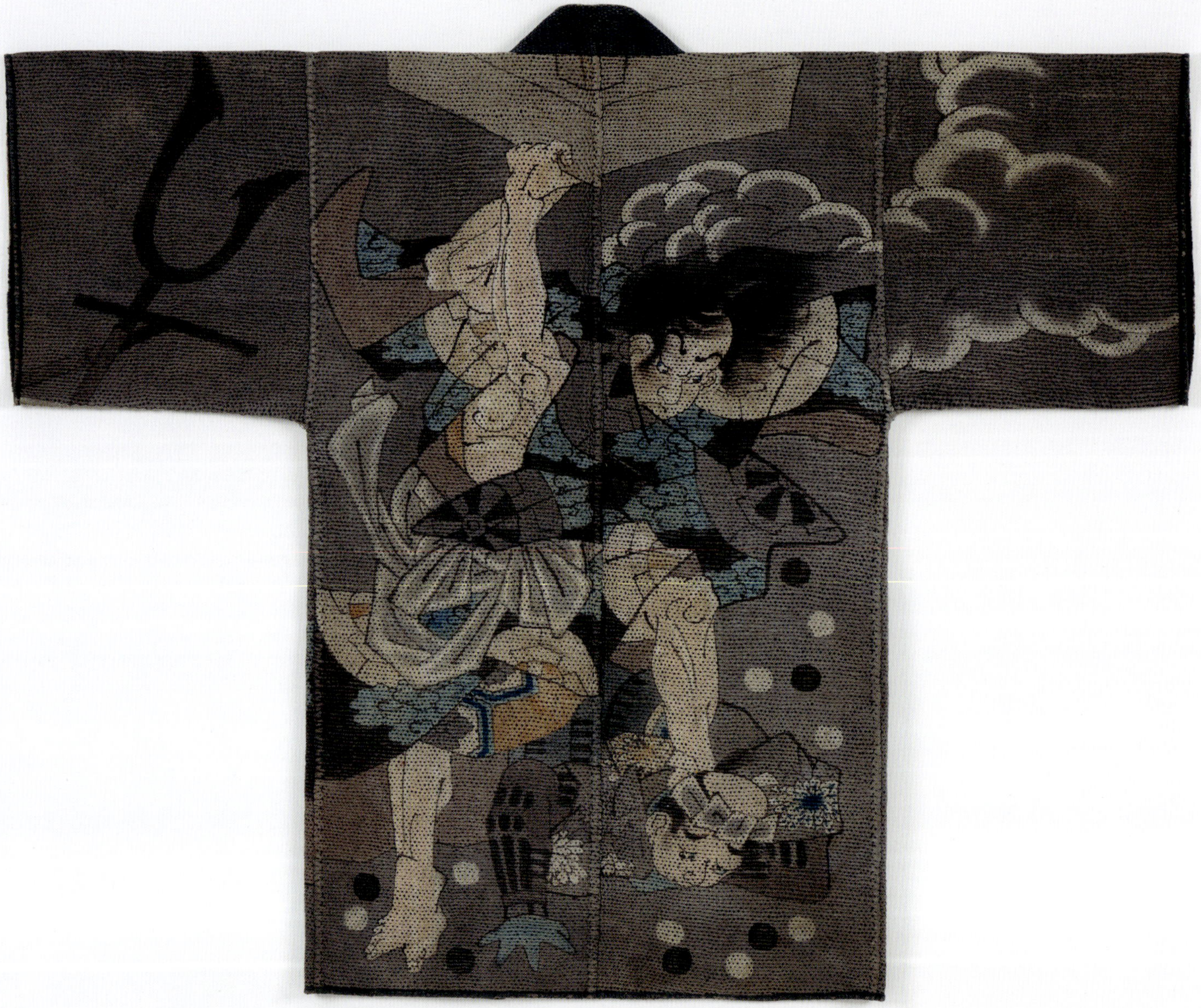

65

Fireman's Coat (*Hikeshi hanten*)

Edo period (1615–1868) or Meiji period (1868–1912), 19th century

Cotton plain weave with rice-paste resist (*tsutsugaki*) and cotton darning stitches (*sashiko*)

125th Anniversary Acquisition. Purchased with funds contributed by the Otto Haas Charitable Trust, The Women's Committee of the Philadelphia Museum of Art, Maude de Schauensee, Theodore R. and Barbara B. Aronson, Edna and Stanley C. Tuttleman, The Hamilton Family Foundation, and Maxine and Howard H. Lewis, 2000-113-14

Fire was a serious threat in nineteenth-century Japanese cities, where houses were densely packed and typically made of wood and paper. The townspeople who served as firefighters struggled to contain frequent infernos, using long hooks to raze burning structures and stop the fire from spreading. Firefighters wore thick, stiff clothing — including coats, hoods, trousers, and gloves — made by layering cotton fabrics that were then quilted with dense lines of running stitches (*sashiko*); these specialized garments were soaked with water before being donned to battle a blaze, helping protect the wearer against intense heat, flames, and falling debris. While practically suited to this hazardous work, firefighters' coats were reversible and thus also reflect the heroic nature of the wearer's occupation. The plain side was out while working, but once the fire was extinguished or on festive occasions such coats were reversed to reveal bold inner designs created using rice-paste resist. The decoration inside often featured forceful creatures, courageous figures, or other imagery that reflected the valor of the wearer.

This coat — somewhat stained and discolored from wear — dynamically depicts a heroic scene made famous by prints and kabuki plays. Loyal samurai Satō Tadanobu (1161–1186), who had selflessly saved the life of his lord, took refuge at the house of his mistress. She betrayed him, however, and he was ambushed as he played the board game Go. Unable to reach his weapons, he fought his way out of the trap with the only thing at hand, the game's heavy wooden table, or *goban*. Here he raises it over his head as the black and white stone game pieces scatter around an attacker he has subdued. Caught again by his enemies the next morning, Tadanobu defended himself until he was badly wounded, ultimately choosing to perish by his own hand. The samurai's battle using the Go table — so well known that he was nicknamed Goban Tadanobu — was a popular motif for firefighters' coats since the tragic hero was an inspiring example of the determination and sacrifice esteemed in both warriors and firefighters. HKH

66

Album of Prints of Kabuki Actors in Their Roles by Hirosada

Konishi Hirosada (also called Gosōtei Hirosada)
(act. 1826–63, d. c. 1865)

Edo period (1615–1868), c. 1847–53

Color woodblock prints, silhouetted (*koban* and *chūban tate-e*), plus 2 brush and color wash drawings; bound and mounted on flecked Japanese paper
Album: 11½ × 7¾ × 2 in. (29.2 × 19.7 × 5.1 cm)

Gift of Jack Shear in memory of Anne d'Harnoncourt, 2008-62-243(1–99)

In this rare album, a collector assembled actor prints (*yakusha-e*) designed by Konishi Hirosada, the most prolific print designer in Osaka in the mid-nineteenth century.[1] Actor prints served as advertisements for kabuki theater houses and also functioned to memorialize particular performances or eminent actors. Prints produced in the Kansai region of Japan, including in the cities of Kobe, Kyoto, and Osaka, are called *Kamigata-e* ("pictures from Kamigata") in reference to the colloquial name of the region. Also known as "Osaka prints" abroad, prints from this region are typically in the *chūban*, or half-block, format and primarily consist of actor prints, a reflection of the artists' consumer base. Although the Tenpō Reforms of 1841–43 had prohibited the sale of actor prints from 1842, stopping their publication for more than five years,[2] the attributed dates of this album are consistent with the resumption of this activity in Osaka and with Hirosada's prolific revival of *nigao-e* (likeness) actor prints.[3]

Kabuki culture was highly interactive, and fans would support their favorite actors by commissioning or creating prints, which they would collect in albums that they could share.[4] This album's owner placed the prints in an accordion format that allowed for showing friends and fellow fans multiple images at a time.

Generally consisting of half-portraits in three-quarter view, Hirosada's portrayals in the album capture the actors' exaggerated facial expressions, expressive gestures, and physical features and attributes as well as their costumes and accoutrements.[5] The right page of the spread illustrated here celebrates the actors Kataoka Gadō II (right) and Nakayama Yoshio III (Nanshi II) in their roles as Genta Kagesue and Umegae, respectively, in the play *Hiragana Seisuiki* (A).[6] On the opposing page, the collector carefully included two playbills commemorating a performance at the Tenman Theater in 1839.

The album owner's enthusiasm and reverence for kabuki is evident throughout the pages. For Hirosada's print featuring Ōkawa Hashizō I, for example, the collector carefully cut around the woodblock-printed clouds and border and affixed a cartouche bearing the actor's name to the flecked paper (B). The owner's identification of each actor throughout the album demonstrates their deep knowledge of the theater and ability to recognize the crests, personal emblems, costumes, and physical characteristics of the performers.[7]

Other pages in the album suggest the collector's tastes and creative interventions. Certain album sheets contain multiple, overlapping actor portraits, creating lively compositions in which prints of actors from different series or productions intermingle on the page (C). As the album reaches a close, an image of a black-clad stagehand, known as a *kuroko*, drawing a curtain closed emphasizes the album's conception as an unfolding and dynamic visual experience. Not only does the album provide a glimpse into the tastes and collecting habits of an individual collector, it also gives a rich sense of one of the many social practices around kabuki theater in which its fans in Osaka fervently engaged. MD

---

1. Keyes 1984, 8. The album includes two drawings and fifteen prints made by other artists.
2. Keyes 1984, 11.
3. Gerstle 2005, 51.
4. Matsudaira 1984, 699.
5. Gerstle 2005, 52.
6. Museum of Fine Arts, Boston, n.d.
7. Keyes 1984, 13.

(A) (right) Utagawa Kunimasu (act. 1830–54), *Actors Kataoka Gadō II as Genta Kagesue and Nakayama Yoshio III as Umegae* (2008-62-243[4]); (left) possibly Konishi Hirosada, two text panels with decorative borders (2008-62-243[5a,b])

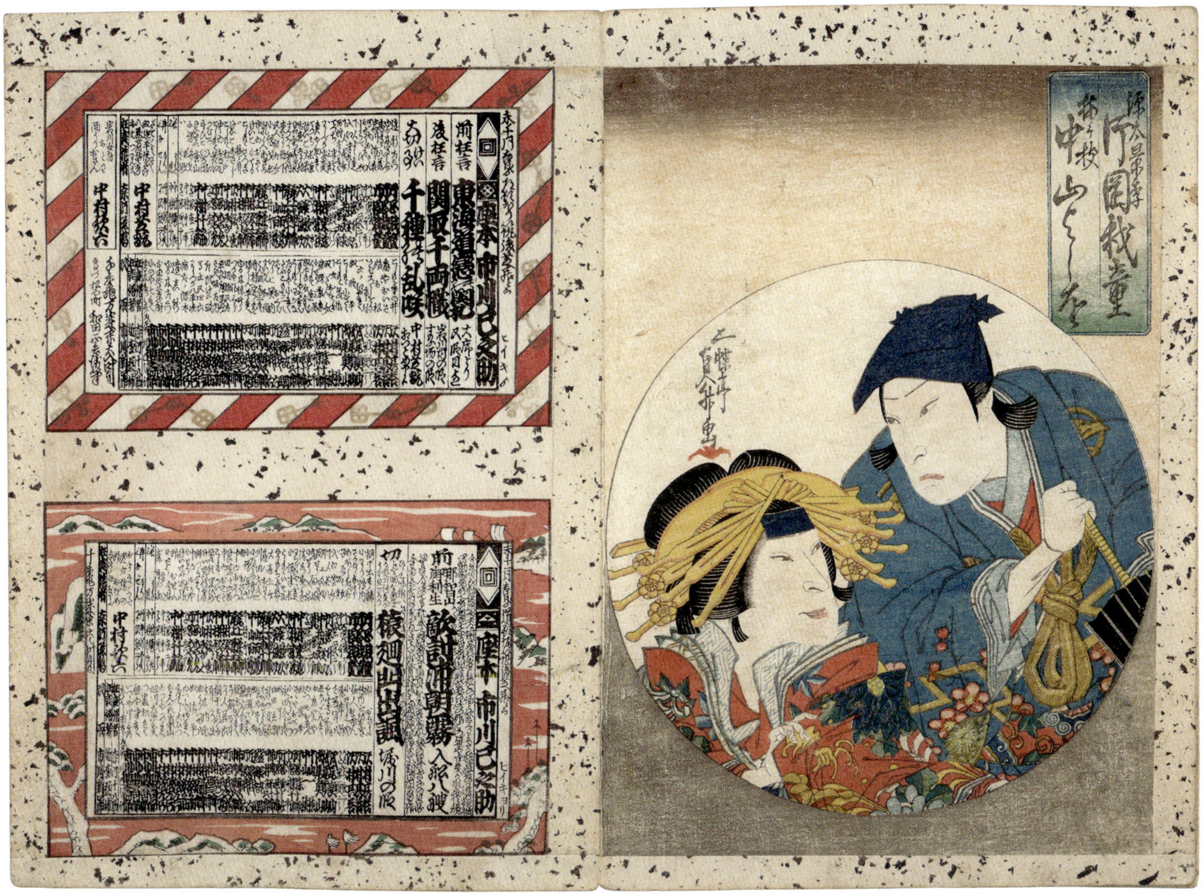

(B) Konishi Hirosada, *Onoe Kikugorō III (Ōkawa Hashizō I) as the Ascetic Priest Nakasaina*, 1848 (2008-62-243[79])

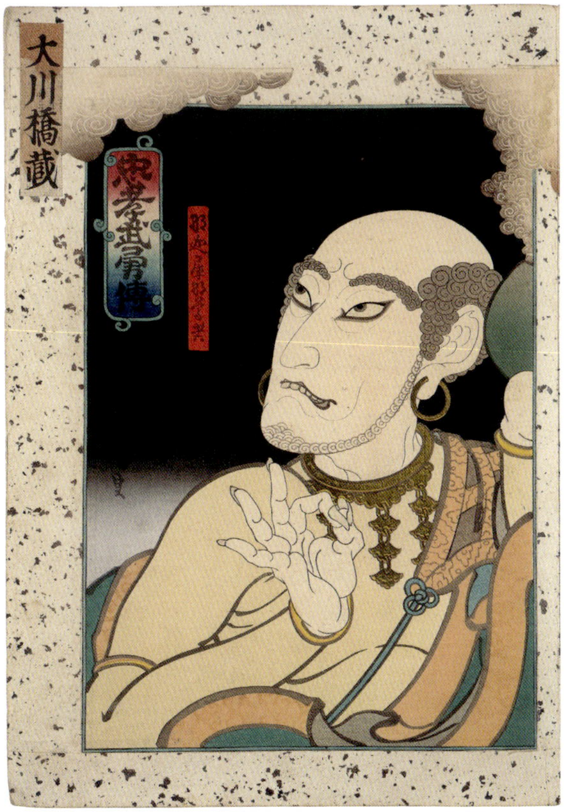

(C) Sadamasu II (act. 1848–49), *Kataoka Ichizō I as Sato Masakiyo* (right) and *Ichikawa Ebijuro IV as Gotobei* (left), 1848 (2008-62-244[30a,b])

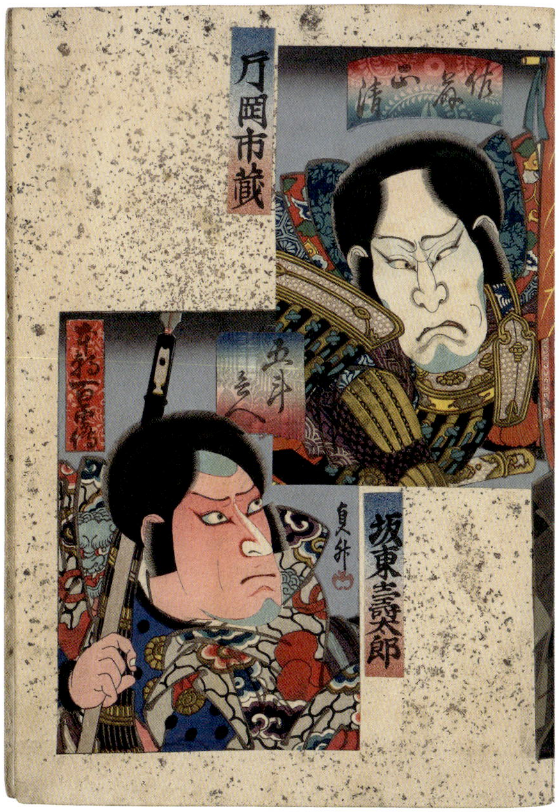

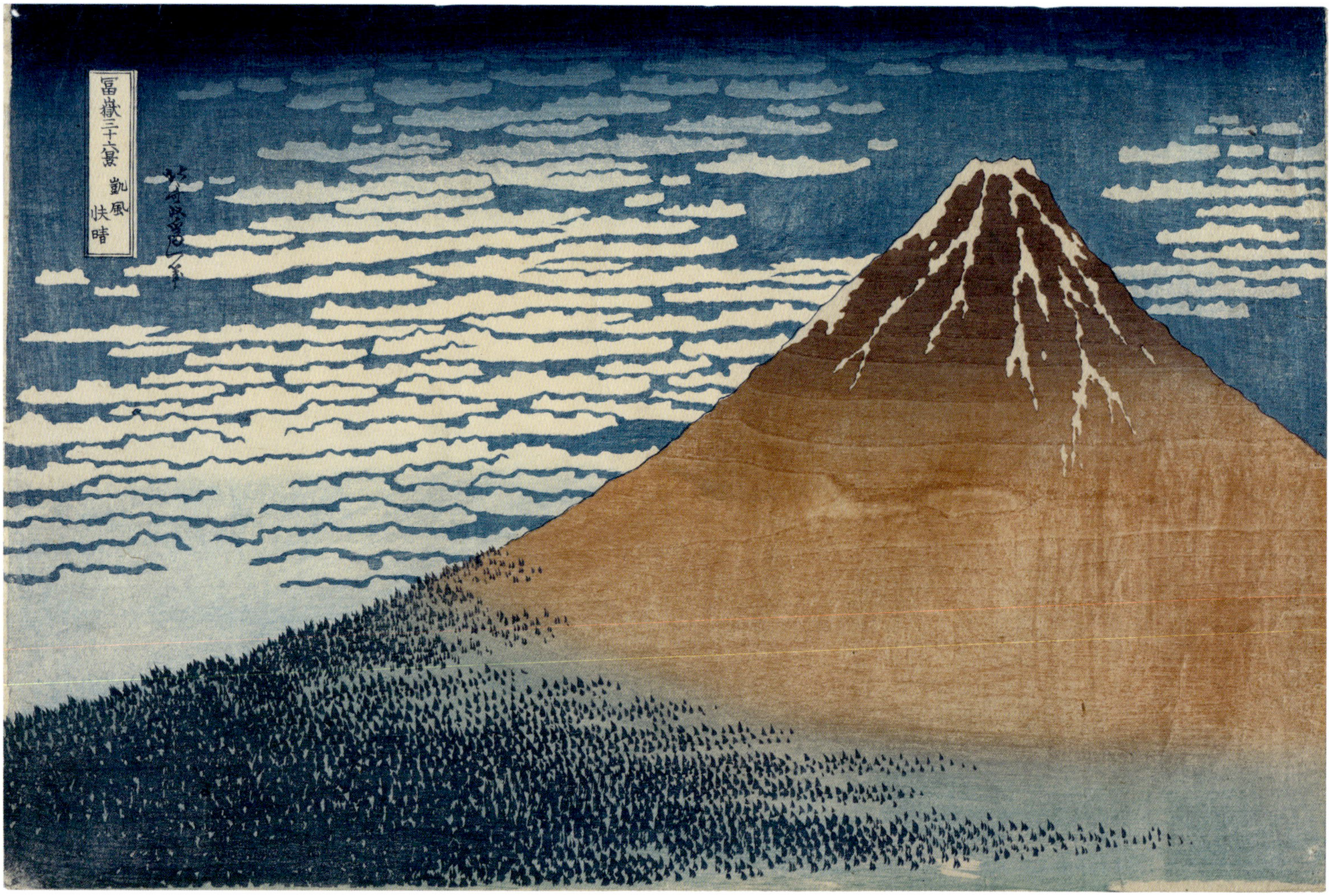
冨嶽三十六景
凱風快晴

67

Fine Wind, Clear Day (*Gaifū kaisei*), also known as *Red Fuji*

Katsushika Hokusai
(1760–1849)

Edo period (1615–1868), c. 1831

From the series *Thirty-Six Views of Mount Fuji* (*Fugaku sanjūrokkei*)

Color woodblock print
10¼ × 15⅛ in. (26 × 38.4 cm)

Gift of Mrs. Moncure Biddle in memory of Ernest Fenollosa, 1958-49-5

In Katsushika Hokusai's famed print of the iconic Mount Fuji, late summer dresses the base of the mountain in rich vegetation, with trees described by rough, clustered strokes carved in dark blue against a field of gentle green. The soft light of sunrise bathes the mountain in a subtle red, while white, cottony clouds appear in the blue sky. The striking blue, printed in *bero-ai* (literally "Berlin blue," or Prussian Blue) was an imported, synthetic pigment that became commercially viable for printing in Japan by the 1830s.[1]

There is a long history of representing Mount Fuji in the Japanese cultural arts. It was first celebrated in poetry in the eighth century, but its proximity to the bustling metropolis of Edo brought the mountain to new prominence during this period. Associated with immortality, the landmark became a popular pilgrimage site.[2]

Hokusai repeatedly returned to Fuji as a subject during his prolific career. *Fine Wind, Clear Day*, colloquially known as *Red Fuji*, is from his famed series *Thirty-Six Views of Mount Fuji*, which proved so popular during its time that the artist and his publisher produced ten additional designs to satisfy the public's desire, bringing the total number to forty-six. Deeply inspired by the mountain, Hokusai designed the illustrated book *One Hundred Views of Mount Fuji* only a few years later.

Hokusai's preoccupation is clear throughout *Thirty-Six Views of Mount Fuji*; the mountain is repeatedly rendered from differing vantage points and in different contexts and seasons. In another print, *The Sazai Hall of the Temple of the Five Hundred Arhats* (*Gohyaku Rakan-ji Sazaidō*), a diminutive Mount Fuji emerges from the horizon (fig. 51). A small crowd of men, women, and children have assembled on the veranda of Sazai Hall, part of the Zen temple Rakan-ji. This popular tourist destination in the city of Edo provided visitors with exceptional views of Mount Fuji from the unusual three-story building. Although the mountain appears in the far distance, a man on the far left points toward the deep blue peak and draws our attention to the true focus of Hokusai's composition.

The museum's impression of *Fine Wind, Clear Day* is particularly exquisite. The clean lines of the print and the delicate appearance of the wood grain indicate that it is an early impression. Although later printings, which exhibit bolder colors and stronger contrasts, seem to have been favored by early foreign collectors, this subtler version is perhaps closer to what was originally intended.[3] QHS

1. Smith 2005, 253.
2. Takeuchi 2002, 28–29.
3. The chronology of different printings and variants of *Fine Wind, Clear Day* has been of great interest to collectors. See Keyes 2007–8; and Nagoya et al. 2013–14, 194.

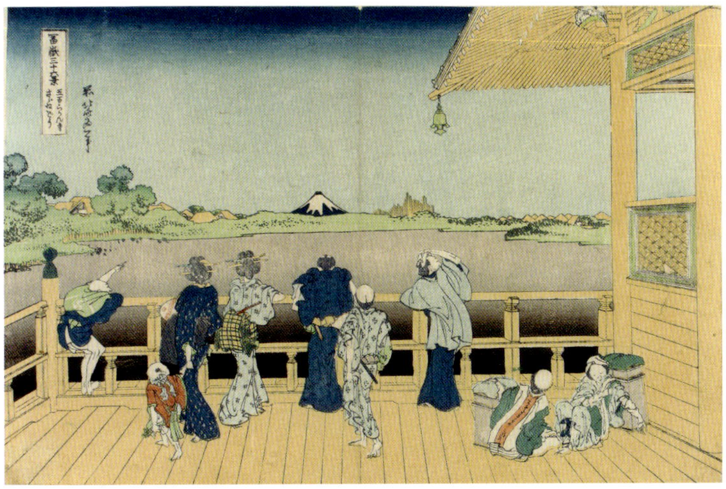

FIG. 51 Katsushika Hokusai. *The Sazai Hall of the Temple of the Five Hundred Arhats* (*Gohyaku Rakan-ji Sazaidō*). Edo period, c. 1831. Color woodblock print, 9¾ × 14¹³⁄₁₆ in. (24.8 × 37.6 cm). Philadelphia Museum of Art: The Samuel S. White 3rd and Vera White Collection, 1967-30-181

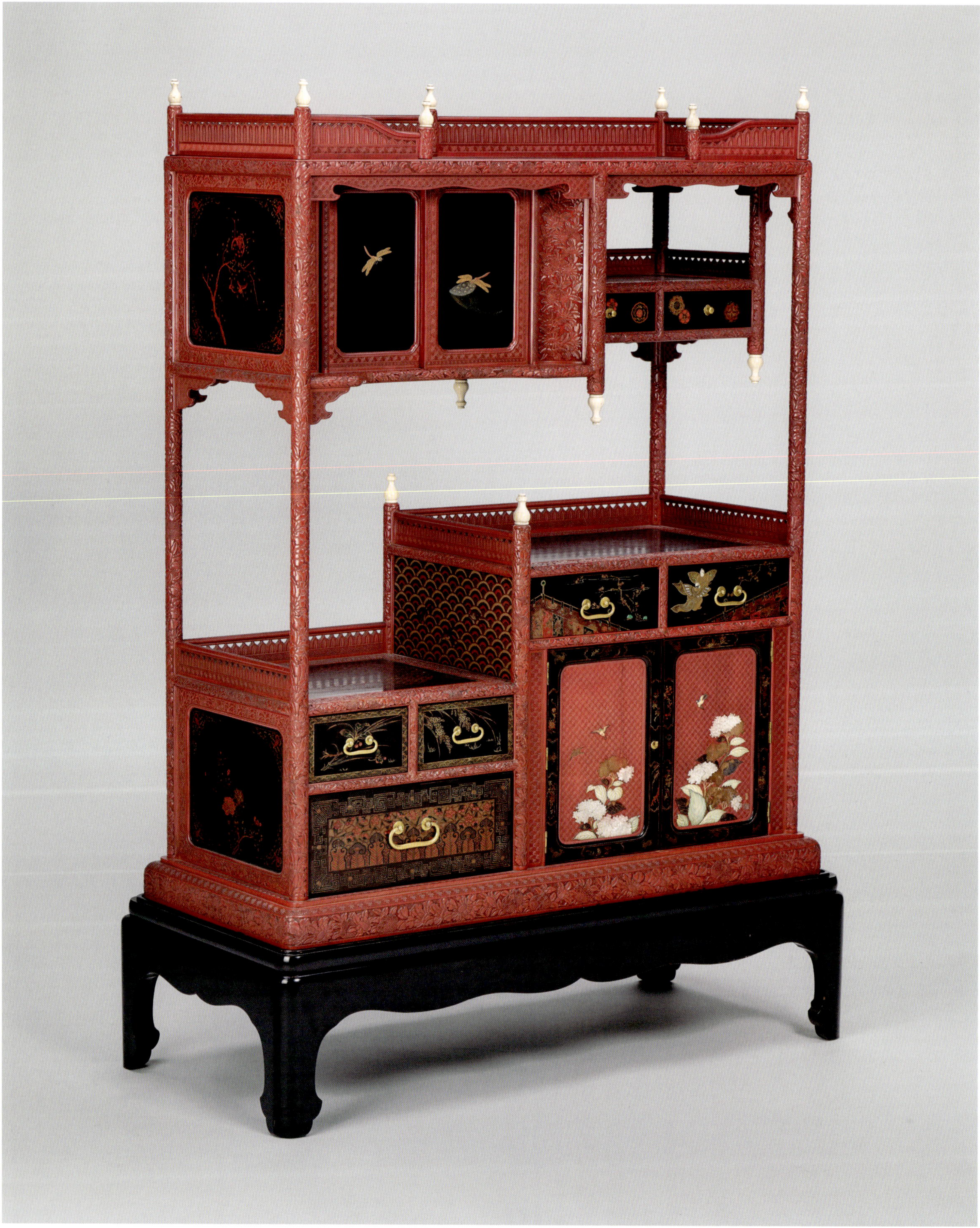

68

Cabinet

Meiji period (1868–1912), late 19th century

Lacquered wood with horn, *raden* (mother-of-pearl), jade, bronze, and malachite inlays; metal fittings; 64½ × 20⅞ × 44¾ in. (163.8 × 53 × 113.7 cm)

Purchased with Museum funds, 1876-1681

This decorative cabinet was exhibited at the 1876 Centennial International Exhibition in Philadelphia. After the Meiji Restoration in 1868, participation in international expositions offered the new government opportunities to show off Japan's national power. A Japanese pavilion was erected in the Philadelphia fair's main exhibition building in Fairmount Park and was used to showcase various arts and crafts including ceramics, lacquerwares, metalwork, and furniture. In addition, carpenters came from Japan to build a traditional Japanese house as a "bazaar," in which Japanese arts and crafts were sold (see fig. 2).[1] This cabinet was shown either in the main building or at the bazaar, and was purchased for the museum after the exposition.

The cabinet has *tuishu* decoration consisting of thickly coated red lacquerware with auspicious patterns of flowers, leaves, and pomegranates carved in relief, as well as black lacquer with patterns in gold and red. The decoration also includes inlaid designs of horn, *raden* (mother-of-pearl), jade, bronze, and malachite made using a technique known as *Shibayama shikki* (Shibayama lacquerware) or *Shibayama zōgan* (Shibayama inlay), developed by the late eighteenth-century artist Shibayama (Onoki) Senzō in Chiba and brought to Yokohama for the export trade following the Meiji Restoration.[2] Shibayama lacquerware is characterized by the three-dimensional appearance of the lacquered surface. With the opening of the Yokohama port in 1859, large numbers of lacquerwares, including Shibayama pieces, were exported to Europe and the United States, and these works became popular with Westerners.

This cabinet has seven drawers of various sizes, two cabinets, and three open shelves. Both doors of the cupboard at top are decorated with a dragonfly made of thick gold lacquer on red lacquer; the right door also features a lotus seedpod created with a delicate feather pattern. The bottom cupboard doors are each decorated with hydrangeas and a small bird in flight inlaid with white shells and ivory. Directly above, two drawers depict a scene from the "Butterflies" chapter of the eleventh-century *Tale of Genji*. Elsewhere on the cabinet the decoration includes the traditional wave pattern known as *seigaiha*, rice ears, pomegranate trees, fruits, and wild roses. Ivory finials are placed at the corners and joints of the cabinet, whose back is decorated with cloud patterns on a black lacquered ground.

Affixed to the cabinet's lower-right front corner is a small tag that reads "Sōichi," which probably records the name of the artist who made this cabinet using a combination of Chinese and Japanese design elements. A lacquer box with floral rondels in mother-of-pearl inlay in the Tokyo National Museum was made by Shibayama Sōichi (b. 1811) in 1892 and exhibited at the World's Columbian Exposition in Chicago in 1893.[3] He may be the same artist who created the Philadelphia Museum of Art's fine examples of Shibayama lacquerware (see also fig. 52). KK

1. Tōkyō Kokuritsu Bunkazai Kenkyūjo Bijutsubu 1997, 209, no. 133.
2. Numata 2005.
3. "Shibayama zōgan kobako, Tokyo-fu, Shibayama Sōichi" (Shibayama small inlay box by Shibayama Sōichi in Tokyo); Tōkyō Kokuritsu Bunkazai Kenkyūjo Bijutsubu 1997, 285, no. O-1457.

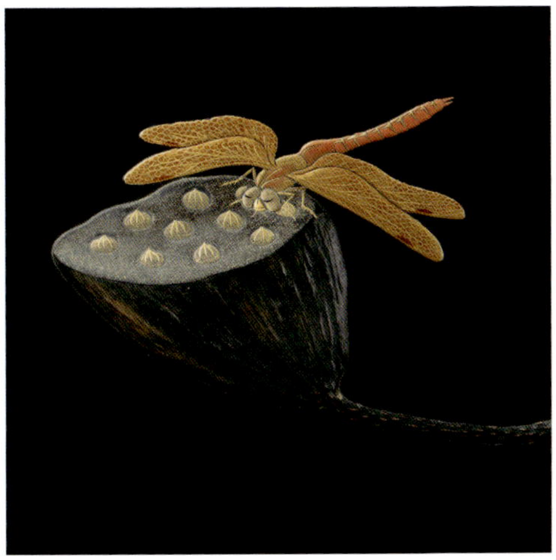

Detail of upper cabinet right-side door

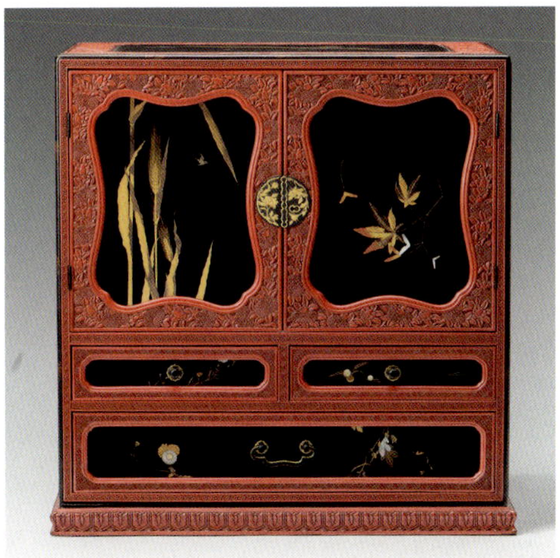

FIG. 52 Cabinet with Designs of Plants of the Four Seasons and Mount Fuji. Meiji period, 19th century. Carved lacquer on wood with painted decoration and *raden* (mother-of-pearl) inlay; metal fittings; 20 7/16 × 12⅝ × 19 in. (51.9 × 32 × 48.3 cm). Philadelphia Museum of Art: Gift of Miss Elizabeth C. Roberts, 1916-237

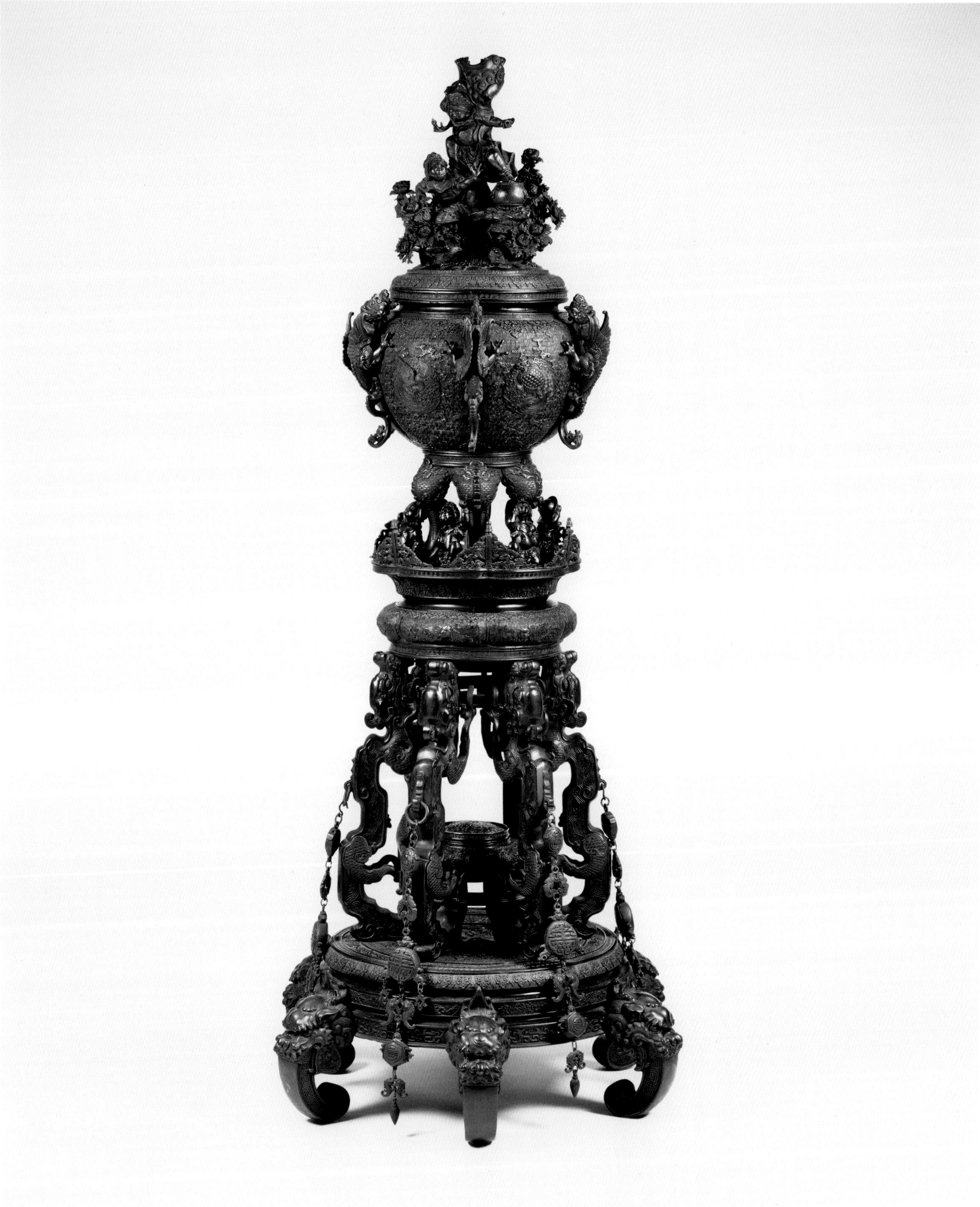

69

Urn and Stand

Meiji period (1868–1912), late 19th century

Cast bronze, 6 ft. 1¼ in. × 35¼ in. (186 × 90 cm)

The George W. B. Taylor Collection, bequest of Mrs. Mary E. Taylor, 1917-158,a;159

"The Japanese exhibit is a mine of wonders. Bronzes of the most exquisite workmanship and immense size, in the shape of animals, men, dragons, temples, vases," wrote Ernest Fenollosa about his impressions of the Philadelphia Centennial International Exhibition of 1876.[1] Indeed, the superb quality of casting and profusion of decorative motifs elicited widespread acclaim.[2]

Over six feet tall, this incense burner is an outstanding example of highly skilled casting, with intricate carved and chased decoration that was labor intensive and involved a team of talented, albeit anonymous metal artisans. The lid features a group of Chinese boys performing a lion dance amid peony blossoms. The Chinese theme continues on the body of the urn with applied dragon handles on a design field of auspicious symbols such as turtles and cranes.

The stand features upright dragons supporting the incense burner, with pendant chains all around and dragon-head feet. Even with the proliferation of ornament, the piece retains an effective overall balance that remains impressive. FF

1. Ernest F. Fenollosa, "Notes on a Visit to Centennial, September–October 1876," Ernest F. Fenollosa Papers, Houghton Library, Harvard University, Cambridge, MA. For more on Fenollosa, see Felice Fischer, "Philadelphia and the Art of Japan," in this volume.
2. For an effusive description, see McCabe 1975, 139.

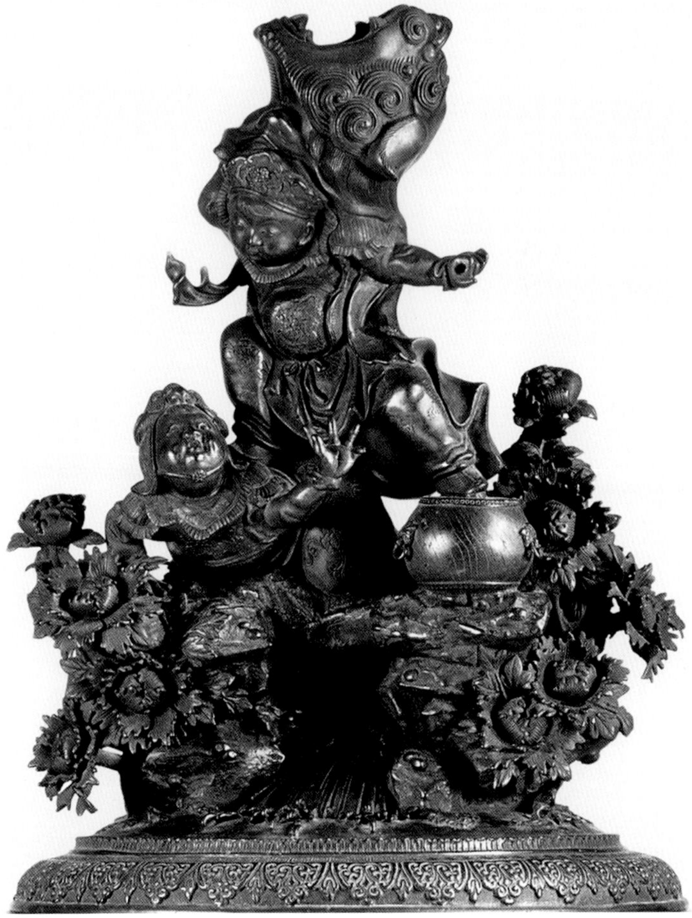

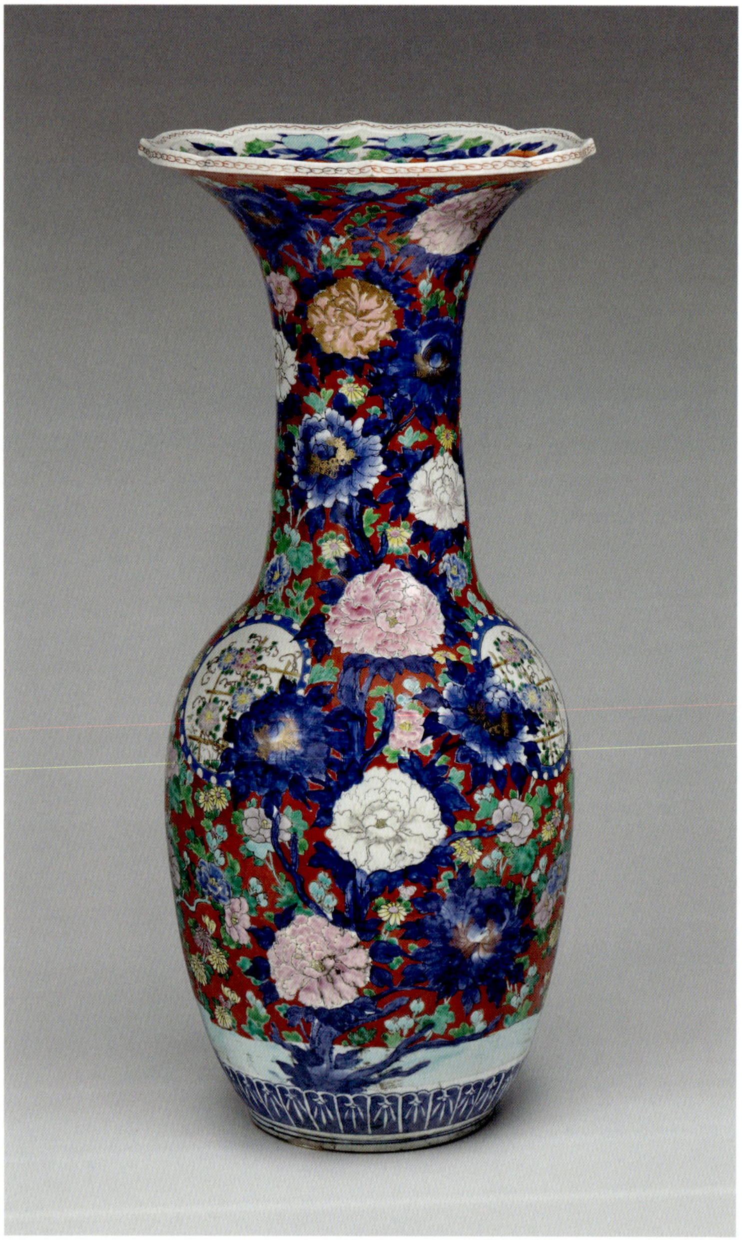

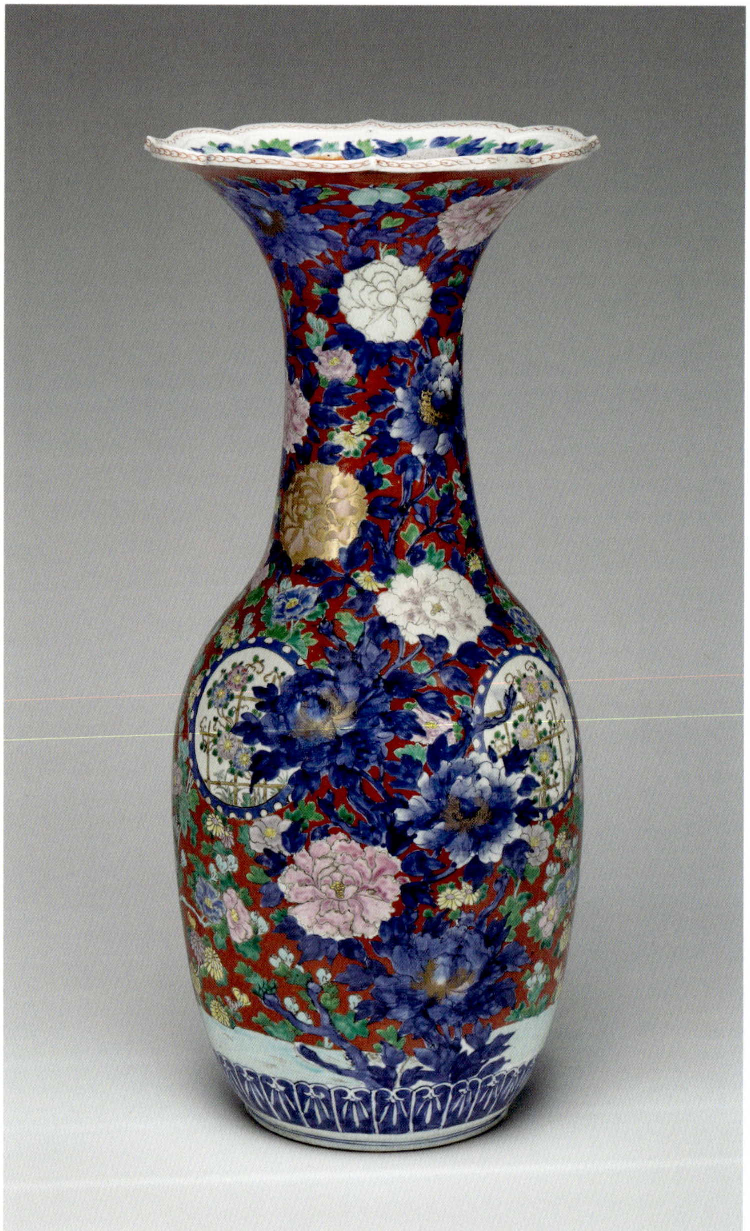

70

Pair of Vases

Fukagawa Eizaemon VIII
(1833–1889)

Meiji period (1868–1912), c. 1868–75

Porcelain with underglaze blue and overglaze enamel and gilt decoration (Arita ware), each: 27½ × 12⅜ in. (69.8 × 31.5 cm)

The General Hector Tyndale Memorial Collection, 1897-353,353a

In preparation for its participation in the first world's fair held in the United States, the Philadelphia Centennial International Exhibition of 1876, the Japanese government solicited crafts nationwide, and a selection was shipped to the exposition. Ceramics filled the largest area in the over seventeen thousand square feet of space allotted the Japanese exhibits, with separate displays for wares from the regional kilns. Among the leading producers of ceramics in the Arita area in Kyushu was the Fukagawa family, headed at that time by Fukagawa Eizaemon VIII, whose signature appears on the base of this pair of vases. In 1875 Fukagawa joined several other manufacturers of ceramics to form a joint company called Kōransha to produce and market their wares for the Centennial Exhibition.[1]

The fair's judges, including General Hector Tyndale, the donor of these vases, acclaimed the technical feats of the Japanese potters, who garnered the lion's share of prizes among the ceramic displays. After the close of the exhibition, Tyndale purchased a large number of ceramics, including this pair of vases, which impressed him not only by their size but by their well-executed design. The vases are decorated with intricate floral motifs in overglaze enamels and gilding along the foliate lip rim. The deep blue underglaze color was obtained from the mineral cobalt. From the 1870s on, synthetic cobalt became popular because of its lower cost, although some potters may have continued to use natural cobalt for important pieces such as these vases. FF

---

1. The partnership dissolved in 1879, and the Fukagawa family has retained the Kōransha name for their ceramic production to the present day.

71

Farming Scenes of the Four Seasons

Kano Sōeki Kagenobu
(act. late 18th–mid-19th century)

Edo period (1615–1868),
late 18th–early 19th century

Ink and color on paper, mounted as a pair of six-fold screens; each: 55⅛ in. × 10 ft. 8¾ in. (140 × 327 cm)

Purchased with the Hollis Fund for East Asian Art Acquisitions, 2016-194-11a,b

The painted decoration on this pair of screens illustrates the farming scenes of the four seasons, an important theme depicted by many Kano-school artists during the Muromachi (1392–1573) and Edo periods. The oldest surviving works with these scenes in Japan are *fusuma* (sliding door) paintings made for the Daisen-in, a sub-temple of the Daitoku-ji in Kyoto. According to historical temple records, the artist Kano Utanosuke Yukinobu (act. first half of the sixteenth century) made the paintings for the building's *rai no ma* (lower room), the reception room closest to the entrance, in 1513; the paintings were later mounted as a set of hanging scrolls, which are now in the Tokyo National Museum.[1]

In China the agricultural ideal that "men till the land and women weave cloth" was pictured as a moralizing image in the imperial court. As governor of Lin'an (present-day Hangzhou), Lou Shou (1090–1162) was concerned with agriculture, and he painted

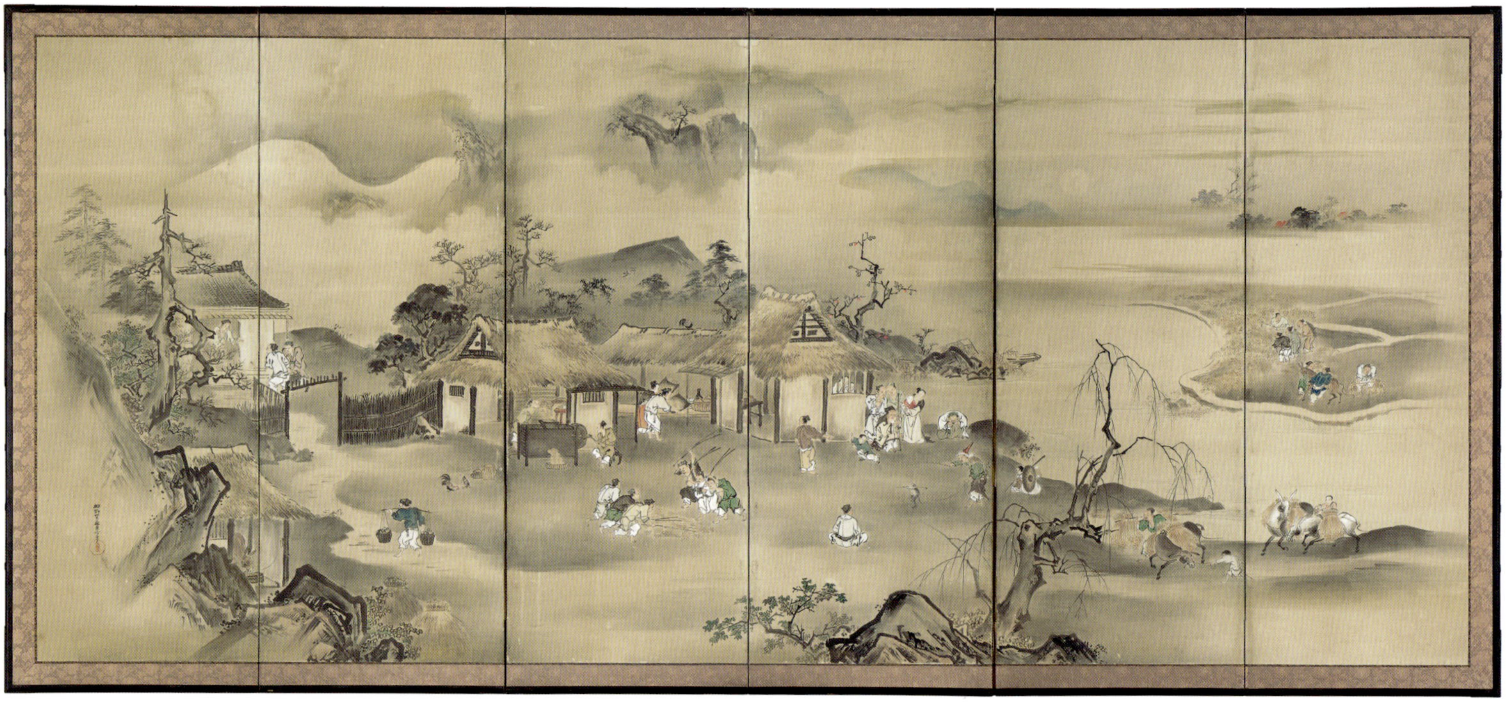

twenty-one scenes of rice cultivation and twenty-four scenes of sericulture (silk farming), each accompanied by eight lines of five-syllable verse. He presented this set of paintings, the *Gengzhi tu* (Pictures of agriculture and sericulture), to Emperor Gaozong (r. 1127–62) in the 1130s. In 1462 the *Gengzhi tu* was published as a set of two printed books, which was circulated widely and exported to Japan. Chinese court painters began to make paintings of these agricultural themes, and a handscroll by Liang Kai (c. 1140–c. 1210) was brought to Japan during the Muromachi period. In Japan the farming scenes were in higher demand than those of sericulture, and the former appeared as an independent subject for paintings on sliding doors, folding screens, and votive tablets.[2]

In the right screen of the museum's pair, Kano Sōeki Kagenobu, a painter who belonged to the Kanda Matsunaga-cho Kano, one of the branches of the Kano family, depicted farmers tilling the fields with water buffalo, soaking and spreading seeds, and replanting seedlings during the spring and summer. The left screen features scenes of harvesting, threshing, milling, and storing the grain in autumn and winter. A talented genre painter, Sōeki Kagenobu focused on the facial expressions and movements of the human figures while following the iconography of earlier painters, as seen here in his lyrical depictions of boys scooping fish from a river and village people sheltering under an umbrella from a sudden summer shower. Another pair of six-fold screens with farming scenes of the four seasons by Sōeki Kagenobu is in a private collection on loan to the Division of Local History of Fujisawa City in Kanagawa.[3]

Sōeki Kagenobu was commissioned for *fusuma* paintings in several rooms of the Hon'maru (Main) and Nishinomaru (Western) palaces of the Edo castle in 1844 and 1852, respectively.[4] However, there is very limited information about the artist. His father was Bokusen Eishin, who was active from about 1830 to 1844.[5] Sōeki Kagenobu seems to have become the head of the Kanda Matsunagacho Kano after his father's retirement or death, and it is likely that he got permission to use his father's artist name of Bokusen. The first appearance of Sōeki Kagenobu's name as Bokusen Sōeki is in the section on the Kano family in the 1840 edition of the *Shūgyoku bukan*, a pocket book containing information on the Tokugawa shogunate bureaucrats. He is listed as the Tokugawa shogunate official painter, documenting him as one of the most important Kano artists of the late Edo period. KK

1. Reizei et al. 1996, 12–17.
2. Philadelphia 2015a, 259.
3. Takahashi 2022.
4. Asaoka 1850.
5. Yamashita 2004, appendix. The name Bokusen Eishin appears from the 1817 until the 1837 editions of the *Shūgyoku bukan* (on this, see text above).

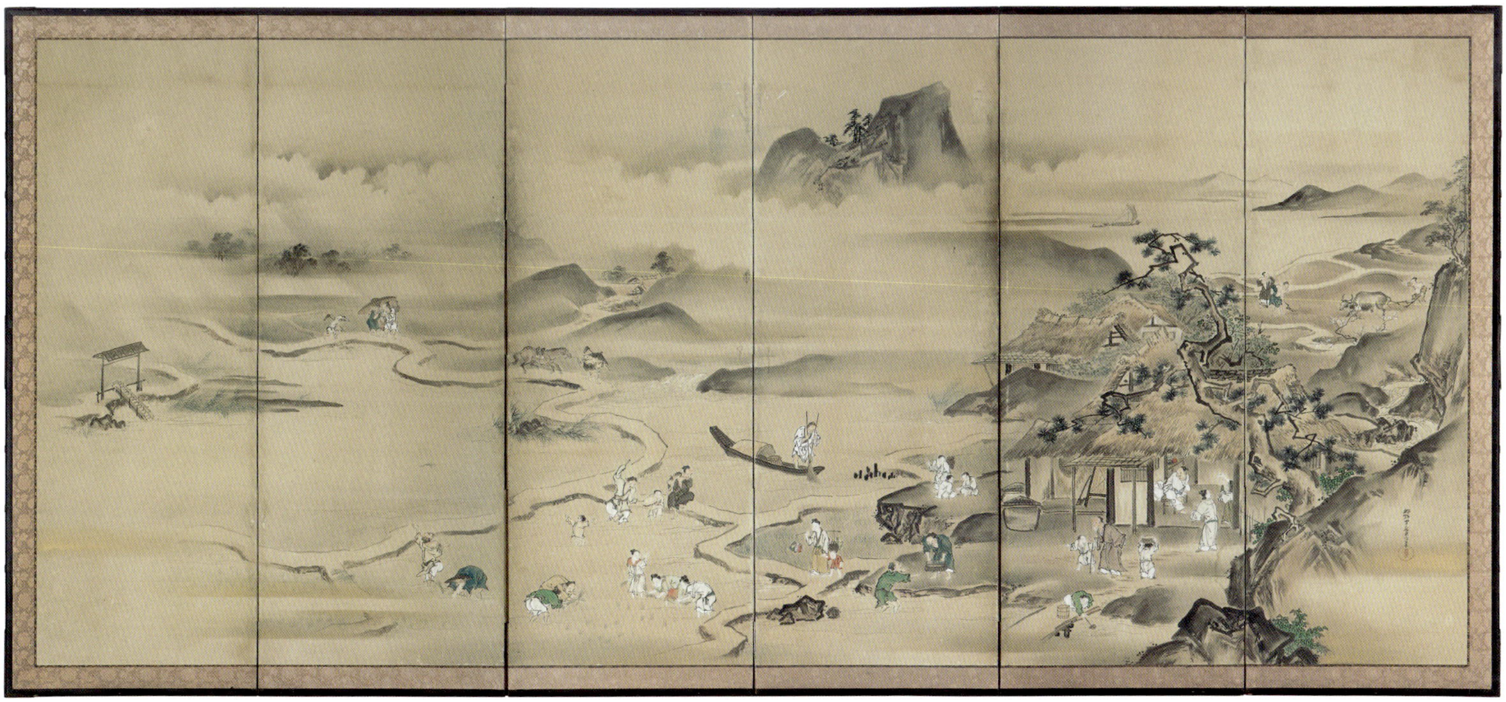

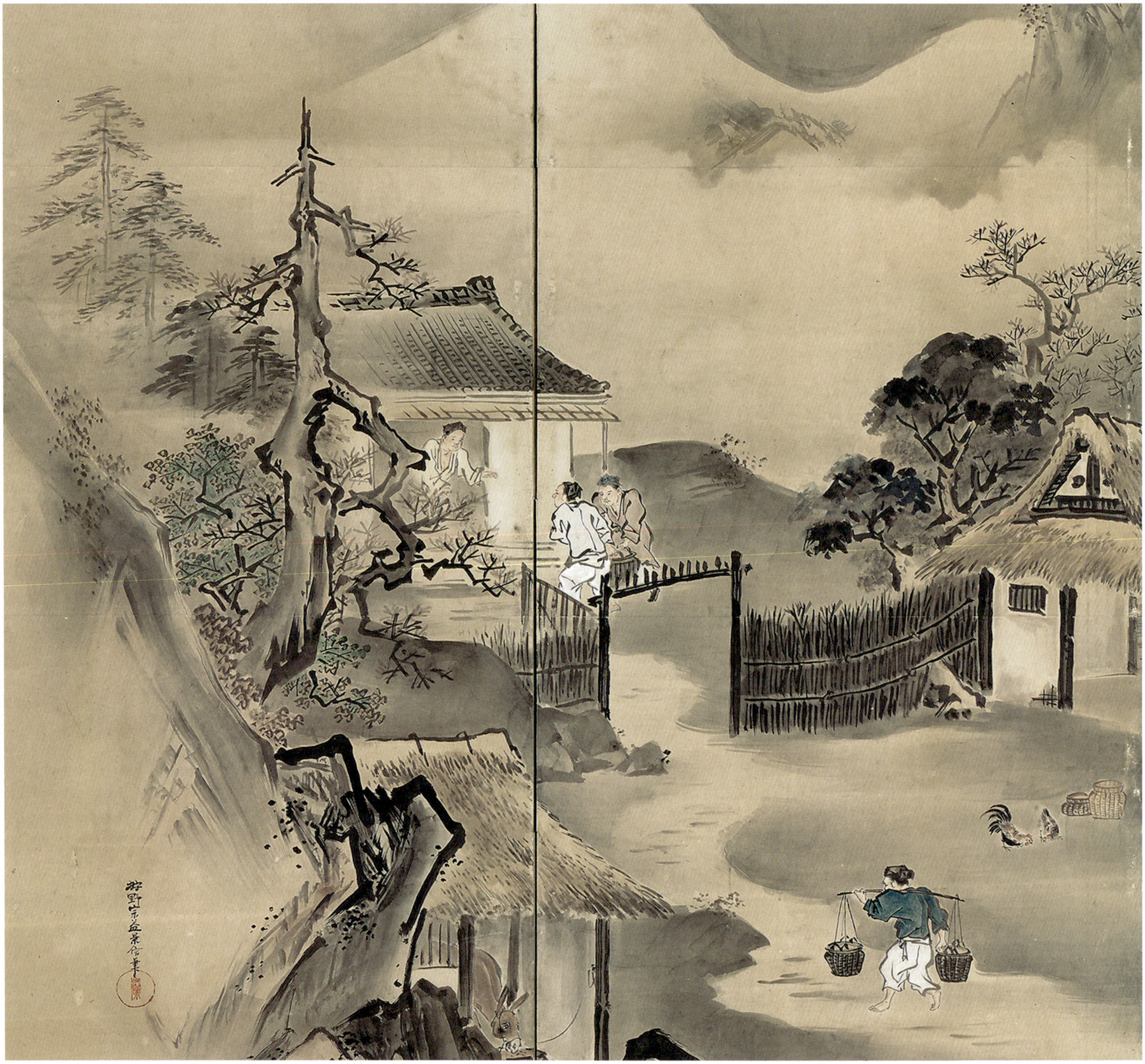

Detail of no. 71 (left screen)

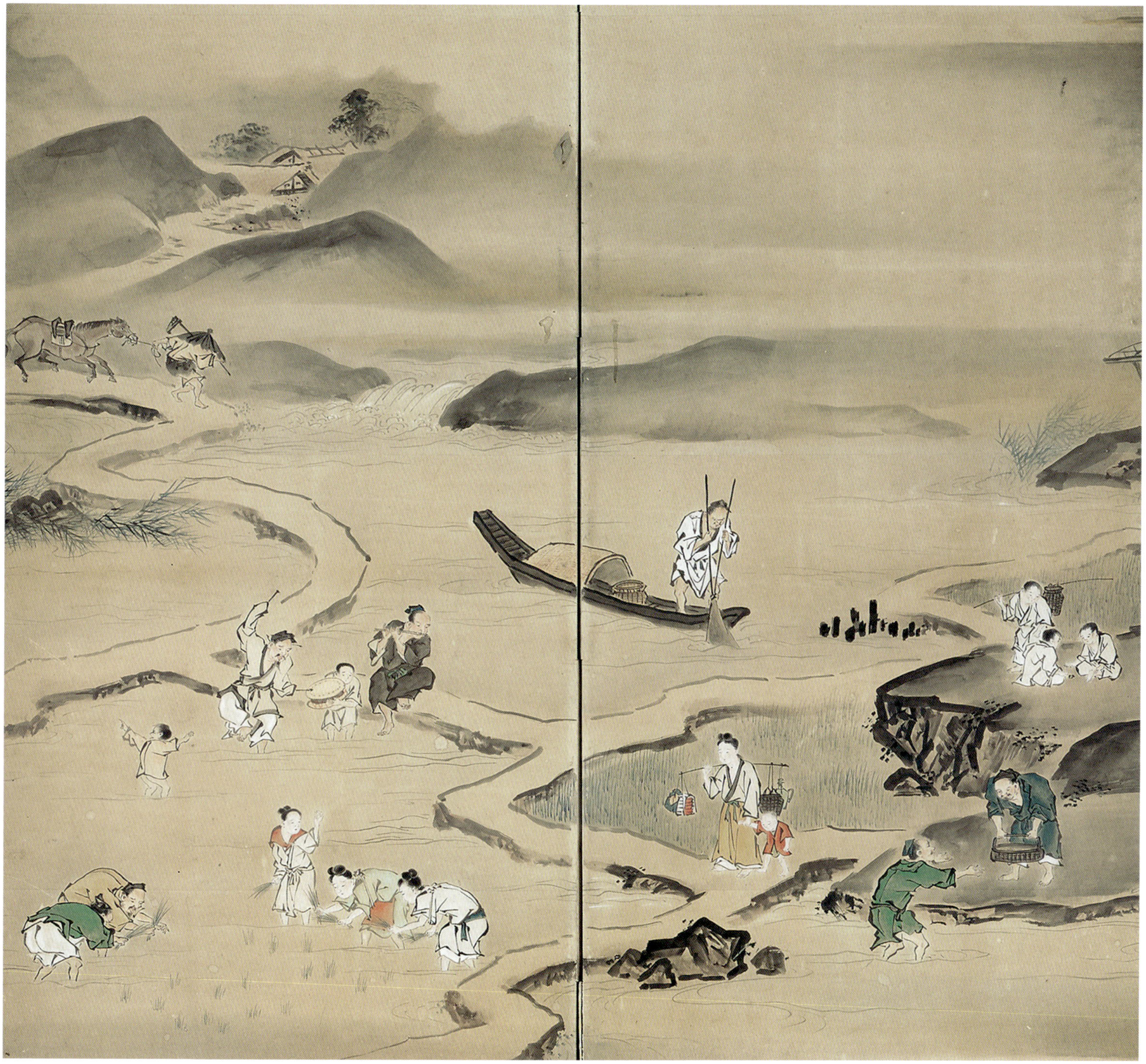

Detail of no. 71 (right screen)

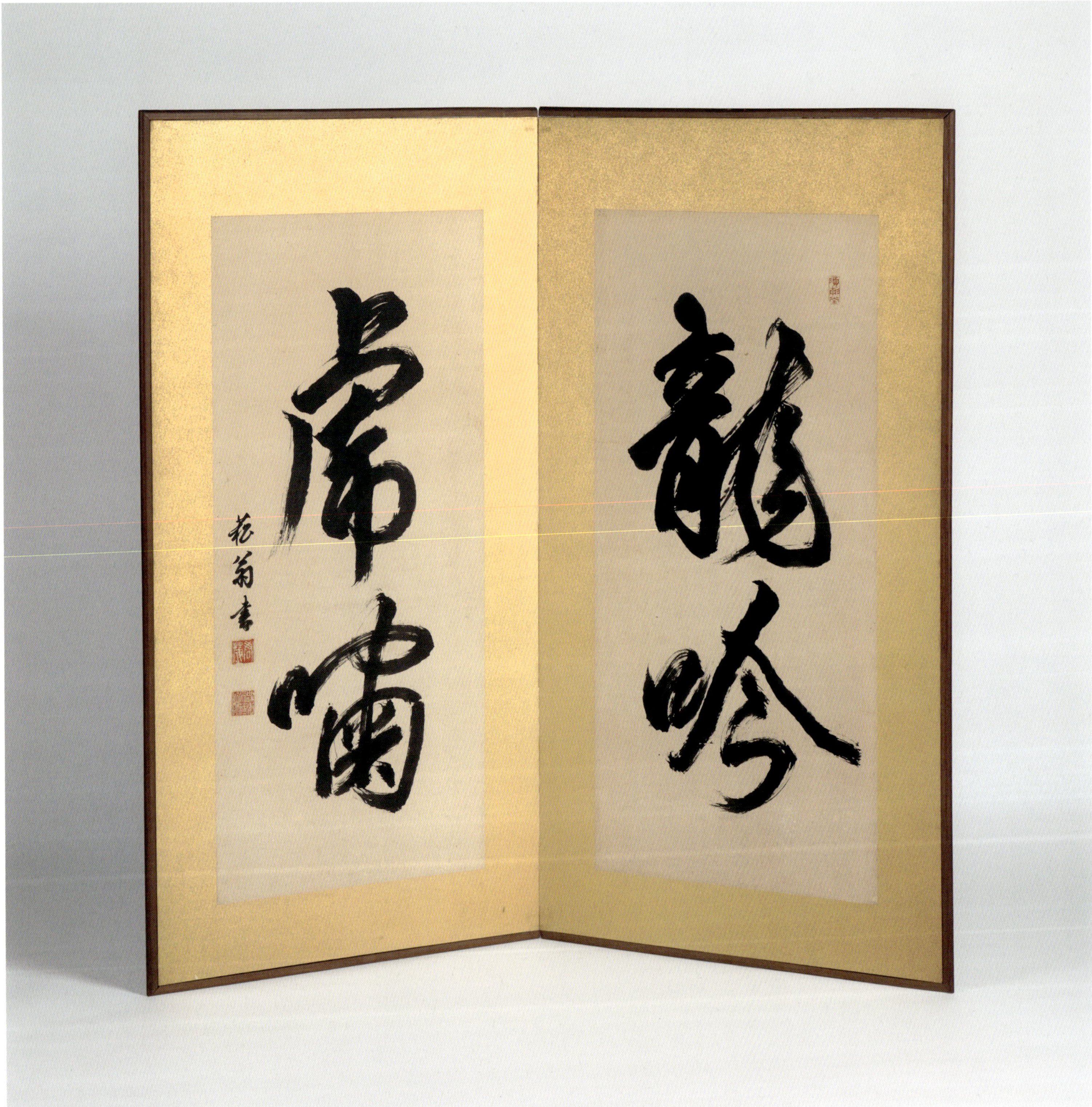
龍吟
虎嘯

72

The Dragon Sings, the Tiger Roars

Nukina Kaioku
(1778–1863)

Edo period (1615–1868), c. 1850

Ink on paper, mounted as a two-fold screen; overall (including frame): 64½ × 66¼ in. (163.8 × 168.3 cm)

Purchased with the George W. B. Taylor Fund, and with funds contributed by Mr. and Mrs. Warren H. Watanabe, funds (by exchange) from the Blanchard Fund and the Thomas Skelton Harrison Fund, and with gifts (by exchange) of Mrs. Frank Thorne Patterson, Mrs. Harald Paumgarten, the Simon A. Stern Collection, Mrs. David Townsend in memory of her husband, and Mrs. Albert Weimer, 1992-13-1

Painter and calligrapher Nukina Kaioku was a leading Confucian scholar in Kyoto. Born to a samurai family, he received a thorough Confucian education and cultivated an appreciation of Chinese calligraphic traditions by following literati masters of the Jin (266–420) and Tang (618–907) dynasties. When he received the Shingon esoteric Buddhist training on Mount Kōya, he also carefully studied the calligraphy of the priest Kūkai (774–835), known as Kōbō Daishi (see no. 16). A broad appreciation of Chinese classical studies and solid artistic practices helped Kaioku develop his calligraphy style, earning him high praise as one of the so-called *Bakumatsu no sanpitsu*, the Three Brushes of the late Edo period.[1]

Calligraphy in the East Asian tradition is valued for revealing the writer's personality or inner mind. In this boldly executed work mounted as a folding screen, Kaioku used his favorite style, the semi-cursive, which calls attention to the force and tension represented in classical writings. The rough and dramatic calligraphy matches well with the size of the screen to make a powerful visual impression. The kanji (Chinese) characters that appear on each panel read "dragon sings" on the right and "tiger roars" on the left. Along the left edge, Kaioku signed Sūō (Old Man Pine), one of the names he used after the age of seventy.

Kaioku's characters are executed in an orthodox Tang-dynasty Chinese writing tradition, clearly influenced by the *karayō* (Chinese) and the *Daishi-ryū* (after Kōbō Daishi) styles of fluent yet exaggeratedly twisted characters. Here the characters for "dragon" and "tiger" take the place of the common depiction of the animals themselves on East Asian screens. The characters for "sings" and "roars" give a sense of sound to the composition. In East Asian Buddhist tradition, the dragon and tiger symbolize spiritual freedom (figs. 53a,b). By creating his own visual and aural images for the two creatures, Kaioku used calligraphy as a verbal sign to invite the viewer's participation in a creative mind-awakening process. YX

1. The other two were Ichikawa Beian (1779–1858) and Maki Ryōko (1777–1843).

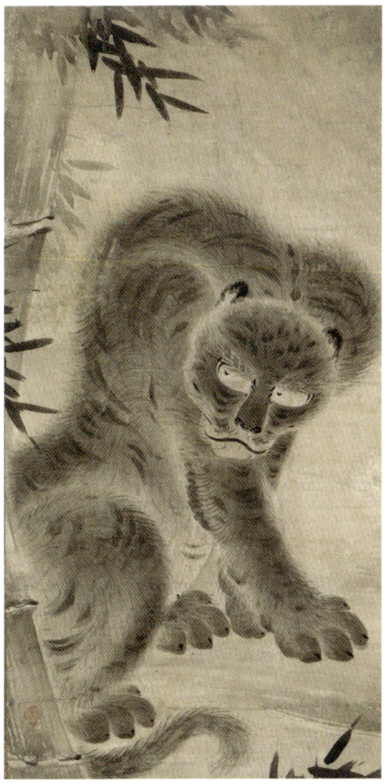

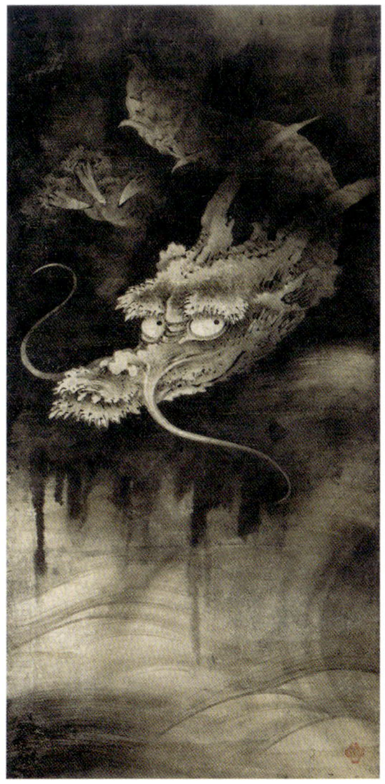

FIGS. 53A,B Attributed to Kano Motonobu (c. 1477–1559). *Tiger* and *Dragon*. Muromachi period (1392–1573), late 15th–early 16th century. Ink and color on paper, mounted as a hanging scroll; each: 33¼ × 17¼ in. (84.5 × 43.8 cm). Philadelphia Museum of Art, 125th Anniversary Acquisition: Purchased with the Edith H. Bell Fund, the Edward and Althea Budd Fund, the Hollis Family Foundation Fund, the J. Stogdell Stokes Fund, and the East Asian Art Revolving Fund, 2000-114-1,2

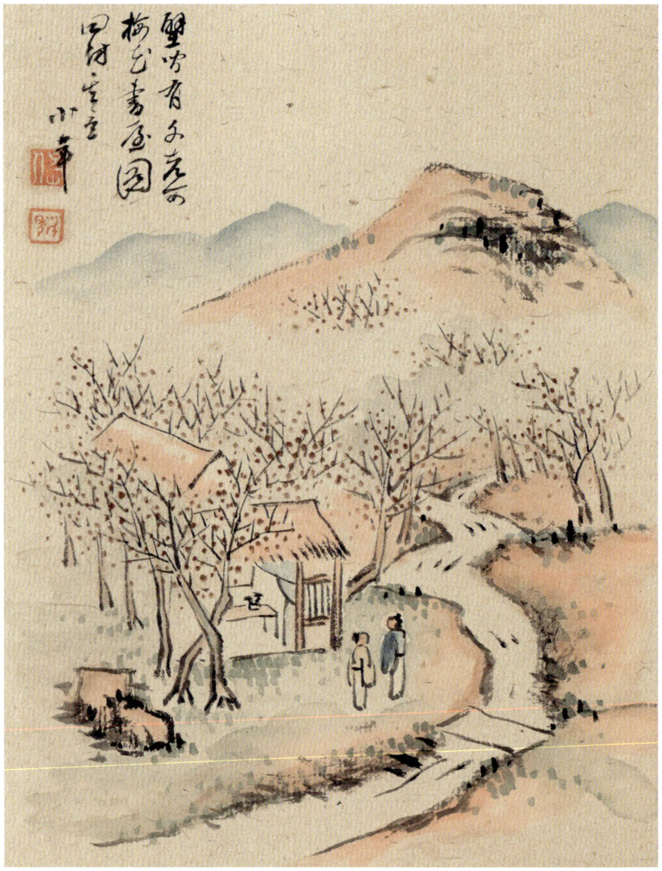

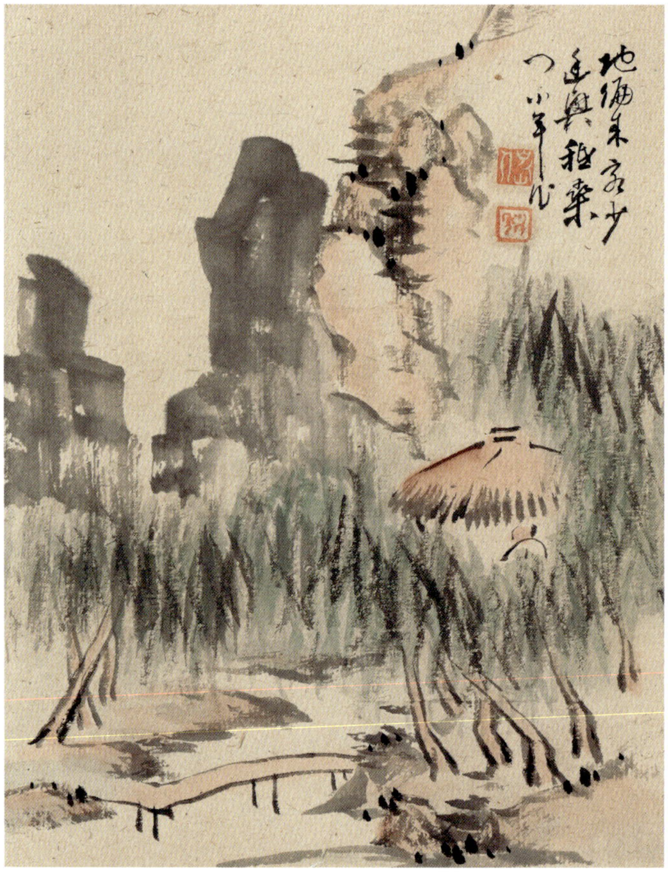

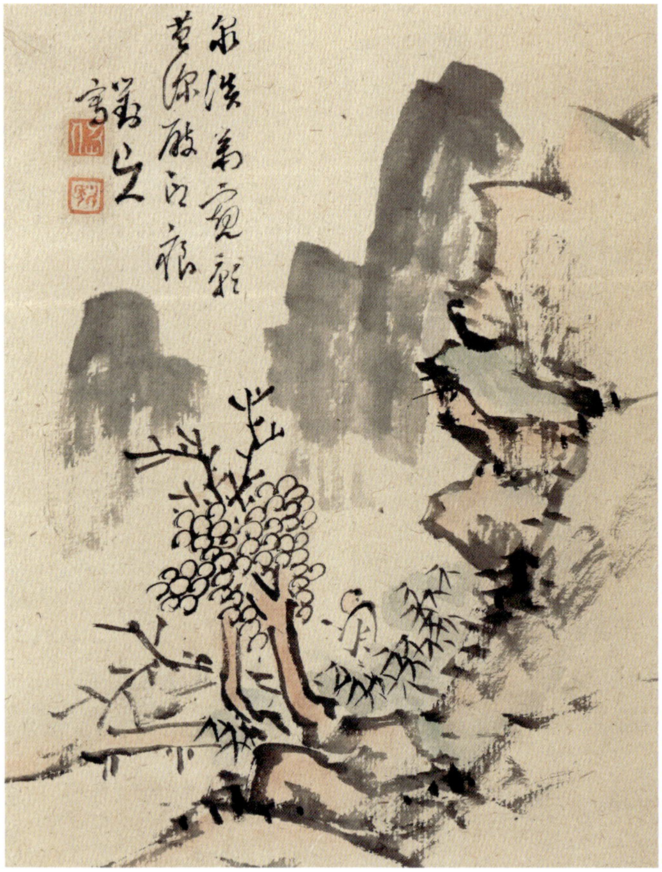

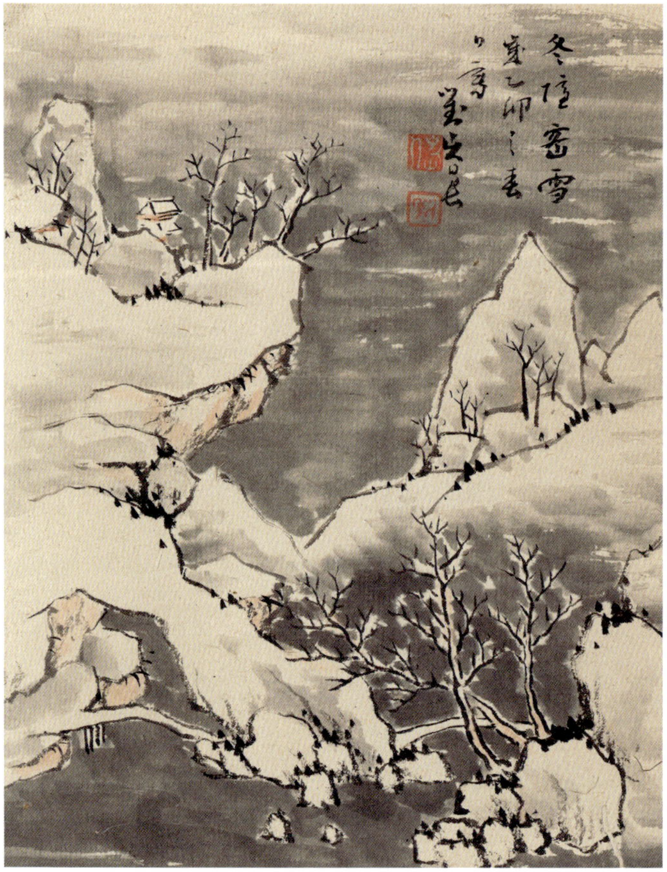

73

Album of Landscapes

Hine Taizan
(1814–1869)

Edo period (1615–1868), 1855

Ink and color on paper, mounted as an album; each leaf: 9½ × 7½ in. (24.1 × 19 cm)

Purchased with funds contributed by Maxine and Howard H. Lewis, and Mr. and Mrs. Peter A. Benoliel, 1998-52-1

Paintings collected within the format of a book-like album are popularly assembled and exchanged among scholar-artists' circles within the East Asian tradition. Such albums often are dedicated to an individual artist or their group for display. While the works in an album are usually small in size, the configuration embeds a sense of intimacy encouraging close appreciation at convivial gatherings. This painting album contains twelve landscapes by the celebrated literati artist Hine Taizan, who was active in Kyoto. He likely completed the paintings after studying the work of old masters, and they were later compiled by acclaimed Japanese calligraphers in the early twentieth century.

The style in which Taizan painted is known as Nanga, or Southern painting, whose liberated and expressive manner was influenced by Chinese literati painting. Taizan was among the literati who shared a profound understanding of Confucian philosophy as embedded in Chinese history, literature, and poetry. He was a student of the renowned Confucian scholar Nukina Kaioku (1778–1863; see no. 72), with whom he also studied calligraphy. In this album, Taizan's paintings and calligraphy work together to demonstrate his appreciation of the natural and spontaneous quality of ink and brush. With his distinctive painting techniques enlivening the poetic sentiment in landscapes, he invites the viewer on a journey across time and space. Beginning in the spring at a plum-sheltered cottage and a remote mulberry-field gate, we then indulge in the refreshing summer views of mountains, streams, and *wutong* trees after rain. Beyond the autumn mist and quiet woods, we hear the songs of hidden birds and a distant temple bell. In winter's darkness, we stop to view the deep moss at the foot of snowy mountain peaks.[1]

Taizan's calligraphic training can be seen in his vigorous diffusion of ink across the landscapes, leading the viewer to experience seasonal changes throughout a single year by opening and folding the album's leaves. The painter and calligrapher Murata Kōkoku (1831–1912), who studied with Taizan under Kaioku, wrote the back colophon in 1889 to express his admiration,[2] while the renowned poet and literati painter Ema Tenkō (1825–1902) signed the front colophon.[3] The title strip of the album's outer cover was signed by the Meiji calligrapher Chō Sanshū (1833–1895).[4] With recognition from these three exceptional artists and calligraphers, this album was preserved as a treasured asset for the appreciation of Taizan's artistic mastery. YX

1. See the Documentation (pp. 257–58) for translations of the paintings' inscriptions.
2. Kōkoku was born in Fukuoka, Kyushu, but mainly lived in Osaka. He studied under the literati painters Hidaka Tetsuō (1791–1871) and Kaioku.
3. Tenkō was a poet and literati painter who studied under the well-known calligrapher and poet Yanagawa Seigan (1789–1858) and served the Meiji government as a historian.
4. One of the outstanding calligraphers of the Meiji period (1868–1912), Sanshū was responsible for the calligraphic exercise books used in Japanese schools.

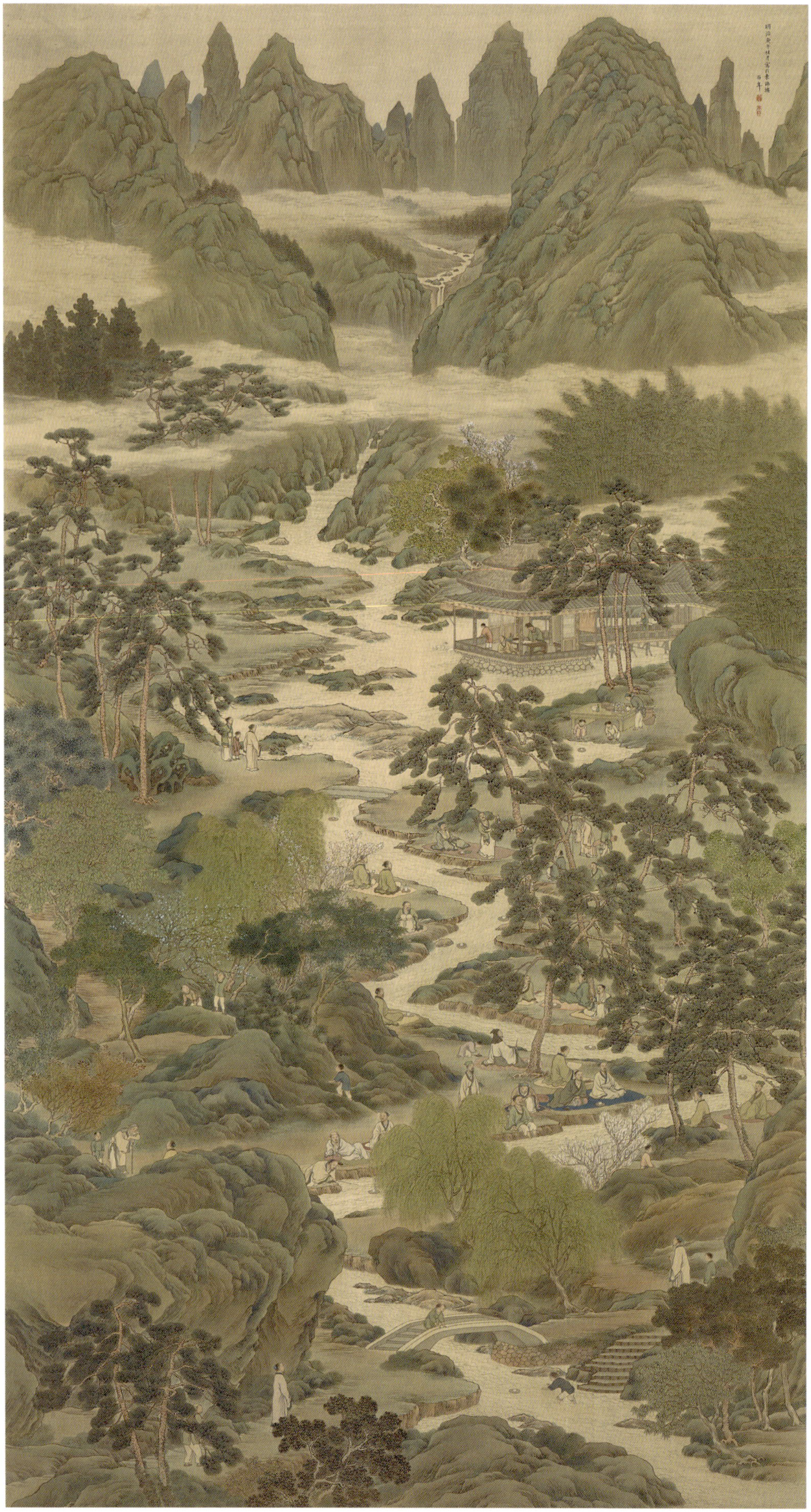

74

Orchid Pavilion Outing

Suzuki Hyakunen
(1825–1891)

Meiji period (1868–1912), 1870

Ink and color on silk, mounted as a hanging scroll; 64½ × 34⅝ in. (163.8 × 87.9 cm)

Gift of Mr. and Mrs. Ralph Balestrieri, 1963-47-1

Suzuki Hyakunen carried the Chinese-style literati painting tradition into the late nineteenth century. He was born in Kyoto as the son of Suzuki Seikai (or Sekō; 1782–1862), a well-known scholar of Confucianism, astronomy, and the art of divination.[1] As a child, Suzuki studied Confucianism and Chinese poetry but also showed a talent for painting, and Seikai asked him to copy maps of the earth for Seikai's study of astronomy. Suzuki was given the artist name Hyakunen by his father around the age of fourteen, and he began his training as a painter by studying with Gantai (1782–1865) and Kishi Renzan (1804–1859). At the age of nineteen, Hyakunen was commissioned by the imperial palace to paint a *sugito* (wooden sliding door) with illustrations of white plum blossoms and a parrot, as well as a pair of screens. In the years following, even after the Meiji Restoration in 1868, he continued to receive imperial orders.[2]

With the opening of the Kyoto Prefectural School of Painting in 1880, Hyakunen was appointed deputy professor of a course on Northern Song–dynasty (960–1127) painting, but he resigned shortly thereafter. He chose to become active as a literati artist (*bunjin*) and traveled across Japan to find subjects for his painting.

The theme of *Orchid Pavilion Outing* derives from an episode on the third day of the third month of 353, when a group of forty-two Chinese poets and scholars met at the Orchid Pavilion in Lanzhu, near Shaoxing in southeast China, to compose poems while seated on the banks of a winding stream. This event became famous through the preface to the collection of poems written by the event's host, Wang Xizhi (303–361), and emerged as a favorite subject for Japanese literati artists into the late nineteenth century (see no. 78, where the scene for the third month depicts a variation on this theme).

Within his dramatic landscape of steep mountains and a meandering stream bordered by pines and willows, Hyakunen carefully depicted a variety of vegetation and human figures. The inscription on the painting reads, "Painted in the eighth month of the kōgo [horse] year of Meiji [1870] by Tōkinrō [Eastern Brocade Tower], Hyakunen." Tōkinrō is Hyakunen's other artist name. In the *Heian jinbutsu-shi* (Who's who in old Kyoto) of the Keiō third edition, published in 1867, Hyakunen's home address is given as Shijō Takakura Nishi (located east of the Nishiki Market). The Chinese characters for "east" and "Nishiki" can be read as "tō" and "kin," from which he may have created the name Tōkinrō. In 1876 Hyakunen's painting *Gunkin-zu* (*Flock of Birds*) was exhibited at the Japanese pavilion of the Centennial International Exhibition in Philadelphia, and his name appears as Kyoto Suzuki Hyakunen in the exhibition list.[3] Hyakunen's paintings were also exhibited at the Pari Nihon Bijutsu Jurankai (Japanese art exhibition in Paris) in 1882 and 1884,[4] which was organized by bureaucrats in Japan's art and culture administration, including Sano Tsunetami (1823–1902) and Kuki Ryūichi (1852–1931). Hyakunen was one of the important representative painters of Japanese art in the early Meiji period. KK

—

1. Akō City 2006, 6.
2. Matsuo 2003.
3. Akō City 2006, 89; Tōkyō Kokuritsu Bunkazai Kenkyūjo Bijutsubu 1997, 219.
4. Akō City 2006, 90.

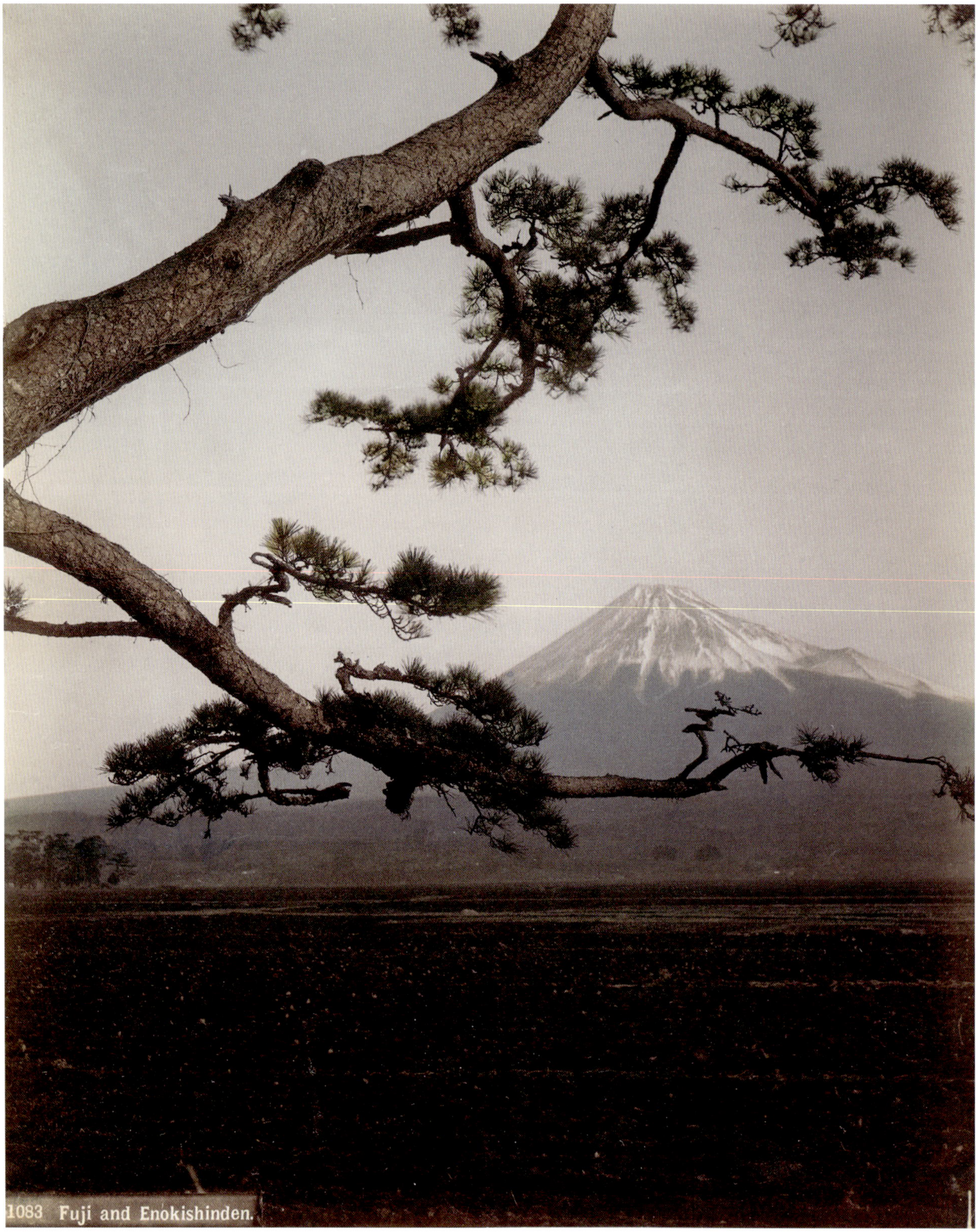
1083 Fuji and Enokishinden.

75

Untitled (Album of Japanese Photographs)

Various Artists

Meiji period (1868–1912), c. 1876–78

Album of albumen silver prints, many hand-colored
Album: 12¾ × 10⁵⁄₁₆ × 2½ in. (32.4 × 26.2 × 6.4 cm)

Gift of an anonymous donor, 2005-186-3

By the mid-nineteenth century, advances in transportation allowed more people in Europe and the United States to explore the world. Travels to new lands were frequently documented in travelogues, diaries, commentaries, and novels, among the most famous examples being Jules Verne's *Around the World in Eighty Days*, first published as a serial in 1872. For many travelers, photography offered an ideal way to record their experiences abroad. Commercial photographers offered high-quality prints of famous places while travelers could also take pictures with their portable cameras. Compiling travel images into albums became a popular practice to remember and show off these journeys.

The 273-page album in the museum's collection includes an array of photographs, the majority of which are views of Japan, although other parts of the world, including China, Egypt, and India, are also represented. The compiler may have traveled to all these locations. Commercially produced by local photographers as souvenirs, all the images were made using the wet-collodion process with glass plates, and many of the prints were meticulously hand-colored. Along the bottom edge of each of the Japanese photographs are a number and descriptive name, which buyers likely used to select the images from a catalogue.

Among the views of the Japanese landscape in this album are places of historical importance and famous landmarks, such as Mount Fuji, as seen in the image illustrated here. Already a popular theme in Japanese landscape imagery, the volcanic mountain was recognized by many foreign travelers as a symbol of Japan. Also represented are everyday scenes that document local customs, occupations, festivals, and seasonal events. Some of the photographs present sights that visitors to Japan would have found exotic, such as women wearing kimono or men in samurai armor. At the same time, images of European-style brick buildings and train stations represent the latest developments of the country's industrialization. Together the images offer multiple perspectives into contemporary Japanese society and culture. NA

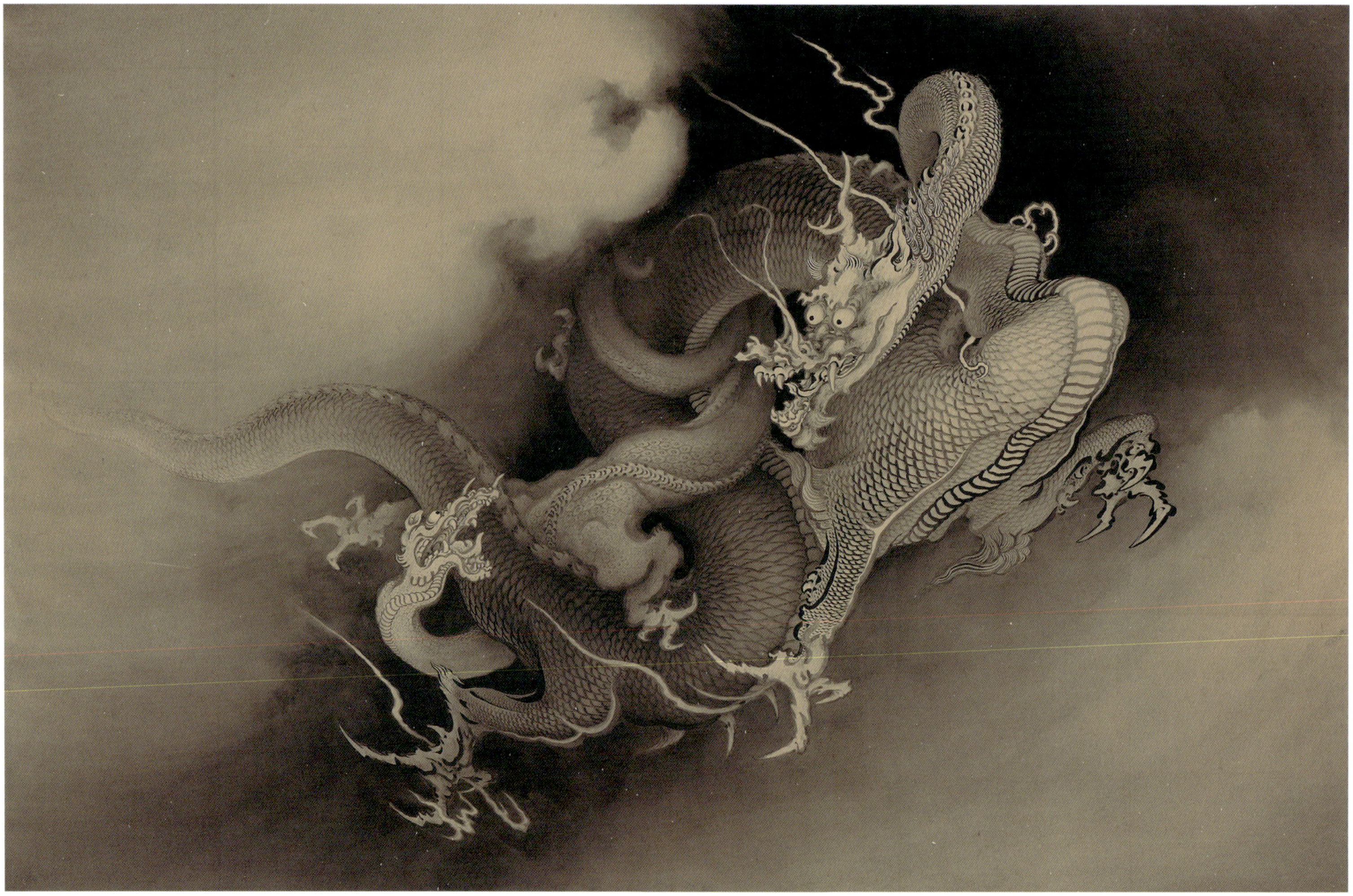

76

Two Dragons in Clouds

Kano Hōgai
(1828–1888)

Meiji period (1868–1912), 1885

Ink on paper, 35½ × 53¼ in.
(90.2 × 135.3 cm)

Gift of Mrs. Moncure Biddle
in memory of her father,
Ernest F. Fenollosa, 1940-41-1

Kano Hōgai exhibited this monumental painting of two dragons in Tokyo in 1886 at the Second Exhibition of the Painting Appreciation Society (Kangakai), of which he was a founding member.[1] It was acquired by the educator and collector Ernest F. Fenollosa (1853–1908) and held pride of place among the art installed at his residence (fig. 54). Fenollosa had been instrumental in founding the Kangakai in 1884, and he promoted the works of contemporary Kano artists such as Hōgai through the society's exhibitions. Fenollosa's ideal was the synthesis of Japanese traditional painting modes with European and American techniques such as perspective, reflected here in Hōgai's masterful fusion of East and West. The use of a Western-style frame to encase a painting on paper emphasizes the intent as well.

The subject of dragons dates back to at least China's Zhou dynasty (c. 1050–256 BCE). Hogai's two dragons writhe with dramatic energy amid swirling clouds in a darkened sky, suggesting a cosmic grandeur. In contrast, the features of the dragons, particularly the minutely described scales, are rendered with naturalistic accuracy (if that term can be applied to mythical animals), flowing with the twists and turns of the creatures' bodies. The sense of three-dimensionality and foreshortening of the dragons' forms reflects Hōgai's familiarity with the use of Western perspective and chiaroscuro, but his use of sumi ink brushed on paper is rooted in Japanese tradition. Hōgai's depiction of an adult as well as a young dragon is unusual and may represent his hope that he would be able to pass on the Kano artistic heritage to a new generation.[2] FF

1. The Kangakai, established in 1884 under the leadership of Ernest Fenollosa and Okakura Kakuzō, aimed to reset the focus of art making and evaluation away from Western-style art to the appreciation of traditional Japanese themes and modes that became known as *nihonga* (Japanese-style painting), in contrast to *yōga* (Western-style painting).
2. This pairing is found in Chinese works such as the thirteenth-century scroll *Nine Dragons*, where it symbolizes the transmission of knowledge from the older dragon to the younger one. See Boston 1997, no. 92.

FIG. 54 Fenollosa residence, Tokyo, c. 1888. Houghton Library, Harvard University, Cambridge, Massachusetts, MS Am 1759 (Box 6:8)

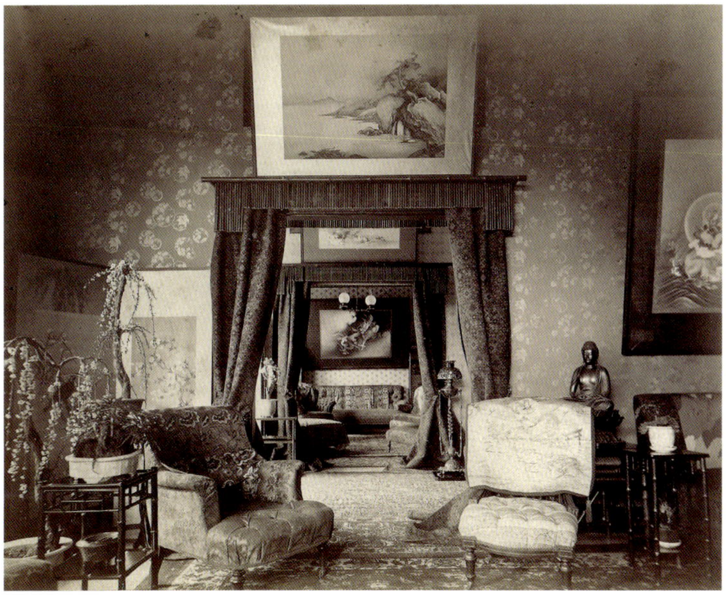

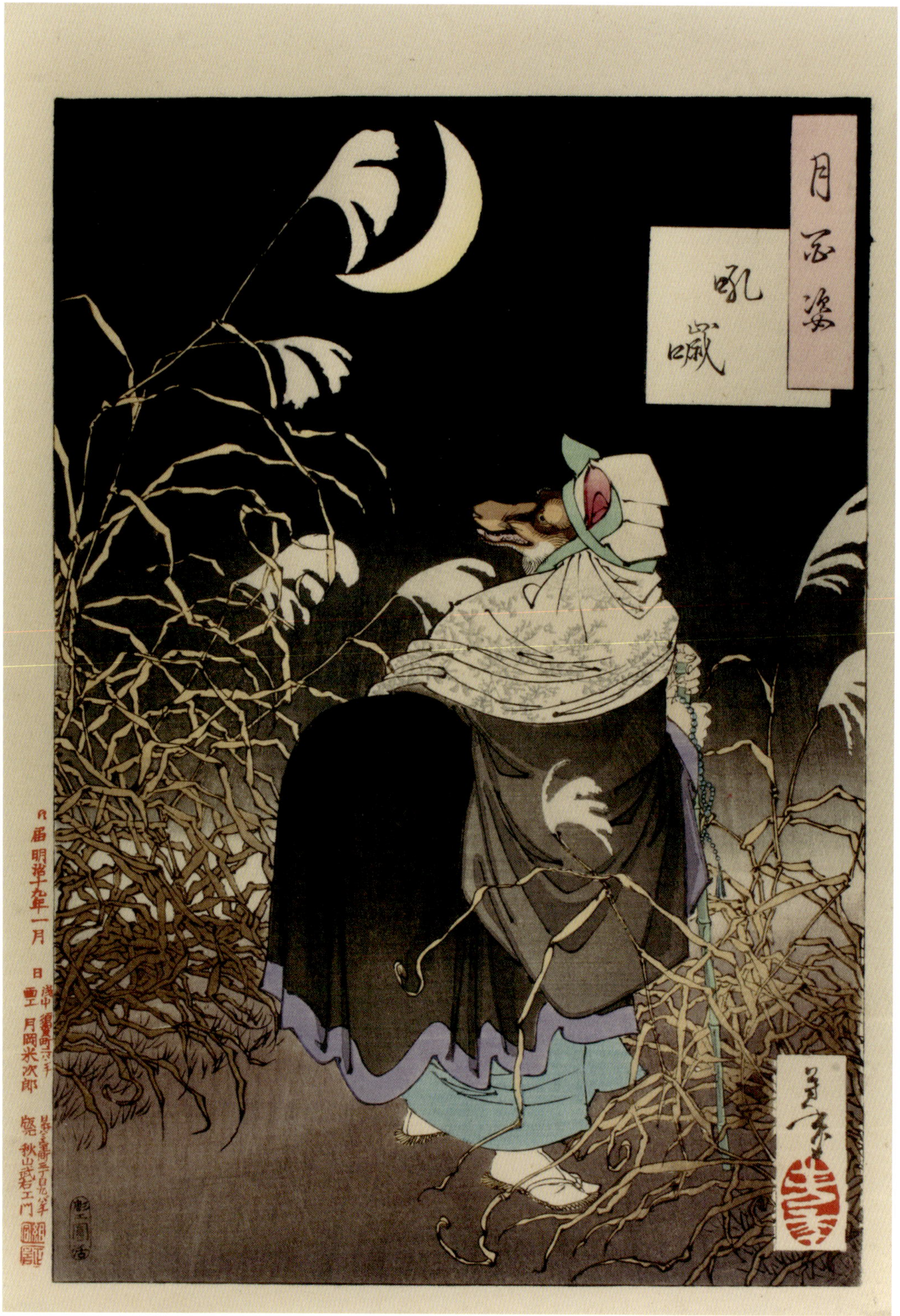

77

The Cry of the Fox (Konkai)

Tsukioka Yoshitoshi
(1839–1892)

Meiji period (1868–1912), 1886

From the series *One Hundred Aspects of the Moon* (*Tsuki hyakushi*)

Color woodblock print, approx. 15½ × 10½ in. (39.4 × 26.7 cm)

Purchased with funds contributed by the E. Rhodes and Leona B. Carpenter Foundation, 1989-47-407

In the fall of 1885, the publisher Akiyama Buemon commissioned Tsukioka Yoshitoshi, a virtuoso draftsperson and skilled painter, to design the series *One Hundred Aspects of the Moon*,[1] a series of one hundred prints whose subjects are based on Chinese and Japanese literature, mythology, theater, or folklore. This print depicts a scene from the *kyōgen* drama *The Cry of the Fox* (*Konkai*),[2] which retells a Japanese folk tale about Hakuzōsu, a shape-shifting *kitsune* (fox spirit). Disguised as the hunter's uncle, the fox visits the hunter and tells him of the virtue of foxes. Realizing that his visitor was not his uncle but rather a fox in human form,[3] the hunter sets a trap, and the fox, lured by the bait, reverts from human manifestation to his true form. Here Yoshitoshi depicted the fox in mid-transformation, its feet and hands still humanlike.[4]

This print features the techniques of *atenashi bokashi* (gradation without definition) and *karazuri* (blind embossing), which is evident inside the ears of grain that are stylized to look like will-o'-the-wisp. The cartouches at upper right bear the series and print titles. The subtle colors of this version are markings of an early impression.

During his lifetime, Yoshitoshi experienced the violent transition of power from Edo- to Meiji-period Japan, followed by the rapid modernization of the country. Discourse with the West had an impact on Japanese print culture, and Yoshitoshi's ability to combine traditional subject matter with Western concepts of space, perspective, and realism is evident throughout the prints in the series.[5] In *Uesugi Kenshin Observing a Flight of Geese* (fig. 55), the black ink silhouetting the birds gently lightens as the flock recedes into the background. Yoshitoshi used the moonlight to model Kenshin's face through shading, and atmospheric perspective foregrounds the figure and imbues the picture with an air of contemplation. The bright colors — pink, yellow, red, and purple — of another print in the series, *Moon of Pure Snow at Asano River: Chikako, the Filial Daughter* (fig. 56), are the result of dyes imported from the West.

Akiyama published an album of the complete set of *One Hundred Aspects of the Moon* in 1892 after Yoshitoshi's death. One such set is in the museum's collection. MD

—

1. Newland 2011, 135.
2. Newland 2011, 137.
3. Stevenson 1992, 96.
4. Hinohara 2017, 54.
5. Uhlenbeck 2011, 14.

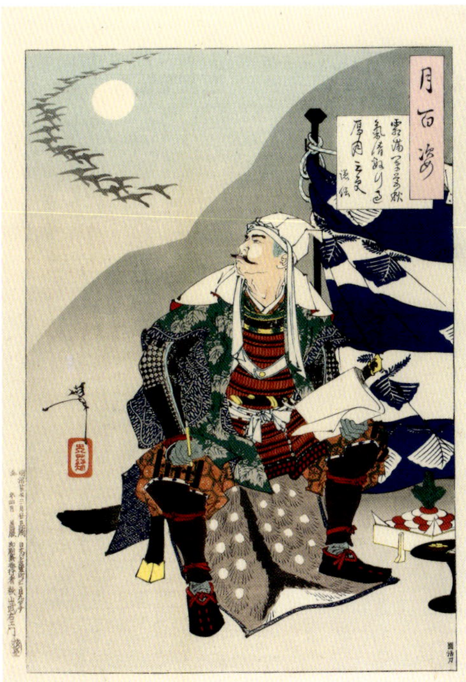

FIG. 55 Tsukioka Yoshitoshi. *Uesugi Kenshin Observing a Flight of Geese*, from the series *One Hundred Aspects of the Moon* (*Tsuki hyakushi*). Meiji period, 1890. Color woodblock print, approx. 15½ × 10½ in. (39.4 × 26.7 cm). Philadelphia Museum of Art: Purchased with funds contributed by the E. Rhodes and Leona B. Carpenter Foundation, 1989-47-476

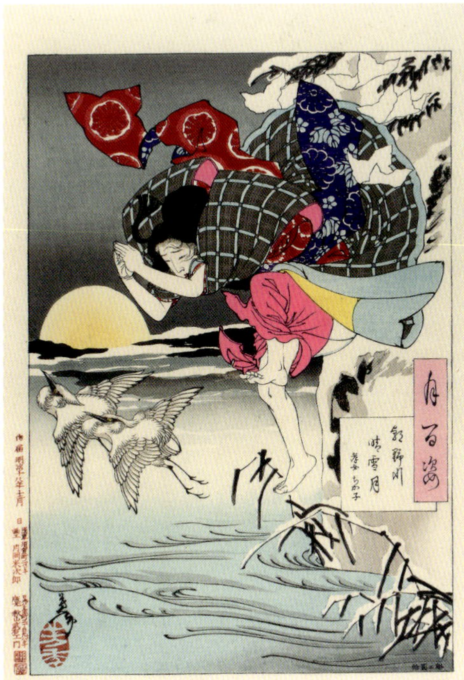

FIG. 56 Tsukioka Yoshitoshi. *Moon of Pure Snow at Asano River: Chikako, the Filial Daughter*, from the series *One Hundred Aspects of the Moon* (*Tsuki hyakushi*). Meiji period, 1885. Color woodblock print, approx. 15½ × 10½ in. (39.4 × 26.7 cm). Philadelphia Museum of Art: Purchased with funds contributed by the E. Rhodes and Leona B. Carpenter Foundation, 1989-47-404

78

The Activities of the Twelve Months

Kawanabe Kyōsai
(1831–1889)

Meiji period (1868–1912), late 19th century

Ink and color on silk, mounted as a pair of six-fold screens; each: 47½ in. × 8 ft. 7 in. (120.7 × 261.6 cm)

Purchased with the Edith H. Bell Fund, 1998-66-1,2

Born into the family of a feudal lord of the Furukawa clan in Shimōsa (now northern Chiba and southern Ibaraki Prefectures), Kawanabe Kyōsai demonstrated his artistic talent from an early age. He became a student of Utagawa Kuniyoshi (1798–1861) at the age of seven and studied ukiyo-e. Kyōsai also learned from the Kano-school artist Maemura Tōwa (d. 1841), and then from Tōwa's teacher, Kano Tōhaku Norinobu (life dates unknown). Tōwa is said to have greatly admired Kyōsai's artistic talent and called him *gaki* (painting demon).[1] In general, mastery of the Kano painting technique required eleven to twelve years, but Kyōsai remarkably completed his study in nine years, and was given a Kano-school diploma and the artist name Kano Tōiku Noriyuki in 1849.[2] He left the Kano school in 1858, and working under the name Seisei Kyōsai, he gained popularity for his ukiyo-e prints. In 1870, having made a caricature criticizing the new Meiji government, he was arrested and imprisoned. He was released the following year and changed his artist name to Kyōsai, in which the Chinese character of *kyō* is different from that in Seisei Kyōsai.

Paintings of the activities of the twelve months date back to the tenth century. Emperor Emeritus Goshirakawa (1127–1192) ordered the *edokoro-azukari* (court painting atelier) to make a set of more than sixty hand-scrolls to record annual court events and seasonal observances. Since then, various kinds of paintings were made and became popular among not only nobles and rulers but also the broader population (see no. 54). During the early Meiji period, depictions of the activities or events of the twelve months reflected aspects of contemporary society.

With his deft brushwork and wry sense of humor, Kyōsai re-created memorable moments of the year, from the first month

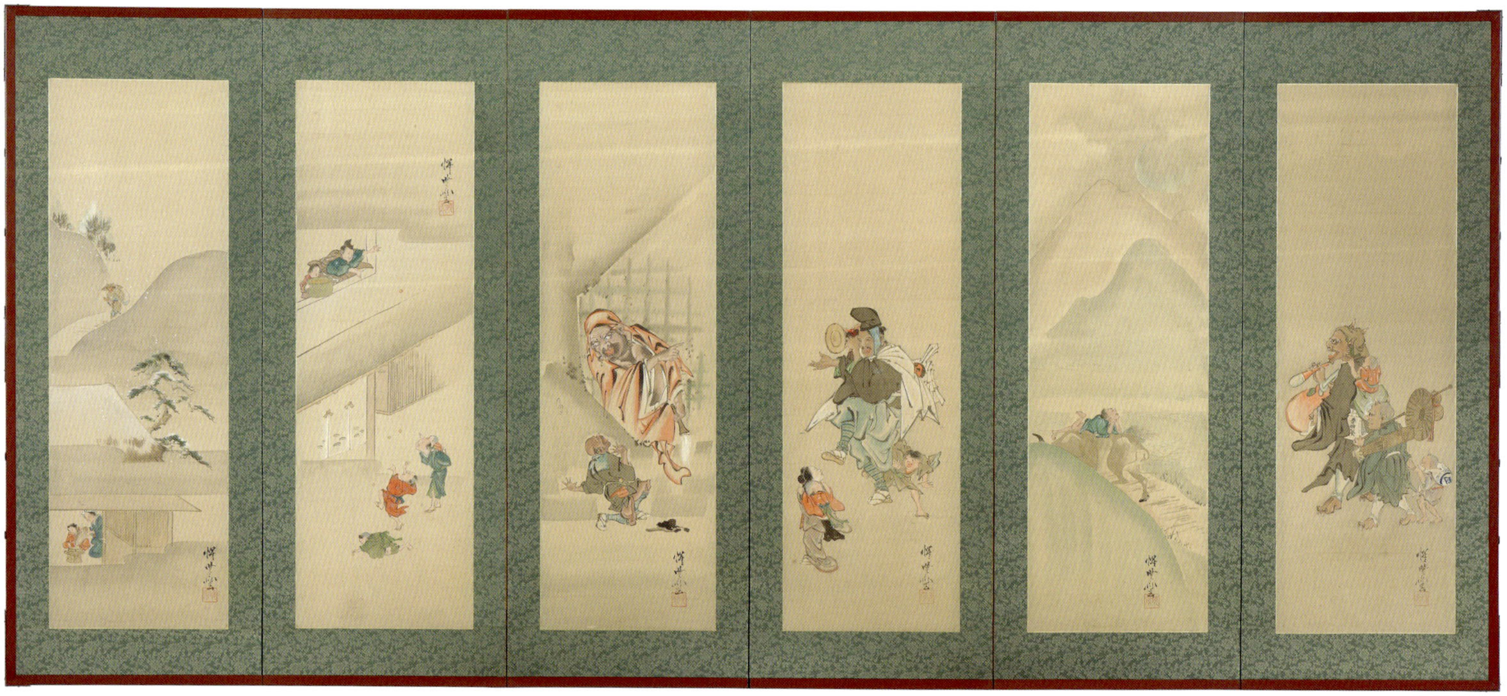

1998-66-2

to the twelfth (reading right to left), on this pair of six-panel screens:[3]

Right screen (1998-66-1)

1. "Banzai" dancers perform traditional New Year's entertainments.
2. An artist sits in front of a painting of Mount Fuji with a dragon engulfed in a smoky haze flying before it. Both the mountain and the mythical creature are auspicious symbols at the start of the year, and perhaps Kyōsai intended this as a self-portrait.
3. Two nobles and a servant sit next to a winding stream, a reference to the activities of the third day of the third month, to drive away evil influences.
4. A running man carries a bucket with a statue of the infant Buddha inside. Buddha's birthday is celebrated on the eighth day of the fourth month.
5. Two priests in white near a Shinto shrine make preparations for the Boy's Day Festival (celebrated on the fifth day of the fifth month), including helping fit a third man with a *tengu* (goblin) mask.
6. Four servants run beside a river. Two carry a chest on a pole, while the third holds a lighted torch and the fourth carries papers and a fan.

Left screen (1998-66-2)

7. A family of *oni* (demons) on a pilgrimage.
8. Lying on the back of his water buffalo, a herd boy gazes at the moon.
9. A street entertainer beats a drum and a boy dances for a young girl with a baby on her back.
10. A frightened worshipper is admonished by Daruma (see no. 9).
11. A man and a child throw persimmons to two children and a man with a baby below. The fruits will then be dried and put on top of two large rice cakes to make a traditional Japanese New Year's decoration called *kagami-mochi*.
12. A mother and child prepare rice grains used in the year-end *oni-bari* (sweeping out the demons) (see the entry for the seventh month above). An unsuspecting demon walks down the path leading to the house.

KK

---

1. Kamiyama 2008.
2. Yamashita 2008.
3. See details of six of the panels on pp. 194–95.

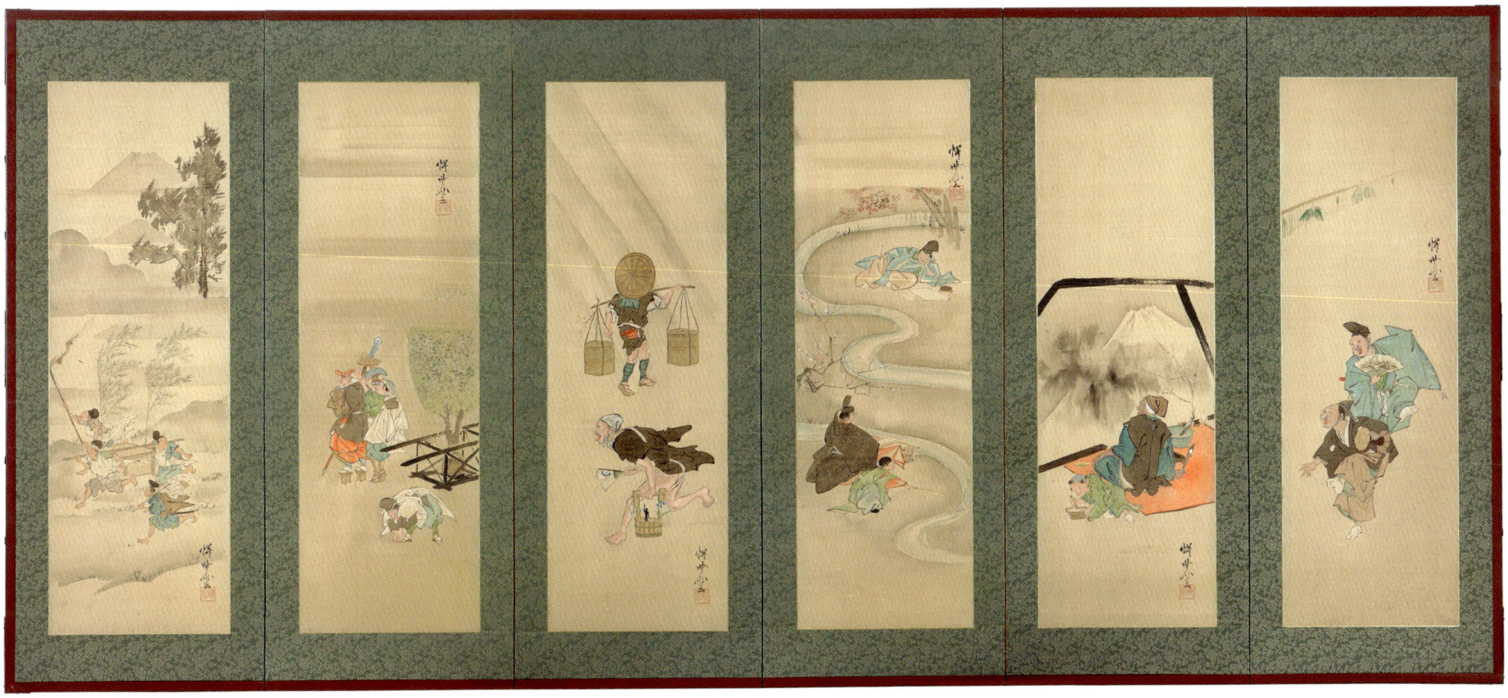

1998-66-1

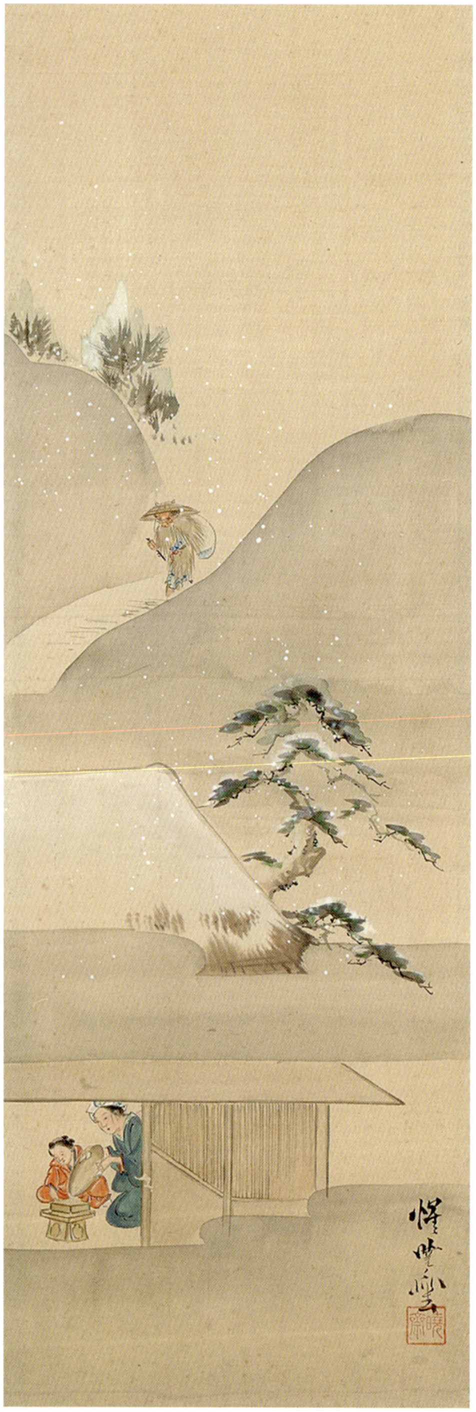

Twelfth month

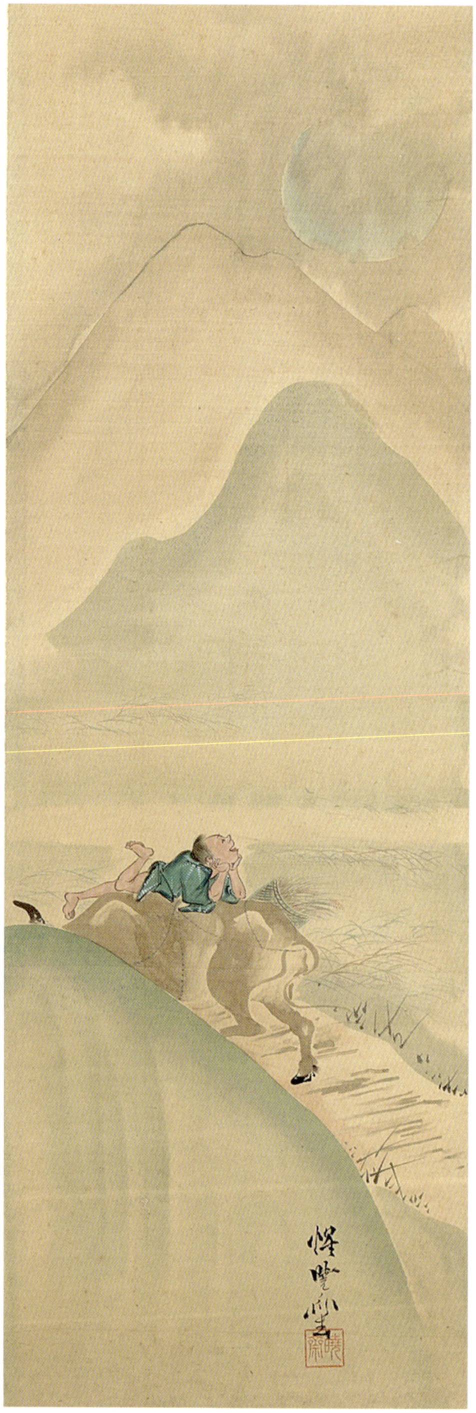

Eighth month

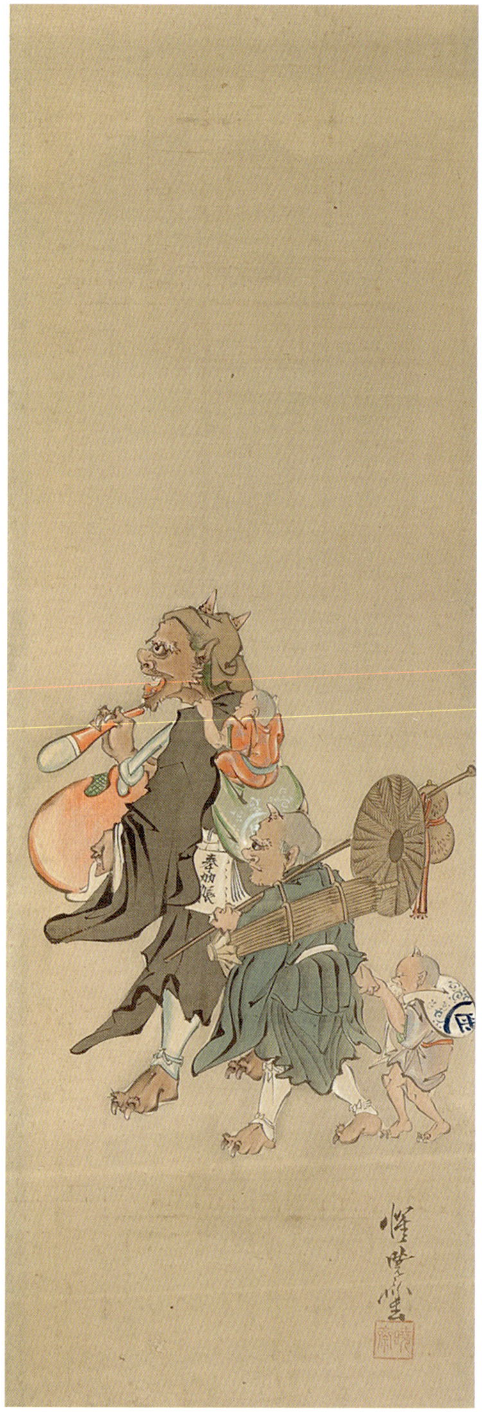

Seventh month

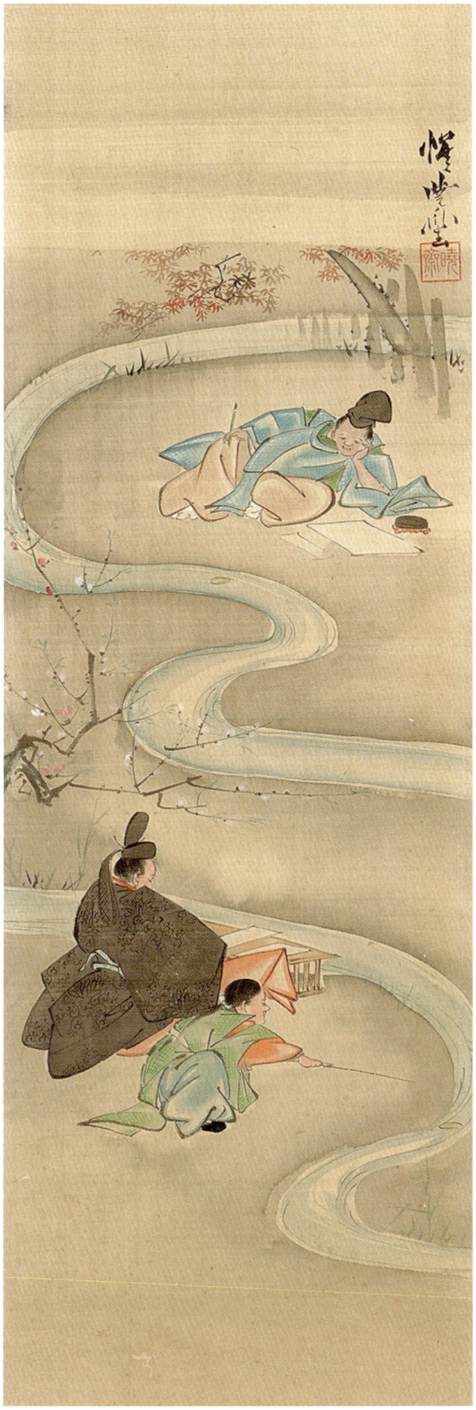

Third month

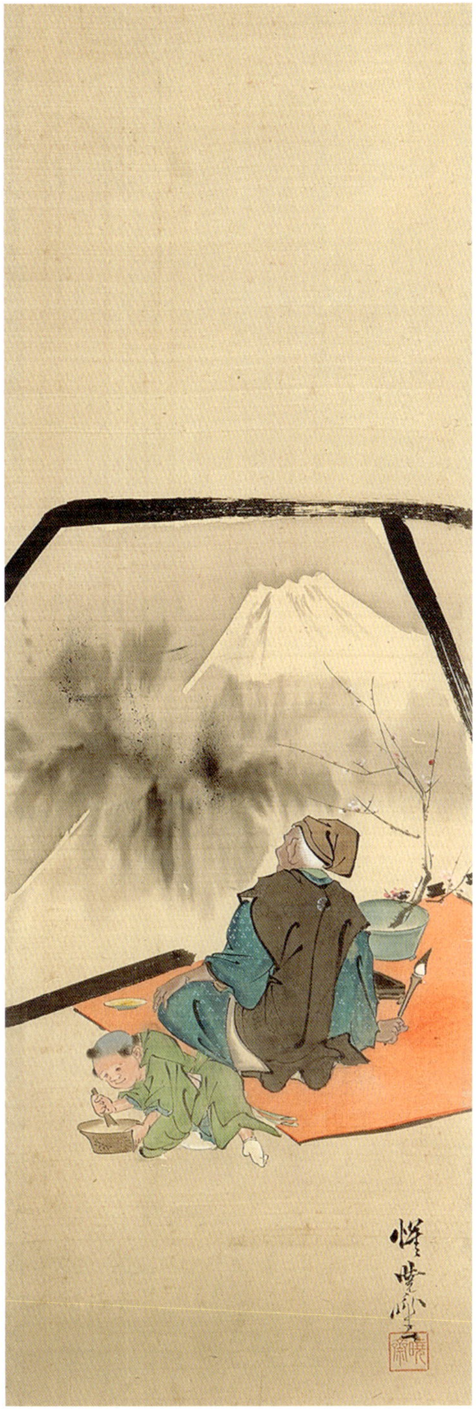

Second month

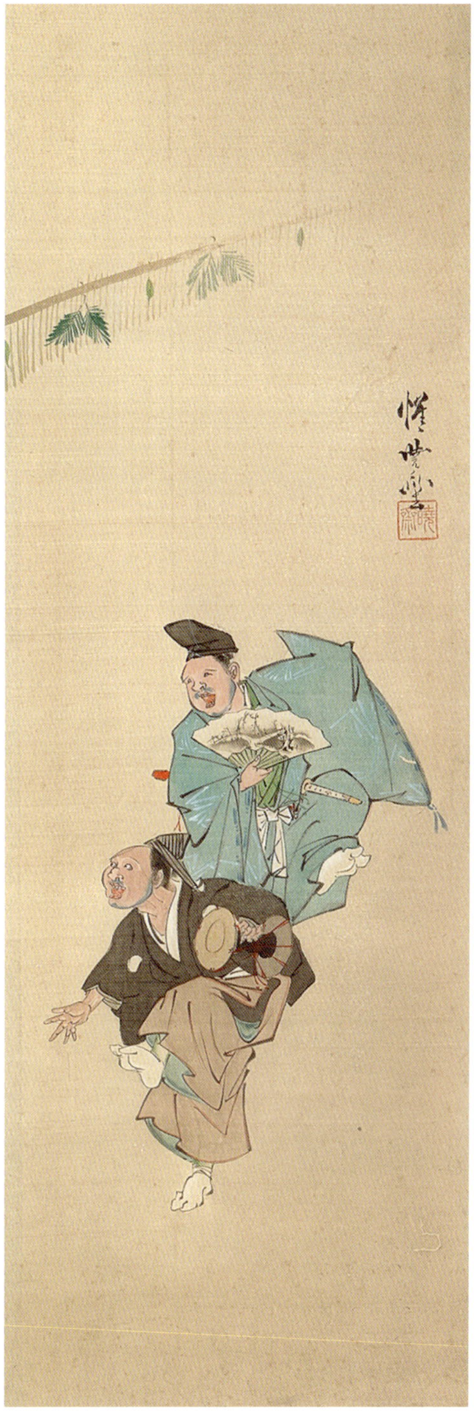

First month

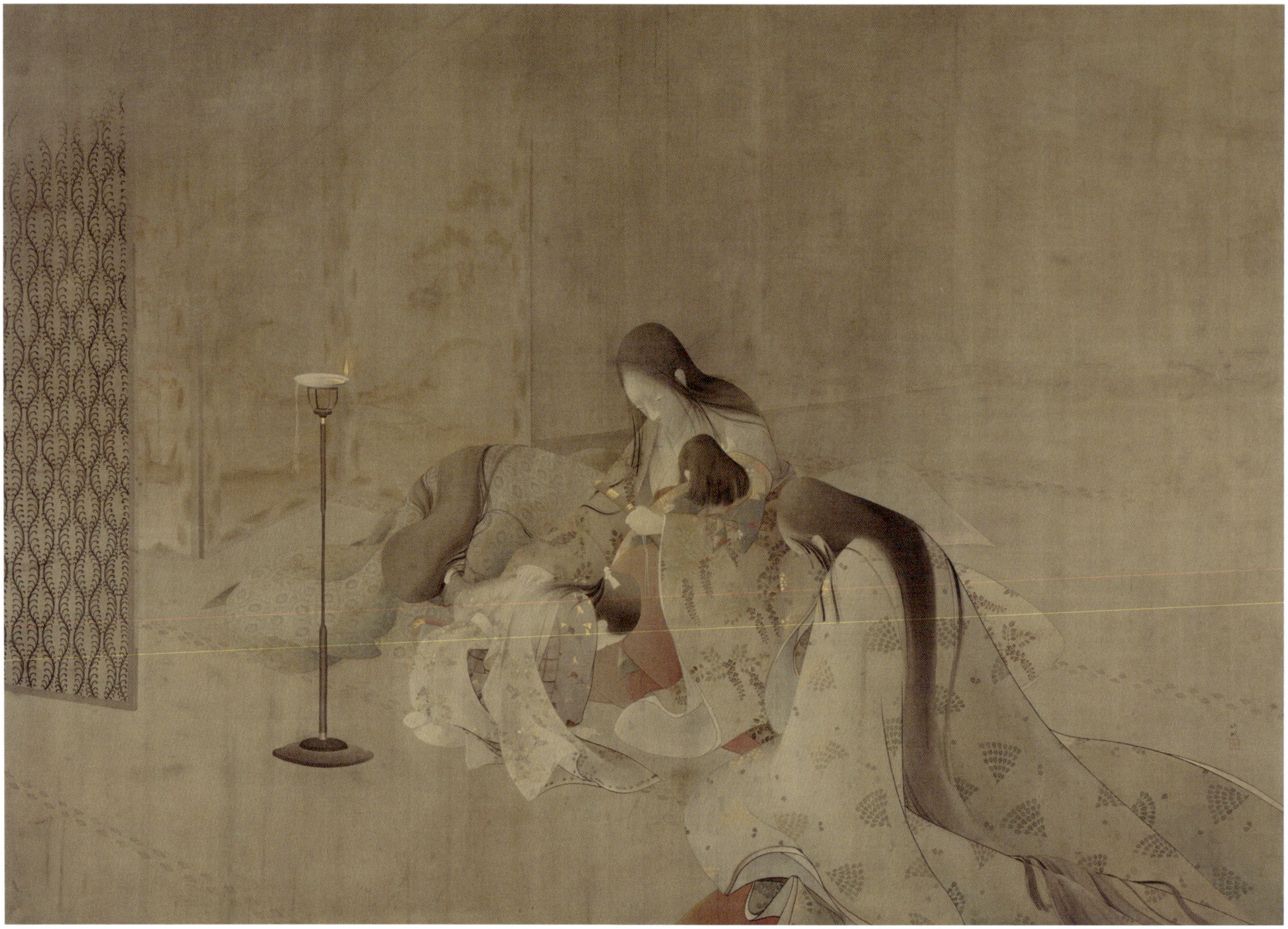

79

Fall of the Castle

Otake Chikuha
(1878–1936)

Meiji period (1868–1912), 1902

Ink and watercolor on silk,
mounted on framed panel
64½ in. × 7 ft. 4⅞ in. (163.8 × 225.7 cm)

The Samuel S. White 3rd and Vera White Collection, 1967-30-281

Fall of the Castle is a large, impressive painting on silk, mounted in a wood frame, made by an artist then in his early twenties. It was shown in the exhibition sponsored by the Japan Art Institute (Nihon Bijutsuin) in the spring of 1902, where it was awarded a silver medal.[1] Otake Chikuha was a protégé of Okakura Kakuzō (1863–1913), and his paintings were shown at the 1900 Exposition Universelle in Paris as well as at the 1904 Louisiana Purchase Exposition in Saint Louis.

The imagery of *Fall of the Castle* is most likely based on an episode in the classic fourteenth-century *Tale of the Heike*. The widow in this scene is bidding farewell to her two children and preparing to cut off her hair as a symbol of entering a Buddhist nunnery, as was customary for aristocratic women in medieval Japan after the death of their husband. While the theme and the dramatic composition of the huddled grieving figures rendered almost life-size have universal appeal, Chikuha has anchored the scene in a specific moment of the Japanese past.[2] The use of a Western-style frame signaled the artist's intent to appeal to a new global audience while simultaneously creating an elegy to traditional ways and mores, which seemed to be in danger of being overwhelmed by ideas newly imported from Europe and the United States.

The piece was acquired by Samuel S. White 3rd (1876–1952) when he visited Japan on business for his family company in 1903.[3] FF

---

1. Ogura et al. 1990, 720.
2. Okakura encouraged depictions of Japanese history during this period of national-identity formation in his editorial for the first issue of the Japanese art magazine *Kokka*, in 1889.
3. The S. S. White Dental Manufacturing Company was founded by White's grandfather and was based in Philadelphia. Since the exhibition in which this painting was featured had closed before White arrived in Japan, it is not clear how or where he saw the painting, but he purchased several others from the same exhibition at that time as well.

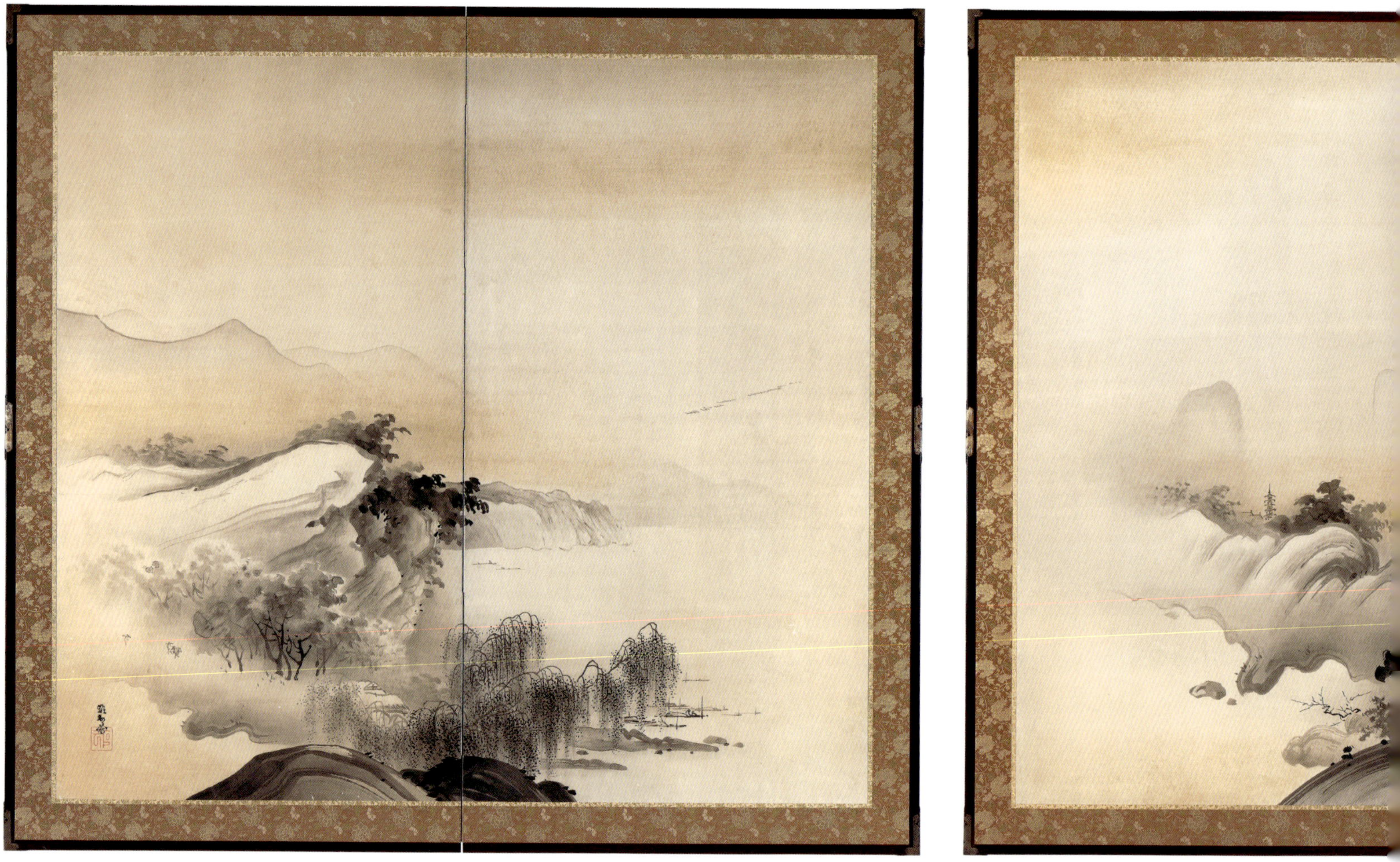

80

Landscape

Hashimoto Gahō
(1835–1908)

Meiji period (1868–1912), c. 1903

Ink and gold on paper, mounted as a pair of two-fold screens; each: $67\frac{11}{16}$ in. × 6 ft. $1\frac{1}{4}$ in. (172 × 186 cm)

Purchased with the Hollis Fund for East Asian Art Acquisitions, 2016-194-12a,b

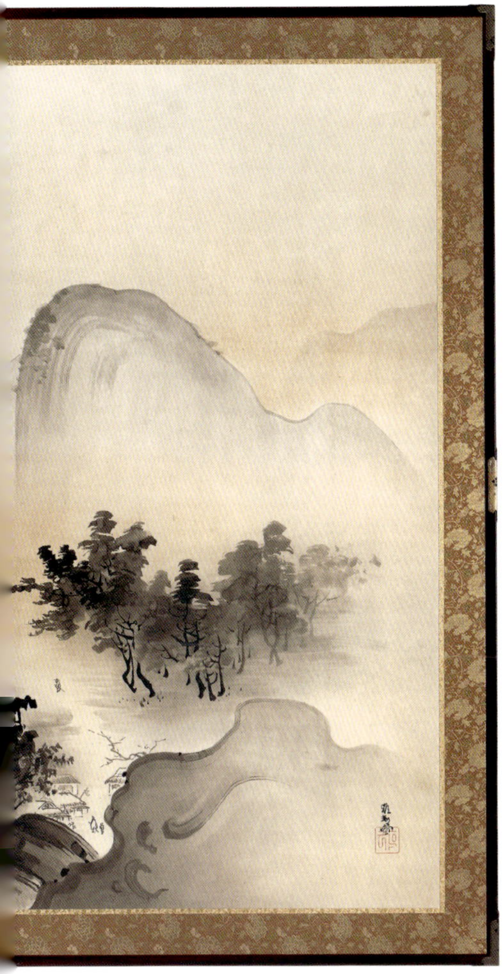

Like his contemporary Kano Hōgai (1828–1888; see no. 76), Hashimoto Gahō was trained in traditional Kano-school painting and was supported by the efforts of Ernest F. Fenollosa in the 1880s during the latter's residency in Japan.[1] Gahō, like Hōgai, experimented with new modes introduced from Western painting such as perspective and naturalistic shading in his works of that period,[2] but later in his career, Gahō returned to his Kano roots, as in this pair of screens.

The weight of each landscape is in the lower, outer corners with soft, graded washes suggesting distant hills, reminiscent of monochrome landscapes by Kano Tan'yū (1602–1674). As part of his early training in the Kano studio system, Gahō had studied and copied sketches from albums by Tan'yū and mastered his brush techniques.[3] Subdued inks and atmospheric washes contrast with darker accents and detailed trees, with one or two figures barely perceptible in the grandeur of the landscape. Although signed, these screens are not dated, but the style is identical to a handscroll of the Eight Views of Xiao and Xiang that Gahō painted in 1903.[4] The landscapes on these screens may in fact refer to passages from the Eight Views. The right-hand screen includes a pagoda, perhaps an allusion to the scene known as "Evening Bell from Mist-Shrouded Temple," and the left-hand screen may reference "Fishing Village in Evening Glow."[5] Whatever the inspiration, Gahō's mastery of ink and brush techniques lends these scenes a fresh, spontaneous effect that still impresses us over a century later. FF

---

1. Fenollosa came to Japan in 1878 at the invitation of the government to teach philosophy at the newly established Imperial University. He became an influential figure in Japanese art circles, promoting the appreciation of traditional Japanese art, which he felt was in danger of being overwhelmed and displaced by ideas and techniques of art being introduced from the West. For more on Fenollosa, see Fischer 1992.
2. See, for example, Philadelphia 2015a, 237 and 284, no. 111.
3. Philadelphia 2015a, 200–201, 275–76, no. 86; and 242, 286, no. 116. Gahō described the studio training of the Kano in an article published in 1889, in the newly founded art magazine *Kokka*.
4. Philadelphia 2015a, 264, no. 55.
5. See no. 82 in this volume.

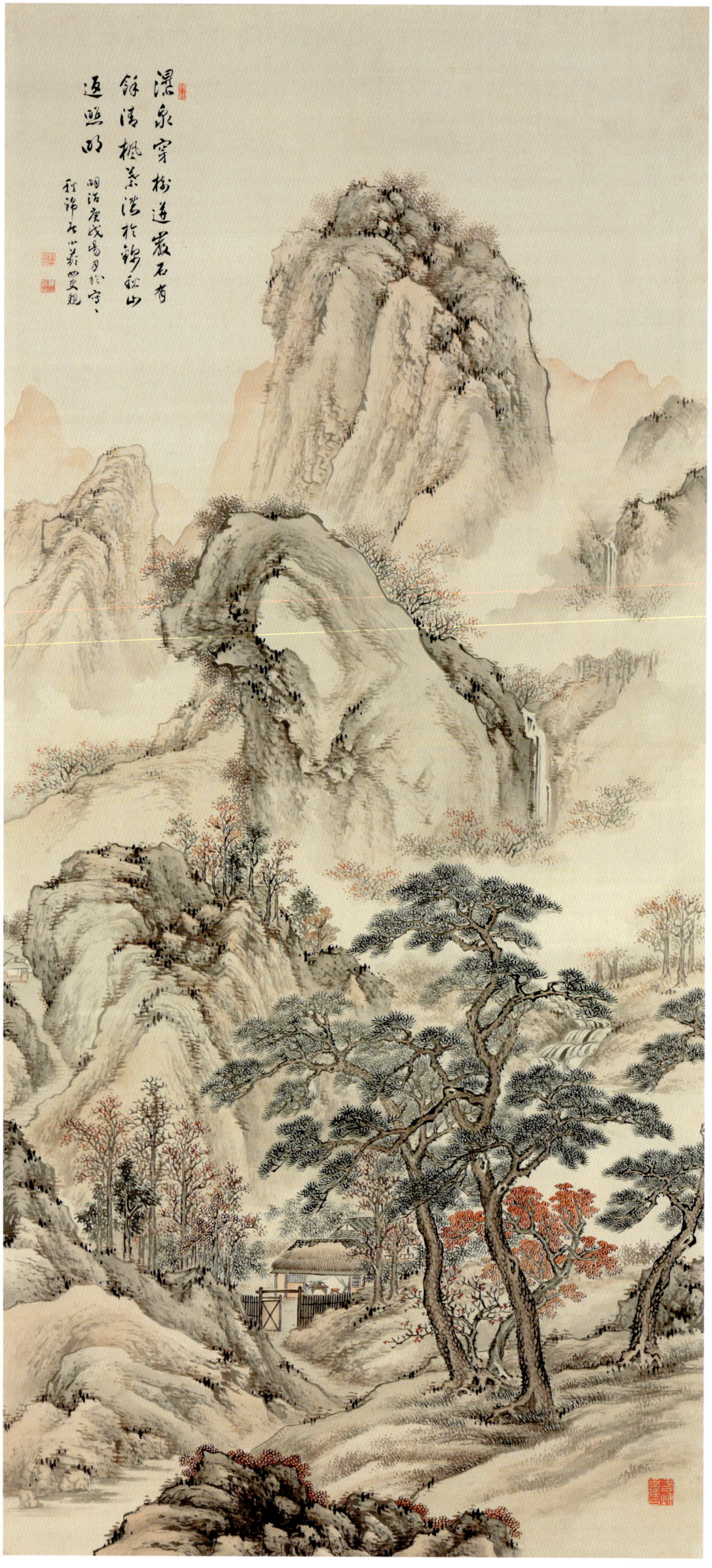

81

Mountains in Autumn

Noguchi Shōhin

(1847–1917)

Meiji period (1868–1912), 1910

Ink and color on silk, mounted as a hanging scroll; 6 ft. 2½ in. × 34 in. (189.2 × 86.4 cm)

Gift of Ralph E. Balestrieri, 1971-267-1

Noguchi Shōhin, one of the most prominent women artists of her time, was born in Nanba, Osaka, as the eldest daughter of Matsumura Shuntai, a Chinese medicine doctor. She was exposed to poetry, calligraphy, and painting during her childhood, which coincided with the end of the Edo period (1615–1868), and showed special talent as a painter. She moved to Kyoto around 1867 to enter the studio of the literati painter Hine Taizan (1814–1869; see no. 73). To support her family after her father died, she made *bijin-ga* (pictures of beautiful young women) that were popular during this time.[1] Shōhin married Noguchi Masaaki (1849–1922), a sake brewer, in 1877. Five years later, in 1882, when their sake business deteriorated and the family was forced to close it, they moved to Tokyo, where Shōhin devoted herself to painting and applied to domestic and international exhibitions. She was invited to exhibit her work at the women's pavilion of the 1893 World's Columbian Exposition in Chicago, where she was awarded a prize for her painting *True View of the Tengu Rocks in Nasu Shiobara*.[2] It is likely that by this point she was no longer making *bijin-ga*.[3]

Shōhin presented her painting to Empress Eishō (1835–1897) and worked for many patrons including the imperial family and the court. In 1889 she became a part-time professor of painting at the Peeress School, which later became Gakushuin Women's College. She was appointed in 1902 to work for the princesses Takedanomiya Masako (1888–1940) and Kanenomiya Fusako (1890–1974), and in 1904 she became the first female imperial household artist.

In this impressive rendering of a mountain landscape in the fall, Shōhin depicted tall pine trees in the foreground, with a small cottage nestled in the valley. In the middle ground she painted a group of small trees amid towering mountains, whose peaks rise toward the heavens. A poem in Chinese composed by the artist appears at the top left and evokes the majesty of the landscape:

A waterfall flows in amongst the trees
and gushes forth again,
The cliffs and rocks have a lingering purity.
With maple leaves as vivid as brocade,
The autumn mountains return to their
bright luster.

Painted seven years before her death at the age of seventy, *Mountains in Autumn* shows her achievement as a literati painter. KK

1. Yamamori 2019, 66.
2. The painting was gifted to the US government, but its current location is unknown. Yamamori 2019, 70.
3. Yamamori 2019, 67.

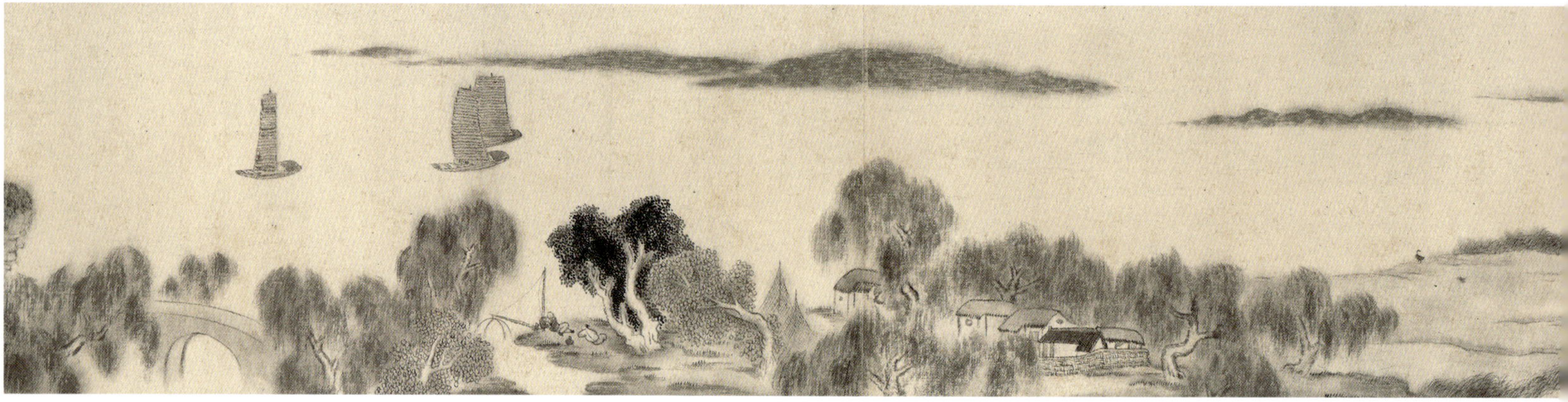

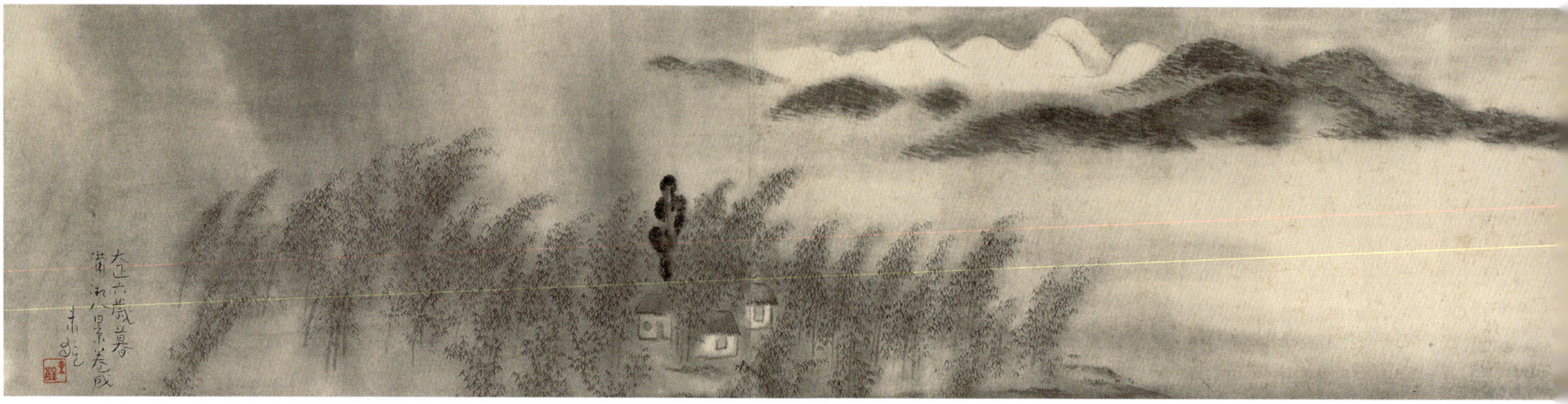

82

Shosho Hakkei (Eight Views of Xiao and Xiang)

Kosugi Hōan Misei
(1881–1964)

Taishō period (1912–26), 1917

Haiku brushed by Matsuse Seisei (1869–1937); title calligraphy by Naitō Konan (1866–1934)

Ink on paper, mounted as a handscroll; with scroll ends: 15⅛ in. × 23 ft. 4¼ in. (38.4 × 711.8 cm)

Purchased with the Henry B. Keep Fund, 2017-104-1

The Chinese theme of Eight Views of Xiao and Xiang (Rivers) has been woven into the cultural fabric of Japanese literature and art since its introduction in the thirteenth century. Inspired by the lush river region of China's Hunan Province, the motif bridges landscape and literature, and first flourished in the hands of Song-dynasty (960–1279) literati painters. Soon, certain "views" became standard compositions celebrated by East Asian artists as cultural symbols. With Japan's 1868 Meiji Restoration, this "foreign" motif fell out of favor and gave way to Japanese-based historical or landscape subjects. But, as the country began looking outward again in the Taishō period, travel increased to Europe, the United States, and other parts of Asia. The traditional view of China as the source of East Asian civilization resurfaced,

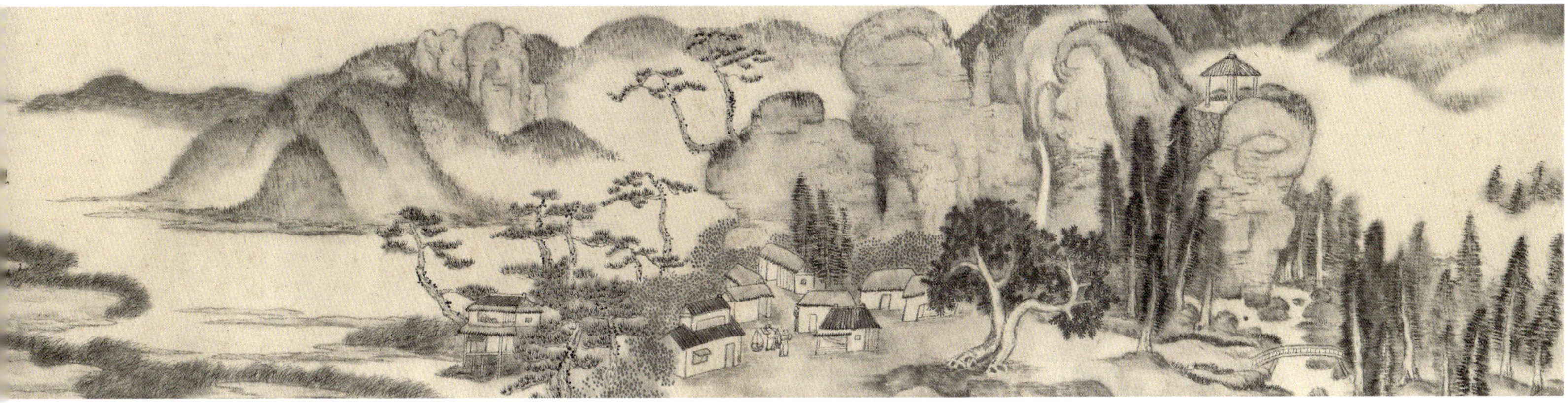

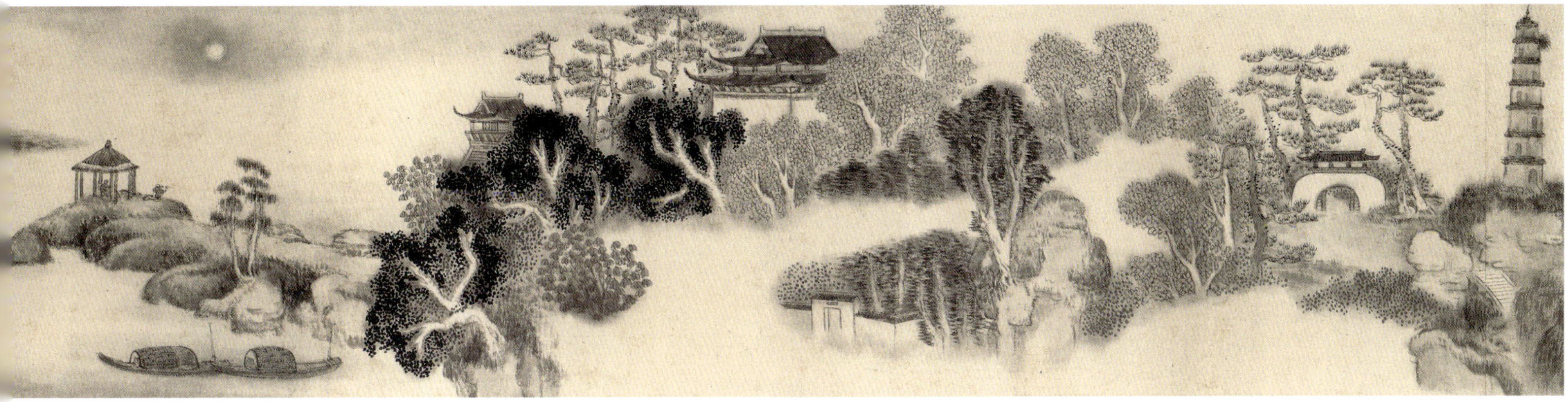

and writers and artists were eager to visit the famed sights of the country, including the Xiao and Xiang Rivers, for inspiration.

Among those travelers was the *nihonga* (Japanese-style painting) artist Kosugi Hōan, or Misei, as he was called then. He was initially trained in Western oil painting, but his study in France in 1913 brought him a renewed appreciation for Japanese art. After his return from Europe the following year, he began to paint in the traditional literati style. Kosugi signed this scroll "recollected in tranquility," indicating that he had painted it after traveling to Hunan Province in the late spring of 1916. He approached the Eight Views theme with a distinguished touch of light brushwork and delicately controlled ink to express the misty atmosphere. A subtle sense of melancholy is evoked as Kosugi's poetic amalgam of scenes extends across this lyrical handscroll, from a mountain market to geese descending on a sandbar, to a fishing village and returning sailboats, through the soundscape of the evening bell from a mist-shrouded temple, to the autumn moon over Lake Dongting, ending with evening snow and night rain over the rivers.

The same sequence of scenes is followed in the colophon by the well-regarded haiku poet Matsuse Seisei, signed a year after the painting itself. He brushed eight haiku to complement the eight scenes that Kosugi depicted,[1] and he wrote his appreciation of the work, which brought back his memories of the Xiao and Xiang Rivers. Noted historian and sinologist Naitō Konan added the title calligraphy of four Chinese characters, "jade-green waters / bright sand," taken from a verse by the Chinese poet Qian Qi (c. 722–780) on the subject of one of the Eight Views, "Wild Geese Descending to a Sandbar." The addition of Naitō's calligraphy gave the scroll an indisputable imprimatur from the foremost China specialist of the day. The joint participation of artist, poet, and historian speaks to the Chinese and Japanese literati tradition of collaborative effort. Such framing enlivens the transmissive function of the Eight Views theme throughout history and identifies all participants as cultivated scholars who contributed to the revival of East Asian culture in the early twentieth century. YX

1. See the Documentation (p. 259) for translations of the haiku.

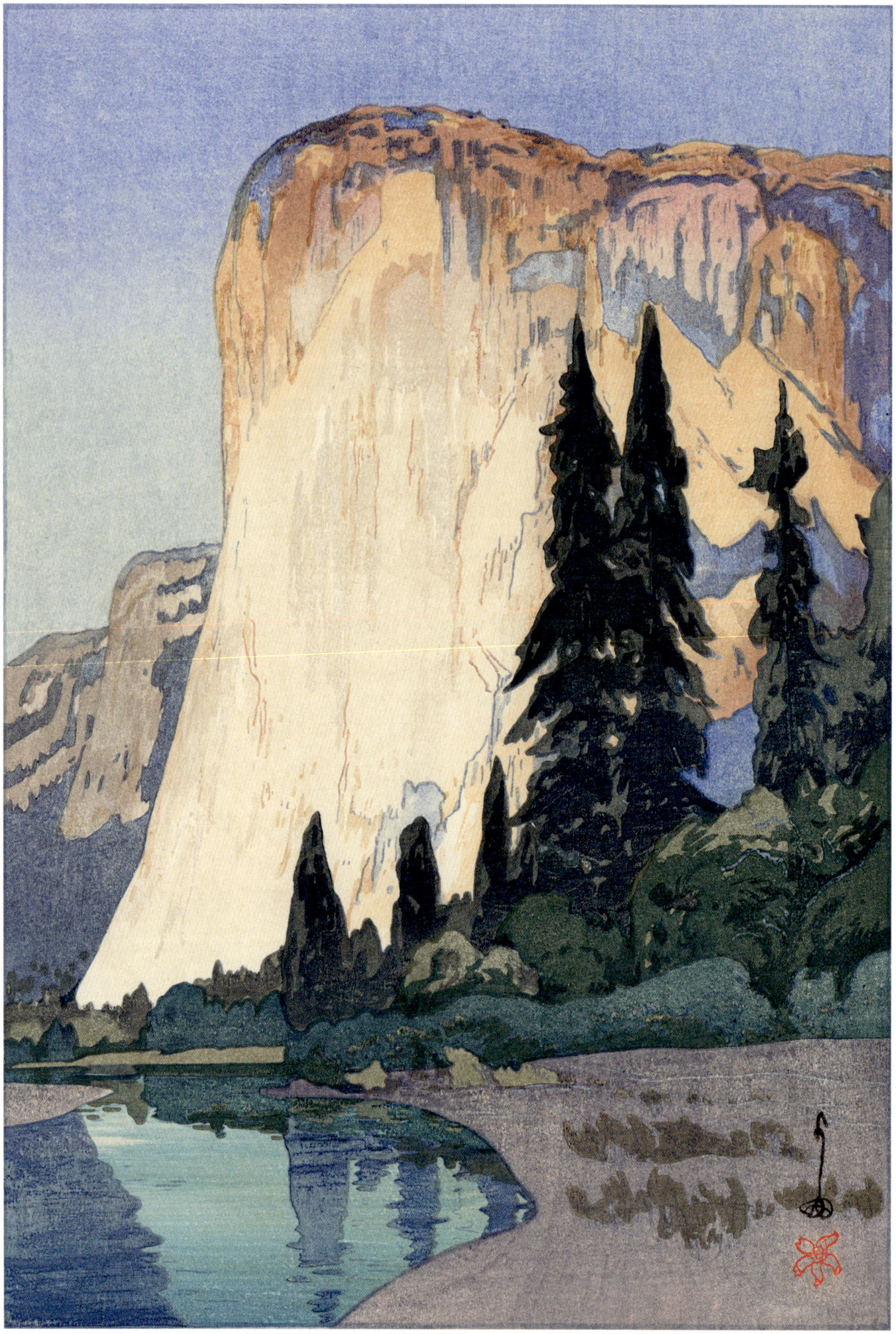

83

El Capitan, Yosemite (Yosemittodani Eru Kyapitan)

Yoshida Hiroshi
(1876–1950)

Taishō period (1912–26), 1925

Color woodblock print
16½ × 10¾ in. (41.9 × 27.3 cm)

Bequest of Althea de B. Budd,
1973-202-39

Famous monuments and landscapes, known as *meisho*, have long been a staple of Japanese literary and pictorial imagination. In the Meiji (1868–1912) and Taishō periods, conventions for representing and selecting these sites changed dramatically. Some artists, such as Kawase Hasui (1883–1957), began to shift away from the established repertoire of places, adventuring into the countryside to capture the melancholy and nostalgia of rural villages (fig. 57).[1] Other artists, including Yoshida Hiroshi, went further, traveling abroad to find new subjects.

After displaying an early talent for art, Yoshida was adopted by Yoshida Kasaburō (1861–1894), who had studied in Tokyo under the Italian painter Antonio Fontanesi (1818–1882). The younger Yoshida later apprenticed with watercolor artist Miyake Katsumi (1874–1954) before beginning to train in European-style oil painting. Yoshida and his contemporaries' paintings drew the attention of important American patrons such as Charles Lang Freer, who financed the first exhibition of Yoshida's work in the United States at the Detroit Museum of Art (now the Detroit Institute of Arts) in 1899.[2] Spurred on by this success, Yoshida was able to finance a grand tour of America, Europe, and North Africa from 1904 to 1906.[3]

Although Yoshida is recognized as one of the most acclaimed masters of the early twentieth-century movement known as *shin hanga* (literally "new print"), his foray into printmaking came later in his life. In 1920 he partnered with the champion of this movement, the publisher Watanabe Shōzaburō (1885–1962), for a series of seven woodblock prints. In 1923, after the devasting loss of his collection of blocks in the Great Kanto Earthquake, Yoshida returned to the US, where he found a public hungry for Japanese prints, and created studies of national landmarks including El Capitan, the Grand Canyon, and Niagara Falls. Motivated by a belief in the singular importance of the hand of the artist, a notion associated with the *sōsaku hanga* (creative prints) movement, he began to self-publish his prints, including scenes of the Japanese Alps (fig. 58).

In this print, Yoshida represented an iconic landmark of California's Yosemite National Park, the soaring El Capitan. To achieve such a sublime conception of the towering monolith, the artist mixed force with finesse, striving to capture the subtlety of watercolor by adeptly modeling the intricate scattering of light across the rock's surface and the chromatic variations in the blue gradations of the sky and water. Yoshida's approval for this print is signaled in the upper-left margin: the term *jizuri* (self-printed) affirms that this impression was executed according to his exacting standards.[4] NP

1. For the potential literary impetus behind this shift, see Goodall-Cristante 1996, 18–19.
2. Yasunaga 2002, 24–25.
3. Yoshida wrote extensively of his travels, as discussed in Merritt 1990, 75–77.
4. On the artist's demanding workshop practice, see Merritt 1990, 78–79; and Till 2007, 15–17.

FIG. 57 Kawase Hasui (1883–1957). *Rain at Soshu Maekawa*, from the series *Views of the Tōkaidō*. Shōwa period (1926–89), 1932. Color woodblock print, 14¼ × 9 7/16 in. (36.2 × 24 cm). Philadelphia Museum of Art: Bequest of Warren H. and Mary I. Watanabe, 2001-138-30

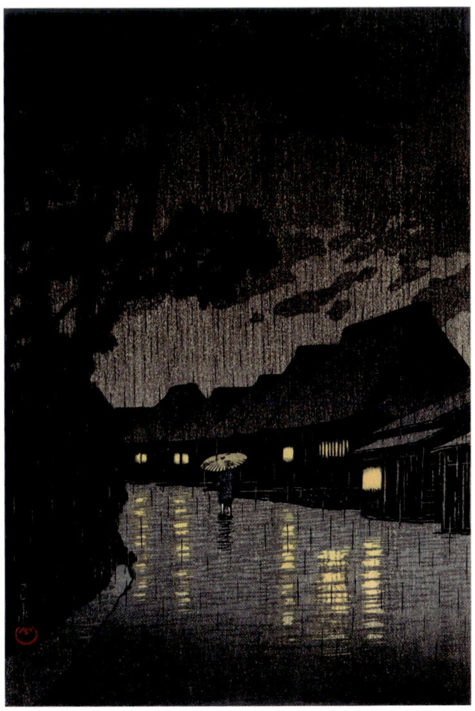

FIG. 58 Yoshida Hiroshi. *Morning at Mt. Tsurugi*, from the series *Twelve Prints of the Japan Alps*. Shōwa period, 1926. Color woodblock print, 14⅝ × 9 13/16 in. (37.1 × 25 cm). Philadelphia Museum of Art: The Samuel S. White 3rd and Vera White Collection, 1967-30-216

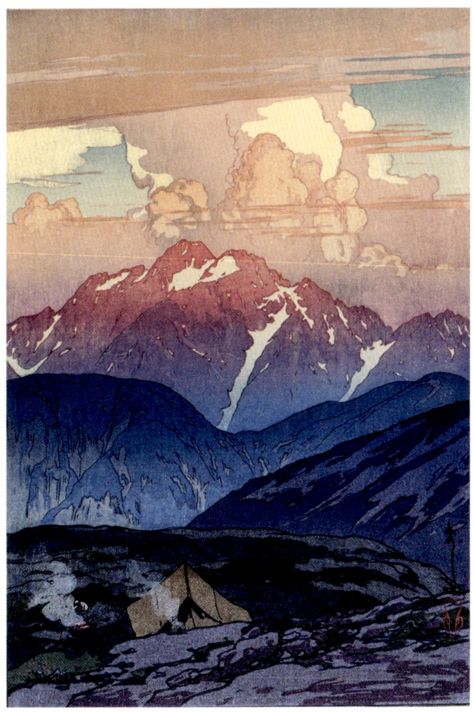

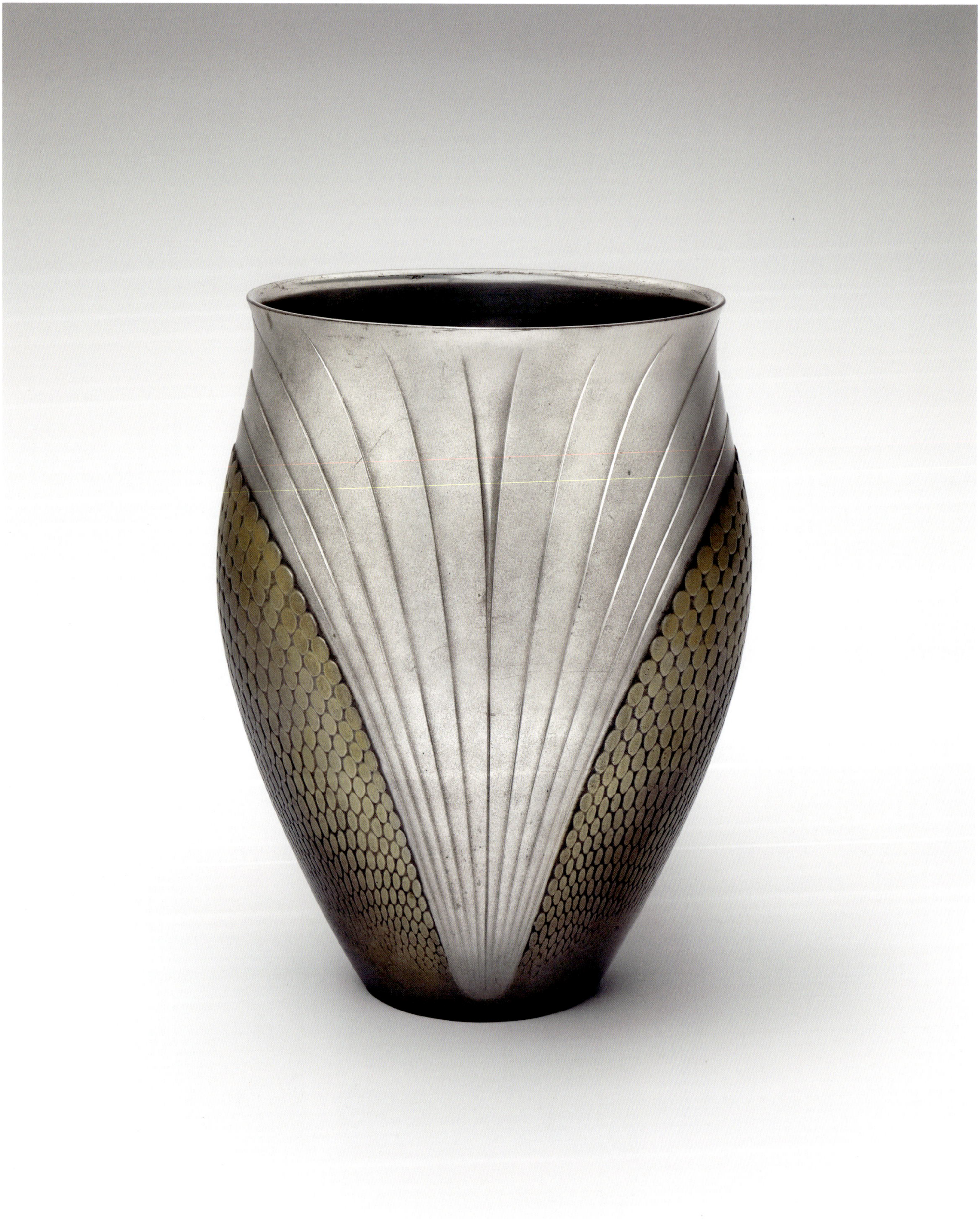

84

Vase

Hyakuse Yamamuro

(1900–1990)

Shōwa period (1926–89), 1937

Yellow and gray bronze with petal motif, 13¼ × 6⅝ in. (33.7 × 16.8 cm)

Gift of the family of Hyakuse Yamamuro in memory of the artist, 1992-8-3

Hyakuse Yamamuro was born in Toyama Prefecture and graduated from the prefectural craft school before moving to Tokyo to study metalworking with the renowned artists Murase Yumin and Unno Senmin at the Tokyo School of Art. He went to work for the Hattori watch company in 1924, where he established the new art section. That same year the Imperial Household Agency designated Yamamuro to oversee and coordinate the gifts distributed on the occasion of the 1928 coronation of the Shōwa emperor, Hirohito (1901–1989).[1]

Yamamuro also created works to commemorate the tenth wedding anniversary of the emperor and empress in 1934. By the 1930s Yamamuro was showing his work in the official Ministry of Education exhibitions; this vase was shown in 1937.[2] The Japanese government chose another of his vases to represent Japanese metalcraft in the 1939 New York World's Fair.[3] Made using traditional Japanese metalworking techniques, Yamamuro's pieces also reflect the modern aesthetic dominant at the time. He cast and incised the form of this vase in yellow and gray bronze in the manner of traditional Japanese metalwork. However, the stylized geometrical decorations, simple shape, and sleek surface reflect the high-style Art Deco designs current in Europe in the 1920s and 1930s. The strong graphic motif in contrasting silver and gold colors displays the understated elegance for which Yamamuro's work was celebrated. FF

1. Among the artists commissioned to create artworks for the 1928 exhibition was Kawai Kanjirō (1890–1966; see no. 85). See Tokyo 2019–20, no. 11.
2. See Philadelphia 2008–9b, 8–14, on the role of government-sponsored exhibitions in promoting crafts.
3. See PMA acc. no. 1992-8-2.

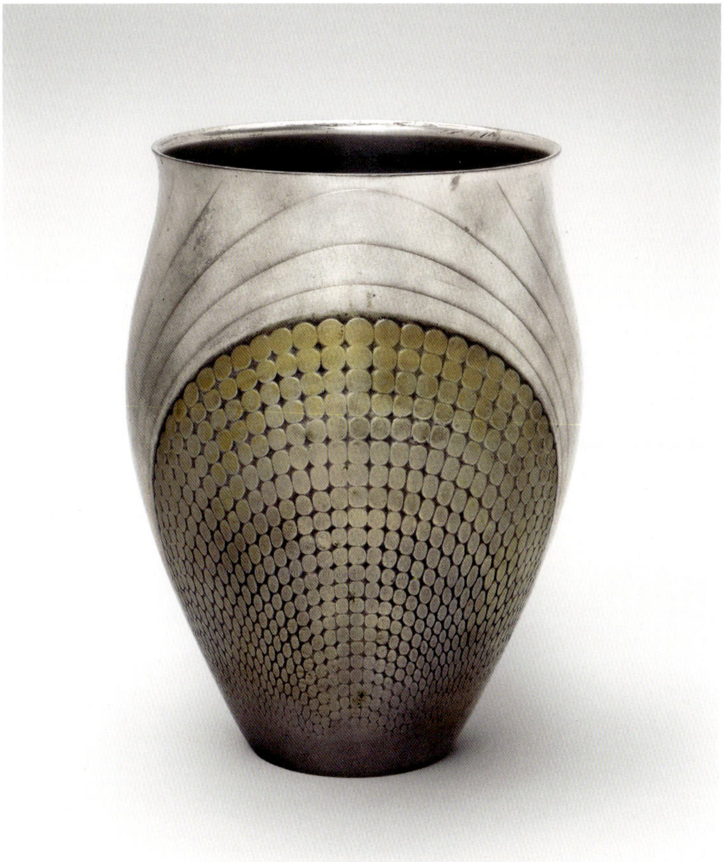

85

Jar

Kawai Kanjirō
(1890–1966)

Shōwa period (1926–89), c. 1938

Earthenware with underglaze iron oxide, copper, and cobalt decoration, 11½ × 11 in. (29.2 × 27.9 cm)

Purchased with funds contributed by Andrea M. Baldeck, M.D., and William M. Hollis, Jr., 2007-34-1

Kawai Kanjirō grew up in Shimane Prefecture, southwest of Kyoto, and in 1910 entered Tokyo Technical College in the ceramic department, where he studied the chemistry of glazes. Kawai continued his research at the Kyoto Municipal Institute of Ceramics, a research and testing facility established in 1896 under the influence of the German chemist Dr. Gottfried Wagner to modernize the Japanese ceramic industry. With his thorough foundation in the science of glazes, Kawai continued creating his ceramic works.

Kawai established his own kiln in Kyoto, called the Shokei-yo, where he worked for the rest of his life.[1] He was especially interested in re-creating certain Chinese glazes, such as celadon, copper red, and iron. The latter was favored by Japanese tea masters and is known as *temmoku* glaze in Japanese. In 1921 he had his first solo exhibition, which included about 180 pieces and was met with great critical success. During his student days Kawai had befriended Hamada Shoji (1894–1978) and through him met Yanagi Muneyoshi (Sōetsu; 1889–1961), the leader of the so-called *mingei* (folk crafts) movement.[2] Traveling to Korea with Hamada and Yanagi, Kawai became enamored with Korean ceramics as well.

This jar combines the Korean "moon jar" form with the Chinese-style *temmoku* glaze. In the wax-resist rondels, Kawai painted semi-abstract designs in underglaze cobalt, copper, and iron. He adhered to the spirit of folk craft by refusing official honors including the prestigious designation of Holder of Intangible Cultural Property, popularly known as Living National Treasure. Kawai left his pieces unsigned, but as this jar attests, his hallmark expression of sophisticated artlessness makes his creations immediately recognizable. FF

1. Designed by the artist in 1937, Kawai's residence, studio, and kiln are now open to the public as the Kawai Kanjirō Memorial Museum.
2. Together they founded the Japan Folk Art Society (Nihon Mingei Kyōkai) in 1934 and the Japan Folk Crafts Museum in 1936 to promote the appreciation of traditional crafts.

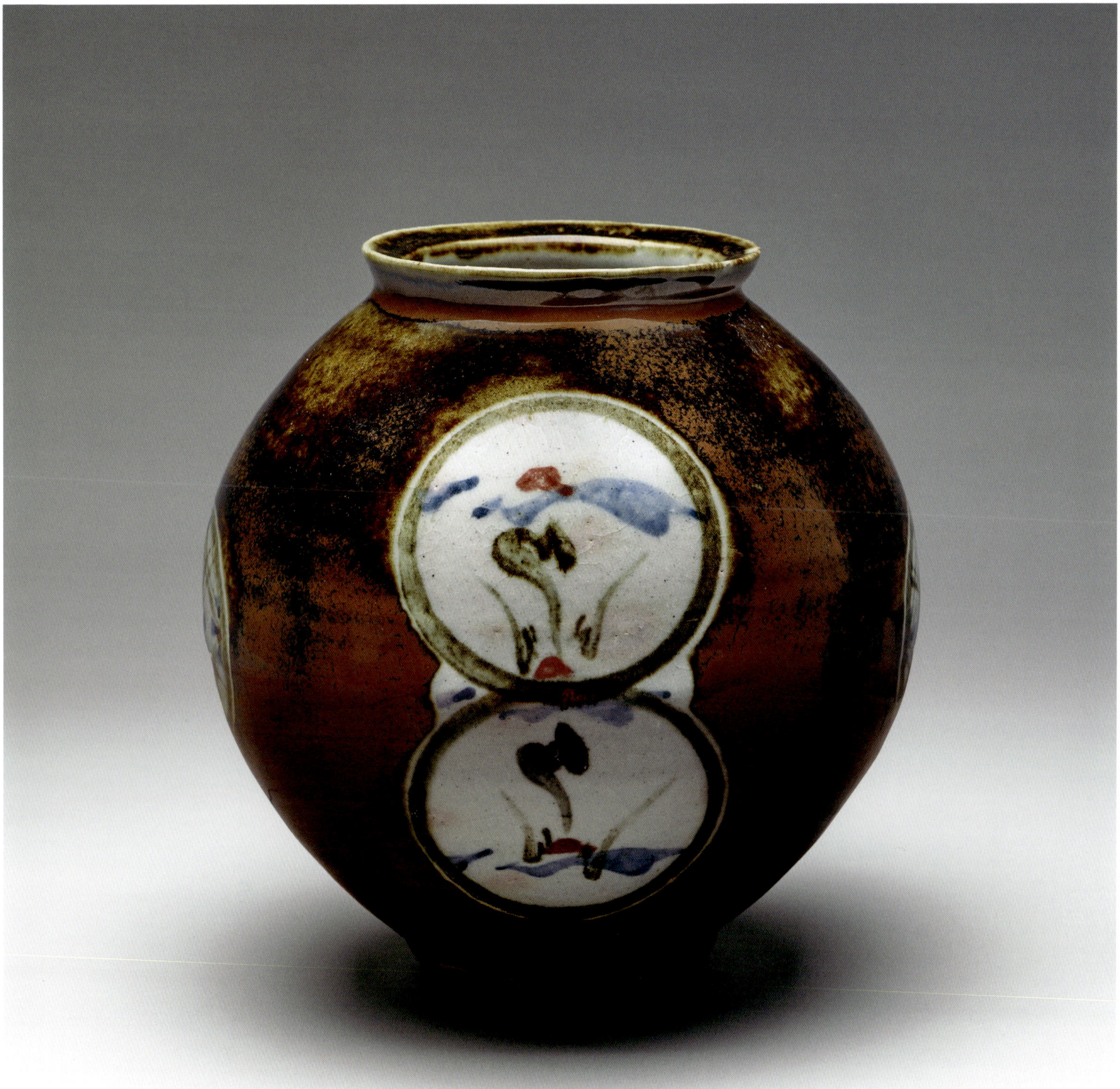

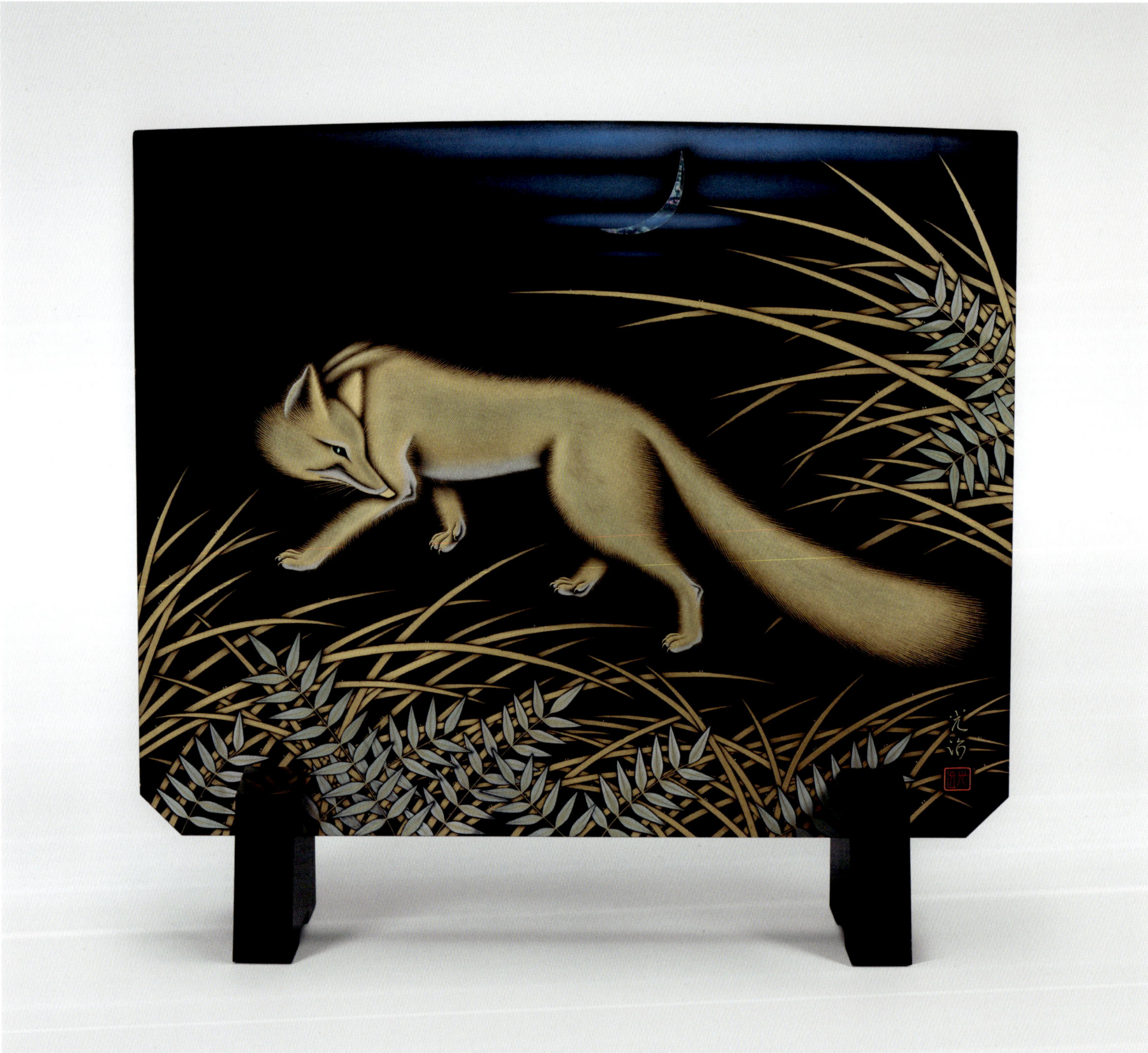

86

Golden Fox Hunting

Itaya Kōji
(1925–2006)

Shōwa period (1926–89), c. 1950s

Lacquer on wood with *chinkin* (incised gold), gold leaf, and inlay of *raden* (mother-of-pearl); single-panel screen (*tsuitate*)
Including feet: 45⅛ × 47¾ × 11 in. (114.6 × 121.3 × 27.9 cm)

Gift of Frederick R. McBrien III, 2006-31-1

The city of Wajima has been known for its high standards of craftsmanship in the production of lacquer since 1397. Lacquer artists have historically specialized in two techniques: *maki-e*, or sprinkled lacquer, which uses a powdered form of gold lacquer; and *chinkin*, or incised gold, which involves incising the design on the lacquer surface and then filling it with gold leaf. The latter technique is particularly difficult and became the hallmark of Wajima lacquerwares. Even a small bowl with *chinkin* decoration can take as long as three months to make, as every step in the process is done by hand and the lacquer must be allowed to dry thoroughly. It probably took the lacquer master Itaya Kōji considerably longer to create this large *tsuitate* (single-panel screen) with a golden fox hunting in the moonlight. Itaya captured the alertness of the animal, which looks back warily as he prowls through the tall grasses. Each hair of the fur and each blade of reed grass is carefully incised and filled with both gold and silver lacquer. The fox's body and tail are done in *maki-e* lacquer, giving the surface a soft appearance that balances the precision of the grasses. The fox's eye and the crescent moon in the night sky are inlaid with mother-of-pearl, reflecting the light. There are blue streaks of clouds in the dark lacquer sky, which is otherwise black.

Itaya was born in and worked most of his life in Wajima. He exhibited frequently in the major craft exhibitions, culminating in him being awarded the Ministry of Education Prize in 1988. A superb example of postwar Japanese lacquer craftsmanship, this screen was most likely made as an exhibition piece sometime in the 1950s. FF

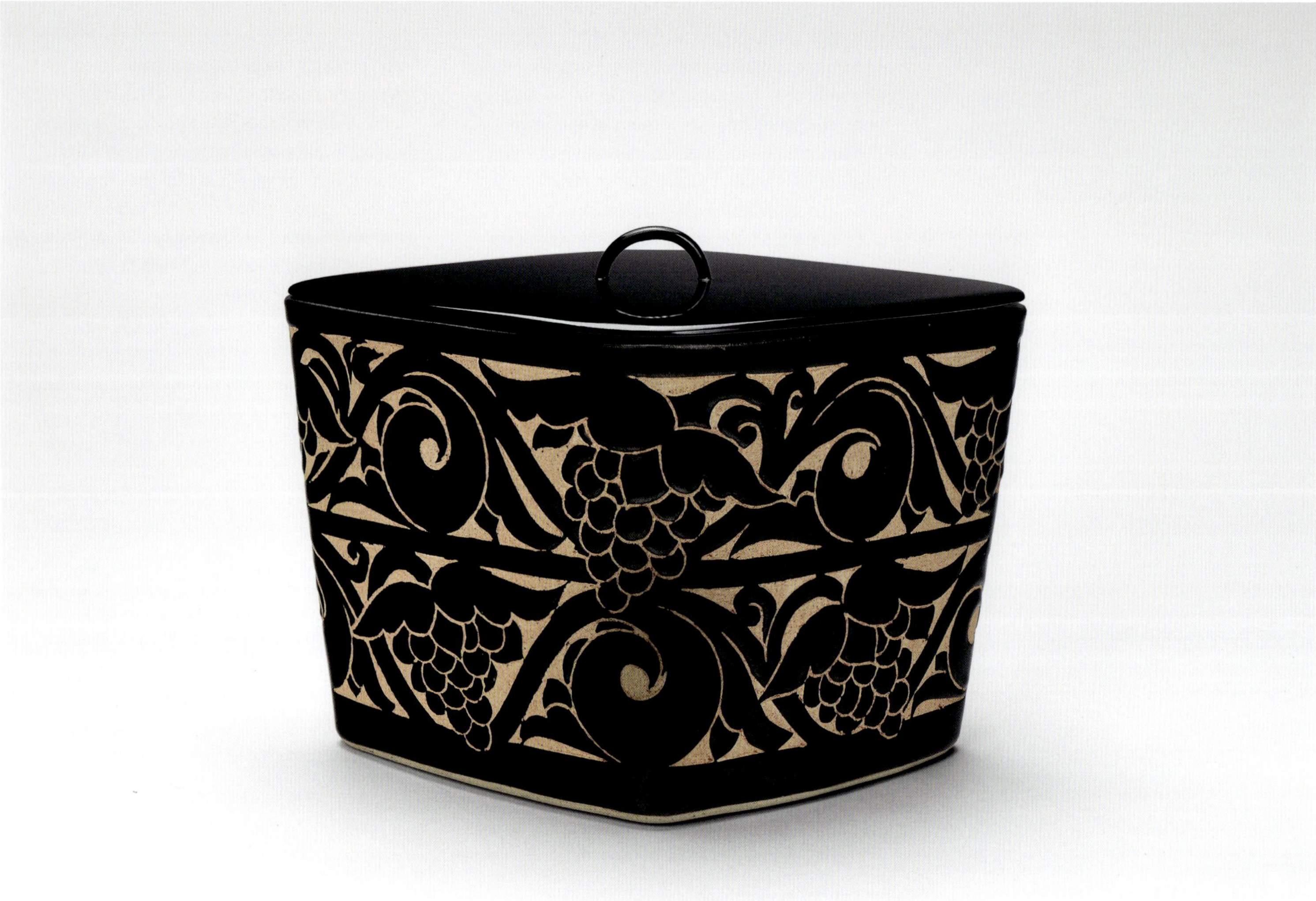

87

Water Container (*Mizusashi*)

Miyanohara Ken
(1898–1977)

Shōwa period (1926–89), 1965

Glazed stoneware; lid: lacquer
6⅞ × 9¾ × 8¼ in. (17.5 × 24.8 × 21 cm)

Gift of Frederick R. McBrien III, 2008-7-9a,b

Trained by the pioneering ceramic masters Itaya Hazan (1872–1963) and Miyagawa Kōzan II (1859–1940), Miyanohara Ken built his first kiln at his home in Tokyo in 1925. He exhibited for the first time in the 1927 Imperial Art Academy Exhibition in Tokyo, and his work was subsequently acquired for the imperial collection.[1] Also in 1927, Miyanohara was a founding member of the Eastern Ceramic Association (Tōtōkai), which sought to raise the status of studio ceramics to a fine art equal to painting and sculpture. He became its head after the death of his mentor, Itaya. From 1929 to 1940, Miyanohara participated in the annual Eastern Ceramic Association exhibitions held at Mitsukoshi Department Store in Tokyo. He moved his kiln several times during World War II, establishing his final one in Chiba Prefecture in 1948, where he created this vessel and worked until his death three decades later.

Throughout his career, Miyanohara experimented freely with techniques and glazes, some modeled on Chinese examples. The chocolate-brown iron glaze on this piece was inspired by Cizhou-style stonewares of the Song dynasty (960–1279). Miyanohara coated the diamond-shaped, hand-molded surface with a thick glaze, and then carved and incised down to the buff clay body to form the grape motif in relief. This is a container for hot water for the tea ceremony and is meant to be handled, so the surface texture is an important element on which Miyanohara focused. With this simple, bold design, the artist transformed a useful vessel into a sculpture that appears to be at once archaistic and modern.[2] FF

1. The Imperial Art Academy Exhibition (Teikoku Bijutsu tenrankai) was one of several important exhibitions for craft artists to achieve official recognition. Miyanohara later was appointed a member of the academy.
2. For another reinterpretation of Chinese glazes, see the jar by Kawai Kanjirō (no. 85).

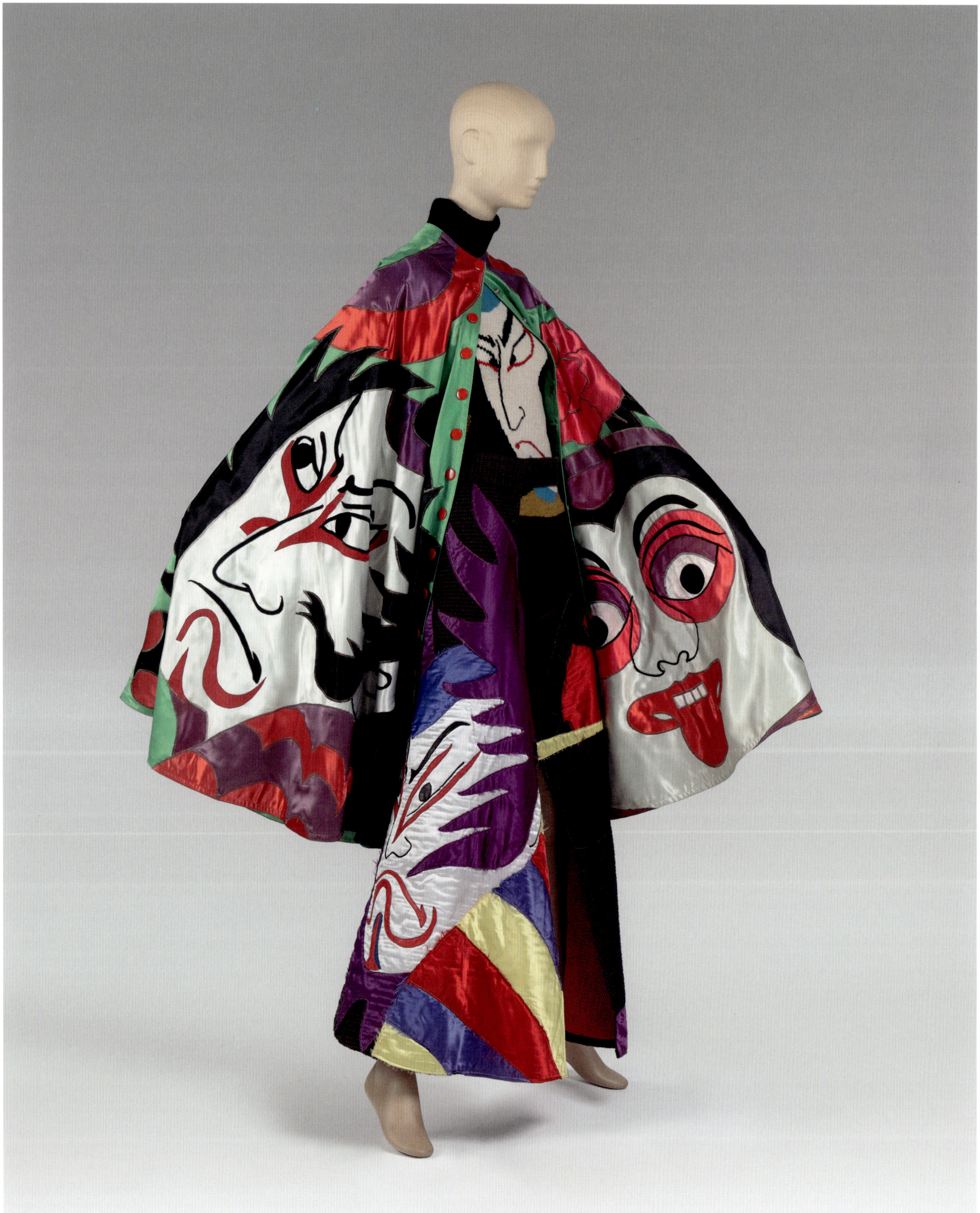

88

Ensemble Consisting of Cape, Bodysuit, and Chaps

Kansai Yamamoto
(1944–2020)

Shōwa period (1926–89), 1971

Wool, synthetic, leather; knit, appliqué

Gift of Hess's Department Store, Allentown, 1974-3-21a–c

In May 1971, Kansai Yamamoto became the first Japanese fashion designer to debut in London. Inspired by kabuki, a classical Japanese form of dance-drama known for its extravagant costumes and exaggerated makeup, and by traditional Japanese dress and ornamentation from workwear to whole-body tattoos, his show was described as "a spectacular coup de théâtre" by the British fashion magazine *Harpers & Queen*.[1]

Featuring flamboyant avant-garde designs, the show was presented at the Great Gear Trading Company on King's Road, a major thoroughfare of London's Chelsea neighborhood and epicenter of the "Swinging London" fashion and cultural scene of the 1960s. Kansai represented the new wave of Japanese fashion designers whose work, while rooted in native traditions, transcended national boundaries with exciting contemporary styles. Among those attending Kansai's 1971 London show was Yvonne Burbage, fashion director of Hess's Department Store in Allentown, Pennsylvania. Burbage was immediately taken by the up-and-coming designer and included him in the store's international imports show of trendsetting fashions for the fall and winter of 1972. The following year, during a buying trip to Asia, Burbage reconnected with Kansai and invited him to create an exclusive collection for Hess's, which was featured in the store's fashion show of contemporary Asian designers that premiered at the newly completed World Trade Center in New York. The collection was later donated to the Philadelphia Museum of Art. Burbage was prescient in her promotion of Kansai, who had also attracted the attention of pop icon David Bowie. A great admirer of Japanese culture, Bowie debuted his androgynous Ziggy Stardust character at New York's Radio City Music Hall in 1973 dressed in womens wear by Kansai provided by stylist Yasuko "Yacco" Takahashin, who had produced the designer's London fashion show. Bowie subsequently commissioned costumes from Kansai for his 1973 *Ziggy Stardust* tour in the United Kingdom and the same year's *Aladdin Sane* shows in the United States.

This ensemble, consisting of a voluminous, brilliantly colored satin cape, bodysuit, and chaps, is one of four outfits from the 1971 fashion show that was featured in *Harpers & Queen*. The appliquéd imagery on the cape and chaps includes kabuki characters in traditional makeup and an emblem of a mask with a protruding tongue, a design often found on Japanese kites; the bodysuit is knitted with the face of a samurai actor. Recalling the quick-change costumes worn in kabuki, the chaps can be easily unsnapped and removed. A pair of Kansai's adaptation of traditional Japanese *okobo* platform sandals, a style worn by geisha during the summer months, is also in the museum's collection (fig. 59). Bowie wore a similar pair of these shoes in a 1973 photograph by Masayoshi Sukita (b. 1938). DB

1. "Kansai Yamamoto Show" 1971, 47.

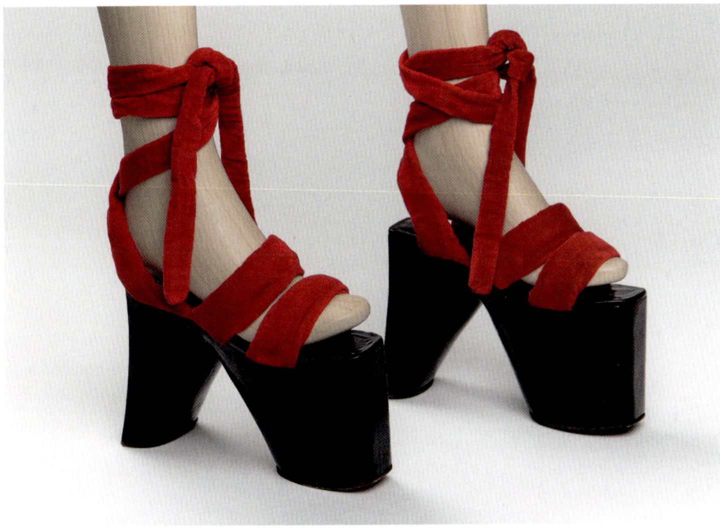

FIG. 59 Kansai Yamamoto. High Platform Shoes. Shōwa period, 1971. *Roiro urushi* (black lacquer) on wood, velvet; H. (back platform): 7½ in. (19.1 cm). Philadelphia Museum of Art: Gift of Hess's Department Store, Allentown, 1974-3-21d,e

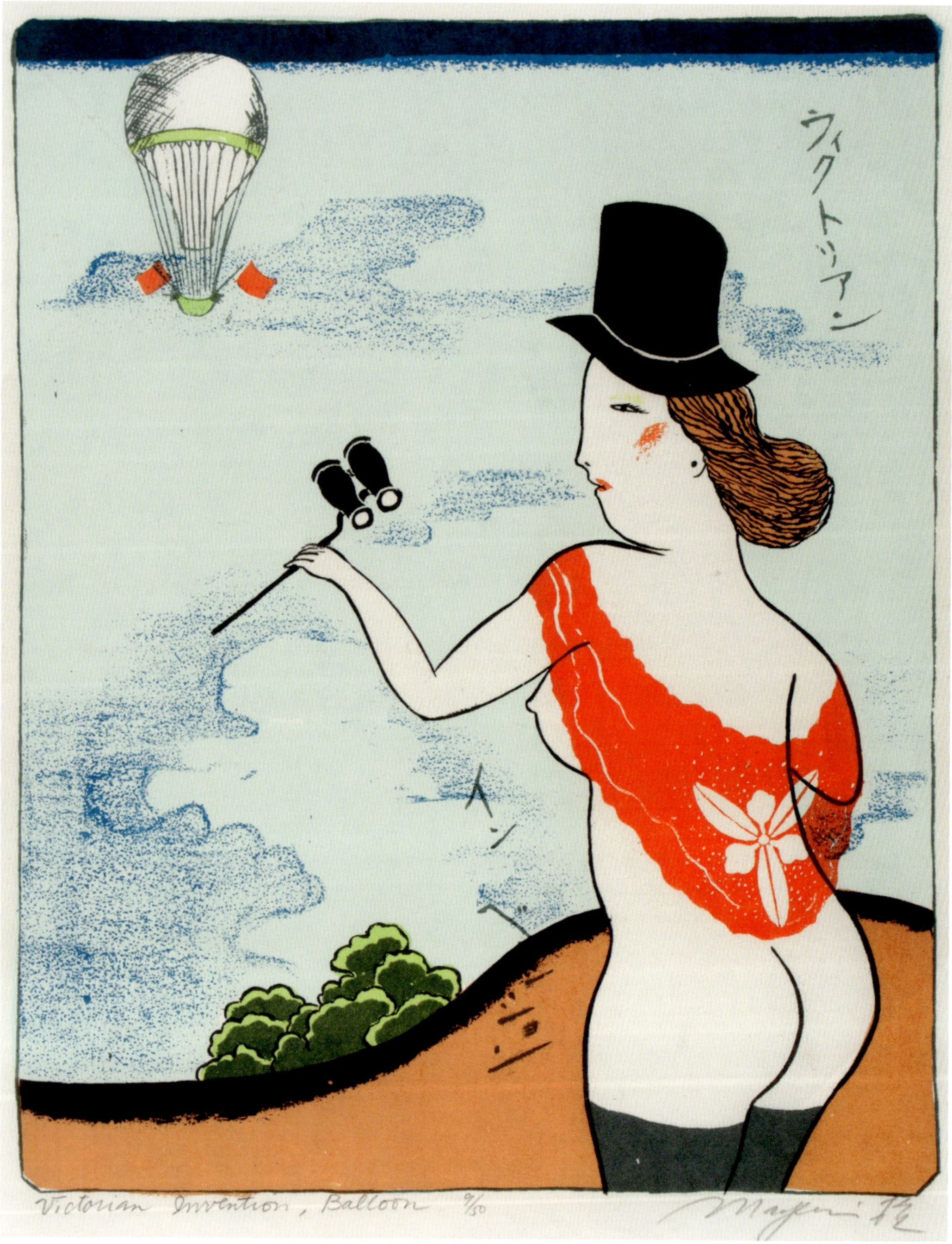

89

Victorian Invention, Balloon

Oda Mayumi
(b. 1941)

Shōwa period (1926–89), 1976

Screenprint; image: 20¾ × 16 in. (52.7 × 40.6 cm)

Gift of Roger Keyes in memory of Kneeland McNulty, 2010-112-1

An auburn-haired woman wearing a top hat lowers her opera glasses so she can gaze at a hot-air balloon in flight. Drawn with confident contour lines and set against an atmospheric sky, the figure is nearly nude, aside from her orange wrap and thigh-high stockings. Contemporary artist Oda Mayumi reimagined the wonder of balloon flight in this hand-pulled screenprint from her series juxtaposing voluptuous figures in proximity with Victorian-era inventions — such as the shower, the telephone, the locomotive, the aerial cycle, and others — as witnesses to modernization.

After graduating from the Tokyo School of Fine Arts (now the Tokyo University of Arts) in 1966, Oda moved to New York, where she studied printmaking at the Pratt Institute. While there she became deeply engaged in anti-war activism, the women's rights movement, and environmentalism, and developed her signature style of female figures as "goddesses" to express these themes. A longtime Zen practitioner, Oda currently resides on her organic farm in Hawai'i, where she continues to paint and make prints.

In this scene, Oda playfully updated a print from more than a century earlier, an impression of which is in the museum's collection. When the first Japanese diplomatic mission traveled to the United States in 1860 (see fig. 1),[1] its members were honored upon their arrival in Philadelphia with the astonishing sight of two hot-air balloons in flight. One of the members drew the scene in his diary, and after its publication, Miyagi Gengyō (1817–1880) made the illustration into a woodblock print (fig. 60), the source for Oda's adaptation. In Japan the subject of hot-air balloon flight became associated with the United States (rather than with France, its place of origin) and often appeared in prints of the 1860s, as in Utagawa Yoshitora's *The Country of America* (fig. 61). Prints depicting the exotic-seeming customs, fashions, practices, and other subjects visible in the port of Yokohama — where citizens from the Five Treaty Nations (France, Great Britain, the Netherlands, Russia, and the US) traded and resided at this time — came to be known as Yokohama pictures (*Yokohama-e*).

This impression shares another link with Philadelphia. In 2010 print scholar Roger Keyes donated it to the Philadelphia Museum of Art in memory of curator Kneeland McNulty (1922–1991). A champion of Japanese prints, McNulty spearheaded the acquisition of the museum's collection of some two hundred Yokohama prints. When McNulty's exhibition of these prints was presented at the Brooklyn Museum in 1972, it was hailed by the *New York Times* as a "surprise, a curiosity, and a delight."[2] Keyes's donation of Oda's vibrant and delightful adaptation thus brings together many threads of Philadelphia history in a single image. JND

1. See Felice Fischer, "Philadelphia and the Art of Japan," in this volume, 13.
2. Canaday 1972, 121.

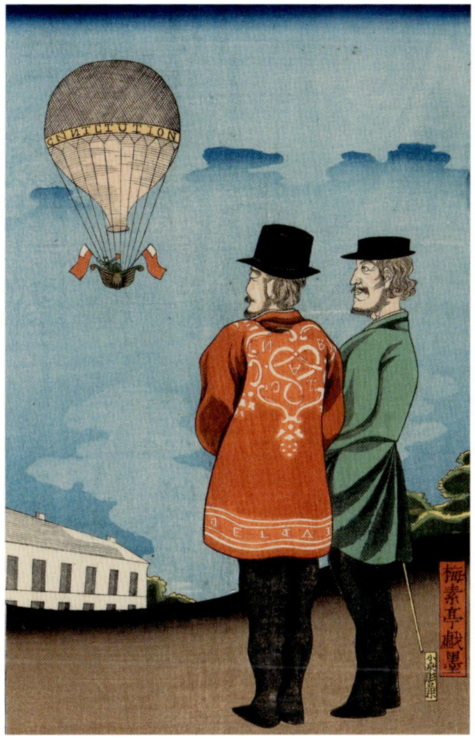

FIG. 60 Miyagi Gengyō (1817–1880). *Picture of a Balloon*, from the series *Camera Views*. Edo period (1615–1868), 1861. Color woodcut, sheet: 14 × 9⅜ in. (35.6 × 23.8 cm). Philadelphia Museum of Art: Purchased with the Lola Downin Peck Fund and with funds contributed by Lessing J. Rosenwald, Mr. and Mrs. Robert A. Hauslohner, Dr. Emanuel Wolff, the Derald and Janet Ruttenberg Foundation, Mrs. Edward G. Budd, Jr., and David P. Willis, 1968-165-26

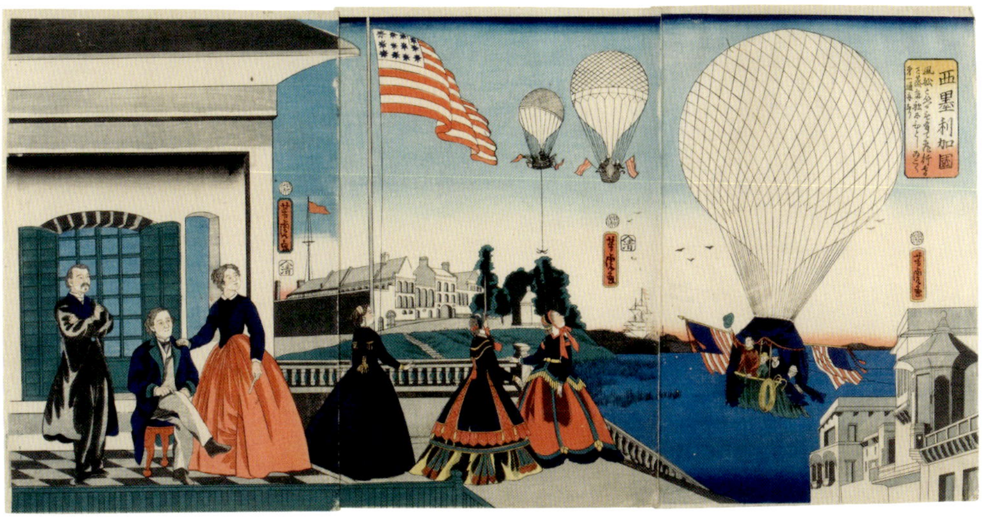

FIG. 61 Utagawa Yoshitora (1836–1887). *The Country of America (People Watching Hot Air Balloons)*. Edo period, 1867. Color woodcut triptych, 14⅜ × 28¾ in. (36.5 × 73 cm). Philadelphia Museum of Art: Purchased with the Lola Downin Peck Fund and with funds contributed by Lessing J. Rosenwald, Mr. and Mrs. Robert A. Hauslohner, Dr. Emanuel Wolff, the Derald and Janet Ruttenberg Foundation, Mrs. Edward G. Budd, Jr., and David P. Willis, 1968-165-108a–c

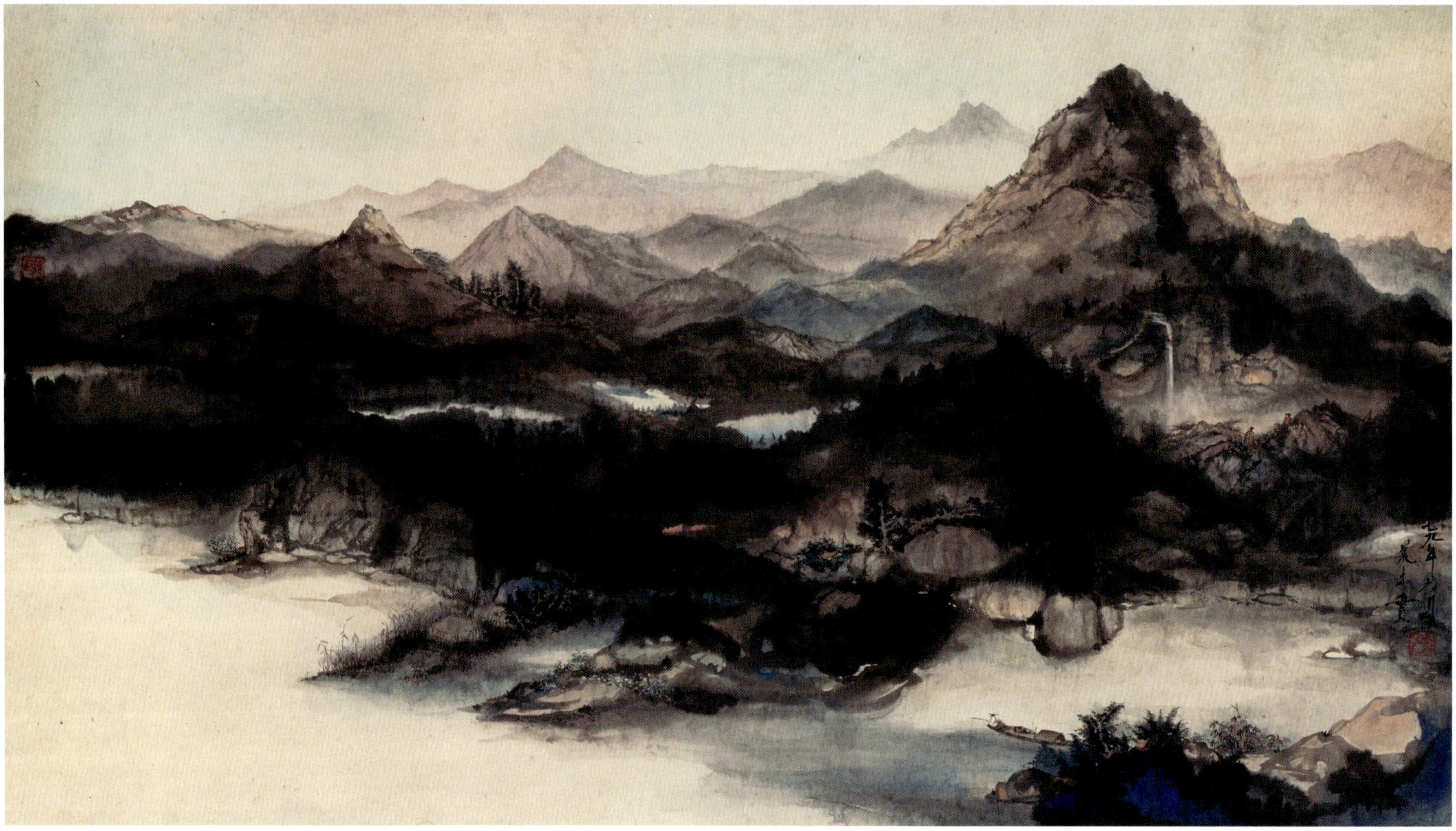

90

Landscape

Minol Araki
(1928–2010)

Shōwa period (1926–89), 1979

Ink and color on paper
36¼ × 63 in. (92 × 160 cm)

Partial gift of David Tausig Frank and Kazukuni Sugiyama and purchased with the Henry B. Keep Fund, 2015-101-1

This impressive landscape is the work of noted industrial designer Minol Araki, whose background was unusually international: he was born to Japanese parents stationed in Manchuria in the city of Dalian. He began his painting studies there under the tutelage of a Chinese family friend, and later studied architecture and design. Araki first set foot on Japanese soil at the age of seventeen, when his family returned to Japan in 1945. He found it a "miniature garden compared with the vastness of China."[1] Araki continued his design studies in Tokyo, where he was exposed to the ideals of the Bauhaus as well as to the ideas and designs of the French-born American industrial designer Raymond Loewy (1893–1986). The latter's influence set Araki on a career in the field, and he opened his own design office, called NOL (from "Minol"), in Japan in 1959.[2]

Araki's design work often took him to Taiwan, where he continued his avocation of painting. On one such visit, he was introduced to the venerable artist Chang Dai-chien (1899–1983), who encouraged Araki in his ink painting experimentation. He developed a style that combines wet-on-wet black and gray ink washes (known as *tarashikomi* in traditional Japanese painting) and finely brushed details. This painting represents a fusion of the dramatic Chinese scenery that surrounded Araki as a child, with echoes of the lower hills and gentle Japanese landscape he experienced as an adult. He did a series of landscapes in this idealized style, the largest of which is called *Hekiba Village* (1985; Minneapolis Institute of Art). While the present work does not have a specific title, it has the "Hekiba" seal that he designed, which links it to the series. Araki sought to remain true to the traditional literati ideal and deliberately stayed outside the Japanese competitive exhibition system, with the first solo exhibition of his work held in museums in Hong Kong, Taipei, and Phoenix in 1998–99.[3] FF

1. Taipei and Phoenix 1998–99, 13.
2. Araki's given name was Minoru, which he anglicized to Minol. In the 1960s he started a second company in New York called PIPA (Personal Interior Products by Araki). A *pipa* is a traditional Chinese musical instrument, whose name is pronounced "hekiba" in Japanese, as reflected by one of the seals on this landscape.
3. Taipei and Phoenix 1998–99.

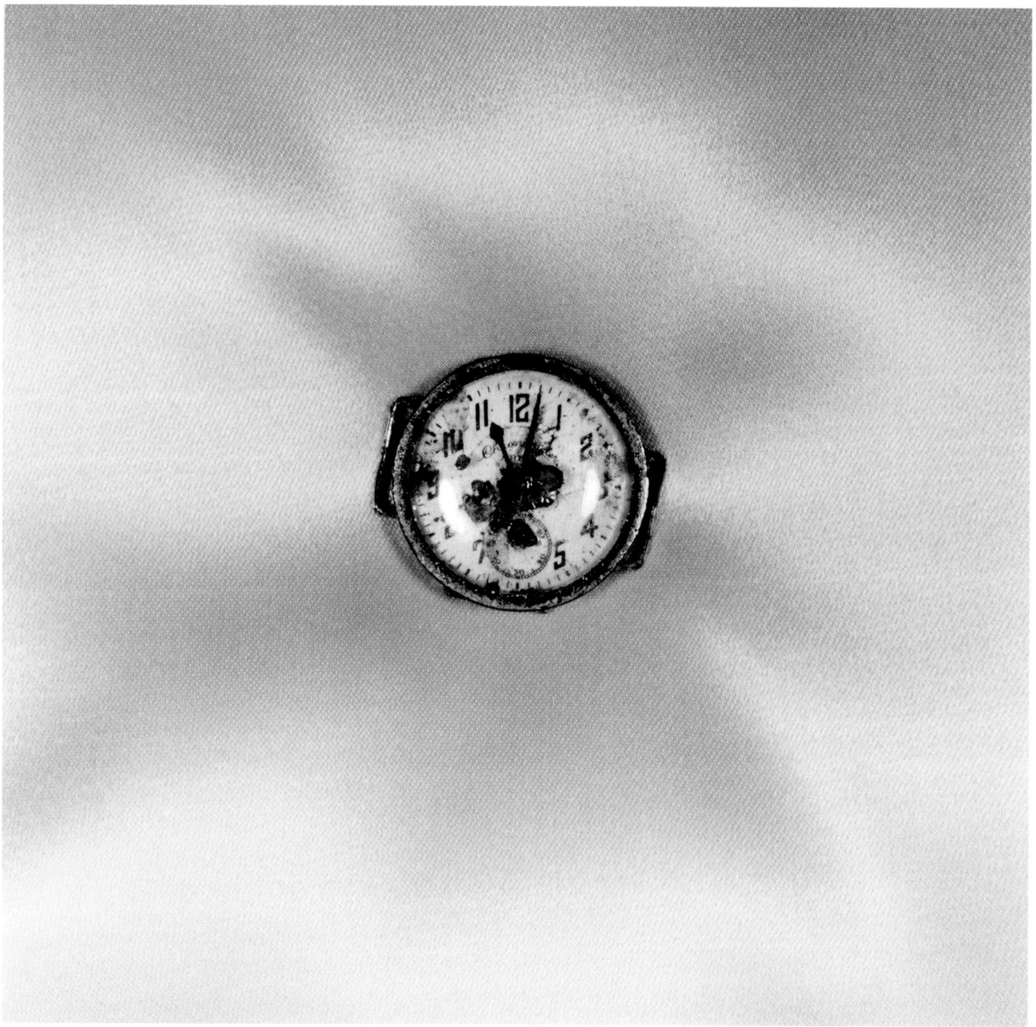

91

A Wristwatch Dug Up in Ueno-machi, approximately 0.7 km from the Epicenter of the Explosion

Shōmei Tōmatsu
(1930–2012)

Shōwa period (1926–89), 1961

Gelatin silver print, $9^{11}/_{16} \times 9^{11}/_{16}$ in. (24.6 × 24.6 cm)

Purchased with funds contributed by the E. Rhodes and Leona B. Carpenter Foundation, 1990-51-109

One of the most important photographers of post–World War II Japan, Shōmei Tōmatsu came of age living near a military base, where he experienced the US occupation of Japan firsthand. Deeply traumatized by the war yet fascinated by the shifting world around him, he began documenting the aftereffects of the conflict and subsequent "Americanization" of Japan, a theme that continued to influence his work for the rest of his career.

In 1961 the Japan Council against Atomic and Hydrogen Bombs sent Tōmatsu to Nagasaki to capture the effects of the atomic bomb dropped there sixteen years earlier, on August 9, 1945. Tōmatsu was shocked to discover that the *hibakusha*, the survivors of the bombing, were continuing to suffer from lingering health problems, the inability to work, and discrimination in marriage due to their exposure to radiation.

The wristwatch in this photograph, one of many objects recovered from the site of the Nagasaki bombing, belonged to one of the day's 73,884 victims.[1] Its stopped time at 11:02 marks the exact moment of the tragedy. Yet what Tōmatsu wanted to capture is how time did not stop for the *hibakusha*; rather, 11:02 is the moment when their suffering began.

To make this image, Tōmatsu placed the wristwatch on a piece of lustrous fabric and used lighting from multiple angles to cast dramatic shadows on the otherwise simple object. The shadows radiating from the watch are reminiscent of the flash of light experienced by victims when the bomb was dropped. Tōmatsu created similar effects in other photographs in the series, including in his close-up of *hibakusha* Senji Yamaguchi's keloid-scarred skin, in which the pattern of light and dark once again evokes the horror of the burst of light (fig. 62). In another image, a melted glass bottle recovered from the site of the bombing appears as if it is a severed body part floating in the sky (fig. 63).

Tōmatsu pioneered a style called *gunsha-shin* (literally "photo constellation") wherein a single image viewed on its own may seem fragmented or abstract, but when the series of photographs is viewed together, the larger meaning becomes manifest, making it an emotionally charged experience for the viewer.[2] Rather than opting for the narrative-driven journalistic style of the older generation of photographers, Tōmatsu, along with contemporaries such as Hosoe Eikō (b. 1933), produced images that are visually aggressive and surreal, often focusing on unsettling details of everyday life in postwar Japan.[3]

Haunted by what he had witnessed in Nagasaki, Tōmatsu continued to document the lives of the *hibakusha* for the next forty years, cultivating lifelong relationships with some of the survivors. EM

1. Tōmatsu 1995, 8.
2. Tsuchiya 2013, 80.
3. Phillips 2004, 52.

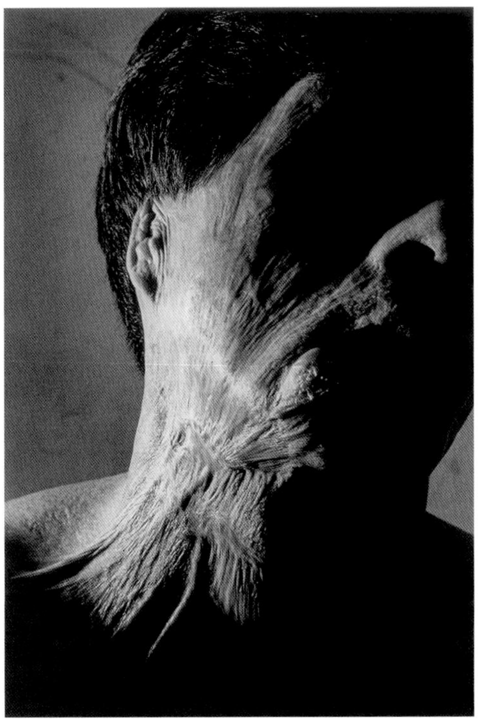

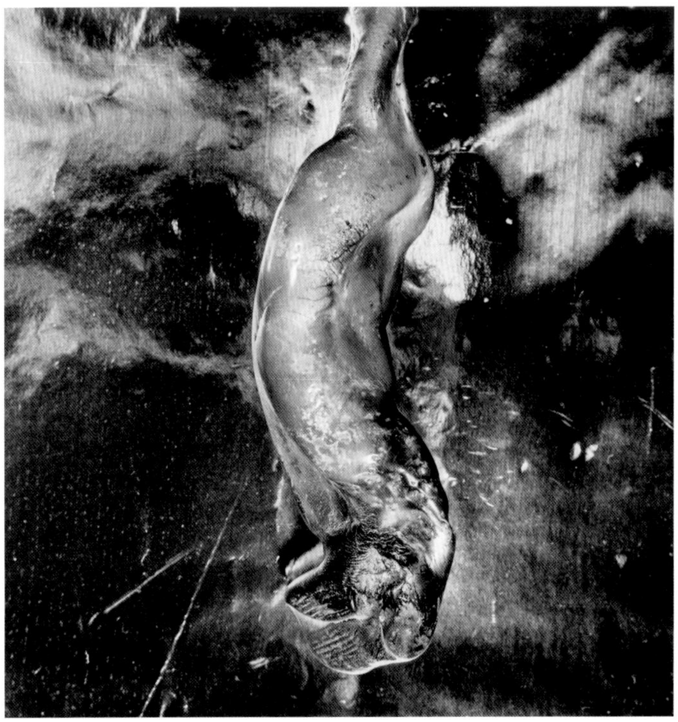

FIG. 62 Shōmei Tōmatsu. *Mr. Senji Yamaguchi*. Shōwa period, 1962. Gelatin silver print, 12⅝ × 85⁄16 in. (32.1 × 21.1 cm). Philadelphia Museum of Art: Gift of the artist, 1990-51-112

FIG. 63 Shōmei Tōmatsu. *Bottle Melted and Deformed by Heat Rays and Fire*. Shōwa period, 1961. Gelatin silver print, 10¼ × 9¾ in. (26 × 24.7 cm). Philadelphia Museum of Art: Purchased with funds contributed by the E. Rhodes and Leona B. Carpenter Foundation, 1990-51-110

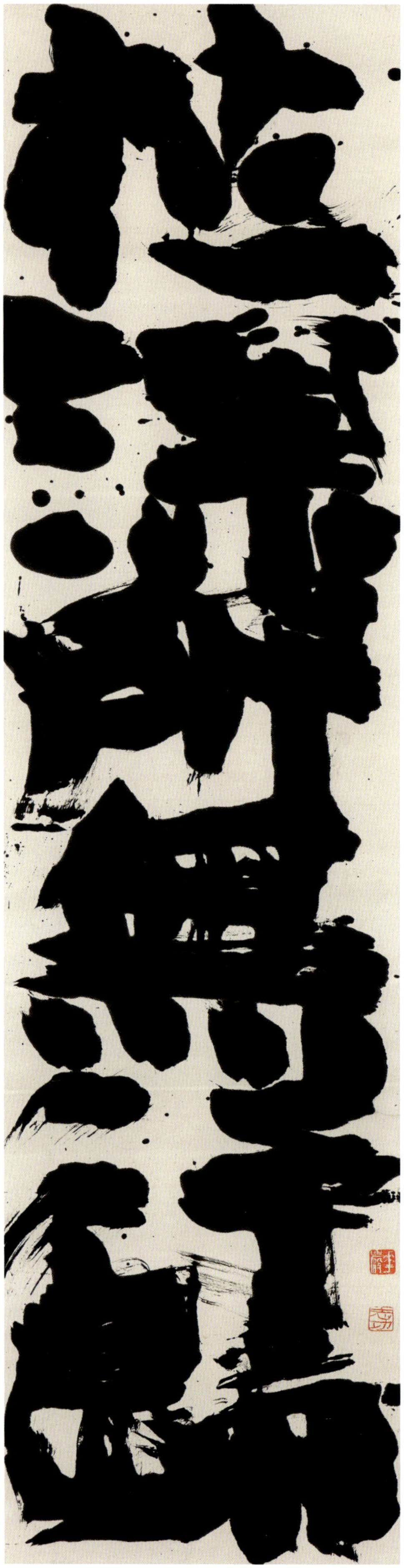

92

No Footprints Show Where Flowers Are Deep

Munakata Shikō
(1903–1975)

Shōwa period (1926–89), 1959

Ink on paper, mounted as a hanging scroll; 53 × 13¾ in. (134.6 × 34.9 cm)

Gift of Carl Zigrosser, 1974-179-5

Munakata Shikō, one of Japan's most celebrated modern print artists of the twentieth century, was born in Aomori to a family of blacksmiths. In 1924, at the age of twenty, he moved to Tokyo to pursue an artistic career, and he became one of the central artists in Japan's *mingei* (folk crafts) movement that began in the late 1920s and was advocated by the philosopher and art critique Yanagi Sōetsu (1889–1961). Munakata revolutionized the concept of traditional Japanese woodcut art, liberating it from the small-scale ukiyo-e format by creating large pieces for screens and wall murals. His artistry earned him worldwide acclaim and top prizes at the São Paulo Biennale in 1955 and the Venice Biennale in 1956. Munakata was equally skilled as a painter in oils and sumi ink, exploring their dynamic material characteristics across media. He was also recognized for the skill with which he depicted varied subject matter, including nature, Buddhism, folk tales, contemporary poetry, and even Western literature.

On his first visit to the United States in 1959, Munakata worked with Philadelphia artist Arthur Flory (1914–1972) to create his first series of lithographs (fig. 64). It was at this time that he brushed *No Footprints Show Where Flowers Are Deep*.[1] The thick, almost abstract lines of the characters were executed with slashing strokes at a furious speed and seem to burst beyond the paper surface. Rendered with an intense concentration of ink, the six-character verse served as Munakata's personal motto and appears repeatedly in his work. It sheds light on the artist's life philosophy: Individual achievements are comparable to footprints left while walking in nature's wilderness, and will soon be erased by falling petals. To leave a trace in one's meandering journey thus requires continuous devotion and determination. The formal composition of this hanging scroll recalls the large-character inscriptions in the Buddhist tradition (see no. 21), functioning as a visual koan that spurred Munakata's artistic inspiration throughout his life.[2] YX/FF

1. Munakata made this calligraphy while a guest at the home of Carl Zigrosser, curator of prints at the Philadelphia Museum of Art. This was in the tradition of Edo-period (1615–1868) literati artists such as Ike Taiga (1723–1776) who would paint "performance" pieces (*sekiga*) on the spot for their hosts.
2. Munakata credited the ceramist Kawai Kanjirō (1890–1966; see no. 85) with imbuing his life with a devotion to Zen Buddhism. See Philadelphia et al. 2002–4, 80–81, no. 7. Munakata's focus was on the *Kegon* (*Flower Garland*) *Sutra*, as attested to by the Kegon seal Munakata carved and stamped on this calligraphy.

FIG. 64 Munakata Shikō. *Calligraphic Design*. Shōwa period, 1959. Printed by Arthur Flory (American, 1914–1972). Lithograph, 15 × 19½ in. (38.1 × 49.5 cm). Philadelphia Museum of Art: Gift of the artist, 1959-95-3

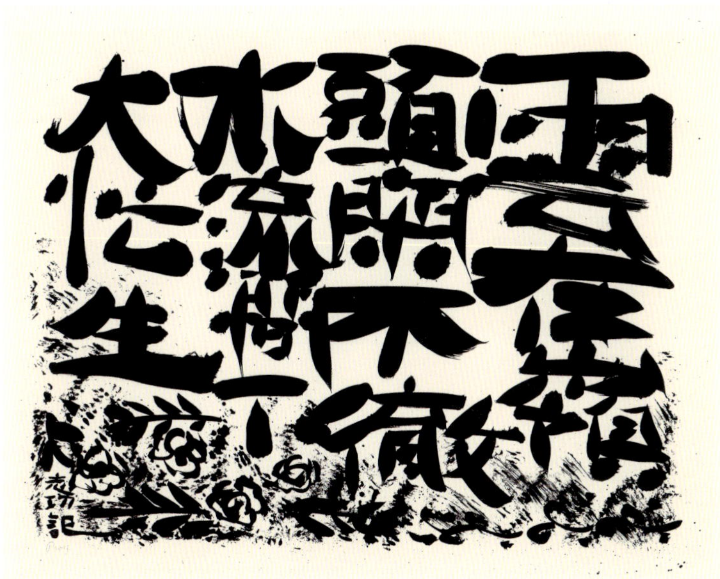

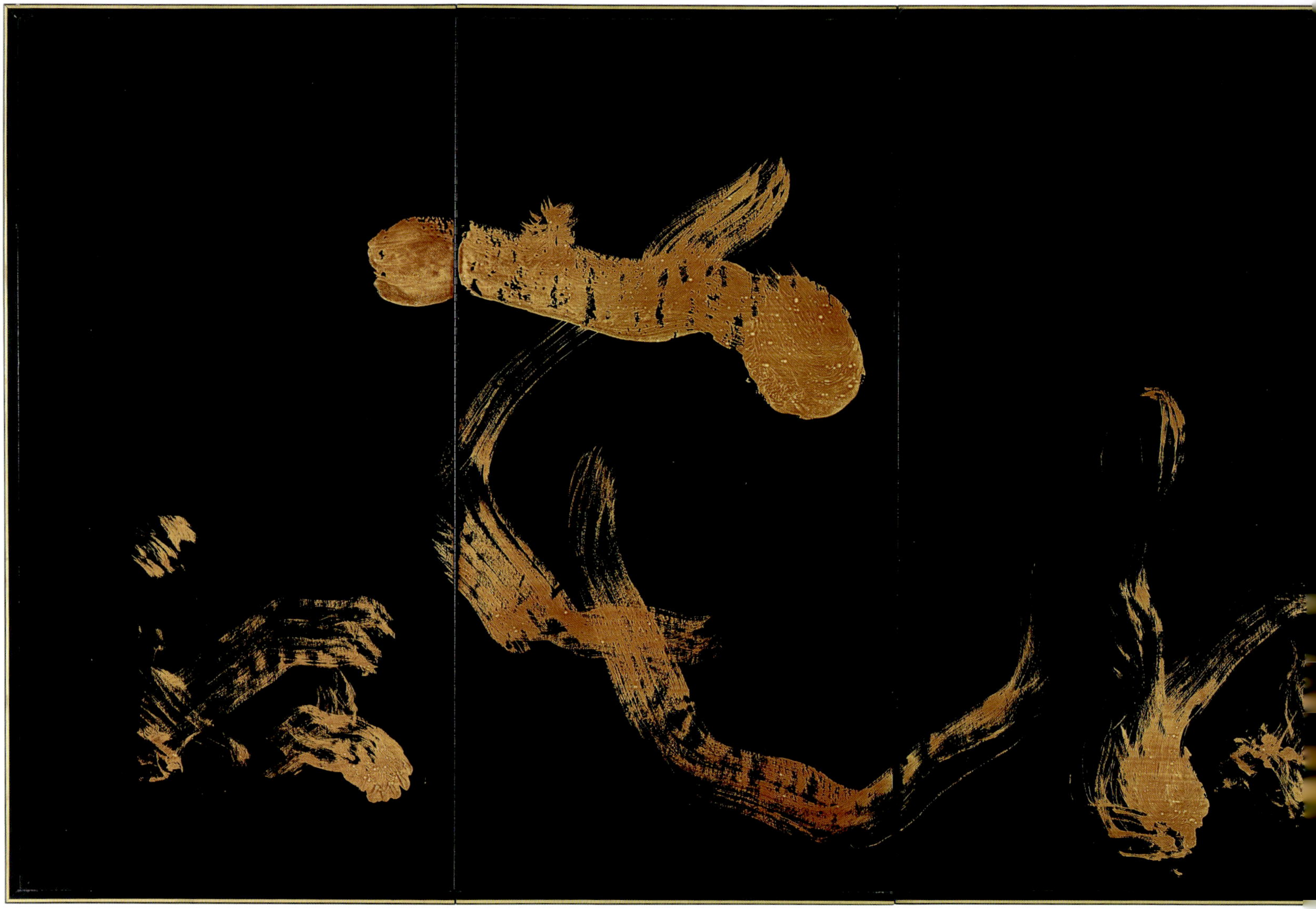

93

Green Willows, Crimson Blossoms

Morita Shiryū
(1912–1998)

Shōwa period (1926–89), 1964

Aluminum-flake pigment in polyvinyl acetate medium, yellow alkyd varnish on black kent paper; mounted as a four-panel screen
42 in. × 7 ft. (106.7 × 213.4 cm)

Purchased with funds contributed by Barbara B. and Theodore R. Aronson, 2009-187-1

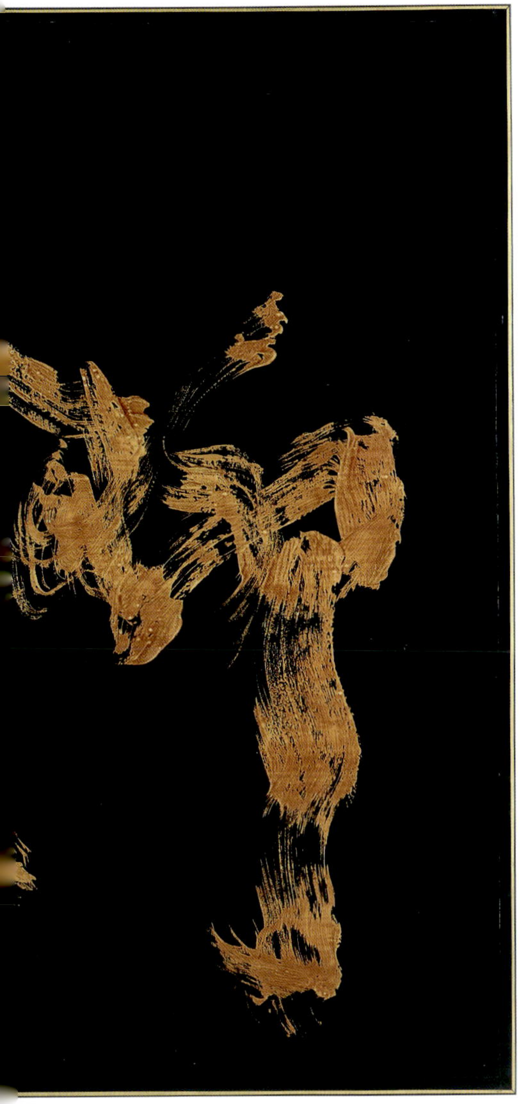

Morita Shiryū was postwar Japan's premier mediator between Japanese calligraphy and Western abstract art. As one of the founders of the group Bokujinkai (People of the Ink) and editor of its journal *Bokubi* (Beauty of ink) in the early 1950s, Morita brought Japanese art and artists to international attention, corresponding with Western artists such as the American painter Franz Kline (1910–1962), whose work appeared in *Bokubi*. While Morita acknowledged the affinities between calligraphic lines and Abstract Expressionism, he stressed that the original meaning of the Japanese characters was still embedded in them.

In his own calligraphy, as seen on this screen, Morita used actual characters but literally pulled them apart to form abstract patterns. The four-character phrase "green willows, crimson blossoms" is almost illegible without the printed title, yet it reflects Morita's deep roots in tradition, in this case, the Zen tradition.[1] The golden characters on a black background may in turn have been inspired by Japanese sutras (see no. 10).

Morita was also experimental in his technique called *shikkin* (lacquer gold). The artist painted the characters with a large brush on a black paper surface with aluminum-flake pigment and then covered the whole with a lacquer varnish. The four panels are joined with metal hinges rather than the traditional paper ones, making the work sturdier and more suitable for a Western setting. Morita's calligraphy met with great international success, but later in his career he seemed to abandon the global dialogue he helped initiate. The phrase on this screen reflects his realization that "East is East and West is West," and that the moment of intersection of the two artistic worlds had passed.[2] FF

---

1. The source of this phrase may be the *Compendium of the Five Lamps*, a compilation of anecdotal biographies of famous Buddhist practitioners in China by the Chinese Zen monk Dachuan Puji (1179–1253). It appears in a dialogue between the Song-dynasty (960–1279) Zen masters Long Huaqiu and Jiuxian Yuxian: "In autumn, mountain and rivers are cold; When spring comes [there are] green willows [and] crimson blossoms," implying that everything has its season and its distinct characteristics. The printmaker Munakata Shikō (1903–1975; see no. 92) employed the same line in his 1959 work *Three Friends of Shikō*. See Philadelphia et al. 2002–4, no. 24.
2. See Bogdanova-Kummer 2020, 119–41.

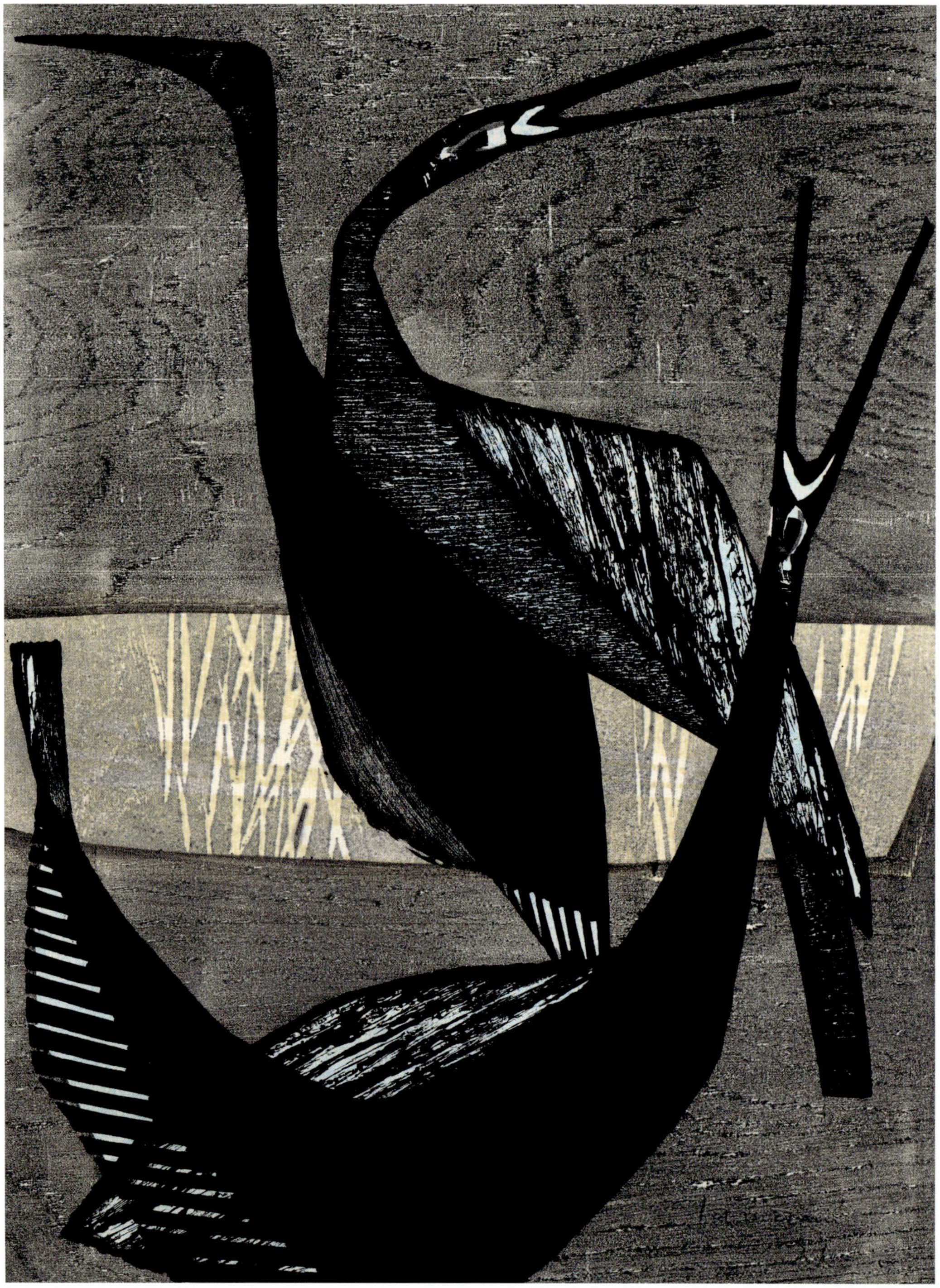

94

Tori B (*Birds B*)

Shima Tamami
(1937–1999)

Shōwa period (1926–89), 1962

From the portfolio *The Modern Japanese Print: An Appreciation*

Edition 52/510

Woodblock print, sheet:
21⅜ × 15¼ in. (54.3 × 38.7 cm)

Gift of Carl Zigrosser,
1964-201-1(6)

In late August 1959, the celebrated novelist James A. Michener invited Carl Zigrosser, curator of prints at the Philadelphia Museum of Art, to be one of the judges for a contemporary Japanese print contest. An ardent collector and promoter of Japanese modern prints in the United States, Michener decided to organize a competition with ten winners, who would each receive a monetary prize and whose original prints would be included as part of a limited-edition book (fig. 65). Zigrosser accepted the offer enthusiastically, and on October 1, 1959, the contest was announced, with Zigrosser, modern print expert Oliver Statler, *Japan Times* art critic Elise Grilli, and collector Nathan Polowetzky as judges.

While the goal was to choose prints that "best represent the richness and power of the modern Japanese print,"[1] in actuality only works that belong to the *sōsaku hanga* (creative prints) movement qualified for submission since the contest rules stated that nominations had to be unpublished works that were self-designed, self-carved, and self-printed.[2] Michener was deeply impressed by the breadth of work created by *sōsaku hanga* artists, who borrowed the best of both Japanese and European printmaking traditions.

The book opens with Hiratsuka Un'ichi's *Byōdō-in, Lakeside*, a graphic black-and-white print characteristic of the artist's later oeuvre (fig. 66). Inspired by the clarity and strength of expression of old Buddhist prints, Hiratsuka printed large black areas several times over to achieve the desired intensity and created jagged lines by digging the chisel sideways while carving. In this print, however, the mass and roughness are masterfully balanced by the delicate iris flowers springing in the center of the image.

For *Tori B* (*Birds B*), Shima Tamami approached the familiar subject of birds as a still life. Using as many as seven blocks — six plywood and one paper — she created diverse woodgrain patterns to covey the feeling of the soft cloudy sky, the ripples on the water, the glossy feathers of one bird, and the mottled coloring of another. According to Michener, the print's subtle play of tones and textures immediately resonated with critics and the public alike.[3]

Published in an edition of 510 copies, the book that encases these prints was made to be a work of art itself. The text was set by hand in Perpetua type on handmade Japanese paper, which was bound in three-colored hemp cloth and housed in a wooden slipcase. After the required number of prints was produced, the blocks were destroyed, making the book a rare collector's item. MP

1. Michener 1968, 55.
2. As opposed to the more traditional system of print production in Japan, in which the artist created the design while the carving and printing were done by professional artisans supervised by the publisher.
3. Michener 1968, 36.

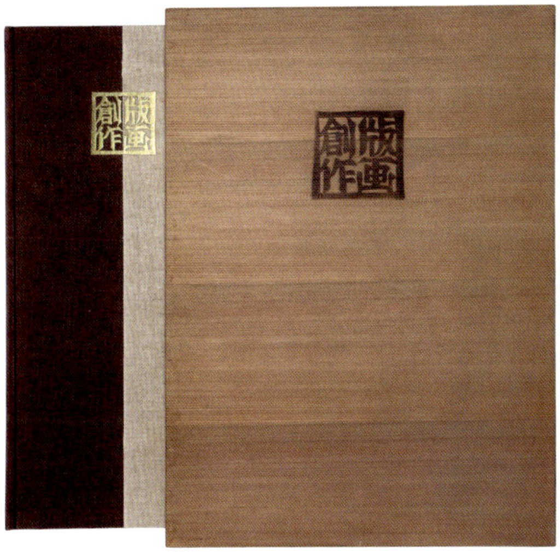

FIG. 65 Various Artists. *The Modern Japanese Print: An Appreciation*. Published by Charles E. Tuttle Company, Tokyo. Shōwa period, 1962. Portfolio of ten prints, 21 7/8 × 15 5/8 × 1 3/16 in. (55.6 × 39.7 × 3 cm). Philadelphia Museum of Art: Gift of Carl Zigrosser, 1964-201-1(1–10)

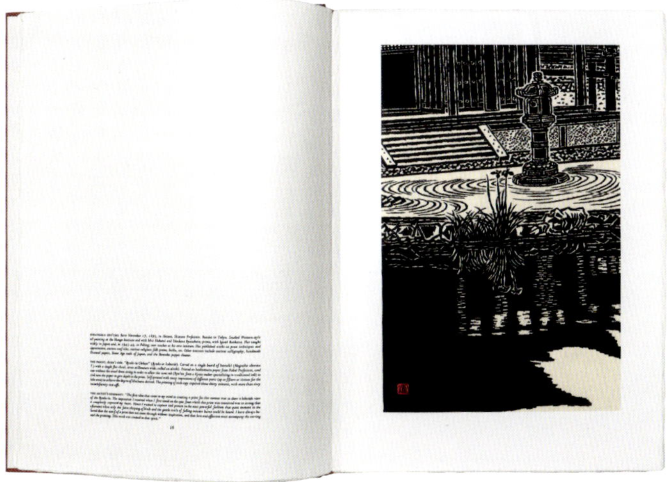

FIG. 66 Hiratsuka Un'ichi (1895–1997). *Byōdō-in, Lakeside*, in the portfolio *The Modern Japanese Print: An Appreciation*. Shōwa period, 1962. Woodblock print, sheet: 21 3/8 × 15 1/4 in. (54.3 × 38.7 cm). Philadelphia Museum of Art: Gift of Carl Zigrosser, 1964-201-1(1)

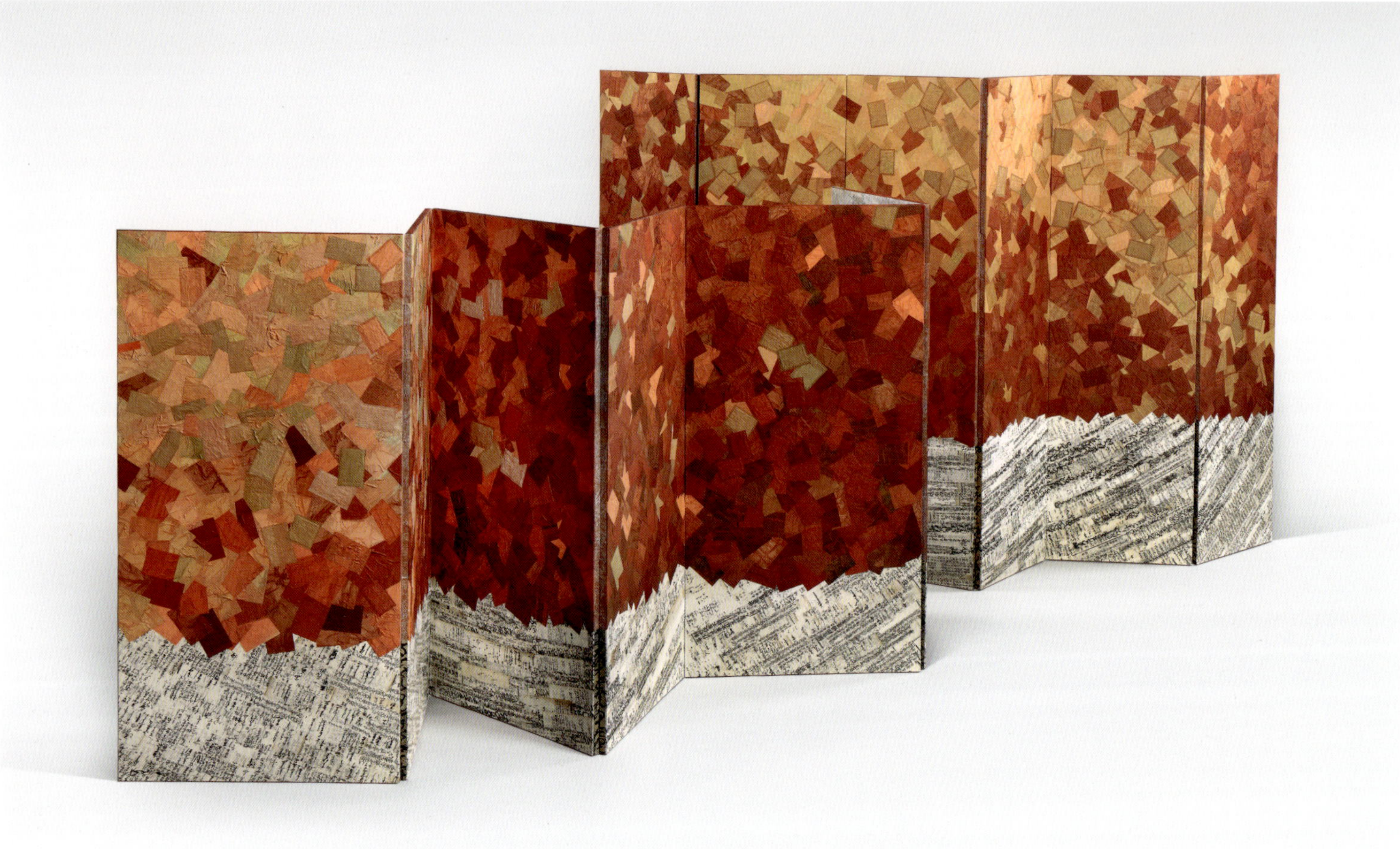

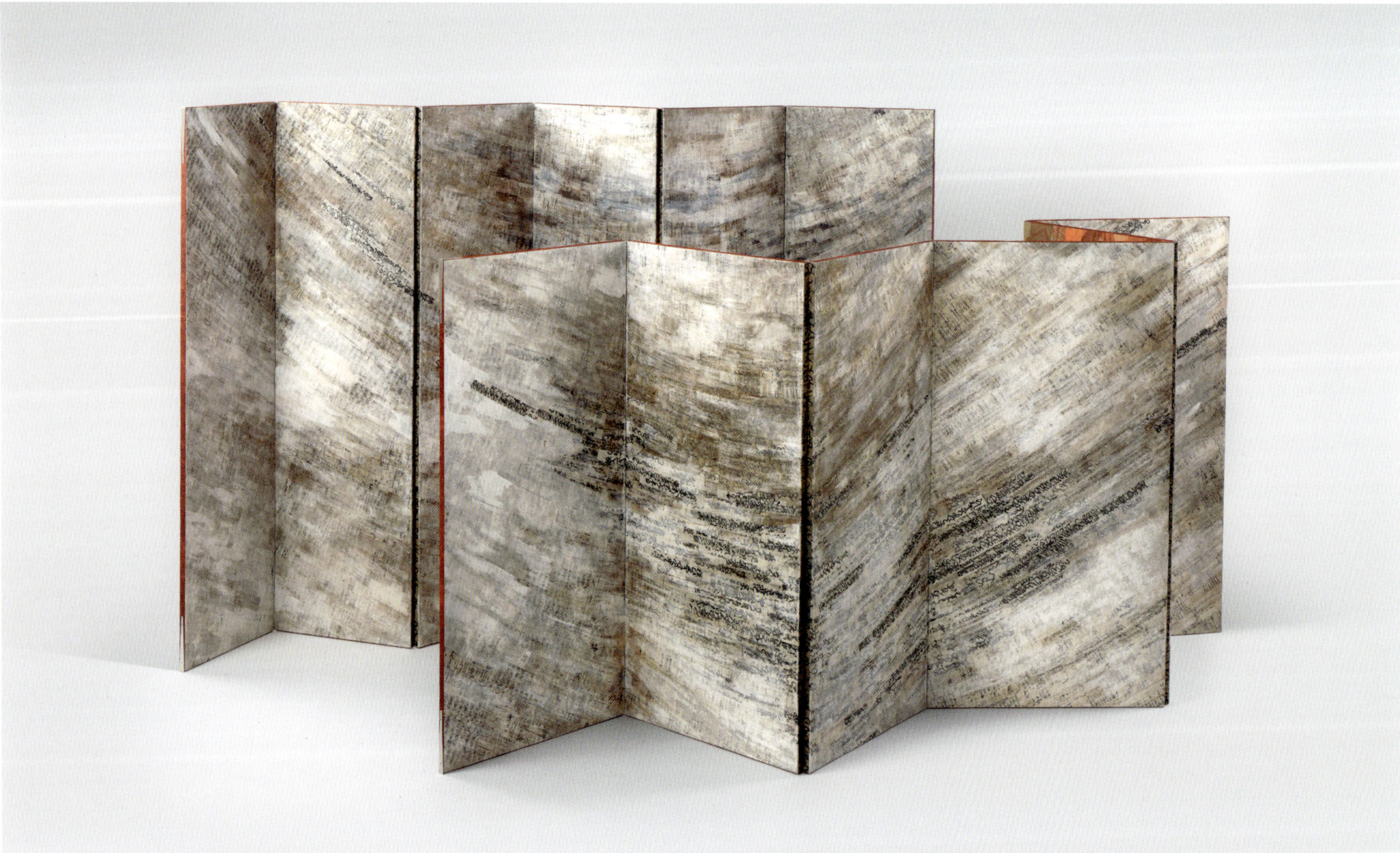

95

Kotodama

Maio Motoko
(b. 1948)

Heisei period (1989–2019), 2008

Silk and paper, mounted as a pair of screens; screen A: 60¹⁄₁₆ in. × 8 ft. 9⅛ in. (152.5 × 267 cm); screen B: 48¹⁄₁₆ in. × 12 ft. ⅛ in. (122 × 366 cm)

Purchased with funds contributed by Mr. and Mrs. Howard H. Lewis and an anonymous donor, 2009-79-1a,b

Folding screens with paper hinges were a Japanese invention and came into widespread use during the sixteenth and seventeenth centuries, when samurai and merchants alike built sumptuous residences during an era of renewed peace that came to be called the Edo period (1615–1868). Screens serve a dual purpose: they are architectural elements and simultaneously a focus for aesthetic contemplation. They divide rooms, provide temporary privacy, or function as backdrops for special occasions. Their painted surfaces run the gamut of Japanese painters' subjects: landscapes, flowers and birds, as well as figures.

It is onto this tradition that Maio Motoko has grafted her unique vision of screens in contemporary life and art. Originally trained in scroll and screen mounting, Maio was led by her curiosity about the traditional formats to explore the techniques used to create them. Her intimate knowledge of the intricacies of production allows her to reinvent the format to suit her own imagination and creativity. She delights in playing with all the possibilities of the screen format, including its physical structure and surface textures.

Called *Kotodama* (The soul of language), this pair of screens is a superb example of Maio's creations. On one side she has layered small scraps of red silk from kimono undergarments over a mulberry-paper surface. The lower part of the screen is covered with fragments of antique paper taken from books or pages from old account ledgers normally used as filler inside screens or sliding doors (see detail below). While traditional screens have plain paper backing, the other side of Maio's screens is completely covered with these word-filled paper scraps, painted over with a pale white wash of shell and walnut oil. The scraps have no meaning by themselves but create a visual world of words.

A playful spirit comes out in *Kotodama* in elements such as the "leaves of words" (*koto no ha*) in the form of poetry playing cards (*karuta*). Such cards are still used in Japanese culture as part of a New Year's game involving the poems from the *Hyakunin isshu* (*One Hundred Poems by One Hundred Poets*). Moreover, the sizes of the two screens are not the same: one is shorter with wider panels than the other. However, they both cover approximately the same amount of surface area. Maio uses tradition and amends it brilliantly, not only in her "inside out" imagery and screen proportions but also in the butterfly hinge technique she developed, which allows the screens to be shown in various configurations. FF

Detail of screen 2009-79-1a, showing scraps of red kimono fabric and fragments of antique paper

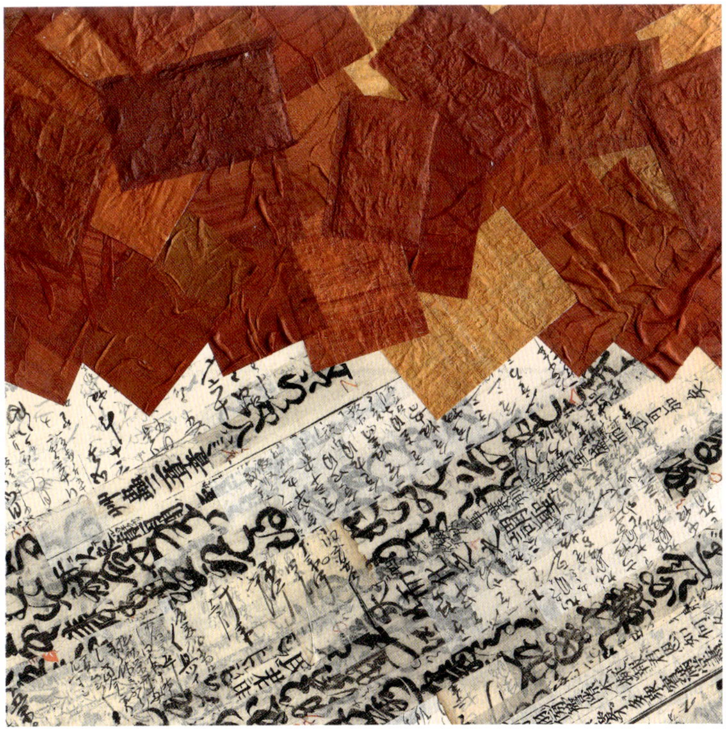

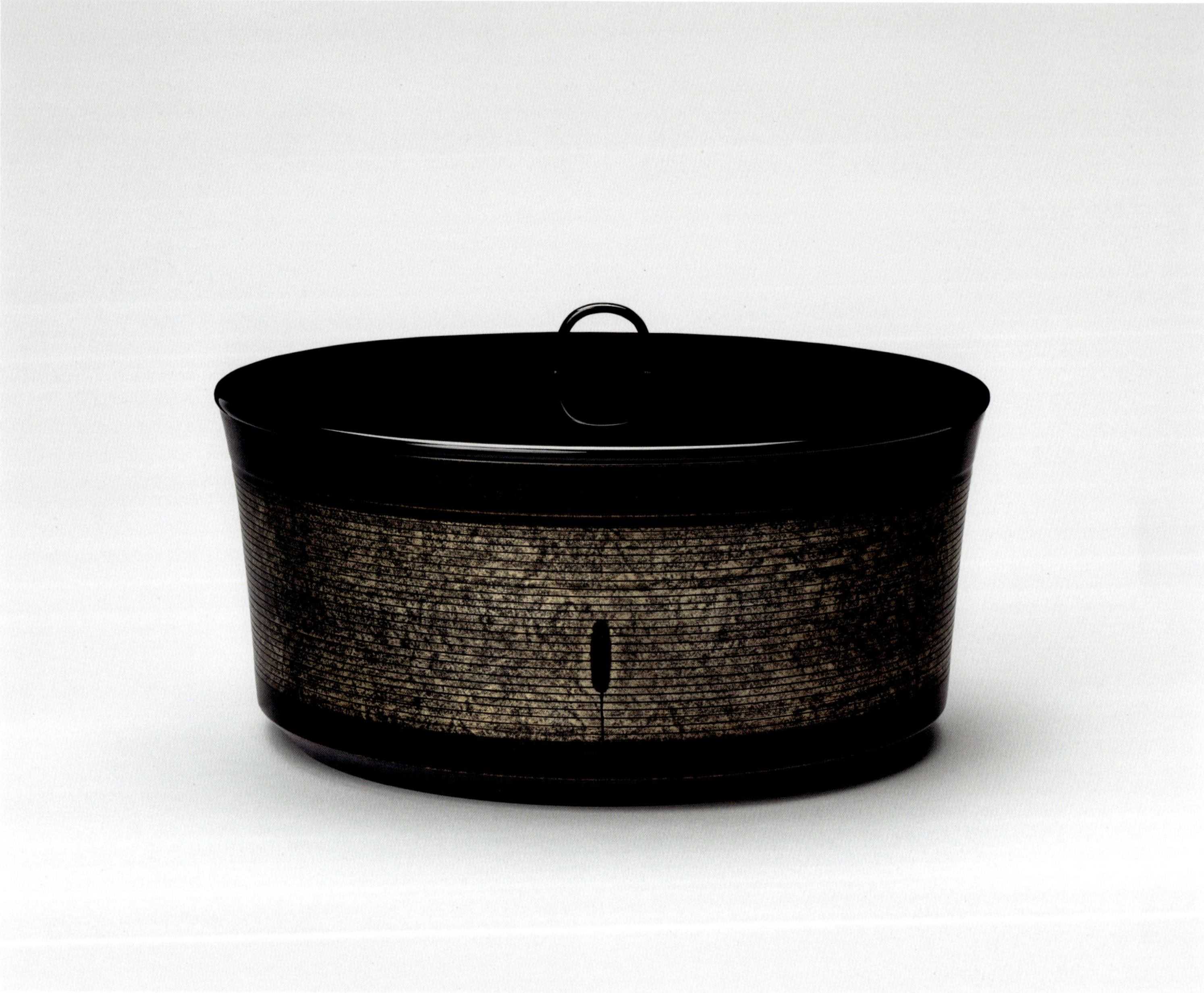

96

Water Container (*Mizusashi*) with Lid

Uozumi Yasuhiko Iraku III
(b. 1937)

Heisei period (1989–2019), 2002

Lid carved by Kawakita Ryōzō (b. 1934)
Lacquer decoration on lid by Shioda Keishirō (1926–2006)

Copper alloy with tin and lead (*sahari*), applied bands of lead; lid: wood, lacquer; 4 × 8⅜ in. (10.2 × 21.3 cm)

Gift of John J. Medveckis, 2002-44-1a,b

Uozumi Yasuhiko, better known by his art name Iraku III, is the third generation of metal artists in his family. He trained with his grandfather Uozumi Iraku I (1886–1964), designated a Holder of Intangible Cultural Property (also known as a Living National Treasure) for his metalcraft skills. Uozumi Yasuhiko succeeded to the Iraku name and built his reputation as an artist employing the copper alloy known as *sahari*. His outstanding skills have been recognized by the government of Japan, which named him as well a Living National Treasure, in 2002. In 2008 he was further acknowledged with the Order of the Rising Sun, Gold Rays with Rosette, awarded by the emperor of Japan for contributions to the arts and culture.

The technique used for producing *sahari* is a traditional one that originated with the production of gongs and bells. For both of these instruments, the metal must be well tempered to withstand hard physical use over a long period of time. The same is true of *mizusashi*, the containers that hold the hot water used in preparing green powdered tea for the tea ceremony. Uozumi incised a precise band of lines around the outer surface of this water container, a difficult feat on the curved body of the piece. *Mizusashi* traditionally have lacquer lids, and the two artists who collaborated to make the lid for this container, Kawakita Ryōzō and Shioda Keishirō, are also both Living National Treasures. FF

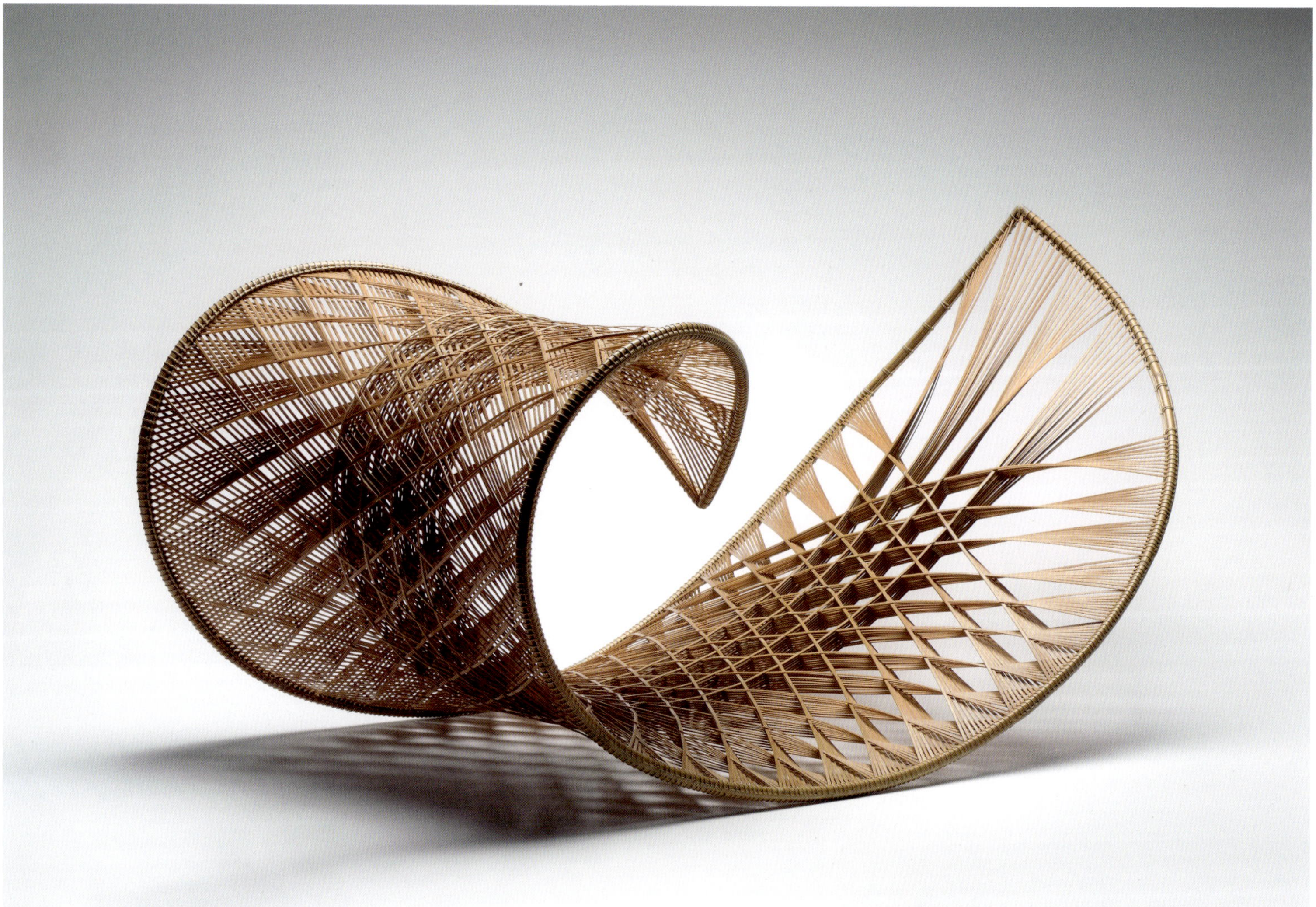

97

Big Wave

Yamaguchi Ryūun
(b. 1940)

Heisei period (1989–2019), 2001

Madake bamboo and rattan
35 × 20¼ × 18½ in. (88.9 × 51.4 × 47 cm)

Gift of Norma Gene Lykes, 2010-178-25

Remnants of baskets have been dated to as early as the Jōmon period, and Japan is home to over six hundred varieties of bamboo.[1] Since it is so plentiful, bamboo has been used for building construction, furniture, basketry, and tea-ceremony implements. Artists who work with bamboo undergo many years of training to develop and hone their skills, often harvesting and preparing the bamboo themselves. Yamaguchi Ryūun lives and works in Beppu, on the southern island of Kyushu, where *madake* bamboo is plentiful. Many famous bamboo artisans have made their home there, including Yamaguchi's mentor, Shōno Shōunsai (1904–1974), who in 1967 became the first bamboo artist to be named Holder of Intangible Cultural Property (popularly known as Living National Treasure) for his skills. After a course of study in the basics of basketry at the Beppu Vocational School, Yamaguchi apprenticed himself to Shōno in 1963, and four years later was given the Award of Excellence at the New Work Exhibition for Bamboo Products. Since then, he has garnered numerous awards, and his work is widely collected both in Japan and abroad.

Working bamboo into sculptural forms is a labor-intensive process, and a piece such as *Big Wave* can take Yamaguchi several months to make. The process begins with the preparation of the bamboo by leaching out oils and sugar from the stalks. Then the artist splits the bamboo into long flexible strips. The complex pattern of lines and crosshatching employed by Yamaguchi reveals how highly attuned he is to the nature of his materials and how far he can literally bend them to his creative will.[2] Yamaguchi titled this work to conjure the surging waves of Katsushika Hokusai's *The Great Wave* with Mount Fuji in the background (fig. 67). With this nearly three-foot-long sculpture, Yamaguchi has joined deep-rooted craft practices and a bold exploration of form. FF

1. The most common type of bamboo is *madake* (*Phyllostachys bambusides*), which is used in this piece. See no. 1 for an example of a Jōmon-period ceramic.
2. Called *sen suji*, or "thousand line," the technique involves weaving the bamboo into parallel lines rather than plaiting it. Rattan is used to tie the junctures of the bamboo strips, as seen in the detail illustrated here.

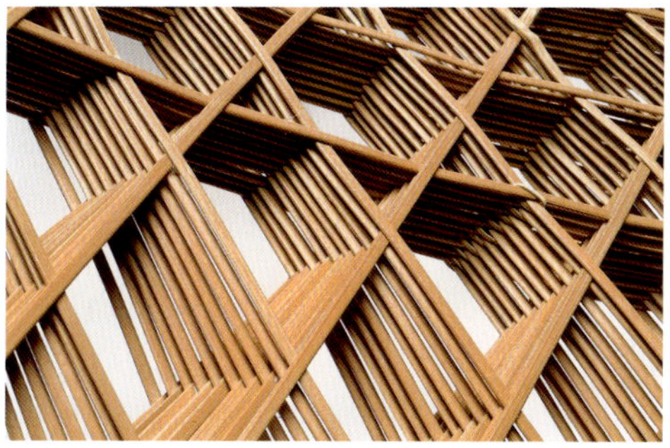

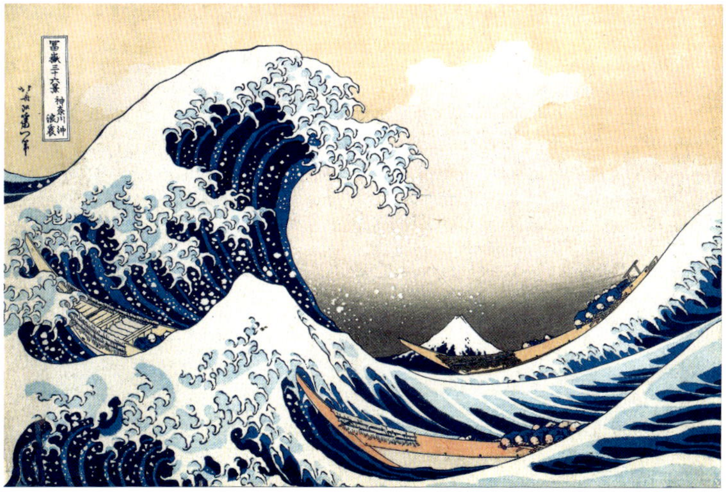

FIG. 67 Katsushika Hokusai (1760–1849). *Under the Wave off Kanagawa* (*Kanagawa oki nami ura*), also known as *The Great Wave*, from the series *Thirty-Six Views of Mount Fuji* (*Fugaku sanjūrokkei*). Edo period (1615–1868), c. 1830–32. Color woodblock print, 10⅛ × 14¹⁵⁄₁₆ in. (25.7 × 37.9 cm). The Metropolitan Museum of Art, New York: H. O. Havemeyer Collection, Bequest of Mrs. H. O. Havemeyer, 1929

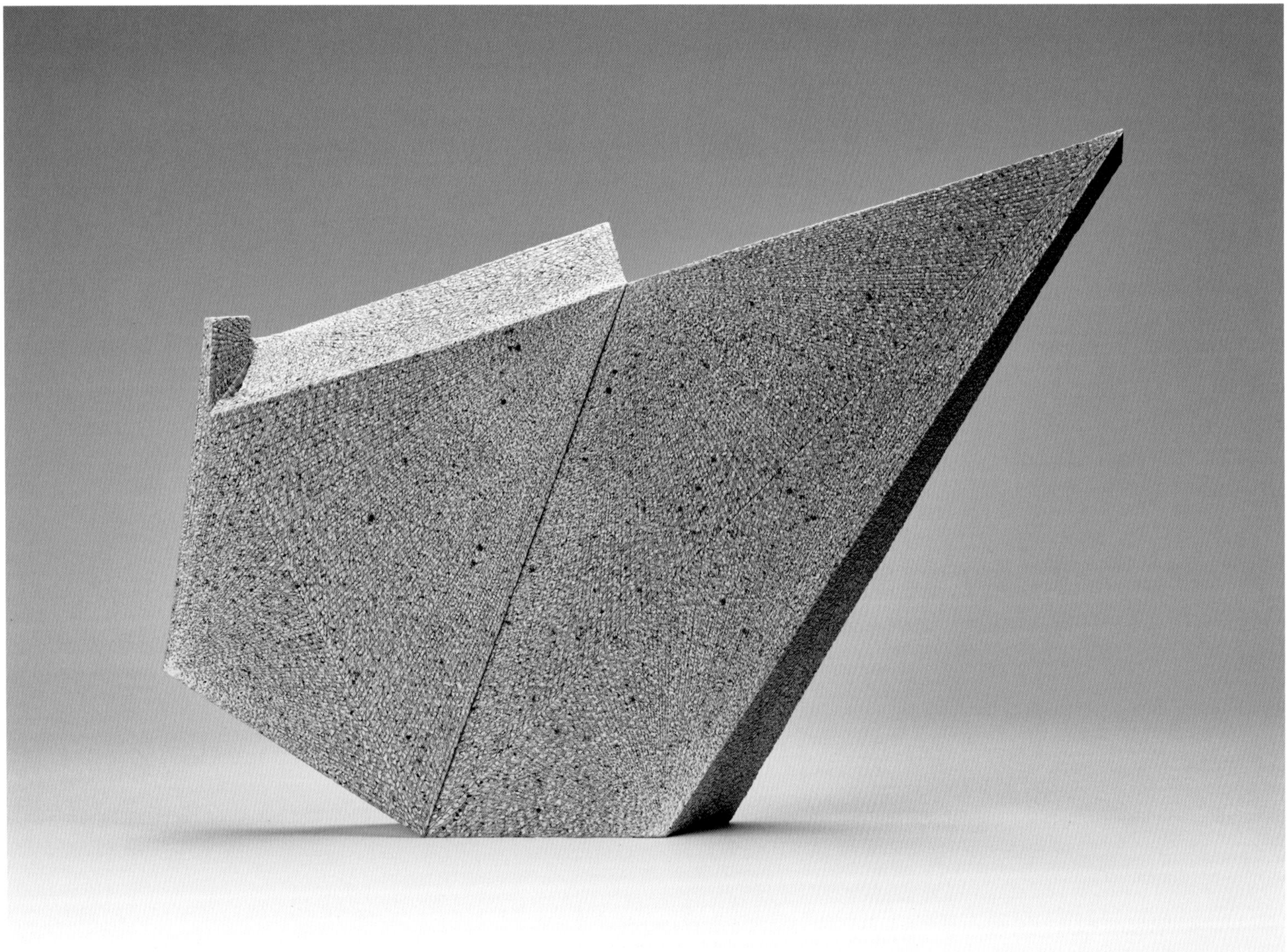

98

Saiseki Zōgan Nōkata (Noh-Inspired Form with Colored Clay Inlays)

Kishi Eiko
(b. 1948)

Heisei period (1989–2019), 2005

Stoneware with colored clay inlay
22⅜ × 30⅝ × 3⅛ in. (56.8 × 77.8 × 7.9 cm)

Gift of Frederick R. McBrien III in memory of Anne d'Harnoncourt, 2009-2-1

The powerful geometric shapes of Kishi Eiko's *Nōkata* series were inspired by actors of the Noh theater in their voluminous, richly embroidered robes (see no. 42). The dynamic balance of this sculpture recalls an actor suddenly frozen in a powerful pose but ready to step forward at any moment and recite his next line. In the artist's words, works from this series display the "inherent tension between tranquility and vibrant energy" in Noh performance, where the held gesture is often more praised than movement.[1]

The work is executed in Kishi's signature *saiseki zōgan* (literally "colored clay inlay") technique. The artist has explained that in devising this technique she was inspired by iridescent insect wings and crystallized rocks. In a laborious process, Kishi prepares chamotte — a coarse grainy clay — in ten different colors and mixes it with fine clay; she then hand builds her sculptures from slabs, leaving the final elegant form thin and hollow. After drying, the form is striated with a *kanna* knife, punctured with a needle, and filled with tiny slips of colored clay to create the mosaic surface. Between firings, Kishi applies a transparent glaze that gives the artwork its shimmering quality. A single object may take three months to complete.

White glaze pools in the corners of the object, from which fine lines radiate like rays of light across the whole surface. The random pockets of blue, yellow, pink, and brownish red that are apparent up close coalesce when one steps back from the work, to reveal the grand design and the artist's keen sense of balance and shape.

Kishi studied art history at Kyoto Seika University but became increasingly interested in ceramic techniques and established her kiln in Kyoto in 1980. The complexity of her technique is even more impressive considering that, unlike many contemporary ceramic artists in Japan, she does not belong to a movement or a lineage and is largely self-taught. Her work has been exhibited extensively in Japan and abroad, and since the mid-1980s she has won numerous awards, including the prestigious Grand Prix at the Asahi Ceramic Art Exhibition in 1985. MP

1. New York 2008, n.p.

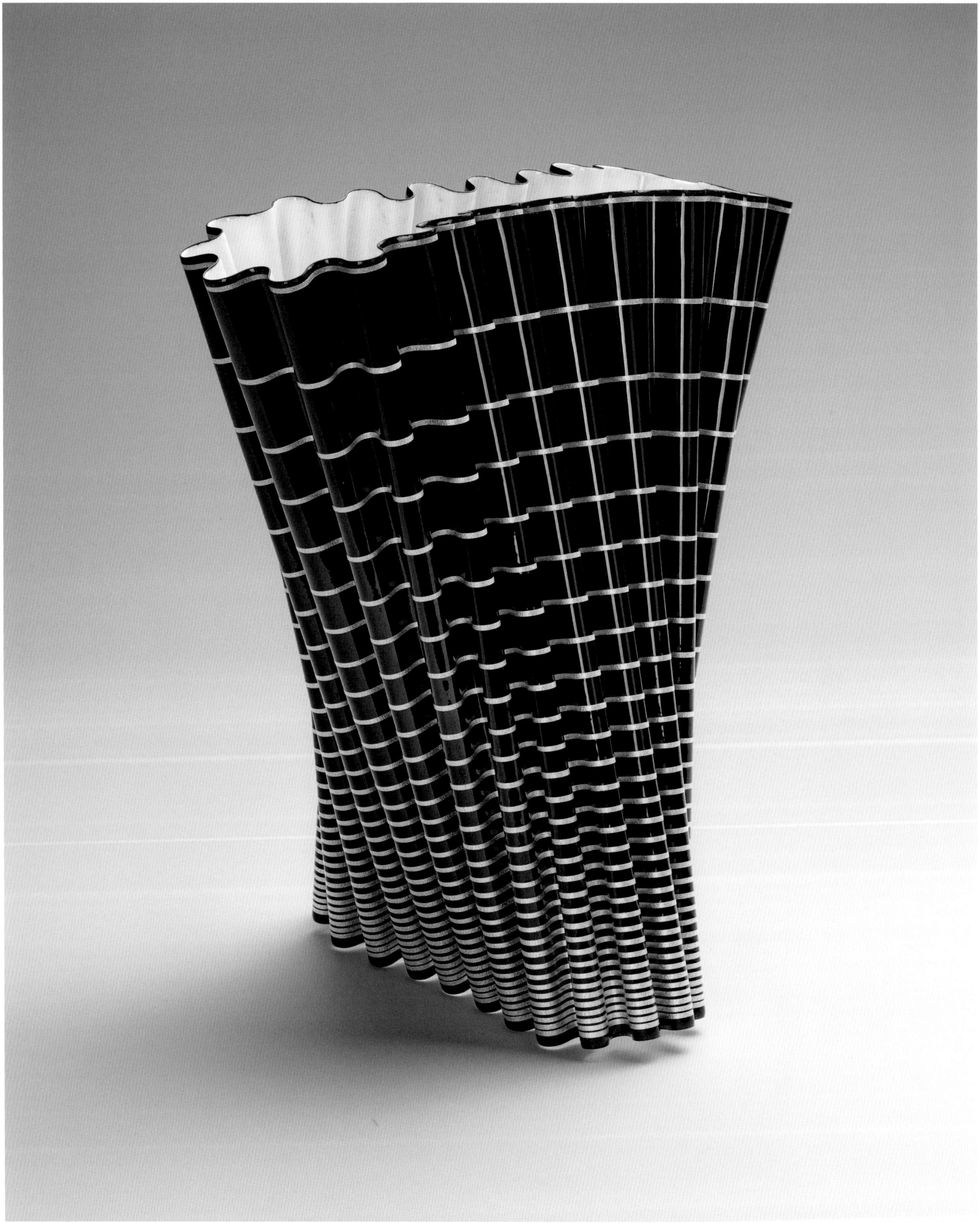

99

Yumegatari (Reverie)

Takeyama Naoki
(b. 1974)

Heisei period (1989–2019), 2013

Enameled copper and silver leaf
15½ × 9½ × 8⅞ in. (39.4 × 24.1 × 22.5 cm)

Purchased with funds contributed by Barbara B. and Theodore R. Aronson and Maxine and Howard Lewis, 2014-34-1

Paper-thin sheets of copper formed into elegant spiraling verticals are the springboards for Takeyama Naoki's creativity. He twists and bends the unfinished copper using no tools other than his hands. Once the desired shape is found, the process of applying enamels begins. A basic color of enamel, blue in this piece, is applied and fired in an electric kiln at about 800 degrees Celsius, and additional hues are blended into successive layers, each of which are again fired, as many as ten to fifteen times. Then the process of adhering the silver-leaf inlay begins: each strip of inlay is individually cut and applied by hand, a painstaking task requiring great concentration and precision. The piece is then fired several more times to ensure that the silver leaf has fused with the enamel base. Each work requires about one month to complete and reveals supreme artistry and craftsmanship in perfect harmony.

The art of enameling, basically fusing glass onto metal, found popularity during the Meiji period (1868–1912), when foreign audiences at the world's fairs admired the enamel pieces exhibited by artists such as Namikawa Yasuyuki (1845–1927).[1] Takeyama studied the traditional methods at the National University of Arts and Music in Tokyo. Although he uses the techniques of his forebears, his sculptural pieces are unique. He emphasizes his engagement with the materials of his craft over the creation of a useful object by omitting a bottom for his pieces and by giving them poetic names, such as *Yumegatari* (*Reverie*). FF

1. See PMA acc. no. 1965-196-1.

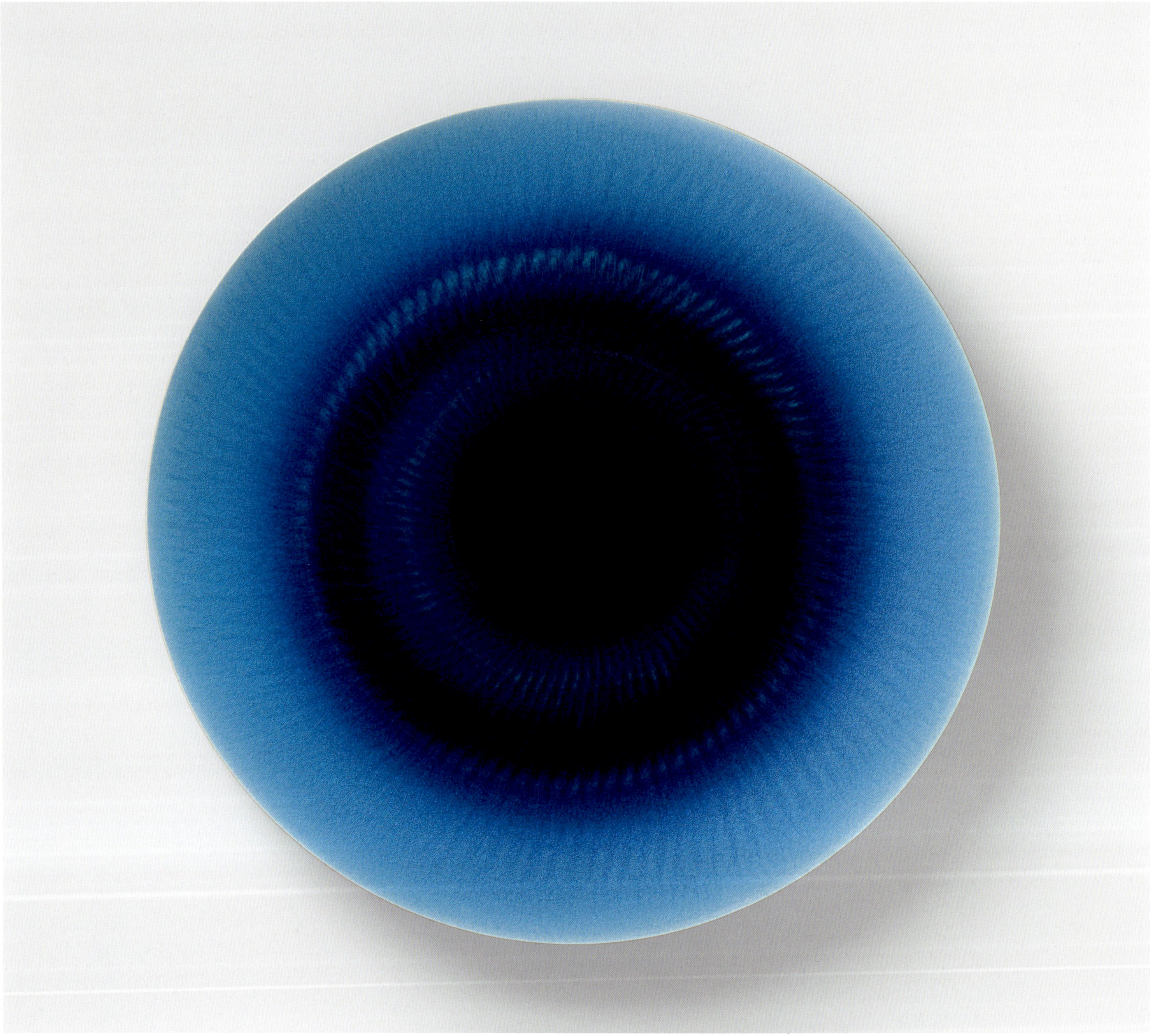

100

Vessel with Blue Glaze

Kimura Yoshiro
(b. 1946)

Heisei period (1989–2019), 2013

Half-porcelain, cobalt blue glaze
2⅞ × 25⅞ in. (7.4 × 65.8 cm)

Purchased with the East Asian Art Revolving Fund, 2018-37-1

Cerulean blue of the sky merges into sapphire purple-blue of the sea, ending in a deep cobalt pool at the center of this extraordinary vessel. Over two feet in diameter, it is one of the largest such chargers made by the ceramist Kimura Yoshiro, who lives and works in Hiroshima. Originally inspired by the azure blue of the Aegean Sea and by the turquoise Persian tile work he saw on his travels, the intense blue glaze Kimura created is the only color he employs for his ceramics. Developed over a long period of experimentation, the glaze is known as "Kimura blue" among aficionados of his work, although he simply calls it "blue glaze" (*hekiyu*). Kimura uses a special tool to carve the rippling pattern onto the wet clay, and then applies the glaze in several layers, repeatedly firing the vessels in his kiln, resulting in subtle, ethereal gradations of color.

Born in Ehime, Kimura moved with his family to the Hiroshima area and attended Okayama Kogyo High School. After graduating college in 1970, he left Japan and traveled extensively throughout Europe and the Middle East. Although he intended to become a Zen Buddhist monk, Kimura changed course after his travels and began his studies of ceramics with the Kutani potter Ito Zojuro. Kimura's outstanding talent was soon recognized when his work was accepted for the Japan Traditional Crafts Exhibition in 1976, and in each of the following twenty-eight years, he won numerous awards and received wide accolades from critics and collectors, both in Japan and abroad.

Kimura's Zen roots are reflected in the simple shapes of his pieces and in the discipline required to produce them. The circular form and gradually deepening blue hues toward the center of this vessel invite concentrated looking akin to meditating on a mandala (see no. 17). FF

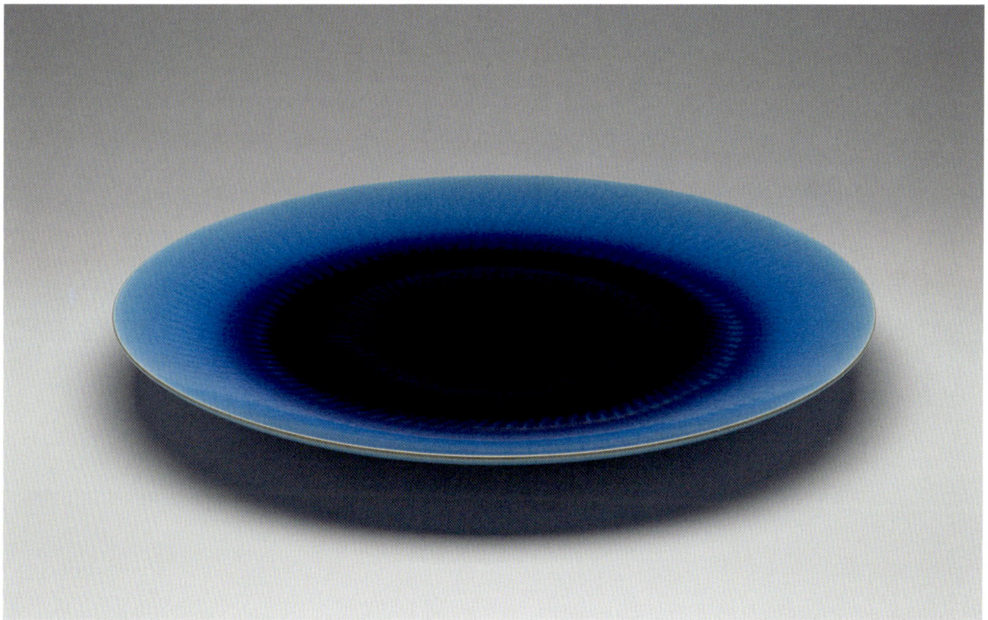

101

Joyfulness in the Sea

Chie Otani

(b. 1951)

Heisei period (1989–2019), 1995

Wax resist dye on cotton, with frame: 9 ft. 2 in. × 39 in. × 6 ft. 6 in. (279.4 × 99.1 × 198.1 cm)

Gift of The Tori Collection, Devault, PA, 2017-133-1a–j

The tradition of embellishing cloth before it is resist-dyed has a long history in Japan, likely dating to prehistory, with more advanced techniques tracing back to China, India, and beyond. There are three resist-dyeing techniques: clamp-resist, tie-resist, and wax-resist. The last of these, known as *rokechi* in Japanese, died out in Japan at the end of the Nara period (710–94); it was revived as *rozome* (*ro* meaning "wax" and *zome* meaning "dyeing") during the early Taishō period (1912–26) by the applied chemist and scholar Tsuruichi Tsurumaki (1873–1942).

By the mid-1990s, contemporary artist Chie Otani was creating between twenty-five and thirty works a year, including large-scale hangings and folding screens, such as *Pleasure in Land and Sea* (1995),[1] using the *rozome* and the challenging *han-bosen* (half-resist) techniques. This latter method is used for shading by varying the thickness and temperature of the wax with pointed or flat brushes to create a barrier during dyeing. Otani works from photographs and sketches, drawing images on the reverse of the fabric before applying her own wax formula, which does not crack like the wax used for the resist technique of Indonesian batik.

Born into a family of musicians and textile artists, Otani studied textile dyeing in college while also working part time for a kimono company. After completing her degree in 1971, she was quickly recognized for her technical skills and unique designs drawn from memories of the Shimane seacoast, where she spent her childhood. She later moved inland to Kyoto, where she maintains her home and studio, and she serves as head of the Dyeing and Weaving Department at the Nara College of Arts. Today she is recognized as one of Japan's preeminent masters of *rozome*.

Joyfulness in the Sea is one of the artist's largest and most complex works, comprising ten overlapping resist-dyed panels that hang from a circular armature. With imagery falling somewhere between reality and a dream, recalling the motion and swirling of the sea, the work embraces the concept of *ki*, the energy or spirit that animates life. DB

---

1. PMA acc. no. 2017-134-1.

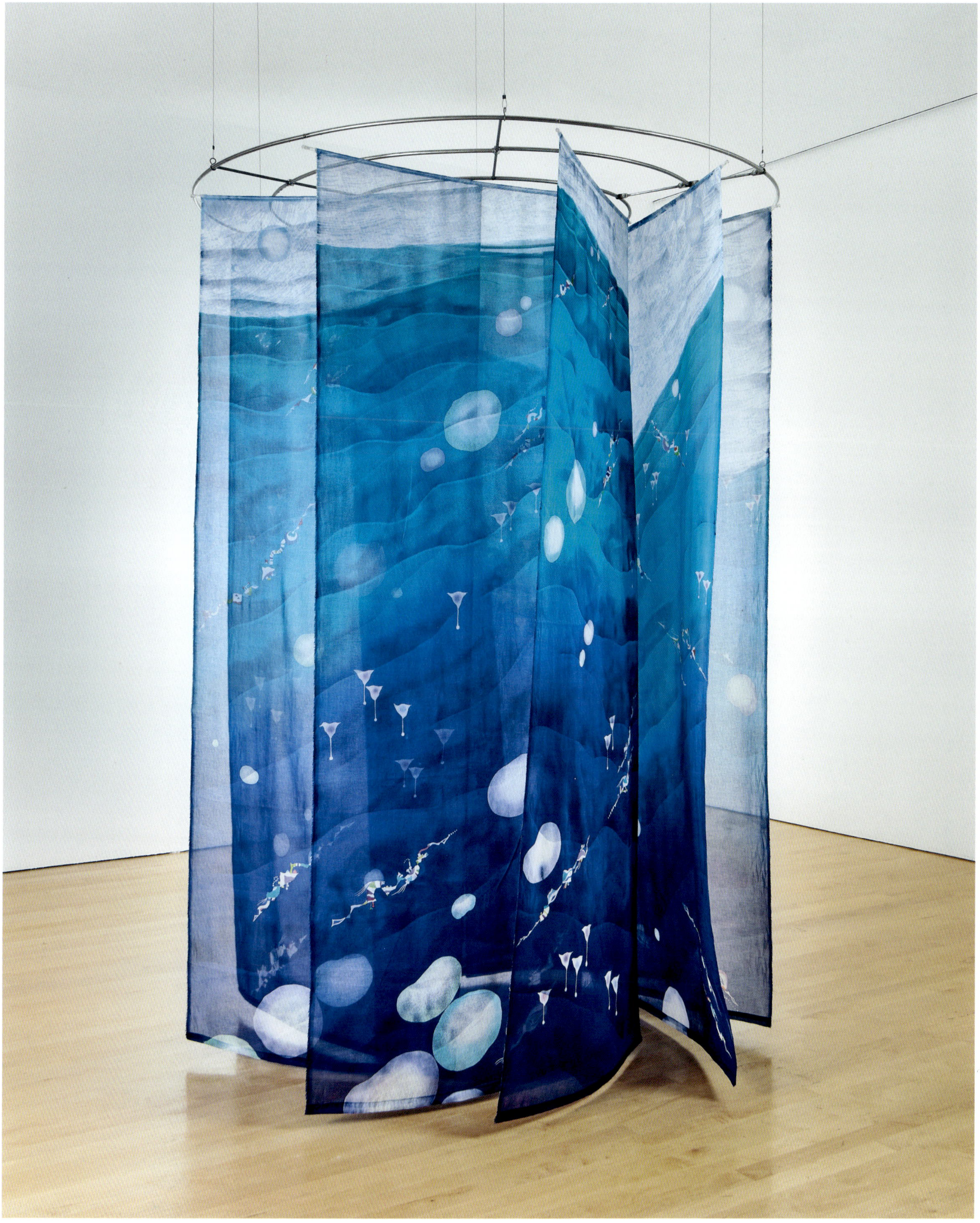

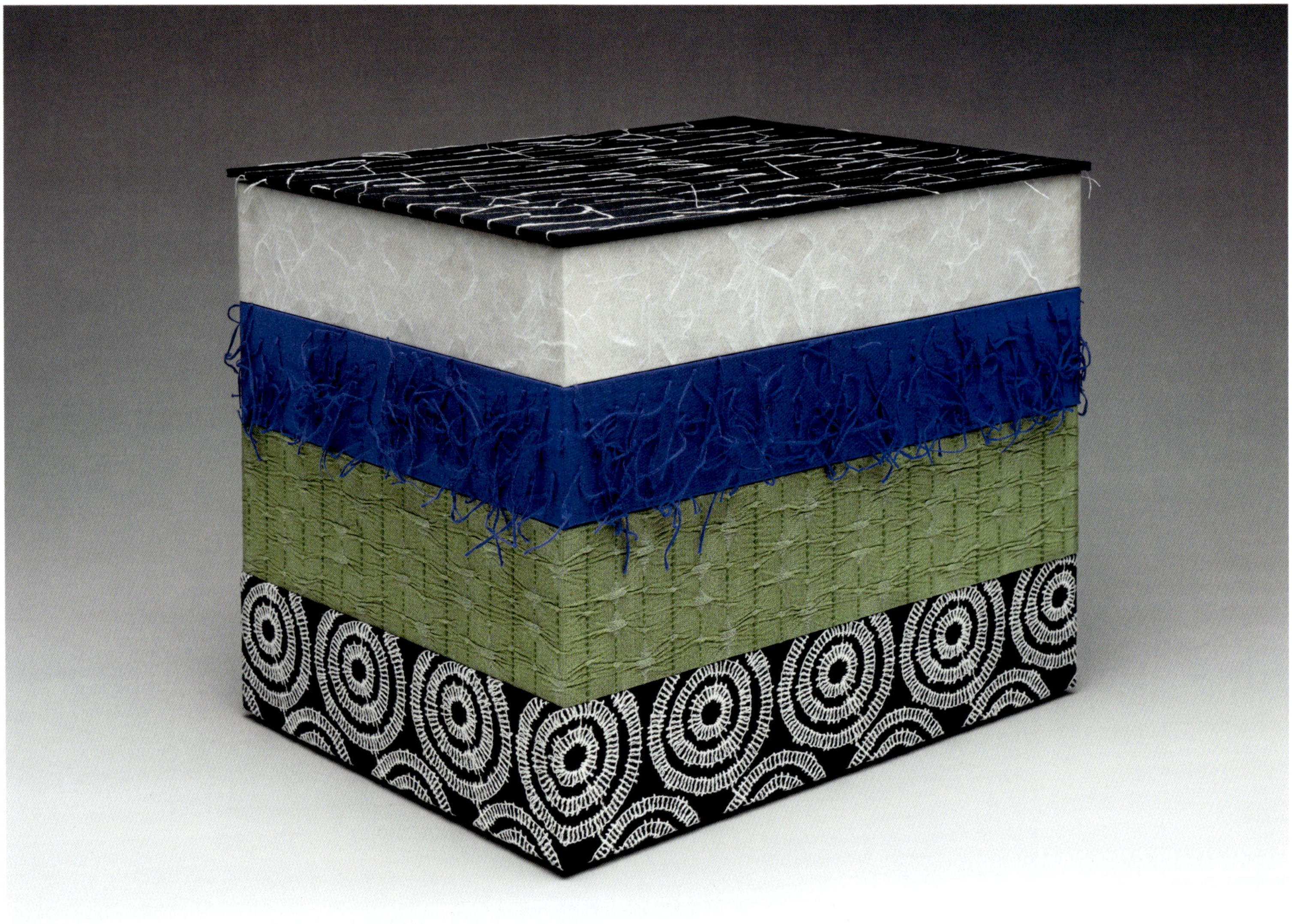

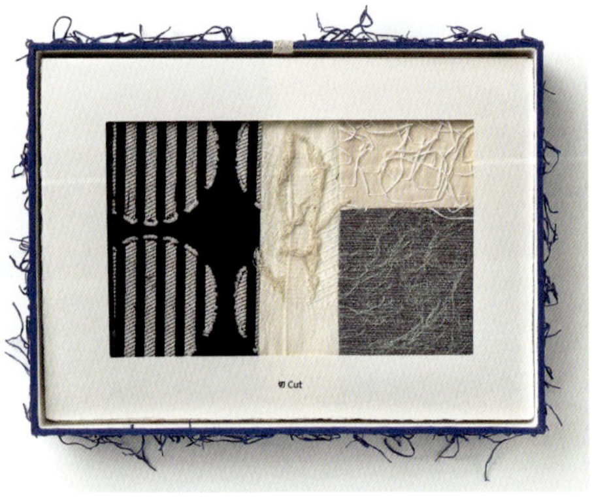

A: Box Two

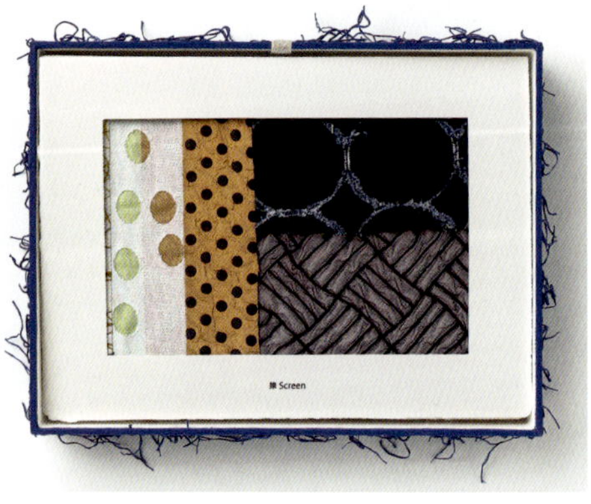

B: Box Two

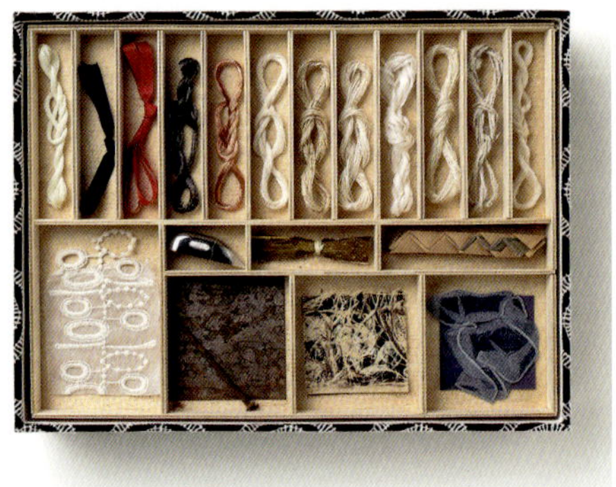

C: Box Four

102

The Nuno Box: Textiles of Reiko Sudo

Reiko Sudo
(b. 1953)

Hesei period (1989–2019), 2017

Made by Paper Hammer Studios (Tieton, Washington, est. 2007) in collaboration with Reiko Sudo
Published by Marquand, division of Lucia | Marquand (Seattle, est. 2006)

Edition 18/50

Mixed media, 11⅛ × 10⅝ × 13¾ in. (28.3 × 27 × 34.9 cm)

Purchased with the Costume and Textiles Revolving Fund and with the Library and Archives Gertrud A. White Memorial Fund, 2018-14-1(1–29k)

Since 1987 Reiko Sudo has served as design director for the textile company Nuno (meaning "cloth" in Japanese), which is renowned for its innovative fabrics that integrate Japan's craft traditions with cutting-edge technologies. Nuno was cofounded in 1984 by Sudo and her mentor, the visionary designer and inventor Junichi Arai (1932–2017), who supplied textiles to avant-garde fashion designers such as Issey Miyake (1938–2022) and Rei Kawakubo (b. 1942) of Comme des Garçons.

The Nuno Box: Textiles of Reiko Sudo was produced by the designer in collaboration with the Seattle-based publisher Marquand in 2017 in a numbered edition of fifty. This handmade "art book" is designed in the form of the classic Japanese four-tiered bento lunch box with each compartment covered in a different Nuno textile. The contents of the boxes serve as a testament to Sudo's innovative textile making, which emphasizes sustainable production. The lid, for example, is covered with Nuno's *Kibiso Cut* cloth that is woven on a mechanized loom from silkworm cocoons, which traditionally were discarded as waste.

Box One contains a booklet with Sudo's autobiography, a list of contents, and three scarves representative of Nuno's approach to textile design and production. The cotton and polyester *Chirimen* scarf (1995) is a translation of the traditional *chirimen* textured silk crepe from the Tango region of Kyoto. The *Tsugihagi* scarf (1997–98), a collaboration between Sudo and designer Kazuhiro Ueno, is made from a patchwork fabric layered between polyester that highlights the company's focus on repurposing textile scraps, while the allover Japanese straw mat pattern of the *Pleat* scarf (1997) disappeared after the cloth's pleats were heat set.

The contents of Box Two document thirty years of Nuno production through fourteen matted collages representing a different material or technique — namely, pleat, pocket, twist, float, cut, embroider, screen, rub, punch, mono, metal, re trad, cocoon, and paper (A, B). Each collage includes four to seven examples of fabrics manufactured between 1987 and 2015. In Box Three a hand-bound sample book of selected fabrics, titled *Nunology*, provides insight into the company's sources of inspiration, design motifs, and technologies. Finally, Box Four contains examples of materials and tools used by Nuno to produce different weaving effects, including various fibers and yarns, rusted nails, aluminum, a nap teaser, and a jacquard punch card (C). DB

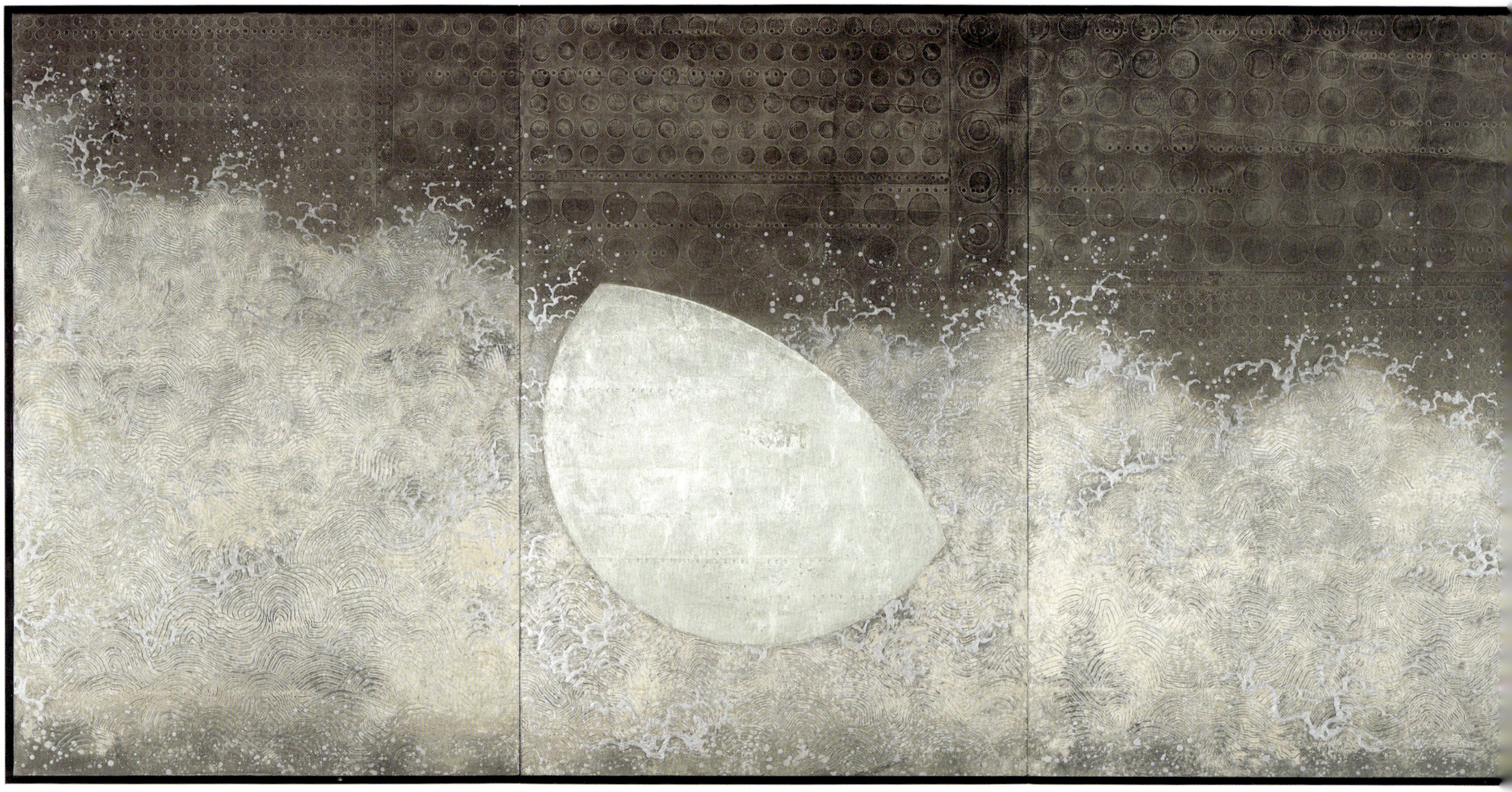

103

Waning Moon

Ken Matsubara
(b. 1948)

Heisei period (1989–2019), 2017

Ink, earth, mica, and white gold on paper, mounted as a set of four *fusuma* (sliding door) panels; 70⅝ in. × 15 ft. 6 in. (179.4 × 472.4 cm)

Purchased with the Henry B. Keep Fund, 2019-210-1a–d

Ken Matsubara lives and works in the mountainous region of Tochigi Prefecture, northeast of Tokyo. Throughout his career he has always worked the local earth and clay into his paintings. Here Matsubara applied a reddish ground layer of iron-rich mud dye called bengala oxide, which he combined with resin over handmade Echigo paper. Although not visible on the finished surface, this layer provides a flexible texture onto which Matsubara applied stamped and combed patterns. Over these he applied additional gray and tan-toned mud dyes to create the sky and waves. The final layers consist of white-gold leaf for the moon and thick mica to accentuate the wave caps. While basing this work on the traditional *fusuma* (sliding door) format, Matsubara also has created novel luminous and mysterious effects.

The four panels that make up *Waning Moon* are part of a larger twenty-four-panel series, *Kūkai's View, Sun and Moon*. Kūkai (also known as Kōbō Daishi; 774–835), the renowned Buddhist monk, poet, and scholar, remains a venerated figure in Japan to this day. In his early twenties, Kūkai spent a period of time in solitary meditation and mantra recitation at Cape Muroto, near the precincts of Zentsū-ji (temple), in Shikoku (see no. 16).[1] In 2015 Matsubara followed in Kūkai's footsteps to meditate and find inspiration for this series.[2] Two years later Matsubara began painting, completing the entire set of *fusuma* in the fall of 2017. As an homage to his inspiration, underneath the painting on each panel Matsubara brushed a poetic text by Kūkai, taken from his *Hizō hōyaku* (The precious key to the secret treasury) (fig. 68).[3]

The waning moon represents the passage of fullness of time in nature, echoed by the life cycle of humans. It often appears as a dramatic silver appliqué on Momoyama-period (1568–1615) screens, referencing the experience of loss explored in *The Tales of Ise* or *The Tale of Genji*. Here the white-gold moon floating amid waves reflects this literary cultural past, as well as the philosophy behind this aesthetic that is rooted in the Buddhist worldview of the transience of life and the endurance of nature. FF

1. Kūkai subsequently traveled to China to study Esoteric doctrines, which he brought back to Japan as founder of the Shingon sect.
2. These paintings were originally commissioned as *fusuma* by Hayashiya Seizo (1928–2017), director of the Musée Tomo in Tokyo and a noted connoisseur of tea wares. They were destined for Jingo-ji in Kyoto, where Kūkai stayed after returning from China. However, Hayashiya passed away before the completion of the works, so the series became available.
3. See the Documentation (p. 261) for a translation of the text inscribed on the museum's *fusuma*. For a translation of Kūkai's complete text, see Hakeda 1972, 157–224. For a video of Matsubara at work, see "Process of Making: Kukai | Sun and Moon," Ippodo Gallery (website), October 1, 2019, https://www.ippodogallery.com/video/9-process-of-making-kukai-sun-and-ken-matsubara/.

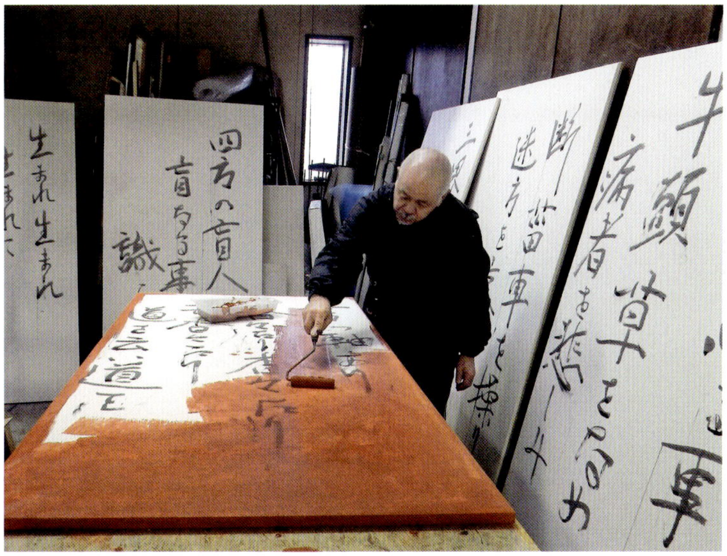

FIG. 68 Calligraphy text of Kūkai's poem partially covered by a layer of bengala oxide. Courtesy Ippodo Gallery, New York

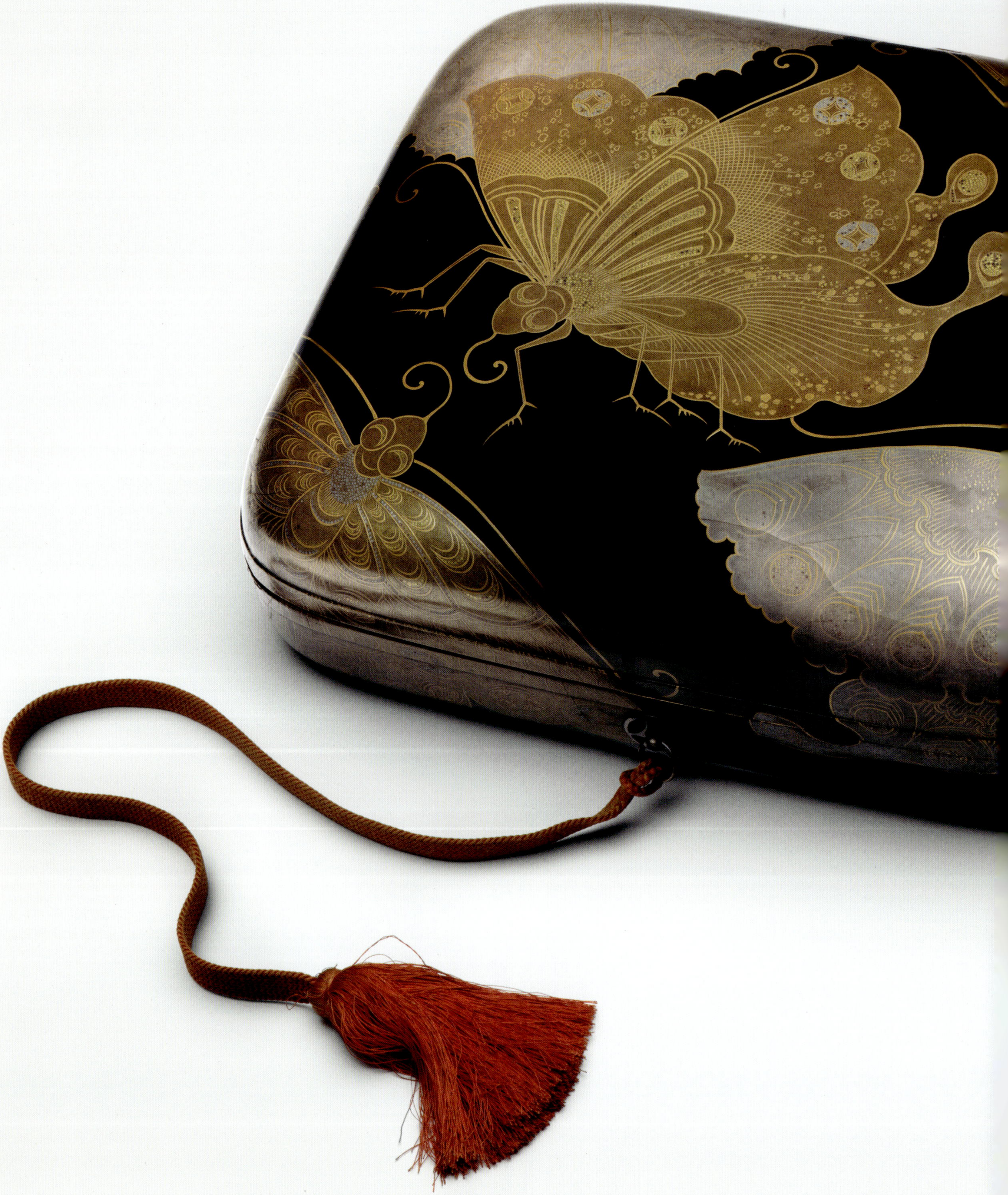

Documentation

1
Jar
1999-130-1

EXHIBITED: New York 1999, 156, no. 44, 288–89; Philadelphia 2002, 2; Philadelphia 2016–17 (no cat.).

PUBLISHED: Cotter 1999, E39; Philadelphia Museum of Art 2014, 2.

2
Pottery Jar with Pedestal and Animal Decoration
2009-80-1

EXHIBITED: Philadelphia 2013 (no cat.).

PUBLISHED: Jenyns 1971, 38, pl. 6B.

3
Tomb Guardian (*Haniwa*)
1963-46-1

EXHIBITED: Philadelphia 2013–14 (no cat.).

4
Kisshōten
2009-78-1

PUBLISHED: Mochizuki 1973, 116, no. 56; Jenkins 1977, 66–67, no. 27; Nishikawa and Sano 1982, no. 32; Philadelphia Museum of Art 2014, 14.

PROVENANCE: Hosomi Family Collection, Izumi-Ōtsu City, Osaka Prefecture, Japan, until 2009.

MARK: [unidentified].

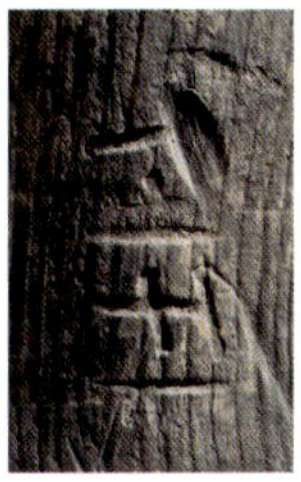

5
Pair of Guardian Lions
F1906-2-1a,b

EXHIBITED: Saint Louis 1904 (not reproduced in the catalogue); Philadelphia 1969 (no cat.); Tokyo 2003, xxv, 161; Philadelphia 2013–14 (no cat.).

PUBLISHED: "Nio-Mon 1906"; Cate 1930b, 26, pl. 6; Shimizu 1980, 100, no. 196, fig. 197; Fischer 1991, 14, fig. 12a,b; Association of Scientific Research 1993, 74, no. 162.

PROVENANCE: Seion-ji, Ibaraki Prefecture, Japan, until 1904; John H. Converse (1840–1910) and Samuel M. Vauclain (1856–1940), Philadelphia, purchased from the Louisiana Purchase Exposition, Saint Louis, 1904.

6
Aizen Myōō
1960-7-1

EXHIBITED: Philadelphia 1990–91 (no cat.); Philadelphia 2013–14 (no cat.).

PUBLISHED: Fischer 1991, 6, fig. 3; Association of Scientific Research 1993, 11, no. 7; Philadelphia Museum of Art 1995, 39; Philadelphia Museum of Art 2014, 26.

PROVENANCE: Possibly Hara Collection.*

* According to a note on a curator card dated to 1960, the year the work was acquired by the museum, in the object file, East Asian Art, Philadelphia Museum of Art.

7
Seated Jizō
1983-16-1

EXHIBITED: Philadelphia 1990–91 (no cat.); San Antonio 2017, 82, 124, pl. 29.

PUBLISHED: Tōkyō Ryōgoku Bijutsu Kurabu 1917, no. 97; Tokyo 1968, 14, no. 1; Fischer 1984, 11, fig. 9; Fischer 1991, 12, fig. 9; Association of Scientific Research 1993, 10, no. 4.

PROVENANCE: Viscount Takahashi Korekiyo (1854–1936), Tokyo, until 1917.

INSCRIBED ON BOX: Attributed to the Takuma [school].*

* The Takuma school was a hereditary school of Buddhist painters active from the late ninth to the late sixteenth century.

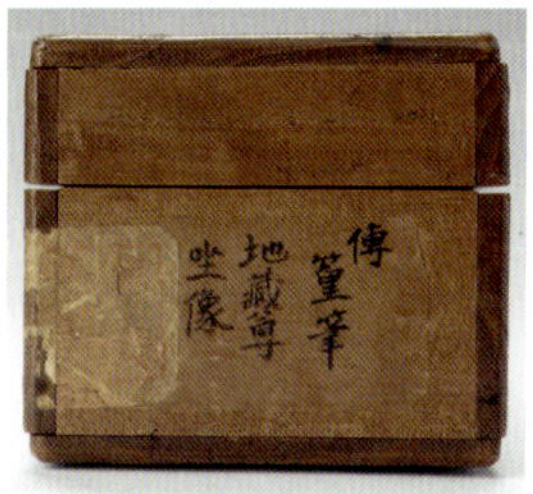

8
Seated Monju
1979-57-1

EXHIBITED: Philadelphia 1980 (no cat.); Philadelphia 1990–91 (no cat.); New York 2016, 72.

PUBLISHED: Ikeda 1941, fig. 39; Fischer 1991, 11, fig. 8; Association of Scientific Research 1993, 72, no. 152; Philadelphia Museum of Art 1995, 40; Philadelphia Museum of Art 2014, 25; Yamaguchi and Miyazaki 2018, 7, 9, 25, figs. 2, 5, 22.

PROVENANCE: Kōfuku-ji, Nara, until 1906; Ikeda Collection, until 1941.

9

Ideal Portrait of Daruma

Kenkō Shōkei (d. 1523)

1928-104-1

EXHIBITED: Philadelphia 1988–89 (no cat.); Philadelphia 1990–91 (no cat.); Philadelphia 2002–3 (no cat.).

PUBLISHED: Fischer 1991, 19, fig. 19; Association of Scientific Research 1993, 16, no. 22.

SEAL: Shōkei.

10

Sutra Fragment

1959-93-89

EXHIBITED: Philadelphia 1990–91 (no cat.); Philadelphia 1998–99 (no cat.).

PUBLISHED: Fischer 1991, 3, fig. 1.

11

Page from the *Anthology of Poems by Thirty-Six Immortal Poets*

1965-77-1

EXHIBITED: New York 1984–85, no. 10; Philadelphia 1996 (no cat.); New York 1997–98b (no cat.); Philadelphia 2000–2001a (no cat.).

PUBLISHED: Philadelphia Museum of Art 1995, 38; Philadelphia Museum of Art 2014, 24.

PROVENANCE: Nishi Hongan-ji, Kyoto, 1549–1929.

12

Ki no Tsurayuki

2013-24-1

EXHIBITED: Tokyo 1986, pls. 59–61; Fukuoka 1991, pls. 25, 26.

INSCRIBED WITH A POEM: For the translation, see p. 57.

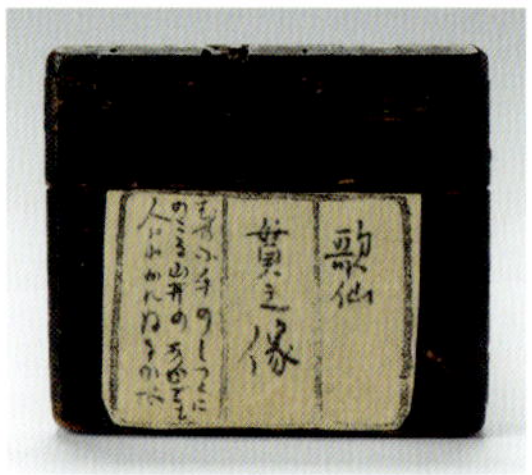

13

Jino-ji engi (Legends of Jin'o-ji)

1962-18-1,2

EXHIBITED: Philadelphia 1990–91 (no cat.); Philadelphia 1996–97 (no cat.).

PUBLISHED: Shimada, Akiyama, and Yamane 1980, nos. 97, 98; Fischer 1991, 16, fig. 14; Association of Scientific Research 1993, 13, nos. 14, 15.

14

Priest Son'i's Visit to the Imperial Palace, from the *Kitano Tenjin engi (Legends of Kitano Tenjin Shrine)*

1929-40-222

EXHIBITED: Philadelphia 1997–98 (no cat.).

PUBLISHED: Fenollosa 1921, 186; Association of Scientific Research 1993, 14, no. 16.

PROVENANCE: V. G. Simkhovitch (1874–1959), New York, until 1929.

15

Chinese Man Releasing a Bird from a Cage

Shikibu Terutada (act. mid-16th century)

1989-78-1

EXHIBITED: Philadelphia 2002–3 (no cat.).

PUBLISHED: Association of Scientific Research 1993, 17, no. 25.

SEALS: Terutada; Ryūkyō.

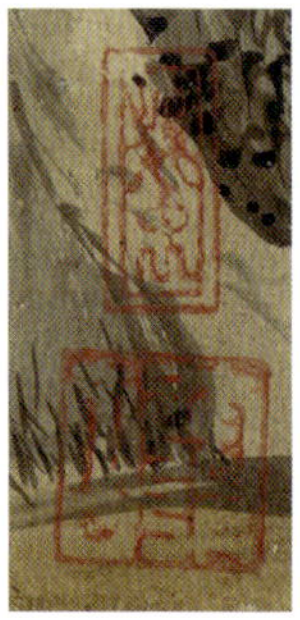

INSCRIBED ON BOX: Kei shōki hitsu.*

* For the meaning of the inscription, see p. 63.

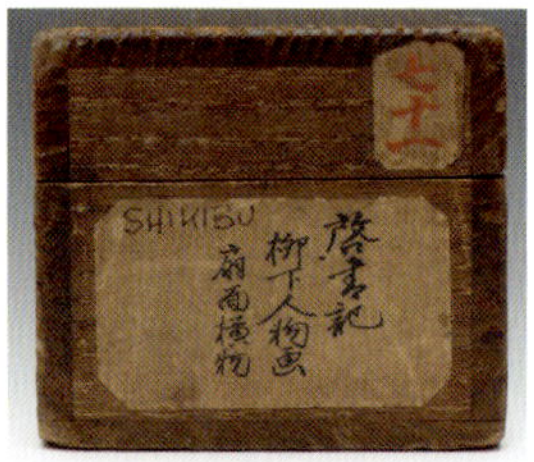

16

Biography of the Great Teacher of Mount Kōya (Kōya Daishi Gyō-jō-e)

1983-83-6

EXHIBITED: Philadelphia 1990–91 (no cat.); Philadelphia 1997–98 (no cat.).

PUBLISHED: Fischer 1991, 17, figs. 15, 16; Association of Scientific Research 1993, 14, no. 17.

INSCRIBED: Fifth day of the tenth month of Kyōhō 4 [1719].

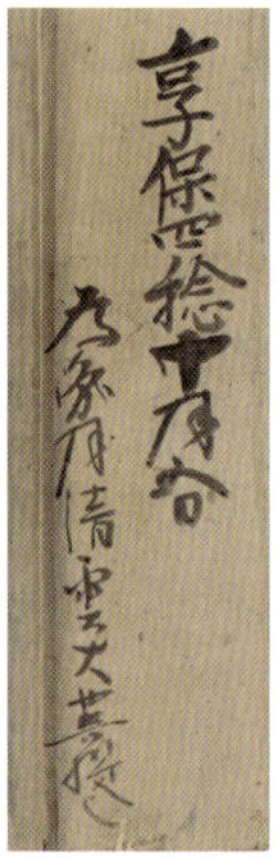

17

Star Mandala

1978-45-2

EXHIBITED: Philadelphia 1980 (no cat.); Philadelphia 1987–88 (no cat.); Philadelphia 1990–91 (no cat.); New York 1997–98a, 43, 124, fig. 42, no. 47; Philadelphia 2013–14 (no cat.).

PUBLISHED: Fischer 1991, 9, fig. 6; Association of Scientific Research 1993, 11, no. 10.

18

Votive Plaques (*Ema*) of a Tiger

1966-118-2

EXHIBITED: Philadelphia 1969 (no cat.); Philadelphia 1987–88 (no cat.); Philadelphia 1989–90 (no cat.); Philadelphia 1997–98 (no cat.); Philadelphia 2013–14 (no cat.).

PUBLISHED: Association of Scientific Research 1993, 65, no. 141.

INSCRIBED: Offered to the honorable shrine; Jōkyō 3, third cyclical year [1686] eighth month, eighth day; Tomizawa town, Tsuyumatsu Rice Shop.

19

Bamboo and Sparrows

Shōkadō Shōjō (1584–1639)

W1972-1-1

EXHIBITED: Philadelphia 1980 (no cat.); Philadelphia 1987–88 (no cat.); Philadelphia 1989–90 (no cat.); Philadelphia 1990–91 (no cat.); Philadelphia 1997–98 (no cat.).

PUBLISHED: Fischer 1991, 20, fig. 21; Association of Scientific Research 1993, 38, no. 80.

PROVENANCE: Shimazu [lord of] Satsuma and Hirase families, present-day Kagoshima Prefecture.*

* An authentication on the box lid by Tayama Hōnan (1903–1980), dated to 1969, provides this provenance.

SIGNED BY THE ARTIST: Inshi Shōjō [Recluse Shōjō].

SEALS OF THE ARTIST: Seiseiō; Shōkadō.

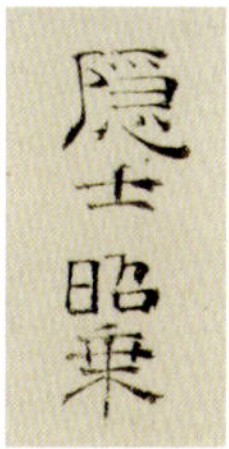

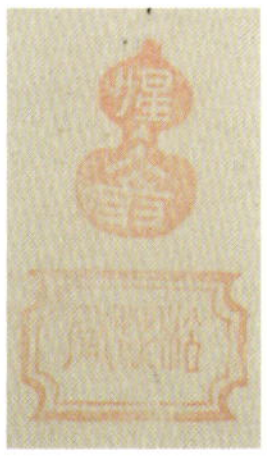

SIGNED BY THE CALLIGRAPHER: Kinshuku Osho.

SEAL OF THE CALLIGRAPHER: Kinshuku.

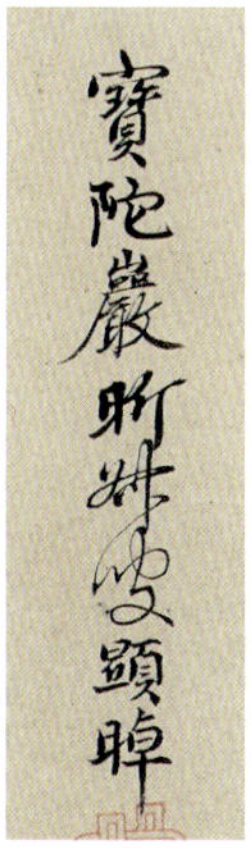

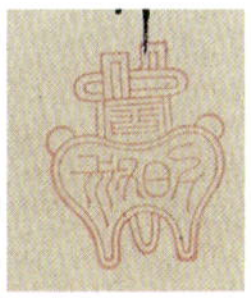

INSCRIBED WITH A BUDDHIST POEM: For the translation, see p. 71.

20

Ink Traces (*Bokuseki*)

1977-164-1(1–15)

EXHIBITED: Philadelphia 1980 (no cat.); Philadelphia 1998–99 (no cat.); Philadelphia 2006–7 (no cat.).

PUBLISHED: Fischer 1991, 23, figs. 24, 25; Philadelphia Museum of Art 2014, 47.

INSCRIBED ON BOX: Ninth month, fifth day [1679].*

* 1679 was the year before Mokuan Shōtō's retirement as abbot, and the year that the Manpuku-ji complex was completed, an event marked by the bell tower's *oni-gawara* (roof tile) naming ritual. This compilation of Ōbaku calligraphies may have been a sort of "Festschrift" to honor Mokuan's achievements.

See p. 250 for illustrations of signatures and seals.

FIFTEEN CALLIGRAPHERS:

1. Mokuan Shōtō (1611–1684)

SIGNED: Ōbaku Mokuan sho.

SEALS: Rinzai shōshū; Mokuan Shōtō; Shōbō eishō.

INSCRIBED:
Verses before sound;
Changes outside the frame.
No obtaining, no losing,
No right, no wrong:
From ancient times
the iron hammer
lacks any grip at all.*

* This is from a poem by the Song-dynasty monk Xueyan Zuqin (1216–1287). The last line literally translates to "the iron hammer lacks any holes at all," a frequently used Zen simile for a situation that gives one no way to "get a grip" on it. Mokuan's calligraphy includes only the poem's second line, "Changes outside the frame."

2. Sokuhi Nyoitsu (1616–1671)

SIGNED AND DATED: [1665]; Sekiju Sokuhi sho.

SEALS: Rinzai sanjū-san sei; Sokuhi; Nyoitsu no in.

INSCRIBED:
That which is mind is
precisely Buddha:
open the seal of mind!
Not the Buddha, *not* the mind:
let your mouth
beam light!
As these flames destroy all
aspects
of "wrong, wrong!"
and "right! right!"—
In life's affairs, a waste
to weigh
your precious
"self-respect."

3. Erin Shōki (1609–1681)

SIGNED: Erin Rōsō sho.

SEALS: Rinzai sanjū-san sei; Erin; Shōki no in.

INSCRIBED:
I have my single fly-whisk—
Using it? I have no special way.
At times I hang it
from branches of
the pines,
It's head hanging,
crown all exposed.

4. Dokutan Shōkei (1628–1706)

SIGNED AND DATED: [1675]; Dokutan.

SEALS: Rinzai shōshū; Dokutan; Shozan shujin.

INSCRIBED:
All day long I watch the
mountains,
never lower blinds.

5. Daibi Shōzen (1616–1673)

SIGNED: Ōbaku Daibi sho.

SEALS: Ōbaku shōshū; Daibi kō; Shōzen no in.

INSCRIBED:
Resting on bamboo bench—
no human footprints
on the moss-grown
path;
Calm night—the clouds open,
moonlight fills the sky.

6. Nangen Shōha (1631–1692)

SIGNED: Ōbaku Nangen sho.

SEALS: Shōbō gan; Shōha no in; Nangen.

INSCRIBED:
PLUM TREE
It has traveled to heaven
above: there is
no other to compete;
And here in the human realm,
it is the first
to bloom in spring.

7. Dokku Shōshi (1624–1688)

SIGNED: Ōbaku Dokku sho.

SEALS: Rinzai shōden; Shōshi; Dokku.

INSCRIBED:
Beyond the clouds dawn
naturally glows above;
Here in the mountains, my
gate is still shut tight.

8. Mujō Shōson (1631–1660)

SIGNED: Ōbaku Mujō.

SEALS: Rin'en ha; Shōson no in; Mujō.

INSCRIBED:
Beyond any sect.

9. Kōsen Shōton (1633–1695)

SIGNED: Ōbaku Kōsen sho.

SEALS: Rinzai shōshū; Ichiji Kōsen; Shōton no in.

INSCRIBED:
LAND All are people of the
Land of Lotus Flowers.*

* That is, the Pure Land of devotional Buddhism.

10. Donzui Shōan (1636–1705)

SIGNED: Juzan Donzui.

SEALS: Shōha gorinkō; Shōan no in; Donzui shi.

INSCRIBED:
Would you see
the Five Elder Peaks
of Lu Mountain?
In this realm,
where on earth
would you *not*
find them?
The tongue is boneless,
anyone can twist it
any way;
"For ironing clothes
or brewing tea,
the water heaters
differ."*

* The last line comes from a poem by the Chinese monk Huikai (1183–1260). Its meaning in this context is unclear. The general idea might be that our ordinary perception and thinking are delusory. All places from this perspective are ultimately the same. Words we speak are undependable and subject to manipulation. Conversely, although boiling water may seem always to be the same, there are differences in how it is done for ironing, for example, or preparing tea.

1. Mokuan Shōtō

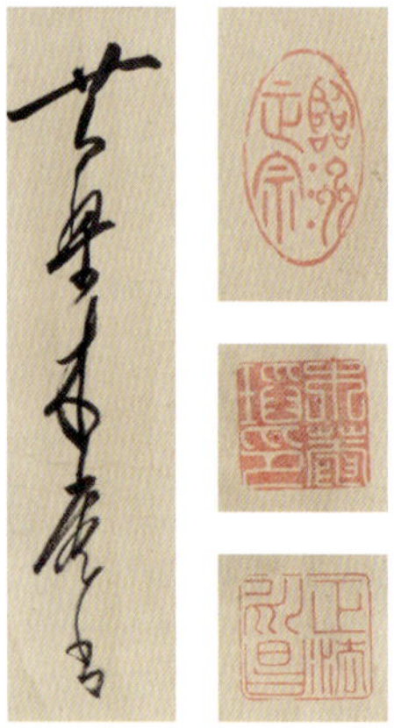

2. Sokuhi Nyoitsu

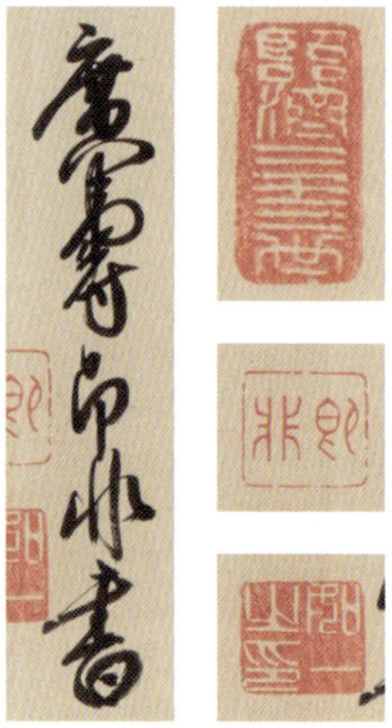

3. Erin Shōki

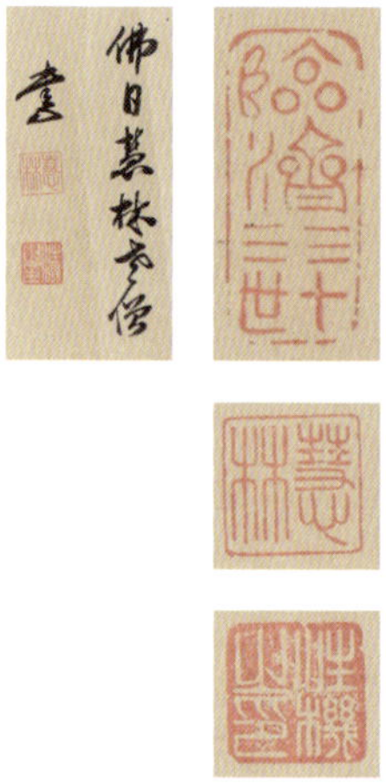

4. Dokutan Shōkei

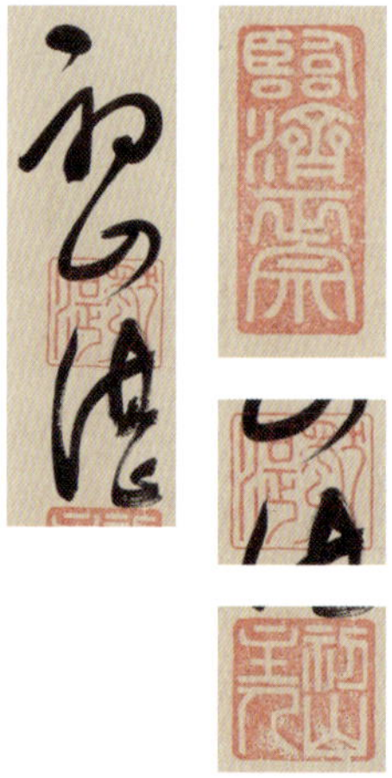

5. Daibi Shōzen

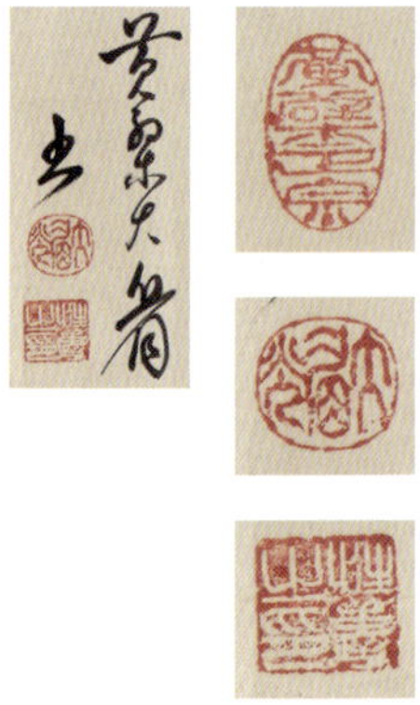

6. Nangen Shōha

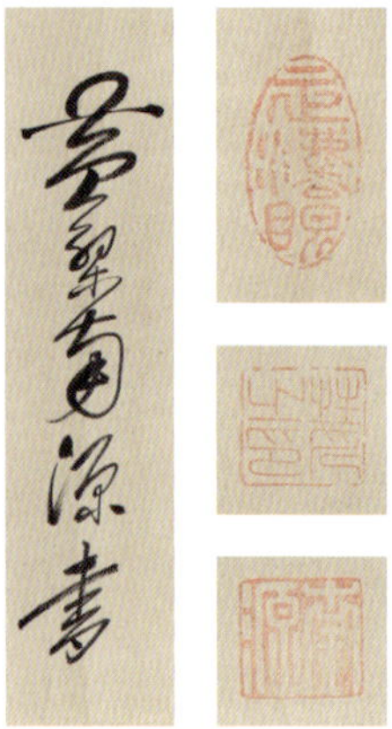

7. Dokku Shōshi

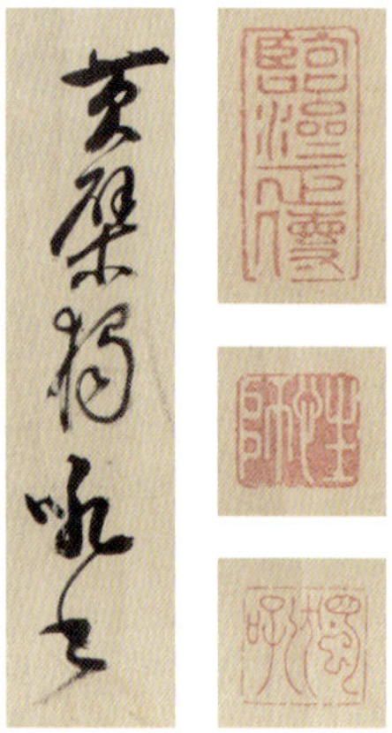

8. Mujō Shōson

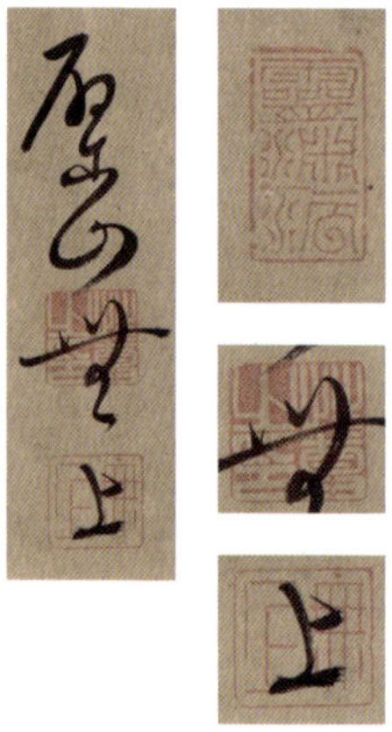

9. Kōsen Shōton

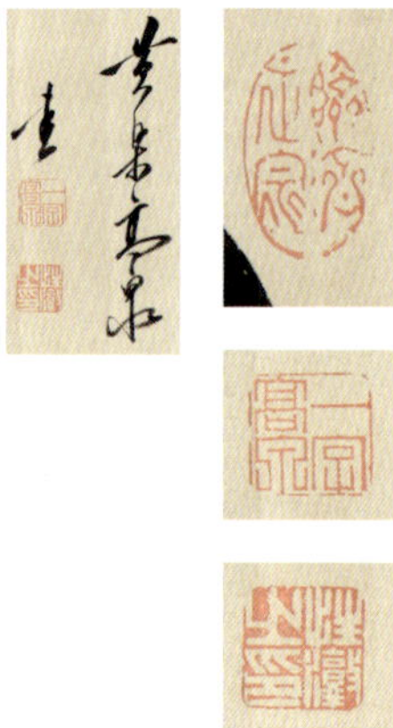

10. Donzui Shōan

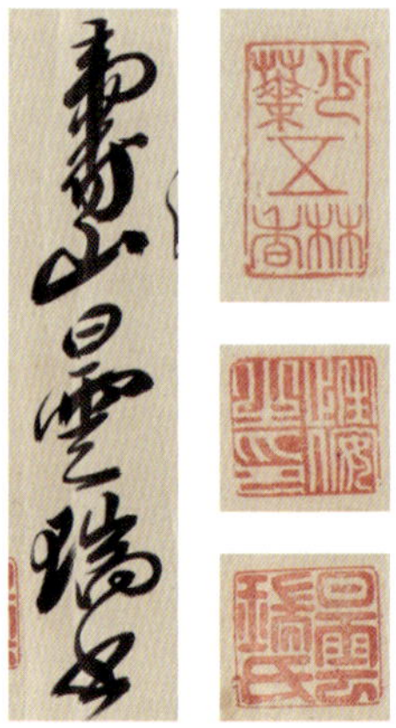

11. Hakugan Shōsetsu

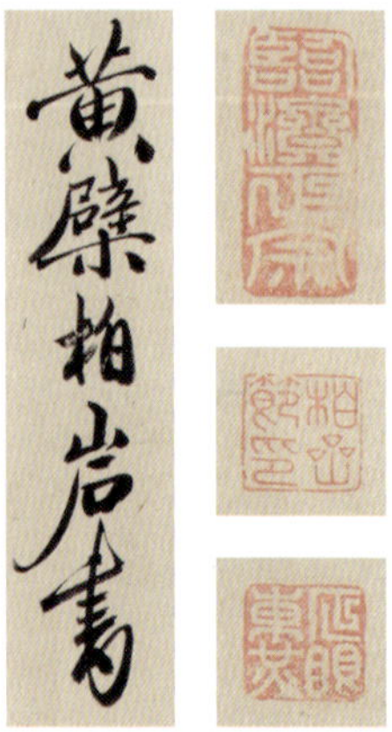

12. Essan Dōshū

13. Yui'i Dōjitsu

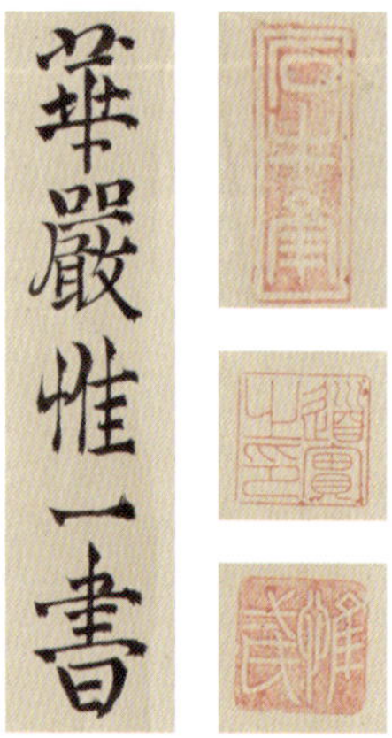

14. Mushin Shōkaku

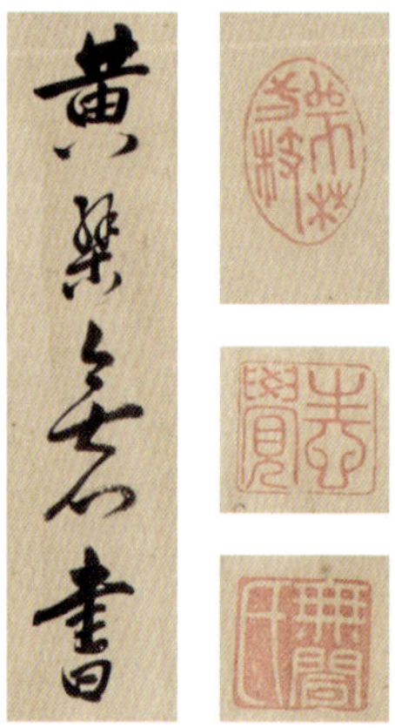

15. Katsuzen Dōwa

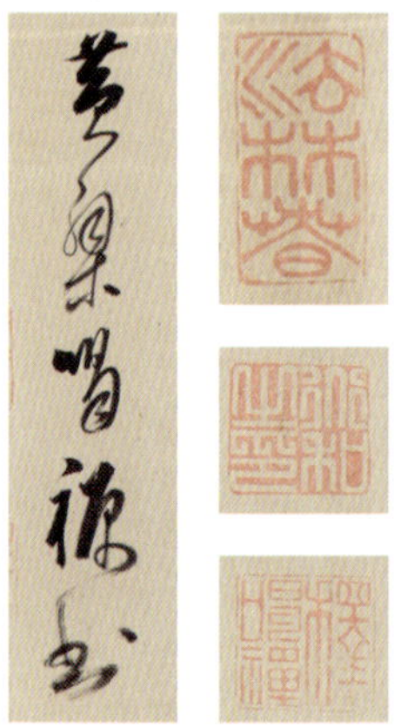

20 (continued)

11. Hakugan Shōsetsu (1634–1673)

SIGNED AND DATED: Ōbaku Hakugan sho [1673].

SEALS: Rinzai shōshū; Hakugan Setsu in; Seigan tōkō.

INSCRIBED:

The sound
of your long whistle
shakes earth
more powerfully
the further it
extends;
How could you realize
that you are still
in the same mountain?

12. Essan Dōshū (1629–1709)

SIGNED: Nangaku Essan sho.

SEALS: Rinzai shōshū; Essan; Dōshū no in.

INSCRIBED:

PINE

Its strong appearance never
changes from then to now:
Its heart of fragrance — who
can match its glory?*

*A couplet from a poem by the great Tang-dynasty master Liu Tsung-yuan/Zongyuan (773–819).

13. Yui'i Dōjitsu (1620–1692)

SIGNED AND DATED: [1677]; Kegon Yui'i sho.

SEALS: Sekigo; Dōjitsu no in; Yui'i shi.

INSCRIBED:

The channeled waters flow on,
all blue and green;
Mountain radiance reflects
the sun's red beams.
I happen by, climb to this
jeweled place,
Gaze far as I can, my feelings
limitless.

14. Mushin Shōkaku (1613–1671)

SIGNED AND DATED: [1668]; Ōbaku Mushin sho.

SEALS: Shirin ikki; Shōkaku; Mumon shi[?].

INSCRIBED:

At the mountain peak,
Zen chambers
pillowed on stone
terrace;
White clouds fly away,
then fly
right back again.
Before the gates a waterfall
spills down
from the void;
Behind the rooms
the hills and peaks
form piling, rippling
waves.
On white walls are pale
depictions
of Buddhas past, present,
future;
From roof-tile vase
fragrance permeates —
a single branch of plum.
Although below
the region of fields is
placid now,
at peace,
It's hard to match
these mountain dwellings,
without a speck of dust.

15. Katsuzen Dōwa (1634–1707)

SIGNED: Ōbaku Katsuzen sho.

SEALS: Hōrinshun; Dōwa no in; Shaku Katsuzen.

INSCRIBED:

LEISURE

From these walls, a few feet
high,
easy to seek
fathoms-tall cliffs;
But with yellow gold, it's hard
to buy
a lifetime of
leisurely peace.

Poems translated and annotated by Jonathan Chaves

21

Myōhō Renge-kyō (Lotus Sutra of the Wonderful Law)

Onkō Jiun (1718–1804)

2002-198-1

EXHIBITED: Philadelphia 2006–7 (no cat.); Philadelphia 2022–23 (no cat.).

SEALS: Kokugō shamon; Jiun.

22

Five Poems

Ryōkan (1758–1831)

2021-112-1

EXHIBITED: Okayama 2017 (no cat.); Tokugawa 2019–20 (no cat.); Tokyo 2021 (no cat.).

PUBLISHED: Satō 1929; Kawaguchi and Iijima 1993, 78–79, 538; Kojima and Sekiya 2017, vol. 1, 120–21, vol. 3, 117.

PROVENANCE: Suzuki Tōken (1794–1851); Suzuki Buntai (1797–1870); Suzuki Juntei (1825–1848); Motoyama Yūkōdō; Nakano Chūtarō (1862–1939); Nakano Shigetaka (d. c. 2015).

SIGNED ON LEFT-MOST PANEL: Shaku Ryōkan sho.

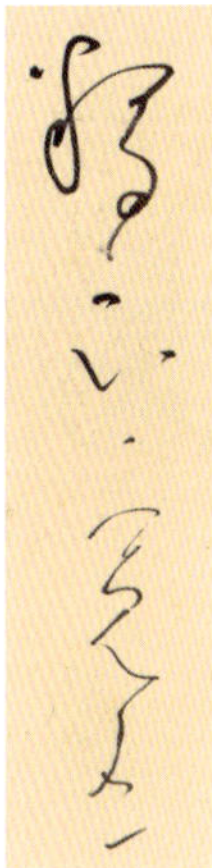

INSCRIBED WITH FIVE POEMS:

1.

Night in spring — I sober up,
then drain what's left
in the jar;
Struck by inspiration, in a
trance
I move my colored brush.
In the past I used to vie
with plum blossoms in
glory,
But that's done now; I'm
getting old,
I yield to you all!

2.

Today I went out begging
for food,
ran into pouring rain;
For a time, I retreated
to an ancient shrine.
What a laugh! With just
one sack
and one begging bowl,
My whole life's been
autumnal wind,
blasting my family's
repute.

3.

My house has a bamboo grove,
Chilly, chilly — thousands
of trees.
They fight to burst out,
covering the path,
Tips tower-slanted,
brushing sky.
Passing through frost,
their spirit doubles,
Seen through mist,
more mysteriously calm.
So suited to the stands
of pine and poplar,
How can the prettiness
of peach and plum
compare?
Trunks so straight,
virtue-knots raised still
higher,
Hearts void, roots stronger
than before.
I love the stolidity of your
pure virtue,
For a thousand autumns,
I hope you will not move.

4.

I just went ahead and shaved
my head
to make myself a monk!
Picking through plants,
examining wind —
been going on for years!
And now I find wherever I go
stuff for brush and paper:
Poems and songs on
calligraphy
are all I have to sing.

5.

What karma, I wonder,
links me so closely
to inkstone and to
brush?
A bout of writing always
followed
by yet another bout!
I just don't know from whom
to get
an answer on all this!
— Maybe The Great Majestic
Harmonious Master
who rules from up in
Heaven!

Poems translated by Jonathan Chaves

23
Shōfuku-ji (Temple of the Attainment of Happiness)

1929-58-1

Permanently on view in Gallery 344 since 1957.

PUBLISHED: Philadelphia Museum of Art 1937, 44–45; Lee 1958a; Fischer 1992, 22, fig. 23.

INSCRIBED ON REVERSE OF SIGNBOARD: [details regarding repairs made to the temple in the seventeenth century].

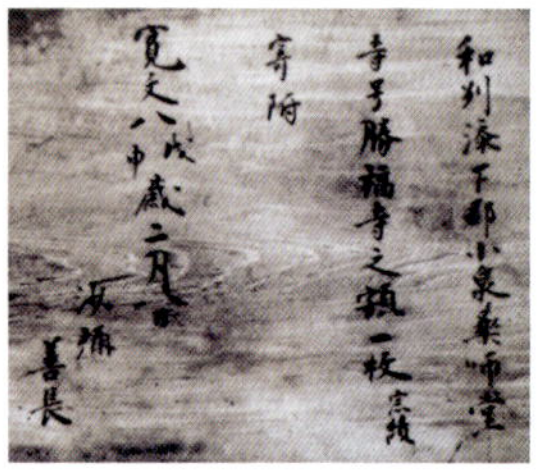

24
Sunkaraku (Evanescent Joys) Ceremonial Teahouse

Ōgi Rodō (1863–1941)

1928-114-1

Permanently on view in Gallery 344 since 1957.

PUBLISHED: Philadelphia Museum of Art 1937, 42–43; Lee 1958b; Philadelphia Museum of Art 1995, 48; Fischer 2017, 1–7, figs. 1, 3–5, 7, 8; Philadelphia Museum of Art 2014, 83; Yoshida 2019, 22–24.

INSCRIBED ON SIGNBOARD: Evanescent Joys.

25
Lantern

2004-179-1

EXHIBITED: Philadelphia 2007–8 (no cat.).

26
Teabowl

2011-47-1

EXHIBITED: Philadelphia 2011–12 (no cat.).

27
Teabowl

1941-87-45

EXHIBITED: Philadelphia 1987–88 (no cat.); Philadelphia 1988–89 (no cat.); Gifu 1997, 114, fig. 69; Philadelphia 2000–2001a (no cat.); Philadelphia 2003–5 (no cat.); Lexington 2007 (no cat.).

28
Jar

2013-25-1

EXHIBITED: Philadelphia 2014 (no cat.).

PUBLISHED: Philadelphia Museum of Art 2014, 24.

MARK: [unidentified kiln mark].

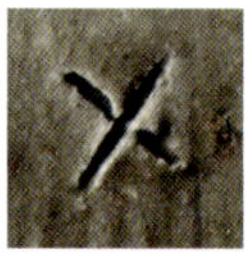

29
Tea Storage Jar (*Chatsubo*)

1955-10-1

EXHIBITED: Philadelphia 1988–89 (no cat.); Philadelphia 1989–90 (no cat.); Philadelphia 1996 (no cat.); New York 2001–2, 101, 121, 178; Lexington 2007 (no cat.).

PUBLISHED: Lee 1955, 33, fig. 1; Philadelphia Museum of Art 1995, 44; Philadelphia Museum of Art 2014, 60.

30
Dishes

Ogata Kenzan (1663–1743)

2002-75-1-5

EXHIBITED: Ithaca and Utica 1973–74, 122, 212, no. 117; Philadelphia 2002, 169, no. 17; Philadelphia 2003–5 (no cat.).

SIGNED: Kenzan.

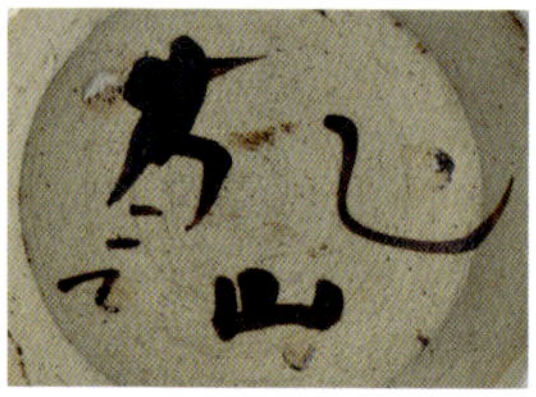

31
Dish

1968-4-1

EXHIBITED: Philadelphia 1987–88 (no cat.); Philadelphia 1988–89 (no cat.).

32
Dish with Design of Birds

2013-20-1

EXHIBITED: Philadelphia 2013 (no cat.).

33
Landscapes of the Four Seasons

School of Sesshū Tōyō (1420–1506)

1929-40-237-40

EXHIBITED: Philadelphia 1996–97 (no cat.); Kyoto and Tokyo 2002, 78.

PUBLISHED: Cate 1930a, 28, fig. 3; Philadelphia Museum of Art 1939, 13; Association of Scientific Research 1993, 20, no. 33.3.

PROVENANCE: Date Family Collection, Sendai, Japan, until c. 1900; V. G. Simkhovitch (1874–1959), New York, until 1929.

34
"Red-Seal" Ship

1953-32-1

EXHIBITED: Toledo 1938, no. 8; Philadelphia 1999–2000 (no cat.); Philadelphia 2011 (no cat.).

PUBLISHED: Association of Scientific Research 1993, 25, no. 44.1; Pegg 2019, 83, fig. 6b.

35
"Red-Seal" Ship

1938-31-1

EXHIBITED: Toledo 1938, no. 9; Philadelphia 1999–2000 (no cat.); Philadelphia 2011 (no cat.).

PUBLISHED: Association of Scientific Research 1993, 25, no. 44.2; Pegg 2019, 82, fig. 6a.

36
Dish

1969-135-1

EXHIBITED: Philadelphia 1984 (no cat.); Philadelphia 2011 (no cat.).

PUBLISHED: Russell 1969, 112.

37
Votive Plaques (*Ema*) of Thirty-Six Immortal Poets

2008-257-1-36

EXHIBITED: Philadelphia 2000–2001a (no cat.); Philadelphia 2002, 170, no. 27; Philadelphia 2006–7 (no cat.); Philadelphia 2010–11 (no cat.).

PROVENANCE: Ōi family.

SIGNED ON REVERSE OF FINAL PLAQUE (2008-257-36): Fujita no zu.

INSCRIBED ON REVERSE OF EACH PLAQUE: Genroku 2, fifth month, auspicious day [1698]; INSCRIBED ON BOX: Ōi [family] collection.

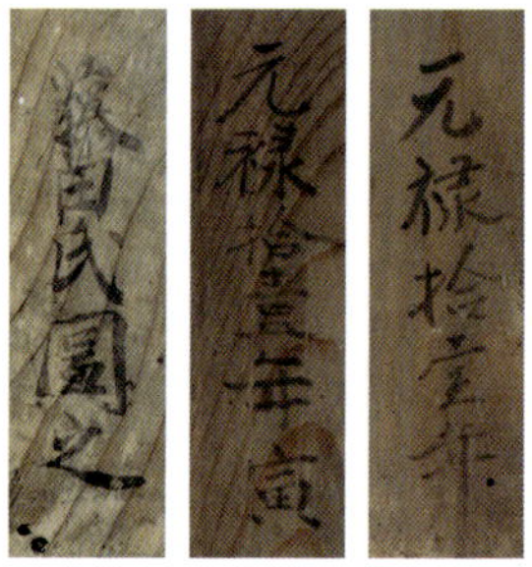

38
Poems from the *Shinkokin wakashū*

Hon'ami Kōetsu (1558–1637)

1999-39-1

EXHIBITED: Philadelphia 2000, 189–91, no. 56; Philadelphia 2002, xiv, 21, 170, no. 25; Philadelphia 2016–17 (no cat.).

PUBLISHED: Masuda 1985; Tokyo 1999a, cat. 44; Philadelphia Museum of Art 2014, 48.

PROVENANCE: Setsu Gatōdō, Tokyo, until 1999.

SEAL OF THE ARTIST: Kōetsu.

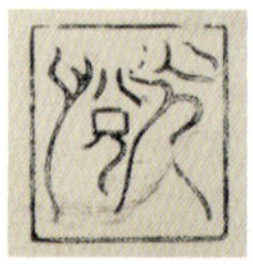

SEAL OF THE PAPERMAKER: Kamishi Sōji.

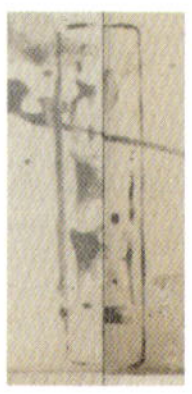

39

Writing Box (*Suzuri-bako*) with Design of a Deer

Attributed to Hon'ami Kōetsu (1558–1637)

1992-7-1a–d

EXHIBITED: Philadelphia 1992–93 (no cat.); Philadelphia 1997–98 (no cat.); Philadelphia 2000, 201, no. 73.

PUBLISHED: Philadelphia Museum of Art 1995, 43.

40

Document Box with Design of Five Butterflies

2004-83-1a,b

EXHIBITED: Philadelphia 2005–6b (no cat.).

PUBLISHED: Philadelphia Museum of Art 2014, 60.

PROVENANCE: Wada Chiman (1835–1910), Zuishin-in temple, Kyoto.*

*Wada was the head priest of the Zuishin-in temple. He was a noted student of Sanskrit and studied calligraphy with Nukina Kaioku (see no. 72).

41

Pair of Flutes (*Nōkan*)

2009-86-1a,b

EXHIBITED: Amsterdam, Düsseldorf, and Philadelphia 1992–93 (not reproduced in the catalogue); Philadelphia 2010–11 (no cat.); Philadelphia 2019a (no cat.).

42

Noh Robe, *Uwagi* (Outer Garment for Female Role), *Karaori* Type

1964-218-1

EXHIBITED: Philadelphia 2000–2001b (no cat.).

PUBLISHED: Blum 1997, 178; Philadelphia Museum of Art 2014, 61.

43

Large Perspective Picture of the Face-Showing at the Stage Performance of a Drama (Shibai kyōgen butai kaomise ōukie)

Okumura Masanobu (1685–1764)

1926-63-20

EXHIBITED: Philadelphia 1931–32 (no cat.); Philadelphia 1966 (no cat.); Philadelphia 1985 (no cat.); Tokyo, Shizuoka, and Osaka 2015, 43, no. 10.

PUBLISHED: Waterhouse 1983, fig. 32; Davis 2021, 55, fig. 15.

SIGNED BY THE ARTIST: The true brush of Hōgetsudō Tanchōsai Okumura Bunkaku Masanobu, originator of the finest Edo pictures.

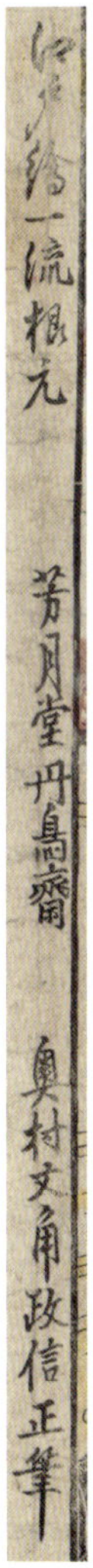

SEAL OF THE ARTIST: Tanchōsai.

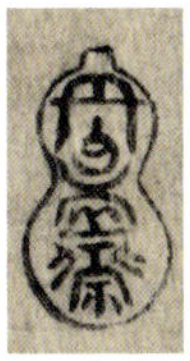

SIGNED BY THE PUBLISHER: Okumuraya Genroku hanmoto.

SEAL OF THE PUBLISHER: [gourd-shaped seal].

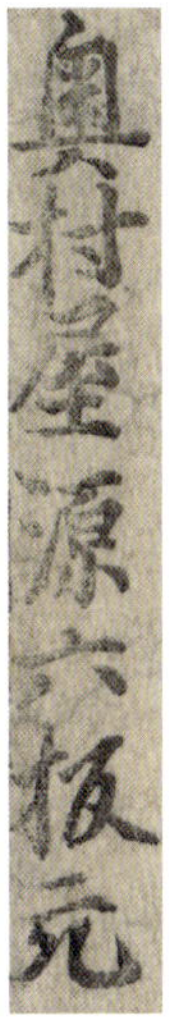

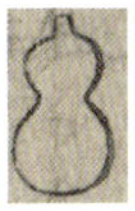

44

Courtesan as Daruma Crossing the River

Suzuki Harunobu (1725?–1770)

1960-17-1

EXHIBITED: Philadelphia 1966 (no cat.); Philadelphia 1970, 90–91, no. 41; Tokyo et al. 1972, no. 12; Philadelphia 1985 (no cat.); Chiba City and Hagi City 2002, 94, no. 87; Tokyo, Shizuoka, and Osaka 2015, 51, no. 19.

PUBLISHED: "Ukiyo-e go daimeisaku shinhakken!" 2020, 9, no. 5.

45

Woman's Kimono (or Robe) (*Kosode*)

1951-42-1

EXHIBITED: Kyoto 1999, 147, no. 70; New York 2001–2, 71, pl. 56.

PUBLISHED: Blum 1997, 182, pl. 341; Kirkham and Weber 2013, 170–71, fig. 7.26.

46

Autumn Flowers

Kitagawa Sōsetsu (act. mid-17th century–early 18th century)

1966-100-1

EXHIBITED: Philadelphia 1996 (no cat.); Philadelphia 2000–2001a (no cat.); Philadelphia 2005–6b (no cat.); Yokohama and Kyoto 2016, 100, no. 65.

PUBLISHED: Association of Scientific Research 1993, 30, no. 63.

PROVENANCE: Mary Cassatt (1844–1926); by inheritance to her niece Ellen Mary Cassatt (Mrs. Horace Binney Hare; 1894–1966), Pennsylvania.

SEAL: Taiseiken.

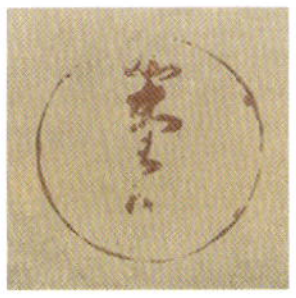

47

Flowers of Spring and Summer

Sōsen (act. 1624–43)

1965-21-1a,b

EXHIBITED: New York 1971, 46, no. 16; Los Angeles and New York 1976–77, 70–71, no. 26; Philadelphia 1987–88 (no cat.); Philadelphia 1996 (no cat.); Philadelphia 2000–2001a (no cat.); Philadelphia 2005–6b (no cat.).

PUBLISHED: Shimada 1969, 76, no. 56, fig. 56; Association of Scientific Research 1993, 28, no. 56.

PROVENANCE: Ikeda Shigeaki (1867–1950).

SIGNED: Sōsen.

SEAL: Sōsen.

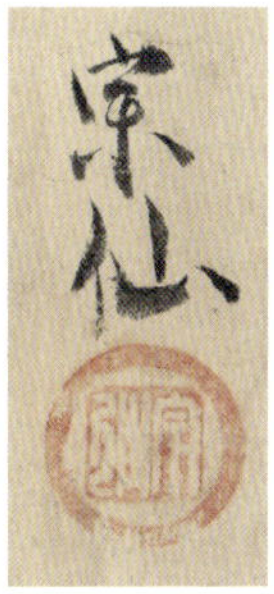

48

Morning Glories

Suzuki Kiitsu (1796–1858)

Kameda Bōsai (1752–1826)

2016-194-7

EXHIBITED: New Orleans 1983–84, 71–72, no. 15; New Orleans, Seattle, and New York 2002–4, 159, 272, pl. 96, no. 92; New York 2012–13, 192, 207, no. 92.

PUBLISHED: Nakamura 1979, 49, no. 79; Yamane 1979, 275, no. 164; Tokyo 1981, 48, no. 38; Kobayashi 1990, 152, 322, 347, no. 259.

PROVENANCE: Manyo'an Collection of Japanese Art, New Orleans, until 2016.

SIGNED: Kiitsu hitsu; Bōsai Rōjin.

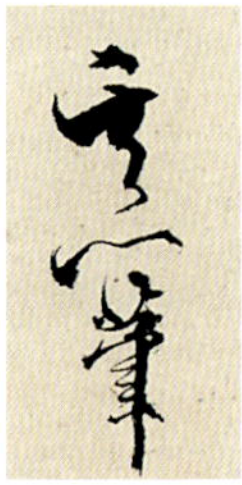

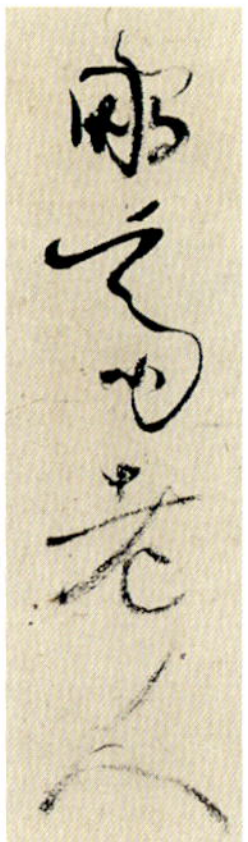

SEALS: Jōun; Chōkō no in.

INSCRIBED WITH A POEM: For the translation, see p. 131.

49

Goshawk Mews

1978-122-1

EXHIBITED: Philadelphia 1980 (no cat.); Philadelphia 1987–88 (no cat.); Philadelphia 1997–98 (no cat.); Boston 2004–5, cover, fig. 6; Philadelphia 2017 (no cat.); Washington and Los Angeles 2019, 188, 191, no. 173.

PUBLISHED: Association of Scientific Research 1993, 21, no. 36; Saunders 2005, 82–92, fig. 7; Callaghan 2019.

PROVENANCE: Akio Saito, Kyoto; Richard Chalfant Gallery, Chadds Ford, Pennsylvania, 1959; Mr. and Mrs. Douglas Cooper, Bryn Athyn, Pennsylvania, until 1978.

50

Flowering Plum Trees in Mist

Ike Taiga (1723–1776)

E1969-1-1,2

EXHIBITED: Philadelphia 1983 (no cat.); Philadelphia 1996 (no cat.); Philadelphia 2007, 164, no. 38; Berkeley 2019–20, 86–87, no. 16.

PUBLISHED: Kurimoto 1957, vol. 5, no. 680; Ooka 1971, 38, 40–44, figs. 4–8; Yamanouchi 1981, fig. 26; Association of Scientific Research 1993, 32, no. 67; Philadelphia Museum of Art 1995, 46; Philadelphia Museum of Art 2014, 75.

PROVENANCE: Possibly Tonomura family;* Hosomi Ryō, Izumi-Ōtsu City, Japan, until 1960s.

* According to the authentication by Hitomi Shōka (see below).

SIGNED ON RIGHT SCREEN: Kyūka Sanshō; ON LEFT SCREEN: Kyūka Sanshō sha.

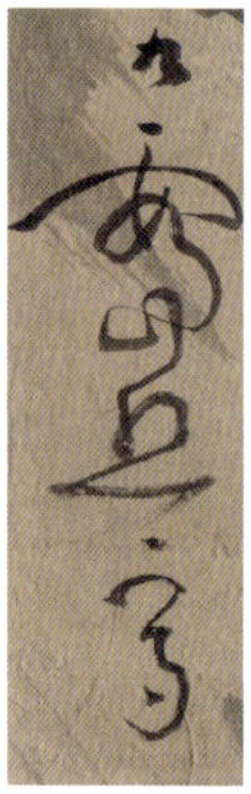

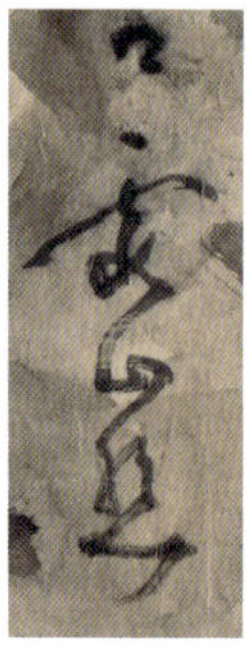

SEALS ON EACH SCREEN: Ike Mumei in; Kashō; Zenshin Sōma Hō Kyūkō.

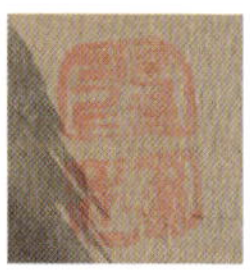

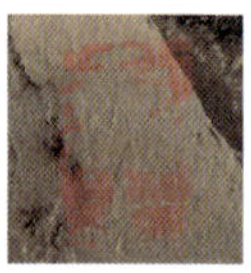

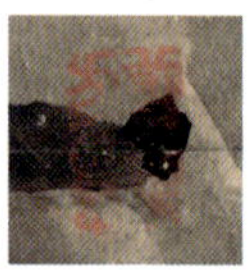

TWO CERTIFICATES OF AUTHENTICATION, DATED TO 1967, PASTED ONTO THE BACKS OF THE SCREENS: One by the artist Hitomi Shōka (1896–1968) and one by the Nanga connoisseur Yamanaka Rankei (1883–1975).

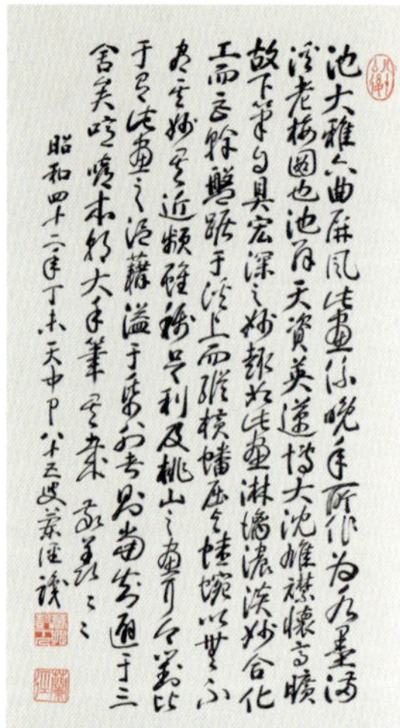

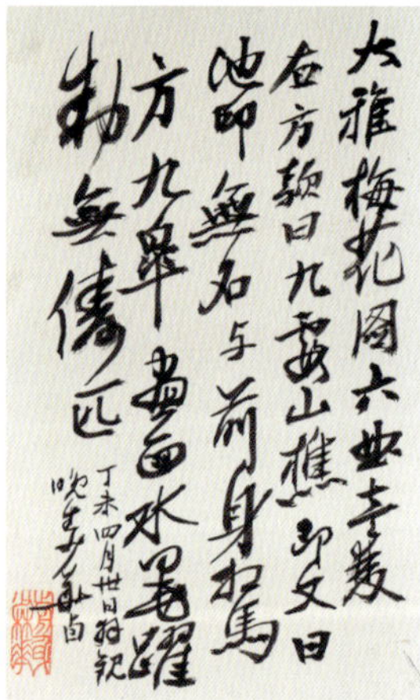

51

Summer Landscape

Tokuyama Gyokuran (1728–1784)

2010-51-1

EXHIBITED: Philadelphia 2013 (no cat.); Berkeley 2019–20, 96–97, no. 21.

PUBLISHED: Mizuo 1957, 70.

SIGNED AND DATED: Gyokuran, Meiwa 1 [1764], seventh month.

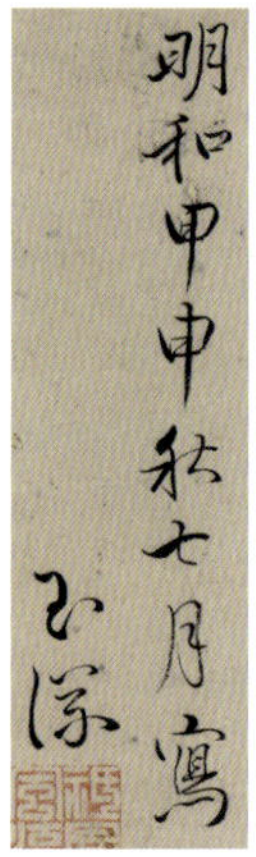

SEALS: Gyokuran; Gyokuran Furyū.

52

Mountain Retreat in Summer

Yosa Buson (1716–1783)

2019-153-1

EXHIBITED: Izumi 1990, 94, 177–78, no. 117; New York 2019a (no cat.).

PUBLISHED: Ogata, Okada, and Sasaki 1998, 86, pl. 363.

PROVENANCE: Kaikodō [gallery], New York; Setsu Gatōdō, Tokyo.

SIGNED: Shunsei.

SEALS: Shunsei shi; Tōsei.

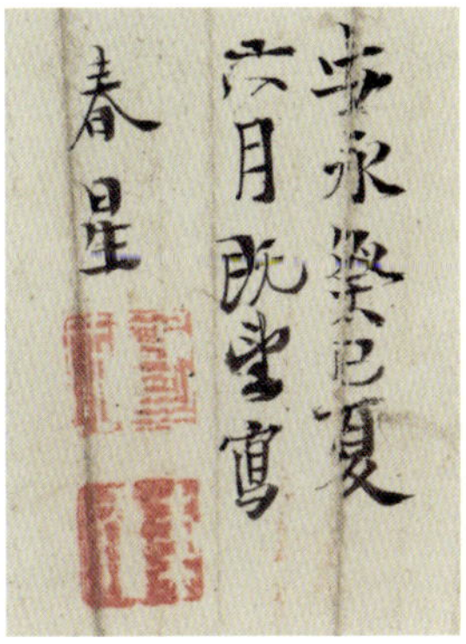

INSCRIBED ON BOX LID: [authentication by Nishimura Nangaku, dated to 1957].

53

Seven Haiku Poets

Matsumura Goshun (1752–1811)

1997-168-1

EXHIBITED: Philadelphia 1998–99 (no cat.); Philadelphia 2000–2001a (no cat.); Philadelphia 2006–7 (no cat.); Berkeley 2019–20, 102–3, no. 24.

SIGNED: Gekkei sha.

SEAL: Goshun no in.

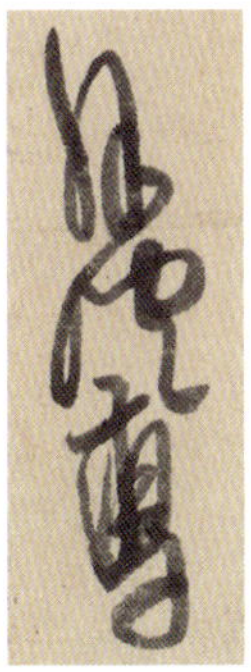

INSCRIBED WITH SEVEN HAIKU.

54

The Activities of the Twelve Months

Nichōsai (Matsuya Heizaburō or Hanzaburō) (b. before 1751, d. 1802 or 1803)

1964-5-1

EXHIBITED: Philadelphia 1990–91 (no cat.); Katonah and Boston 1996, 84–85, no. 31; Philadelphia 1997–98 (no cat.); Philadelphia 1999–2000 (no cat.); Philadelphia 2010–11 (no cat.).

PUBLISHED: Chinese Art Society of America 1962, 112, fig. 30; Fischer 1991, 18, fig. 17; Association of Scientific Research 1993, 42, no. 93.

PROVENANCE: Hagiwara Hiromichi (1815–1863); Sakai Shōtō, Kobe, Japan, until 1924.

SEAL AT UPPER RIGHT: Manji sakazuki; SEALS AT LOWER LEFT: Sō ni arazu, Zoku ni arazu. Sake wo motte Na to nasu; Nichō sai-bō.

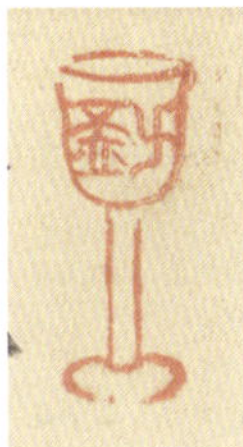

55

Recumbent Bull

Soga Shōhaku (1730–1781)

1971-11-1

EXHIBITED: Philadelphia 1980 (no cat.); Philadelphia 1987–88 (no cat.); Philadelphia 1997–98 (no cat.).

PUBLISHED: Association of Scientific Research 1993, 40, no. 86.

SIGNED: Jasokuken Mahito zu.

SEAL: Jasokuken Shōhaku.

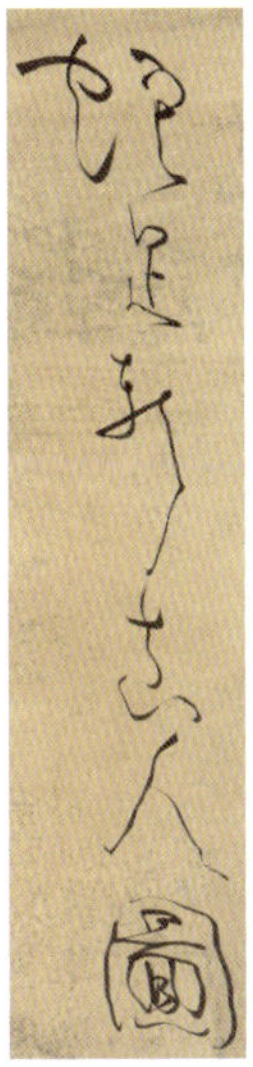

56

Grapes

Itō Jakuchū (1716–1800)

1965-70-1

EXHIBITED: Philadelphia 1987–88 (no cat.); Philadelphia 1989–90 (no cat.); Philadelphia 1996 (no cat.); Kyoto 2000, 228, 350, 388, 395, no. 89; Fukushima 2019, 20, 162.

PUBLISHED: Association of Scientific Research 1993, 39, no. 83.

SEALS: Tō Jokin azana Keiwa; Jakuchū Kōji.

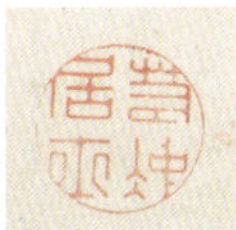

57

Morning Glories

Itō Jakuchū (1716–1800)

1965-71-1

EXHIBITED: Philadelphia 1987–88 (no cat.); Philadelphia 1989–90 (no cat.); Philadelphia 1996 (no cat.); Kyoto 2000, 229, 350, 388, 395, no. 90; Fukushima 2019, 21, 162.

PUBLISHED: Association of Scientific Research 1993, 39, no. 84.

SEALS ON EACH SCROLL: Jokin; Jakuchū koji.

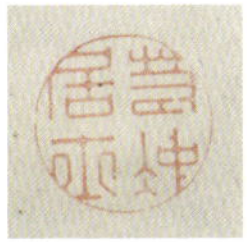

58

Woodcutter and *Fisherman*

Nagasawa Rosetsu (1754–1799)

2010-27-1,2

Not previously exhibited or published.

SIGNED ON EACH SCROLL: Rosetsu sha.

SEAL ON EACH SCROLL: Gyo.

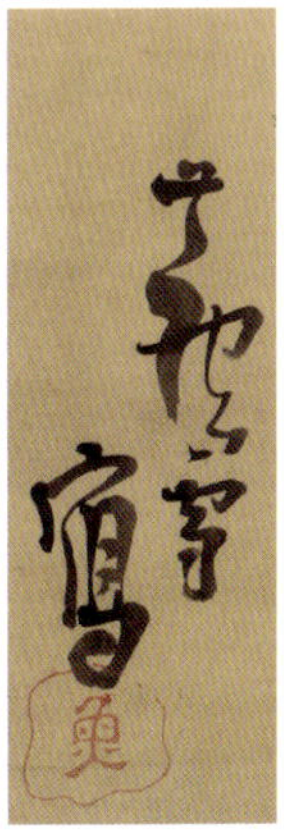

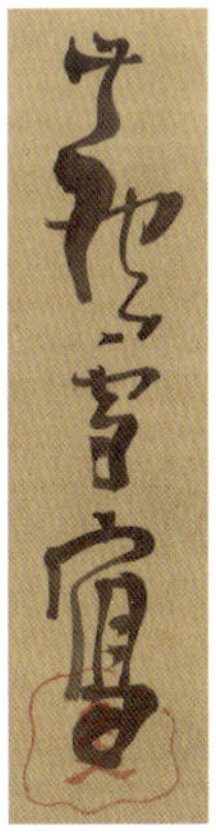

59

Summer Landscape

Tani Bunchō (1763–1840)

1976-193-1

EXHIBITED: Philadelphia 1977, no. 112; Philadelphia 1980 (no cat.); Philadelphia 1996–97 (no cat.); Philadelphia 2006–7 (no cat.).

PUBLISHED: Association of Scientific Research 1993, 33, no. 71.

SIGNED: Bunchō.

SEAL: Gagakusai.

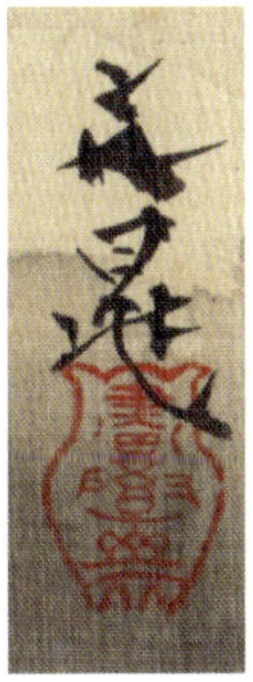

60

Three Pairs of Sliding Doors (*Sugito*)

1966-211-5a,b;6a,b;7a,b;8a,b;15 a,b;16a,b

EXHIBITED: Philadelphia 1969 (no cat.); Philadelphia 1989–90 (no cat.); Philadelphia 1997–98 (no cat.); Philadelphia 2015a, 193, 274, no. 82.

PUBLISHED: Association of Scientific Research 1993, 46–47, nos. 99-2, 99-3, 99-4, 99-5, figs. 99.5–.12; 51, nos. 99-12, 99-13, figs. 99.25–.28.

61

Short Sword (*Wakizashi*)

Attributed to Inoue Kunisada II (1630–1682)

1964-178-30

Not previously exhibited or published.

CERTIFICATE OF AUTHENTICATION: Purchased in Japan by Capt. E. L. Zalinski U.S.A. (ret'd). Swords were inspected by Chikayoshi Honami Hereditary Imperial Sword Official, Prof. Sakur[a]i, Instructor of sword making, Imperial School of Fine Arts, and Mr. Yoda of Tokio [*sic*]. Swords were only purchased on which the above mentioned agreed as to the name of maker. Age is given for 1896.

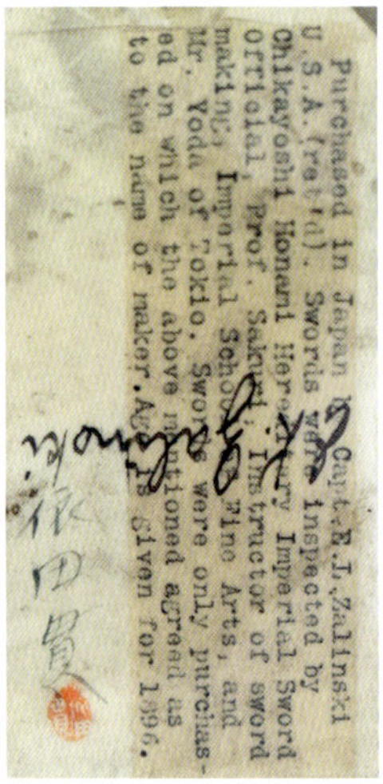

62

Dragon *Menuki*

1972-167-1a,b

EXHIBITED: Philadelphia 1980 (no cat.); Philadelphia 1987–88 (no cat.); Philadelphia 1997–98 (no cat.).

63

Figure of a Beckoning Cat (*Maneki neko*)

1984-107-1

EXHIBITED: Philadelphia 1987–88 (no cat.); Philadelphia 1997–98 (no cat.).

PUBLISHED: Association of Scientific Research 1993, 76, no. 163.

64

Futon Cover

2000-113-35

EXHIBITED: Philadelphia 2002, 79, no. 7.

PUBLISHED: Philadelphia Museum of Art 2014, 82.

65

Fireman's Coat (*Hikeshi hanten*)

2000-113-14

EXHIBITED: Philadelphia 2002, 78, no. 7; Philadelphia 2019a (no cat.).

PROVENANCE: Harry G. C. Packard (1914–1991), Kyoto.

66

Album of Prints of Kabuki Actors in Their Roles by Hirosada

Konishi Hirosada (also called Gosōtei Hirosada) (act. 1826–63, d. c. 1865)

2008-62-243(1–99)

Not previously exhibited or published.

2008-62-243(4):
SIGNED: Gochōtei Sadamasu ga.
SEAL: [bat-shaped seal].

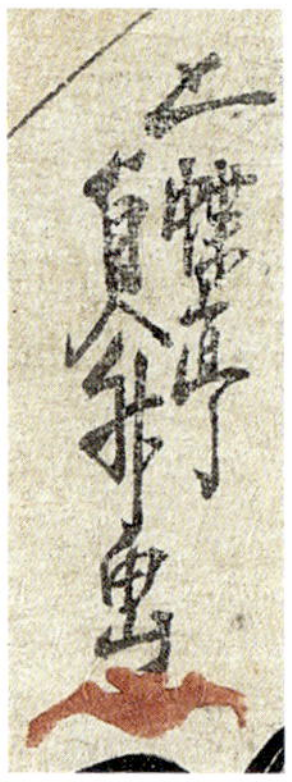

2008-62-243(30B):
SIGNED: Sadamasu.
SEAL: [bat-shaped seal].

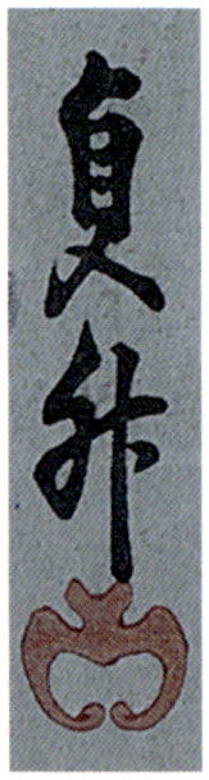

2008-62-243(79):
SIGNED: Hirosada.

67

Fine Wind, Clear Day (*Gaifū kaisei*), also known as *Red Fuji*, from the series *Thirty-Six Views of Mount Fuji* (*Fugaku sanjūrokkei*)

Katsushika Hokusai (1760–1849)

1958-49-5

EXHIBITED: Philadelphia 1966 (no cat.); Philadelphia 1976–77 (no cat.); Tokyo, Shizuoka, and Osaka 2015, 143, no. 114.

PROVENANCE: Harry Parsons Garland (1859–1935) and Edith (Pew) Garland (1869–1938), Saco, Maine; Garland sale, Parke-Bernet Galleries, New York, April 12, 1945; Mrs. Moncure Biddle (Brenda Fenollosa Biddle; 1883–1959), Philadelphia.

SIGNED: Hokusai aratame Iitsu hitsu.

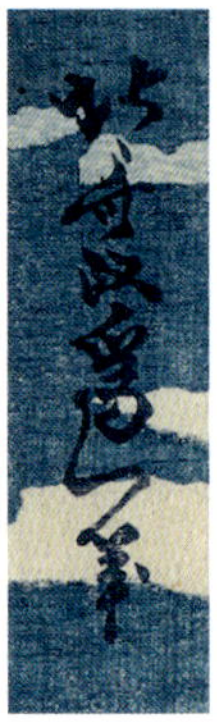

68

Cabinet

1876-1681

EXHIBITED: Philadelphia 1876 (not reproduced in the catalogue); Philadelphia 2001–2 (no cat.); Los Angeles 2005, 98, fig. 2; Ithaca and Sacramento 2016–17 (not reproduced in the catalogue).

PUBLISHED: Barber 1906, 25; Hiesinger 2011, 34, no. 24.

69

Urn and Stand

1917-158,a;159

EXHIBITED: Philadelphia 1876 (not reproduced in the catalogue); Washington 1976–96 (no cat.); Philadelphia 2001–2 (no cat.); Tokyo, Osaka, and Nagoya 2004–5, 31, no. I-57; Los Angeles 2005, 33, no. 46; Ithaca and Sacramento 2016–17 (not reproduced in the catalogue).

PUBLISHED: Fischer 2002, pl. II.

70

Pair of Vases

Fukagawa Eizaemon VIII (1833–1889)

1897-353,353a

EXHIBITED: Philadelphia 1876 (not reproduced in the catalogue); Philadelphia 2001–2 (no cat.).

PUBLISHED: Fischer 2002, 103, pl. 11.

PROVENANCE: General Hector Tyndale (1821–1880), Philadelphia, purchased from the Centennial International Exhibition, Philadelphia, 1876.

MARK ON BASE OF EACH VASE: Hichōzan Fukagawa zō.

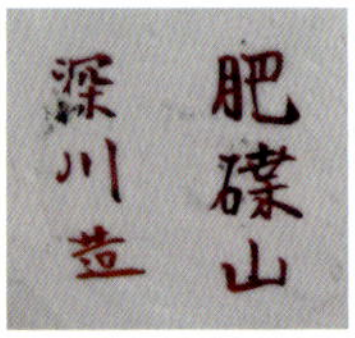

71

Farming Scenes of the Four Seasons

Kano Sōeki Kagenobu (act. late 18th–mid-19th century)

2016-194-11a,b

EXHIBITED: Jerusalem and Houston 2014–15, 77–78.

SIGNED ON EACH SCREEN: Kano Sōeki Kagenobu hitsu.

SEAL ON EACH SCREEN: Fujiwara.

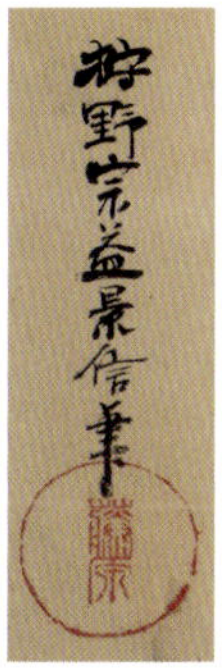

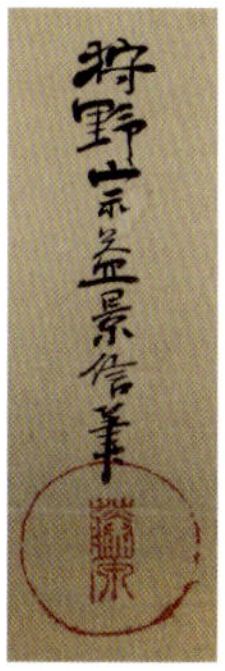

72

The Dragon Sings, the Tiger Roars

Nukina Kaioku (1778–1863)

1992-13-1

EXHIBITED: Philadelphia 1992–93 (no cat.); Philadelphia 1998–99 (no cat.); Philadelphia 2002–3 (no cat.); Philadelphia 2006–7 (no cat.); Philadelphia 2022–23 (no cat.).

SIGNED: Written by Sūō.

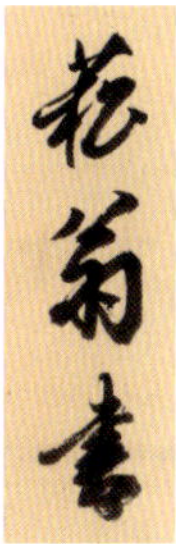

SEAL ON RIGHT PANEL: Shūseidō.

SEALS ON LEFT PANEL: Kunmo; Seimi honpaku sakusa.

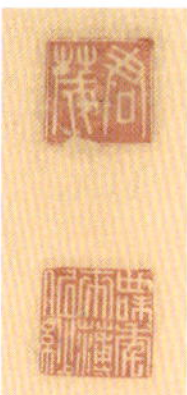

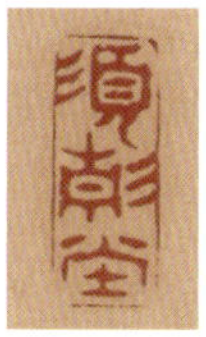

73

Album of Landscapes

Hine Taizan (1814–1869)

1998-52-1

EXHIBITED: Philadelphia 1998–99 (no cat.); Philadelphia 2006–7 (no cat.).

INSCRIPTIONS, SIGNATURES, AND SEALS:

On outer cover title strip:

INSCRIBED BY CHŌ SANSHŪ (1833–1895): Album of landscapes painted by Taizan.

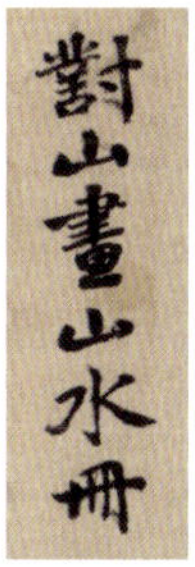

SIGNED: Sanshū.
SEAL: Sanshū.

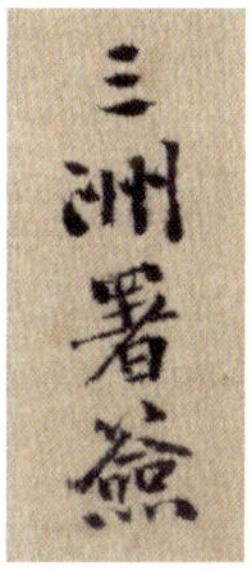

Front colophon:

INSCRIBED BY EMA TENKŌ (1825–1902): Made this title in October of the Year of the Rat [1900]. The brush comes and creates.

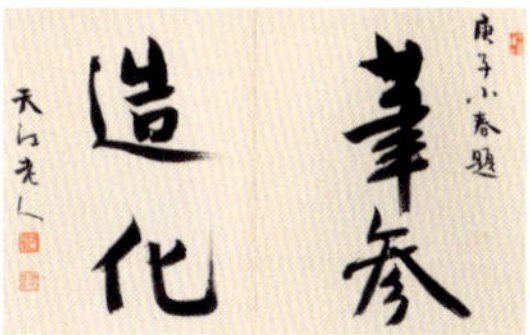

SIGNED: Tenkō Rōjin.

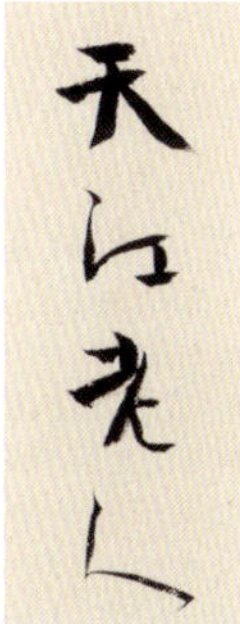

SEALS: Shiji baichū; Ema Seikin; Kō shi saku.

Back colophon:

INSCRIBED BY MURATA KŌKOKU (1831–1912): Twelve leaves of landscape painting by Hine Taizan. They have variety in each composition and are excellent. Perhaps he may have done them after studying old masters' works. However, he absorbed and fused them well. Other contemporary painters cannot equal Taizan. I, Kōkoku, burnt incense and admired this album; at last, I wrote the colophon. Winter day in the boar year Meiji 32 [1899] at Gomizenbō in Kōjimachi in Tokyo.

SIGNED: Kōkoku Murata Shuku.

SEALS: Murata Shuku in; Kōkoku.

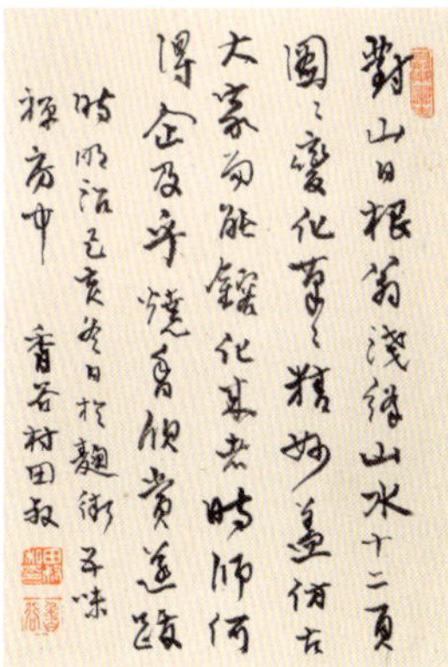

Twelve landscape painting calligraphies by Hine Taizan:

1.
SIGNED: Shōnen.
SEALS: Taizanjin; Shōnen.

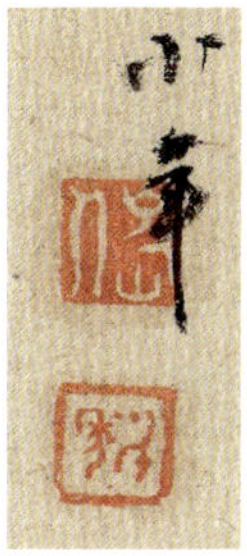

INSCRIBED:
Hanging on the wall is the *Painting of the Plum Blossom Study*, so I have infused this work with his "brush feeling."*

* The artist of the work may have been Wen Zhengming (1470–1559).

2.
SIGNED: Shōnen sha.
SEALS: Taizanjin; Shōnen.
INSCRIBED:
The place, remote, visitors
are few.
There are hidden joys through
the mulberry-field gate.*

* This is a couplet from a poem by the great Song-dynasty poet Wang Anshi (1021–1086).

3.
SIGNED: Shōnen.
SEALS: Taizanjin; Shōnen.
INSCRIBED:
Summer Mountains
after Rain.

4.
SIGNED: Painted by Taizanjin.
SEALS: Taizanjin; Shōnen.
INSCRIBED:
Willows Shading Stones in
a Stream.

5.
SIGNED: Shōnen.
SEALS: Taizanjin; Shōnen.
INSCRIBED:
Wutong Trees after Rain.

6.
SIGNED: Taizanjin sha.
SEALS: Taizanjin; Shōnen.
INSCRIBED:
Though the water over rocks
does make a noise,
It's nothing like the sound
of wheels and hooves.

7.
SIGNED: Shōnen.
SEALS: Taizanjin; Shōnen.
INSCRIBED:
Summer Dawn So Refreshing.

8.
SIGNED: Taizan Hinaga.
SEALS: Taizanjin; Shōnen.
INSCRIBED:
Water here aplenty, clouds
are nil;
The ten thousand sounds
in this place, purified.

9.
SIGNED: Shōnen.
SEALS: Taizanjin; Shōnen.
INSCRIBED:
Beyond the mist, the sound
of the great bell;
A mountain monk, alone,
returns to the temple.*

* This couplet is by the major Ming-dynasty poet Gao Qi (1336–1374).

73 (continued)

10.
SIGNED: Shōnen sha.
SEALS: Taizanjin; Shōnen.
INSCRIBED:
The hidden birds don't sing,
the woods are still.*

* This verse is in the relatively rare six-character meter.

11.
SIGNED: Taizanjin sha.
SEALS: Taizanjin; Shōnen.

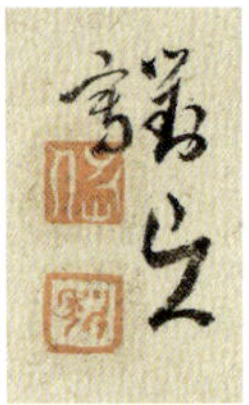

INSCRIBED:
The stream is calm; birds peer
at reflections;
The moss is deep; clogs
imprint their steps.*

* This couplet is by the Song-dynasty poet Zhao Bian (1008–1084).

12.
SIGNED: Taizanjin Hinaga.
SEALS: Taizanjin; Shōnen.

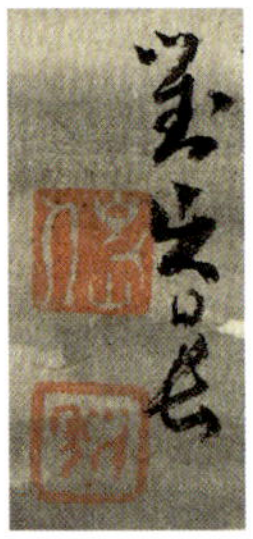

INSCRIBED:
Snow on Peaks in Winter
Darkness.

Landscape painting calligraphies translated and annotated by Jonathan Chaves

74
Orchid Pavilion Outing
Suzuki Hyakunen
(1825–1891)
1963-47-1

EXHIBITED: Ithaca et al. 1980–81, 64–65, no. 23; Philadelphia 2002–3 (no cat.).

SEALS: Tōkinrō; Hyakunen.

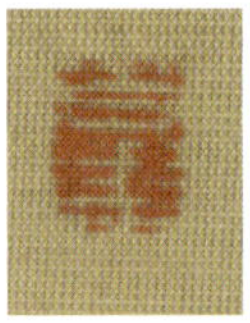

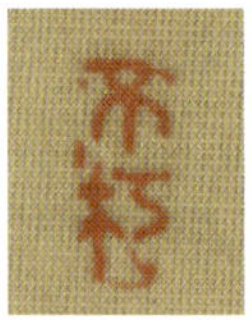

INSCRIBED: Painted in the eighth month of the kōgo [horse] year of Meiji [1870] by Tōkinrō [Eastern Brocade Tower], Hyakunen.

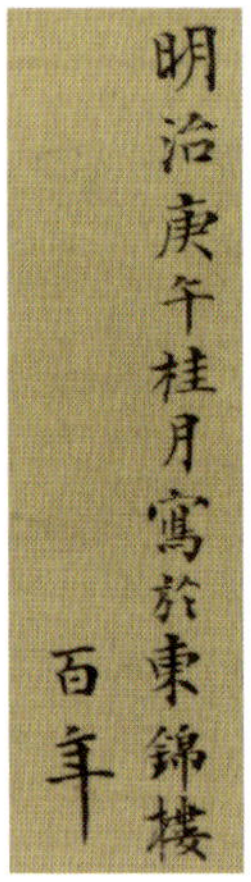

75
Untitled (Album of Japanese Photographs)
Various Artists
2005-186-3

Not previously exhibited or published.

76
Two Dragons in Clouds
Kano Hōgai (1828–1888)
1940-41-1

EXHIBITED: Tokyo 1886 (no cat.); Cleveland 1916, 192, no. 6; Philadelphia 1969 (no cat.); Philadelphia 1983 (no cat.); Tokyo, Shimonoseki, and Kyoto 1988–89, 66–67, no. 63; Berlin 1993–94, 189, fig. 158, 509, no. 16/12; Ibaraki 1997, 33, 160, no. 8; Fukui 2013, 49, no. 34; Philadelphia 2015a, 60, 245, 287, no. 119.

PUBLISHED: Hosono 1978, 198, pl. 95; Nihon Bijutsuin 1989, 68–69, 468, no. 57; Fischer 1992, 12, fig. 12; Association of Scientific Research 1993, 107, no. 105; Philadelphia Museum of Art 1995, 47; Foxwell 2008, 282–83, 514, fig. 4.6; Philadelphia Museum of Art 2014, 80; Foxwell 2015, 102–3, fig. 3.14.

PROVENANCE: Ernest F. Fenollosa (1853–1908); by inheritance to his daughter, Brenda Fenollosa Biddle (1883–1959), Philadelphia.*

* When Biddle donated this painting to the museum in 1940, she commissioned a brass plaque for the frame that reads, "In Memory of Ernest F. Fenollosa, for whom this picture was painted by Kano Hōgai (1828–1888)."

77
The Cry of the Fox (*Konkai*), from the series *One Hundred Aspects of the Moon* (*Tsuki hyakushi*)
Tsukioka Yoshitoshi
(1839–1892)
1989-47-407

EXHIBITED: Philadelphia 2019a (no cat.).

PUBLISHED: Keyes 1982, 478.13.

SIGNED BY THE ARTIST: Yoshitoshi.

SEAL OF THE ARTIST: Yoshitoshi.

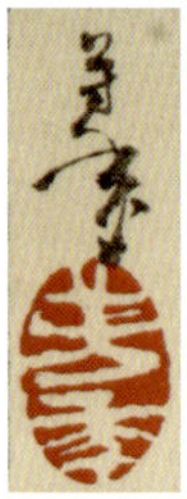

SEAL OF THE CARVER: Chōkō Enkatsu.

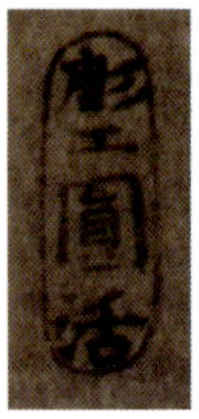

SIGNED BY THE PUBLISHER: Akiyama Buemon.

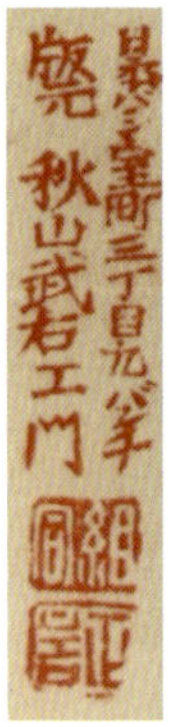

SEALS OF THE CENSOR: kumiai [association]; akashi [proof].

78
The Activities of the Twelve Months
Kawanabe Kyōsai
(1831–1889)
1998-66-1,2

EXHIBITED: Philadelphia 1999–2000 (no cat.); Philadelphia 2010–11 (no cat.).

SIGNED ON EACH PANEL: Seisei Kyōsai ga.

SEAL ON EACH PANEL: Kyōsai.

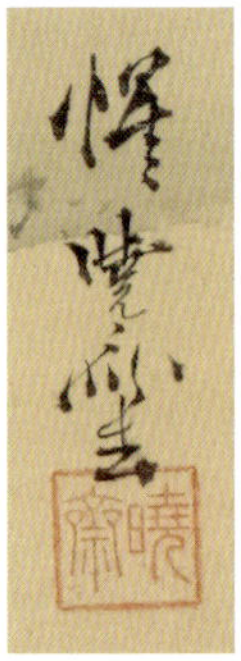

79
Fall of the Castle
Otake Chikuha (1878–1936)
1967-30-281

EXHIBITED: Philadelphia 2018–19 (no cat.).

PUBLISHED: Gardiner 1968, 139, 148, no. 303; Ogura et al. 1990, 720; Association of Scientific Research 1993, 57, no. 114.

SIGNED: Chikuha.

SEAL: Chikuha.

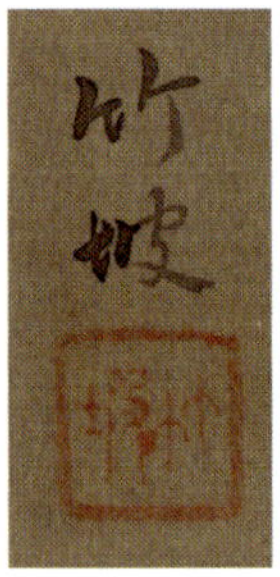

80

Landscape

Hashimoto Gahō (1835–1908)

2016-194-12a,b

EXHIBITED: Jerusalem and Houston 2014–15, 76–79; Philadelphia 2018–19 (no cat.).

PROVENANCE: Manyo'an Collection of Japanese Art, New Orleans, until 2016.

SIGNED ON EACH SCREEN: Gahō-zu.

SEAL ON EACH SCREEN: Kokki.

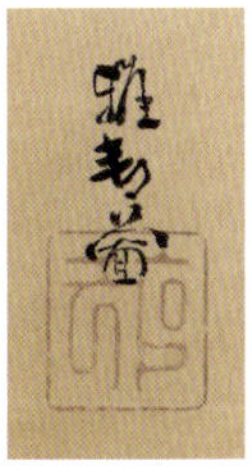

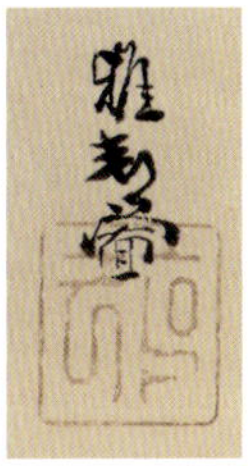

INSCRIBED ON WOOD STORAGE CASE: Authentication by the artist's son, Shūhō (1881–1947), dated to Shōwa 9 [1934].

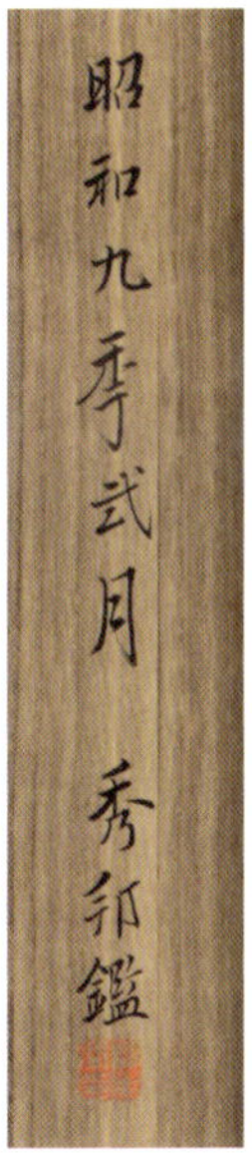

81

Mountains in Autumn

Noguchi Shōhin (1847–1917)

1971-267-1

EXHIBITED: Philadelphia 1980 (no cat.); Ithaca et al. 1980–81, 78–79, no. 32; Lawrence and Honolulu 1988, 179, no. 87; Philadelphia 1996–97 (no cat.); Philadelphia 2018–19 (no cat.).

PUBLISHED: Association of Scientific Research 1993, 56, no. 110.

SIGNED: Autumn leaves in the mountains are depicted by Ms. Shōhin herself.

SEALS: Chōsei Kakei; Noguchi Shin'in; Shōhin Joshi; Shunjū Kajitsu Ōshi.*

* The phrase *Shunjū Kajitsu Ōshi*, which translates to "many fine days in spring and autumn," is probably from the poem "[Joy of] Migration" by the Chinese poet Tao Yuanming (365–427).

INSCRIBED WITH A POEM: For the translation, see p. 201.

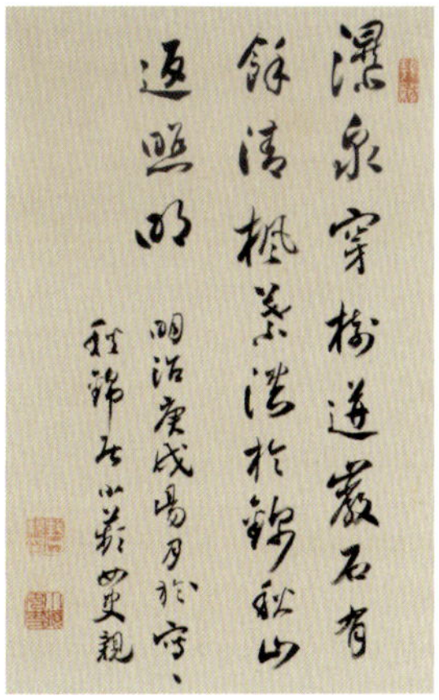

82

Shosho Hakkei (Eight Views of Xiao and Xiang)

Kosugi Hōan Misei (1881–1964)

Haiku brushed by Matsuse Seisei (1869–1937)

Title calligraphy by Naitō Konan (1866–1934)

2017-104-1

EXHIBITED: Tokyo 1919, 1029–30; Philadelphia 2018–19 (no cat.).

SIGNED BY THE ARTIST: Misei.

SEAL OF THE ARTIST: Misei.

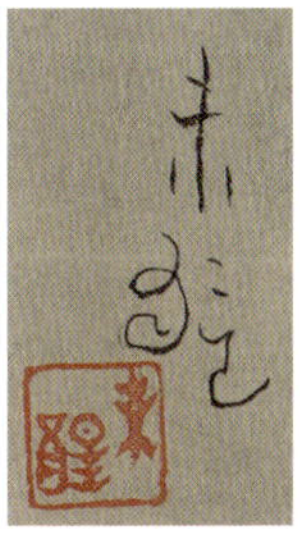

SIGNED BY THE TITLE CALLIGRAPHER: Konan sakyū.

SEALS OF THE TITLE CALLIGRAPHER: Hōbakai; Tōryō.

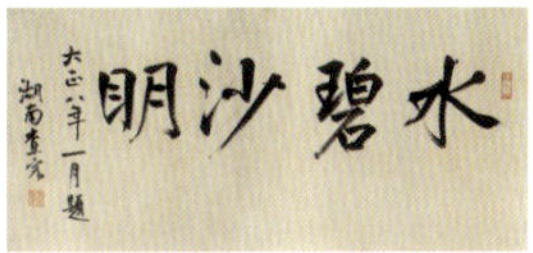

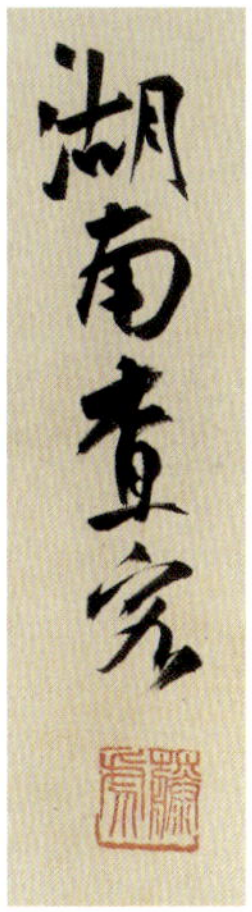

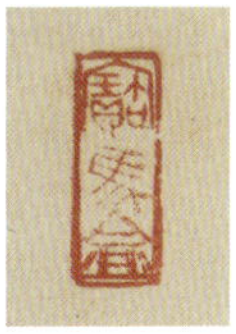

SIGNED BY THE HAIKU CALLIGRAPHER: Seisei.

SEAL OF THE HAIKU CALLIGRAPHER: Manji.

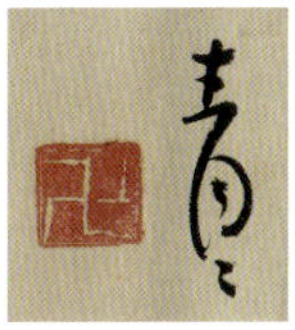

INSCRIBED WITH EIGHT HAIKU:

1.
clear autumn day / as pine trees are standing tall / a sense of respite

2.
this moment's desire / only to the wild geese / can it be known

3.
the sun is setting / over roses of Sharon / a fisherman's fence

4.
returning boats / the peaceful tranquility / of the island shore

5.
mosquitoes under the bell / the expanse / of the evening sea

6.
a thousand miles of moonlight / the sound of a flute / in early evening

7.
leaves are rustling / the horizon / snow capped

8.
early winter clouds / drip through the long autumn night / maddening

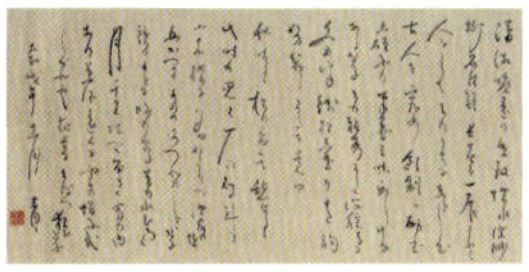

Haiku translated by Sonia Coman

83

El Capitan, Yosemite (Yosemittodani Eru Kyapitan)

Yoshida Hiroshi (1876–1950)

1973-202-39

EXHIBITED: Philadelphia 2015b, 21.

SIGNED: Yoshida.

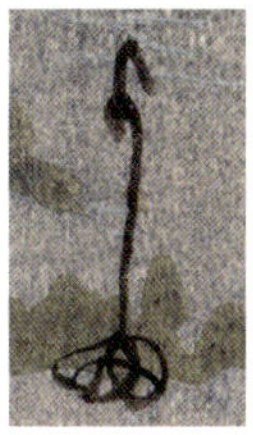

SEALS: [flower-shaped seal]; jizuri [self-printed].

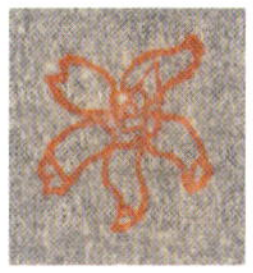

INSCRIBED: Hiroshi Yoshida.

84

Vase

Hyakuse Yamamuro (1900–1990)

1992-8-3

EXHIBITED: Tokyo 1937 (no cat.); Philadelphia 1992–93 (no cat.); Philadelphia 2016–17 (no cat.).

SIGNED ON BASE: Hyakuse.

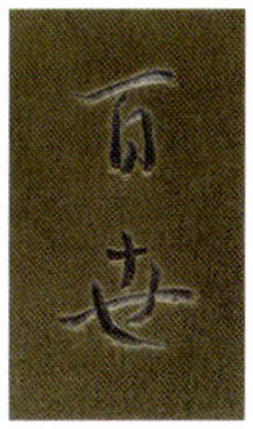

85
Jar
Kawai Kanjirō (1890–1966)
2007-34-1
EXHIBITED: Philadelphia 2007–8 (no cat.).

86
Golden Fox Hunting
Itaya Kōji (1925–2006)
2006-31-1
EXHIBITED: Philadelphia 2008–9b, 32, no. 38, pl. 16; Philadelphia 2009 (no cat.).
PUBLISHED: Philadelphia Museum of Art 2014, 80.
PROVENANCE: Kagedo Japanese Art [gallery], Orcas, Washington, until 2006.
SIGNED: Kōji.
SEAL: Kōji.

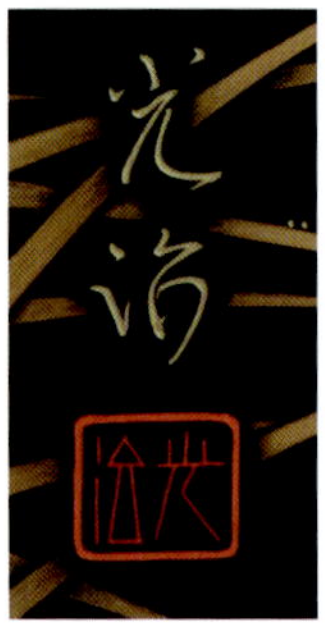

87
Water Container (*Mizusashi*)
Miyanohara Ken (1898–1977)
2008-7-9a,b
EXHIBITED: Tokyo 1966, no. 175; Tokyo 1999b, no. 115; Philadelphia 2008–9b, 38, no. 45, pl. 22.
PUBLISHED: Cline and Knospe 2007, 175, no. 185.
MARK ON BASE: Ken.

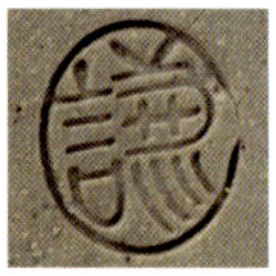

INSCRIBED ON LID OF INNER FITTED WOOD BOX: Carved glazed grape design water jar; ON UNDERSIDE OF LID: Fuchiku kiln.

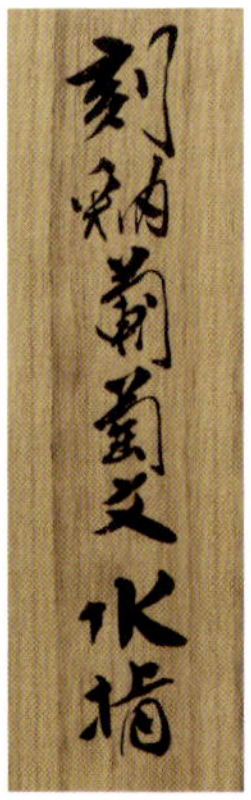

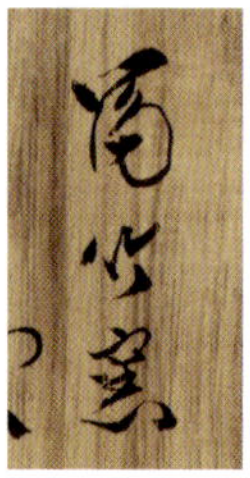

SIGNED ON UNDERSIDE OF LID: Ken.
SEAL ON UNDERSIDE OF LID: Ken.

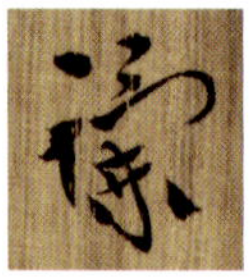

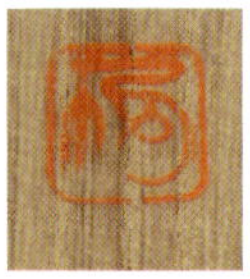

88
Ensemble Consisting of Cape, Bodysuit, and Chaps
Kansai Yamamoto (1944–2020)
1974-3-21a–c
EXHIBITED: Kyoto, Los Angeles, and Brooklyn 1996–99, 168, fig. 118; Philadelphia 2008–9a (no cat.).
PUBLISHED: “Kansai Yamamoto Show” 1971, 50–51.

89
Victorian Invention, Balloon
Oda Mayumi (b. 1941)
2010-112-1
Not previously exhibited or published.
SIGNED: Mayumi.

90
Landscape
Minol Araki (1928–2010)
2015-101-1
EXHIBITED: Taipei and Phoenix 1998–99, 131, no. 17.
SIGNED AND DATED: Year 79, sixth month Araki Minoru.

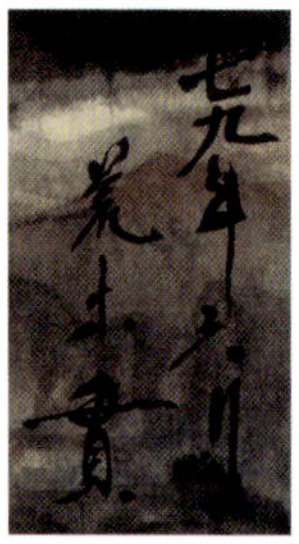

SEALS: MA; Hekiba.

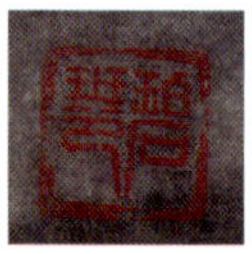

91
A Wristwatch Dug Up in Ueno-machi, approximately 0.7 km from the Epicenter of the Explosion
Shōmei Tōmatsu (1930–2012)
1990-51-109
EXHIBITED: Oxford, London, and Philadelphia 1985–86, 34; Philadelphia 1999 (no cat.); Philadelphia 2019b (no cat.).
SIGNED AND DATED ON VERSO: ’85 Tom.

92
No Footprints Show Where Flowers Are Deep
Munakata Shikō (1903–1975)
1974-179-5
EXHIBITED: Philadelphia 1980 (no cat.); Philadelphia 1988–89 (no cat.); Philadelphia 1990–91 (no cat.); Philadelphia 1998–99 (no cat.); Philadelphia et al. 2002–4, 38, fig. 13.
PUBLISHED: Munakata 1961, frontispiece; Fischer 1991, 26, fig. 28; Philadelphia Museum of Art 1995, 47.
SEALS: Kegon; Shikō.

93
Green Willows, Crimson Blossoms
Morita Shiryū (1912–1998)
2009-187-1
EXHIBITED: Philadelphia 1998–99 (no cat.).
PUBLISHED: Inada 2019, 153, 562, 636, no. XVII-498.
SIGNED ON PAPER LABEL ON BACK OF SCREEN: Morita Shiryū.
SEAL ON PAPER LABEL ON BACK OF SCREEN: Sei no ji.

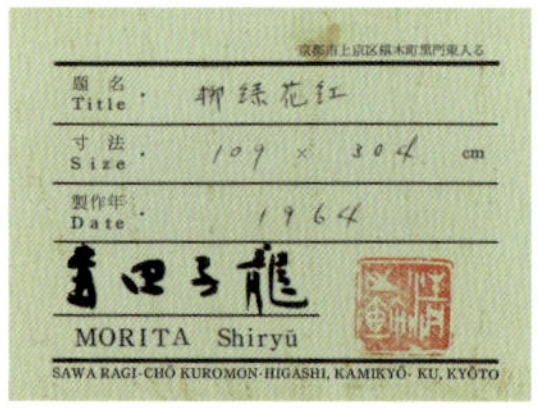

PROVENANCE: Yamada Art Gallery, Kyoto; sold to Mrs. H. Gates (Lally) Lloyd, Philadelphia, 1964.*

* Information from Mrs. Lloyd’s daughter Mrs. Minney Robb, who was living in Japan at the time of her mother’s visit there in 1964 and accompanied her mother to the Yamada Art Gallery in Kyoto, which was holding a solo exhibition of Morita Shiryū’s work, *Morita Shiryū shosaku-te* (Exhibition of Morita Shiryū calligraphic works). Mrs. Minney Robb, telephone conversation with Felice Fischer, 2021.

94
Tori B (*Birds B*), from the portfolio *The Modern Japanese Print: An Appreciation*
Shima Tamami (1937–1999)
1964-201-1(6)
COLOPHON OF PORTFOLIO SIGNED BY AUTHOR: James A. Michener.

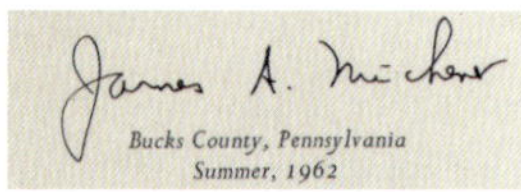

95

Kotodama

Maio Motoko (b. 1948)

2009-79-1a,b

EXHIBITED: Philadelphia 2012 (no cat.); Philadelphia 2016–17 (no cat.).

PUBLISHED: Lesley Kehoe Galleries 2008, 24–31; Philadelphia Museum of Art 2014, 421.

96

Water Container (*Mizusashi*) with Lid

Uozumi Yasuhiko Iraku III (b. 1937)

2002-44-1a,b

EXHIBITED: Kanazawa 2002 (no cat.); Philadelphia 2003–5 (no cat.); Philadelphia 2005–6a (no cat.); Philadelphia 2016–17 (no cat.); Shizuoka 2018 (no cat.).

SIGNED ON BOX: Iraku.

SEAL ON BOX: Iraku.

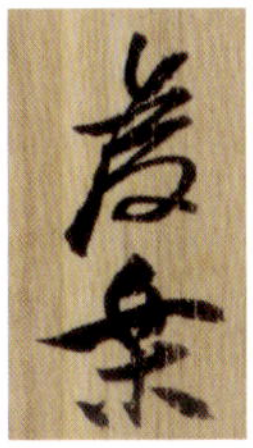

INSCRIBED ON BOX: Sahari water container with linear motif.

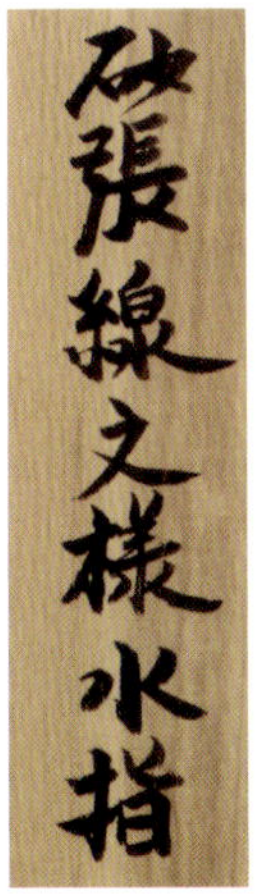

97

Big Wave

Yamaguchi Ryūun (b. 1940)

2010-178-25

EXHIBITED: Philadelphia 2012 (no cat.); Philadelphia 2016–17 (no cat.).

98

Saiseki Zōgan Nōkata (Noh-Inspired Form with Colored Clay Inlays)

Kishi Eiko (b. 1948)

2009-2-1

EXHIBITED: New York 2008, n.p.; Philadelphia 2010–11 (no cat.); Philadelphia 2012 (no cat.); Philadelphia 2016–17 (no cat.).

PUBLISHED: Yanagi 2008, 1–3.

INSCRIBED ON BASE: July 2005 saku Eiko Kishi; Eiko [artist's seal].

SIGNED ON LID OF FITTED BOX: Kishi Ei.

SEAL ON LID OF FITTED BOX: Eiko.

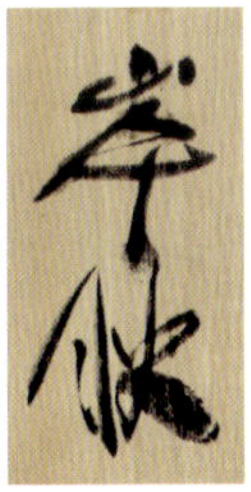

99

Yumegatari (Reverie)

Takeyama Naoki (b. 1974)

2014-34-1

EXHIBITED: Philadelphia 2016–17 (no cat.).

SIGNED ON INTERIOR BOTTOM: Takeyama 831.

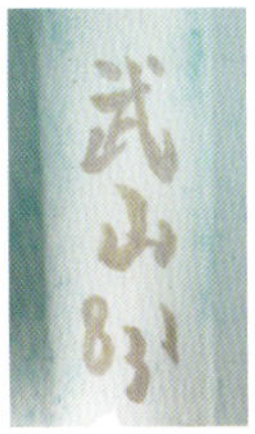

SIGNED ON BOX LID: Takeyama Naoki.

SEAL ON BOX LID: Take.

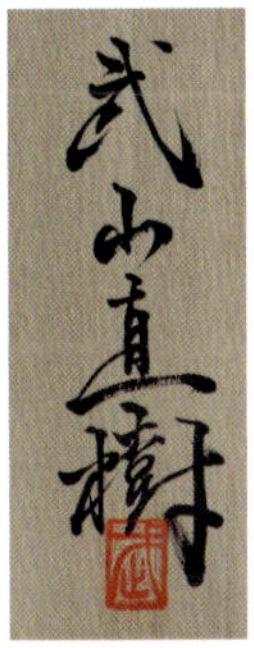

INSCRIBED ON BOX LID: Yumegatari.

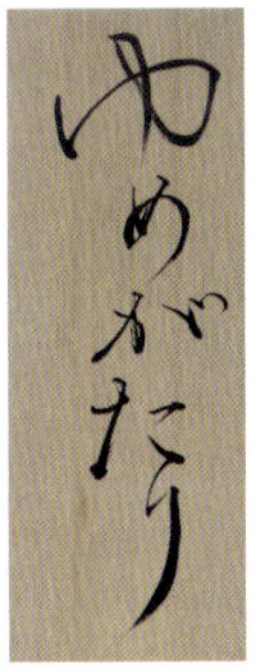

100

Vessel with Blue Glaze

Kimura Yoshiro (b. 1946)

2018-37-1

EXHIBITED: Tokyo 2013–14 (no cat.); Philadelphia 2019–22 (no cat.).

SIGNED ON BASE: Kimura Yoshiro.

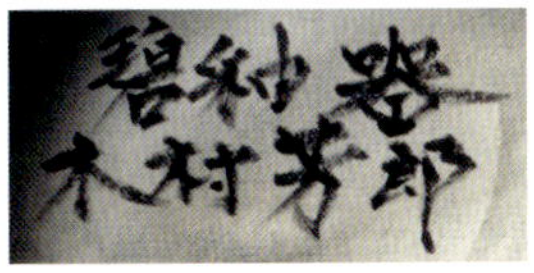

SIGNED ON BOX LID: Kimura Yoshiro.

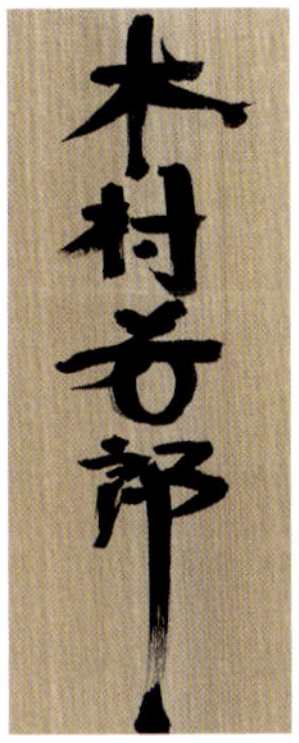

SEAL ON BOX LID: Yoshiro.

101

Joyfulness in the Sea

Chie Otani (b. 1951)

2017-133-1a–j

Not previously exhibited or published.

102

The Nuno Box: Textiles of Reiko Sudo

Reiko Sudo (b. 1953)

2018-14-1(1–29k)

Not previously exhibited or published.

103

Waning Moon

Ken Matsubara (b. 1948)

2019-210-1a–d

EXHIBITED: New York 2019b (no cat.).

INSCRIBED ON OBVERSE, THEN PAINTED OVER:

The Precious Key to the
Secret Treasury
From the dim, remote, and
immemorial past,
Texts are transmitted in
a thousand and ten
thousand tomes,
Elucidating Buddhist and
non-Buddhist teachings.
Abstruse, obscure, and
indistinct
Are a hundred opinions and
theories,
Each claiming to be the
final way.
Copying and reciting until
one's death,
How can one penetrate the
ultimate Source?
I do not know, however
I ponder.
The Buddha, I believe, had
no mind for this.
He took pity on diseased
minds
And taught them to take
medicinal herbs as Shen
Nung did.
Out of compassion, he
showed the direction to
the lost,
As did the Duke of Chou by
making the compass-cart.
But deranged men do not
perceive their madness;
The blind are unaware of
their blindness.
Born, reborn, and still born
again,
Whence they have come they
do not know,
Dying, dying, and dying yet
again,
Where they go in the end they
do not know.

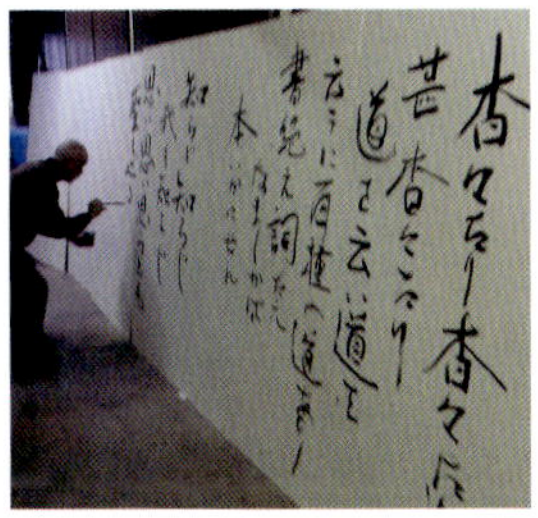

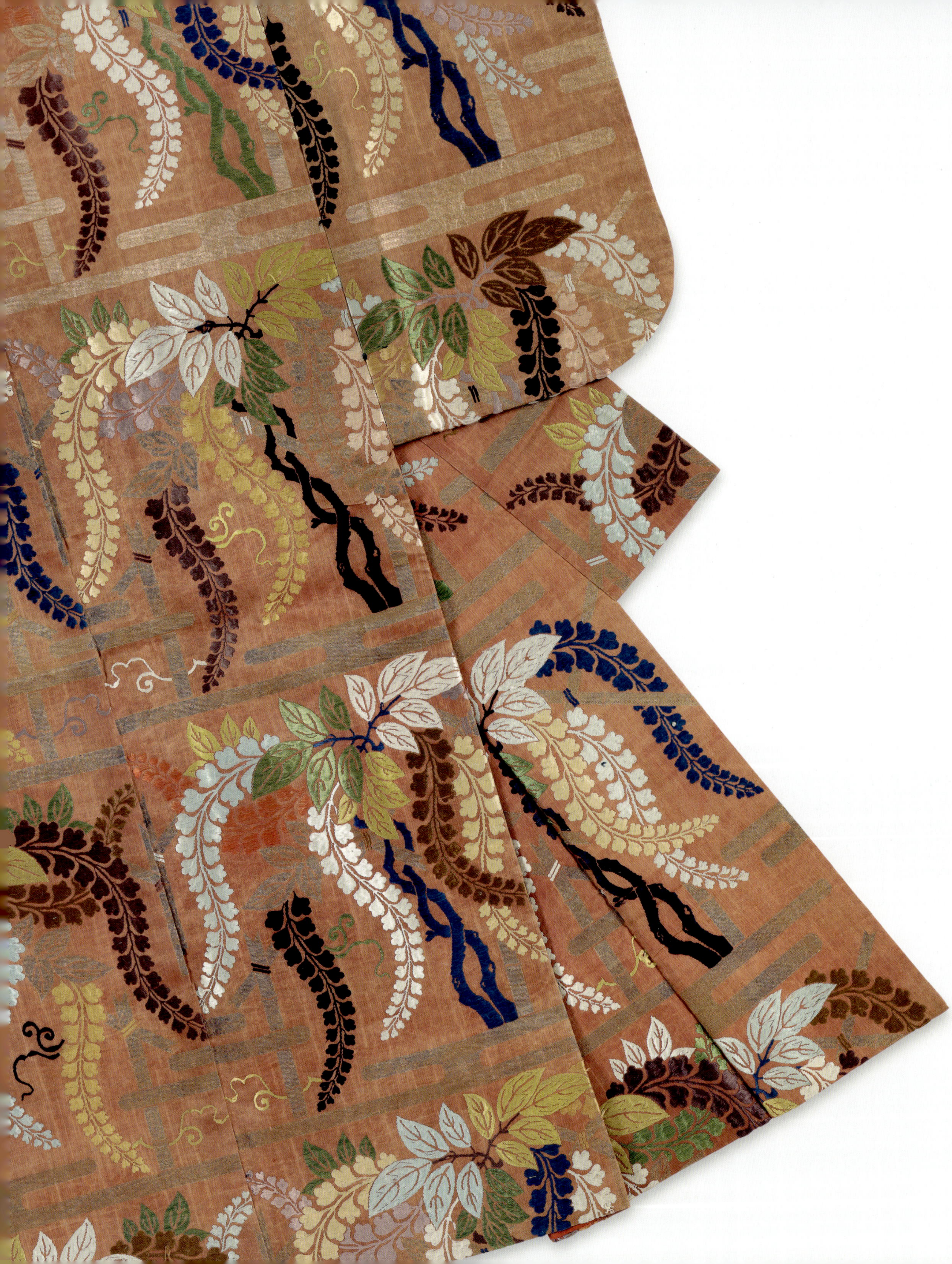

References

Exhibitions

Akō City 2006
Suzuki Hyakunen Shōnen: Akō yukari no gaka [Suzuki Hyakunen and Shōnen: Painters in Akō]. Akō City Tabuchi Museum of Art, November 2–December 17, 2006. Catalogue. Akō-shi: Akō Shiritsu Bijutsu Kōgeikan Tabuchi Kinenkan, [2006].

Amsterdam, Düsseldorf, and Philadelphia 1992–93
Beauty & Violence: Japanese Prints by Yoshitoshi, 1839–1892. Van Gogh Museum, Amsterdam, April 17–June 28, 1992; Kunstmuseum Düsseldorf, September 6–October 18, 1992; Philadelphia Museum of Art, December 19, 1992–March 14, 1993. Catalogue by Eric van den Ing and Robert Schaap. Bergeyk, Netherlands: Society for Japanese Arts, 1992.

Arita 2012
Shōgunke kenjō no Nabeshima Hirado Karatsu: Seikōnaru yakimono / Ceramics for the shogunate. Kyushu Ceramic Museum, Arita, October 6–November 25, 2012. Catalogue. Arita: Saga Kenritsu Kyūshū Tōji Bunkakan, 2012.

Atami 1999
Kōetsu to nō: Kareinaru utaibon no sekai; Tokubetsuten [Kōetsu and Noh: The great world of Noh libretti; Special exhibition]. MOA Museum of Art, Atami, October 29–December 1, 1999. Catalogue by Yukihiroshi Tanaka, Kondō Machiko, and Nakamoto Kumiko. Shizuoka: MOA Bijutsukan, 1999.

Berkeley 2019–20
Hinges: Sakaki Hyakusen and the Birth of Nanga Painting. Berkeley Art Museum and Pacific Film Archive, University of California, October 2, 2019–February 2, 2020. Catalogue by Julia M. White. Berkeley: University of California Press, 2019.

Berlin 1993–94
Japan und Europa, 1543–1929. Martin Gropius Bau, Berlin, September 12, 1993–January 9, 1994. Catalogue by Doris Croissant et al. Berlin: Berliner Festspiele, Argon, 1993.

Bonn 2003
Japans Schonheit, Japans Seele: Meisterwerke aus dem Tokyo National Museum. Kunst- und Ausstellungshalle der Bundesrepublik Deutschland, Bonn, August 29–October 26, 2003. Catalogue. Bonn: Kunst- und Ausstellungshalle der Bundesrepublik Deutschland, 2003.

Boston 1997
Tales from the Land of the Dragons: 1,000 Years of Chinese Painting. Museum of Fine Arts, Boston, April 13–July 20, 1997. Catalogue by Wu Tung. Boston: Museum of Fine Arts, 1997.

Boston 2004–5
Pursuits of Power: Falconry and the Samurai, 1600–1900. Museum of Fine Arts, Boston, December 17, 2004–June 6, 2005. Brochure by Rachel Saunders. Boston: Museum of Fine Arts, 2004.

Chiba City and Hagi City 2002
Suzuki Harunobu. Chiba City Museum of Art, September 14–October 20, 2002; Hagi Uragami Museum, Hagi City, November 2–December 8, 2002. Catalogue by Kobayashi Tadashi. N.p.: Chiba City Museum of Art and Hagi Uragami Museum, 2002.

Cincinnati 2009–10
Decoded Messages: The Symbolic Language of Chinese Animal Painting. Cincinnati Art Museum, October 9, 2009–January 3, 2010. Catalogue by Hou-mei Sung. New Haven, CT: Yale University Press, 2009.

Cleveland 1916
The Inaugural Exhibition of Cleveland Museum. Cleveland Museum of Art, June 6–September 20, 1916. Catalogue. Cleveland: Cleveland Museum of Art, 1916.

Fukui 2013
Okakura Tenshin: 150th Anniversary Okakura Tenshin Retrospective. Fukui Fine Arts Museum, November 1–December 1, 2013. Catalogue by Sasaki Miho, Shiino Akifumi, and Nagano Eishun. Fukui: Fukui Fine Arts Museum, 2013.

Fukuoka 1991
Kasen-e [Images of the Immortal Poets]. Fukuoka Prefectural Museum of Art, January 4–February 3, 1991. Catalogue. Fukuoka: Fukuoka Prefectural Museum of Art, 1991.

Fukushima 2019
Ito Jakuchū: A Prayer for Recovery Following the Great East Japan Earthquake. Fukushima Prefectural Museum of Art, March 26–May 6, 2019. Catalogue by Kano Hiroyuki. Fukushima: Fukushima Prefectural Museum of Art, 2019.

Gifu 1997
Special Exhibition for the 15th Anniversary of the Museum of Fine Arts, Gifu: Oribe, (Re) Searching "Oribeism." Museum of Fine Arts, Gifu, October 1–December 20, 1997. Catalogue by Takeuchi Jun'ichi. Gifu: Museum of Fine Arts, 1997.

Gifu 2005
Mino kotō ten: Momoyama jidai–Edo jidai zenki [Mino ancient pottery exhibition: Momoyama period–early Edo period]. Gifu Prefectural Ceramics Museum, June 1–September 4, 2005. Catalogue. Gifu: Gifu-ken Tōji Shiryōkan, 2005.

Ibaraki 1997
Tenshin to Izura no sakkatachi: Ibaraki-ken Tenshin Kinen Izura Bijutsukan kaikan kinenten [Tenshin and his colleagues of Izura: Tenshin Memorial Museum of Art, Ibaraki]. Tenshin Memorial Museum of Art, Ibaraki, November 8–December 14, 1997. Catalogue. Ibaraki: Tenshin Memorial Museum of Art, 1997.

Ithaca and Sacramento 2016–17
JapanAmerica: Points of Contact, 1876–1970. Herbert F. Johnson Museum of Art, Cornell University, Ithaca, NY, August 27–December 18, 2016; Crocker Art Museum, Sacramento, CA, February 12–May 27, 2017. Catalogue by Nancy E. Green and Christopher Reed. Ithaca, NY: Herbert F. Johnson Museum of Art, Cornell University, 2016.

Ithaca and Utica 1973–74
Asian Art: A Collector's Selection. Herbert F. Johnson Museum of Art, Cornell University, Ithaca, NY, October 17–November 25, 1973; Munson-Williams-Proctor Institute, Utica, NY, December 16, 1973–January 13, 1974. Catalogue by Martie W. Young. Ithaca, NY: Office of University Publications, Cornell University, 1973.

Ithaca et al. 1980–81
Imperial Japan: The Art of the Meiji Era (1868–1912). Herbert F. Johnson Museum of Art, Cornell University, Ithaca, NY, April 16–June 29, 1980; Munson-Williams-Proctor Institute, Utica, NY, August 17–October 19, 1980; Cincinnati Art Museum, November 14, 1980–January 4, 1981; Portland Art Museum, OR, January 23–March 1, 1981. Catalogue by Frederick Baekeland. Ithaca, NY: Herbert F. Johnson Museum of Art, Cornell University, 1980.

Izumi 1990
Tokubetsuten: Ōgi-e; Nihon, Chūgoku, Chōsen Hantō [Special exhibition: Fan paintings from Japan, China, and the Korean peninsula]. Kubosō Memorial Museum, Izumi, 1990. Catalogue. Izumi: Kubosō Memorial Museum, 1990.

Jerusalem and Houston 2014–15
Unfolding Worlds: Japanese Screens from the Gitter-Yelen Collection. Israel Museum, Jerusalem, June 7–November 8, 2014; Museum of Fine Arts, Houston, February 28–May 9, 2015. Catalogue by Miriam Malachi. Jerusalem: Israel Museum, 2014.

Kanazawa 2002
58th Annual Contemporary Art Exhibition. Ishikawa Prefectural Museum of Art, Kanazawa, April 6–11, 2002. No cat.

Kanazawa 2003
Ishikawa no kasen ema: Shunki tokubetsuten [Votive plaques of poets in Ishikawa Prefecture: Special summer exhibition]. Ishikawa Prefectural History Museum, Kanazawa, April 19–May 25, 2003. Catalogue. Kanazawa-shi: Ishikawa Kenritsu Rekishi Hakubutsukan, 2003.

Katonah and Boston 1996
Object as Insight: Japanese Buddhist Art & Ritual. Katonah Museum of Art, NY, January 14–March 17, 1996; Museum of Fine Arts, Boston, April 19–June 30, 1996. Catalogue by Anne Nishimura Morse and Samuel Crowell Morse. Katonah, NY: Katonah Museum of Art, 1995.

Koka 2004
Kenzan: Yūsui to fūga no sekai / Kenzan: A World of Quietly Refined Elegance. Miho Museum, Koka, September 1–December 15, 2004. Catalogue. Shigaraki: Miho Museum, 2004.

Kyoto 1999
Miyako no mōdo: Kimono no jidai; Tokubetsu tenrankai / Kyoto Style: Trends in 16th–19th Century Kimono; Special Exhibition. Kyoto National Museum, October 19–November 23, 1999. Catalogue. [Kyoto]: Kyoto Kokuritsu Hakubutsukan, [1999].

Kyoto 2000
Special Exhibition: Jakuchū! 200th Anniversary of His Death. Kyoto National Museum, October 24–November 26, 2000. Catalogue by Kano Hiroyuki. Kyoto: Kyoto National Museum, 2000.

Kyoto and Tokyo 2002
Sesshū: Botsugo 500-nen tokubetsuten [Sesshu: Master of ink and brush; 500th anniversary exhibition]. Kyoto National Museum, March 12–April 7, 2002; Tokyo National Museum, April 23–May 19, 2002. Catalogue by Oguri Toshiyuki et al. Tokyo: Tokyo National Museum; Kyoto: Kyoto National Museum, 2002.

Kyoto, Los Angeles, and Brooklyn 1996–99
Japonism in Fashion. Kyoto Costume Institute, August 28–November 24, 1996; Los Angeles County Museum of Art, March 16–June 15, 1998 (as *Japonism in Fashion: The Influence of Japan on Western Dress*); Brooklyn Museum, November 20, 1998–February 14, 1999 (as *Japonism in Fashion: Japan Dresses the West*). Catalogue by the Kyotō Costume Institute and the Brooklyn Museum of Art. Brooklyn: Brooklyn Museum, 1998.

Lawrence and Honolulu 1988
Japanese Women Artists, 1600–1900. Spencer Museum of Art, Lawrence, KS, April 2–May 22, 1988; Honolulu Academy of Arts, September 21–October 23, 1988. Catalogue by Patricia Fister. Lawrence: Spencer Museum of Art, University of Kansas, 1988.

Lawrence and New Orleans 1978
Obaku: Zen Painting and Calligraphy. Helen Foresman Spencer Museum of Art, University of Kansas, Lawrence, April 8–May 31, 1978; New Orleans Museum of Art, June 15–August 6, 1978. Catalogue by Stephen Addis. Lawrence, KA: Helen Foresman Spencer Museum of Art, 1978.

Lexington 2007
Tea Treasures from East to West. Reeves Museum of Ceramics, Lexington, VA, February 2–June 15, 2007. No cat.

Los Angeles 1985
Japanese Ink Painting. Los Angeles Museum of Art, March 10–May 12, 1985. Catalogue by Miyajima Shin'ichi and Sato Yasuhiro. Los Angeles: Los Angeles County Museum of Art, 1985.

Los Angeles 2005
Japan Goes to the World's Fairs: Japanese Art at the Great Expositions in Europe and the United States, 1867–1907. Los Angeles County Museum of Art, May 26–October 10, 2005. Catalogue by Sara Cody et al. Los Angeles: Los Angeles County Museum of Art, 2005.

Los Angeles and New York 1976–77
Birds, Beasts, Blossoms, and Bugs: The Nature of Japan. University of California, Los Angeles, March 30–May 23, 1976; Asia House Gallery, New York, October 6–December 4, 1977. Catalogue by Harold P. Stern. New York: Harry N. Abrams, 1976.

Nagoya 2013
Kyodai jōkaku Nagoya-jō: Nagoya-jō tokubetsuten [Giant Nagoya Castle: Special exhibition]. Nagoyajō Tenshukaku, October 12–November 24, 2013. Catalogue. Nagoya: Nagoya Castle Office, 2013.

Nagoya et al. 2013–14
Bosuton bijutsukan ukiyoe meihinten: Hokusai / Hokusai from the Museum of Fine Arts, Boston. Nagoya/Boston Museum of Fine Arts, Nagoya, December 21, 2013–March 23, 2014; Kobe City Museum, April 26–June 22, 2014; Kitakyushu Municipal Museum of Art, Riverwalk Gallery, July 12–August 31, 2014; Ueno Royal Museum, Tokyo, September 13–November 9, 2014. Catalogue by Sarah Thompson, Nagata Seiji, and Iwakiri Yuriko. Tokyo: Nihon Keizai Shinbunsha, 2013.

New Orleans 1983–84
A Myriad of Autumn Leaves: Japanese Art from the Kurt and Millie Gitter Collection. New Orleans Museum of Art, November 13, 1983–April 22, 1984. Catalogue by Stephen Addiss. New Orleans: New Orleans Museum of Art, 1983.

New Orleans, Seattle, and New York 2002–4
An Enduring Vision: 17th- to 20th-Century Japanese Painting from the Gitter-Yelen Collection. New Orleans Museum of Art, August 31–October 26, 2002; Seattle Asian Art Museum, April 10–June 15, 2003; Japan Society, New York, March 15–July 10, 2004. Catalogue by Lisa Rotondo-McCord. New Orleans: New Orleans Museum of Art, 2002.

New York 1971
Rimpa: Masterworks of the Japanese Decorative School. Japan Society, New York, fall 1971. Catalogue by Harold P. Stern. New York: Japan Society, 1971.

New York 1979
Journey of the Three Jewels: Japanese Buddhist Paintings from Western Collections. Asia House Gallery, New York, fall 1979. Catalogue by John Rosenfield and Elizabeth ten Grotenhuis. New York: Asia Society, 1979.

New York 1984–85
Masters of Japanese Calligraphy, 8th–19th Century. Asia Society and Japan House, New York, October 4, 1984–January 6, 1985. Catalogue by John M. Rosenfield and Yoshiaki Shimizu. New York: Asia Society and Japan House, 1984.

New York 1997–98a
Mandala: The Architecture of Enlightenment. Asia Society and Tibet House, New York, September 24, 1997–January 4, 1998. Catalogue by Denise Patry Leidy and Robert A. F. Thurman. New York: Asia Society and Tibet House, 1997.

New York 1997–98b
The Resonant Image: Tradition in Japanese Art. Metropolitan Museum of Art, New York, October 21, 1997–April 26, 1998. No cat.

New York 1999
In the Company of Spirits. Kaikodo, New York, March 16–April 17, 1999. Catalogue in *Kaikodo Journal* (Spring 1999): 63–319.

New York 2001–2
Traditional Japanese Design: Five Tastes. Japan Society Gallery, New York, September 26, 2001–January 6, 2002. Catalogue by Michael Dunn. New York: Japan Society and Harry N. Abrams, 2001.

New York 2003–4
Turning Point: Oribe and the Arts of Sixteenth-Century Japan. Metropolitan Museum of Art, New York, October 21, 2003–January 11, 2004. Catalogue edited by Miyeko Murase. New York: Metropolitan Museum of Art; New Haven, CT: Yale University Press, 2003.

New York 2008
Rays of Light: The Intricate Ceramic Art of Kishi Eiko. Joan B. Mirviss Ltd., New York, March 15–19, 2008. Dealer flyer.

New York 2009–10
Art of the Samurai: Japanese Arms and Armor, 1156–1868. Metropolitan Museum of Art, New York, October 21, 2009–January 10, 2010. Catalogue edited by Morihiro Ogawa. New York: Metropolitan Museum of Art, 2009.

New York 2012–13
Designing Nature: The Rinpa Aesthetic in Japanese Art. Metropolitan Museum of Art, New York, May 26, 2012–January 13, 2013. Catalogue by John T. Carpenter. New York: Metropolitan Museum of Art, 2012.

New York 2016
Kamakura: Realism and Spirituality in the Sculpture of Japan. Asia Society Museum, New York, February 9–May 8, 2016. Catalogue by Ive Covaci. New York: Asia Society Museum, 2016.

New York 2019a
Summerfest. Kaikodo, New York, June 3–August 16, 2019. No cat.

New York 2019b
Kūkai: Sun and Moon. Ippodo Gallery, New York, October 10–November 22, 2019. No cat.

Okayama 2017
Benevolent Priest Ryōkan. Okayama Prefectural Museum of Art, September 29–November 5, 2017. No cat.

Oxford, London, and Philadelphia 1985–86
Black Sun: The Eyes of Four. Museum of Modern Art, Oxford, December 8, 1985–February 9, 1986; Serpentine Gallery, London, April 5–May 11, 1986; Philadelphia Museum of Art, August 9–October 26, 1986. Catalogue by Mark Holborn. New York: Aperture, 1986.

Philadelphia 1876
The Centennial International Exhibition. Philadelphia, May 10–November 10, 1876. Official catalogue by United States Centennial Commission. Philadelphia: John R. Nagle and Co., 1876.

Philadelphia 1931–32
Japanese Color Prints from the Henry LaBarre Jayne Memorial Collection and from Recent Gift by Miss Elsie Biddle Robinson. Philadelphia Museum of Art, December 1931–January 3, 1932. No cat.

Philadelphia 1966
Japanese Master Prints. Philadelphia Museum of Art, February 7–March 20, 1966. No cat.

Philadelphia 1969
The Animal Kingdom. Philadelphia Museum of Art, March 13–April 16, 1969. No cat.

Philadelphia 1970
Suzuki Harunobu: Bicentenary Exhibition of Prints and Illustrated Books. Philadelphia Museum of Art, September 18–November 22, 1970. Catalogue by Jack Hillier. Philadelphia: Philadelphia Museum of Art, 1970.

Philadelphia 1976–77
First Impressions. Philadelphia Museum of Art, November 27, 1976–January 30, 1977. No cat.

Philadelphia 1977
Gifts to Mark a Century: An Exhibition Celebrating the Centennial of the Philadelphia Museum of Art. Philadelphia Museum of Art, February 18–March 20, 1977. Catalogue. Philadelphia: Philadelphia Museum of Art, 1977.

Philadelphia 1980
Far Eastern Art Department: Recent Acquisitions. Philadelphia Museum of Art, February 8–April 20, 1980. No cat.

Philadelphia 1983
100 Years of Acquisitions. Philadelphia Museum of Art, May 7–July 3, 1983. No cat.

Philadelphia 1984
Dutch Tiles. Philadelphia Museum of Art, March 18–May 13, 1984. No cat.

Philadelphia 1985
Fleeting Moments: Japanese Prints from the Collection. Philadelphia Museum of Art, March 23–May 19, 1985. No cat.

Philadelphia 1987–88
The Arts of Edo. Philadelphia Museum of Art, September 1987–July 1988. No cat.

Philadelphia 1988–89
The Arts of Tea. Philadelphia Museum of Art, September 15, 1988–July 15, 1989. No cat.

Philadelphia 1989–90
Theme and Variation: Japanese Design Motifs. Philadelphia Museum of Art, September 15, 1989–July 15, 1990. No cat.

Philadelphia 1990–91
Japanese Buddhist Art. Philadelphia Museum of Art, August 15, 1990–August 15, 1991. No cat.

Philadelphia 1992–93
Recent Acquisitions in Japanese Art. Philadelphia Museum of Art, July 15, 1992–July 15, 1993. No cat.

Philadelphia 1996
Japan in Flower. Philadelphia Museum of Art, February 25–March 3, 1996. No cat.

Philadelphia 1996–97
Japanese Landscapes. Philadelphia Museum of Art, October 8, 1996–July 31, 1997. No cat.

Philadelphia 1997–98
Frolicking Animals. Philadelphia Museum of Art, September 26, 1997–August 2, 1998. No cat.

Philadelphia 1998–99
Ink Traces: East Asian Calligraphy. Philadelphia Museum of Art, August 11, 1998–August 2, 1999. No cat.

Philadelphia 1999
Passages: Photographs from the Collection. Philadelphia Museum of Art, June 5–November 14, 1999. No cat.

Philadelphia 1999–2000
Fun & Games in Japanese Art. Philadelphia Museum of Art, August 14, 1999–June 18, 2000. No cat.

Philadelphia 2000
The Arts of Hon'ami Kōetsu: Japanese Renaissance Master. Philadelphia Museum of Art, July 29–October 29, 2000. Catalogue by Felice Fischer. Philadelphia: Philadelphia Museum of Art, 2000.

Philadelphia 2000–2001a
Japanese Nō Costumes from the Collection. Philadelphia Museum of Art, May 27, 2000–May 20, 2001. No cat.

Philadelphia 2000–2001b
Tea, Poetry, and Rimpa: Works from Japan. Philadelphia Museum of Art, July 1, 2000–April 29, 2001. No cat.

Philadelphia 2001–2
West Meets East: China and Japan at the Centennial Exhibition. Philadelphia Museum of Art, May 10, 2001–June 26, 2002. No cat.

Philadelphia 2002
Gifts in Honor of the 125th Anniversary of the Philadelphia Museum of Art. Philadelphia Museum of Art, September 29–December 8, 2002. Catalogue by Alice O. Beamesderfer. Philadelphia: Philadelphia Museum of Art, 2002.

Philadelphia 2002–3
Translations and Transformations: Chinese Themes in Japanese Art. Philadelphia Museum of Art, November 30, 2002–October 31, 2003. No cat.

Philadelphia 2003–5
Libations: Wine and Tea in East Asia. Philadelphia Museum of Art, November 3, 2003–May 15, 2005. No cat.

Philadelphia 2005–6a
Contemporary Crafts from the Collection. Philadelphia Museum of Art, March 19, 2005–August 20, 2006. No cat.

Philadelphia 2005–6b
Kachō-ga: Flowers and Birds in Japanese Art. Philadelphia Museum of Art, May 28, 2005–September 24, 2006. No cat.

Philadelphia 2006–7
Japanese Literati Culture in the Edo Period. Philadelphia Museum of Art, October 7, 2006–November 11, 2007. No cat.

Philadelphia 2007
Ike Taiga and Tokuyama Gyokuran: Japanese Masters of the Brush. Philadelphia Museum of Art, May 1–July 22, 2007. Catalogue by Felice Fischer and Kyoko Kinoshita. Philadelphia: Philadelphia Museum of Art, 2007.

Philadelphia 2007–8
Cornucopia: Recent Acquisitions in Japanese Art. Philadelphia Museum of Art, November 24, 2007–November 16, 2008. No cat.

Philadelphia 2008–9a
Hello! Fashion: Kansai Yamamoto, 1971–1973. Philadelphia Museum of Art, May 24, 2008–August 2009. No cat.

Philadelphia 2008–9b
The Art of Japanese Craft: 1875 to the Present. Philadelphia Museum of Art, December 6, 2008–September 13, 2009. Catalogue by Felice Fischer. Philadelphia: Philadelphia Museum of Art, 2008.

Philadelphia 2009
A Director's Vision: The Legacy of Anne d'Harnoncourt. Philadelphia Museum of Art, April 25–July 19, 2009. No cat.

Philadelphia 2010–11
Pleasures and Pastimes in Japanese Art. Philadelphia Museum of Art, January 9, 2010–January 2011. No cat.

Philadelphia 2011
Kobe: Japan's Window on the World. Philadelphia Museum of Art, March 26–October 2, 2011. No cat.

Philadelphia 2011–12
A Taste for Tea in Japan. Philadelphia Museum of Art, October 8, 2011–March 2012. No cat.

Philadelphia 2012
Craft Spoken Here. Philadelphia Museum of Art, May 5–August 12, 2012. No cat.

Philadelphia 2013
First Look: Collecting for Philadelphia. Philadelphia Museum of Art, July 13–September 8, 2013. No cat.

Philadelphia 2013–14
Guardians Galore: Protecting the East. Philadelphia Museum of Art, October 21, 2013–October 16, 2014. No cat.

Philadelphia 2014
Making a Classic Modern: Frank Gehry's Master Plan for the Philadelphia Museum of Art. Philadelphia Museum of Art, June 26–September 1, 2014. No cat.

Philadelphia 2015a
Ink and Gold: Art of the Kano. Philadelphia Museum of Art, February 16–May 10, 2015. Catalogue by Felice Fischer and Kyoko Kinoshita. Philadelphia: Philadelphia Museum of Art, 2015.

Philadelphia 2015b
A Sense of Place: Modern Japanese Prints. Arthur Ross Gallery, University of Pennsylvania, Philadelphia, April 9–June 21, 2015. Catalogue edited by Julie Nelson Davis. Philadelphia: Department of the History of Art at the University of Pennsylvania, 2015.

Philadelphia 2016–17
Designing Japan. Philadelphia Museum of Art, December 6, 2016–September 14, 2017. No cat.

Philadelphia 2017
Wild: Michael Nichols. Philadelphia Museum of Art, June 27–September 17, 2017. No cat.

Philadelphia 2018–19
Philadelphia Collects Meiji. Philadelphia Museum of Art, September 1, 2018–August 11, 2019. No cat.

Philadelphia 2019a
Yoshitoshi: Spirit and Spectacle. Philadelphia Museum of Art, April 16–August 18, 2019. No cat.

Philadelphia 2019b
Photography and Memory. Philadelphia Museum of Art, August 2–October 23, 2019. No cat.

Philadelphia 2019–22
Kōgei: Art Craft Japan. Philadelphia Museum of Art, August 31, 2019–April 4, 2022. No cat.

Philadelphia 2022–23
Ink and Brush: The Beauty and Spirit of Japanese Calligraphy. Philadelphia Museum of Art, 2022–April 30, 2023. No cat.

Philadelphia et al. 2002–4
Munakata Shikō: Japanese Master of the Modern Print / Munakata Shikō ten: Munakata Shikō seitan hyakunen jinen. Philadelphia Museum of Art, July 27–November 10, 2002; Los Angeles County Museum of Art, December 5, 2002–March 2, 2003; Miyagi Museum of Art, Sendai, April 5–June 15, 2003; Takaoka Art Museum/Fukumitsu Art Museum, June 21–July 27, 2003; Aomori Prefectural Museum, August 2–September 15, 2003; Nara Prefectural Museum of Art, September 27–November 16, 2003; Bunkamura Museum of Art, Tokyo, November 22, 2003–February 1, 2004; Museum of Art, Ehime, February 13–March 28, 2004. Catalogue edited by Robert T. Singer and Kakeya Nobuho and translated by Maya M. Hara and Ogata Mikako. Kamakura: Munakata Museum, 2002.

Saint Louis 1904
Louisiana Purchase Exposition. Saint Louis, April 30–December 1, 1904. Catalogue. Saint Louis: Official Catalogue Company, 1904.

San Antonio 2017
Heaven and Hell: Salvation and Retribution in Pure Land Buddhism. San Antonio Museum of Art, June 10–September 3, 2017. Catalogue by Erin Kathleen Murphy et al. San Antonio: San Antonio Museum of Art, 2017.

Seattle 2007–8
Japan Envisions the West: 16th–19th Century Japanese Art from Kobe City Museum. Seattle Art Museum, October 11, 2007–January 6, 2008. Catalogue edited by Yukiko Shirahara. Seattle: University of Washington Press, 2007.

Shizuoka 2018
Living National Treasure Exhibition. Museum of Modern Art, Shizuoka, 2018. No cat.

Taipei and Phoenix 1998–99
Minol Araki. National Museum of History, Taipei, Taiwan, December 24, 1998–January 17, 1999; Phoenix Art Museum, May 15–July 18, 1999. Catalogue by Claudia Brown, Richard Barnhart, and Steven D. Owyoung. Phoenix: Phoenix Art Museum, 1999.

Tokugawa 2019–20
Ryōkan: The Man and His Calligraphy. Tokugawa Art Museum, November 16, 2019–January 31, 2020. No cat.

Tokyo 1886
Second Painting Appreciation Society Exhibition. Kangakai, April 1886. No cat.

Tokyo 1919
5 Nihon Bijutsuin ten [The fifth exhibition of the Japan Art Institute]. Takenodai Exhibition Hall, Ueno Park, Tokyo, February 1–10, 1919. Catalogue in *Nihon Bijutsuin hyakunen shi* [The hundred-year history of the Japan Art Institiute], vol. 4. Tokyo: Nihonbijutsuin, 1994.

Tokyo 1937
Mombushō Bijutsu tenrankai [Ministry of Education art exhibition]. Tokyo, 1937. No cat.

Tokyo 1966
15 Goto ten [The fifteenth exhibition of modern Japanese paintings and sculpture]. Tokyo Art Club, April 1966. Catalogue. Tokyo: Tokyo Art Club, 1966.

Tokyo 1968
Tōbi tokubetsuten (*Art Dealers' Fair and Exhibition in Tokyo*). Tokyo Art Club, 1968. Catalogue. Tokyo: Kyuryudo, 1968.

Tokyo 1981
Sakai Hōitsu to Edo Rimpa [Sakai Hōitsu and Edo Rimpa]. Suntory Museum of Art, Tokyo, May 19–June 28, 1981. Catalogue. Tokyo: Bijutsukan, 1981.

Tokyo 1986
Sanjurokkasen-e [Images of the Thirty-Six Immortal Poets]. Suntory Museum of Art, Tokyo, September 12–October 19, 1986. Catalogue. Tokyo: Santorī Bijutsukan, 1986.

Tokyo 1999a
Kōetsu to Sōtatsu. Suntory Museum of Art, Tokyo, June 1–July 11, 1999. Catalogue. Tokyo: Santorī Bijutsukan, 1999.

Tokyo 1999b
Geidai bijutsukan shozō meihin-ten: Kaikan kinen / Selected Masterpieces from the University Art Museum, Tokyo National University of Fine Arts and Music: Grand Opening Exhibition. Tokyo University of the Arts, October 5–December 5, 1999. Catalogue. Tokyo: Tōkyō Nihon keizai shinbunsha and NHK, 1999.

Tokyo 2003
Kamakura: Zen no genryū / Kamakura: The Art of Zen Buddhism. Tokyo National Museum, June 3–July 13, 2003. Catalogue by Tatsumichi Keiko. Tokyo: Nihon Keizai Shinbunsha, 2003.

Tokyo 2013–14
Nihon dentō kogeiten [Sixtieth Japan traditional arts and crafts exhibition]. National Museum of Modern Art, Tokyo, December 21, 2013–February 23, 2014. No cat.

Tokyo 2018
Shin Momoyama no chatō / Momoyama Tea Utensils: A New View. Nezu Museum, Tokyo, October 20–December 16, 2018. Catalogue. Tokyo: Nezu Bijutsukan, 2018.

Tokyo 2019–20
Tairei: Keishuku no katachi / Art Works to Celebrate the Enthronement Ceremonies. Museum of the Imperial Collections, Tokyo, September 21, 2019–January 19, 2020. Catalogue. Tokyo: Sannomaru Shōzōkan, 2019.

Tokyo 2021
Ryōkan (Part 2): Poet with the Heart and Spirit of the Japanese. Eisei Bunko Museum, Tokyo, April 24–August 1, 2021. No cat.

Tokyo et al. 1972
Zaigai ukiyo-e meisaku ten [Exhibition of ukiyo-e masterpieces from foreign collections]. Matsuzakaya Department Store, Tokyo, January 4–16, 1972; and four other locations of Matsuzakaya Department Stores in Shizuoka, Fukuoka, Nagoya, and Osaka, through February 27, 1972. Catalogue by Muneshige Narazaki. Japan: Nihon Ukiyo-e Kyōkai, 1972.

Tokyo, Osaka, and Nagoya 2004–5
Commemorating the 2005 World Exposition, Aichi, Japan: Arts of East and West from World Expositions, 1855–1900: Paris, Vienna and Chicago. Tokyo National Museum, July 6–August 29, 2004; Osaka Municipal Museum of Art, October 5–November 28, 2004; Nagoya City Museum, January 5–March 6, 2005. Catalogue. Tokyo: NHK, NHK Promotions, Nihon Keizai Shimbun, 2004.

Tokyo, Osaka, and Shizuoka 2017
Tagane no hana: Mitsumura korekushon no tōsōgu; Tokubetsuten / Pinnacle of Elegance: Sword Fittings of the Mitsumura Collection; Special Exhibition. Nezu Museum, Tokyo; Osaka Museum of History; Sano Art Museum, Shizuoka. Catalogue by Nezu Bijutsukan. Tokyo: Nezu Bijutsukan, 2017.

Tokyo, Shimonoseki, and Kyoto 1988–89
Kano Hōgai Exhibition in Commemoration of the Centenary of His Death. Yamatane Museum of Art, Tokyo, October 22–November 20, 1988; Shimonoseki City Art Museum, January 5–February 12, 1989; Kyoto National Museum, March–April 1989. Catalogue. Shimonoseki: The Museum, 1989.

Tokyo, Shizuoka, and Osaka 2015
Harunobu ichiban! Sharaku niban! Firaderufia Bijutsukan ukiyoe meihinten, nishikie tanjō 250-nen / Ukiyo-e Masterpieces from the Philadelphia Museum of Art Featuring Harunobu, Sharaku, and More! Exhibition on the 250th Anniversary of the Birth of Nishiki-e. Mitsui Memorial Museum, Tokyo, June 20–August 16, 2015; Shizuoka City Museum of Art, August 23–September 27, 2015; Abeno Harukas Art Museum, Osaka, October 10–December 6, 2015. Catalogue. Osaka: Yomiuri Shinbunsha, 2015.

Toledo 1938
A Special Exhibition of Japanese Art: Examples of Screen Painting, Fan Painting and Lacquer-Work from the Collections of Museums and Private Owners. Toledo Museum of Art, OH, January 1938. Catalogue. Toledo, OH: Toledo Museum of Art, 1938.

Washington 1976–96
1876: A Centennial Exhibition. Smithsonian Institution, Washington, DC, May 11, 1976–August 10, 1996. No cat.

Washington 2001–2
The Potter's Brush: The Kenzan Style in Japanese Ceramics. Freer Gallery of Art, Arthur M. Sackler Gallery, Smithsonian Institution, Washington, DC, December 9, 2001–October 27, 2002. Catalogue by Richard L. Wilson and Saeko Ogasawara. Washington, DC: Freer Gallery of Art and Arthur M. Sackler Gallery, Smithsonian Institution, 2001.

Washington and Los Angeles 2019
The Life of Animals in Japanese Art. National Gallery of Art, Washington, DC, May 5–July 28, 2019; Los Angeles County Museum of Art, September 8–December 8, 2019. Catalogue by Robert T. Singer and Kawai Masatomo. Washington, DC: National Gallery of Art, 2019.

Yokohama and Kyoto 2016
Mearī Kasatto ten / Mary Cassatt Retrospective. Yokohama Museum of Art, June 25–September 11, 2016; National Museum of Modern Art, Kyoto, September 27–December 4, 2016. Catalogue by Pamela A. Ivinski et al. Tokyo: NHK Puromōshon, 2016.

Publications

Aikawa 1819a
Aikawa Min'wa. *Hengaku kihan, shohen* [Model of tablets, vol. 1]. Kyoto: Yoshino-ya, Ōtani ihei, 1819.

Aikawa 1819b
Aikawa Min'wa. *Hengaku kihan, nihen furoku* [Model of tablets, vol. 2 appendix]. Kyoto: Yoshino-ya, Ōtani ihei, 1819.

Aimi 1938
Aimi Kōu. "Sōsetsu, Sōsetsu to Sōsen." *Nihon bijutsu Kyokai hōkoku* [Japan Art Association report] 48 (1938): 15–20.

Akiyama 1969
Akiyama Terukazu. "Jin'o-ji engi emaki no fukugen no kōsatsu: Iiwayuru Kōnin Shōnin eden o megutte" [The reconstruction and study of the illustrated history of the Jin'o-ji temple: On the illustrated biography of the monk Kōnin]. In *Emakimono* [Narrative scroll painting], 98–113. Vol. 3 of *Zaigai Nihon no hihō* [Japanese art: Selections from Western collections], edited by Shimada Shūjirō. Tokyo: Shōgakukan, 1969.

Asaoka 1850
Asaoka Okisada. *Koga bikō* [Biographies of painters]. N.p., 1850.

Association of Scientific Research 1993
Association of Scientific Research on Historic and Artistic Works of Japan. *Firaderufia Bijutsukan: Kaiga chōkoku* (*Painting and Sculpture of Philadelphia Museum of Art*). Vol. 3 of *Kaigai shozai Nihon bijutsuhin chōsa hōkoku* (*Catalogue of Japanese Art in Foreign Collections*). Tokyo: Kobunkazai kagaku kenkyūkai, 1993.

Barber 1906
Barber, Edwin A., ed. "Japanese Lacquers." *Bulletin of the Pennsylvania Museum* 4, no. 14 (April 1906): 24–25.

Blair 2011
Blair, Heather. "Zaō Gongen: From Mountain Icon to National Treasure." *Monumenta Nipponica* 66, no. 1 (2011): 1–47.

Blum 1997
Blum, Dilys. *The Fine Art of Textiles: The Collections of the Philadelphia Museum of Art*. Philadelphia: Philadelphia Museum of Art, 1997.

Bogdanova-Kummer 2020
Bogdanova-Kummer, Eugenia. *Bokujinkai: Japanese Calligraphy and the Postwar Avant-Garde*. Leiden, Netherlands: Brill, 2020.

Callaghan 2019
Callaghan, Sarah, ed. "The Life of Animals in Japanese Art." *Asian Art Newspaper* 22, no. 6 (Summer 2019): 14–15.

Canaday 1972
Canaday, John. "When East Met the West — in Prints." *New York Times*, December 17, 1972, 121, 132.

Castiglioni 2015
Castiglioni, Andrea. "Ascesis and Devotion: The Mount Yudono Cult in Early Modern Japan." PhD diss., Columbia University, 2015.

Cate 1930a
Cate, Philip Harding. "Four Landscape Scrolls of the Seasons by Sesshu." *Bulletin of the Pennsylvania Museum* 25, no. 135 (May 1930): 26–31.

Cate 1930b
Cate, Philip Harding. "Japanese Sculpture." *Bulletin of the Pennsylvania Museum* 26, no. 137 (December 1930): 17–28.

Chinese Art Society of America 1962
Chinese Art Society of America. "Oriental Art Recently Acquired by American Museums." *Archives of the Chinese Art Society of America* 16 (1962): 104–24.

Clements and Sang 2022
Clements, Rebekah, and Seung Yeon Sang. "Stories of Clay: Discovering Choson Korean Potters in Tokugawa Japan." Aftermath of the East Asian War of 1592–1598. 2022. https://aftermath.uab.cat/stories-of-clay/.

Cline and Knospe 2007
Cline, Jeffery, and William Knospe. *Breaking Light: Arts of 20th-Century Japan*. Seattle: Kagedo Japanese Art, 2007.

Cort 1992
Cort, Louise Allison. *Seto and Mino Ceramics*. Washington, DC: Freer Gallery of Art, Smithsonian Institution, 1992.

Cotter 1999
Cotter, Holland. "Dizzying Realm of Asian Art." *New York Times*, March 26, 1999, E37, E39.

Daiten 1875
Daiten Kenjō. "Tō Keiwa gaki" [Record of paintings by Tō Keiwa (Ito Jakuchū)]. *Shōun seikō* [Manuscripts in cloudlets] 8 (1875): n.p.

Davis 2021
Davis, Julie Nelson. *Picturing the Floating World: Ukiyo-e in Context*. Honolulu: University of Hawai'i Press, 2021.

Doi 1980
Doi, Tsugiyoshi. *Sanraku to Sansetsu*. Nihon no Bijutsu 172. Tokyo: Shibundō, 1980.

Fenollosa 1921
Fenollosa, Ernest F. *Epochs of Chinese and Japanese Art*. Vol. 1. New York: Frederick A. Stokes Co., 1921.

Fischer 1984
Fischer, Felice. "Seated Jizō." *Philadelphia Museum of Art Bulletin* 80, nos. 343–44 (Summer/Fall 1984): 9–11.

Fischer 1991
Fischer, Felice. "Japanese Buddhist Art." *Philadelphia Museum of Art Bulletin* 87, no. 369 (Winter 1991): 1–27.

Fischer 1992
Fischer, Felice. "Meiji Painting from the Fenollosa Collection." *Philadelphia Museum of Art Bulletin* 88, no. 375 (Autumn 1992): 1–24.

Fischer 2002
Fischer, Felice. "The Centennial Exhibition, the Philadelphia Museum of Art, and Hector Tyndale." *Magazine Antiques* (March 2002): 96–103.

Fischer 2017
Fischer, Felice. "Sunkarakuan: A Teahouse for Philadelphia." *Orientations* 48, no. 6 (November/December 2017): 1–7.

Fischer 2019
Fischer, Felice. "Unfolding Hyakusen's Legacy." In *Hinges: Sakaki Hyakusen and the Birth of Nanga Painting*, edited by Julia White, 23–31. Exh. cat. Berkeley: UC Berkeley Art Museum and Pacific Film Archive; Oakland: University of California Press, 2019.

Foxwell 2008
Foxwell, Chelsea. "Kano Hōgai (1828–88) and the Making of Modern Japanese Painting." PhD diss., Columbia University, 2008.

Foxwell 2015
Foxwell, Chelsea. *Making Modern Japanese-Style Painting: Kano Hogai and the Search for Images*. Chicago: University of Chicago Press, 2015.

Gardiner 1968
Gardiner, Henry G. "The Samuel S. White, 3rd, and Vera White Collection." *Philadelphia Museum of Art Bulletin* 63, nos. 296–97 (Winter 1968): 71–150.

Gerstle 2005
Gerstle, C. Andrew. *Kabuki Heroes on the Osaka Stage, 1780–1830*. Honolulu: University of Hawai'i Press, 2005.

Goodall-Cristante 1996
Goodall-Cristante, Hollis. "*Shin-Hanga*: Traditional Prints in a New World." In *Shin-Hanga: New Prints in Modern Japan*, by Kendall H. Brown and Hollis Goodall-Cristante, 11–34. Exh. cat. Los Angeles: Los Angeles County Museum of Art in association with University of Washington Press, 1996.

Graybill 1983
Graybill, Maribeth. "*Kasen-e*: An Investigation into the Origins of the Tradition of Poet Pictures in Japan." PhD diss., University of Michigan, 1983.

Guth 1993
Guth, Christine. *Art, Tea, and Industry: Masuda Takashi and the Mitsui Circle*. Princeton, NJ: Princeton University Press, 1993.

Hakeda 1972
Hakeda, Yoshido S. *Kūkai*. New York: Columbia University Press, 1972.

Hickman 1998
Hickman, Money L. "Takada Keiho and Soga Shōhaku." In *Soga Shōhaku*, edited by Nobuo Tsuj, 16–24, 189. Exh. cat., Chiba City Museum of Art and Mie Prefectural Art Museum. Tokyo: Asahi Shimbun, 1998.

Hiesinger 2011
Hiesinger, Kathryn B. *Collecting Modern: Design at the Philadelphia Museum of Art Since 1876*. Philadelphia: Philadelphia Museum of Art, 2011.

Hinohara 2017
Hinohara, Kenji. *Tsukioka Yoshitoshi: Tsuki hyakushi* (*One Hundred Views of the Moon*). Kyoto: Seigensha, 2017.

Hosono 1978
Hosono Masanobu. *Edoganō to Hōgai* [Edo Kano and Hōgai]. Tokyo: Shogakukan, 1978.

Ikeda 1941
Ikeda Shōtarō, ed. *Ikeda Daisendō kobijutsu shūhō* [Old art treasures of Ikeda Daisendō]. Vol. 2. Osaka: Ikeda Daisendō, 1941.

Inada 2019
Inada Sōsai, ed. *Morita Shiryū Catalogue Raisonné: 1952–1998*. Kyoto: Sōryūsha, 2019.

Iwao 1985
Iwao, Seiichi. *Shuinsen bōekishi no kenkyū* [A study on the history of the red-seal ship trade]. Rev. ed. Tokyo: Yoshikawa Kōbunkan, 1985.

Jenkins 1977
Jenkins, Donald. *Masterworks in Wood: China and Japan*. Portland, OR: Portland Art Museum, 1977.

Jenyns 1971
Jenyns, Soame. *Japanese Pottery*. London: Faber and Faber, 1971.

Kaminishi 2021
Kaminishi, Ikumi. "Furuta Oribe: Controversial Daimyo Tea-Master." In *The Tokugawa World*, edited by Gary P. Leupp and Demin Tao, 685–704. London: Routledge, 2021.

Kamiyama 2008
Kamiyama, Fumiko. "Hyōden: Kyōsai ga kataru Kyōsai" [A critical biography: Kyōsai talks about Kyōsai]. In *Kawanabe Kyōsai: Kisō no tensai eshi* [Kawanabe Kyōsai: A genius painter of strange ideas], edited by Toshinobu Yasumura, 146. Tokyo: Heibonsha, 2008.

Kanagawa Kenritsu Kanazawa Bunko 2011
Kanagawa Kenritsu Kanazawa Bunko, ed. *Aizen Myōō: Ai to ikari no hotoke* [Aizen Myo-o: Love and anger]. Kanagawa: Kanagawa Kenritsu Kanazawa Bunko, 2011.

Kanō 1693
Kanō Einō. *Honchō gashi* [Japanese painting history and theory]. Vol. 3. 1679. Reprint, [Kyoto]: Yoshinoya Sōbē, [1693].

Kanō 2005
Kanō Hiroyuki. "Burai to iu yuetsu: Soga Shōhaku he no shiza" [The pleasure of being a rascal: A perspective on Soga Shōhaku]. In *Soga Shōhaku: Burai to iu yuetsu* [Soga Shōhaku: The pleasure of being a rascal], 15–18. Exh. cat. Kyoto: Kyōto Kokuritsu Hakubutsukan, 2005.

"Kansai Yamamoto Show" 1971
"The Kansai Yamamoto Show." *Harpers & Queen*, July 1971, 46–51.

Kawaguchi and Iijima 1993
Kawaguchi Seitei and Iijima Tachio, eds. *Ryōkan bokuseki taikan* [Collection of Ryōkan's calligraphy]. Tokyo: Chūō Kōron Bijutsu Shuppan, 1993.

Keene 1993
Keene, Donald. *Seeds in the Heart: Japanese Literature from Earliest Times to the Sixteenth Century*. New York: Henry Holt, 1993.

Keyes 1982
Keyes, Roger. *Courage and Silence: A Study of Life and Color Woodblock Prints of Tsukioka Yoshitoshi, 1839–1892*. PhD diss., Union for Experimenting Colleges and Universities, 1982.

Keyes 1984
Keyes, Roger. "Hirosada: Ōsaka Print Designer." In *Hirosada: Ōsaka Printmaker*, edited by Jane K. Bledsoe, 8–25. Exh. cat. Long Beach: University Art Museum, California State University, 1984.

Keyes 2007–8
Keyes, Roger. "Pink Fuji: The Print Hokusai Saw." *Impressions* 29 (2007–8): 68–75.

Kinoshita 2007
Kinoshita, Kyoko. "The Life and Art of Tokuyama Gyokuran." In *Ike Taiga and Tokuyama Gyokuran: Japanese Masters of the Brush*, by Felice Fischer and Kyoko Kinoshita, 33–51. Exh. cat. Philadelphia: Philadelphia Museum of Art, 2007.

Kinoshita 2019
Kinoshita, Kyoko. "Study of the Red-Seal Ship Screens in the Collection of the Philadelphia Museum of Art: The Relationship between the Red-Seal Ship Screens and the Votive Tablets in the Kiyomizu Temple." *Kashima bijutsu kenkyū* [Kashima art research] 36 (2019): 507–18.

Kirkham and Weber 2013
Kirkham, Pat, and Susan Weber, eds. *History of Design: Decorative Arts and Material Culture, 1400–2000*. New York: Bard Graduate Center, 2013.

Kline 2000
Kline, A. S. *Like Water or Clouds: The T'ang Dynasty and the Tao*. Luxembourg: Poetry in Translation, 2000.

Kobayashi 1990
Kobayashi Tadashi, ed. *Seasonal Flowering Plants and Birds*. Vol. 2 of *Rimpa Painting*. Kyoto: Shikosha, 1990.

Kojima and Sekiya 2017
Kojima Masayoshi and Sekiya Tokue, eds. *Ryōkan ibokushū: Sono hito to sho* [Collection of the Ryōkan posthumous calligraphy: The man and his writing]. 3 vols. Kyoto: Tankōsha, 2017.

Kurimoto 1957
Kurimoto Kazuo, ed. *Ike-no Taiga gafu* [Album of works of Ike-no Taiga]. 5 vols. Tokyo: Chūō Kōron Bijutsu Shuppansha, 1957.

Lee 1955
Lee, Jean Gordon. "Recent Acquisitions in the Department of Far Eastern Art." *Philadelphia Museum Bulletin* 50, no. 245 (Spring 1955): 33–39.

Lee 1958a
Lee, Jean Gordon. "Shofuku Ji." *Philadelphia Museum of Art Bulletin* 53, no. 256 (Winter 1958): 36–38.

Lee 1958b
Lee, Jean Gordon. "Sun Ka Raku." *Philadelphia Museum of Art Bulletin* 53, no. 256 (Winter 1958): 39–42.

Lesley Kehoe Galleries 2008
Lesley Kehoe Galleries. *Japanese Works of Art 2008*. Melbourne, Australia: Lesley Kehoe Galleries, 2008.

Masuda 1985
Masuda Takashi. "Shinshutsu no Kōetsu no wakakan" [Newly discovered poetry scroll by Kōetsu]. *Sumi*, no. 55 (July 1985): 124–27.

Matsudaira 1984
Matsudaira, S. "*Hiiki Renchū* (Theatre Fan Clubs) in Osaka in the Early Nineteenth Century." *Modern Asian Studies* 18, no. 4 (1984): 699–709.

Matsuo 2003
Matsuo, Yoshiki. "Zusho to Hyakunen: Suzuki-ha no tanjō" [Zusho and Hyakunen: The birth of Suzuki school]. *Bulletin of University Art Museum of Kyoto City University of Arts* 13 (2003): 15–25.

McCabe 1975
McCabe, James D. *The Illustrated History of the Centennial Exhibition*. 1876. Philadelphia: National Publishing Company, 1975.

McKelway 2018
McKelway, Matthew P. "Rosetsu's Signature and Seals." In *Rosetsu: Ferocious Brush*, by Matthew McKelway and Khanh Trinh, 276–85. Exh. cat., Museum Rietberg, Zurich. Munich: Prestel, 2018.

"Memorial" 2002
"Memorial: Laurance P. Roberts '29." *Princeton Alumni Weekly*, March 2002. https://paw.princeton.edu/memorial/laurance-p-roberts-%E2%80%9929.

Merritt 1990
Merritt, Helen. *Modern Japanese Woodblock Prints: The Early Years*. Honolulu: University of Hawai'i Press, 1990.

Michener 1968
Michener, James A. *The Modern Japanese Print: An Appreciation*. Rutland, VT: C. E. Tuttle, 1968.

Miyatake 1911
Miyatake Gaikotsu. *Sōkō: Naniwa meika bosho-ki* [Draft of the record of famous families' cemeteries in Naniwa]. Osaka: printed by the author, 1911.

Mizuo 1957
Mizuo Hiroshi. "'Summer Landscape' by Ike Gyokuran." *Kokka*, no. 779 (1957).

Mochizuki 1973
Mochizuki Shinjyo, ed. *Shoka aizo Nihon Bukkyo bijutsu hiho* [Japanese Buddhist art objects in private collections]. Tokyo: Sansaisha, 1973.

Moriyama 2016
Moriyama Eiichi. "Surviving Castles and Abolished Castles: When Did Castles Cease?" Report of the Research Symposium on the Preservation and Utilization of Historic Sites, Nara National Research Institute for Cultural Properties. 2016.

Morse 1901
Morse, Edward S. *Catalogue of the Morse Collection of Japanese Pottery*. Cambridge, MA: printed at the Riverside Press, 1901.

Munakata 1961
Munakata Shikō. *The "Way" of the Woodcut*. Brooklyn: Pratt Adlib Press, 1961.

Museum of Fine Arts, Boston, n.d.
Museum of Fine Arts, Boston. "Actors Kataoka Gadō II as Genta Kagesue and Nakayama Yoshio III as Umegae." Museum of Fine Arts, Boston (website). Accessed September 19, 2022. https://collections.mfa.org/objects/460677/actors-kataoka-gado-ii-as-genta-kagesue-and-nakayama-yoshio.

***Nada Sakai Shōtō-shi shozō-hin nyūsatsu* 1924**
Nada Sakai Shōtō-shi shozō-hin nyūsatsu [Auction of Mr. Sakai Shōtō collection in Nada]. [Kobe]: Osaka Bijutsu Club, 1924.

Nakamura 1979
Nakamura Tanio. *Hōitsu-ha kachō gafu* [Hōitsu school flowers and birds]. Vol. 4. Kyoto: Shikōsha, 1979.

Nakanishi 2009
Nakanishi Kaoru, ed. *Tanba no meitō / Old Tamba*. Tokyo: Kyūryūdō, 2009.

Newland 2011
Newland, Amy Reigle, ed. *Yoshitoshi: Masterpieces from the Ed Freis Collection*. Leiden: Hotei, 2011.

Nihon Bijutsuin 1989
Nihon Bijutsuin, ed. *Nihon Bijutsuin hyakunenshi* [Centennial history of the Japan Art Institute]. Vol. 1, pt. 1. Tokyo: Nihon Bijutsuin, 1989.

"Nio-Mon" 1906
"Nio-Mon, or Temple Gate." *Bulletin of the Pennsylvania Museum* 4, no. 13 (January 1906): 12.

Nishikawa and Sano 1982
Nishikawa Kyotaro and Emily J. Sano. *The Great Age of Japanese Buddhist Sculpture, AD 600–1300*. Fort Worth: Kimball Art Museum, 1982.

Numata 2005
Numata, Hideko. "Shibayama Zaiku nitsuiteno kisokenkyū: Yokohama to no kankei wo chūshin ni" [Fundamental research on Shibayama Zaiku: Focusing on his connection to Yokohama]. *Yokohama bijutsukan Yokohama shimin gyararī kenkyū kiyō / Bulletin of the Yokohama Museum of Art and the Civic Art Gallery* 7 (2005): 59–76.

Ogata, Okada, and Sasaki 1998
Ogata Tsutomu, Okada Akiko, and Sasaki Jōhei. *Buson zenshū: Kaiga, iboku* [Complete works of Buson: Paintings and calligraphies]. Vol. 6. Tokyo: Kodansha, 1998.

Ogura et al. 1990
Ogura Yuki et al., eds. *Nihon bijutsuin hyakunenshi* [One hundred years of the Japan Art Institute]. Vol. 2a. Tokyo: Nihon Bijutsuin, 1990.

Okada 2014
Okada Azusa. "Revolution and Meanings of Flower-Grass Paintings with 'Inen' Seal around Sōsetsu School in the 17th Century: Focusing on the Demander and the Influence on Japanese Art after the 18th Century." *Faculty of Integrated Arts and Social Sciences Journal* (Japan Women's University) 20 (2014): 231–48.

Okano 2017
Okano, Tomoko. *Suzuki Kiitsu: Edo Rinpa no kishu / Suzuki Kiitsu: Standard-Bearer of the Edo Rimpa School*. Tokyo: Yomiuri Shimbun, 2017.

Ooka 1971
Ooka, Dianne T. "Ike-No Taiga: Paintings in the Collection." *Philadelphia Museum of Art Bulletin* 66, no. 305 (July–September 1971): 28–44.

Ōta 1986
Ōta Nanpo. *Kaigen kikō* [New era travelogue]. Vol. 8 of *Ōta Nanpo zenshū* [Ōta Nanpo complete books], edited by Giichirō Hamada. Tokyo: Iwanami Shoten, 1986.

Pankenier 2013
Pankenier, David W. *Astrology and Cosmology in Early China: Conforming Earth to Heaven*. New York: Cambridge University Press, 2013.

Pegg 2019
Pegg, Richard A. "Early Edo Maritime Trade: Red-Seal System Maps and Ships." *Orientations* 50, no. 3 (May–June 2019): 78–85.

Philadelphia Museum of Art 1937
Philadelphia Museum of Art. "[Museum Rooms and Decorative Elements]." *Bulletin of the Pennsylvania Museum* 32, no. 174 (May 1937): 2–48.

Philadelphia Museum of Art 1939
Philadelphia Museum of Art. "New Sections." *Philadelphia Museum Bulletin* 34, no. 181 (March 1939): 3–15.

Philadelphia Museum of Art 1995
Philadelphia Museum of Art. *Philadelphia Museum of Art: Handbook of the Collections*. Philadelphia: Philadelphia Museum of Art, 1995.

Philadelphia Museum of Art 2014
Philadelphia Museum of Art. *Philadelphia Museum of Art: Handbook*. Philadelphia: Philadelphia Museum of Art, 2014.

Phillips 2004
Phillips, Sandra S. "Currents in Photography in Postwar Japan." In *Shomei Tomatsu: Skin of the Nation*, edited by Leo Rubinfien, Sandra S. Phillips, and John W. Dower, 42–57. Exh. cat. San Francisco: San Francisco Museum of Modern Art in association with Yale University Press, 2004.

Reizei et al. 1996
Reizei, Tamehito, et al. *Mizuho no kuni Nihon: Shiki Kōsaku-zu no Sekai* [Land of Mizuho, Japan: The world of four seasons farming map]. Kyoto: Tankō-sha, 1996.

Russell 1969
Russell, John C. (Mrs.). "The Women's Committee." *Philadelphia Museum of Art Bulletin* 64, no. 301 (October–December 1969): 112–13.

"Ryaku-nenpu" 2005
"Ryaku-nenpu / Soga Shōhaku to sono jidai" [Abbreviated chronology / Soga Shōhaku and his times]. In *Shōhaku Show*, 388–89. Exh. cat. Kyoto: Kyoto National Museum, 2005.

Satō 1929
Satō Kichitarō, ed. *Ryōkan ibokushū* [Collection of the Ryōkan posthumous calligraphy]. Tokyo: Daiichi Shobō, 1929.

Saunders 1964
Saunders, E. Dale. *Buddhism in Japan with an Outline of Its Origins in India*. Philadelphia: University of Pennsylvania Press, 1964.

Saunders 2005
Saunders, Rachel. "Pursuits of Power: Falconry in Edo Period Japan." *Orientations* 36, no. 2 (2005): 82–92.

Shimada 1969
Shimada Shūjirō, ed. *Zaigai hihō: Ōbei shūzō nihon kaiga shūsei (Shōheiga rinpa bunjinga)* [Japanese paintings in Western collections (Screen paintings, Rimpa, literati paintings)]. Vol. 2. Tokyo: Gakushū Kenkyūsha, 1969.

Shimada, Akiyama, and Yamane 1980
Shimada Shūjirō, Akiyama Terukazu, and Yamane Yūzō, eds. *Zaigai Nihon no shihō—Emaki* [Japanese art: Selections from Western collections, narrative scroll painting]. Vol. 2. Tokyo: Mainichi Shinbun-sha, 1980.

Shimizu 1980
Shimizu Zenzō. "Amerika, Kanada ni aru Nihon chōkoku" [Japanese sculpture in the United States and Canada]. *Ars Buddhica* 128 (January 1980): 98–117.

Shively 1964–65
Shively, Donald H. "Sumptuary Regulation and Status in Early Tokugawa Japan." *Harvard Journal of Asiatic Studies* 25 (1964–65): 123–64.

Smith 2005
Smith, Henry. "Hokusai and the Blue Revolution." In *Hokusai and His Age: Ukiyo-e Painting, Printmaking, and Book Illustration in Late Edo Japan*, edited by John T. Carpenter, 252–59. Amsterdam: Hotei, 2005.

Sōma 1928
Sōma Ryōfu. *Ryōkan ibokushū* [Ryōkan's posthumous writings]. Tokyo: Daiichi Shobō, 1928.

Stevenson 1992
Stevenson, John. *Yoshitoshi's One Hundred Aspects of the Moon*. Redmond, WA: San Francisco Graphic Society, 1992.

Takahashi 2022
Takahashi, Osamu. "Edo bakufu goyō eshi Kano Kagenobu (Kano Sōeki) hitsu *The Farming Scenes of the Four Seasons* to no taiwa" [Dialogue of *The Farming Scenes of the Four Seasons* by Edo shogunate official painter Kano Kagenbu (Kano Sōeki)]. *Tokyo Joshidaigaku Kyōshoku gakugeiin katei* [Bulletin of the teacher training and obtaining curator's certificate courses of Tokyo Woman's Christian University] (2022): 62–83.

Takakusu et al. 1977
Takakusu, Junjiro, et al., eds. *Taishō Shinshū Daizōkyō* [Index to the Taisho Tripitaka]. Vol. 24. Tokyo: Taisho Shinshu Daizokyo Kankokai, 1977.

Takeuchi 2002
Takeuchi, Melinda. "Making Mountains: Mini-Fujis, Edo Popular Religion and Hiroshige's 'One Hundred Famous Views of Edo.'" *Impressions* 24 (2002): 24–47.

Till 2007
Till, Barry. *Shin Hanga: The New Print Movement of Japan*. San Francisco: Pomegranate, 2007.

Tōkyō Kokuritsu Bunkazai Kenkyūjo Bijutsubu 1997
Tōkyō Kokuritsu Bunkazai Kenkyūjo Bijutsubu, ed. *Meijiki bankoku hakurankai bijutsuhin shuppin mokuroku* [List of art objects exhibited at the world expositions during the Meiji period]. Tokyo: Chūō Kōron Bijutsu Shuppan, 1997.

Tōkyō Ryōgoku Bijutsu Kurabu 1917
Tōkyō Ryōgoku Bijutsu Kurabu. *Dai nikai Akaboshi ke shozohin nyusatsu* [The second auction preview of the Akaboshi family collection]. Tokyo: Tōkyō Ryōgoku Bijutsu Kurabu, 1917.

Tōmatsu 1995
Tōmatsu, Shōmei. *Nagasaki <11:02> 1945-nen 8-gatsu 9-nichi / Nagasaki, 11:02, August 9, 1945*. Tokyo: Shinchōsha, 1995.

Tsuchiya 2013
Tsuchiya Seiichi. "'Toki' no montāju: Tōmatsu Shōmei ron" [Montage of "time": Tōmatsu Shōmei theory]. *Gendai shisō* [Contemporary thought] 41, no. 6 (2013): 78–85.

Tsuji 2019
Tsuji, Nobuo. *Kyoto jūhasseiki Kyoto gadan: Shōhaku, Jakuchū, Ōkyo tachi no sekai* [Artists' world in Kyoto in the eighteenth century: Shōhaku, Jakuchū and Ōkyo]. Tokyo: Kōdansha, 2019.

Uhlenbeck 2011
Uhlenbeck, Chris. "The Phases in the Career of Tsukioka Yoshitoshi: A Print Designer in a Time of Change." *Yoshitoshi: Masterpieces from the Ed Freis Collection*, edited by Amy Reigle Newland, 8–24. Leiden: Hotei, 2011.

"Ukiyo-e go daimeisaku shinhakken!" 2020
"Ukiyo-e go daimeisaku shinhakken!" [Five newly discovered ukiyo-e masterpieces!]. *Shūkan Nippon no ukiyo-e 100* [Weekly Japanese ukiyo-e 100] 5, no. 9 (2020): 6–9.

Warner 1958
Warner, Langdon. *The Enduring Art of Japan*. New York: Grove, 1958.

Waterhouse 1983
Waterhouse, David. *Early Japanese Prints in the Philadelphia Museum of Art*. Toronto: University of Toronto, York University Joint Centre on Modern East Asia, 1983.

Waterhouse 2013
Waterhouse, David. *The Harunobu Decade: A Catalogue of Woodcuts by Suzuki Harunobu and His Followers in the Museum of Fine Arts, Boston*. 2 vols. Leiden: Hotei, 2013.

Wilson 1991
Wilson, Richard L. *The Art of Ogata Kenzan: Persona and Production in Japanese Ceramics*. New York: Weatherhill, 1991.

Yamaguchi and Miyazaki 2018
Yamaguchi Ryūsuke and Miyazaki Motoko. "The Transfer of Buddhist Sculptures from Kōfukuji in the Meiji Era and Their Locations Today: Source-Study Research Conducted Using Old Photographs at Kōfukuji." *Museum: The Bimonthly Magazine of the Tokyo National Museum*, no. 676 (October 2018): 5–57.

Yamamori 2019
Yamamori, Yayoi. "Noguchi Shōhin no sansui-ga, shinkei-zu to sonogo no tenkai" [Noguchi Shōhin's landscape paintings, true-view paintings, and later developments]. In *Noguchi Shōhin: Josei nangaka no kindai* [Noguchi Shōhin: Modern times of female Nanga painter], 66–71. Exh. cat. Tokyo: Kōsetsu Memorial Museum, Jissen Women's University, 2019.

Yamane 1979
Yamane Yūzō, ed. *Rinpa kaiga zenshū: Hōitsu-ha* [Rimpa paintings: Hōitsu school]. Vol. 5. Tokyo: Nihon Keizai Shinbunsha, 1979.

Yamanouchi 1981
Yamanouchi Chōzō. *Nihon Nanga-shi* [The history of Japanese Nanga painting]. Tokyo: Ruri Shobō, 1981.

Yamashita 1985
Yamashita Yuji. "Shikibu Terutada no kenkyū: Kantō suibokuga ni kansuru hito kōsatsu" [Research on Shikibu Terutada: A study on Kantō ink painting]. *Kokka*, no. 1084 (1985): 11–31.

Yamashita 1992
Yamashita Yuji. "Shikibu Terutada sairon" [Revisiting Shikibu Terutada]. *Kokka*, no. 1161 (1992): 11–27.

Yamashita 2004
Yamashita, Yoshiya. "Ketteiban Kano-ha keizu" [Definitive edition of the genealogy of the Kano school]. In *Kano-ha ketteiban* [Kano school definitive edition], edited by Yuji Yamashita, n.p. [appendix]. Tokyo: Heibonsha, 2004.

Yamashita 2008
Yamashita, Yoshiya. "Kyōsai ga Kano-ha kara etamono" [What Kyōsai gained from the Kano school]. In *Kaiga no bōkensha Kyōsai: Kindai e kakeru hashi; Tokubetsu tenrankai botsugo 120-nen kinen* [Kyōsai, bridge to modernity: Kyōsai's adventures in painting; Commemorating the 120th memorial of Kawanabe Kyōsai], edited by Kyōto Kokuritsu Hakubutsukan, 24–30. Exh. cat. Kyoto: Kyōto Kokuritsu Hakubutsukan, 2008.

Yanagi 2008
Yanagi, Harumi. *Contemporary Ceramics, Winter 2008*. Kyoto: Gallery MIKI, 2008.

Yasunaga 2002
Yasunaga, Koichi. "Lofty Mountains and Misty Valleys: The Art and Life of Yoshida Hiroshi." In *A Japanese Legacy: Four Generations of Yoshida Family Artists*, by Laura W. Allen et al., 23–70. Exh. cat. Minneapolis: Minneapolis Institute of Art, 2002.

Yoshida 2019
Yoshida Hiroyuki. *Tea Men Born from Nakama: Ōgi Rodō and Ōgi Seisai*. Nakamashi: Nakamashi kyōiku iinkai, 2019.

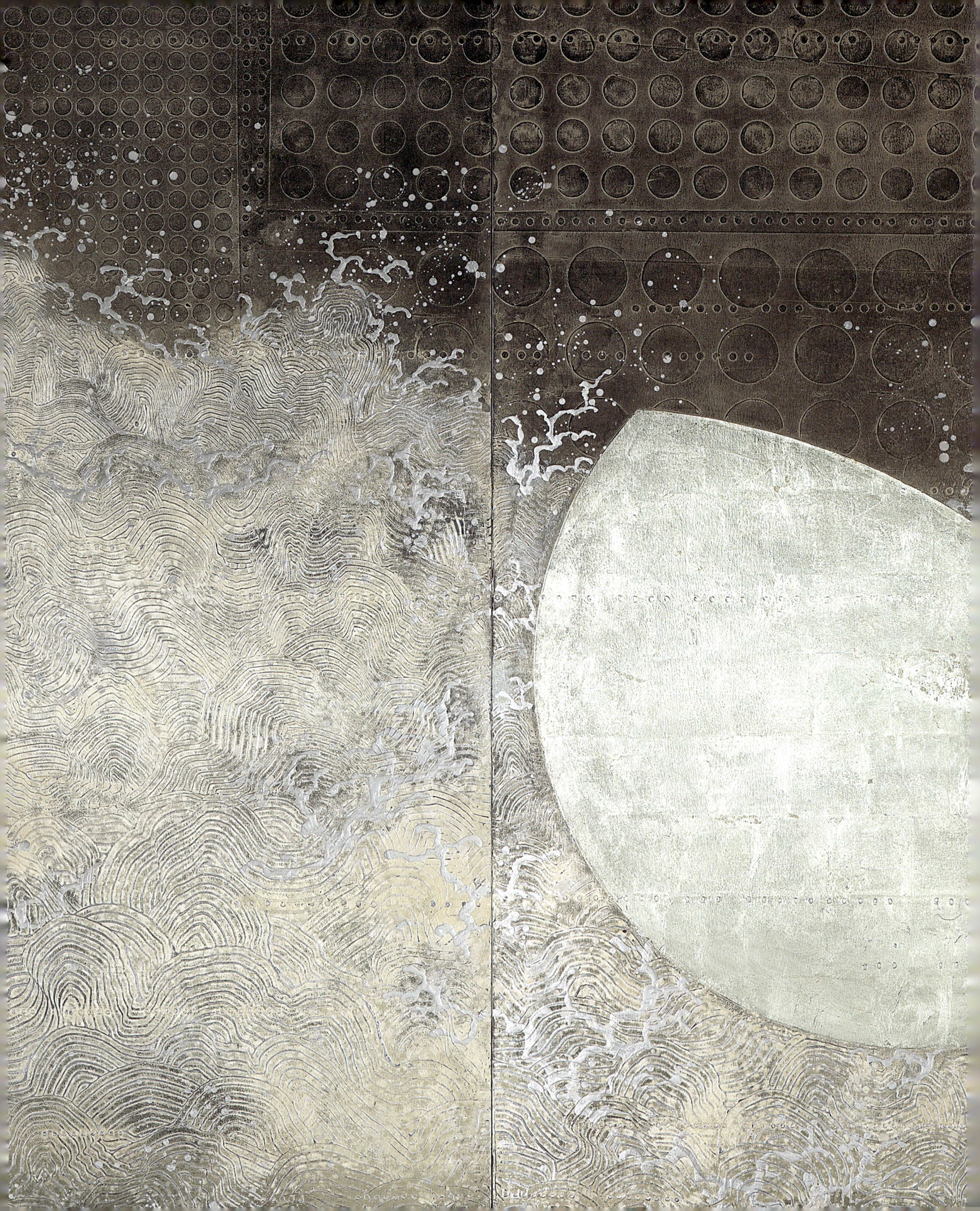

Selected Index

Page numbers in **bold** indicate illustrations.

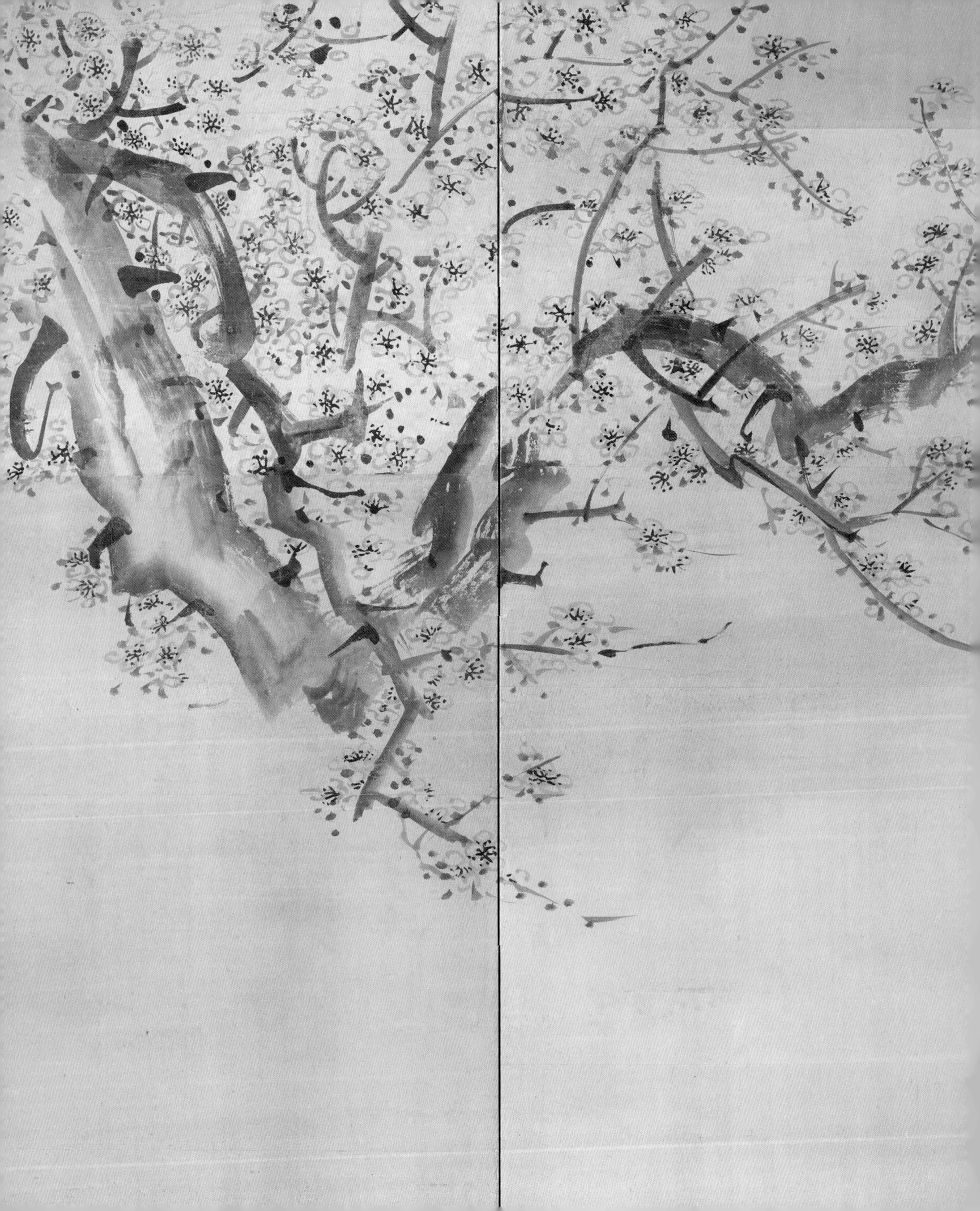

Display Images

Front cover: Shōkadō Shōjō (1584–1639), *Bamboo and Sparrows* (detail), c. 1638 (see no. 19)

Page 2: *Ki no Tsurayuki* (detail), early 14th century (see no. 12)

Page 4: Ōgi Rodō (1863–1941), Sunkaraku (Evanescent Joys) Ceremonial Teahouse (interior view), c. 1917 (see no. 24)

Page 6: *Goshawk Mews* (detail), c. 1675 (see no. 49)

Page 12: Hon'ami Kōetsu (1558–1637), Poems from the *Shinkokin wakashū* (detail), early 17th century (see no. 38)

Pages 32–33: Hashimoto Gahō (1835–1908), *Landscape* (detail), c. 1903 (see no. 80)

Page 246: Document Box with Design of Five Butterflies (detail), 17th–18th century (see no. 40)

Page 262: Noh Robe, *Uwagi* (Outer Garment for Female Role), *Karaori* Type (detail), 1750–1850 (see no. 42)

Page 272: Ken Matsubara (b. 1948), *Waning Moon* (detail), 2017 (see no. 103)

Page 278: Ike Taiga (1723–1776), *Flowering Plum Trees in Mist* (detail), c. 1750 (see no. 50)

Back cover: Ogata Kenzan (1663–1743), Dishes (detail), 1712–31 (see no. 30)

Photography Credits

Photographs were supplied by the owners and/or the following:

Houghton Library, Harvard University, Cambridge, Massachusetts: fig. 54

Idemitsu Museum of Arts, Tokyo: fig. 30

Ippodo Gallery, New York: fig. 68

Kyoko Kinoshita: figs. 22a–c

Kiyomizu Temple, Kyoto: figs. 38, 39

Library of Congress, Prints and Photographs Division, Washington, DC: fig. 3

The Metropolitan Museum of Art, New York: figs. 37, 67

Minneapolis Institute of Art: fig. 31

Museum of Fine Arts, Boston: fig. 49

National Museum of Asian Art, Freer Gallery of Art, Washington, DC: figs. 35, 36

National Museum of Asian Art Archives, Washington, DC: fig. 6

Philadelphia Inquirer, photograph by Michael Bryant: fig. 17

This publication was made possible by the Neubauer Family Foundation to honor Dr. Felice Fischer, Curator Emerita of Japanese and East Asian Art and former Luther W. Brady Curator of Japanese Art and Senior Curator of East Asian Art at the Philadelphia Museum of Art, who has guided the museum's exploration of Japanese art since 1972 and was recognized in 2013 by Japan with the Order of the Rising Sun, Gold and Silver Rays, the country's oldest international honor (1875), for her prodigious accomplishments in fostering cultural exchange.

Produced by
Publishing Department
Philadelphia Museum of Art
Kathleen Krattenmaker
Director of Publishing
2525 Pennsylvania Avenue
Philadelphia, PA 19130-2440
philamuseum.org

Distributed by
Yale University Press
302 Temple Street
P.O. Box 209040
New Haven, CT 06520-9040
yalebooks.com/art

Library of Congress Control Number: 2023931575

ISBN 978-0-87633-300-6

Printed and bound in Spain

Edited by
Sarah Noreika and Mary Cason

Production by
Richard Bonk

Design and composition by
Joseph Cho and Stefanie Lew
Binocular, New York

Photography by
Joseph Hu, Tim Tiebout, and Graydon Wood

Index by
Barbara L. Phillips and Holly Chen

Separations and printing by
Brizzolis, Madrid

Bound by
Méndez, Madrid

See page 279 for cover illustrations, display images, and photography credits.